BLACK ART AND AESTHETICS

ALSO AVAILABLE FROM BLOOMSBURY

African American Philosophers and Philosophy, by John H. McClendon III
and Stephen C. Ferguson II
Architecture in Black, by Darell Wayne Fields
The Cultural Promise of the Aesthetic, by Monique Roelofs
The Paralysis of Analysis in African American Studies, by Stephen C. Ferguson II
Working Aesthetics, by Danielle Child

BLACK ART AND AESTHETICS

Relationalities, Interiorities, Reckonings

EDITED BY
MICHAEL KELLY and
MONIQUE ROELOFS

BLOOMSBURY ACADEMIC
LONDON • NEW YORK • OXFORD • NEW DELHI • SYDNEY

BLOOMSBURY ACADEMIC
Bloomsbury Publishing Plc
50 Bedford Square, London, WC1B 3DP, UK
1385 Broadway, New York, NY 10018, USA
29 Earlsfort Terrace, Dublin 2, Ireland

BLOOMSBURY, BLOOMSBURY ACADEMIC and the Diana logo are trademarks
of Bloomsbury Publishing Plc

First published in Great Britain 2024

Cover design by Louise Dugdale
Cover image © 2023 The Estate of Terry Adkins / Artists Rights Society (ARS), New York

ISBN: HB: 978-1-3502-9463-9
        PB: 978-1-3502-9462-2
        ePDF: 978-1-3502-9461-5
        eBook: 978-1-3502-9460-8

Typeset by RefineCatch Limited, Bungay, Suffolk
Printed and bound in Great Britain

To find out more about our authors and books visit www.bloomsbury.com
and sign up for our newsletters.

CONTENTS

ILLUSTRATIONS

All images are provided in black and white in the main text, adjacent to where they are discussed. Color images appear additionally in one of the three color plate sections. The page numbers below refer to the black and white versions.

Plates

Black and White Figures

ACKNOWLEDGEMENTS

The texts below have originally appeared in previous publications. The editors and publisher gratefully acknowledge the permission granted to reproduce the copyrighted material in this book.

Evie Shockley, "buried truths" and "cogito ergo loquor" from *semiautomatic* © 2017 by Evie Shockley. Published by Wesleyan University Press. Reprinted with permission.

Evie Shockley, "dependencies" and "ode to my blackness" from *the new black* © 2011 by Evie Shockley. Published by Wesleyan University Press. Reprinted with permission.

Simone White, "go to jail," in *or, on being the other woman*. Copyright 2022, Duke University Press. All rights reserved. Reprinted by permission of the publisher.

The W. E. B. Du Bois quote in Simone White's epigraph in "go to jail" originally appeared in *The Philadelphia Negro: A Social Study* by W. E. B. Du Bois published by University of Pennsylvania Press in 1899.

Mabel O. Wilson, "White by Design," in *Among Others: Blackness at MoMA*, eds. Darby English and Charlotte Barat (New York: Museum of Modern Art, 2019), 100–109.

Wangechi Mutu, "Making Histories: Wangechi Mutu in Conversation with Isaac Julien and Claudia Schmuckli," in *I Am Speaking, Are Your Listening?*, 37–47, edited by Claudia Schmuckli and published by the Fine Arts Museums of San Francisco and DelMonico Books / DAP in 2021.

Kevin Quashie, "Aliveness and Aesthetics," in *Black Aliveness, or A Poetics of Being*, 57–82. Copyright 2021, Duke University Press. All rights reserved. Republished by permission of the copyright holder, and the Publisher.

Aracelis Girmay, excerpt and "the black maria" from *the black maria*. Copyright © 2016 by Aracelis Girmay. "Kingdom Animalia," "Elegy," and "Ars Poetica" from *Kingdom Animalia*. Copyright © 2011 by Aracelis Girmay. All reprinted with the permission of The Permissions Company, LLC on behalf of BOA Editions, Ltd., boaeditions.org.

Sarah Elizabeth Lewis, "Groundwork: Race and Aesthetics in the Era of Stand Your Ground Law," *Art Journal*, 79, no. 4 (2020): 92–113.

Claudia Rankine, excerpts from *Citizen: An American Lyric*, 69–76. Copyright © 2014 by Claudia Rankine. Excerpts from *Don't Let Me Be Lonely: An American Lyric*, 127–131. Copyright © 2004 by Claudia Rankine. All reprinted with the permission of The Permissions Company, LLC on behalf of Graywolf Press, graywolfpress.org and Penguin UK.

PREFACE: BLACKNESS, WHITENESS, AND CURATORIAL CARE

Michael Kelly & Monique Roelofs

Why an anthology of Black aesthetics? Why now? Why these particular authors, artists, and poets? Why these two editors?

I.

Black Art and Aesthetics: Relationalities, Interiorities, Reckonings has a genealogy that highlights the striking transformation in contemporary Black aesthetics over the last two decades and that, in turn, helps to explain the rationale, timing, and editorship of this anthology. In 2017, we organized a Questioning Aesthetics Symposium on "Black Aesthetics" at Hampshire College, in Amherst, Massachusetts. It was held in celebration of the renaissance of Black aesthetics evident in a number of texts, published between 2010 and 2016, that develop the field in largely unprecedented ways.[1] What were these texts responding and giving rise to, whether in academia or in society at large? What were the different senses and practices of Black aesthetics operating across a range of disciplines, making Black aesthetics an exemplar of transdisciplinary aesthetics? How is this exemplar challenging and transforming the field of aesthetics? What unprecedented models of creation, reflection, and everyday agency are becoming critical for contemporary Black aesthetics? How are these models related to earlier stages of Black aesthetics? Many of the symposiasts are contributors here, but we also invited many new people who also inspired the symposium or who have shaped contemporary Black aesthetics.[2]

At the same time, the 2017 symposium was a follow-up to a 2009 symposium on "Is There a Black Aesthetics?" held at the University of North Carolina at Charlotte.[3] One revealing contrast between the two symposia helped to generate this anthology. Whereas a number of participants or audience members in the first symposium were rightfully suspicious of aesthetics because of its history of anti-Black racism, those involved in the second symposium eight years later fully revalorized, redefined, and retooled the "critical edge" of aesthetics, as Hortense Spillers would call it.[4] In short, they embrace a revisioned aesthetics as a site of critical cultural change and a direly needed source of social alternatives. They also insisted that Black aesthetics has its own independent history that should not be overshadowed by the tendency of modern Western aesthetics to exclude it.[5] With contributions from a wide variety of artists, poets, and theorists alike, *Black Art and Aesthetics: Relationalities, Interiorities, Reckonings* demonstrates that there is no longer any question that Black aesthetics is not only thriving today but that, given how the contributors here invoke many of their predecessors, it also has had a rich history simultaneous with modern aesthetics.

One of the prominent philosophical and political concerns in the 2017 symposium was the common expectation among some critics and practitioners of Black art and aesthetics that "resistance" be its explicit goal, which often results, however, in the reception of Black art and aesthetics being more political than aesthetic. A powerful rejoinder to this expectation in that symposium and subsequently in this anthology has been to resist resistance, because making resistance to anti-Black racism the centerpiece of meaningful practices in Black art and aesthetics entails that racists continue to overdetermine those practices and elides or downplays other important dimensions of Black cultural production.[6] The force of resistance and alternatives to it are captured by the lyrics of Sun Ra's "Saga of Resistance," written much earlier at the height of the Civil Rights Movement in 1968, when a prominent form of contemporary Black aesthetics was thriving. He described an awareness that "I cannot be what you will," so he resisted, determined to be much more "What I will," which implies the self-determination (autonomy) of Black being that, in turn, generates Black art, culture, and aesthetics: interiority seeking objective expression mediated by relationality. If self-determination sounds too utopian, it is and is not. In the 1968 volume *Black Fire: An Anthology of Afro-American Writing*, James. T.

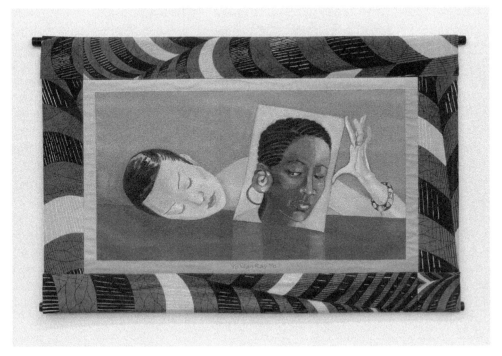

Plate 1 Emma Amos, *Yo Man Ray Yo*, 2000. Copyright 2022, Emma Amos. Licensed by VAGA at Artists Rights Society, New York.

Stewart says in the opening essay that, even if Black artists cannot create "a forever," they can "create forever," if they create "as change": "Creation is itself perpetuation and change is being."[7] Such creations are the materiality of Black art and culture enacting multifarious forms of Black relationality and interiority. Together, these aesthetic and ontological strategies also demand forms of "reckoning" with racism within society, not just within art and aesthetics—new ways of imagining and realizing racial justice. Hence, with our title and subtitle, *Black Art and Aesthetics: Relationalities, Interiorities, Reckonings*, we underline these three strategies and allude also to their generative entwinements, which we clarify further in the Introduction.

II.

Now that the genealogy and rationale of this anthology are clearer, we would like to take a moment to comment on our white editorial positionality as organizers of the earlier symposia and now as editors of *Black Art and Aesthetics: Relationalities, Interiorities, Reckonings*.

Addison Gayle, editor of the classic *The Black Aesthetic* anthology published in 1971, envisioned a day when anthologies of Black art, culture, or aesthetics would be edited, introduced, and written solely by Black writers, critics, theorists, and artists. By contrast, this new anthology has two white editors with a mostly Black cast of writers, philosophers, poets, theorists, and artists. For some reviewers and readers, this racial composition may imply a step backward in the battle to overcome anti-Black racism in aesthetics, art, publishing, and elsewhere. For others, this very criticism might itself be problematic if it implies a kind of essentialism in the ostensible form of a liberatory politics of identity. So, are we, as white editors, reinstating a racist hierarchy? Or, are we helping to foster a philosophical discussion of Black aesthetics without corralling it into white aesthetics? What is the right balance in the case of an anthology on Black art and aesthetics today?

We continue to struggle with these issues, as we recognize that we assume editorial positions inside a terrain in which racial identity has important epistemic, social, political, ethical, and aesthetic implications. We write, think, and relate to others and ourselves in ways marked by white privilege. Our presence as embodied persons in the academy and the society at large contributes to problematic structures of whiteness, even if we also work to disrupt them. We organize symposia and this anthology in ways assisted by our white powers. We give form to our white agency in our creativity, imagination, and orientations toward the world. Our response to our racial positionality, while recognizing that whiteness carries a force apart from our intentions, has been to adopt a mode of agency and address where we are working with the Black artists, scholars, activists, curators, students, readers, and cultural workers from whom we have learned over the years while being entangled with Black aesthetics. The authors, artists, and poets of *Black Art and Aesthetics: Relationalities, Interiorities, Reckonings* have graciously entrusted us with the responsibility to curate, that is, to care for, their beautiful work on its way into the world. Let us now carry that trust and care forward toward our audience: we count on you to further give shape to the tonality, form, and modes of address of this book. After all, these aesthetic elements will disclose and realize themselves gradually in the course of the book's engagement with you, its readers, and in your engagements with it, and with one another. The ultimate adjudication of this anthology's success lies not with us but with the readers and the future voices of Black aesthetics.

III.

We believe that in addition to our long-standing engagements with Black aesthetics, the mode of address we have designed, and our hope that the texts and images in *Black Art and Aesthetics: Relationalities, Interiorities, Reckonings* will speak for themselves, the following philosophical and pedagogical considerations lend support to the editorial roles we have carved out. Black artists and aestheticians are revalorizing, reinventing, and reinvigorating the entire field of aesthetics today. Contemporary artistic and aesthetic practices are deeply, ineluctably, and positively marked by Black aesthetics. If Black aesthetics was once excluded from the history of modern Eurocentric aesthetics, it is now at the forefront of aesthetics. If aesthetics is critical thinking, imagining, and making in and about art, culture, design, everyday life, and nature, Black aesthetics is today the exemplar of the "critical edge," as it was already for Gayle: "Represented in this anthology is not the best critical thought on the subject of the Black Aesthetic, but critical thought that is among the best."[8]

Thus, an outsider position to Black aesthetics today is either unavailable or simply undesirable. Our strategy as editors has been to draw on philosophical resources from our transdisciplinary aesthetic training and from the many multiracial aesthetic dialogues, interactions, symposia, and experiences over several decades that we have been fortunate to be a part of. Again, we hope to contribute collaboratively to the best of our ability to the advancement of Black aesthetics. As Paul C. Taylor, one of the authors here, observes, the interdisciplinary project of Black aesthetics includes participants of all races and having a Black identity is not a prerequisite for participation in this project.[9] Similarly, artists and theorists such as Audre Lorde, Stuart Hall, Henry Louis Gates, Jr., and Linda Martín Alcoff make us hopeful about the coalitional possibilities of white critical agency in the context of Black art and aesthetics.[10]

In addition, we have been teaching Black aesthetics for a number of years, but could not find a contemporary anthology for our students. Assigning mainly single, disparate articles weakens the case for the centrality and exemplarity of Black aesthetics, and assigning multiple books risks not reflecting the copious range of Black aesthetics, as we could assign only a few of the many books written in the field just in the last dozen years. This anthology remedies these pedagogical concerns, too.

IV.

Gayle posed a challenge to Black aesthetics in 1971, which helps to clarify how we understand aesthetics for purposes of *Black Art and Aesthetics: Relationalities, Interiorities,*

Reckonings, though of course we do not imagine we can speak for the contributors here. "A critical methodology," and this anthology comprises many of them, "has no relevance" to Black communities unless it aids its members "in becoming better than they are," which is to say, becoming who they are. So, a principal question here is not merely "how beautiful is a melody, a play, a poem, or a novel, but how much more beautiful" any work of art has made the lives of Black people and communities. The transformative potential of Black art and aesthetics is not the endeavor of art and aesthetics alone, as Frederick Douglas recognized while lecturing on aesthetics during the Civil War, because it requires concrete changes in social-political reality. But this endeavor is what has driven this anthology's investigation of the life-affirming, change-making "skeleton architecture of our lives" that generates and sustains Black art and aesthetics.[11] If Sylvia Wynter is right that the legacy of the Black aesthetics and the Black Arts Movements "lay not in the answers that their theoreticians and artists gave, but in the central questions that they have posed to the large society," then we conclude with one last question, raised by Wangechi Mutu, a contributor here: "So what is this conversation really about?"[12]

Notes

1   The 2017 symposium was made possible by the generous support of almost thirty programs, departments, and offices at Hampshire College and its partners in the Five College Consortium of Western Massachusetts: Amherst College, Mt. Holyoke College, Smith College, the University of Massachusetts at Amherst, and the Five College Lecture Fund. The symposium was also co-funded by the Transdisciplinary Aesthetics Foundation and the American Society for Aesthetics. In addition, the symposium liaised with concurrent exhibitions by Kara Walker and Caitlin Cherry at the University Museum of Contemporary Art at the University of Massachusetts, Amherst; and with the annual Eric Schocket lecture by poet/theorist Fred Moten in the School of Humanities, Arts, and Cultural Studies at Hampshire College.

   To name only a few texts in the period 2010–2016: GerShun Avilez's *Radical Aesthetics and Modern Black* Nationalism (Urbana: Illinois University Press, 2016); Jeremy Matthew Glick's *The Radical Tragic: Performance, Aesthetics, and the Unfinished Haitian* Revolution (New York: NYU Press, 2016); Phillip Brian Harper's *Abstractionist Aesthetics: Artistic Form and Social Critique in African American Culture* (New York: New York University Press, 2015); Amy Ongiri's *Spectacular Blackness: The Cultural Politics of the Black Power Movement and the Search for a Black* Aesthetic (Charlottesville: University of Virginia Press, 2010); Kevin Quashie's *The Sovereignty of Quiet: Beyond Resistance in Black Culture* (New York: Routledge, 2012); Evie Shockley's *Renegade Poetics: Black Aesthetics and Formal Innovation in African American Poetry* (Iowa City: University of Iowa Press, 2011); Paul C. Taylor's *Black is Beautiful: A Philosophy of Black Aesthetics* (Malden, MA: Wiley Blackwell, 2016); and Michelle Wright's *Physics of Blackness: Beyond the Middle Passage Epistemology* (Minneapolis: University of Minnesota Press, 2015).

   There are other texts on Black aesthetics just before and after this period, though some are less explicit about embracing Black aesthetics. See, for example, Moten, *In the Break: The Aesthetics of the Black Radical Tradition* (Minneapolis: University of Minnesota Press, 2003). More recently, Moten has argued that "when you talk about the aesthetic, you've got to talk about it in its interinanimative autonomy vis-à-vis the political. Moten, in "Not In Between," in *Black and Blur* (*Consent not to be a single being*, vol. 1) (Durham, NC: Duke University Press, 2017), 19–34; 26. See also Amber Jamilla Musser, *Sensual Excess: Queer Femininity and*

Brown Jouissance (New York: New York University Press, 2018); Tina M. Campt, *A Black Gaze: Artists Changing How We See* (Cambridge: MIT Press, 2021); Samantha A. Noël, *Tropical Aesthetics of Black Modernism* (Durham: Duke University Press, 2021); Alessandra Raengo, "Blackness, Aesthetics, Liquidity," in *liquid blackness* 2 (2014). https://liquidblackness.com/liquid-blackness-journal-issue-2 (last accessed June 29, 2023); and the liquid blackness project and journal, since 2021 titled *liquid blackness: journal of aesthetics and black studies*.

Also, there are certainly examples of a Black aesthetics in previous decades, if it is understood as critical, theoretical discussions confirming the importance of Black art and culture. Hortense Spillers makes this point clearly, if indirectly, while speaking about Black culture—Hortense J. Spillers, "The Idea of Black Culture," *The New Centennial Review* 6, no. 3 (2006): 7–28. For another example, see Trey Ellis, "The New Black Aesthetic," *Callaloo* 38 (Winter 1989): 233–43. But we have in mind an additional task: aesthetic *theory*. As Lewis Gordon points out after praising the work of Hazel V. Carby, Paul Gilroy, Kobena Mercer, and others in Black cultural studies, "Missing in much of this literature . . . is an actual *theory of aesthetics*," because, we would add, cultural studies has long been largely anti-aesthetic. By aesthetics, Gordon means "the realm of the sensory and symbolic life through which human beings in effect make themselves at home with reality," which he regards as "central to what it means to live a human life." Lewis Gordon, "Black Aesthetics, Black Value," *Public Culture* 30, no. 1 (2017): 19–34; 20, 24. Cultural studies in the twenty-first century of course has substantially discarded its earlier opposition to aesthetics, as exemplified, for example, by L. H. Stallings, *Funk the Erotic: Transaesthetics and Black Sexual Cultures* (Urbana, Chicago, and Springfield: University of Illinois Press, 2015).

2   For videos of the talks at the Hampshire College Black aesthetics symposium, please see: https://transaestheticsfoundation.org/qas-black-aesthetics-hampshire-college-march-31-april-1-2017/. See also: https://sites.hampshire.edu/blackaesthetics/.

3   The symposium was organized by Professors Jae Emerling, Robin James, and Michael Kelly with the support of a Chancellor's Diversity Grant from the University of North Carolina, Charlotte. Monique Roelofs, who then was editing a special issue of *Contemporary Aesthetics* on aesthetics and race that included work on Black aesthetics (*Contemporary Aesthetics*, Special Volume 2 (2009), *Aesthetics and Race: New Philosophical Perspectives*), one of the main speakers.

4   Hortense J. Spillers, "The Idea of Black Culture," *The New Centennial Review* 6, no. 3 (2006): 7–28; 26.

5   See, for example, Simon Gikandi, *Slavery and the Culture of Taste* (Princeton: Princeton University Press, 2011). This transformation of Black aesthetics mimics a wider transformation of aesthetics today: a field once considered ideological by its critics is now a thriving transdisciplinary field with some of its former critics as prominent voices. See, for example: decolonial aesthetics (e.g., Gayatri Chakravorty Spivak, *An Aesthetic Education in the Era of Globalization* (Cambridge: Harvard University Press, 2012); and carceral aesthetics (e.g., Nicole Fleetwood, *Marking Time: Art in the Age of Mass Incarceration* (Cambridge: Harvard University Press, 2020).

6   As Quashie demonstrates persuasively in *The Sovereignty of Quiet*.

7   James T. Stewart, "The Development of the Black Revolutionary Artist," in *Black Fire: An Anthology of Afro-American Writing*, Amiri Baraka and Larry Neal, eds. (Baltimore, MD: Black Classic Press, 2007 [1968]), 3–10; 4.

8   Addison Gayle, Jr., introduction to *The Black Aesthetic* (New York: Doubleday, 1971), xv–xxiv; xxii.

9   Paul C. Taylor, "Black Reconstruction Aesthetics," *Debates in Aesthetics* 15, no. 2 (2020): 9–47; 38–39.

10 Audre Lorde grounds the possibilities of coalition on an affirmation of differences, understood intersectionally and as a source of polarities that sparks creativity. Audre Lorde, "The Master's Tools Will Never Dismantle the Master's House," in *Sister Outsider: Essays and Speeches* (Freedom, CA: The Crossing Press, 1984), 110–113; and "Age, Race, Class, and Sex: Women Redefining Difference," in *Sister Outsider*, 114–123. Stuart Hall associates a critical Black cultural politics of difference that employs immanent rather than transcendent criteria of aesthetic value—in other words, a form of Black aesthetics—with a project that builds solidarities, identifications, and common struggles, as it "works with and through differences." Hall, "New Ethnicities," in *Stuart Hall: Critical Dialogues in Cultural Studies*, ed. David Morley and Kuan-Hsing Chen (New York: Routledge, 1996), 441–449; 444. Concerned about the current prevalence of cultural policing and underscoring his own and W. E. B. Du Bois's reading beyond identitarian lines, Henry Louis Gates, Jr., in his remarks at the 2021 PEN America Literary Gala, embraces the capacities of social identities to "connect us in multiple and overlapping ways" while cautioning that these identities "are not protected but betrayed when we turn them into silos with sentries" and that cordoning them off from each other "sells short the human imagination" (Henry Louis Gates, "Henry Louis Gates, Jr. on Literary Freedom as an Essential Human Right," *New York Times*, October 12, 2021 [online]). For an analysis of whiteness and a discussion of the roles that white people can play in coalitional struggles aimed at realizing a just communal future, see Linda Martín Alcoff, *The Future of Whiteness* (Malden, MA: Polity, 2015).

11 For Audre Lorde, whose wonderful phrase we transpose to the context of Black aesthetics here, poetry engenders this architecture, as she discusses in her account of this form's vital importance, specifically in the lives of black women and to their capacities to create social change for the better. Audre Lorde, "Poetry Is Not A Luxury," in *Sister Outsider*, 36–39; 38.

12 Sylvia Wynter, "Black Aesthetics and the Black Arts Movement," in the *Encyclopedia of Aesthetics*, ed. Michael Kelly (New York: Oxford University Press, 2014), 391. Wangechi Mutu, "Wangechi Mutu in Conversation with Isaac Julien and Claudia Schmuckli," in *I Am Speaking, Are Your Listening?* (San Francisco and New York: Fine Arts Museums of San Francisco and Delmonico Books, 2021), 37–47; 45. This interview is reproduced in this anthology.

INTRODUCTION: REVALORIZING BLACK AESTHETICS

Michael Kelly & Monique Roelofs

Black art and aesthetics have had racialized histories because of anti-Black racism, yet they now have a commanding presence in the artworld, in everyday culture and society, and in academia.[1] *Black Art and Aesthetics: Relationalities, Interiorities, Reckonings* is a collective, polyphonous expression of the present state of Black art and aesthetics against the background of their histories and with an eye toward their futures.

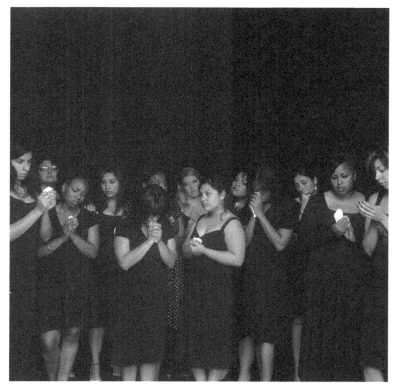

Figure I.1 Carrie Mae Weems, *Looking Forward, Looking Back, from Constructing History: A Requiem to Mark the Moment*, 2008. Archival pigment print, 60 × 50 inches (print). Copyright Carrie Mae Weems. Courtesy of the artist and Jack Shainman Gallery, New York.

I. The Idea of Black Aesthetics

While the histories of Black art and Black aesthetics are clearly intertwined, though different, the sense of those histories being racialized is arguably more discursively explicit in the history of Black aesthetics, so that is our initial focus. Black aesthetics has been racialized because anti-Black racism has had a deep history within modern Western aesthetics. For example, David Hume, one of the early aestheticians in the 18th century, believed that "There scarcely ever was a civilized nation" or any arts created by the "negro" complexion, because "negroes" are "naturally inferior to the whites." Similarly, Immanuel Kant proclaimed in the same period that the white race "contains all incentives and talents in itself"; by contrast, the "Negro race . . . acquire[s] culture, but only a culture of slaves; that is, they allow themselves to be trained."[2] Not only do people interpellated as Black allegedly lack aesthetic taste and judgment, according to these and other philosophers, they also lack the "mental capacities," such as reason, to engage in arguments against such bald-faced prejudices. As Cornel West concludes, "the very structure of modern discourse *at its inception* produced forms of . . . aesthetic and cultural ideals which require the constitution of the idea of white supremacy."[3] There might seem to be no path for Black aesthetics.

Yet, a major strategy in response to the prejudices of modern Western aesthetics has been to performatively defy them by engaging in art, taste, judgment, and reason. The history of such performativity is the history of Black art and aesthetics, although, to avoid being associated with modern aesthetics, Black aesthetics understandably has often had other names with diverse purposes and methods, such as Black studies or cultural studies. In the arts, the more familiar names have been the Harlem Renaissance, Negro Art, Negritude, Black culture, or Black Arts Movement. The spirit of this defiant, anti-aesthetic history was captured in the 1960s by Larry Neal's manifesto for the Black Arts Movement: "the Western aesthetic has run its course; it is impossible to construct anything meaningful within its decaying structures. We advocate a cultural revolution in art and ideas."[4] The aim is to avoid becoming trapped in what Frantz Fanon would call "a borrowed aesthetic."[5]

The anti-Black racism within modern Western aesthetics poses a dilemma. Anybody who engages in modern aesthetics would seem to countenance or endorse its anti-Black racism, even if they are individually self-consciously critical of it, because the racism operates at systemic conceptual levels, so long as taste and beauty are racialized. At the same time, anybody who completely disavows modern aesthetics to avoid its racism would seem to be complicitous with anti-Black racism, as such a disavowal is indiscernible from the racist ideology that Blacks are incapable of art, beauty, and aesthetics.[6] What are the options to escape this dilemma?

Start by asking: Why let anti-Black racists determine whether Black aesthetics exists or not, or what it should be? Why not refuse the refusal of "that which has been refused to you," in Fred Moten's words?[7] After all, as Moten expresses in the same dialogue with Saidiya Hartman on anti-Black racism just quoted, "anybody who thinks they can come even close to understanding how terrible the terror has been without understanding how beautiful the beauty has been against the grain of that terror, is wrong."[8] But if Black beauty is needed in some form to understand the terror of anti-Black racism that would seem to eclipse the very possibility of Black beauty, then aesthetics would appear to be imperative as a way to secure and sustain the cognitive as well as affective dimensions of such understanding and to disclose the eclipsed beauty and the denied being it implies. Without mentioning aesthetics explicitly, Hartman identifies "the collective wealth of the enslaved," such as "the capacity and knowledge and arts and tradition that crossed the water" with which the enslaved "were endowed and which would enable them to persist and endure."[9] Similarly, in Sylvia Wynter's analysis of the Black arts movement in the 1960s, "Black is Beautiful" explicitly "served as the common thread unifying the continuum of approaches to the quest for a Black aesthetic. These approaches ranged from the more political, which saw the aesthetic as a mere function of the broader struggle, to the hegemonically aesthetic, which saw the mainstream aesthetics as *the* central site of the struggle."[10] The Black lifeworld implies Black beauty implies Black aesthetics. Emphasizing continuity while respecting rupture and difference, Margo Natalie Crawford argues that what links Black aesthetics today to the Black Arts movement and, in turn, to the Harlem Renaissance — and perhaps, to a lesser extent, to the entire history of Black aesthetics — is the "push to the mixed media, abstraction, satire, and sheer experimentation."[11]

A principal way to counter the anti-Black racist narrative within aesthetics, and to negate the denial of being to Blacks that underlies it, is to revalorize Black art, beauty, and aesthetics and thus repossess Black being. In Frederick Douglass's words: "The process by which man is able to invent his own subjective consciousness into the objective form [picturing], considered in all its range, is in truth the highest attribute of man's nature. All that is really peculiar to humanity . . . proceeds from this one faculty or power."[12] And as if to demonstrate what he meant by objective form and that Blacks possessed the faculty to express it, Douglass himself became the most photographed human in the United States in the nineteenth century as well as arguably the first Black aesthetic theorist. Later, W. E. B. Du Bois makes a similar argument tying together Black art and Black being, aesthetics and ontology: "until the art of the Black folk compells [sic] recognition they will not be treated as human."[13] Continuing in this vein, Alain Locke argued in the early twentieth century, "even ordinary living has epic depth and lyric intensity" for people under social pressure and "this, their material handicap, is their spiritual advantage" that takes the form of art.[14] In the twenty-first century, Achille Mbembe also defends the importance of Black art as well as Black reason: "For communities whose history has long been one of debasement and humiliation, religious and artistic creation has often represented the final defense against the forces of dehumanization."[15] All of these writers and theorists confirm Audre Lorde's insight, and practice, that "poetry is not a luxury."[16]

Still, what is to be done about the systemic anti-Black racism within modern aesthetics? Where do figurations of "Blackness" and, more broadly, Black cultural productions have any valence not determined by anti-Black racism, given how pervasive it has been in history and even in the conceptual structure of aesthetics? Once it is possible to see, in Amanda Gorman's 2021 Presidential Inaugural words — echoing Douglass and Du Bois, as well as Maya Angelou and Toni Morrison — that "the norms and notions of what just is isn't always justice," where can Black artists and aestheticians find light "in this never ending shade" in everyday life, ontologically as well as politically?[17] What is Blackness, ontologically and experientially? Are we rather in an anticipatory era of Black post-Blackness? When is aesthetics *Black*? If, as Teju Cole poetically argues, "Turns out Black is multifarious and generative. It is capacious and dissenting," what does aesthetics have to do with not just Black everyday life but also Black futurity—"There Are Black People in The Future," as Alisha B. Wormsley's Pittsburgh billboard assures some and warns others?[18] How can Black artists and aestheticians get outside of being left outside of aesthetics and now be at home uncannily inside of aesthetics that is less, if not yet no longer, constituted by Blacks being outside? These questions, to be addressed manifestly and latently in *Black Art and Aesthetics: Relationalities, Interiorities, Reckonings*, link Black aesthetics to ontology, as the core of anti-Black racism is to deny being (humanity) to Blacks, making the task of Black aesthetics to (re)possess Black being while revalorizing Black beauty.

It is thus time to revalorize Black aesthetics, to repossess territory that Blacks were unfairly dispossessed of centuries ago, though they never relinquished it. In Wynter's words again: "The central contribution of the Black aesthetic and Black Arts Movements was . . . linked to the revalorizing turn they made to the hitherto despised African-derived tradition, and their recognition of . . . *an alternative cultural and aesthetic tradition*."[19] *Black Art and Aesthetics: Relationalities, Interiorities, Reckonings*, building on past efforts, is a contribution to such revalorization, though we want to be clear that it has been

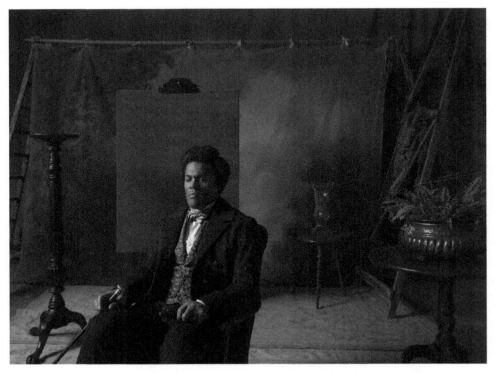

Plate 2 Isaac Julien, *J. P. Ball Studio, 1867 Douglass (Lessons of the Hour)*, 2019. Framed photograph on gloss inkjet paper mounted on aluminum. Courtesy of the artist and Victoria Miro, London/Venice.

underway as long as the devalorization has been the order of the day in the modern regime of Western aesthetics. Black aesthetics has always already existed in modernity, even though it generally went unrecognized within modern aesthetics, even though it was as invisibilized as the Blacks who created it, as Du Bois has argued: "the literary output of the American Negro has been large and creditable, although, of course, comparatively little known."[20] For example, Phillis Wheatley created poetry, but there are some reports that before she was allowed to publish it under her own name, she first had to prove before an official tribunal that included the Governor of Massachusetts that, despite being Black and allegedly lacking being because she had been enslaved, she was capable of writing poetry.[21] That meta-step, though an egregiously unjust process imposed by anti-Black racism, was also a confirmation of Black art and aesthetics, as it introduced the critical voice of a Black poet in defiance of all philosophical, political, and religious prejudices that sought to invisibilize her work. As Douglass might say, Wheatley was not only a commodity that spoke, but a commodity that wrote poetry *and* a commodity that could make a case that she could write poetry.

Douglass and Du Bois continue to be insightful and instructive on the need to revalorize aesthetics, because they developed theories of aesthetics, albeit under other names, and always while under the duress of anti-Black racism. Douglass developed his aesthetic theory over the course of four lectures delivered during the US Civil War. He believed that publicly philosophizing about pictures was a vital part of his self-representation as a human who should not be enslaved, as he once had been for eighteen years. In turn, Douglass's aesthetic theory, a theory of picture making encompassing all the arts plus other forms of speech and action, was self-consciously enacted as a vital part of his famed abolitionism.[22]

For his part, Du Bois spoke explicitly about the need for beauty in the same text where he first introduced the concept of double consciousness, that is, of Blacks knowing themselves to be human while being treated inhumanely and experiencing themselves through that lens: "What has this Beauty to do with the world? What has Beauty to do with Truth and Goodness," which he clarifies as "the facts of the world" and "the right actions of men," respectively? He confidently answers his own question, saying that Beauty, Truth, and Goodness in the "here and now" are "unseparated and inseparable."[23] Du Bois continues: "it is the bounded duty of Black America to begin this great work of the creation of Beauty, of the preservation of Beauty, of the realization of Beauty, and we must use in this work all the methods that men have used before."[24] As aesthetics is one of the methods for creating, preserving, and realizing beauty, Du Bois is revalorizing Black aesthetics. In doing so, he shares Douglass's insight that Black aestheticians, like Black artists, have a secret power to "see what ought to be by the reflection of what is, and endeavor to remove the contradiction."[25] Along with Black art, Black aesthetics challenges the facticity and historicity of anti-Black racism, its ontological foundations as well as its historical manifestations. In Du Bois's own version, what Black artists see is "what the world could be if it were truly a beautiful world," where a beautiful world is also a truly just world.[26] A critical task of Black aesthetics is to exercise and sustain that untapped power, that shaded vision, that terrorized beauty, that deferred justice. To give up on aesthetics would be to let all this beauty and justice go unrealized. This is why Douglass and Du Bois proposed, in effect, that the Black anti-aesthetic—a natural response to the anti-Black racism inscribed within aesthetics—yield to a new Black aesthetics to enable a beautiful, if future, world to emerge in defiance of, but without being overdetermined by, enslavement, racism, white supremacy, and all their historical forms: lynching, Jim Crow laws, police brutality, mass incarceration, tools of hyper-surveillance, voter suppression, and other forms of anti-Black racism.

More recently, Hortense Spillers has made a similar, indirect case for Black aesthetics, starting from the argument that Black culture, or more accurately Black diasporic culture, "is born in the penumbra of the official cultures that are historically emergent at a particular moment that we could rightly call modernity."[27]

> In a sense, if there is no black culture, or no longer black culture (because it has "succeeded"), then we need it now; and if that is true, then perhaps black culture—as the reclamation of the critical edge, as one of those vantages from which it might be spied, and no longer predicated on "race"—has yet to come.[28]

Spillers proposes that the concept of Black culture be reintroduced today after being overshadowed by premature victory laps following the Civil Rights Movement in the 1960s, which lead to Black culture being expected to be assimilable within American culture. Why Black culture again? Because Black culture, "having imagined itself as an *alternative* statement, as a *counter*statement to American culture/civilization, or Western culture/civilization, more generally speaking, identifies the cultural vocation as the space of 'contradiction, indictment, and the refusal'."[29] That is, Black culture is the voice of the negation and critique of American culture/civilization so long as it perpetuates anti-Black racism and, worse, so long as it is constituted by it. The contradiction between freedom and enslavement that Douglass and others have argued is written into the American Constitution is embodied in American culture. In this light, Black culture stands as the negation of that contradiction, just as the Black-designed National Museum of African American Culture and History stands as the negation—qua dialogic equal—of the white-stoned Washington Monument on the National Mall in Washington, DC. Black aesthetics, like Black culture, is the "reclamation of the critical edge," which Spillers articulates by linking Du Bois and the Frankfurt School of critical theory, particularly Herbert Marcuse.[30]

But critique, directed at American culture or modern aesthetics, is not the only rationale for Black culture or aesthetics, as negation in Black aesthetics is at the same time Black expression: Black is beautiful. In *The Invisible Man*, Ralph Ellison offers a version of the subtlety of negation: "And while fiction is but a form of symbolic action, a mere game of 'as if', therein lies its true function and its potential for effecting change. For at its most serious, just as is true of politics at its best, it is a thrust toward a human ideal. And it approaches that ideal by a subtle process of negating the world of things as given in favor of a complex of man-made positives."[31] In a similar spirit of constructive negation, the editor and authors of *The Black Aesthetic* anthology did not only smash the idols of Western aesthetics because of their anti-Black racism, they also espoused a new set of rules "by which Black literature and art is to be judged and evaluated," as Du Bois had proposed earlier in his "Criteria of Negro Art."[32] In addition, Black art has to engage in what Du Bois provocatively called "propaganda," meaning that Black artists have to seize the ideological power of art to address and redress concerns of the Black lifeworld, just as whites have been using art for their own concerns and lifeworld.[33] Art and aesthetics are tools of empowerment, which is precisely why whites have tried to take them away from Blacks since modern art and aesthetics began. And this is why Black art and aesthetics need to be revalorized and repossessed.

Thus, the forerunners to the present anthology enacted the power of Black art and aesthetics, and did so without worrying about recognition from the relevant institutions of their times. The kind of power at stake here was articulated by James Baldwin, speaking about the relationship between the rise of Black language and the conditions from which it arises: "A language comes into existence by means of brutal necessity," such as "the horrors of the American Negro's life," "and the rules of the language are dictated by what the language must convey."[34] The new Black aesthetics, like any new Black language, must therefore have enough plasticity regarding its rules, forms, and contents to convey

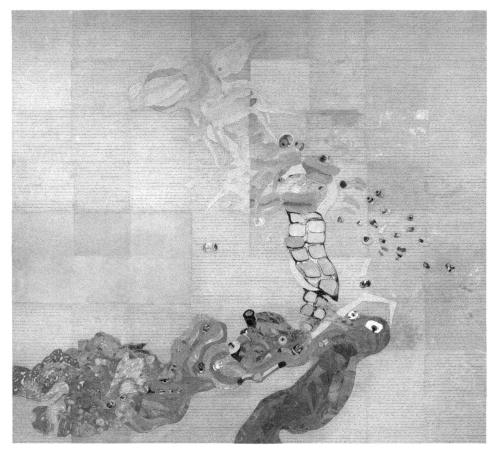

Plate 3 Ellen Gallagher, *Dew Breaker*, 2015. Copyright Ellen Gallagher. Courtesy of the artist and Hauser & Wirth. Photo: Ernst Moritz.

what must be conveyed while refusing to be restricted by anti-Black racism. Developing the language analogy further, Baldwin continues: "People evolve a language in order to describe and thus control their circumstances, or in order not to be submerged by a reality that they cannot articulate. (And, if they cannot articulate it, they are submerged.)"[35] Revalorized Black aesthetics celebrates and sustains the genealogy and promise of Black art, language, and culture.

II. Residual Skepticism About Black Aesthetics

Some critics of Black aesthetics, such as Afropessimists, may reject the optimism of revalorized Black aesthetics because it implies redemption, but redemption, according to Frank Wilderson III, is "the narrative inheritance of humans. There is no denouement to social death."[36] That is, because Blacks are not considered human in the mainstream Western narrative of modernity, there could be critique in Black aesthetics but without any expectation of redemption: "the violence that saturates Black life isn't threatened with elimination just because it is exposed."[37] Clearly, the challenge to consider Blacks human is monumental, as it first requires a redefinition of what it means to be human, if the extant conception of a human is predicated on the denial of humanity to Blacks.[38] So, in effect, the "human" world as we know it would first have to end: "Anti-Black violence is a paradigm of oppression for which there is no coherent form of redress, other than Frantz Fanon's 'the end of the world'."[39] Yet, even Wilderson acknowledges that anti-Black racism and the world built on its shoulders was constructed "by the violence and imagination of other sentient beings," so it can be destroyed, deconstructed, displaced.[40] He warns, however, that the price of such destruction is exorbitantly high, as "the first step toward the destruction is to assume one's position (*assume, not celebrate or disavow*), and then burn the ship or the plantation, in its past and present incarnations, from the inside out."[41] This abolitionist position is not unlike what the editor and authors of the 1971 *The Black Aesthetic* anthology seemed to advocate in their critique of aesthetics (and of American culture and society more generally), or that Amiri Baraka imagined in his more impassioned poems in the 1960s, when he envisioned that the world itself would be a Black poem, a poem spoken by "All Black People."[42]

However, as Spillers argues, the Afropessimist position risks being conservative unless it is taken as the point of departure rather than as the point of arrival for Black culture or, here, Black art and aesthetics.[43] Moreover, the cautionary tale of Afropessimism— "Afropessimism is not an ensemble of theoretical interventions that *leads* the struggle for Black liberation"[44]—is, we believe, arguably always already present in Black aesthetics because, since at least Douglass, aesthetics has been characterized as the "endeavor" to remove contradictions (e.g., between freedom and enslavement) rather than as the claim to have removed them already, if ever. In Douglass's case, he recognized theoretically as well as experientially that the Emancipation Proclamation and the 13–15th Amendments were only the departure points of Black freedom. At the same time, he also understood the need to redefine what it means to be human: A human "does not take things as he finds them, but goes to work to improve them. Tried by this text, too, the negro is a man."[45] This definition of a human complements Black aesthetics because Douglass argues that by the cultivation of the faculty of picture making, a human possesses "the marvelous power of enlarging the margin and extending the boundaries" of their existence.[46] Black art and aesthetics are ways to be human ontologically as they are ways to improve existence historically, albeit always with a recognition of the ongoing endeavor they entail.

The ontological point of contention in the exchange with Afropessimism, which has implications for the viability of revalorized Black aesthetics, seems to be the following. While to be an enslaved person is to be considered not only a nonhuman but also a nonbeing, as there is no other mode of being available to the enslaved, is there a state of Black being prior to or sustainable in the wake of enslavement?[47] That is, is this lack an irredeemable ontological condition, a mode of social death whose only sanctuary is death, as Wilderson argues?[48] Or is Black being independent of enslavement enough that enslavement is a state of "loss" of Black being rather than a state of "absence" of Black being that is irredeemable?[49] These are clearly difficult questions. But Black aesthetics provides a path to answer them. For example, according to Hartman, the "terror and violence" inflicted on blacks during chattel enslavement was necessary "to convert persons into commodities and units of currency"; that is, enslavers had to extract value from Blacks as humans and thus negate their being to enslave them (before they could then extract surplus value from them as unpaid laborers qua commodities within capitalism).[50] While Hartman adds that such extraction and negation have "defined blackness" ever since, seemingly agreeing with the Afropessimists, she also acknowledges, as we saw earlier, that enslaved persons retained human capacities that enabled them to "persist and endure" despite their commodity status.[51] Insofar as the enslaved retained these capacities, they retained their being, they remained human. When they exercised these capacities, they were practicing aesthetics and enacting their humanity—as Douglass, Du Bois, Lorde, Wynter, and others argue.

It is impossible to practice Black aesthetics without Black being, so, if we can point to Black aesthetics, we are pointing at the same time to Black being.[52] This is what enabled Douglass, Du Bois, Lorde, Spillers, and many others to revalorize Black aesthetics, knowing that to do so would also be to repossess Black being, cutting to the core of anti-Black racism, as it denied aesthetics to enslaved persons because it denied being to them. One major implication of these points for Black art and aesthetics is that they are not generated by Black *non*being, as if they were compensatory silver linings in the otherwise cruel existence of enslavement and its wake today, in the sense, say, people argue that enslavement generated the blues that generated jazz and other forms of Black music.[53] According to Kevin Quashie, it is critical in Black aesthetics to be "cautious about the declarative assertion of nonbeing and its slippery poetics."[54] Rather, Black being generated Black aesthetics, even under enslavement. Black aesthetics *is* Black being. So, Black aesthetics is relatively independent of enslavement. In Moten's words: "Black art neither sutures nor is sutured to trauma."[55] Thus, remembering Claudia Rankine's point that "Black 'hope' is different from American optimism," Black aesthetics is thus arguably beyond or otherwise outside the binary of optimism and pessimism.[56]

As editors, we thus agree that it is important to revalorize Black aesthetics, despite the above skepticism and the lingering fact that modern Western aesthetics has been and may remain racist, so that we can appreciate and sustain the long-standing as well as current forms of Black art and aesthetics. Only by critiquing and transforming aesthetics can we apprehend and sustain the counter-phenomena of Black art and aesthetics and their contemporary heirs, including what Denise Ferreira da Silva calls "blackness's creative capacity."[57] In doing so, it is important to reiterate that Black art and aesthetics were always already present during their absence from the histories of modern Western art and aesthetics. As Locke argues in the case of art, the Western world did not know or acknowledge that Africans had been capable artists with their "own art techniques and traditions" long before chattel enslavement separated "the Negro artist" from their art.[58] To cite a recent discussion within aesthetics, Paul C. Taylor offers in *Black is Beautiful: A Philosophy of Black Aesthetics* "a reconstructive survey of the black aesthetic tradition[s] in the vocabularies of largely English-language philosophy" as a way of transforming aesthetics, not just as a strategy for including Black aesthetics within that tradition.[59] In effect, he calls that tradition to task for failing to recognize Black aesthetics and for not understanding and acknowledging that its failure has been constitutive of its own history — i.e., contemporary Western aesthetics.[60] When that understanding and acknowledgement happen, aesthetics will no longer be the same epistemically and ontologically in its conditions, conceptual structure, aspirations, and affects. No longer sidelined, Black aesthetics will take center stage once it is revalorized. Just as Spillers argues that Black culture *is* culture, Black aesthetics *is* aesthetics.[61] This marks a major transformation of aesthetics, even if the transformation is admittedly still a work in progress, even a dream.[62] For the time being, *Black Art and Aesthetics: Relationalities, Interiorities, Reckonings* can at least be a stand-in for the transformation that, in Spillers's words again, "has yet to come."

An insistence on what is to come similarly characterizes Mbembe's reflections on aesthetics in engagement with current geopolitical, technological, ecological, and financial conditions.[63] Analogously marking the end of the hegemony of Eurocentric, anti-African, and anti-indigenous aesthetics and sketching a transformation that is in process and partially yet to occur, he argues that "Africa is firmly writing itself within a new and decentered but global history of the arts."[64] He regards Africa as a "geoaesthetic category" and offers Afropolitanism as an aesthetic and cultural sensibility that comprises "a migrant and circulatory form of modernity . . . at the intersections of multiple encounters with multiple elsewheres."[65] Given the resonance of African and Afrodiasporic art—produced significantly but not exclusively by Black artists—with "*the digital spirit of our times,*" he predicts that "the art of the twenty-first century will be Afropolitan."[66] He looks to art as a generator of new, radically democratic imaginaries of life, associating the at once ongoing and historical "project of the Africa to come" with the "project for a full human life and for the future world."[67] In Mbembe's vision, African people are actors and keepers of a history of the world outside Africa as they enact an Afropolitan aesthetics enmeshed in a plurality of mutually imbricated worlds. In short, Afropolitan aesthetics for Mbembe is aesthetics.[68] The worlds it carries and projects encompass the planet. In his approach, varieties of Black art and aesthetics undergo a revalorizing reconceptualization.

To be clear, the goal of the revalorization of Black aesthetics is not merely that aesthetics be inclusive of Black aestheticians, although, as we have seen, modern Western aesthetics

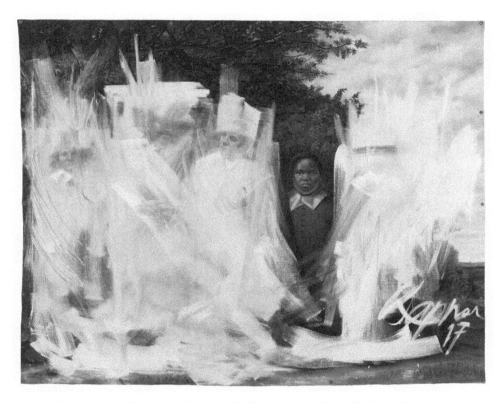

Plate 4 Titus Kaphar, *Shifting the Gaze*, 2017. Oil on canvas 83 × 103 1/4 in. Brooklyn Museum, William K. Jacobs Jr., Fund, 2017.34. Copyright Titus Kaphar.

was constituted in part by its exclusion of Black artists, writers, and aestheticians— just as Morrison argues that U.S. literature has been constituted over the same historical period by its exclusion and marginalization of Black writers and its distancing figuration of blackness within the white American imaginary.[69] Neither aesthetics nor literature is necessarily transformed merely by including Blacks today, because the rhetoric of inclusion perpetuates languages of property and transparently legible differences that underwrite both enslavement and the exclusion of Blacks from culture, art, and aesthetics. That is, the languages of exclusion and inclusion are both based on a false presumption of white people's proprietary rights and semiotic control over aesthetics, much like their self-proclaimed property rights and representational/symbolic power over the enslaved, as if white aestheticians should decide who is and is not to be included in or excluded from aesthetics, the way they decided whether Wheatley was "really" a poet.[70] Furthermore, inclusion in its own right, as is widely recognized, does not revise the *terms* of participation, risking, as Lorde might put it, our "merely settling for a shift of characters in the same weary drama."[71] In this light, the separatist Black aesthetics that Neal and Addison Gayle proposed in the 1960s, promoting Black beauty as an aesthetic analog of Black power, could be understood as a strategy to escape the exclusion/inclusion binary, that is, as a strategy to ensure that Black aesthetics is free from the penumbras cast by anti-Black racist aesthetics and, more generally, to shift attention to the normative, experiential, social, and racial terms on which Black aesthetics is lived and being created.[72] This kind of strategy liberates Black aesthetics from the dilemma posed at the start of this introduction. It complements, even opens up the possibility of, other strategies in Black aesthetics comprising *Black Art and Aesthetics: Relationalities, Interiorities, Reckonings*.

III. Relationalities, Interiorities, Reckonings

Returning to the challenging summative question of this anthology raised earlier—Can Black artists and aestheticians get outside of being left outside of aesthetics and now be at home inside of aesthetics that is less, if not yet no longer, constituted by Blacks being outside?—it is clear there are many ways to answer it, because the genealogies of contemporary iterations of Black aesthetics are geographically, politically, aesthetically, and metaphysically varied, complex, competing, and intersecting. Accordingly, this anthology is polyvocal. While it assumes "resistance" to anti-Black racism, because anti-Black racism and resistance to it go hand in hand, it also recognizes that resistance takes many forms and that it is not the only way to revalorize Black aesthetics and repossess Black being. For example, Quashie's aesthetic-ontological concept of "aliveness" articulates a conception of Black being independent of resistance, which is at the same time compatible with resistance at an ontological rather than political level: "every black text rests on a quiet premise of black humanity—that the text and its aesthetics *assume* being."[73] His earlier book, *The Sovereignty of Quiet,* makes a persuasive case for "quietude" as a major aesthetic concept. So, resistance to resistance yields a positive in Black aesthetics: not only a recognition of the lived experience of anti-Black racism, but the need to undercut it by any means necessary using, among other strategies, the resources of aesthetics. The loosening of the expectation of resistance, in other words, reveals that Black art and culture enact both the vibrant creativity and critical capacities found in relationality and interiority. This example explains how the concepts of interiority and relationality and their embodiments have come to signify two complementary, nonexclusive aesthetic strategies that indirectly contribute to resistance.

To continue with the idea of ontological resistance, the "relationality" (or sociality, community) created against the grain of enslavement is at the same time a mode of being, as it marks a refusal to be determined by all the insidious modes of racism pervasive in everyday Black lives.[74] Taylor opens his book, *Black is Beautiful: A Philosophy of Black Aesthetics*, by discussing an account of enslaved Africans who fashioned their hair with chards of glass while on an enslaver's ship. Upon the ship's arrival in the Americas, the enslaver asked the captain what he had done to the enslaved people's hair, and the captain said, defensively but revealingly, they did it to themselves—and the "it" is relationality implying Black art and aesthetics qua Black being.[75] In a recent art exhibition and catalog, *Collages*, Lorna Simpson continues to showcase the aesthetic importance of the relationality of Black hair by including "A Selection of Phrases Culled the Advertising that Originally Accompanied Many of the Images that Appear with the Collages."[76] The

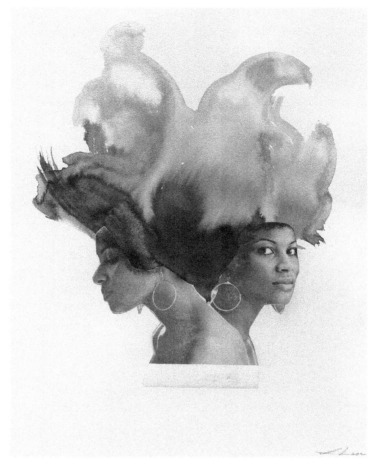

Plate 5 Lorna Simpson, *Touching*, 2012. Collage and ink on paper, 11 3/16 × 8 11/16. Framed: 12 5/8 × 10 1/8 × 1 1/2 in. Copyright Lorna Simpson. Courtesy of the artist and Hauser & Wirth.

selection begins with "Put on your Afro Pony-Tail and swish those superflies away," reminds us in the middle that "A beautiful head of hair is never an accident," and ends with "Reveal the beauty that you conceal."[77]

A few more examples of interiority and relationality would also be helpful here, starting with Alice Walker's writing, as she has been an enduring inspiration for Black art and aesthetics. She venerated the creative capabilities of her mother, who, as seen through the daughter's eyes, immersed her children in a world of stories and also shared the flowers she grew in her garden with her neighbors. Her aesthetic capabilities and practices sustained self-other relations in a manner that supported Black women's self-preservation and communal flourishing, all while serving as a mainstay of resistance against racism.[78] The soul of these relations is interiority, a source of strength delimiting the reach of anti-Black racism. Similarly, Angela Y. Davis (whose work is included here) uncovers the relational affiliations across boundaries of race, class, and gender, and sexuality engendered by the work of women blues singers, such as Gertrude "Ma" Rainey, Bessie Smith, and Billie Holiday, who embody critical, feminist forms of aesthetic consciousness— interiority—that are communicable and relatable across cultural divides.[79] In both Walker's and Davis's examples, one an artist and the other a philosopher, resistance is taken as a given, a silent partner with far-reaching creative echoes. The question is how best to be and to relate, not only to resist. And this illustrates, again, how the concepts of relationality and interiority emerged from the 2017 symposium (see preface above) as open-ended, nonbinary sources of resistance and resistance to resistance, and comprise pivotal points of Black aesthetics.[80]

The powers of interiority and relationality are also exemplified in Lorde's writings, as she offers philosophical insights into how freedom emerges from reordered types of social relationality, mutual interdependencies, and affirmations of feelings that effect alterations in the actual conditions of existence marking the lives of Black women.[81] Lorde understands poetry as a potentially nonreactive form that can sustain the confidence in resistance at moments when other forms of resistance run into obstacles.[82] To clarify, she believes it is incumbent on us to construe and apprehend difference as a font of polarities that foster creativity rather than as a mere deviation from a received white masculinist norm—heterosexualist, ageist, and middle class.[83] In a move that is critical for Black aesthetics, she delineates an important role for poetry in this difference-affirming process of producing freedom:

> We can train ourselves to respect our feelings and to transpose them into a language so they can be shared. And where that language does not yet exist, it is our poetry which helps to fashion it. Poetry is not only dream and vision; it is the skeleton architecture of our lives. It lays the foundations for a future of change, a bridge across our fears of what has never been before.[84]

Relationality, Lorde shows, is freed up when relations enacting trajectories of interiority and self-determination can undermine racism without resisting it directly. Here, too, "forever creation" as change is a key (see preface above). The present anthology offers many other examples of poetry—by Aracelis Girmay, Benjamin Krusling, Claudia Rankine, Evie Shockley, and Simone White—indebted, if only indirectly, to Lorde, where revalorized Black aesthetics is central in reimagining, reexperiencing, and rearticulating Black relationalities, interiorities, and reckonings.[85]

Complementing relationality, "interiority," in one prominent line of thought, is the home of the self, person, and subjectivity relatively free from racism without any naïveté about its pervasiveness. Interiority is repossessed as part of the repossession of Black being after they were both denied as even possibilities by anti-Black racism.[86] If interiority is a sanctuary, it is not a solipsistic trap. That is, interiority as we understand it does not exemplify what Christopher Freeburg calls "epistemic estrangement," namely, a *separation* between the self and any other, which he thinks is positive and even "a crucial part of the black aesthetics' philosophical force."[87] By contrast to estrangement, we understand "interiority" as a way both to re-establish relations between self and other and between Black subjects and potentially collective Black politics, albeit without assuming these relations are inherent or given.[88] Quashie articulates this understanding of interiority through his concept of "quietude": Quiet is "a metaphor for the full range of one's inner life—one's desires, ambitions, hungers, vulnerabilities, fears. The inner life is not apolitical nor without social value, but neither is it determined entirely by publicness."[89] With such interiority, Black aesthetics is (re)gained.

Another line of reflection on interiority complicates the link with subjectivity just described, on account of the racializing production of subjectivity in Western philosophy and under coloniality. According to Ferreira da Silva, reason in its capacity of *"universal poesis"* has endowed white masculinity with a sovereignty and interiority that it withholds from the white subject's racialized other, who is produced as an "affectable thing."[90] In the sculptures, and especially the vessels, of Simone Leigh, Amber Jamilla Musser finds an Afro-fabulist performance of objecthood that creates opaque interiors and that, through its address to corporality and the senses rather than to recognition- and desire-based visual registers, enacts a nonuniversal onto-epistemology of race.[91] This performance engages aspects of race that fall outside of regimes of discipline, in a mode of personification, and without "presuming that we know precisely what race itself means," thus engaging in a practice of myth making that is also a form of feminist theorizing.[92] Interiority, here, is a matter of material, affective, and sensory circulations that sidesteps

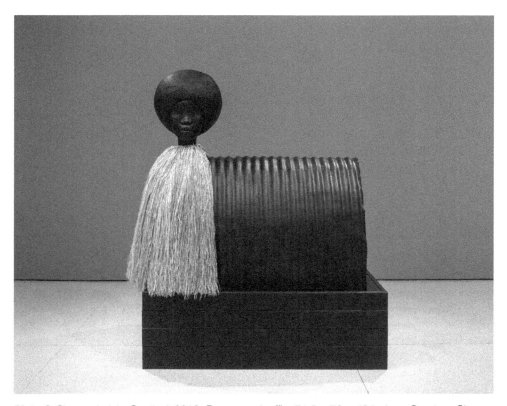

Plate 6 Simone Leigh, *Sentinel*, 2019. Bronze and raffia, 71.5 × 72 × 42 inches. Courtesy Simone Leigh and Matthew Marks Gallery.

certain, though we would argue not necessarily all, logics of subjectivity. Like the approach to interiority that foregrounds the movements of subjectivity, however, this performative focus, likewise, ties interiority to aesthetics and relationality.[93]

The bonds between the aesthetics, interiority, and relationality are also visible in Harney and Moten's notion of the uncanny, "prophetic organization" of the undercommons.[94] They explore an aesthetic sociality in the undercommons where poetry and music mediate interiority as (common) feeling. In their gorgeous description, this is "a way of feeling through others, a feel for feeling others feeling you. This is modernity's insurgent feel, its inherited caress, its skin talk, tongue touch, breath speech, hand laugh."[95] This feel and this feeling "(for) each other" withstand the denial of "sentiment, history and home" in the confinement of "the ship, the boxcar, the prison, the hostel."[96] Aesthetics, seen here as a medium of interiority and relationality, unfolds at a distance from the politics of the nation-state and the home conceived of on a model of possession, a site of settlement.[97] Conceptually, current artistic and theoretical figurations of relationality, interiority, and aesthetic mediation thus shape the ground for a renewed understanding of Black aesthetics.

At the same time, while we agree with Stephen Best that artists should be free from constraining and melancholic conceptions of Blackness as "authenticity, tradition, and legitimacy," we do not subscribe to his "aesthetics of the intransmissible" based on the idea that a work of art is inherently ineffable, even unintelligible. Such aesthetics risks eliminating the possibility of establishing any relations between the self and other, or subject and world.[98] Here, the price for revalorizing Black aesthetics may be unnecessarily high, as it risks severing connections between interiority and relationality. Best seems willing to incur this price by arguing that "whatever blackness or black culture is, it cannot be indexed to a 'we'—or if it is, that 'we' can only be structured by and given in its own negation and refusal," for in the archives of enslavement and of Black history generally, "we discover not who we are but how 'we' are not."[99] He thus seems to turn the negative dialectic integral to Black aesthetics against itself, potentially forfeiting its future in order to sever its melancholic ties to an irretrievable yet inescapable past of enslavement. By contrast, the sense of negation and contradiction in Black aesthetics as far back as Douglass are meant to capture the negative dialectic Best has in mind without short-circuiting Black aesthetics in the process.

Following Douglass, interiority is a constellation of "thought pictures" awaiting objective expression through the mediation of relationality. That is, interiority is linked to the possibility and conditions of its expression in two senses. Interiority serves as a necessary sanctuary so long as the relations comprising the external world are at all shaped by anti-Black racism. But interiority also remains oriented to the very world in which it has been *dis*oriented because of anti-Black racism, making it "multiply oriented," in the words of Daphe Lamothe (a contributor here).[100] Interiority—understood here as the self, subject, person—makes its sanctuary a site or source of creativity, insisting on having the freedom to express its creativity through Black art and aesthetics. Thus, Black interiority seeks Black relationality, and Black relationality presupposes Black interiority. This entanglement takes a form that manifests how both have been denied or constrained by anti-Black racism while also reflecting an ontological intertwinement of interiority and relationality that exceeds racist reductions.

And why turn to art when faced with such denials or constraints? To answer, we can point to the account of the emancipatory dimension of art offered by Fumi Okiji (a contributor here): "Art has a crucial role to play as a sanctioned, cordoned-off site where people are able to fulfill those impulses that have been all but expelled from other areas of life."[101] Langston Hughes similarly understood the power of art: "We younger Negro artists who create now intend to express our individual dark-skinned selves without fear or shame."[102]

In turn, relationality and interiority combined enact a demand for a "reckoning" about anti-Black racism, which Black Lives Matter and other groups have made manifest in the streets and other venues all over the world. Aesthetics is part of this reckoning, not only in demanding it but in contributing to it, because the reflectively critical dimensions of everyday life and art embodied in interiority and relationality are vital to actualizing justice. In Douglass's words, "As to the moral and social influence of pictures, it would be hardly extravagant to say of it, what Moore has said of ballads, give me the making of a nation's ballads and I care not who has the making of its laws."[103] While art and aesthetics alone cannot create justice, and nobody argues they can, justice is not possible without art and aesthetics—because they enact and sustain visions of justice and freedom yet to be realized in society.

"Relationalities, Interiorities, and Reckonings" is thus the subtitle of this anthology, representing the many trajectories of Black aesthetics. The overall aim here is to revalorize

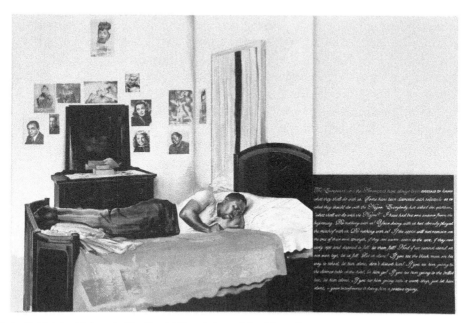

Plate 7 Meleko Mokgosi, *The Social Revolution of Our Time Cannot Take Its Poetry from the Past but Only from the Poetry of the Future*, 8, 2019, 2 panels. Oil on canvas, permanent gold marker on canvas, 98 × 145 3/8 × 3 inches (framed). Copyright Meleko Mokgosi. Courtesy of the artist and Jack Shainman Gallery, New York.

Black art and aesthetics. If this seems impossible, then we turn to Baldwin again: "in our time, as in every time, the impossible is the least that one can demand—and one is, after all, emboldened by the spectacle of . . . American Negro history . . ., for it testifies to nothing less than the perpetual achievement of the impossible."[104]

IV. Summaries of Texts

To capture the texture of the conceptual lineages threading through the essays and artworks, along with an array of standpoints within and about aesthetics, we have organized the contributions in the anthology along five intersecting axes or groupings:

    I.   Blackness as Aesthetic Strategy
    II.   Black Art Spaces
    III. Making Histories, Creating Worlds
    IV. Groundings, Transpositions, Breaks
    V.   Callings

Collectively, the essays and artworks revalorize aesthetics as critical imagining, making, and thinking in and about art, culture, nature, design, and everyday life as expressions and invocations of Black life experiences in all their political, ethical, social, and ontological complexity. Complexity is a central concept here, pointing to the complexity of Blackness and the complexity of aesthetics needed to articulate and reflect it. For this reason, we have included a transdisciplinary array of contributions by philosophers, literary theorists, cultural theorists, art historians, poets, musicians, painters, and others. While most authors and artists are African-American, some are African. Some are queer, some straight, some nonbinary. Some have a long history with aesthetics, some are new to the field. Some are academics, some not. And the complexity multiplies further as soon as these groupings intersect and bear new fruit.

Underscoring the complexity, the anthology comprises works by a number of artists. Five poets—Girmay, Krusling, Rankine, Shockley, and White—are offering poems that may intersect indirectly with other chapters (e.g., thematizing connections between naming, presence, and bodies; the relation between literary and visual color to think about sociality in racialized society; the space and time of interpretation and pain as compared to those of other kinds of action). Five visual artists—Theaster Gates, Meleko Mokgosi, Wangechi Mutu, Nell Painter, and Kara Walker—either present images of their work, explore its aesthetics, participate in an interviews, or pursue different combinations of these options. The social-practice artist Gates engages in self-reflection about the political-economic risks of conserving and redeploying John Johnson's four-million image library as part of a Black Image Corporation in Chicago. Mokgosi immerses himself in the chemistry of pigments to explore how best, from the perspective of a Botswanian painter now living in the US, to represent a Black allegorical subject without an overdetermining racist sense of Blackness hampering its signification. Mutu rewrites the history of art embodied in museums by engaging in dialogues with historical artworks and museums, while helping to rewrite the contemporary history of African art. Just as Black art is a way of "writing" Black history for Painter, herself a historian as well as a painter, Black aesthetics is an integral part of the creation of history. Architect and architectural theorist Mabel O. Wilson documents how buildings, exhibitions, and archives institute racial distinctions between "black and other bodies and white ones," and demonstrates the power of modern architecture to create whiteness "by design." Walker's images re-envision concepts and meanings embodied in a colonialist public monument and the languages informing reflection on history.

Three musicians—Vijay Iyer, George E. Lewis, Fumi Okiji—write about aesthetic issues raised within the larger context of the kinds of improvisatory music they perform. Iyer proposes that we listen to Black performance as a site of Black speculative musicalities or, in other words, forms of relationality that engender new possibilities for "Black life and Black subjectivities" as well as future ways "of being human together." Lewis associates the field of new music with an intercultural, impure, historically contingent identity and highlights how Afrodiasporic contemporary classical composition is a global practice stretching across the Americas, Europe, Asia, and Africa. Drawing on composer/theorist Olly Wilson and art historian Robert L. Douglas, among others, Lewis cites a number of distinctive characteristics marking this worldwide Afrodiasporic aesthetics, such as, notably, heterogeneity and multidominance, and shows how "both black lives and black liveness matter in new music." Okiji distinguishes the concept of "aesthetic form" from "musical form" in the music of Ornette Coleman and others against the background of Theodor Adorno's critique of jazz. As it turns, out, the music she discusses embodies what Adorno expects from modern music, not only more than he ever imagines but perhaps more than the music he preferred in contrast to jazz.

Theorists and historians, some of whom are primarily artists, analyze particular art works while enacting different aesthetic strategies within Black aesthetics, making it happily nigh impossible to separate aesthetic theory and practice. We already discussed Quashie's work on aliveness as a poetics of being. To introduce other theory/practice examples, GerShun Avilez favors "fragmentation" over coherence in Danez Smith's poetry capturing the vulnerability of the Black queer experience. Also addressing vulnerability, Deborah Goffe, a dancer, reflects on auto-ethnographic strategies in contemporary dance used simultaneously for personal stories, inherited legacies, and reclamation of relational curatorial frameworks. Thomas F. DeFrantz, also a dancer, examines why Black social dance replenishes with an inevitable, dissident inevitability. Shifting back to poetry, Jeremy Matthew Glick explains the concept of "immersive particularity" and why it is especially important in Black aesthetics. Paul C. Taylor transposes core Afropessimist ideas into a Deweyan vocabulary of phenomenological reflection on experience that affirms the importance of ethical and aesthetic responsibility yet calls into question the usefulness of the term pessimism. James Haille, III analyzes the difficulty that Black artists face while working within the constraints of an artworld that seems open to Black artists but has yet to figure out how to understand and appreciate their work. In a reading of what she describes as the post-soul aesthetic of the memoir *Ordinary Light* by author Tracy K. Smith, Daphne Lamothe understands Black life-writing, as exemplified by Smith, as a form of aesthetic self-fashioning, yielding nuanced and open-ended understandings of Black womanhood at the turn of a new millennium. Focused on the everyday, and viewing Blackness "under an 'ordinary light,'" this process of imaginative exploration, according to Lamothe, renders Blackness "more opaque and less transparent, less easily digested and more layered and multi-valenced." Moving to theater, Mickaella Perina presents Aimé Césaire's plays as a medium though which to engage critically with the world and advance social justice using an assemblage of the aesthetics of resistance, difference, and relationality. Sarah Elizabeth Lewis analyzes contemporary art in the age of stand-your-ground laws, which serve as cruel realities in the everyday lives of Blacks harassed by other citizens as well as by the police and highlights the revisioning of such groundings of subjectivity in the aesthetics of contemporary Black art, including Mark Bradford, Amy Sherald, Hank Willis Thomas, and Kehinde Wiley. Angela Y. Davis introduces the notion of "soft aesthetics," in contrast to more politically explicit art, as a more effective strategy for raising people's consciousness about social injustice, whether apartheid, mass incarceration, or other forms of anti-Black racism.

VI. Conclusion

Today, Black writers, artists, theorists, and everyday people are developing aesthetics in ways that are less separatist than they were in 1971, when *The Black Aesthetic* anthology appeared, which means that, while the contributors here are as critical of aesthetics as their predecessors were, they are less inclined to disavow the field. Forgiving or forgetting aesthetics for being racist is not an option, but disavowing aesthetics is also not an option, we believe, and the contributors in *Black Art and Aesthetics: Relationalities, Interiorities, Reckonings* share some version of this belief. There will be Black aesthetics in the future.

Notes

1   The authors in the current anthology were given a choice to use 'Black' or 'black' in their respective chapters. The preference is split roughly evenly.

2   David Hume, "Of National Characters" (1753), in David Hume, *Selected Essays*, ed. Stephen Copley and Andrew Edgar (Oxford: Oxford University Press, 1998), 113–25, note 120, p. 360; Immanuel Kant, *Lectures on Anthropology*, ed. Allen W. Wood and Robert B. Louden, trans. Robert B. Louden (Cambridge: Cambridge University Press, 2007), 320–1; Akademie Ausgabe of Kant's Gesammelte Schriften, AA 25:1187). Immanuel Kant proclaims, "The Negroes of Africa have by nature no feeling that rises above the trifling. . . . So fundamental is the difference between these two races [whites and Blacks] of man, and it appears to be as great in regard to mental capacities [e.g., judgment] as in color." Immanuel Kant, "Of National Characteristics," in *Observations on the Feeling of the Beautiful and Sublime*, trans. John T. Goldthwait (Berkeley: University of California Press, 1960 [1764]), 110–11.

At the same time that early modern aestheticians were racist, aesthetic reasoning emerged as a complement to scientific reasoning and, according to Nell Painter (a contributor here), played a key role in the development of race theory in the eighteenth century by introducing "aesthetic judgments into [race] classification." For example, J. F. Blumenbach, who first developed the term "Caucasian," still in use today to categorize white people, interjected "aesthetic judgments into [race] classification" by arguing that whites were superior because of their beauty. Nell Irvin Painter, *The History of White People* (New York: W. W. Norton, 2010), 79.

3 Cornel West, "A Genealogy of Modern Racism," in *Race Critical Theories: Text and Context*, ed. Philomenna Essed and David Theo Goldberg (Malden, MA: Blackwell, 2002), 90. Lewis Gordon expresses a similar worry, but without drawing the same conclusion: "A problem with constructing black aesthetics is whether *aesthetics* has been so colonized that its production would be a form of colonizing instead of decolonizing practice." Lewis Gordon, "Black Aesthetics, Black Value," *Public Culture* 30, no. 1 (2017): 19–34, 9, 24.

4 Larry Neal, "The Black Arts Movement," in *The Black Aesthetic*, ed. Addison Gayle, Jr. (New York: Doubleday, 1971), 257–74; 258. To achieve the goal of creating art that speaks directly to the needs and aspirations of Black America, he advocated that Black artists develop "a separate symbolism, mythology, critique, and iconology." More recently, Amy Ongiri has argued that the Black Arts Movement in the 1960s "linked the articulation of the radical political ethos of Black Power to a radically transformative culture of oppositional creativity," linking black experiences with black aesthetics, overthrowing existing cultural norms and creating new ones. *Spectacular Blackness: The Cultural Politics of the Black Power Movement and the Search for a Black Aesthetic* (Charlottesville: University of Virginia Press, 2010), 18, 52, 89, 115.

5 Frantz Fanon, *The Wretched of the Earth*, trans. Richard Philcox (New York: Grove, 2004).

6 Simon Gikandi develops a two-part strategy for understanding Black aesthetics. He first describes the "nonidentical twins" of "slavery and the culture of taste" or aesthetics, as if they were inseparable. *Slavery and the Culture of Taste* (Princeton: Princeton University Press, 2014), xii. Then, Gikandi makes a powerful case for the critical relevance of aesthetics today: "the site in which the Black body was imprisoned" was also "the conduit for its liberation," creating a "counterculture" of taste (13).

7 Moten—Duke Lecture, "The Black Outdoors." See also Stefano Harney and Fred Moten, *The Undercommons: Fugitive Planning and Black Study* (New York: Minor Compositions, 2013), 96.

8 Moten, Duke Lecture, "The Black Outdoors." In Hartman's words: "The beauty of this *black thing* borne of terror." "Dead Book Remains," in Okwui Enwezor, *Grief and Grievance: Art and Mourning in America* (New York: Phaidon and New Museum, 2022), 117–21; 119.

9 Hartman, "Dead Book Remains," in *Grief and Grievance*, 119.

10 Sylvia Wynter, "Black Aesthetics and the Black Arts Movement," in the *Encyclopedia of Aesthetics*, ed. Michael Kelly (New York: Oxford University Press, 2014), 386.

11 Margo Natalie Crawford, *Black Post-Blackness: The Black Arts Movement and Twenty-First Century Aesthetics* (Urbana: University of Illinois Press, 2017), 3–4 and passim. For Crawford, Black post-Blackness is "the circular inseparability of the lived experience of blackness and the translation of that lived-experience into the world-opening possibilities of art" (2).

12 Frederick Douglass, "Lecture on Pictures" (1861), in John Stauffer, Zoe Trodd, and Celeste-Marie Bernier, *Picturing Frederick Douglass: An Illustrated Biography of the Nineteenth Century's Most Photographed American*, revised edition (New York: Liveright Publishing, 2018), 126–41; 133. James B. Haile, III (a contributor here) explains well how Douglass's concept of picture making is meant to encapsulate all art, not just photography, and thus the concept depicts all aesthetic expression: "The element out of which photographs spring—that is, the element of their *production* (inverting subjective consciousness to objective form) and *consumption* (recognition of the objective form as expressive of one's subjective ideal)—does not strictly belong to photography, but, broadly speaking, belongs to aesthetic expression. Aesthetic expression, in short, is that through which we transform our multitudinous

experiences into meaningful expression to organize our social, political, private and public worlds." James B. Haile, III, "On Heroism," https://sites.hampshire.edu/blackaesthetics/files/2016/12/haile-on_heroism.pdf. See also Michael Kelly, "Frederick Douglass's Prospective Aesthetic Theory," *Critical Philosophy of Race* 9, no. 2 (2021): 240–69.

13 W. E. B. Du Bois, "Criteria of Negro Art," in *W. E. B. Du Bois: Writings* (New York: Library of America, 1986), 1002.

14 Alain Locke, "Negro Youth Speaks" (1925), in *The Black Aesthetic*, 16–22; 17, 18, 21, 23.

15 Achille Mbembe, *Critique of Black Reason*, trans. Laurent DuBois (Durham: Duke University Press, 2017), 173.

16 Audre Lorde, "Poetry is Not a Luxury," in *Sister Outsider: Essays and Speeches* (Freedom, CA: The Crossing Press, 1984).

17 Amanda Gorman, "The Hill We Climb," in Amanda Gorman, *The Hill We Climb: An Inaugural Poem for the Country* (New York: Viking, 2021), 11–12.

18 Teju Cole, "The Blackness of the Partner," in *Black Paper* (Chicago: University of Chicago Press, 2021), 149. He continues" "Those who have to learn Black also expand what Black can be. My pain is Black pain, my joy is Black joy, my individuality is Black."
   See https://alishabwormsley.com/. Wormsley discusses this work in *Black Futures*, ed. Kimberley Drew and Jenna Wortham (New York: One World/Random House, 2020), 44–47. The rest of this volume is, as the title implies, focused on the future, starting from a current paradox about Black lives: "We have never been more empowered and yet, in many ways, are still so disenfranchised" (xiii). The volume comprises ample documentation of contemporary Black art and culture.

19 Wynter, "Black Aesthetics and the Black Arts Movement," 391.

20 W. E. B. Du Bois, "The Negro in Literature and Art," in *The New Negro: Readings on Race, Representation, and African American Culture, 1892–1938*, ed. Henry Louis Gates, Jr. and Gene Andrew Jarrett (Princeton: Princeton University Press, 2007), 301. Du Bois adds: "To appraise rightly this body of art one must remember that it represents the work of those artists only whom accident set free" (302).

21 For an account of Wheatley's tribunal, see Henry Louis Gates, Jr., *The Trials of Phillis Wheatley: America's First Black Poet and Her Encounters with the Founding Fathers* (London: Civitas Books, 2010). See also David Waldstreicher, *The Odyssey of Phillis Wheatley: A Poet's Journey through American Slavery and Independence* (New York: Farrar, Strauss and Giroux, 2023).

22 Douglass, "Pictures and Progress," in Stauffer, Trodd, and Bernier, *Picturing Frederick Douglass*, 161. For analysis of this point, see Kelly, "Frederick Douglass's Prospective Aesthetic Theory."

23 Du Bois, "Criteria of Negro Art," 995. Their inseparability becomes clearer as Black artists face their "own past as a people," as the "past is taking on form, color, and reality," "we are beginning to be proud" (996).

24 Du Bois, "Criteria of Negro Art," 1000. To explain what he means by beauty, he gives four examples; (1) The Cologne Cathedral"; (2) a village of the Veys in West Africa; (3) Venus of Milo; and (4) "a single phase of music in the Southern South," of the type discussed in "The Sorrow Songs," the last chapter of *The Souls of Black Folk* (995).

25 Douglass, "Pictures and Progress," in Stauffer, Trodd, and Bernier, *Picturing Frederick Douglass*, 161.

26 Du Bois, "Criteria of Negro Art," 994.

27 Spillers, "The Idea of Black Culture," 21.

28 Hortense J. Spillers, "The Idea of Black Culture," *The New Centennial Review* 6, no. 3 (2006): 7–28, 26.

29 Spillers, "The Idea of Black Culture," 25.

30 Spillers, "The Idea of Black Culture," 25–26. See also her online lecture on the "The Idea of Black Culture" at the University of Waterloo, March 19, 2013: https://www.youtube.com/watch?v=P1PTHFCN4Gc [accessed January 17, 2022].

  While comparing Du Bois's and Marcuse's ideas of culture, Spillers says what they had in common was "the encounter with the extreme," enslavement and anti-Black racism for one and the extermination of the Jews for the other. They wrote "as though their very lives depended on it" and turned specifically to culture because it offers not an escapist "realm of ghosts and illusions" but because it sustains, and insists on the realization of, "historical possibilities." Spillers, "The Idea of Black Culture," 15–16.

31 Ralph Ellison, *Invisible Man* (New York, Vintage Books,1952).

32 Addison Gayle, Jr., "Cultural Strangulation: Black Literature and the White Aesthetic," in *SOS—Calling All Black People,* 161. Du Bois does not identify specific criteria but says instead: "The ultimate judge has got to be you and you have got to build yourselves up into that wide judgment, that catholicity of temper which is going to enable the artist to have his widest chance for freedom. We can afford the Truth. White folk today cannot" ("Criteria of Negro Art," 1001). "We must come to the place where the work of art when it appears is reviewed and acclaimed by our own *free and unfettered judgment*. And we are going to have a real and valuable and eternal judgment only as we make ourselves free of mind, proud of body and just of soul to all men" (1001–02; italics added).

  For a discussion of the search for new criteria of Black aesthetics within the Black Arts Movement, see Wynter, "Black Aesthetics and the Black Arts Movement," in *Encyclopedia of Aesthetics*, 383–92.

  The issue here is establishing not only criteria for judging Black art but also expressive features of making Black art. See, for example, Zora Neale Hurston, "Characteristics of Negro Expression" (1934), in *The New Negro: Readings on Race, Representation, and African American Culture, 1892–1938*, ed. Henry Louis Gates, Jr. and Gene Andrew Jarrett (Princeton: Princeton University Press, 2007), 355–64.

33 "Thus all art is propaganda" and "I do not give a damn for any art that is not used for propaganda" ("Criteria of Negro Art," 1000). In the context, "propaganda" means that art is inseparable from truth and goodness, and it challenges the propaganda "of people who believe white blood divine, infallible and holy" and who deny blacks the right to their own propaganda. That is, art is propaganda for truth and goodness (justice). But it is also propaganda "for gaining the right of black folk to love and enjoy," as blacks are "inspired with new ideals for the world," the cry for freedom ("Criteria of Negro Art," 1000, 1001).

  Du Bois's sense of art as propaganda is not unlike Malcom X's belief about culture: "Culture is an indispensable weapon in the freedom struggle. We must take hold of it and forge the future with the past. *By Any Means Necessary (Malcolm X Speeches and Writings)* (New York: Pathfinder Press, 1992).

34 James Baldwin, "If Black English Isn't a Language," *New York Times* (July 29, 1979), 133. For the reference to "horrors" that provoke "the Negro idiom," see *The Fire Next Time*, in James Baldwin: *Collected Essays*, ed. Toni Morrison (New York: Library of America, 1998), 287–347; 326.

35 Baldwin, "If Black English Isn't a Language," 132. For a recent discussion of the relevance of Baldwin to critical race theory today, see Eddie S. Gaude, Jr., *Begin Again: James Baldwin's America and Its Urgent Lessons for our Own* (New York: Crown, 2020).

36 Frank B. Wilderson III, *Afropessimism* (New York: Liveright Publishing, 2020), 325.

Other critics, such as Gates, Jr., worry that Black aesthetics implies essentialism, but Evie Shockley, a contributor here, has a strategic response to this line of criticism: "Eschewing racial essentialism, but maintaining a healthy respect for 'the integrity of . . . black cultures', I suggest that the term 'black aesthetics', from which many contemporary critics have distanced themselves, need not be inevitably linked to static understandings of how blackness is inscribed in literary texts. Instead, what is called for is a redefinition of the term, one that makes it descriptive, rather than prescriptive." Shockley, *Renegade Poetics: Black Aesthetics and Formal Innovation in African American Poetry*, 7, 198. She continues: "the 'black' in the conception of 'black-aesthetics' . . . describes the subjectivity of the African American writer—that is, the *subjectivity produced* by the experience of identifying or being interpolated as 'black" in the U.S.—actively working out a poetics in the context of a racist society. Black aesthetics are a function of the writing process, are contingent, and must be historicized and contextualized with regard to period and place, and with regard to the various other factors that shape the writer's identity, particularly including gender, sexuality, and class as well" (9).

Again eschewing racial essentialism, Michelle Wright argues that, as Blackness is not biological in origin but socially and discursively constructed, it is best to approach it as a "when" and a "where" instead of a "what." Putting discourses on space-time from physics into conversation with works on identity from the African Diaspora, Wright explores how Middle Passage epistemology subverts racist assumptions about Blackness, yet its linear structure inhibits the kind of inclusive epistemology of Blackness needed in the twenty-first century. She then engages with bodies frequently excluded from contemporary mainstream consideration: Black feminists, Black queers, recent Black African immigrants to the West, and Blacks whose histories may weave in and out of the Middle Passage epistemology but do not cohere to it. Michelle Wright, *The Physics of Blackness: Beyond the Middle Passage Epistemology* (Minneapolis: University of Minnesota Press, 2015).

37 Wilderson, *Afropessimism*, 171, 174, 314, 225. See also Jared Sexton, who similarly argues that Black life "is not social, or rather that black life is *lived* in social *death*." "The Social Life of Social Death: On Afro-Pessimism and Black Optimism," in *InTensions Journal* 5 (Fall/Winter 2011), 29.

38 Wilderson, *Afropessimism*, 331.

39 Wilderson, *Afropessimism*, 171.

40 In Douglass's words: "It was not *color*, but *crime*, not *God*, but *man*, that afforded the true explanation of the existence of slavery; nor was I long in finding out another important truth, viz: what man can make man can unmake." Frederick Douglass, *My Bondage and My Freedom*, in *Frederick Douglass: Autobiographies*, ed. Henry Louis Gates (New York: Library of America, 1994), 179.

41 Wilderson, *Afropessimism*, 103.

42 Amiri Baraka, "Black Art" (1965), in *Black Fire: An Anthology of Afro-American Writing*, ed. Amiri Baraka and Larry Neal (Baltimore: Black Classic Press, 2007), 302–03.

43 Spillers, online discussion, "Afropessimism and Its Others: A discussion between Hortense J. Spillers and Lewis R. Gordon," May 17, 2021 (accessed January 18, 2022): https://www.youtube.com/watch?v=Z-s-Ltu06NI. Spillers asks whether current iterations of Afropessimism spring from "philosophies of European exhaustion" (e.g., Arnold Toynbee, Oswald Spengler, et al.)

44 Wilderson, *Afropessimism*, 173.

45 Douglass, "The Claims of the Negro Ethnologically Considered," 225–26.

46 Douglass, "Life Pictures" (transcript), 35.

47 Moten discusses a similar question when he asks whether the commodity that speaks—e.g., Douglass's Aunt Hester and Douglass himself—is able to do so because it was once not a commodity, giving it value before being reduced to exchange value as a commodity. See Moten, "Resistance of the Object: Aunt Hester's Scream," in *In the Break: The Aesthetics of the Black Radical Tradition* (Minneapolis: University of Minnesota Press, 2003), ch. 1. Our response to Moten's question is that an enslaved person is a human before it becomes a commodity qua enslaved and is reduced to its exchange value in the system of chattel enslavement. That is the only way we see to explain how an enslaved commodity can defy the logic of capitalism and speak in ways other commodities cannot. On questions and possibilities of being and "new ways of being in the world," see Lorde, "Age, Race, Class, and Sex: Women Redefining Difference," in *Sister Outsider*, 121; and "The Master's Tools Will Never Dismantle the Master's House," in *Sister Outsider*, 111.

48 Hartman similarly argues: "The intimacy with death that was first experienced in the hold continues to determine black existence." But does she believe that the only sanctuary is death? "Dead Book Remains," in *Grief and Grievance*, 117. Hartman, elsewhere, offers "critical fabulation" as a counter-narration to the "death sentence" or the "tomb," that is the archive of enslavement. Critical fabulation is an exercise of the imagination that aspires to "paint as full a picture of the lives of the captives as possible." In this fashion, it observes aesthetic impossibilities inherent in the archive while also pushing back against these limits. What emerges from this form of narration, which anticipates future freedom rather than give freedom priority to captivity or enslavement, is a present marked and interrupted by loss and exposed in its intimacy "with the lives of the dead." This intimacy, at the same time, involves the uptake by the living of the "claim" the dead make on us and of the "demand . . . to imagine a future in which the afterlife of slavery has ended." This, emphatically, is a future beyond social death. Hartman, "Venus in Two Acts," *Small Axe* 26 (2008): 1–14, 2, 4, 9, 11, 13. While Hartman is reluctant to associate critical fabulation with narrative enactments of beauty and poetics, both aesthetics and beauty centrally shape the black radical visions of the future disclosed by the counter-narratives of her book *Wayward Lives, Beautiful Experiments: Intimate Histories of Riotous Black Girls, Troublesome Women, and Queer Radicals* (New York: Norton, 2019). Here, in an outright embrace of black art and aesthetics, the focus is on the "beautiful experiments" through which young black women between 1890 and 1935 practiced freedoms and made life into "an art" (xiv).

49 Wilderson distinguishes between loss and absence in *Afropessimism*, 16, 46, 176.

50 Hartman, "Dead Book Remains," in *Grief and Grievance*, 118.

51 Hartman, "Dead Book Remains," in *Grief and Grievance*, 119.

52 Along with Black aesthetics comes Black reason, whose primary activity, according to Mbembe, is "fantasizing," that is, "gathering real or attributed traits, weaving them into histories, and creating images." Mbembe, *Critique of Black Reason*, 27.

53 See, for example, Clyde Woods's analysis of the blues in his *Development Arrested: The Blues and Plantation Power in the Mississippi Delta* (London: Verso Book, 1998/2017): "The blues became an alternative form of communication, analysis, moral intervention, observation, celebration for a generation that had witnessed slavery, freedom, and unfreedom in rapid succession between 1860 and 1875" (36).

54 Kevin Quashie, *Black Aliveness, or a Poetics of Being* (Durham: Duke University Press, 2021), 8. He is trying to "surpass terror as the uninflected language of black being" (9). "An antiblack world expects blackness from black people; in a black world, what we expect and get from black people is beingness" (10).

55 Fred Moten, *Black and Blur* (*Consent not to be a single being*, vol. 1) (Durham: Duke University Press, 2017), ix.

56 Claudia Rankine, *Don't Let Me Be Lonely: An American* Lyric (Minneapolis: Graywolf Press, 2004), 21.

57 Denise Ferreira da Silva, "1 (life) ÷ 0 (blackness) = ∞ − ∞ or ∞/∞: On Matter Beyond the Equation of Value," *E-flux journal* 79 (February 2017). On Ferreira da Silva's critical, "poethical," and transformative approach to aesthetics in relation to the creativity of Black women and in particular contemporary Black women artists such as Otobong Nkanga and Simone Leigh, see Denise Ferreira da Silva, "How," *E-flux journal* 105 (December 2019).

58 Alain Locke, *Negro Art: Past and Present* (Eastford, CT: Martino Fine Books, 1936/2020), 1, 7. Locke makes the further argument that Negro art came into its own in the 20th century in part because American artists were determined to distinguish themselves from European art traditions (43–58).

59 Paul C. Taylor, *Black is Beautiful: A Philosophy of Black Aesthetics* (London: Wiley Blackwell, 2016), 69.

60 More generally, Black aesthetics, for Taylor, involves a project of reconstruction geared toward racial and other forms of social justice and democracy, within and beyond philosophy. Paul C. Taylor, "Black Reconstruction Aesthetics," *Debates in Aesthetics* 15, no. 2 (2020): 9–47.

61 Similarly, Moten equates "the most exciting and generative advance in black critical theory" with "critical theory," in "Blackness and Nothingness (Mysticism in the Flesh)," in *The South Atlantic Quarterly* 112, 4 (Fall 2013), 737. In this context, he is speaking specifically about Afropessimism in the work of Frank B. Wilderson III and Jared Sexton.

62 On the sense of "dream" here, see Zora Neale Huston: "Ships at a distance have every man's wish on board. For some they come in with the tide. For others they sail forever on the horizon, never out of sight, never landing until the Watcher turns his eyes away in resignation, his dreams mocked to death by Time. That is the life of men. Now, women forget all those things they don't want to remember, and remember everything they don't want to forget. The dream is the truth. Then they act and do things accordingly." Zora Neale Hurston, *Their Eyes Were Watching God* (New York: HarperCollins, 2006 [1937]), 1.

63 Achille Mbembe, *Out of the Dark Night: Essays on Decolonization*, trans. Daniela Ginsburg et al. (New York: Columbia University Press, 2021).

64 Mbembe, *Out of the Dark Night*, 221; see also 215.

65 Mbembe, *Out of the Dark Night,* 221.

66 Mbembe, *Out of the Dark Night,* 221; see also 213.

67 Mbembe, *Out of the Dark Night*, 229–30.

68 Mbembe, *Out of the Dark Night,* 215.

69 Toni Morrison, *Playing in the Dark: Whiteness and the Literary Imagination* (New York: Vintage, 1993), 3–17. More precisely, Morrison explores how, in the United States, by way of invisibilization and silence, white constructions of blackness pervading literary practice allow "the black body a shadowless participation in the dominant cultural body" (10). Morrison's intervention is to shift the critical attention from imagined blackness to the white selves doing the imagining (17, 90).

70 For a critique of contemporary racializing logics of inclusion/exclusion under the rubric of cultural difference and their presuppositions of transparency, see Denise Ferreira da Silvia, "'Bahia Pêlo Negro': Can The Subaltern (Subject of Raciality) Speak?," *Ethnicities* 5, no. 3 (2005): 321–42. From a different angle, Okwui Enwezor objects to practices of Western ratification of work by African artists and to constructions of difference on Western terms. In response to these routines, he advocates a "delocalization and decentring of the centre." Okwui Enwezor, "Between Worlds: Postmodernism and African Artists in the Western Metropolis," in *Reading the Contemporary: African Art from Theory to the Marketplace*, ed. Olu Oguibe and Okwui Enwezor (Cambridge: MIT Press, 2000), 248–49. Dismantling notions of cultural purity and wholeness and underscoring the presence of African artists and their art in Western metropolitan spaces, Enwezor repudiates the practice of rendering "the value of their

work . . . contingent on the display of an 'authenticity' certified, codified and ratified by an adjudicating tribunal" and challenges deployments of difference "as a determining criterion for their inclusion within the pantheon of contemporary cultural producers" (272–73).

71 Lorde, "Uses of the Erotic," 59.

72 Crawford similarly argues: "When cultural nationalism is improvised, it is always on the verge of becoming something that is closer to an aesthetic than a programmatic ideology. The 'post' in black post-blackness is, partially, post-ideological blackness." *Black Post-Blackness: The Black Arts Movement and Twenty-First Century Aesthetics*, 217.

73 Quashie, *Black Aliveness*, 2.

74 On the connection between "relation," "being," and aesthetics see Édouard Glissant, *The Poetics of Relation*, Betsy Wing, trans. (Ann Arbor: University of Michigan Press, 1997), 29, 150–55, 185–88, 203. On relationality and aesthetics, see also Kobena Mercer, *Travel & See: Black Diaspora Art Practices since the 1980s* (Durham, NC: Duke University Press, 2016), 10, 28, 30; and Monique Roelofs, *The Cultural Promise of the Aesthetic* (New York: Bloomsbury, 2014).

75 Taylor, *Black is Beautiful*, 1–2.

76 Lorna Simpson, *Collages*, intro. Elizabeth Alexander (San Francisco: Chronicle Books, 2018). According to Alexander, "Black women's hair is epistemology, but we cannot always discern its codes" (1, but unpaginated). And she adds that the "universal governing principle" of Simpsons's collages is "the black and boisterous" hair.

77 In the National Museum of African American History and Culture in Washington D.C., there is a display called "Black is Beautiful," which includes a 1960s image of Marsha Hunt along with these words: "Crowning Glory. After appearing in the London production of hair in 1968, Marsha Hunt and the image of her large Afro became an international icon of Black beauty."

78 Alice Walker, "In Search of Our Mothers' Gardens," in *In Search of Our Mothers' Gardens: Womanist Prose by Alice Walker* (San Diego: Harcourt Brace Jovanovich, 1983).

79 Angela Y. Davis, *Blues Legacies and Black Feminism: Gertrude "Ma" Rainey, Bessie Smith, and Billie Holiday* (New York: Random House, 1998).

80 On relationality as a core constituent of the notion of the aesthetic and of different historical and contemporary forms of aesthetics, Black, white, and Latin(x) American, see also Roelofs, *The Cultural Promise of the Aesthetic* and *Arts of Address: Being Alive to Language and the World* (New York: Columbia University Press, 2022).

81 Lorde, "Poetry Is Not A Luxury," "Master's Tools," 111–13, "Age, Race, Class, and Sex: Women Redefining Difference," 121–23, "Uses of the Erotic." Quashie discusses Lorde's essay on poetry in connection with his concept of "aliveness" and relationality, but he understands aliveness specifically "as a term of relation where the focus is on one's preparedness for encounter rather than on the encounter itself. In this way, to be in relation is to be in the embodied sociality of one's readiness." Quashie, *Aliveness*, 21.

82 Lorde, "Poetry Is Not A Luxury," 37–38.

83 Lorde, "Master's Tools," 111, "Age, Race, Class, and Sex, 116." Lorde, in this context, like Baldwin, deploys the language of necessity—the necessity of poetry as well as interdependency ("Poetry Is Not A Luxury," 37, "Master's Tools," 111).

84 Lorde, "Poetry," 37–38.

85 Several very recent, if brief, discussions of the aesthetics of Black art outside the academic setting have also inspired *Black Art and Aesthetics: Relationalities, Interiorities, Reckonings*, confirming its timeliness if not its urgency. Lorna Simpson, whose art is reproduced here, and the poet Elizabeth Alexander spoke at the Whitney Museum of Art (July 18, 2018) in New York

City about their collaborative art project and publication, *Collages*. They emphasized the need to discuss Simpson's art—and, implicitly, the work of all contemporary Black artists—in aesthetic terms, such as the role of aesthetic form in critically engaging our disparately shared, dysfunctional contemporaneity. Simpson also spoke specifically about the central role of interiority in her work, which is an important aesthetic concept with a genealogy extending back to the origins of modern aesthetics. The same kind of critique of the undervaluing of aesthetics was raised in a profile of Carrie Mae Weems in the *New York Times Style Magazine*: "marginalization, being categorized as 'Black artist' or 'woman artist' rather than simply *artist*, is something Weems has dealt with her entire career." Megan O'Grady, "How Carrie Mae Weems Rewrote the Rules of Image-Making," *New York Times Style Magazine* (15 October 2018).

"The painter Norman Lewis rarely complained in public about the singular struggles of being a Black artist in America. But in 1979, dying of cancer, he made a prediction to his family. 'He said to us, 'I think it's going to take about 30 years, maybe 40, before people stop caring whether I'm Black and just pay attention to the work',' Lewis's daughter, Tarin Fuller, recalled recently." Quoted in Randy Kennedy's "Black Artists and the March Into the Museum," *New York Times* (28 November 2015).

In Fred Wilson's catalog for his "Afro Kismet" exhibition, he explains how he uses "beauty in the service of meaning." Among other works, the show comprises a number of Black chandeliers, which he describes as meditations "on death, on blackness, on beauty"— meditations on Black aesthetics. Several essays in the catalog for the "We Wanted a Revolution: Black Radical Women 1965–85" exhibition at the Brooklyn Museum embrace the notions of Black feminist aesthetic experiences and interventions, asserting the compatibility of Black aesthetics and Black activism. *We Wanted a Revolution: Black Radical Women, 1965–85—A Sourcebook*, ed. Catherine Morris and Rujeko Hockley (Brooklyn Museum and Duke University Press, 2017).

Also, the recent Tate Modern and Brooklyn Museum exhibition, *Soul of a Nation: Art in the Age of Black Power*, comprised art from 1963–1983, a distinctive historical period covering the civil rights movement. But its organizing principle was not chronological. Rather, the principle was the "different aesthetic strategies and debates circulating around what it meant to be a Black artist" during that period. *Soul of a Nation: Art in the Age of Black Power*, ed. Mark Godfrey and Zoé Whitley (London and New York: Tate Gallery and Distributed Art Publishers, 2017), 14. The 2019 Venice Biennale foregrounded a number of Black artists, prominently featuring works by Henry Taylor, Njideka Akunyili Crosby, Michael Armitage, Julie Mehretu, Arthur Jaffa, Otobong Nkanga, John Akomfrah, Felicia Abban, Zanele Muholi, and Martin Puryear (US Pavilion), among others, and lodging Black art firmly in the center of the debates about the turbulent times we live in today. We mention these numerous examples as evidence of the contemporary, widespread interest in Black aesthetics as a complement to, and as rigorously interwoven with, concerns about social justice, corroborating that the moment seems right for the deeper discussions of Black aesthetics presented in this anthology.

More recent examples include: *Among Others: Blackness at MoMA*, ed. Darby English and Charlotte Barat (New York: Museum of Modern Art, 2019); *Reconstructions: Architecture and Blackness in America*, ed. Sean Anderson and Mabel O. Wilson (New York: Museum of Modern Art, 2021). Of course, the COVID-19 pandemic interrupted art exhibitions since March 2020, and they are only beginning to re-emerge to pre-pandemic levels in 2022–2023. Of note, as we come out of this rupture, are Simone Leigh's show *Sovereignty* for the U.S. pavilion at the 2022 Venice Biennale, along with her works for that Biennale's International Exhibition and her 2023 show at ICA Boston, and Wangechi Mutu's exhibition *Intertwined* at the New Museum in New York (2023).

We have also been inspired by the recent anthology, *The Fire This Time: A New Generation Speaks about Race*, ed. Jesmyn Ward (New York: Scribner, 2016), which is of course a reconsideration of Baldwin's *The Fire Next Time*. Just as the essays in Ward's anthology were organized in three groups, "Legacy, Reckoning, and Jubilee," we hope to capture the same temporal trio of past, present, and future with the texts and artworks in *Black Art and Aesthetics: Relationalities, Interiorities, Reckonings*: implicitly or explicitly critiquing the anti-Black racist (and colonialist) legacy of aesthetics; utilizing aesthetics to reckon with the present struggles against racism, which Black Lives Matter and other activist groups are leading; yet also defending the important role of imagination in critical resistance, whether in prisons or elsewhere, as Davis has passionately argued (see her essay in this volume).

86 Richard Wright provides an account of the relative freedom of Black writers. To say "no" to injustice and "yes" to "the faint stirrings of a new and emerging life," Black writers need: (A) "perspective": "that part of a poem, novel, or play which a writer never puts directly upon paper"; "that fixed point in intellectual space where a writer stands to view the struggles, hopes, and sufferings of his people." (B) The functional, professional "autonomy" of their craft. In short, Black writers are "being called upon to do no less than create values by which [their] race is to struggle, live and die." Wright, "Blueprint for Negro Writers," reprinted in *The Black Aesthetic*, 315–26; 334, 339, 340, 341, 343. Originally published in *New Challenge* 2 (1937): 53–65.

87 Christopher Freeburg, *Black Aesthetics and the Interior Life* (Charlottesville: University of Virginia Press, 2017), 3–4. He makes this argument in an effort to "decouple black subjects' inherent connection to collective black politics," as if such separation and decoupling were necessary prices to pay to revalorize Black aesthetics (110). Freeburg uses Glenn Ligon's *Untitled* (1988), which displays the words "I *AM* A Man," as a primary example of a separation between the Black subject and Black politics. It is worth briefly mentioning two alternative approaches to the links between aesthetics and politics. Jeremy Matthew Glick argues that in the Black Radical Tradition in aesthetics "the aesthetic properties bound to this cluster of dramatic works [C.L.R. James, Édouard Glissant, Lorraine Hansberry, et al.] offers up political insight and constitutes a field ripe for speculative thinking on the interrelationship between Black radical pasts, presents, and futures, as well as the continued relevance of leaders and masses in Black revolutionary struggle." Glick, *The Black Radical Tragic: Performance, Aesthetics, and the Haitian Revolution* (New York: NYU Press, 2016), 3. In GerShun Avilez's words, "Aesthetic radicalism describes the artistic inhabiting and reconfiguring of political radicalism." That is, as a strategy for doing black aesthetics, the suggestion is to engage in "disruptive inhabiting" of aesthetics in relation to black nationalism and artistic experimentalism, combined with intersectional theory, queer theory (queer of color critique), and critical race theory along with close analyses of works by contemporary artists. GerShun Avilez, *Aesthetics and Modern Black Nationalism* (Urbana: University of Illinois Press, 2016).

88 Lorde is a crucial proponent of the links between interiority, aesthetics, and politics signaled here. Lorde, "Uses of the Erotic: The Erotic as Power," in *Sister Outsider*, 55–56, 59, and "Poetry is not a Luxury," 37. A coincidence of a reconceptualized aesthetics with inwardness, a sociality, and a decolonizing orientation toward "social (juridic, economic, ethical) context," emerges furthermore in Ferreira da Silva, "How."

89 Kevin Quashie, *The Sovereignty of Quiet: Beyond Resistance in Black Culture* (New York: Routledge, 2012), 6. An aesthetic of quiet entails "a black expressiveness without publicness as its forbearer, a black subject in the undisputed dignity of its humanity" (26).

90 Denise Ferreira da Silva, *Toward a Global Idea of Race* (Minneapolis: University of Minnesota Press, 2007), 31.

91 Amber Jamilla Musser, "Toward Mythic Feminist Theorizing: Simone Leigh and the Power of the Vessel," *differences* 30, no. 3 (2019): 63–91.

92 Musser, "Toward Mythic Feminist Theorizing," 88.

93   See also Amber Jamilla Musser, *Sensual Excess: Queer Femininity and Brown Jouissance* (New York: New York University Press, 2018).

94   Harney and Moten, *The Undercommons*, 42.

95   Harney and Moten, *The Undercommons*, 98.

96   Harney and Moten, *The Undercommons*, 98; see also 97–99.

97   Harney and Moten, *The Undercommons*, 18–20, 96–97, 139–40. In *Black and Blur*, Moten takes a more expansive view of aesthetic politics, tracing manifold aesthetic-political strategies in the arts and pointing to "the interinanimative autonomy of the aesthetic and the politico-economic" (23).

98   Stephen Best, *None Like Us: Blackness, Belonging, Aesthetic Life* (Durham: Duke University Press, 2018), 22.

99   Best, *None Like Us,"* 132.

100   Daphne Lamothe, *Inventing the New Negro: Narrative, Culture and Ethnography* (Philadelphia: University of Pennsylvania Press, 2008): "New Negro literature [Harlem Renaissance, early 20th century; term introduced by Alain Locke] is . . . disorienting (or, more accurately, multiply oriented) in that its creators produce multiple, fluid, and dynamic portraits of African America, depictions that resist absolutist thinking about the other. Thus, even as they respond to and challenge stereotypical presentations of African Americans as subhuman and inferior, they resist questions of truth and illusion, authenticity and falsity, and turn our attention to a redefinition of truth as multiply unfolding and composed of a constellation of interconnected concepts and experiences" (3).

101   Fumi Okiji, *Jazz as Critique: Adorno and Black Expression Revisited* (Stanford: Stanford University Press, 2018), 35.

102   Langston Hughes, "The Negro Artist and the Racial Mountain" (1926), in *The Black Aesthetic*, ed. Addison Gayle, Jr., 167–72; 172. He continues: "If white people are pleased we are glad. If they are not, it does not matter. We know we are beautiful. And ugly too. The tom-tom cries and the tom tom laughs. If colored people are pleased we are glad. If they are not, their displeasure doesn't matter either. We build our temples for tomorrow, strong as we know how, and we stand top of the mountain, free within ourselves."

103   Frederick Douglass, "Lecture on Pictures" (1861).

104   Baldwin, *The Fire Next Time*, 46. In a related vein, Sun Ra said: "The impossible attracts me," "because everything possible has been done and the world didn't change." Quoted in Hua Hsu, "How Sun Ra Taught Us to Believe in the Impossible," New Yorker (July 5, 2021): https://www.newyorker.com/magazine/2021/07/05/how-sun-ra-taught-us-to-believe-in-the-impossible.

PART ONE

BLACKNESS AS AESTHETIC STRATEGY

1

COLORING HISTORY, THEORY, AND PAINTING

Meleko Mokgosi

Is it possible for the visual representation of the so-called Black subject to function metaphorically not necessarily symbolically, and therefore communicate without the politics of blackness overdetermining any signification or the semiotic activity within any reading? How does it happen that blackness mainly produces normative iterations of difference and semi-polysemy, whereas whiteness easily allows polysemy and normativity?

I. Blackness and Polysemy

I came to these questions through two paths, first by looking specifically at how certain painters represent Black bodies; and second, through the ways in which living in America as an immigrant from Africa has affected my ideas of representation. As a painter that is invested in the representation of subjects from southern Africa, I had never thought twice about the idea of blackness until only a few years ago. Before this, the subjects I represented were not Black or native but simply subjects or Africans; these are subjects that I have always understood from a perspective of a not-exclusively racialized perspective of the world, primarily because back home (in Bostwana) around ninety-four percent of the people in the community are dark-skinned: so members of parliament, the president, doctors, teachers, bankers, truck drivers, et al. have dark skin, or "Black." In this context, occupying a body with dark skin is normal, it is not felt through the racializing history of colonialism or the trans-Atlantic enslavement trade. For this reason, and many others, a dark-skinned person grows up loving their dark skin, embracing it, being comfortable in it, and therefore does not feel over-policed or threatened by how they might be perceived. Of course, this does not mean there are no problems caused by issues of class, gender, sexuality, ethnicity, race, colonialism, and so forth.[1]

All of this was unsettled by how my subjecthood was interpellated in the American context where the polysemy of blackness is reduced by whiteness to occupy the vitriolic and racist stereotypes that feeds the fears and paranoias of those who identify exclusively with whiteness. Put differently, it was not until I came to the U.S. when I became fully aware of my blackness. My aim here is to explore these histories and frameworks as well as the idea that color is a material object that can be used to unfold the political implications, processes, and tools that are used to render representations. Specifically, I will briefly look at two artists' work, present some ideas about my project, and then work through the proposal that the articulation of Black skin is to an extent imbued with an examination of whiteness. My argument is that the process or techniques of painting, which fall within the non-mimetic,[2] should be thought of as equally meaningful as the mimetic the non-mimetic, defined loosely as institutional framing devices—is contingent upon precedents from any field that is referenced through the artwork. In many ways, the non-mimetic is a pathway that reveals institutional interventions that the artist is trying to make; interventions that are not limited to mimesis or representational protocols.

II. Conventions and Interventions

So, how does one learn how to recreate flesh tones on canvas? To go about this, the painter needs to tackle both the foundation that the paint sits on and the combination and chemistry of paints. If you were interested in figurative painting in art school, the first formulae you would be taught would be specific ways of preparing the ground, and color mixing—experimenting with: hue, value, saturation, chroma, tinting, shades, and tones. Conventionally, a painting ground is prepared depending on whether the artist will be using acrylic or oil paint. Both tend to require that the artist apply at least four layers of primer or gesso, ideally allowing each layer to completely dry and sanding lightly. Primer and gesso have historically looked white because they both contain chalk, white pigment, and some kind of synthetic or organic binder. Not only does the white ground provide the highest points of contrast, but is also allows more luminosity with how it interacts with light moving through the paint in addition to allowing the artist the freedom to rework the surface as many times as he or she wants. At face value, the white of the ground which receives these representations could be seen as neutral and not carrying much rhetorical or ideological value, however any artist would be remiss if they did not account for the semiotic value and resonance of the whiteness of the primer or gesso in relation to the history of the practice, especially given the fact that a large majority of paintings in the Western canon are made on white primed canvas. Therefore, there are conceptual and political implications of the use of a white ground to construct representations of the human subject, some of which will be detailed below.

After preparing the painting surface, compositions, and so forth, the artist then utilizes another academic formula to realistically render human flesh: namely, magenta, yellow, and white. For example, one foundational combination you could use is cadmium red, yellow ochre, and titanium white; or raw sienna, cadmium red, and titanium white; or raw umber, yellow ochre, and burnt sienna. I need not stress that titanium white, flake white, and zinc white are all necessary colors in every combination. After modeling, and building volume and texture, the painter then progresses to the satisfying process of glazing, which is used to add nuance and translucency to the surface of the painted skin. Here, the painter manipulates translucent and transparent colors so that light is made to reflect and refract in such a way that the color on the canvas mimics the translucency of the skin, showing the veins, muscles, and bone structure beneath the skin. This is why figurative painters love oil paint; it is quite the opposite of acrylic paint, which sits flat on the surface.

Altering or rejecting these established and academic methods of painting has political and aesthetic implications, both of which will be explored below through the work of Kerry James Marshall and Adriana Varejão. In many instances, artists make specific decisions in terms of the tools that are used to construct particular kinds of representations, even if it means creating some tools from scratch. For many artists, the way in which someone is represented is important because how one is perceived and treated is informed by how one looks. Subjectivity is therefore not just a theoretical thing about identitarian politics; it is a felt, somatic, and a visual thing. For this reason, figurative painters continuously work on creating visual languages that are in line with their conceptual framework. Deviating from academic painting formulae was one of my primary goals over ten years ago. The beige color of cotton duck canvas became an important ground to construct Black skin tones. In constructing my skin tones, I use a clear ground that allows the texture and color of cotton duck canvas to show through, therefore become the highest point of contrast. Although this technique is effective because the texture and warmth of cotton duck canvas is ideal for rendering specific skin tones, one of the side effects of this method is that there is no room for error and over-painting, which could be useful to hide mistakes, too. It is virtually impossible to mimic the texture and color of cotton duck canvas, so once paint is applied on top it, there is no turning back. Another interesting development from disavowing the white primer is that I mainly paint by removing paint to create volume as opposed to additive painting. That is, because I rely on the beige of the canvas as the lightest point, I cannot use white paint at all to render Black skin, otherwise it obstructs the surface of the cotton duck canvas. Put another way, by building the skin tones using only four colors (raw umber, burnt umber, raw sienna, and burnt sienna) plus the beige canvas means that I have strategically gotten rid of using white paint to also create highlights. Defined loosely, highlights are the points at which light touches the surface of an object therefore illuminating it and giving it visibility, rendering it legible to others. It would not be a stretch here to also interpret "light" as a metaphor connected to specific politics, just as darkness is connected to the politics of blackness and the creation of the African savage in race discourse.

III. Blackened Blackness

Kerry James Marshall engages with the representation of the Black body in a way that highlights the darkness of blackness, literally using black paint to create a flattened and solid diagrammatic skin tone with little interest in realism. His formulations of painting skin is configured in high contrast and contradiction to academic conventions of painting skin tones, therefore creating images that bring into sharp focus the history of painting and how this history as a representational space has continuously foreclosed other subjects of human history.

It is no secret that the economy of painting skin tones was originally developed to render Caucasian skin. While some painters may choose to not directly engage with these

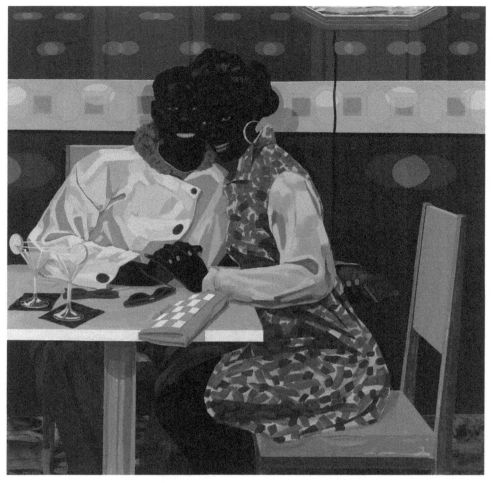

Plate 8 Kerry James Marshall, *Untitled (Club Couple)*. Acrylic on PVC panel. Copyright Kerry James Marshall. Courtesy of the artist and Jack Shainman Gallery, New York.

histories and epistemological representational tools, there remains a continuous reconciliation of what employing these protocols and participating in the discourse exactly mean, if we are to agree that these forms of representation that spoke more to whiteness occupy a large part of the constellation of discursive fields that come after European colonial projects, the Trans-Atlantic enslavement trade, globalization, finance capital, and neo-imperialism. Both Marshall and Varejão's work show how artists challenge and overcome specific aesthetic and institutional forces in order to expose their limitations as well as point to residues of Eurocentrism and whiteness in the construction of representations in Fine Arts.

As a figurative painter, Marshall is quick to point out two driving points. First, he argues that many Black artists tend to shy away from painting the Black subject because of the supposed limitations of blackness, which is said to block the viewer from having the full aesthetic experience of the art object. In other words, the painted Black subject limits the art object and also flattens the artist into the baggage that comes with this blackness, because it becomes hard to see how the artist has nothing to do with the idea of blackness that he or she is representing. Second, Marshall specifically outlines his project as one that was compelled by the limitations of art history and cultural production to show representations with which he as an African American could identify. His paintings, mostly done in acrylic paint, do not use realistic rendering of skin tone or skin texture. The black figure is rendered with the weight of a black marble sculpture, and stylized towards the aesthetics of socialist realism sculptures/monuments. The answer to what seems like a disregard for the complexity and specificity of skin tone is counter-intuitive; namely, that for Marshall, the figure is painted black to highlight blackness; and when it is highlighted, the viewer can acknowledge blackness and move onto more analysis of the painting. This idea is the painterly equivalent of the theoretical procedure of *sous rature* because it conveys the numerous over-exposures and challenges that come with representation. As previously stated, it is understood that blackness as a contemporaneous idea related to identity politics is located within the notion of race, which is in turn produced by race discourse. So to highlight the subject as solidly Black—since again when someone is said to be black they are not actually black—Marshall literalizes this signifier to reveal the fact that this subject can only be thought of within this limited and asymmetrical framework. In other words, this painterly sous rature exposes the limitations and absurdity of blackness within the confines of race discourse, makes it hyper-visible, cancels it out, yet proposes that not only is this blackness inadequate to understanding any kind of subjectivity, but this blackness should be immediately overlooked—the viewer should focus on other things happening in the painting. Therefore, literal blackness is made to argue that the concept of blackness in general is inadequate yet necessary.

Marshall also paints with only acrylic paint, which is somewhat considered with less seriousness by many painters because of its flatness, "graphic quality," and quick drying time. As a water-based paint, acrylic is easy to clean and does not contain any toxins or require specific ventilation for work areas. And although it takes about fifteen to twenty minutes for a layer of acrylic paint to dry, it is virtually impossible to remove acrylic paint from a surface once it has dried. Attempting to remove acrylic paint with soap or solvents will only damage the actual surface the paint is on. Additionally, it has a polymer emulsion binder, making it elastic, crack resistant, and unlikely to yellow over time. These aesthetic and chemical properties, I believe, are important in the interpretation of the images, especially given the fact that they are used to render Black skin. For example, it can be argued that the permanence and resilience of material such as acrylic can be read as a metaphor for the African American experience within U.S. history—experiences and subjecthoods that are central to the foundation of the country, its economy, and political systems. Regardless of how many efforts are made to downplay the importance of African Americans in U.S. history, as well as the continued efforts to disregard and not recognize the systemic and institutionalized violences and injustices that are perpetrated in the name of whiteness, the African American subject will always persist along-side various Othered subjectivities, and their constitutive role cannot be erased or obscured from the fabric of this nation.

The Black figure in Marshall's work is stylized and to an extent, it is essentialized—the nuance and texture of the skin is overshadowed by literalizing blackness through black

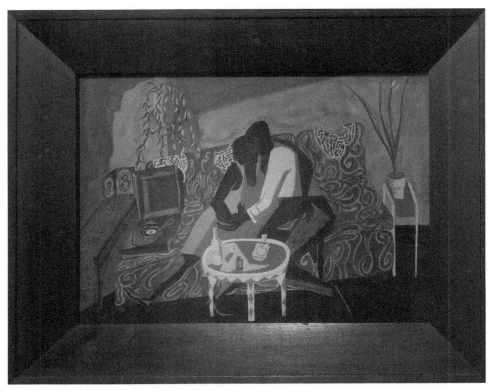

Plate 9 Jacob Lawrence, *The Lovers*, 1946. Copyright 2023, The Jacob and Gwendolyn Knight Lawrence Foundation, Seattle / Artists Rights Society, New York. Courtesy of Jonathan Boos Gallery.

pigment; the skin is made diagrammatic—i.e., it is solid Black with slight grey highlights. This flattened and diagrammatic skin tone is presented first as a synecdoche and then as a metonym of something that is presented as real, thus mimicking the perception of Black skin in the real world. No doubt, an important precedent for this trope is seen in the work of Jacob Lawrence, who specifically set out to flatten the skin tone of the Black subject so as to create a universalizable Black subject not necessarily tied down by race discourse. However, Marshall's Black subject presents race first and foremost. Race then is something that viewer has to acknowledge and move beyond in the service of creating a more complex reading of the situation. Yet highlighting the body in this way is key because the visual field plays a significant part in how race discourse functions. I quote Jennifer Gonzalez at length:

"The body is the site where race discourse is seen to play out because it is where race is presumed to reside. As an artifact of cultural framing, the human body is the object that must always display its signs. There is no escape from the fact of its "epidermalized" status; the materiality of the body is understood to offer a continuous surface of legible information. The "raced" body, as generations of theorists have argued, is a reified body, a body that has become an object in the process."[3]

Consequently, I propose that Marshall's blackening of the Black body points the viewer to the fallacy and limitations of signifying systems that take their cue from and depend on race discourse for meaning-making. In addition, it is important that Marshall examines blackness with the use of specific black pigment on a two-dimensional surface because the technical and chemical properties of the pigment itself carries additional weight. Creating predominant black pigments such as Bone Black, Black Oxide, Ivory Black, Mars Black, chromatic Black, and Black Spinel is complex. To quote the manufacturer of Rublev bone black: "it is an opaque cool black, fine grained with good tinting strength. Bone black, also known as 'bone char' or 'animal charcoal', is produced by charring animal bones. The bones are heated to high temperatures without oxygen. Bone black consists mainly of calcium phosphate and a smaller amount of carbon." As a result, each black produces different effects; for example, natural black oxide is as deep but because it is an oxide, it has greater tinting strength and dries matt, whereas bone black is more transparent but dries deeper. The combination of these various black pigments or paints result in producing a very nuanced and complex representation of a diagrammatic or stylized Black skin tone; and these complexities should then be mapped on to ontological and existential questions regarding the Black subject because they speak to the important issues around the constructed-ness of blackness, and its polysemy: ideas that Adriana Varejão examines at great length in one of recent project, "Polvo."

Although Varejão has employed similar technical and conceptual concerns as Marshall, her focus has however been on the colonial and decolonization histories of Brazil. For her project, "Polvo," Varejão began with a 1976 Brazilian household survey conducted by the Brazilian Institute of Geography and Statistics, which posed the question: "What is your colour?" The survey was meant to counteract the official Brazilian census, which categorized people into five different groups according to their skin color: white, black, red, yellow, and brown. The survey ended up producing 135 distinct terms such as: "Fox on Fire Red, Angry Sulphur, Milky Coffee, Snow White, Faded Fawn, Steady Colour, Big Black Dude, Buffed, and Sun Kissed." The title of the project, which is Portuguese for "octopus," gestures toward melanin, the primary substance that makes up octopus ink; and, of course, the substance responsible for pigmentation in human skin.

To realize the project, Varejão commissioned the fabrication of the thirty-three oil color tubes that were displayed in a vitrine, in addition to enlisting an "academic painter" to paint portraits of her using these unique skin colors. Afterward, Varejão painted the color splotches on the portraits. The portraits are said to have been inspired by "casta" paintings—which were used to document South American people in terms of racial purity, with emphasis on the darkness of skin pigmentation; the darker the skin, the more impure the subject. The main categories for this color system were black, white, red, brown, or yellow. The thirty-three oil colors produced for the project are not typical flesh tone paints or tints, but rather they are specific pre-mixed flesh tones that can be used directly on a surface. Here, the artist not only bypasses the academic formulae of color mixing to achieve flesh tones, she has also claimed the representational means of production by manufacturing her own oil paints. This is significant for two reasons. First, artists do not have much say on how or why pigments are made by art supply companies. The formulae and techniques used to create pigments, binders, and paint mediums by paint supply companies are virtually not connected to many artists. So, unless you want to grind your own pigments and create your own binders, you accept and work with whatever color you buy from the store. Therefore, as an artist you have no say as to what a brown or orange or yellow or red should look like as it is made in the factory. Second, Varejão, like Marshall, invented painting techniques that negate the academic formula of painting human flesh. However, unlike him, she did not do it through color choice or color mixing; rather, her strategy was to make an intervention in the economic and commercial production of pigments and paint. Put another way, the artist changed the terms within the means of production.

Despite the resources invested in the production of the skin tone paint tubes, Varejão has argued that the name of the color plays a bigger role. The color of the pigment in the tube, she offers, is less important than the name given to the color by the specified subject who has decided to provide that descriptive name to their skin tone. Taking this together, the artist then seems to be making a counter-intuitive argument regarding the relationship between linguistics and semiotics. Whereas the linguistic description—with all of its baggage as well as cultural, historical, and contextual specificity—would usually be given priority in terms of trying to understand the rhetorical effect of the signifier; here, Varejão prioritizes the linguistic play undertaken by the individual subject who constructs their interpretation of their skin tone outside the boundaries of race discourse, while at the same time gesturing toward acquiring agency for an otherwise othered subject that would not ordinarily be given such discursive and intellectual space or authority. Additionally, engaging with the creation of categories and the ways in which knowledge production is shaped and organized—the artist fosters a decentralizing practice of racial and ethnic categorization.

In many aspects of representation, color and colorism play a crucial role. In race discourse, skin pigmentation is the primary mechanism through which traits and biases are artificially constructed. And in Brazil, the history of colorism is as complex as in many parts of the world—complexities detailed below by the artist:

> The issue of racial identity is still very controversial in Brazil. Although Brazil is known and exalted for its supposed racial democracy, the truth is that we are quite a racist country. We've never had the racial segregation in an official way as it happened in the United States, or as the apartheid in South Africa, but we have always faced quite strong racial discrimination. Brazil still has very little social mobility. Races are mixed, but hierarchies remain.[4]

IV. Whiteness is not a Color

I focused on these two artists, and also on some of my work, as a way to show how artists challenge and overcome specific aesthetic and institutional forces in order to expose their limitations as well as point to residues of Eurocentrism and whiteness in the construction of representations.

All in all, I wish to propose that the use of black or brown paint to represent blackness, or rather the preoccupation with representing Black skin within a tradition that is

Eurocentric and geared to representing white subjects, the aims of these projects, seem to also interrogate whiteness,[5] which can be taken as a specific form of Eurocentricity. This strategy, I think is obvious, you highlight something and its effects by actually hiding it. The Black and brown body, which has been cancelled out on many occasions, takes center stage, and in rendering these subjects through complex methods that reject and challenge institutionalized forms of painterly production, it becomes impossible to imagine the white counterpart. Therefore, this blackness and brown-ness actually put into question both the practice of whiteness that led to the continual erasure of marginalized subject positions, and the manner in which subjects that identify with blackness/brown-ness are essentialized and not given their due recognition as equals.

Again, the commitment to certain representations of Black skin with paint points to the need for examining the idea and practice of whiteness, and using this to develop more specificity in understanding this taken-for-granted racial non-category that is actually foundational for how race is perceived. This is an important yet difficult challenge because being black or white here in the U.S. automatically and symbolically functions as a trigger of associations that place you in either the group whose ancestors were enslaved for generations, or the other group whose ancestors benefited handsomely from turning black muscle and bone into profit, or put otherwise—the other group that strategically dehumanized and chained generations of another people, confining them only to forced manual labor and denying them the slightest possibility of ever counting as human. So, to be American, and again this is not a judgment, is to be brought up with a racialized perspective of the world. And the politics of these works show that one of the aims in aesthetic practice is to collectively undermine this perception and agree that a good number of people have to find ways to repay their ancestral debts.

Notes

1   Although it is conventional knowledge, it worth stating here that what I am pointing to is the fact that blackness as it is currently understood is tied to the idea of race, which comes from race discourse. Therefore, the concept of race can only exist in so much as it is constructed through race discourse, itself a construct of bogus European imperialistic pseudo-scientific considerations. Put otherwise, race and race discourse have become conventions that are the center through which people locate themselves in relation to established discursive frameworks. However the history, experiences, and subjectivities of the dark-skinned African subject precede race discourse together with race and the blackness that comes with it all. It goes without saying that there exists various modes of intersectionality with all subject formations, and this intersectionality—although not always visible, should signal towards the notion that there is no finite interpretation and experience of what is understood as blackness through race discourse.

2   Developed by Meyer Schapiro in his seminal essay, "On Some Problems in the Semiotics of Visual Art: Field and Vehicle in Image-Signs," in *Netherlands Quarterly for the History of Art* 6, no. 1 (1972–1973), 9–19.

3   Jennifer A. González, *Subject to Display: Reframing Race In Contemporary Installation Art* (Cambridge: MIT Press, 2008), 4

4   *New Waves: Contemporary art and the issues shaping its tomorrow*, ed. Marta Gnyp (Milano: Skira, 2021).

5   Cheryl Harris rightly argues that whiteness is a form of capital that is not always apparent but
         can be traded in at any time—Harvard *Law Review* 106, no. 8 (June 1993): 1707–91.
         Therefore, and here I quote another text: to treat whiteness as the unspoken norm is to fail to
         see precisely how those who are perceived as white have come systematically to acquire this
         capital, buttressed by the particularities of the law. Homi Bhabha goes on to state that
         whiteness is held up by, quote, "the histories of trauma and terror that whiteness must
         perpetrate and from which it must protect itself; the amnesia it imposes on itself; and the
         violence it inflicts in the process of becoming a transparent and transcendent force of
         authority." "The White Stuff," *Artforum* (May 1998): 21–24.

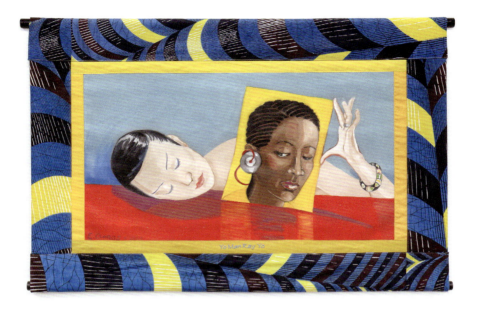

Plate 1 Emma Amos, *Yo Man Ray Yo*, 2000. Copyright 2022, Emma Amos. Licensed by VAGA at Artists Rights Society, New York.

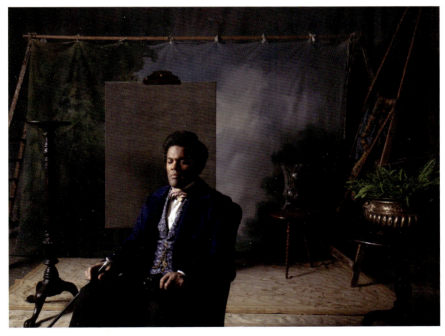

Plate 2 Isaac Julien, *J. P. Ball Studio, 1867 Douglass (Lessons of the Hour)*, 2019. Framed photograph on gloss inkjet paper mounted on aluminum. Courtesy of the artist and Victoria Miro, London/Venice.

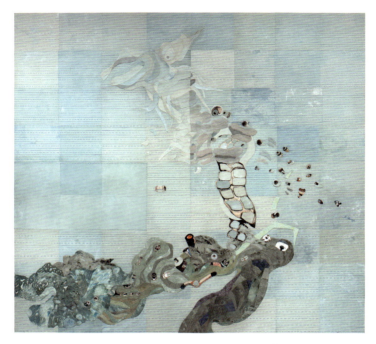

Plate 3 Ellen Gallagher, *Dew Breaker*, 2015. Copyright Ellen Gallagher. Courtesy of the artist and Hauser & Wirth. Photo: Ernst Moritz.

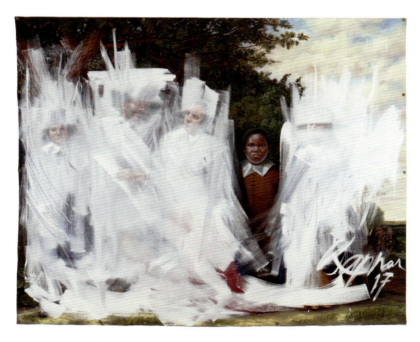

Plate 4 Titus Kaphar, *Shifting the Gaze*, 2017. Oil on canvas 83 × 103 1/4 in. Brooklyn Museum, William K. Jacobs Jr., Fund, 2017.34. Copyright Titus Kaphar.

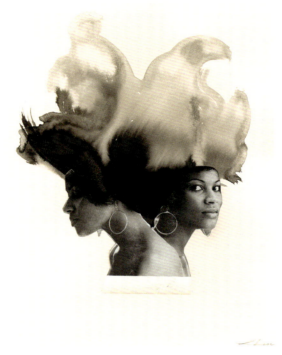

Plate 5 Lorna Simpson, *Touching*, 2012. Collage and ink on paper, 11 3/16 × 8 11/16. Framed: 12 5/8 × 10 1/8 × 1 1/2 in. Copyright Lorna Simpson. Courtesy of the artist and Hauser & Wirth.

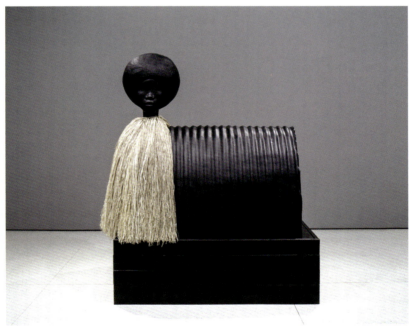

Plate 6 Simone Leigh, *Sentinel*, 2019. Bronze and raffia, 71.5 × 72 × 42 inches. Courtesy Simone Leigh and Matthew Marks Gallery.

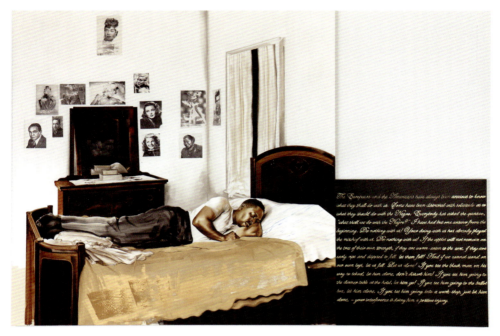

Plate 7 Meleko Mokgosi, *The Social Revolution of Our Time Cannot Take Its Poetry from the Past but Only from the Poetry of the Future*, 8, 2019, 2 panels. Oil on canvas, permanent gold marker on canvas, 98 × 145 3/8 × 3 inches (framed). Copyright Meleko Mokgosi. Courtesy of the artist and Jack Shainman Gallery, New York.

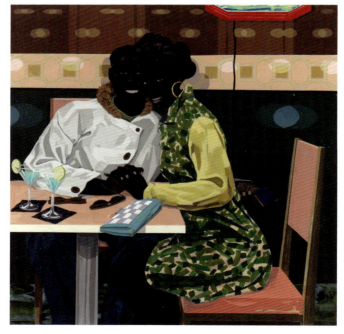

Plate 8 Kerry James Marshall, *Untitled (Club Couple)*. Acrylic on PVC panel. Copyright Kerry James Marshall. Courtesy of the artist and Jack Shainman Gallery, New York.

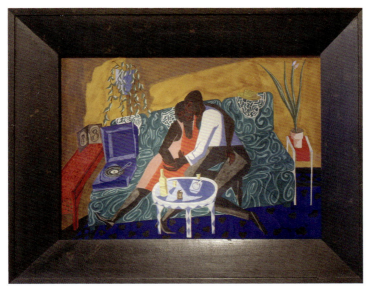

Plate 9 Jacob Lawrence, *The Lovers*, 1946. Copyright 2023, The Jacob and Gwendolyn Knight Lawrence Foundation, Seattle / Artists Rights Society, New York. Courtesy of Jonathan Boos Gallery.

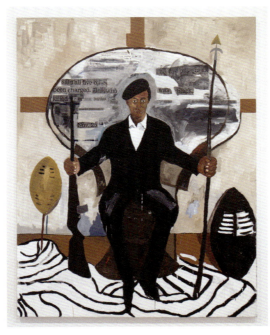

Plate 10 Henry Taylor, *Huey Newton*, 2007. Acrylic and collaged photocopies on canvas, 94 5/8 × 76 1/4 inches. Copyright Henry Taylor. Courtesy of the artist and Hauser & Wirth.

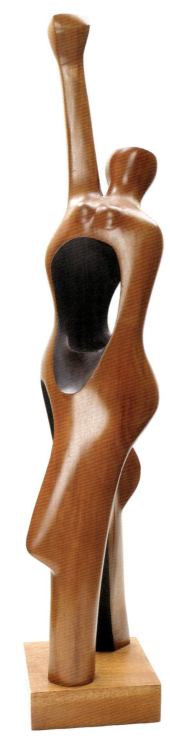

Plate 11 Elizabeth Catlett, *Homage to My Young Black Sisters*, 1968. Copyright 2022, Mora-Catlett Family. Licensed by VAGA at Artists Rights Society, New York.

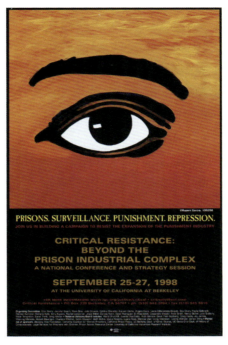

Plate 12 Rupert Garcia, *Critical Resistance* poster, 1998, 17 × 11 inches. Courtesy of the University Archives & Special Collections Department, Joseph Healey Library, University of Massachusetts, Boston: Stephen Lewis Poster collection.

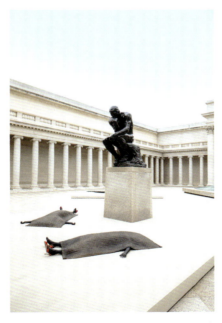

Plate 13 Wangechi Mutu, Installation shot, *I Am Speaking, Are You Listening?* Exhibition, Legion of Honor, San Francisco. From *Wangechi Mutu: I am Speaking, Are you Listening?* Edited by Claudia Schmuckli and published by the Fine Arts Museums of San Francisco and DelMonico Books/DAP in 2021. Photo: Gary Sexton.

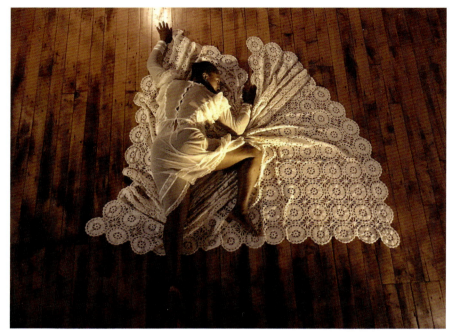

Plate 14 Deborah Goffe, *Privy*, 2016. Photo by Kelly Silliman. Courtesy of Scapegoat Garden, Inc.

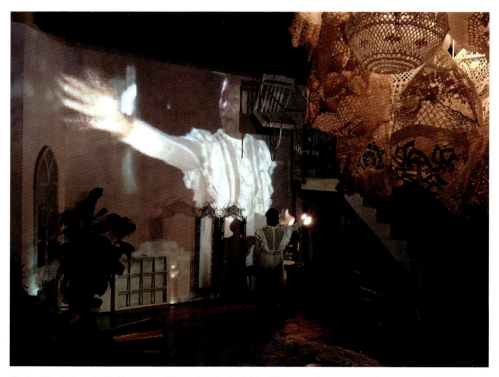

Plate 15 Deborah Goffe, *Privy*, 2016. Photo by Kelly Silliman. Courtesy of Scapegoat Garden, Inc.

2
FROM *THE NEW BLACK* AND
FROM *SEMIAUTOMATIC*
Evie Shockley

ode to my blackness

you are my shelter from the storm
                        and the storm
my anchor
                    and the troubled sea

                *   *   *

night casts you warm and glittering
upon my shoulders   some would
say you give off no heat   some folks
can't see beyond the closest star

                *   *   *

you are the tunnel john henry died
            to carve
i see the light
            at the end   of you   the beginning

                *   *   *

i dig down deep and there you are   at the root of my blues
you're all thick and dark, enveloping   the root of my blues
seem like it's so hard to let you go   when i got nothing to lose

                *   *   *

without you, i would be just

                    a self of my former shadow

buried truths

are you not the sweet to rave on
and on about, the smart in
the sore, the phantasy so near,
so far from dark disney's phantom?

are you not the cold drama doing hot duty, the remedy aloe
salving new york city's forty-one
gaping pus-filled wounds?

are you not the river jordan
we must cross this very day, visceral evidence of florida's abyss?

are you not the crimson mark
circling the crater white brits dug in
the brown earth of tottenham?

are you not the handfuls of rice
thrown up in cleveland's tame air,
a cloud raining sharply down
that will not be swept away?

are you not the filamentary niche, a
sign of how fear will make bride
of blood, how it motors cities,
flaming, right off the map?

are you not the silvery key, a
raft rigged with new vines, buoyed
by bronzeville's kitchenette arias?

are you not the atmospheric
rush to infuse lungs dying to garner
inspiring staten island breezes?

are you not the fertile mystery cajoling hope, despite narrow ills, on
a half-plucked wing and a half-heard
prayer in lima, ohio's wasted land?

are you not the jet stream germane
to the question of whose scar becomes whose scare, screams or tires
peeling on greater toronto streets?

are you not the music's ignition,
the beat, the bass, and the bell
sounding new york's belated alarm?

are you not the young life ready
to explode from the wet shell of gray
into riotous mobtown flower?

—after keorapetse kgositsile

dependencies

visiting monticello was
an education   of course   you
named your home in a romance
language   spent 40 years
constructing it   and the myth
of yourself

we hold these truths

(freedom)

you designed your home on aesthetic
and scientific principles   maximizing   space
in the main house   by placing
the dependencies   beneath   and behind
it   built into the hillside   half
underground

to be self

*These "dependencies," or areas for domestic work, served as points of
intersection between Jefferson's family and enslaved people, and were
instrumental to the functioning of the house.*

-evident, that

i hear you loved
wine (we have that in common)
you had a cellar full of french
vintage you drew up
to the dining room   via
a dumbwaiter that ran between
you and the person
waiting (dumbly) below   to set
the dark bottles   in place

all men are

i hear you had
sally hemmings   i hear you
and she   had
six children   thus making a dependency
of your bedroom (another part
of the house   rarely seen)

created equal and are

(free)

you had james   (another
hemmings) to travel   to paris
to study french cuisine   to cook
for you   for wages
during your years in france

endowed

_Monticello, which means "little mountain" in Italian, was a house,
an ornamental landscape, a diverse community that included as many
as 140 enslaved men, women, and children, and a plantation._

by their creator

as president   you sent lewis
and clark west   they returned
with maps   american elk antlers   native
american art painted on dried buffalo
hide   you placed
these items on your walls
for the edification of your visitors

with certain in alien able

you founded the university
of virginia   from your notes
students would learn they must compete
with the oorang-ootan   for
the negress's favors   from your life
they would learn

rights, that among

like you   i read   the poetry
of that good christian   phillis wheatley
her ode to george washington   the one
who freed his slaves

these are   life

you promised james hemmings
his freedom   if he would
return with you from france
(where he was   free) and teach   (enslaved)
others the french style of cooking
i hear   you were as   good
as your   word

liberty

James Hemmings trained his brother Peter, completed an inventory of the kitchen, and left Monticello in February 1796. Word came in 1801 that he had "committed an act of suicide."

                                                 and   [what was it locke said?]

your pen   successfully severed
religious belief   from civic life
you drafted the   declaration of   independence
this is the legacy   you left
to the country   to your creditors
you left   130 black people   enslaved
in payment of debts

                                          the pursuit   **of happiness**

in some world   an even
newer one   i might have liked you
and you might have liked
(not fancied)   me
we might have shared   a bottle
a conversation   some poems
in this world   i prefer your   words
depending   on them   to be
better   than you

cogito ergo loquor

some brutalities are unspeakable, and we shouldn't force ourselves to speak of them.
                      —ching-in chen

i think, therefore i am.
                    —rené descartes

i.

i could speak of the economic fist that slammed
   into the body of the elderly woman downstairs ::
used to be downstairs : taking her time but not
   taking help bringing in the groceries : lucky to
live in a first-floor apartment :: less lucky now :
   she learned how many more dollars a month

above her rent the building owners need to turn
　　~~a trick~~ a profit :: did they foresee how many
slow steps she'd take to find a new home ? did
　　they bruise their tight red knuckles ?: the grey
powdering the half-nappy pony-puff she pulled
　　her hair into bought her a little time but what
will it get her on the open market ?: her eviction
　　was the fourth bomb dropped this month in
the war on poverty the wealthy are waging on my
　　block : in which i am a diplomat and a survivor.

ii.

to speak of *fists* is not to speak of *fistulas* : false
　　cognates we might misrecognize as kin :: the
latter comes from latin and a word meaning *pipe*
　　or *tube* but the one does not lead necessarily
to the other :: as anarcha's doctor taught us : right
　　after swearing the hypocritic oath : fistulas are
torn tissue : as in : a passage between the urethra
　　and the vagina :: as one cannot close the vulva at
will this causes : in terms of plumbing : a leak ::
　　i do not mention this to be vulgar : *vulgar* and
vulva being another case of fake cousins kissing
　　:: anarcha's condition resulted from slave labor :
the difficult delivery of a tiny new hand unto its
　　master :: o there are other causes : ask the war-
weary women of the congo :: but upon advice
　　and consideration i will not speak of them.

iii.

nor should we force ourselves to be silent ::
　　unmentionables once were underwear : where
were the worst brutalities then ?: buried under
　　under in the most vulnerable organs and held
down by that busy muscle the tongue :: in
　　silence *unspeakable* becomes *unthinkable* : a word
like *numberless* that runs *can't* into *won't* :: some
　　unthinkable things i just keep tninking about :
a 7-year-old girl and a gang rape facilitated by
　　her 15-year-oid sister for money : a 95-year-old

floridian woman stripped of her wet diaper
    by airport security : a congolese man who wears
pads meant for menstrual blood after years as
    a prisoner of war : companies seeking off-shore-
drilling permits while uncontrollable oil is still
    ravaging an ecosystem :: thinkable : unthinkable.

iv.

perhaps *unimaginable* should stand between
    ourselves and the worst :: if i spare myself
and you : gentle reader : if i spare us the graphic
    details will we still write checks to fund the less
poetic work of others ?: or is *checks* itself too far
    from lyrical for your taste ?: palatable poetry
comes in fewer flavors than edible cuisine : yet
    taste and *palatable* swing between the tongue
and the mind : a dance this poem has already
    performed :: can we empathize without taking
on the trauma ?: can we pursue cognition by
    a path that cuts through the body but bypasses
the gut ?: i must insist that my need for shelter :
    clean air & water : dignity : good food : security
: love : peace : and joy exists in you and every
    you : us : humans :: we are not false cognates.

3

ART AND NEGATIVE DIALECTICS: ON SOFT AESTHETICS[1]

Angela Y. Davis

This is an exciting moment. We are here in Oakland, and it is May 1, International Workers Day. We gather on colonized land, the land of the Ohlone. A place with a very rich history, a place where 50 years ago the Black Panther Party was founded. We are here in Oakland among artists, other cultural workers, educators, activists, organizers. We are here in Oakland where we all know that Black lives matter. Oakland is the home of Oscar Grant, of Occupy, of Critical Resistance, of Black Lives Matter. The Transgender, Gender-Variant, and Intersex Justice Project is physically located across the bay, but has a very strong presence in the Oakland abolitionist movement. And so Oakland is an amazing place, it's an amazing place for the anti-policing, anti-prison, restorative justice and radical education movements, for disability justice movements, for environmental movements, for food sovereignty movements. Oakland is a place where art and politics are always clashing, always interacting, and frequently converging.

No radical social transformation is ever imaginable without the pivotal role of art and culture. The theme of this conference is power, and of course since we're in Oakland, we cannot help but add "to the people"—power to the people, power to the people! And thus we remember the founding of the Black Panther Party fifty years ago. Bobby Seale and Huey Newton were students at Merritt College when they founded the Black Panther Party in 1966.

This is an image created by Henry Taylor in 2007, one of the countless number of artists inspired by the Black Panther Party, to call for radical change through their art practices (Plate 10). Elizabeth Catlett is a prime example. This is her 1993 *Homage to the Panthers*. And this is the wood sculpture that is entitled *Black Unity*, which she made in 1968, but you have to see the other side of the fist [shows the two side-by-side faces forming the obverse]. See? And this one, *Homage to My Young Black Sisters*, presaging Black Lives Matter and its distinctly feminist and queer dimension (Plate 11).

Of course, it's impossible to evoke visual art related to the Black Panther Party without acknowledging Emory Douglas, who represents the enduring legacy of the Black Panther Party. And this is the logo he created, inspired by the Lowndes County Freedom

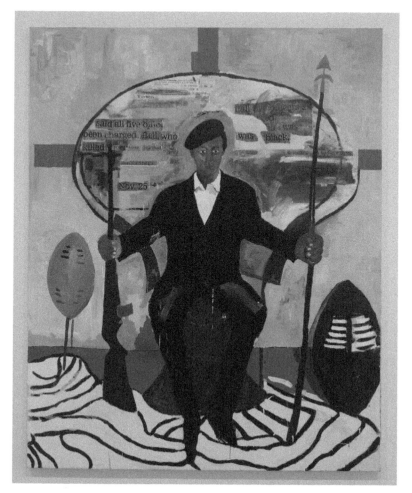

Plate 10 Henry Taylor, *Huey Newton*, 2007. Acrylic and collaged photocopies on canvas, 94 5/8 × 76 1/4 inches. Copyright Henry Taylor. Courtesy of the artist and Hauser & Wirth.

Democratic Party in Alabama, competing, of course, with the elephant and the donkey. Emory's work was widely circulated through the Black Panther Party newspaper. ["Mannenberg" begins.]

Abdullah Ibrahim is playing in the background ("Mannenberg") and speaking in an interview:

> We were in Cape Town at a recording studio and it was just at the time of what came to be known as the Soweto uprising. . . . I don't know where it came from "ba boo ba do de . . ." and then the musicians picked it up, and then we got a little bridge going off that, "da da ba da dum . . ." and we recorded it. I think it was about 17 minutes. And that's just one take, and then we went back to record the other music. But we kept on thinking, well something has happened with that recording that we just

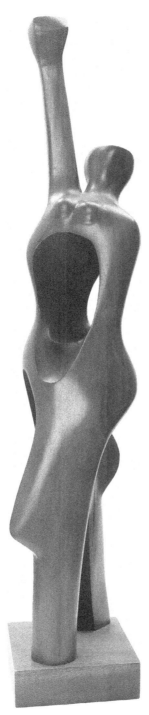

Plate 11 Elizabeth Catlett, *Homage to My Young Black Sisters*, 1968. Copyright 2022, Mora-Catlett Family. Licensed by VAGA at Artists Rights Society, New York.

need to. . . . So, we asked the engineer to play it back, and we realized what had happened is that it captured the spirit and the mood of the nation at that time . . . and it was confirmation and affirmation of our cultural and political inheritance, and the public or the people picked up the song and it was played and sung everywhere, and in some regard it has become almost like an unofficial anthem, national anthem of South Africa.

According to Ibrahim, when Mandela heard the recording of "Mannenberg," which was smuggled into Robben Island Prison, he said "liberation is near." In describing his own approach to art, Ibrahim notes that often times in order to generate the power that we need, softness is required. He says, "softness overcomes the hardness. Even in that horrendous system that we lived under in South Africa, we learned from our parents and grandparents and our teachers that softness will overcome."

As I listen to Ibrahim it becomes clear to me why this conference, *Open Engagement*, is so important. The conference offers us possibilities of collective reflection and the softness he evokes is precisely a place of reflection, a place of imagination, a place of possibility. A song, an image, or any other work of art can push us to travel to universes beyond, to places animated by freedom and justice. And not primarily in the sense of discovering the *fact* of freedom and justice once and for all, but rather in the sense of discovering a motion, a constant motion, a constant movement that is both comforting and troubling, the sense that whenever we land, wherever we land, we have to continue to move.

["Waters from an Ancient Well" by Abdullah Ibrahim begins.] Some of you might recognize "Waters from an Ancient Well." So, art plays a pivotal role in shaping the awareness of people who can change the world. The philosopher Herbert Marcuse once pointed out that "[a]rt . . . can contribute to changing the consciousness and drives of the men and women [and all] who [can] change the world."[2] There is an affinity here between art and critical engagements with the world. Whether implicitly or explicitly, art challenges the status quo, it challenges the world as it is. Both art and critical theory direct our attention away from what is, away from the given, away from the *facticity* of the world, and they point elsewhere. They point elsewhere towards possibility. And this happens through the power of negation. If, according to Marcuse, art is negation and possibility, and if critical theory relies on negative dialectics to focus our attention on and beyond *what is* in order to make room for *what might be*, then one can argue that this is precisely the power we need to generate: critical engagements, critical theory, critical resistance.

Almost 20 years ago, I became involved in a movement we called Critical Resistance: Beyond the Prison Industrial Complex. Some of you may remember the poster that circulated in connection with the conference. This image was created by Rupert Garcia, a well-known Bay Area artist and co-founder of Galería de la Raza. In all of our organizing to bring people together from all over the world to initiate a conversation about dismantling the prison industrial complex, what constituted the beginnings of the current abolitionist movement, perhaps the most interesting and most intense conversations revolved around the role of visual art and the politics of representation. In exploring how we wanted to publicly represent this new movement, there were those who assumed that, of course,

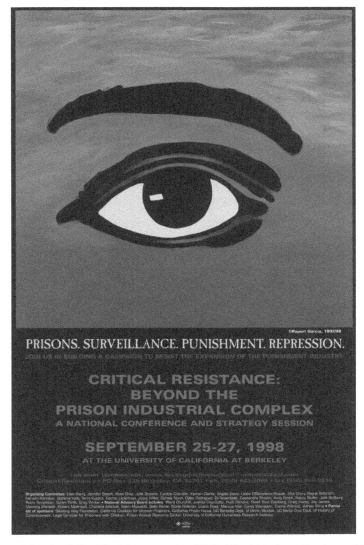

Plate 12 Rupert Garcia, *Critical Resistance* poster, 1998, 17 × 11 inches. Courtesy of the University Archives & Special Collections Department, Joseph Healey Library, University of Massachusetts, Boston: Stephen Lewis Poster collection.

we would rely on images of bars and chains. But we fought about this assumption. Some insisted that if the poster contained bars and chains and depictions of objects that effectively convince people that they are already aware of the nature of jails and prisons, they will walk past the poster without giving it another thought. We needed an image that would speak to them in a different way, an image that would provoke them to thought from the outset.

I've been friends with the artist Rupert Garcia for many years, so I approached him about ideas for a poster that would not include the usual bars, chains, handcuffs, etc.

Eventually, he offered us an image of an enormous eye painted against a bright yellow orange background (Plate 12). He characterized it as the eye of surveillance, of carceral supervision, but also the eye that envisions the future because the backdrop is a beautiful sunrise. Precisely because this was an image encouraging engagement and reflection, I am sure that played a major role in attracting the 3,500 people who attended the conference, ten times as many as we were initially expecting.

I have been talking about critical thinking, critical theory, critical resistance. If Ibrahim tells us that power does not always have to be aggressive and destructive, that it can be soft and transformative and interdisciplinary and reflexive, and it can help transform our worlds and purge them of domination and oppression and make them more habitable for human and all other beings, this means that critical power, critical resistance rely on and educate the imagination. The imagination is as central to the production of knowledge, to our thought processes as it is certainly central to the process of producing and engaging with art.

When I was a young graduate student, I found it very helpful to study Immanuel Kant— and, parenthetically, I decided to include these observations in my talk today because I have recently encountered students who are reluctant to read the work of thinkers whom they refer to as "dead white men." Of course, it may very well be the case that much of that work will not necessarily enlighten us, but we have to realize that this is the world we live in, and it is incumbent upon us to understand its intellectual foundations—especially if we are setting out to change the world. I am not at all embarrassed to say that I found Kant provocative, and useful. I was especially impressed by the way he maps out a pivotal position for aesthetics, precisely because art and the aesthetic judgment are able to represent freedom in a way that is impossible using ordinary language and discourse. In the *Critique of Judgment* he argues that freedom is a moral concept, but beauty can be the symbol of morality. The ability to be moved by a work of art or something that is beautiful points to a human capacity to use the imagination in a way that is not confined to our usual cognitive processes. One of the major deficiencies in public education is the failure to teach children the value of the imagination. Art can teach us lessons that are nowhere else to be found, knowledges that have always eluded conceptual thought that can only be rendered possible through art. I am referring to the epistemological value of art.

Let me refer to Marcuse again, who in his last book, *The Aesthetic Dimension: Toward a Critique of Marxist Aesthetics*, wrote,

> Inasmuch as art preserves, with the promise of happiness, the memory of the goals that failed, it can enter, as a "regulative idea," the desperate struggle for changing the world. Against all fetishism of the productive forces, against the continued enslavement of individuals by objective conditions (which remain those of domination) art represents the ultimate goal of all revolutions: the freedom and the happiness of the individual.[3]

This is the power of art. Art can inspire people to struggle for economic and political and educational and sexual power. If we want to talk about the struggle to change the world, this requires us to engage with power. This requires us to bring politics into the frame.

Therefore I would like to move toward a discussion of the Black radical tradition where art, philosophical perspectives, and politics have always been enmeshed. The most consistent philosophical theme in the history of Black people in this hemisphere has been the quest for freedom. It has always been taken for granted that the United States of America is the oldest democracy in the world, and that France is the second oldest, right? But we know that both American and French democracies recognized no contradiction between their endorsement of enslavement and the enslavement trade, on the one hand, and their proclamations of human equality, on the other. These democracies were therefore inherently elitist. Elitist democracy sounds like an oxymoron, doesn't it? But this is the secret of Western democracies: they have always been democracies of the minority.

On the other hand, the Haitian revolution lead by Toussaint Louverture produced the world's first non-racial democracy. Interestingly, in the 1805 Haitian constitution conceived by Jean-Jacques Dessalines, all citizens regardless of their racial background were designated as "Black." "In this manner," I'm quoting the political theorist, Siba N'Zatioula Grovogui, "'black' became a symbol around which to organize national solidarity and public life. As a result, 'black' thus was not an exclusionary category . . . . [B]y this constitutional gesture, the 'black' majority welcomed all others to rejoice in the identity of the majority."[4]

From the very beginning, the subject of democracy has been raced as white. The subject of human rights has been clandestinely raced as white. So, Grovogui asks: Why cannot we imagine humanity as exemplified by those who have been most suppressed, as exemplified by those who have had to rely on their own collective struggle for freedom to define the very meaning of humanity? Why is it so difficult to envision Black humanity as representative of all humanity that can aspire toward universality? Haiti's constitution proclaimed all citizens to be Black by virtue of their citizenship. If our "freedom dreams," to use Robin Kelley's wonderful phrase, can be enriched by this proposition, what happens if we imagine Black women as the measure of humanity? Racial hierarchies were temporarily overturned by the Haitian revolution, establishing a goal toward which we continue to aspire today—one of those unfulfilled promises to which Marcuse was referring.

If racial hierarchies need to be overturned, so too do gender hierarchies. Zora Neale Hurston reminded us that the Black woman is the mule of the world. So, what if the mules of the world become the very measure of humanity? This would be real power. And this is the question that has been posed by the Black Lives Matter movement.

This is why we need to make Hillary Clinton accountable. And especially accountable for her recent unconscious invocation of the racist history of the colonization of North America when she suggested [in 2016] that she would have no problems dealing with Donald Trump because, and I quote, "I have a lot of experience dealing with men who sometimes get off the reservation in the way they behave and they speak." It is increasingly recognized that such metaphors serve as incontrovertible evidence of the racism that has shape U.S. culture, and Clinton was the target of much criticism for her casual use of such a term. While her national political director issued an apology, she herself failed to take advantage of what could have certainly been a teachable moment. Clinton could have lead the country in a conversation about the extent to which racism against indigenous people has become so embedded in the collective psyche that we don't recognize it. I have raised this issue because I personally think that she might indicate that she is committed to challenging anti-indigenous racism by working for the freedom of Leonard Peltier. It has been 40 years since he was arrested in connection with the struggles at Wounded Knee. So, here is an image of Leonard Peltier. And here are some of his paintings, some of the works he has produced during the four decades he has been behind bars. And I couldn't resist showing this poster. "And we are still here."[5] Indigenous people are always represented as having disappeared, as invisible.

When Trayvon Martin was killed in 2012, I thought about David Hammons's 1993 installation that was entitled *In the Hood*, and it seems as if this work quietly presaged the racist murder of Trayvon Martin as well as the responses of the Dream Defenders and Black Lives Matter. For those who argue that Black Lives Matter is a slogan and concept based on a narrow and particular portion of humanity, it might help to recognize that no one who has not already been identified as white has been welcomed into whiteness, but blackness has a much further reach than its own racial implications. Recall the Haitian Constitution's redefinition of blackness. A visit to the Black Lives Matter website reveals demands that particularize even further the importance of recognizing the way racism works: if Black lives matter, Black women matter, Black girls matter, Black gay lives matter, Black bi lives matter, Black boys matter, Black queer lives matter, Black men matter, Black lesbians matter, Black trans lives matter, Black immigrants matter, Black incarcerated lives matter, Black differently abled lives matter. Yes, Black lives matter. Latinx, Asian American, Native American, Muslim, poor, and working class white people's lives matter. There are many, many more particular instances that we would have to name before we can ethically and comfortably claim that all lives matter.

I don't think it is coincidental that one of the cofounders of Black Lives Matter, Patrisse Cullors, is a performance artist. She understands the importance of challenging what you might call the tyranny of the universal and the way in which the universal can conceal internal racialization, in, for example, the notion that "all lives matter." Cullors understands the role that art can play in overturning conceptual and material hierarchies that produce relations of domination. She was a member of a delegation that visited Palestine in December 2014 to express solidarity between the Black movement in the U.S. and the struggle for justice in Palestine. And picture maps depicting Palestinian land in 1948, and Palestine in 2014. Which, parenthetically, makes it difficult to even imagine a two-state solution. Where, exactly, would the second state be located, given the colonization of virtually all of Palestine? Picture an image with the words, "Ferguson is Palestine, Palestine is Ferguson."

Cullors and artists in the Black Lives Matter movement understand how important it is to contest what Gayatri Spivak calls the "privatization of the imagination." Art can educate the imagination. It is interesting that at least within the U.S., the contemporary struggles against racist violence have entered the realm of popular music and jazz. From Janelle Monae's 2015 single, *Say Her Name (Hell You Talmbout)*, we heard Common and John Legend's "Glory" as we gathered this evening. And of course everybody knows Kendrick Lamar's *The Blacker the Berry*. It was remarkable, wasn't it, that we were able to see his performance during the Grammys on prime-time network television. While I loved the performance, I have critiques as well. We should all recognize that it's possible to be supportive and to be critical at the same time. And so with Lamar, the performance was absolutely amazing. Particularly since we have rarely if ever seen visual representations of people in prison with that kind of power. But when he closes with an image placing Compton on the map of Africa it seems to me that he minimizes the significance of the continent of Africa. As people of African descent, we have to recognize that the meaning of Africa is far greater than its role as an important element of our origin story. Struggles that are unfolding in Africa for justice and for freedom have the potential to change the world.

I suppose I could also talk about Beyoncé, but everybody is talking about Beyoncé, so I don't think you need my ideas. However, since you're encouraging me, I suppose I can also repeat that one can intensely appreciate an aesthetic experience and at the same time be ambivalent about it. So, I can appreciate the openings that have been created as a result of Beyoncé's work, but I cannot ignore the corporate capitalist dimension that I would subject to rigorous critique. I was planning to mention the jazz trumpeter Terence Blanchard's album, *Breathless*, inspired by Eric Garner's plea, "I can't breathe." And of course, we have to pay tribute to Prince. I remember when Prince was asked to present the album of the year at the Grammys, and he said quite simply, "like Black lives and books, albums also matter." A quiet and powerful statement.

Last year we observed the 100th anniversary of the birth of Billie Holliday [1915]. Her music continues to be heard both in its original versions and through others such as Cécile Mclorin Salvant, many of whose performances this year have been organized around Lady Day's music. But of course I cannot fail to mention Nina Simone. When we speak about the way in which art can generate the power to contest the status quo, we have to evoke Simone, who, in her own words, devoted her art entirely to the struggle. Those of us who were inspired by her in earlier years are very happy that she is becoming popular among a new generation. For some the anthem of the freedom movement was "We Shall Overcome," but for many of us it was, "Mississippi Goddamn!" Simone definitely urged us to stretch our imagination when she sang, "I wish I would know how it would feel to be free." Lauryn Hill is the featured artist on a new release that pays tribute to Simone. And perhaps not so incidentally, Lauryn Hill also narrates Göran Olsson's new documentary on Frantz Fanon entitled *Concerning Violence*.

A number of recent visual art exhibitions have asked us to revisit the relationship between art and struggle. The 2011–2012 Hammer Museum *Now Dig This!: Art and Black Los Angeles 1960–1980*, curated by Kellie Jones, included work by Charles White, Betye Saar, Noah Purifoy, John Outterbridge, Samella Lewis, Marie Johnson, and many others. One of the artists featured in that exhibition was Hammons, whom I evoked earlier in relation to his 1990s installation *In the Hood*, the disembodied hooded sweatshirt. Hammons has described his own practice as "tragic magic," tragic magic in which he takes the "discarded vestiges of Black life, and transforms them, restoring to them a lost potency reinvested with the power of the fetish."[6] His work simultaneously evokes profound grief and quiet joy at the possibility of reawakening. In fact, much of the work in this exhibition, produced during what is taken to be the most combative phase of the Black Liberation movement, does not appear to promote impulsive militancy, but rather demands deep reflection. The catalogue cover reproduces the lithograph Charles White offered to the committee organized around the demand for my freedom. It depicts a Black woman and a red rose and is entitled *Love Letter #1*. The committee created postcards bearing this image on one side and a letter to then Governor Ronald Reagan on the other calling upon him to release me on bail. The first line of the message is "Because we love justice and freedom."

Continuing with this theme of political prisoners, I am reminded that Herman Wallace's time in Angola prison, eventually including 41 years in solitary confinement, inspired the artist Jackie Sumell to ask a simple question in 2003: "What kind of house does a man who has lived in a 6 ft. by 9 ft. cell for over 30 years dream of?" This image is of the installation, and that is the cell he lived in. He imagined a house with flowers and grass—not that distinctive a house, but someplace peaceful where he could be with his family and friends. You may know that when Herman was finally released on October 1, 2013, he died three days later. This was both a defeat and a history.

I will wind up my remarks by emphasizing the importance of these times. In many ways we have been waiting for this moment for decades. The turn towards freedom struggle in art and music, in theater, in visual art signals a historical conjuncture where radical change is being recognized as a real possibility. I say *possibility*, which does not mean that it will happen as a matter of course; it will not happen if we do not make it happen. But this is precisely the time to become involved in the many and varied ways we can promote an equitable future.

But let us remember that as we are currently engaging with racist violence in this country, similar struggles are unfolding in other places. In Europe, the immigration crisis has reached massive proportions. They are witnessing a postcolonial revenge. We in the U.S. should pay attention because this country is certainly not immune when it comes to responsibility for the current refugee crises in Europe. Who invaded Iraq, who invaded Afghanistan, who is responsible for the upsurges in Syria? Yes, racism is a global phenomenon.

And the power of art, art as power, can help us to decolonize our minds, in the way that Ngũgĩ Wa Thiong'o insisted decades ago. We are witnessing the popularization of more complex analyses of racism and misogyny, especially those that have developed within the context of Black and women of color feminisms, and these approaches can assist us to understand how deeply racist violence is embedded in our country's historical, economic, and ideological structures. These new ways of talking about racism, especially the structural and institutional essence of racism, can help us to grasp the global reach of our struggles. This is how we might recognize our responsibility to end the occupation of Palestine, particularly given the extent to which the U.S. government is the main financial backer of the occupation and considering the ways Islamophobia has begun to redefine the terrain of racism.

Deeper understandings of racist violence arm us against deceptive solutions. When we are told that our response to racist police violence in our communities should be to call for "better" police, who will refrain from attacking young Black and Brown people, we should counter with the recognition that the institution itself is saturated with violence. Racist police violence will continue, until we recognize and begin to transform its structural character. When we are told that we need better prisons, we should respond by saying that a better prison is no prison. This is a period in which we are called upon to reimagine security and call for abolition of policing and imprisonment as we know them today. We say demilitarize the police, disarm the police, abolish the institution of the police as we know it, and abolish imprisonment as the dominant mode of punishment.

But that is just the beginning of our struggle for power, justice, and sustainability. Let us reflect on how we might promote this process of radical change. I end with *Liberation Over Gangsterism* by Christian Scott aTunde Adjuah featuring Elena Pinderhughes, on flute. [music plays.] Thank you.

Notes

1   This essay was first delivered as a Keynote Lecture at the "Open Engagement 2016: Power" conference held on May 1, 2016, at the Oakland Museum of California. It was edited for the present volume. For the full lecture with a question and answer segment, see: https://youtu. be/oqC6T4oooCE [Editors' note]. I would like to express my gratitude to René de Guzman and Jen de los Reyes, and all of the other organizers of this conference for inviting me to participate in these creative deliberations on the theme of power. And I understand that this conference initiates a three-year cycle of gatherings: this year [2016] on the theme of power in Oakland; next year on the theme of justice in Laquan McDonald's Chicago, where the city government seriously needs to learn some lessons on the meaning of justice; and the following year in New York on sustainability; and of course the environmental movements, water and food movements, constitute ground zero of the quest for social justice. The children of Flint Michigan are teaching us that we can no longer even take water for granted.

2   Herbert Marcuse, *The Aesthetic Dimension*: *Toward a Critique of Marxist Aesthetics* (Boston: Beacon Press, 1978), 32–3.

3   Marcuse, *The Aesthetic Dimension*, 69.

4   Siba N'Zatioula Grovogui, "To the orphaned, dispossessed, and illegitimate children: Human rights beyond republican and liberal traditions," *Indiana Journal of Global Legal Studies*, Vol. 18, No. 1 (Winter 2011), 41–63; 58.

5   The poster displayed during the lecture depicts indigenous people and the words, "Homeland Security: Fighting Terrorism since 1492": https://www.northernsun.com/Homeland-Security-Sticker-%285094%29.html. And "We Are Still Here" is on the cover of Dick Bancroft and Laura Waterman Wittstock's book, *We Are Still Here: A Photographic History of the American Indian Movement* (Nepean, Ontario: Borealis Books, 2013). [Editors' note]

6   David L. Smith, "David Hammons: Spade Worker," in *Yardbird Suite, Hammons 93*, ed. Deborah Menaker Rothschild (Williamstown, MA: Williams College Museum of Art, 1994). See also: https://artmap.com/zwirnerwirthny/exhibition/david-hammons-2006?print=do.

4

EMBRACING INJURY: BLACK QUEER BODIES AND POETIC EXPERIMENTATION

GerShun Avilez

Afro-Pessimism has become a dominant, though contested, strain of theory within African American Studies in the twenty-first century.[1] This school of thought involves a critical emphasis on injury and social death as the dominant ways to articulate the state of Black being within the context of ongoing anti-Black racism. Such racism can seem so totalizing that it can be difficult to imagine full Black subjectivity or Black identity outside of the constraints of racialized oppression, hence Afro-*Pessimism*. One may wonder what—if any—relationship exists between this critical discourse and trends in contemporary artistic production. In other words, to what extent do artists explore the social threats of social death? Furthermore, and perhaps more important, how might artists aestheticize notions of social death in ways that may move beyond the bounds of critical culture? To address these questions, I turn to the writing of performance poet Danez Smith, specifically their *Don't Call Us Dead: Poems*.[2] Smith embraces physical and emotional vulnerability in a way that seems to mirror the discourse around social death, but the artist recasts such vulnerabilities as valuable sites of subject formation and artistic innovation.[3] In addition, Smith couples their thinking about racial identity with an exploration of queer sexuality and embodiment, elements very nearly absent from many considerations of social death, in rethinking the social meaning of vulnerability.

I argue that the realities of anti-Black racism and homophobia become the basis for a reformulation of identity instead of primarily mechanisms for objectification in Smith's poems. The paradigm of the Black-body-as-object integral to the logic of social death becomes a vehicle for creation, a pathway rather than an unsurmountable fact. In addition, Smith illustrates how illness and desire give shape to the experience of vulnerability, and they provide a language for documenting this impact. As I explore this artistic project of embracing vulnerability, I also show how this vulnerability gets translated into experimental poems. Smith's poems map the queer body onto the space of the page. Part of my argument is that Smith's attention to Black queer vulnerability puts him in a genealogy of Black queer artists concerned with the vicissitudes of Black experience. Specifically, I connect Smith's work to that of Melvin Dixon and Sharon Bridgforth, particularly in terms of these writers' experimental aesthetic projects. Following such writers, Smith offers a rendering of the aesthetics of queerness and suggests that poetic fragmentation becomes the most effective way to capture the complexity of queer life. Smith presents a series of structural strategies to convey the social significance of non-normativity and minority status. In the final analysis, Smith's innovative poetry collection is a meditation on the value of embracing vulnerability for the queer subject and offers significant insight into the critical exploration of injury to contemporary Black queer writing.

There are two dominant impulses in *Don't Call Us Dead*. The first is the desire to illuminate the significance of racism and the social and affective legacies of enslavement. This impulse is paired with the goal of conveying the experience of living with HIV. Thinking about racism alongside the stigmatization of HIV/AIDS allows Smith to think about different expressions of embodied injury and to explore the seeming ubiquity of threat and death for subjects who sit at the intersections of minority status. Part of what Smith tries to achieve in their poems is the translation of the implicit idea of duality that comes from thinking about racism and homophobia-tinged stigma around illness. The experimental form of many of the poems can be thought of as registering the poet's engaging performances of the pieces on the page, as Smith is a performance poet. However, the structure of the poems, as I will show, also reflects a desire to capture this double vision and the multi-faceted nature of injury onto the pages of the collection.

The poem "Everyday is a Funeral & a Miracle," which sits at the heart of the collection, provides an overview of the conceptual project of the collection as a whole in that it illustrates a triangulation of AIDS, social threat, and poetic experimentation. The poem presents a speaker talking about his life and connects himself to Black figures such as Tamir Rice and Rekiya Boyd, both of whom were shot by police officers. Following this connection, the speaker insists that "some of us are killed in pieces, some of us all at once."[4] The point is that Rice and Boyd are killed all at once because of the fatal gunshots. The speaker is one who is symbolically killed in pieces as his body becomes overwhelmed with AIDS, which is referenced in the next stanza. It is important to note that the poem is a segmented poem that conflates sexual desire with the threat of death. Although it is segmented, there are not numbered sections as in the poem "seroconversion," to which I will return. Instead, the sections of the poem are separated or differentiated by two slash lines (//). This structural division appears in other poems in the collection: "you're dead, America," "not an elegy," "blood hangover," "crown," "recklessly," and "summer, somewhere." Therefore, the slash lines represent a dominant method for crafting individual poems. Smith primarily writes segmented poems. This structural element (//) instantiates the idea of being in pieces, or having one's body broken literally by a bullet and figuratively by an illness; in addition, the insistence on using double lines encapsulates the idea of duality that undergirds the collection.

The ideas of corporeal segmentation and dual threat are most powerfully linked in a few lines near the end of the poem: "I got this problem: I was born / Black & faggoty / they sent a boy / when the bullet missed."[5] This assertion shows that there are dual (or perhaps multiple) kinds of threats the speaker faces: social and personal. Implicitly, the speaker faces the same kind of vulnerability from the state that Rice and Boyd faced. In addition, the poem suggests that intimacy itself presents a parallel kind of material threat through the possibility of contraction of HIV. Being "Black & faggoty" renders one vulnerable. Furthermore, part of the point that Smith makes is that whether we like it or not, desire and our emotional connections are caught up in a web of power structures and social dynamics. The U.S. government may not have invented AIDS, but the social and political neglect of its development over decades and the lack of access to treatment for many people hastened the spread of the virus and has effectively created (the context for) the rates of high infection among Black Americans.[6] The government's neglect made it possible for the "boy" in the poem to accomplish the task of the bullet.

What I am trying to point out is that aesthetic attention to AIDS — particularly in thinking about the biology of the virus — in the context of anti-Black violence yields artistic experimentation and significant social theorizing. In this way Smith builds on the work of earlier artists living with AIDS that theorized the condition, especially Melvin Dixon. In fact, I think of much of *Don't Call Us Dead* as a rewriting or reformulation of Dixon's posthumously published poetry collection *Love's Instruments*, which explores the experience of living with AIDS in a number of the poems alongside meditations on the possibilities of and parameters on Black gay life.[7] Dixon's "Heartbeats" is perhaps the most well-known poem in *Love's Instruments*. The poem consists of forty lines of mostly iambic dimeter.[8] The meter of the poem is meant to mimic the two-part pumping action of the heart muscle with two complete beats (four symbolic contractions) per line: "Work out. Ten Laps / Chin ups. Look Good / [. . .] Sore throat. Long Flu."[9] The poem tracks a person's transition from a healthy body to a body living with HIV. Though the terms HIV, AIDS, or virus never appear in the poem, Dixon's diction actively seeks to suggest that the central figure has been exposed: "hard nodes," Whites low," "Loose stools," "Weight Loss." Part of what the poem reflects is the collective social silence around infection. There was of course neglect on the part of the state and the media, as Cathy Cohen so carefully proves.[10] However, because there was so much stigma around HIV and AIDS, the disease was talked about in whispers. Seeing someone's weight loss or an engorged gland communicated something even if nothing was said out loud. The poem models this reading of the illness through the body without explicit communication.

More important, through this poem, Dixon performs the monumental task of putting the reader within the body of the person living with HIV. The meter of the poem is the heart beat of an individual with HIV. We not only experience the progression of the illness as the chin ups (the exercise) transmogrify into keeping one's chin up because of depression. Our speech and breath become the beats of a failing heart. The metrical design forges an intimacy between the reader and the HIV+ body. We are inside that body — the rhetorical move stages an imagined intimacy that few would be so willing to risk in life or even in their imaginations. Every syllable that we that we state moves us closer to the final breath of the last line: "breathe out." As a whole the poem moves from a place of control to uncertainty. The iambic dimeter lines get replaced by trochaic dimeter lines meaning that there is a structural move in terms of syllabic stress from rising action to falling action. In addition, question marks emerge in the final few lines suggesting the idea of uncertainty. These ideas of falling and uncertainty indicate the presence of death but through the poetic design situate the reader as adjacent to, intimate with, and inside the space of the dying.

My goal is to position Dixon as a primary interlocutor for Smith, as both think about the Black queer body and the impact of HIV on the perception of that body as well as the experience of inhabiting that body. Smith's poem "seroconversion" helps to illuminate this connection. The idea of seroconversion, which denotes transitioning from being HIV- to HIV+, is an important linkage between the 1996 collection and the 2017 collection in that one way of reading "Heartbeats" is as a poetic translation of seroconversion. The shifts in language, meter, and syntax are designed to register graphically the move of the body's status from seronegative to seropositive. Smith's "Seroconversion" is a serial poem made up of a succession of retellings of the encounter that results in infection and conversion; however, none of the encounters actually details a sexual encounter. The fifth and final section begins by asserting, "one day, the boy with the difficult name / laid with a boy who shall remain nameless in the sun."[11] This laying together described in the stanza ends with an ambiguous object rising from ashes, blood-sucking ticks moving toward one of the boys, and a name being called out from dirt. The ticks and dirt suggest both blood and death; however, the poem never loses its focus on intimacy. The narrative that begins as a scene of intimacy is overwhelmed by confusing and disruptive imagery that suggests the emergence of a *different* kind of intimacy: the two bodies are replaced by creatures moving toward one of the bodies and the earth being familiar enough with an individual to call him by his name. Smith moves away from the literal and toward the fabular. The reader encounters princesses, deities, animal viscera, and other powerful and evocative imagery in place of scenes of unprotected sex.

It is noteworthy that Smith chooses to write this poem as a sequence poem. As I have mentioned, the collection as a whole illustrates their interest in segmented poetic structure, but the presentation of the poem in terms of sections is relevant to the meditation on seroconversion. Although the poem is a sequence poem—a poem of five section that appears to be moving in a distinct direction, the poem itself is not sequential. As the reader moves across the five sections, there is not a progressive move toward an idea. Moreover, the sections do not necessarily relate to nor do they grow out of each other. Each section of the poem is a retelling of the same scene as opposed to a progressive movement. The reader keeps returning instead of moving forward. We find a series of retellings as opposed to the clear progress narrative that constitutes the poem "Heartbeats." Why resist the progress narrative the seroconversion itself implies? One way of thinking about this approach is that it provides multiple perspectives and impressions of the same moment. To some extent, time has stopped for the persona and the reader as the retellings turn again and again to the scene of seroconversion. Smith keeps returning attention to the site of transmission complicating it by linking together through the metaphorical imagery ideas about pleasure, confusion, misunderstanding, pain, transformation, and identification. It is a scene of jumbled meaning that never moves past that understating.

The poem "litany with blood all over" picks up where "seroconversion" leaves off and further works through the conceptual terrain laid down by "Heartbeats." If "Heartbeats" situates the reader inside the HIV+ body through metrical design, "litany with blood all over" does so through the graphic presentation of the poem. "litany with blood all over" enhances the thinking in "seroconversion" by exploring the social implications of what are referred to as "test results." The speaker suggests that their test results do not only register serostatus but that they also say something about their personality and character traits. From there, the poem shifts to contemplate the individual who exposed the speaker to the virus. Conflating imagery of a wedding and a funeral, sexual intimacy becomes a means of connecting the two intimate figures while also registering contradictory meanings. The speaker insists that a metaphorical husband has left them "with child." Infection is metaphorized as pregnancy, confusing notions of life and death. The sense of confusion becomes the primary visual strategy of the poem. Smith ends the poem with the repetition of the phrases "my blood" and "his blood." The two phrases initially appear as "my blood his blood" and then later as "his blood my blood." On one hand, the repetition of this phrasing is meant to give substance to the idea of a litany, a series of call and response statements in a religious space. The back-and-forth represents the serial or repeated intimacy with each phrase standing in for the body of each man. The use of the term "litany" also suggests that there is something spiritual about the intimacy or that it effects a connection that moves beyond the body. We also might think about the phrases as suggesting that there are two (or multiple) voices here, each repeating one or both of the phrases. On the other hand, because initially the phrases appear as "my blood his blood" and then later as "his blood my blood" (before being further jumbled), we might consider it as a purposeful chiasmus to emphasize notion of confusion and mixing. Such rhetorical and structural chiasmatic crossings, which is supposed to represent the commingling of life essences, continue to happen until there is no structural integrity to the words. I cannot fully replicate these confused crossings here, but Smith writes the words on top of each other until it is difficult to distinguish individual letters.

Smith does not just repeat the phrases ("my blood" and "his blood") over and over again; the two phrases are scattered all over the page and become mixed together by being written over and against one other. By the end of the last page of the poem, it is difficult to discern the words and phrases. Visual images of long, undulating lines appear where there was once clear text. On one hand, this technique reminds one of the opening to Toni Morrison's novel *The Bluest Eye*, which relies upon the steady compression of text into a mass of letters, as well as some of Glenn Ligon's large-scale prints, which often features texts blurring together on canvas such as *Black Like Me No. 2* (Figure 4.1) or *Untitled: Four Etchings*. Both Morrison and Ligon call attention to literacy, reading, and language as they explore complexities of racism and sexism in Black life. Smith also seeks to question the ability of normative orthography to convey meaning for those that sit at the intersection of multiple sites of oppression. However, there is something else at stake in Smith's poetic experiment. Their crossings and commingling of the words are supposed to represent visually infected blood and suggest that there is something unreadable or perhaps unspeakable about the intimacy and the subjects involved in it. We are offered a peek inside an HIV-positive body. The reader is allowed to bear witness simultaneously to queer intimacy and to infection. Even in the twenty-first century a significant amount of stigma surrounds queer and seropositive subjects. Smith, then, crafts an aesthetic project out of the space of stigma by translating the site of stigma into an experimental graphic image.

My point here is that through this poem Smith calls for a visualizing and embracing of social injury, which is what stigma embodies and represents. However, they do not rest at injury. Injury is a source of creation and meaning in the poem. I am calling attention to a

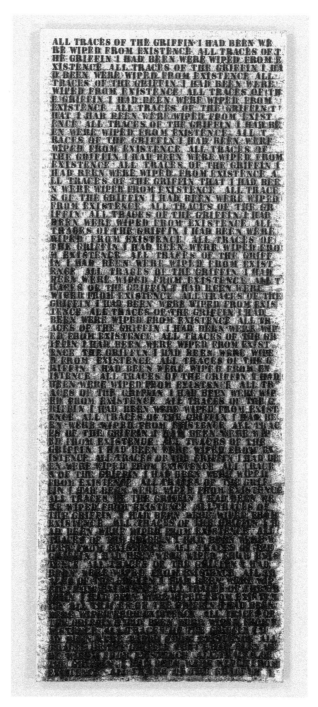

Figure 4.1 Glenn Ligon, *Untitled (Black Like Me #2)*, 1992. Oil stick and gesso on canvas. Collection of Hirshhorn Museum and Sculpture Garden, Smithsonian Institution, Museum Purchase, 1993. Copyright Glenn Ligon. Courtesy of the artist; Hauser & Wirth, New York; Regen Projects, Los Angeles; Thomas Dane Gallery, London; and Chantal Crousel, Paris.

complex relationship to injury that is articulated throughout the volume. Injury is a means of stigmatization and a source of creativity. One might think about this strategy in terms of a disidentification with injury and death.[12] In fact, I have used this framework before to think about complex means of affiliation, especially by minoritarian subjects.[13] Though that analytical lens is relevant, I believe Smith is up to something else that has implications far beyond disidentification.

I rely upon two primary critical interlocutors to make sense of Smith's poetic embrace of injury: Dagmawi Woubshet and Darius Bost. In his book *The Calendar of Loss*, Woubshet examines writings by Black authors during what he calls the early era of AIDS.[14] He focuses on how people mourning the loss of others depicted their own imminent deaths. They were grieving the loss of intimates as they grieved their own impending deaths. Examining authors such as Dixon, he sees these double-grieving writers as "disprized mourners," those who society has devalued because they have AIDS and are queer. This disprized mourner experiences serial loss as well as multiple forms of social neglect. The speakers in Smith's poems might be thought of as disprized mourners that are contemplating their own approaching deaths. Moreover, the idea of seriality is integral to Smith's poetics as the serial poems illustrate. Serialized loss and threat provide the foundations for Smith's construction of the poetic personas. Though writing at a different historical moment, well after the early era of AIDS, Smith's work resonates with that of the writers Woubshet examines.

In his book *Evidence of Being*, Bost explores a similar historical moment to Woubshet, but he is more interested in how Black gay authors think about violence in relationship to their subjectivity.[15] He explains, "AIDS-infected Black gay bodies often signify as absence and negation in dominant scholarly and popular chronologies of antiBlack violence—slavery, lynching, mass incarceration, and police brutality. As such, a framework is necessary for thinking about how Black gay men's marginalization within Black communities intensifies their precarity."[16] The framework he goes on to suggest is one related to secondary marginalization but that he terms "internal structural antagonism."[17] With this idea he aims to describe how anti-Black racism penetrates Black communities and shapes intramural interactions; in addition, he is pointing to how multiple kinds of alienation contour the structural experience of Black gay life. I think this idea of internal structural antagonism might offer a useful way to think about the complex kinds of poetic strategies Smith employs in *Don't Call Us Dead*. For example, the playful manipulation of "my blood" and "his blood" in "litany" might be thought of as an artistic translation of the idea of internal(ized) structural antagonisms.

The critical work of Woubshet and Bost offers us a set of methods to characterize Smith's poems, and because both turn their attention to the writing of gay men in the 1980s, we can further connect Smith's twenty-first century projects to the writing of artists of the recent past in order to begin to recognize a genealogy—I will return to this idea below. That being said, I do think that Smith's work moves in a different direction than the artists Woubshet and Bost examine. Although the disprized mourners and the subjects of internal structural antagonisms do describe Smith's personas well, I do not think the earlier authors showcase the embrace and re- articulation of injury as explicitly as Smith does. In fact, the embracing and redefining of injury is Smith's primary artistic strategy.[18] This strategy is best epitomized in a line from the epic poem that begins the collection "summer, somewhere": "don't call / us dead, call us alive someplace better."[19] The sentence, which occupies a line and a half, provides the title for the collection and summarizes the intellectual project of the poems as a whole. The demand not be to called dead but to be seen and described as being "alive someplace better" accomplishes a couple of conceptual tasks. On one hand, it engages the critical conversations around social death in Black critical culture. Rather than fully embrace the idea of social death and offer what one might think of as an Afro-Pessimist view or completely reject the tenets of social death and put forward a more Afro-Optimist view, Smith lingers in between. The speaker of the poem does not deny symbolic or material death. The speaker insists that we develop a new language to describe the state of Blackness even if that state is surrounded by violence and fatality. Smith's speaker calls for a re-framing of injury and a redefining of it. It is not a flat refusal of injury but a wish to define oneself outside of familiar, destructive parameters. I see this move as embodying injury but a move to do so that involved self-definition. Thinking back to the "litany" poem, perhaps the reason that we cannot legibly make out the final page has to do with the fact that we need a new way of reading the poem, of reading Black queer bodies. Smith's method is not meant to supply us with that new way but rather to make legible our inability to recognize the subjective space of Black queerness. From this perspective, it is our way of reading that is disprized and our assumptions that cause the destructive antagonisms. In making visible the commingling of blood and the site of stigma, Smith makes evident our complicity in creating such stigma. More important, the only way that they can make this point is through formal manipulation of their poems.

Although thus far I have emphasized Smith's aesthetic connections to 1980s/90s writers such as Dixon, there is a more recent writer whose art sets more of the conceptual groundwork for Smith's poetic enterprise while also emphasizing the constructive recognition of injury, highlighting a genealogy of innovative Black queer art. I turn to the work of Sharon Bridgforth, especially her performance novel *love/conjure blues*.[20] Bridgforth claims that *love/conjure blues* has the qualities of poetry, performance, and the novel. The value of Bridgforth's work is that it makes the reader conscious about questions of form and generic distinction by existing in between distinct categories. Anyone familiar with her work knows that Bridgforth is invested in transforming form. In connecting her work to Smith's poetry, my goal is not to lock the *love/conjure blues* into one generic mode (by comparing it to poetry and emphasizing its poetic elements), but rather to interrogate the possibilities of the mode, what fits into this category, and how the question of the poetic or the poem-like fits into the discussion.

Bridgforth describes this piece itself as exploring "a range of possibilities of gender expression and sexuality within a rural/Black working class context."[21] She accomplishes this goal by portraying a large cast of "mens womens some that is both some that is neither" not only through diction that reflects regional dialect, but also by manipulating the graphic presentation of the text. Throughout *love conjure/blues*, Bridgforth italicizes some sections, puts others in bold, and uses a dozen different fonts that signal shifts in character, attitude, or tone. The graphic and generic complexity of Bridgforth's work is an expression of the positionality of the Black queer subject, which is her declared focus. Some of these graphic manipulations are difficult to describe exactly, but the discussion of the relationship between the characters booka change and his lover joshua davis provides a sense of the different treatments of the written word that occur throughout the work:

this is how booka change and joshua davis found each
other. in
blistering sun/working days never ending/backs bent
in toil/in
the company of men they claimed each other
declared themselves
adorned each other with words. united
in heart/booka change and joshua davis married one the
other
with a poem.
love
you
live with
me
love
you
live
with
me[22]

In this section about booka chang and davis, there is a shift to italics and to mostly monosyllabic lines. This textual change marks the movement from a description of the men's relationship to a lyric interpretation of their vows as well as a movement from a third-person narration to a first- hand account. Here and throughout the text, prosaic moments transform into poetic moments and all are contained in a work that the author insists is unceasingly "performative." Bridgforth relies upon generic complexity and the manipulation of the graphic presentation of her words to express Black queerness in a way that prefigures what Smith would do years later.

To reiterate, Bridgforth is not only writing about men and women but also "the both and the neither," so she must adopt a formal practice that can convey this unsettling of social and personal boundaries of identity. The graphic architecture of the language houses and delineates such subject positions. In other words, Bridgforth's subject matter itself necessitates a manipulation of the form. The attention to queers of color yields formal and generic experimentation. In addition, it is vital to keep in mind Bridgforth's insistence that her novel "places the fiction-form *inside* an African-American voice."[23] She insists that she shapes the content and the structural elements by being attentive to an African-American register and material existence. Such attention to the African-American voice and its relationship to artistic practices calls to mind a much earlier work that one might not think to connect to Bridgforth: Sara Webster Fabio's 1970 essay "Tripping with Black Writing."[24] Fabio, who is connected to the Black Arts Movement of the 1960s and 70s, argues that artistic awareness of the structure of "Black language" has determined and must continue to inform Black artistic production. She calls for artists to employ what she describes as "Black perspective, Black aesthetic, Black rhetoric, [and] *Black language*" in their works.[25] As opposed to seeing this call as limiting, artists such as Bridgforth find inspiration in and recognizes the possibilities of such a focus. Bridgforth's emphasis on a Black *queer* perspective means that she is building on and departing from Fabio's Black Arts Movement investment in capturing cultural perspective and language by also thinking about queer communities.[26]

Bridgforth is not only concerned with the value of Black language. An interest in the social realities of Black subjects coincides with and enhances the organizing frame of a Black idiom. One of the speaker's emphasizes the importance of the frame of violence for making sense of Black queer life:

> **we is peoples borned to violence. not our making and**
> **not our choosing. just the world we came to. fighting**
> **like animals leashed in a pen. maimed if we don't**
> **win. killed if we don't fight. so we been**
> **perfecting/fighting to win**
> **the whole of our time here. and though violence is**
> **not our first nature sometimes**
> **violence boils the blood/explodes in the veins.**
> **sometimes violence**
> **shows up unexpected**
> **and just claims a nigga.**[27]

It becomes clear that the Black bodies that populate the poetic world of *love conjure/blues* face bodily harm and physical threats. There are descriptions of violence throughout the text, as when Bitty gets into an altercation with Nigga Red over a shared woman, Peachy Soonyay. However, the speaker is not simply referencing the seemingly-random occurrence of violence in the lives of the characters. Rather, she is charting the particularly "nigga" experience of rarely having full control over one's life or one's body within the social matrix ("**sometimes violence / shows up unexpected / and just claims a nigga**"). Bridgforth attempts to capture linguistic *and* experiential Blackness in her text, which defies simple generic categorization. In fact, it is this social identity that is at stake in the textual performance of queerness. Blackness is an aesthetic strategy here. It is both the subject and the governing methodology. Moreover, the passage indicates the inevitability of violence and the need to prepare oneself for this fact of life. What I am trying to think through here is the relationship between questions of form and considerations of positionality. I want to suggest that form can function as a means of translation. Form does not only convey meaning, it transforms it. Thinking about Smith in light of Bridgforth allows one to see a discernible tradition of inventing new forms and finding innovative ways to inhabit familiar ones.

Again, Bridgforth recognizes the inevitability of violence. The "blues" in the title, with its connotations of melancholy and dejection, is in part a reflection of this idea. However, acknowledging this reality, the fact that you could be "claimed," does not pre-empt the possibilities of pleasure or the re-imagining of bonds of affiliation—the "love" of the title. Perhaps the most important word in the title is the word "conjure," with its sense of transformation and change. The queer intimacy can change or reform the socially-constructed blues that permeates the imagined community within the performance novel. Bridgforth calls attention to the inescapable realities of violence so that she can transform the site of pain into something else.

Along the same lines, Smith details the ubiquity of violence and death in poem after poem for the Black queer subject to undermine its presence and gesture toward other ways of thinking. In the final piece in the collection, "dream where every Black person is standing by the ocean," Smith sets a scene in which Black people ask a personified ocean about all of their ancestors "swallowed" during the Middle Passage and later acts of racialized violence. The ocean responds that by now those bodies lost to the water have disintegrated and been drunk by the living. One of the figures hears this statement, yells "Emmett," and spits. Then a young man begins crawling to the shoreline. This young man can be read as representing Emmett Till brought back to life. Emmett Till was a fourteen-year old boy who was a victim of anti-Black violence in 1955. He was lynched and thrown into the Tallahatchie River. Through the imagery of swallowing, the poem suggests the internalization of trauma, which is made literal here as the woman spits out Till's (living) body. Accordingly, Emmett has always been with us; this social injury, which his death signifies, is inside of us. Nevertheless, our "shouts" (perhaps metaphors for actions *and* writings) may help to right the wrongs of the past. Social injury may have been internalized, we might carry it around within our bodies, but it is perhaps possible to cast it out and recast it just as the living Emmett joins the other Black people on the shore. Again, it is the fabular to which Smith turns to explore the parameters of racialized violence. The curious poem relies heavily on anaphora; each line begins with an ampersand (&) suggesting ideas of continual return through the structural presentation. Ideas of return and continuation are presented in a poem that is initially about the permanence of historic loss. However, the anaphoric structure, with its constant returns and repetitions, perhaps foreshadows the metaphoric rebirth in the closing lines, thus receding away a loss that must be total. The collection ends with this image of rebirth, but this image occurs through the presentation of serial violence and death.

How do we imagine Black queer existence? Smith, like Dixon and Bridgforth before them, indicates that this imagining must be done through the lens of vulnerability to some extent. Such vulnerability cannot necessarily be denied, but Smith shows us that it can be written and re-imagined. One must take up injury to disarm it. Through this idea we come to appreciate the work of Smith and queer artists creating before them. If we are to take seriously the tenets of social death and the impact on anti-Black racism in the contemporary moment, we must also come to understand how artist imagine ways through such realities. Their fragmented and segmented poetic projects come to stand in for the threatened queer body, but the artworks themselves do not only relay notions of injury. Black queer writers like Smith offer artistic production as a space that may be beyond injury—perhaps the only such space possible for racial and sexual minorities.

Notes

1   For discussions of the critical terrain of Afro-Pessimism as well as its origin points, see Orlando Patterson, *Slavery and Social Death: A Comparative Study* (Cambridge: Harvard University Press, 2018, 2nd ed.); Jared Sexton, "The Social Life of Social Death: On Afro- Pessimism and Black Optimism," in *Time, Temporality and Violence in International Relations: (De)fatalizing the Present, Forging Radical Alternatives* (New York: Routledge, 2017), 62–75.; Frank Wilderson, *Red, White, and Black: Cinema and the Structure of U.S. Antagonisms* (Durham: Duke

University Press, 2010); and Calvin Warren, *Ontological Terror: Blackness, Nihilism, and Emancipation* (Durham: Duke University Press, 2018).

2   Danez Smith, *Don't Call Us Dead: Poems* (Minneapolis: Graywolf Press, 2017).

3   Smith prefer the use of the pronouns they/their/them. I reproduce that usage when writing about them.

4   Smith, *Don't Call Us Dead*, 65.

5   Smith, *Don't Call Us Dead*, 66.

6   See Linda Villarosa, "America's Hidden H.I.V. Epidemic: Why Do America's Black Gay and Bisexual Men Have a Higher H.I.V. Rate than Any Country in the World?" in *The New York Times Magazine*, June 6, 2017: https://www.nytimes.com/2017/06/06/magazine/americas-hidden-hiv-epidemic.html

7   Melvin Dixon, *Love's Instruments* (Sylmar, CA: Tía Chucha Press, 1995).

8   One should not lose sight of the fact that this poem made up of (mostly) iambic dimeter couplets is a forty-line poem. One might think of each line as representing the forty weeks of human gestation.

9   Dixon, *Love's Instruments*, 67.

10 Cathy Cohen, *Boundaries of Blackness: AIDS and the Breakdown of Black Politics* (Chicago: University of Chicago Press, 1999).

11 Smith, *Don't Call Us Dead*, 39.

12 See José Esteban Muñoz, *Disidentifications: Queers of Color and The Performance of Politics* (Minneapolis: University of Minnesota Press, 1999).

13 See GerShun Avilez, *Radical Aesthetics and Modern Black* Nationalism (Urbana: University of Illinois Press, 2016).

14 Dagmawi Woubshet, *The Calendar of Loss: Race, Sexuality, and Mourning in the Early Era of AIDS* (Baltimore: Johns Hopkins University Press, 2015).

15 Darius Bost, *Evidence of Being: The Black Gay Cultural Renaissance and the Politics of Violence* (Chicago: University of Chicago Press, 2018).

16 Bost, *Evidence of Being*, 14.

17 For explanations of secondary marginalization, see Cohen, *Boundaries of Blackness*.

18 One might venture to say that this shift has to do with the treatments that are available now that were unavailable twenty years ago. However, the fact that many Black communities have little access to such drugs puts pressure on this assessment, but it does not completely undermine it.

19 Smith, *Don't Call Us Dead*, 3.

20 Sharon Bridgforth, *love/conjure blues* (New Orleans: Redbone Press, 2004).

21 Bridgforth, *love/conjure blues,* ii.

22 Bridgforth, *love/conjure blues,* 70–71.

23 Bridgforth, *love/conjure blues,* vii.

24 Sara Webster Fabio, "Tripping with Black Writing," in *The Black Aesthetic*, ed. Addison Gayle (New York: Doubleday, 1971), 173–81.

25 Fabio, "Tripping with Black Writing," 180 (emphasis added).

26 I emphasize Fabio here, but there are a number of theorists of the Black aesthetic who reflect similar concerns. In many ways the period lays the groundwork for the concern with Black writing and communities among queer artists in the 1980s, when Dixon is producing.

27 Bridgforth, *love/conjure blues,* 2 (sic). The text is in bold in the original.

5

AFRODIASPORIC AESTHETICS IN CLASSICAL AND EXPERIMENTAL MUSIC AFTER 1960

George E. Lewis

I. Introduction

The train of thought that resulted in this essay began in 2017 at the Berliner Festspiele, when I attended a concert of the music of the queer African American composer, pianist, vocalist and conductor Julius Eastman (1940–1990), a featured and highly anticipated event at the Maerzmusik Festival für Zeitfragen (Festival for Time Issues). After a turbulent creative and personal life, Eastman died homeless and practically destitute, with most of his scores and papers considered lost.[1] However, around the time of this concert, a number of lost Eastman works had been unearthed, due in large measure to the relentless musicological sleuthing of composer Mary Jane Leach, a central figure in Downtown experimentalism. The result has been new performances and recordings worldwide, and a rapid accretion of posthumous acclaim that has been described by some as "Eastmania."

While I was listening to these performances of Eastman's work, some of which I had heard in concert while he was alive, it suddenly occurred to me that most of the audience members and critics celebrating (and in some cases, denigrating) him had probably never heard the work of any other black composer. That wasn't their fault—how could they have done so? Certainly, despite decades of associations in Europe since 1976, and having lived on the continent for five years in the 1980s, I had seen only two concerts of the music of Afrodiasporic contemporary composers: this one by Eastman, and a set of solo works by Alvin Singleton and Maurice Weddington, performed at IRCAM by bass clarinetist Harry Sparnaay sometime in the mid-1980s.

The inevitable outgrowth of that silence of whiteness is what musicologist Dana Reason has called "the myth of absence," the spurious claim that there are, in fact, no Afrodiasporic composers of any consequence, and thus, nothing at all to hear.[2] However, at the Eastman concert I could not escape the feeling that the Berlin audience, one of the most sophisticated and committed in the world, was hungry for a radical diversification of this putatively all-white field, while perhaps not suspecting that there were lots of black composers out there who the curators, historians, critics, and academicians simply weren't talking about. Indeed, despite the enormous influence of Afrodiasporic music-makers around the world, and the fact that Afrodiasporic classical composition is an international practice, with important work coming out of North America, South America, Europe, the UK, Scandinavia, and Africa, this absence of blackness was by no means anomalous in the European contemporary music scene.[3]

By 2018, in the internationally experienced wake of Black Lives Matter, some influential stakeholders in the field of contemporary music admitted publicly that they could do better. During 2017 and 2018, I was part of "Defragmentation," a project on "Curating Contemporary Music" supported by the Kulturstiftung des Bundes (German Federal Cultural Foundation), and involving four major European contemporary music festivals. Defragmentation was "aimed at enduringly establishing the debates currently ongoing in many disciplines on gender and diversity, decolonization and technological change in institutions of New Music." The Darmstadt Ferienkurse 2018, one of the oldest and most important festivals for contemporary music in Europe (and indeed the world), produced the centerpiece of the Defragmentation events, a four-day conference on the topic that included lectures, panels, workshops, and listening spaces.[4]

The German new music group Ensemble Modern's November 2020 livestreamed Afro-modernism concert at Philharmonie Essen, performed without audience under COVID-19 regulations, was one of the first portrait presentations of the work of Afrodiasporic composers to be presented in Europe.[5] Just two weeks later, the London Sinfonietta presented the livestreamed concert "Yet Unheard: Music by emerging and established black composers."[6] Björn Gottstein, then artistic director of the Donaueschinger Musiktage, the oldest contemporary music festival in the world and a key participant in Defragmentation, appeared on the Ensemble Modern's November 2020 live-streamed Afro-Modernism Symposium to admit publicly that the Donaueschinger Musiktage had never programmed a black composer in its entire hundred-year history, until 2020.

What has come to be known retroactively as Western Art Music is said to be a Eurodiasporic music that is performed and composed around the world. However, as musicologist David R.M. Irving notes, "WAM [Western Art Music]--if we can call it that— has been entangled with the rest of the world's societies for the last half-millennium, to varying degrees, and in different shapes and forms. It cannot be studied in a vacuum; it must be situated in a global ontological framework of connected histories."[7]

In spite of clear evidence of unprecedented levels of global movement and intensive cultural interactions through music for the past half-millennium, WAM is still often seen as a culturally exclusive and elite artform, owing in large part to the ways in which it is represented in academic and public discourse, and in reverential and museum-like performances. It is often assumed, by default, to represent the pinnacle of indigenous Western European musical expression, and to embody a pan-European creative disposition . . . I locate this tendency within the ideas of essentialism, exceptionalism, and Eurocentrism in music historiography and discourse, and the continuing desire by musicologists, ethnomusicologists, and independent scholars to see WAM as "exceptional" and "unique," rather than thoroughly contingent on global processes and constitutive of a clear set of environmental, social, political, economic, intellectual, and religious circumstances.[8]

In his 1949 essay, The Main Stream of Music," the musicologist Donald Francis Tovey presciently suggested that that an absence of stable canon would come to mark the contemporary musical landscape. "At the present day all musicians feel more or less at sea, and not all of us are good sailors," Tovey wrote. [9] One of the key outcomes of this condition is that twenty-first century new music is becoming ever more marked by a condition of créolité.[10] *Éloge De La Créolité,* an influential 1989 manifesto crafted by Caribbean writers Jean Bernabé, Patrick Chamoiseau, and Raphaël Confiant, begins with this ringing declaration: "Neither Europeans, nor Africans, nor Asians, we proclaim ourselves Creoles. This will be for us an interior attitude – better, a vigilance, or even better, a sort of mental envelope in the middle of which our world will be built in full consciousness of the outer world."[11]

According to these writers, "Creoleness is an annihilation of false universality, of monolingualism, and of purity."[12] Elaborating on their claim that "The world is evolving into a state of Creoleness," the authors write,

> The son or daughter of a German and a Haitian, born and living in Peking, will be torn between several languages, several histories, caught in the torrential ambiguity of a mosaic identity. To present creative depth, one must perceive that identity in all its complexity. *He or she will be in the situation of a Creole!*"[13]

Indeed, Bernabé, Chamoiseau, and Confiant have warned that "Our aesthetics cannot exist (cannot be authentic) without Creoleness."[14]

Along related lines, African composers have theorized their engagement with European and other world musical forms as a kind of intercultural encounter. The Nigerian Akin Euba, one of the most influential Afrodiasporic composers of his generation, wrote in 1988,

> More and more Africans, therefore, live in a bicultural sphere. . .A realistic approach to contemporary Africa must therefore accept traditional cultures as the basis of African society, and at the same time, recognize the possibilities and creative energies that Africa contributes to a coexistence of cultures in all spheres of life.[15]

For Euba, the result of the intercultural encounter is "a new type of composer, using a musical language based partly, but not exclusively, on that of European art music."[16] Kofi Agawu, among other African musicologists, has traced the historical development of this new kind of composer:

> What kind of heritage do these composers possess? The first thing to note is that the heritage is multiple and eclectic. It stems from community-based traditional music (music with the strongest claims to being of pre-European origin--like the Agbadza dance referred to earlier), modifications of this tradition into neo-traditional forms; the ubiquitous popular music of Cuban, American and British origins; and, perhaps most

important. . .selected European repertories, including hymns, simple classics, Gilbert and Sullivan operas, and a little encounter with the music of 20th-century composers.[17]

Declaring that he regards intercultural music as "the great event of the 21st century," Euba maintains that "No longer shall the spirit of Europe dictate trends; world cultures should work side by side and with each other on an equal footing.[18] Euba, who taught for nearly two decades at the University of Pittsburgh, noted a key reason for what we today see as the myth of absence of Afrodiasporic composers: "One of the main demands of interculturalism is also directed at music education in Europe. While education in Africa and Asia is oriented towards interculturalism, in Europe it is still strictly Eurocentric. "[19]

In that light, we can see why, according to Irving, "WAM is caught in a paradox: that of claims for uniqueness being pitted simultaneously against clear evidence of its internal (and internalized) hybridity."[20] Thus, what the new music field needs now is to recognize its place in the world as exemplifying a mosaic identity that recognizes historical, geographical and cultural cross-connections--not so much to achieve diversity as to pursue a new complexity that can yield that greater creative depth. Adopting a mental envelope of creolization would allow contemporary classical music to renounce its self-image as the celebration of a whiteness-based European sonic diaspora, an identity politics that, as with other addictions, operates with deadly effect.

Accordingly, according to Agawu,

notions of "whiteness" or "Europeanness" will not be wielded as self-evident categories when it comes to creativity. Creative practices are fields of possibility, fields that may be tagged with different colors--black, brown or yellow--according to desire and context. In this way, African composers will not be forced into a defensive mode when it comes to justifying their work; they will not be sent on a wild goose chase looking for "non-white" or "authentic" or "African" spaces that they'll be told are their own. All spaces are "potentially" African.[21]

In this way, we can understand Afrodiasporic contemporary composition as manifesting a stance of incredulity regarding narratives of genre and cultural purity.

II. Observations on an Afrodiasporic aesthetic in contemporary music

Over a period of two decades, the African American composer Olly Wilson (1937–2018) produced a quartet of articles that, in retrospect, can be seen as having exercised enormous influence in proposing an African-American musical aesthetic in contemporary classical music.[22] Wilson's motivation was to locate African American music as a form of art with an Afrodiasporic origin point. Thus, what he hears as similarities between "sub-Saharan" African music and African American musics such as jazz, blues, and related forms indicates to him that "The significant role of music in sub-Saharan African cosmology, coupled with the obvious historical-cultural connection of peoples of African descent throughout the world, suggests that all peoples within this diaspora share common modes of musical practice."[23] Wilson sensibly grounds this observation in the fact that "musicologists may still speak intelligently of broad general qualities that characterize western European music notwithstanding the importance of cultural distinctions within a large population mass sharing a geographically defined region."[24]

Wilson also recognizes the fact that cultural traditions are permeable: "Black American music has both influenced and been influenced in several ways by non-black musical traditions. Therefore it is difficult to pinpoint precisely the essential qualities that make this music part of a larger African or black music tradition."[25] While this implies that outsider/insider distinctions can be tenuous, Wilson nonetheless identifies

> a distinct set of musical qualities which are an expression of the collective cultural values of peoples of African descent. This musical tradition has many branches which reflect variations in basic cultural patterns over time, as well as diversity within a specific time frame. However, all of these branches share, to a greater or lesser extent, a group of qualities which, taken together, comprise the essence of the black musical tradition.[26]

Identifying "shared conceptual approaches to music making" in Afrodiasporic music-making, Wilson maintains that "An analysis of any genre of black music will reveal the existence of demonstrable musical characteristics that consistently reflect the presence of these underlying conceptual approaches."[27] Wilson's understanding of these approaches is worth citing at length:

1   The approach to the organization of rhythm is based on the principle of rhythmic and implied metrical contrast. There is a tendency to create musical structures in which rhythmic clash or disagreement of accents is the ideal; cross-rhythm and metrical ambiguity are the accepted and expected norm.

2   There is a tendency to approach singing or the playing of any instrument in a percussive manner; a manner in which qualitative stress accents are frequently used.

3   There is a tendency to create musical forms in which antiphonal or call-and-response musical structures abound. These antiphonal structures frequently exist simultaneously on a number of different architectonic levels.

4   There is a tendency to create a high density of musical events within a relatively short musical time frame--a tendency to fill up all of the musical space.

5   There is a common approach to music making in which a kaleidoscopic range of dramatically contrasting qualities of sound (timbre) in both vocal and instrumental music is sought after. This explains the common usage of a broad continuum of vocal sounds from speech to song. I refer to this tendency as "the heterogeneous sound ideal tendency."

6   There is a tendency to incorporate physical body motion as an integral part of the music making process.

By 1992, Wilson has subsumed all of the above characteristics as part of his notion of the "heterogeneous sound ideal" that he identifies as his fifth tendency: "The desirable musical sound texture is one that contains a combination of diverse timbres," and a "fundamental bias for contrast of color--heterogeneity of sound rather than similarity of color or homogeneity."[28]

Wilson appears cautious in not directly describing this sound ideal as an aesthetic. However, an influential 1991 essay by art historian Robert L. Douglas, seeking central characteristics of an African American aesthetic in the visual arts, proposes something quite similar to Wilson's ascription of heterogeneity. While Douglas does not reference Wilson's work, he cites music as an example, through Alan P. Merriam's description: "African music is distinguished from other world traditions by the superimposition of several lines of meter."[29] Douglas sees this musical practice as exhibiting "multidominant elements," or what I want to call "multidominance." Douglas uses the multidominance concept to contextualize the work of the Africobra artists, including Jeff Donaldson, Wadsworth Jarrell, Jae Jarrell, Barbara Jones-Hogu, and others.[30] What Wilson describes as "tendencies," Douglas describes as "predispositions":

> The predisposition to apply colors in layers, the multiple use of colors in intense degrees, or the multiple use of textures, design patterns, or shapes, is fundamental to African art while also being universal elements in the formation of any visual art. Likewise, rhythm is fundamental to the formation of music, and the predisposition to use multiple types of rhythm in musical construction speaks equally to a distinctive aesthetic as does the multiple use of visual elements.[31]

In an essay from 2000, I place both Wilson and Douglas in intersection with art historian Robert Farris Thompson, who sees the black Atlantic visual tradition as displaying "a propensity for multiple meter."[32] Among many examples, Thompson cites Akan *asadua* cloth, woven using narrow, multistrip patterns: "[A]s multiple meter distinguishes the traditional music of black Africa, emphatic multistrip composition distinguishes the cloth of West Africa and culturally related Afro-American sites."[33]

Barbara Jones-Hogu summarized Africobra visual aesthetics in ways that resonate with Wilson, Thompson, and Douglas:

> FREE SYMMETRY, the use of syncopated rhythmic repetition which constantly changes in texture, shape, form. .MIMESIS at MID-POINT, design which marks the spot where the real and the unreal, the objective and the non-objective, the plus and the minus meet. .a point exactly between absolute abstraction and absolute naturalism. . . . . .VISIBILITY, clarity of form and line based on the interesting irregularity one senses in a freely drawn circle or organic object. . . . . .LUMINOSITY, "Shine," literal and figural, as seen in the dress and personal grooming of shoes, hair (process or Afro), laminated furniture, faces, knees, or skin. . . . . .COLOR, Coolade color, bright colors with sensibility and harmony.[34]

We can fuse Douglas's notion of "the multiple use of colors in intense degrees" and Wilson's references to the desirability of diverse timbres and textures into Hogu's reference to "shine," which Jeff Donaldson calls "a big one. . .a major quality," comparing it to "the rich lustre of a just-washed "Fro."[35]

Wilson presents numerous examples of the heterogeneous sound ideal in a wide range of African and African American musical practices, with the curious exception of African and African American classical and contemporary music—his own primary field. His 1970 orchestra work *Voices*, however, exemplifies many of the tendencies he identifies.[36] The work begins with swirling repetitive sonic behaviors, static without while dynamic within, with interjections from drums and percussion. Ingenious, uncanny effects, such as whistling by members of the orchestra, are only one part of an overall heterogeneity of sound and color that rules this piece.

The main direction in this essay, then, is taken directly from Wilson's piece. Through examples from the work of a diverse (and by no means exhaustive) range of Afrodiasporic contemporary composers, I want to identify aesthetic directions that appear frequently in Afrodiasporic contemporary classical music, whether as "predispositions," "tendencies," or "propensities." In 2001, Nigerian musicologist Bode Omojola cited his fellow Nigerian, composer and ethnomusicologist Akin Euba, as "the foremost Nigerian composer of piano music and the man who first advanced the concept of African pianism."[37] Euba first articulated the concept of African pianism in 1970, as a concept allied with his proto-creolizing notion of interculturalism:

For those composers interested in cross-cultural musical synthesis, there is a line of evolution in the use of the Western Pianoforte in combination with African drums and other instruments of percussion. The Piano already displays certain affinities with African music, and by creating a type of African Pianism to blend with African instruments it should be possible to achieve a successful fusion.[38]

As the equally influential musicologist-composer J.H. Kwabena Nketia observed in the preface of the score for his own *African Pianism: Twelve Pedagogical Pieces*,

African pianism refers to a style of piano music which derives its characteristic idiom from the procedures of African percussion music as exemplified in bell patterns, drumming, xylophones and mbira music. It may use simple or extended rhythmic motifs or the lyricism of traditional songs and even those of African popular music as the basis of its rhythmic phrases.[39]

Most attractive to many composers was the concept's agnosticism with regard to tonality. Nketia observes that:

Its harmonic idiom may be tonal, atonal, consonant or dissonant in whole or in part, depending on the preferences of the composer, the mood or impressions he wishes to create to heighten or soften the jaggedness of successive percussive attacks. In this respect, the African composer does not have to tie himself down to any particular school of writing, if his primary aim is to explore the potential of African and tonal usages.[40]

Euba's African pianism developed into a highly influential form. Writing in 1988. the composer elaborated on his successful conception in ways that resonate with Wilson's identification of the percussive manner of performance as central to an Afrodiasporic heterogeneous sound ideal:

> The piano, being partially a percussive instrument, possesses latent African characteristics. Techniques in the performance of xylophones, thumb pianos, plucked lutes, drum chimes, for which Africans are noted, and the polyrhythmic methods of African instrumental music in general would form a good basis for an African pianistic style.[41]

Euba's *Igbá Kerin--Àwon Abàmì Eye* ("Supernatural Birds"), a movement from his 1964 work "Four Pictures from Oyo Calabashes," constitutes a remarkable forty-second distillation of his conception.[42] A more extended view of the concept appears in Joshua Uzoigwe's *Agbigbo* (2003) for solo piano. This twelve-minute excursion by Uzoigwe (1946–2005), who Euba calls "one of the major figures in the neo-African school of composition," [43] eschews conventional Western styles, forms, and techniques to express a kind of circularity of form reminiscent of an eternal recurrence, realized with a deliberately extreme and highly focused economy of means.[44]

In introducing his theory of multidominance, Douglas recalls from his art-student days that "most African-American artists with Eurocentric art training will reveal that they received similar instructions, such as 'tone down your colors, too many colors'."[45] These "helpful" pedagogical interventions were presented as somehow universal and transcendent, rather than as emanating from a particular culturally or historically situated worldview, or as based in networks of political, economic, or social power. Thus, Wilson's observation that Afrodiasporic sonic expression favors "heterogeneity of sound rather than similarity of color or homogeneity," makes common cause with Donaldson's ecstatic exhortation of "*Color color* Color color that shines, color that is free of rules and regulations. . .Color that is expressively awesome. . .superreal color. . .Color that is as bright as the color dealing on the streets of Watts and the Southside. . .in Roxbury and in Harlem, in Abijan. . .in Bahia, in Dakar."[46]

The repeated invocation of "color" in Donaldson's remark leads me to an initial identification of the role of repetition in Afrodiasporic sonic aesthetics, one that I will follow up on in my discussion of specific works. James A. Snead's complex and influential 1981 article, "On Repetition in Black Culture," epigraphically cites Søren Kierkegaard's famous essay: "Repetition is reality and it is the seriousness of life. He who wills repetition is matured in seriousness. . .Repetition is the new category which has to be brought to light." Snead sees this passage as challenging a dominant nineteenth-century Western belief that "there is no repetition in culture, but only a difference, defined as progress and growth."[47]

As Africobra artist Wadsworth Jarrell recounts, "We used John Coltrane as one of the models. . .We were creating sheets of color like Coltrane was creating sheets of sound."[48] Coltrane was also a signal influence on and proponent of early musical minimalism, one still largely unacknowledged in many music histories. Coltrane's 1960 recording of *My Favorite Things* (particularly the McCoy Tyner solo) is essentially a minimalist improvisation using repetition as a primary element.[49] Coltrane's use of repetition precedes that of Steve Reich and Philip Glass, and is roughly coterminous with that of La Monte Young and Terry Riley, both soprano saxophonists who, like many, were taken with Coltrane's sound on that instrument.[50]

By 1965, however, Coltrane had developed a relentlessly intense, freely fractal, nonlinear and nonmetric repetition music, one that featured a kind of ecstasy and "shine" that was obviously attractive to the Africobra artists, with their deployment of Jones-Hogu's notion of "syncopated rhythmic repetition." Robert Farris Thompson's memorable description of Mande-culture textile work as "Round Houses and Rhythmized Textiles" makes the direct connection between these visual rhythms of repetition and both African and African-American music.[51]

Examples of repetition-based forms and structures abound in Afrodiasporic contemporary music. In Eleanor Alberga's Suite from *Dancing With the Shadow* (1990), for flute, clarinet, violin, cello, piano, and percussion, repetition is a constant presence, whether quick and fleeting, as in the clarinet and piano, or repeated and stabbing, as in the percussion. Afrodiasporic references abound, as in the "Jonkonnu Festival" moment in the piece, which references Alberga's native Jamaica,[52] and the bell patterns in the percussion. The creolizing impact of the piece infuses classical music with new histories of sound and expression.

The Egyptian Halim El-Dabh, whom Akin Euba in 1970 called perhaps the most important African composer, created the electronic work *Ta'bir al-Zar* ("The Expression of Zar") in a radio studio in Cairo, a half-decade before the advent of musique concrete. El-Dabh, who went on to realize important work in the 1960s at the Columbia-Princeton Electronic Music Studios as part of a prolific career as composer and ethnomusicologist, was recognized as the "father of African electronic music" at the 2005 UNYAZI Electronic Music Festival in Johannesburg, the first event of its kind on the continent.[53] His *Voyages* series of ensemble works deploy heterogeneous forms of repetition with improvisation and multidominance.[54]

Since the early 1980s, Anthony Davis's music harnesses the powers of strong, memorable melodies carried by tricky polyrhythms. Manifesting a multidominance of cultural reference, Davis's music features forms of repetition that are strongly informed not only by Afrodiasporic aesthetics, but also by Javanese and Balinese musical culture. In the opera *Amistad* (1996), Davis deploys cycles within cycles, superimposing complex, overlapping, syncopated gestures and metric blocks of meaning of differing durations upon each other that recall Thompson's notion of rhythmized textiles. Act I, Scene 1, "The Unknown Is My Realm," underpins a virtuosic tenor aria with music marked by constant motion and kaleidoscopic permutation; the musical structure seems to refuse any notion of rest. Motives appear and reappear in ever-shifting guises, and palindromes, sudden inversions, and laminar displacements abound.[55]

In Allison Loggins-Hull's 2020 work *The Pattern*, for flute, clarinet, violin, cello, piano, and percussion, radical timbral differences are deployed, and repetition, implied metrical contrasts, and sudden interjections of seemingly incommensurate materials are key features that recur in different guises throughout the work.[56]

Alvin Singleton's 1979 chamber ensemble work *Again* uses repetition of composite musical behaviors rather than patterns. The score example shows one such behavior state among many that comprise the work.

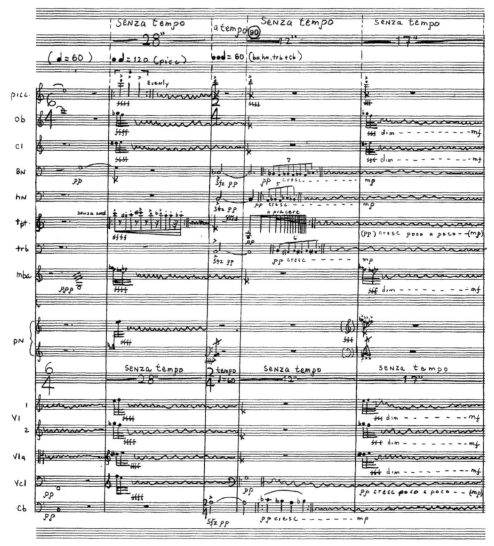

Figure 5.1 Alvin Singleton, *Again*, 1979, for chamber orchestra. Copyright 1979 by Schott Music Corporation, New York, NY. All Rights Reserved. Used by permission of Schott Music Corporation, New York, NY.

In contrast, the score of Wadada Leo Smith's *Gondwana: Earth* (2022), for solo cello, three ensembles, and conductor, embeds complex repetition into the score. In an expression of Wilson's heterogeneous sound ideal, each performer or ensemble can exercise agency in the real time of performance as to how the repeat notation in a given passage is to be interpreted.

Tania León's music is well described by musicologist Jason Stanyek in terms that center the work's origin in processes of sonic creolization. "All at once," Stanyek notes, "this is music of the Americas, of the trans-Atlantic world, of the Cuban diaspora, of the

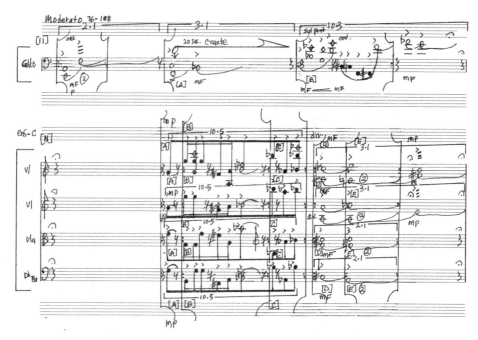

Figure 5.2 Wadada Leo Smith, *Gondwana: Earth*, 2022, for solo cello, three ensembles and conductor. Copyright Wadada Leo Smith. Score excerpt reproduced by permission of the composer.

European avant-garde. It is pan-Latin, local, intercultural, cosmopolitan, indigenous, global, transcendent, grounded."[57]

What we hear in León's five-movement work *Rítmicas* for chamber ensemble is a complex evocation of multidominance and the heterogeneous sound ideal, achieved through the use of multi-directional rhythms and complex metrical contrast, driven by the congas and other drums, with off-meter interjections and "response without call" commentary.

According to the program notes, "*Rítmicas* was inspired by the legacy and the title of a work by Cuban composer, violinist and conductor Amadeo Roldan, who in 1930 wrote the first symphonic pieces to incorporate Afro-Cuban percussion instruments." León's notes affirm the work's Afrodiasporic provenance, basing the sonic behavior

> on a rainbow of polyrhythmic inventions emerging from the Son and Guaguancó clave pattern . . . a fundamental African-derived rhythmic device which consists of the addition of irregular pulses repeated as a persistent structure—ostinato—throughout a piece. This rhythmical tool creates and instills music with a sense of energetic groove and can be found in the music of Cuba, Puerto Rico, throughout the rest of the Caribbean basin, in Brazil, in Latin America and in sub-Saharan cultures.[58]

Andile Wiseman Khumalo's 2020 work *Invisible Self,* for chamber ensemble with piano soloist, visits related ground to *Rítmicas* from the standpoint of Khumalo's native South Africa. In an expression of the "no margin, no center" aspect of multidominance, Khumalo writes that "though the piano is the central object, it is not viewed differently from the

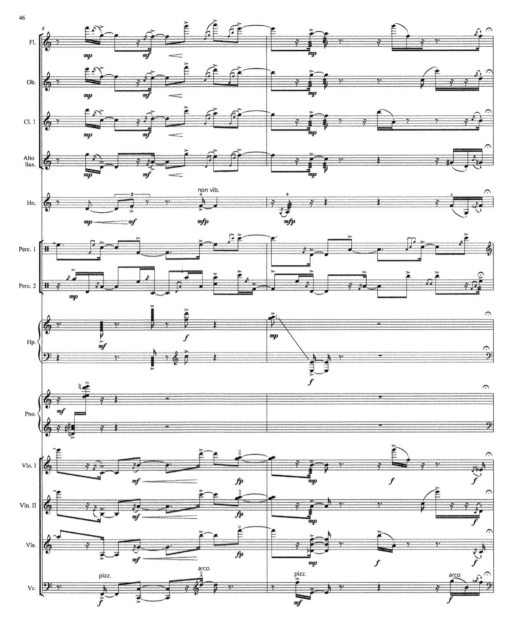

Figure 5.3 Tania León, *Rítmicas*, 2019, for chamber orchestra. Copyright Tania León. Score excerpt reproduced by permission of the composer.

whole ensemble, which is the metaphorical representation of the environment from which the object finds itself in."[59]

That metaphorical environment is marked by a process of identity transformation:

The piece was inspired by the tension between the "migrant" Africans and Africans within South Africa, that led to the xenophobic attacks that have dominated the South

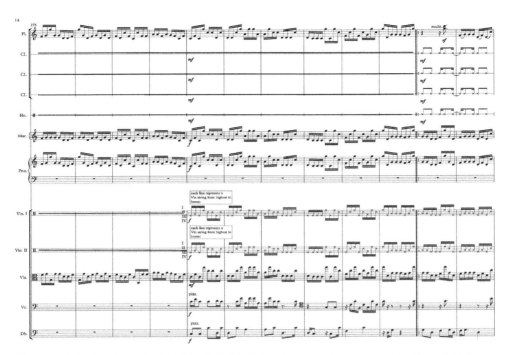

Figure 5.4 Andile Khumalo, *Invisible Self*, 2020, for piano and large ensemble. Copyright Andile Khumalo. Score excerpt reproduced by permission of the composer.

African social landscape in recent years. Of course one asks: What is a migrant African, in Africa? And according to whom do we define foreign-ness or the "other" as Africans in Africa. . .I constantly feel like, I don't recognize whom we have become--or have my travels distorted the reality of who I thought was, a definition of the African-ness or in other words the concept of "UBUNTU" as we know it in Zulu culture? So in short, the work is about IDENTITY. How we perceive whom we are, based on what people see versus whom we are based on our internal Self.[60]

Before George Floyd, there was Sandra Bland--and far too many others. In July 2015, the 28-year-old African American Chicago native, looking to take up a new job, was found hanged in a Texas jail cell, three days after her arrest on a pretextual traffic stop. Presciently, in a Facebook video posted shortly before her death, she remarked, "In the news that we've seen as of late, you could stand there, surrender to the cops, and still be killed."[61] The African American Policy Forum coined the Twitter hashtag #SayHerName to call attention to police violence targeting black women.[62]

Courtney Bryan's *Yet Unheard* (2016) for soprano, chorus, and orchestra, premiered on the first anniversary of Bland's death, was a musical response to that call. The text, by Sharan Strange, is a sustained and shocking testimony, which Bryan imbues sonically with freely fractal repetition to indicate an eternal recurrence of the same baleful tales of loss, violence, and racism:

The police made a yoke
I could not slip. I tell you, I willed
myself to live! as my life was
clipped.
And what was the crime?
I dared to resist
society's murderous design.[63]

The effect is reminiscent of the fourth movement of John Coltrane's *A Love Supreme* (1964), titled "Psalm," in which the saxophonist prosodically "recites" his own prayer and testimony. The link to the Gambian griots is evident in both.[64]

One can compare this with another great musical evocation of resistance, Wendell Logan's 1989 orchestral setting of Robert Hayden's 1962 poem *Runagate, Runagate*.[65] The word "runagate" refers to a runaway enslaved person, and the work's depiction of fugitivity is marked by repetition, blues elements in the voice, quick changes of mood, sharp contrasts, and apparent incommensurabilities of color, texture, and rhythm.

In composer, visual artist, and saxophonist Matana Roberts's *Coin Coin Chapter Three, River Run Thee* (2015), testimony is central to the work. *Coin Coin* is a series of extended works that use texts, field recordings, voice, instruments, and visual elements to explore history, memory, legacy, family, sexuality, and myth in the American Afrodiaspora, exemplifying the power of the mobile, multi-voiced creative artist to infuse history with the spiritual, where black lives, past and present and future, are crucially at stake.[66]

John Coltrane's incorporation in his music of what some commentators decried as sheer noise recalls the characterization of virtually every form of Afrodiasporic music, whether classical, folk, or popular, as noise. As historian Jon Cruz notes, the history of this trope in the United States dates back at least as far as the enslavement period: "Prior to

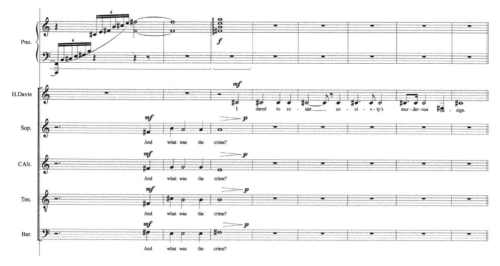

Figure 5.5 Courtney Bryan, *Yet Unheard*, 1978, for chamber orchestra, chorus, and voice soloist, libretto by Sharan Strange. Copyright Courtney Bryan. Score excerpt reproduced by permission of the composer.

the mid-19th Century black music appears to have been heard by captors and overseers primarily as noise--that is, as strange, unfathomable, and incomprehensible."[67] For his part, Robert L. Douglas compares Eurocentricity in art training to its counterpart in music, which in his view does not equip its students to hear music with multidominant rhythmic and melodic elements as anything but "noise," "frenzy" or perhaps "chaos."[68]

Olly Wilson makes a similar point about an eighteenth-century observer's description of a black musical festivity in Newport, Rhode Island: "Every voice in its highest key, in all the various languages of Africa, mixed with broken and ludicrous English, filled the air." Wilson points out that the observer's remark reveals that this kind of sound is "uncommon in his cultural experience. He does not understand that an ensemble of contrasting timbres is highly desirable from an African aesthetic viewpoint."[69] As Cruz points out, to hear only noise is "tantamount to being oblivious to the structures of meaning that anchored sounding to the hermeneutic world of the slaves," remaining "removed from how slave soundings probed their circumstances and cultivated histories and memories."[70]

Thus, a kind of retention dynamic seems to explain in some measure the dovetailing of the myth of Afrodiasporic absence in classical music with tropes in critical reception that framed black composers as out of place, out of their depth, or literally out of their minds—or even all three at once. As Chuck D of Public Enemy put it, "Writers treat me like Coltrane, insane."[71] In full recognition of the disapprobation of their music by powerful sectors of the dominant culture of their own day, hip-hop appropriated and ironicized this trope, challenging themselves, their listeners and their detractors with their explicit intention and exhortation to "bring the noise."[72] In this way, noise becomes an aspect of social aesthetics, as well as aesthetics in the more traditional sense, available for deployment by Afrodiasporic composers.

The metaphor of the assemblage has gradually supplanted that of the network in actor network theory, particularly in the writing of Georgina Born, for whom fundamental processes of mediation and remediation, bricolage and improvisation, become articulated through sound and image.[73] For Gilles Deleuze, an assemblage is "a multiplicity which is made up of many heterogeneous terms and which establishes liaisons, relations between them."[74] From the theoretical perspective of Bruno Latour's actor-network theory, materials and sounds, encountered at particular architectonic levels in an assemblage, can be regarded as actants with agency. Assemblages of actants, whether in a physical work of art, a piece of music, or in other mutually articulated social/material formations, exhibit contingency, heterogeneity, nonlinearity, and the emergence of overall agency. In other words, these objects—whether organized in sonic or visual form—can have objectives of their own.[75]

Noah Purifoy (1917–2004) was a key initiator of the African American assemblage art movement in Southern California in the 1960s and 70s, along with Betye Saar, John Outterbridge, and David Hammons. Purifoy's large outdoor sculptures, often composed from ironic recycling of junkyard gleanings such as hubcaps and old toilets, exemplify how assemblages of actants, whether in a physical work of art or in other mutually articulated social/material formations, exhibit contingency, heterogeneity, nonlinearity, and emergence.[76]

Also relevant to a discussion of Afrodiasporic aesthetics in music is Michael Gallope's understanding of Deleuze and Felix Guattari's basic notion of *agencement* (which has been translated into English, with some slippage in meaning, as "assemblage") as "a

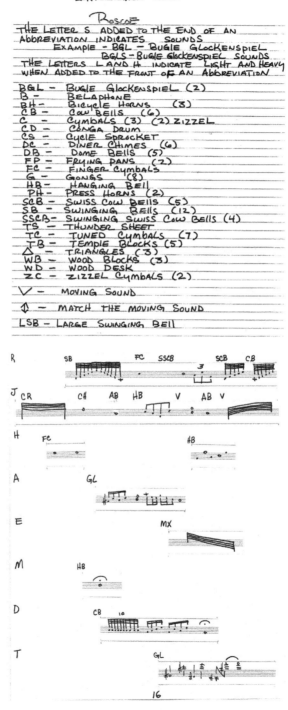

Figures 5.6a, 5.6b Roscoe Mitchell, *The Maze*, 1978, for eight percussionists. Copyright Roscoe Mitchell. Score excerpt reproduced by permission of the composer.

material being that is fundamentally the product of relation, exterior connection, change, and even corruption— not genesis, essence, purity or autonomy."[77] The complex relation between musical elements that characterizes heterogeneity and multidominance leads to the notion of a sonic assemblage that is always in motion—a virtual physicality that resonates with Wilson's notion of the Afrodiasporic "tendency to incorporate physical body motion as an integral part of the music making process."

An extended example of this assemblage orientation is Roscoe Mitchell's composition *The Maze* (1978), a meditative, twenty-minute work written for eight "percussionists." In fact, only two of the performers—Famoudou Don Moye and Thurman Barker—were primarily active as percussionists. The others—Anthony Braxton, Douglas R. Ewart, Malachi Favors, Joseph Jarman, Henry Threadgill, and Mitchell himself—perform on their personal assemblages, including Braxton's set of large, carefully tuned trash cans, and Threadgill's "hubkaphone," a collection of tuned hubcaps. The result sounds as much like the individual voices of the musicians as the compositional voice of Mitchell.[78] *The Maze* was an obvious outgrowth of the early music of the Art Ensemble of Chicago, a group founded by Mitchell, whose work incorporated not only woodwinds and saxophones, brass, and strings, but also a vast complement of harmonicas, tambourines, whistles, bells, gongs, washboards, and other miscellaneous percussion.

Homunculus C.F. for 10 percussionists (1960) is a singular work in the repertoire of Julia Perry (1924–1979). Perry attended the Juilliard School of Music, studied with Nadia Boulanger and Luigi Dallapiccola, received two Guggenheim Fellowships, and won prizes for her compositions in the US and Europe. Nonetheless, within a decade after her passing, little more was heard of her work for many years, a situation which is only now becoming ameliorated.[79] The harp and vibraphone passages in *Homunculus C.F.* recall African pianism *avant la lettre*, developing a series of repetitions and temporal juxtapositions into a ritual march whose harp passages recall the Ennanga music of Uganda, which William Grant Still also explored in his *Ennanga* (1956), for harp, piano, and strings.[80]

III. Conclusion

It should be made plain that these identified characteristics of Afrodiasporic aesthetics must be viewed as culturally contingent, historically emergent, and linked to situated structures of power and dialogue, rather than taken as prescriptive, somehow received, or functioning as a sonic litmus test for each and every Afrodiasporic musical work. Moreover, Afrodiasporic aesthetics are by no means limited to composers of Afrodiasporic provenance. For example, we can find these characteristics explicitly adopted in the "saturation" music of Raphaël Cendo and Franck Bedrossian. Thomas Meyer notes that Bedrossian refers to the Afrodiasporic, not only in titles such as *Swing* or *Charleston*, but also in his music, "in the rhythmic impulsivity or the high tempo that puts it close to free jazz. He says that Anthony Braxton influenced him more than Brian Ferneyhough, whose music he got to know late."[81]

As Bedrossian has noted regarding noise,

Knowing that the instrumental world, as it has been conceived within the Western tradition, tends to exclude or hide complex sounds from instrumental possibilities, an approach that includes them and gives them musical functions allows composers to transcend categories, to play with the thresholds of perception, and to modify or even subvert the hierarchies within musical discourse.[82]

The example of Public Enemy shows that noise can subvert many kinds of social as well as musical hierarchies.

We can also locate the Afrodiasporic in the music of Louis Andriessen. The aesthetics of multidominance are to be found not only in the music, but in the Heiner Goebbels-directed Park Avenue Armory production of his magisterial non-opera, *De Materie* (1988), which treated supertitle texts not as background information or running commentary, but as rhythmically and metrically vital elements in their own right, refusing hierarchies between the visual and the sonic.[83] Despite Andriessen's cryptic remark that in this work, shipbuilding serves as "a musical metaphor for the eruption of intellectual, and also physical, violence,"[84] Maja Trochimczyk hears *De Materie*'s long and overtly violent series of percussively dominated choral accents in the first movement merely as "nails rammed into a ship's hull."[85] However, the accents can easily be read, not only as the hammering together of a ship, but also as a sublimated depiction of the appalling violence and objectification of human beings on enslavement ships that attended not just the building of European nations, but even--in a staggering moral contradiction—the emergence of the Enlightenment.

De Materie presents its avatar for the 17th century philosopher David Gorlaeus as a tenor, presenting his still-developing *Idea Physicae* in a slow, mournfully blues-inflected melody, floating atop a pan-tonal sea of flatted fifths. In the next movement, in which the avatar for the mystic Hadewijch calls for submission to the will of God, Andriessen's melodic setting of her ancient Dutch text presents still more bebop-like flatted fifths, evoking tones that could have been sung by Mahalia Jackson. And then, there are what Andriessen calls the "terrifying blue columns" of his large ensemble work *De Tijd* (1980), which I refer to as "blues columns" due to their stacked dominant seventh construction.[86]

In the end, this inquiry is not in search of an essential "black sound." Instead, I proceed from an understanding that Afrodiasporic contemporary music comes from a different history and experience of the world, while being extensively variegated in its own forms. Musicologist Guthrie P. Ramsey has defined Afro-modernism as "how Blacks throughout the world responded to the experience of modernity, globality, and anti-colonialism as well as the expanded sense of experimentation and visibility of Black expressive culture."[87] For Kofi Agawu, the art music of Africa stands as a

significant but much less visible response to colonialism than its popular music counterpart. Just as creative writers like Ngugi, Achebe, Armah, and Soyinka drew on European traditions of poetry and the novel, using a "European" language albeit one inflected by various African languages, so composers like Ayo Bankole (Nigeria), Cyprien Rugamba (Rwanda), Nicholas Z. Nayo (Ghana), and Justinian Tamusuza (Uganda), among many others, have sought to write "classical" music for nonparticipating audiences, music that might be regarded as the African equivalent of Bach, Beethoven, and Brahms."[88]

Thus, as Agawu puts it, "[I]nstead of imagining an art music tradition purged of ostensible European influence—that's simply a chimera—we're better off recognizing ways in which African composers have sought change from within, transforming existing materials and practices (the things they came to meet) in response to new awakenings and stimuli."[89] Or, as Muhal Richard Abrams, co-founder of the Association for the Advancement of Creative Musicians, said so well: "We know that there are different types of black life, and therefore we know that there are different kinds of black music. Because black music comes forth from black life."[90]

Thus, while I fully recognize that this short essay only scratches the geographical surface of a worldwide Afrodiasporic aesthetics, I wish to affirm that both black lives and black liveness matter in new music.

Notes

1   For a diverse set of writings on Eastman, see Renée Levine Packer and Mary Jane Leach, eds., *Gay Guerrilla: Julius Eastman and His Music* (Rochester: University of Rochester Press, 2016).

2   Andreas Kolb, "Den Mythos der Abwesenheit Widerlegen: MaerzMusik-Kurator George Lewis Über den Schwerpunkt „Tele-Visions"," *Neue Musikzeitung* 68 (March 2019), https://www. nmz.de/artikel/den-mythos-der-abwesenheit-widerlegen.

3   For a discussion of this absence and what might be done about it, see Hannah Kendall, Harald Kisiedu, and George Lewis, "There Are Black Composers in the Future: A Wide-Ranging Discussion about the Past, Present, and Future of Contemporary Music," in *Dynamic Traditions: Global Perspectives on Contemporary Music*, ed. Elisa Erkelenz and Katja Heldt (Stuttgart: SWR, 2021), 143–58. A recent binilgual (English/German) edited volume addressing these issues is *Composing While Black: Afrodiasporische Neue Musik Heute/Afrodiasporic New Music Today*, ed. Harald Kisiedu and George E. Lewis (Hofheim: Wolke Verlag, 2023).

4   The Defragmentation initiative is discussed in George E. Lewis, "A Small Act of Curation," in *Curating Contemporary Music*, ed. Lars Petter Hagen and Rob Young, vol. 44, 2020, https:// www.on-curating.org/issue-44-reader/a-small-act-of-curation.html.

5   "Afro-Modernism in Contemporary Music: Concert and Symposium as Livestreams," Ensemble Modern, November 7, 2020, https://www.ensemble-modern.com/en/news/2020-11-05/afro-modernism-in-contemporary-music.

6   "Yet Unheard: Music by Emerging and Established Black Composers," London Sinfonietta, November 25, 2020, https://londonsinfonietta.org.uk/channel/video/performance-yet-unheard.

7   David R.M. Irving, "Rethinking Early Modern 'Western Art Music': A Global History Manifesto," *IMS Musicological Brainfood* 3, no. 1 (2019): 8.

8   Ibid., 7.

9   Donald Francis Tovey, *The Main Stream of Music and Other Essays* (Cleveland and New York: Meridian Books, 1949), 351.

10 For an initial discussion of creolization in classical music, see George E. Lewis, "The Situation of a Creole," *Twentieth Century Music* 14, no. 3 (2017): 442–46.

11 Jean Bernabé, Patrick Chamoiseau, and Raphaël Confiant, *Éloge De La Créolité, édition bilingue français/anglais*, trans. M. B. Taleb-Khyar (Paris: Gallimard, 1993), 75.

12 Ibid., 90.

13 Ibid., 112.

14 Ibid., 89.

15 "Immer mehr Afrikaner leben daher in einem bi-kulturellen Bereich. . .Ein realistischer Zugang zum heutigen Afrika muß also die traditionellen Kulturen als Grundlage der afrikanischen Gesellschaft akzeptieren und gleichzeitig die Möglichkeiten und kreativen Energien erkennen, die Afrika zu einem Miteinander der Kulturen in allen Lebensbereichen beiträgt." Akin Euba, "Der Afrikanische Komponist in Europa: Die Herausforderung des Bi-Kulturalismus," trans. Marion Diederichs-Lafite, *Österreichische Musikzeitschrift* 43, no. 7–8 (1988): 404.

16 „. . .ein neuer Komponisten-Typ, der sich einer Musiksprache bedient, die teilweise, aber nicht ausschließlich, auf dem der europäischen Kunstmusik basiert." Ibid.

17 Kofi Agawu, "African Art Music and the Challenge of Postcolonial Composition," in *Dynamic Traditions: Global Perspectives on Contemporary Music*, ed. Elisa Erkelenz and Katja Heldt (Stuttgart: SWR, 2021), 181.

18 "das große Ereignis des 21. Jahrhunderts. . .Nicht länger soll der Geist Europas die Trends diktieren, die Weltkulturen sollen gleichberechtigt neben- und miteinander wirken." Euba, "Der Afrikanische Komponist in Europa: Die Herausforderung des Bi-Kulturalismus," 406. On interculturalism in African contemporary music, see also Godwin Sadoh, "Intercultural Creativity in Joshua Uzoigwe's Music," *Africa: Journal of the International African Institute* 74, no. 4 (2004): 633–61.

19 "Eine Hauptforderung des Interkulturalismus richtet sich auch an die Musikausbildung in Europa. Während die Ausbildung in Afrika und Asien am Interkulturalismus orientiert ist, ist sie in Europa noch strikt eurozentriert." Euba, "Der Afrikanische Komponist in Europa: Die Herausforderung des Bi-Kulturalismus," 406.

20 Irving, "Rethinking Early Modern 'Western Art Music': A Global History Manifesto," 9.

21 Agawu, "African Art Music and the Challenge of Postcolonial Composition," 186.

22 Olly Wilson, "The Significance of the Relationship between Afro-American Music and West African Music," *The Black Perspective in Music* 2, no. 1 (1974): 3–22; Olly Wilson, "Black Music as an Art Form," *Black Music Research Journal* 3 (1983): 1–22; Olly Wilson, "The Black-American Composer and the Orchestra in the Twentieth Century," *The Black Perspective in Music* 14, no. 1 (1986): 26–34; Olly Wilson, "The Heterogeneous Sound Ideal in African-American Music," in *Signifyin(g), Sanctifyin', and Slam Dunking: A Reader in African American Expressive Culture*, ed. Gena Dagel Caponi (Amherst: University of Massachusetts Press, 1999), 157–171.

23 Wilson, "The Heterogeneous Sound Ideal in African-American Music," 158.

24 Ibid. David R. M. Irving has periodized this the origins of this generalization as part of a project in the construction of pan-European identity. See David R.M. Irving, "Ancient Greeks, World Music, and Early Modern Constructions of Western European Identity," in *Studies on a Global History of Music: A Balzan Musicology Project*, ed. Reinhard Strohm (London and New York: Routledge, 2018), 21–41.

25 Wilson, "Black Music as an Art Form," 2.

26 Ibid.

27 Wilson, "Black Music as an Art Form," 3.

28 Olly Wilson, "The Heterogeneous Sound Ideal in African-American Music," 160.

29 Alan P. Merriam, "African Music," in *Continuity and Change in African Cultures*, ed. William Bascom and Melville Herskovits (Chicago: University of Chicago Press, 1959), 129, quoted in Robert L. Douglas, "Formalizing an African-American Aesthetic," *New Art Examiner* 18, no. 10 (1991): 18.

30 George E. Lewis, "Purposive Patterning: Jeff Donaldson, Muhal Richard Abrams and the Multidominance of Consciousness," *Lenox Avenue*, no. 5 (1999): 64.

31 Douglas, "Formalizing an African-American Aesthetic," 18–19.

32 Robert Farris Thompson, *Flash of the Spirit: African and Afro-American Art and Philosophy* (New York: Vintage, 1983), xiii.

33 Thompson, *Flash of the Spirit*, 208.

34 Barbara Jones-Hogu, "The History, Philosophy and Aesthetics of AFRI-COBRA," in *AFRI-COBRA III* (Amherst: University Art Gallery, 1973), 1. Quoted in Kirstin L. Ellsworth, "Africobra and the Negotiation of Visual Afrocentrisms," *Civilisations* 58, no. 1 (2009): 29–30.

35 Jeff Donaldson, "Africobra—African Commune of Bad Relevant Artists: Ten in Search of a Nation," *Black World*, October 1970, 85.

36 This performance of Wilson's *Voices* was presented by the Boston Sympony Orchestra, conducted by Seiji Ozawa, on February 19, 1977: https://www.youtube.com/watch?v=AGVcgFPCRAI.

37 Bode Omojola, "African Pianism as an Intercultural Compositional Framework: A Study of the Piano Works of Akin Euba," *Research in African Literatures* 32, no. 2 (2001): 153.

38 Akin Euba, "Traditional Elements as the Basis of New African Art Music," *Africa Urban Notes* 10, no. 4 (1970): 55.

39 Emmanuel Boamah, "The Concept of African Pianism," *Legon Journal of the Humanities*, no. 23 (2012): 142–43.

40 Quoted in Boamah, "The Concept of African Pianism," 143.

41 Quoted in Omojola, "African Pianism as an Intercultural Compositional Framework: A Study of the Piano Works of Akin Euba," 157.

42 William Chapman Nyaho, "Igbá Kerin," in *Kete: Piano Music of Africa and the African Diaspora* (MSR Classics, 2020), digital download.

43 Akin Euba, "Remembering Joshua Uzoigwe: Exponent of African Pianism," *Journal of the Musical Arts in Africa* 2, no. 1 (2005): 84.

44 This performance is by Darryl Hollister, performed at Churchill College at the University of Cambridge in 2005: https://www.youtube.com/watch?v=gSyoz6900PI.

45 Douglas, "Formalizing an African-American Aesthetic," 18.

46 Donaldson, "Africobra—African Commune of Bad Relevant Artists: Ten in Search of a Nation," 86.

47 James A. Snead, "On Repetition in Black Culture," *African American Review* 50, no. 4 (2017): 649.

48 Graham Lock, "Wadsworth Jarrell and AFRICOBRA: Sheets of Color, Sheets of Sound: An Interview with Graham Lock," in *Hearing Eye: Jazz and Blues Influences in African American Visual Art*, ed. Graham Lock and David Murray (New York: Oxford University Press, 2008), 155.

49 Hear John Coltrane, *My Favorite Things*, compact disc (Atlantic 13420, 1961).

50 For an account of Coltrane's impact on early minimalist composers, see Edward Strickland, *Minimalism: Origins* (Bloomington: Indiana University Press, 1993).

51 Thompson, *Flash of the Spirit: African and Afro-American Art and Philosophy*, 194–222.

52 This is a reference to Jonkonnu by the Government of Jamaica: https://jis.gov.jm/information/25daysofchristmas/jonkonnu-day-2/.

53 George E. Lewis, "Recharging Unyazi 2005," *Herri*, no. 4 (2020), https://herri.org.za/4/george-lewis/.

54 Hear Halim El-Dabh, "Voyages for Orchestra," in *Halim El-Dabh: Music Compositions Throughout the Years* (CD Baby, 2009), compact disc.

55 Anthony Davis, *Amistad: An Opera in Two Acts*, compact disc (New World Records, 1996).

56 This video of a performance of *The Pattern* presents the full, scrolling score: https://www.youtube.com/watch?v=nhsZ7oPq0dE.

57 Quoted in George E. Lewis, "Lifting The Cone of Silence From Black Composers," *New York Times*, July 3, 2020, https://www.nytimes.com/2020/07/03/arts/music/black-composers-classical-music.html.

58 Program note, Tania León, *Ritmicas* (New York and Hamburg: Peer Music Classical, 2019), music score.

59 Program note, Andile Wiseman Khumalo, *Invisible Self*, 2020, music score.

60 Ibid.

61 Adeel Hassan, "The Sandra Bland Video: What We Know," *New York Times*, May 7, 2019, https://www.nytimes.com/2019/05/07/us/sandra-bland-brian-encinia.html.

62 *Say Her Name: Resisting Police Brutality Against Black Women* (African American Policy Forum and Center for Intersectionality and Social Policy Studies, 2015), http://static1.squarespace.com/static/53f20d90e4b0b80451158d8c/t/560c068ee4b0af26f72741df/1443628686535/AAPF_SMN_Brief_Full_singles-min.pdf.

63 Sharan Strange, *Yet Unheard* (unpublished libretto, 2016).

64 This performance of *Yet Unheard* is by the La Jolla Symphony & Chorus, conducted by Steven Schick; Helga Davis, soprano: https://www.youtube.com/watch?v=dsSENWpYqFw.

65 To read Hayden's *Runagate, Runagate*, visit https://www.poetryfoundation.org/poems/52947/runagate-runagate. To hear Logan's work, visit https://www.youtube.com/watch?v=uTf1fPswqeo .

66 Matana Roberts, *Coin Coin, Chapter Three: River Run Thee* (Constellation, 2015), compact disc.

67 Jon Cruz, *Culture on the Margins: The Black Diaspora and the Rise of American Cultural Interpretation* (Princeton: Princeton University Press, 1999), 43.

68 Douglas, "Formalizing an African-American Aesthetic," 18.

69 Wilson, "The Heterogeneous Sound Ideal in African-American Music," 164.

70 Cruz, *Culture on the Margins: The Black Diaspora and the Rise of American Cultural Interpretation*, 47.

71 "Don't Believe The Hype" is the third track on the rap group Public Enemy's album, *It Takes a Nation of Millions to Hold Us Back* (Def Jam/Universal, 1988), digital.

72 "Bring the Noise" is the second track on the rap group Public Enemy's now classic album, *It Takes a Nation of Millions to Hold Us Back* (Def Jam/Universal, 1988), digital.

73 Georgina Born and Andrew Barry, "Music, Mediation Theories and Actor-Network Theory," *Contemporary Music Review* 37, no. 5–6 (2018): 443–87.

74 Gilles Deleuze and Claire Parnet, *Dialogues II*, trans. Hugh Tomlinson and Barbara Habberjam, revised edition (New York: Columbia University Press, 1977), 52.

75 Bruno Latour, *Reassembling the Social: An Introduction to Actor Network Theory* (Oxford: Oxford University Press, 2005), 63–86.

76 Noah Purifoy, Franklin Sirmans, and Yael Lipschutz, *Junk Dada* (Munich: DelMonico, in association with the Los Angeles County Museum of Art, 2015).

77 Michael Gallope, "George Lewis: Temporal Assemblages as Critical Forms (Liner Note)" (New World Records 80792, 2017), 8.

78 Roscoe Mitchell, *L-R-G; The Maze; S II Examples* (Nessa 14, 1978), compact disc.

79 See Helen Walker-Hill, "Julia Perry," in *From Spirituals to Symphonies: African-American Women Composers and Their Music* (Urbana and Chicago: University of Illinois Press, 2007), 93–133.

80 See Gerhard Kubik, "Ennanga Music," *African Music* 4, no. 1 (1966): 21–24. For an analysis of *Homunculus C.F.*, see Mildred Denby Green, "A Study of the Lives and Works of Five Black Women Composers in America" (unpublished D.Mus.E, diss., University of Oklahoma, 1975). A performance of the Still work may be viewed at https://www.youtube.com/watch?v=5HIQiD5Y0VI.

81 Thomas Meyer, "Nimm Dein Eden sonstwohin: Zur Musik von Franck Bedrossian" (Kairos, 2019). Booklet for Franck Bedrossian, *Twist, Edges, Epigram* (Kairos, 2019, compact disc)

82 Aaron Cassidy and Aaron Einbond, eds., "Interview with Franck Bedrossian," in *Noise In and As Music* (Huddersfield: University of Huddersfield Press, 2013), 172.

83 Meyer, "Nimm Dein Eden sonstwohin: Zur Musik von Franck Bedrossian."

84 Yayoi Uno Everett, *The Music of Louis Andriessen* (Cambridge: Cambridge University Press, 2006), 118.

85 Maja Trochimczyk, "Andriessen and the Art of Composing," in *The Music of Louis Andriessen* (New York and London: Routledge, 2002), 277, Kindle edition.

86 For a discussion of these "blue columns," see Robert Adlington, "Counting Time, Countering Time: Louis Andriessen's 'De Tijd,'" *Indiana Theory Review,* 22, no. 1 (2001): 1–35.

87 Katelyn Silva, "On Afro-Modernism and Music," March 30, 2018, https://omnia.sas.upenn.edu/story/afro-modernism-and-music.

88 Kofi Agawu, *Representing African Music: Postcolonial Notes, Queries, Position* (New York: Routledge, 2003), 16.

89 Agawu, "African Art Music and the Challenge of Postcolonial Composition," 185.

90 Quoted in Bert Vuijsje, *De Nieuwe Jazz: Twintig Interviews Door Bert Vuijsje* (Baarn: Bosch & Keuning, 1978), 199.

Works Cited

Adlington, Robert. "Counting Time, Countering Time: Louis Andriessen's 'De Tijd.'" *Indiana Theory Review*, 22, no. 1 (2001): 1–35.

Agawu, Kofi. "African Art Music and the Challenge of Postcolonial Composition." In *Dynamic Traditions: Global Perspectives on Contemporary Music*, edited by Elisa Erkelenz and Katja Heldt, 179–88. Stuttgart: SWR, 2021.

———. *Representing African Music: Postcolonial Notes, Queries, Position*. New York: Routledge, 2003.

Bernabé, Jean, Patrick Chamoiseau, and Raphaël Confiant. *Éloge De La Créolité, Édition bilingue français/anglais*. Translated by M. B. Taleb-Khyar. Paris: Gallimard, 1993.

Boamah, Emmanuel. "The Concept of African Pianism." *Legon Journal of the Humanities*, no. 23 (2012): 141–54.

Born, Georgina, and Andrew Barry. "Music, Mediation Theories and Actor-Network Theory." *Contemporary Music Review* 37, no. 5–6 (2018): 443–87.

Cassidy, Aaron, and Aaron Einbond, eds. "Interview with Franck Bedrossian." In *Noise In and As Music*, 171–72. Huddersfield: University of Huddersfield Press, 2013.

Coltrane, John. *My Favorite Things*. Compact disc. Atlantic 13420, 1961.

Cruz, Jon. *Culture on the Margins: The Black Diaspora and the Rise of American Cultural Interpretation*. Princeton: Princeton University Press, 1999.

Davis, Anthony. *Amistad: An Opera in Two Acts*. Compact disc. New World Records, 1996.

Deleuze, Gilles, and Claire Parnet. *Dialogues II*. Translated by Hugh Tomlinson and Barbara Habberjam. Revised edition. New York: Columbia University Press, 1977.

Donaldson, Jeff. "Africobra—African Commune of Bad Relevant Artists: Ten in Search of a Nation." *Black World*, October 1970, 81–89.

Douglas, Robert L. "Formalizing an African-American Aesthetic." *New Art Examiner* 18, no. 10 (1991): 18–24.

El-Dabh, Halim. "Voyages for Orchestra." In *Halim El-Dabh: Music Compositions Throughout the Years*. CD Baby, 2009. compact disc.

Ellsworth, Kirstin L. "Africobra and the Negotiation of Visual Afrocentrisms." *Civilisations* 58, no. 1 (2009): 21–38.

Ensemble Modern. "Afro-Modernism in Contemporary Music: Concert and Symposium as Livestreams," November 7, 2020. https://www.ensemble-modern.com/en/news/2020-11- 05/afro-modernism-in-contemporary-music.

Euba, Akin. "Der Afrikanische Komponist in Europa: Die Herausforderung des Bi-Kulturalismus." Translated by Marion Diederichs-Lafite. *Österreichische Musikzeitschrift* 43, no. 7–8 (1988): 404–7.

———. "Remembering Joshua Uzoigwe: Exponent of African Pianism." *Journal of the Musical Arts in Africa* 2, no. 1 (2005): 84–88.

———. "Traditional Elements as the Basis of New African Art Music." *Africa Urban Notes* 10, no. 4 (1970): 52–63.

Everett, Yayoi Uno. *The Music of Louis Andriessen*. Cambridge: Cambridge University Press, 2006.

Gallope, Michael. "George Lewis: Temporal Assemblages as Critical Forms (Liner Note)." New World Records 80792, 2017.

Green, Mildred Denby. "A Study of the Lives and Works of Five Black Women Composers in America." Unpublished D.Mus.E, diss., University of Oklahoma, 1975.

Hassan, Adeel. "The Sandra Bland Video: What We Know." *New York Times*, May 7, 2019. https://www.nytimes.com/2019/05/07/us/sandra-bland-brian-encinia.html.

Irving, David R.M. "Ancient Greeks, World Music, and Early Modern Constructions of Western European Identity." In *Studies on a Global History of Music: A Balzan Musicology Project*, edited by Reinhard Strohm, 21–41. London and New York: Routledge, 2018.

———. "Rethinking Early Modern 'Western Art Music': A Global History Manifesto." *IMS Musicological Brainfood* 3, no. 1 (2019): 6–10.

Jones-Hogu, Barbara. "The History, Philosophy and Aesthetics of AFRI-COBRA." In *AFRI-COBRA III*, 1–5. Amherst: University Art Gallery, 1973.

Kendall, Hannah, Harald Kisiedu, and George Lewis. "There Are Black Composers in the Future: A Wide-Ranging Discussion about the Past, Present, and Future of Contemporary Music." In *Dynamic Traditions: Global Perspectives on Contemporary Music*, edited by Elisa Erkelenz and Katja Heldt, 143–58. Stuttgart: SWR, 2021.

Khumalo, Andile Wiseman. *Invisible Self*, 2020. music score.

Kolb, Andreas. "Den Mythos der Abwesenheit Widerlegen: MaerzMusik-Kurator George Lewis Über den Schwerpunkt „Tele-Visions"." *Neue Musikzeitung* 68 (March 2019). https://www.nmz.de/artikel/den-mythos-der-abwesenheit-widerlegen.

Kubik, Gerhard. "Ennanga Music." *African Music* 4, no. 1 (1966): 21–24.

Latour, Bruno. *Reassembling the Social: An Introduction to Actor Network Theory*. Oxford: Oxford University Press, 2005.

León, Tania. *Ritmicas*. New York and Hamburg: Peer Music Classical, 2019. music score.

Lewis, George E. "A Small Act of Curation." In *Curating Contemporary Music*, edited by Lars Petter Hagen and Rob Young, Vol. 44, 2020. https://www.on-curating.org/issue-44- reader/a-small-act-of-curation.html.

——. "Lifting The Cone of Silence From Black Composers." *New York Times*, July 3, 2020. https://www.nytimes.com/2020/07/03/arts/music/black-composers-classical-music.html.

——. "Purposive Patterning: Jeff Donaldson, Muhal Richard Abrams and the Multidominance of Consciousness." *Lenox Avenue*, no. 5 (1999): 63–69.

——. "Recharging Unyazi 2005." *Herri*, no. 4 (2020). https://herri.org.za/4/george-lewis/.

——. "The Situation of a Creole." *Twentieth Century Music* 14, no. 3 (2017): 442–46.

Lock, Graham. "Wadsworth Jarrell and AFRICOBRA: Sheets of Color, Sheets of Sound: An Interview with Graham Lock." In *Hearing Eye: Jazz and Blues Influences in African American Visual Art*, edited by Graham Lock and David Murray, 150–70. New York: Oxford University Press, 2008.

London Sinfonietta. "Yet Unheard: Music by Emerging and Established Black Composers," November 25, 2020. https://londonsinfonietta.org.uk/channel/video/performance-yet-unheard.

Merriam, Alan P. "African Music." In *Continuity and Change in African Cultures*, edited by William Bascom and Melville Herskovits. Chicago: University of Chicago Press, 1959.

Meyer, Thomas. "Nimm Dein Eden sonstwohin: Zur Musik von Franck Bedrossian." Kairos, 2019.

Mitchell, Roscoe. *L-R-G; The Maze; S II Examples*. Nessa 14, 1978. compact disc.

Nyaho, William Chapman. "Igbá Kerin." In *Kete: Piano Music of Africa and the African Diaspora*. MSR Classics, 2020. digital download.

Omojola, Bode. "African Pianism as an Intercultural Compositional Framework: A Study of the Piano Works of Akin Euba." *Research in African Literatures* 32, no. 2 (2001): 153–74.

Packer, Renée Levine, and Mary Jane Leach, eds. *Gay Guerrilla: Julius Eastman and His Music*. Rochester: University of Rochester Press, 2016.

Public Enemy. "It Takes a Nation of Millions to Hold Us Back." Def Jam/Universal, 1988, digital.

Purifoy, Noah, Franklin Sirmans, and Yael Lipschutz. *Junk Dada*. Munich: DelMonico, in association with the Los Angeles County Museum of Art, 2015.

Roberts, Matana. *Coin Coin, Chapter Three: River Run Thee*. Constellation, 2015. compact disc.

Sadoh, Godwin. "Intercultural Creativity in Joshua Uzoigwe's Music." *Africa: Journal of the International African Institute* 74, no. 4 (2004): 633–61.

Say Her Name: Resisting Police Brutality Against Black Women. African American Policy Forum and Center for Intersectionality and Social Policy Studies, 2015. http://static1.squarespace.com/static/53f20d90e4b0b80451158d8c/t/560c068ee4b0af26f7 2741df/1443628686535/AAPF_SMN_Brief_Full_singles-min.pdf.

Silva, Katelyn. "On Afro-Modernism and Music," March 30, 2018. https://omnia.sas.upenn.edu/story/afro-modernism-and-music.

Snead, James A. "On Repetition in Black Culture." *African American Review* 50, no. 4 (2017): 648–56.

Strange, Sharan. *Yet Unheard*. unpublished libretto, 2016.

Strickland, Edward. *Minimalism: Origins*. Bloomington: Indiana University Press, 1993.

Thompson, Robert Farris. *Flash of the Spirit: African and Afro-American Art and Philosophy*. New York: Vintage, 1983.

Tovey, Donald Francis. *The Main Stream of Music and Other Essays*. Cleveland and New York: Meridian Books, 1949.

Trochimczyk, Maja. "Andriessen and the Art of Composing." In *The Music of Louis Andriessen*. New York and London: Routledge, 2002. Kindle edition.

Vuijsje, Bert. *De Nieuwe Jazz: Twintig Interviews Door Bert Vuijsje*. Baarn: Bosch & Keuning, 1978.

Walker-Hill, Helen. "Julia Perry." In *From Spirituals to Symphonies: African-American Women Composers and Their Music*, 93–133. Urbana and Chicago: University of Illinois Press, 2007.

Wilson, Olly. "Black Music as an Art Form." *Black Music Research Journal* 3 (1983): 1–22.
——. "The Black-American Composer and the Orchestra in the Twentieth Century." *The Black Perspective in Music* 4, no. 1 (1986): 26–34.
——. "The Heterogeneous Sound Ideal in African-American Music." In *Signifyin(g), Sanctifyin', and Slam Dunking: A Reader in African American Expressive Culture*, edited by Gena Dagel Caponi, 157–171. Amherst: University of Massachusetts Press, 1999.
——. "The Significance of the Relationship between Afro-American Music and West African Music." *The Black Perspective in Music* 2, no. 1 (1974): 3–22.

PART TWO
BLACK ART SPACES

6

SEE ME HERE: DEFINING BLACK SPACE AT THE INTERSECTION OF ARTISTIC AND CURATORIAL PRACTICES IN *PRIVY*

Deborah Goffe

In 2010, having found safe distance from the whirlwind life circumstances I had experienced over the previous three years, I embarked on a process to craft shared experience from those threads of my own. The work would unfold over the next several years with one mistimed attempt after another to bring the project to fruition. Time and again, I found that the conditions of my environment could not meet the work where it wanted to be. So, I toiled and waited, while other projects served as laboratories to test ideas, methods, and frameworks on safe(r) ground. This prolonged building and aggregating of materials and processes reached its critical mass on the evening of December 16, 2016. With a group of twenty-five guests gathered in my home to witness the experience, I performed *Privy* as an assemblage of dance, story, song, site-responsive installation, and dinner party for the first time.

Just shy of ten years earlier, my body had betrayed me. In that betrayal, I found myself navigating a healthcare system that had no place for me, a family medical history deemed none of my business, and the reality that my body might not always submit to my will. I was growing aware of patterns and legacies that aligned my body with larger networks of Black and brown women's bodies. The only way I could imagine engaging a dialogue with that network of women, or to make our dialogue visible, was to do so through my own body in performance.

So, when those twenty-five guests gathered in my home in 2016, I had envisioned the evening as a site-specific installation of sorts, one in which my home served as an immersive world made manifest by the accumulated research, movement phrases, choreographic structures, text, songs, soundscapes, images and objects I had gathered over the years. With this assemblage, I hoped to break something open by calling each of these objects, memories and movement patterns forth with enough frequency, or force . . . or perhaps *quiet*. I hoped to test the notion of performance space as social space, attend to the risks and benefits of revealing one's vulnerabilities in this public/private

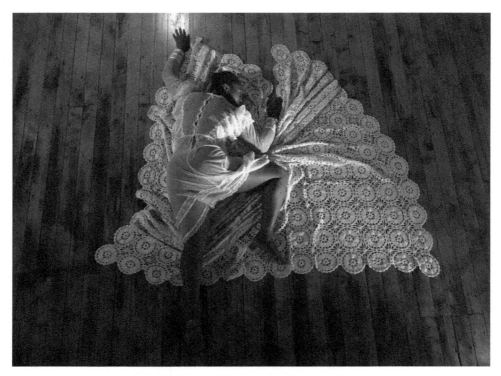

Plate 14 Deborah Goffe, *Privy*, 2016. Photo by Kelly Silliman. Courtesy of Scapegoat Garden, Inc.

moment, and on some level, resolve my nagging compulsion to tease out the events of one long year in my life through movement. Alongside those priorities, I sought an exchange with people through a practice of connection, and collective attention to the ways we might hold space for others' vulnerabilities in this and other contexts.

Privy is both a time machine and a map, marking ties to events and locations that have fed its emergence. Its process stretches back and forth across small New England cities and towns from Connecticut to Maine, and subtly reaches into family histories and geographies across the Atlantic. This work now rests (if only for this moment) in my current habitat in Holyoke, Massachusetts—homeland of the Nipmuc and Pocumtuc. Small cities, like the one I live in, often lack the infrastructure or inclination to support and nurture local performance making, and this is especially true for artists from marginalized communities within those locales. It is not uncommon for dance artists to assume the responsibility of presenting their own work—securing the means, venue, and audience. Depending on the context, this practice may be met with praise or suspicion as it threatens to bypass processes that would affirm its value in the eyes of established gatekeepers. However, when I've turned this lens back on my personal artistic trajectory, I recognize the environments of care—curatorial care—necessary to meaningfully incubate new work. I have learned to provide that care for myself and fellow artists when established systems fail to do so. *Privy* called for a considered frame of its own making—one that would enable the work's growth, hold nurturing space for my vulnerability as its maker, and likewise build the infrastructure necessary to make that work manifest. Through this evolving relationship to time and place, I actualize a practice that is at once curatorial and artistic.

Frames Matter

This inclination to simultaneously build the work, its frame, and its environment has been informed by my ongoing study of arts ecosystems and the strategies dance artists employ to navigate those structures. My focus has been particularly trained on the strategies employed by dance artists working outside perceived cultural centers, and the colonizing drives that define and enclose the very idea of *a center* in the first place. For artists working in geographies like those in which I live, the dynamism of their work is often out of step with assumptions about the possibilities and impossibilities of that dynamism. For artists of color, the impact of limiting perceptions of place are often compounded exponentially. For these reasons, I have nurtured a practice that recognizes and foregrounds the cultural dynamism operating right in front of me, though often outside established gatekeeping structures. This practice has continually increased my attentiveness to the ways artists bend the constitutive parts of arts ecologies to their individual and collective wills, thereby defining the means by which their work manifests in the world. They navigate, circumvent, and intervene in raced, gendered, sexed, classed, geographic, and institutionally-biased systems of marginalization, nesting their own ecological configurations within, under, and against prescribed frameworks. In this vast resourcefulness—drawing lines of connection from within cultural, business and educational sectors, familial and social networks, and far beyond—artists generate their own abundance. I recognize this cultural abundance all around me, even as it is all too often rendered invisible by dominant modes of cultural perception. Nonetheless, attention to the quality and direction of my own seeing has defined environments of care that I now recognize and value as a most urgent form of curatorial practice.

To thrive, artists need and deserve considered environments of care with the capacity to hold the full integrity of their work. I see curatorial practice as a kind of connective tissue, bridging the gaps between artists, their work, audiences, and infrastructures in space and time. But who is afforded a curator's care? Who defines the conditions of care (the artist, curator, or audiences), by what means, and in what spaces? From my observations of artists and their environments, it is clear that if artists *are* making art, someone is fulfilling these curatorial functions on their behalf in some fashion—regardless of whether these functions are fulfilled through formal curatorial positions, distributed among artists' networks, or assumed by artists themselves.

While invoking curatorial practices, I am acutely aware of the risks inherent in invoking *curation* at this time in history when it would seem curators, or people who curate, are ubiquitous. From YouTube platforms to web-based retail subscriptions, everything is curated, and everyone is a curator. If, as the current state of media democratization seemingly implies, everyone's voice carries equal weight regardless of established expertise, perhaps all voices are rendered meaningless. However, rigorous curatorial frameworks can function as systems of care and nurturance, especially when this care is distinguished from infantilization: artists do not need a parental figure to rescue them. Instead, I have committed to setting aside my artistic cravings from time to time in order to hold space for other artists to do the work we collectively need them to do—to travel to other realms and to come back whole. I hold onto the hope that someone will do that for me on occasion as well. Some have.

It is in the context of this artist-centered *nesting* of interconnected relationships, resources, and affiliations—or *nested arts ecosystems,* as I've come to call them—that my evolving curatorial frame has emerged, and which hones my own active engagement in similarly nested artistic activities. My hybrid identities, roles, and relationships to locality—black, woman, dance artist, educator, curator, scholarly interpreter, and resident of New England—have necessitated my own intervening strategies. *Privy* has functioned as a vital space of experimentation through which I actively integrate my artistic practice, the overlapping ecosystems I find myself operating within, and the invisibilities that have compelled me to define a space of my own.[1] Perhaps this approach to curatorial choreography is an ethos that responds to the pressures uniquely dealt to dance and performance makers of color. *Privy* has been a space to build my own frame—to hold the process, the work, the performance encounter, and my Black body on my own terms.]

Framing Black Space

As the daughter of Jamaican immigrants, I have found that sometimes colloquialisms say it best. In Jamaican patois, "see me here" is a reply to the call "Where are you?" I have a vivid image in my mind of a little Debbie, embroiled in some mischief in some corner of the house, and upon hearing my mother call out for me, I respond by peeking out from around that corner to sing, "see me here." In truth, this vivid image probably portrays a much better behaved cousin than me. My more likely response to my mother was "what," although my memory is better served by countering the reality of my Americanized gruffness with this more romanticized image of childhood. Now as an adult, my mother and I often use patois as a bonding language. Guiding me through the syntax, cadences and idioms of the dialect has been one of the many ways she has remained my teacher as she ages. However, speaking patois in public is still a relatively transgressive act for her. For my family, who remember Jamaica before its independence from British colonial rule, patois is a language reserved for one's inner circle—those made privy, one's family.

Likewise, "see me here" strikes me as an apt frame for a pattern that has emerged in my choreographic process in recent years. In answer to internal and external pressures to account for the relationship between my identities and my artistic voice, I have developed a habit of foregrounding particular identity markers as a way of confronting those who witness my work—insisting they consider the associations placed on bodies in performance, and the ways their reading of a work is informed by those associations. *Privy*, is an invitation to see me here as I locate my experiences in my own body, and as a center of collective awareness for a moment. I have come to understand that much of the labor of dance making is predicated on the body as an expressive vessel with its own lived and inherited experience, in action, through space and time, in relationship to itself and other bodies, and within a frame. That frame is shaped by each body's unique features, the discrete spaces they occupy, and the world those bodies are born out of, and into, anew each time the dance moment is revisited. Within and beyond that frame, a network of interdependent associations can also be found. *My body is source material.*

Mine is a Black and female body. With those assertions, I affirm the body-centered, relational, temporal, and political realities of dance practice. *Dance making is world making.* However, in my grappling with choreographic and curatorial frames, particularly as they relate to my work in developing *Privy,* I have questioned the blackness of the dancing itself—so often deemed too Black or not Black enough in performance and social contexts throughout my life. In my experience, the idea of *Black dance* has often been attributed to a narrow set of movement vocabularies, methodologies, and contexts fixed in time, geography, imagination, or reach. In other instances, Black dance has been invoked as a counter to established systems of exclusion. In *How to See a Work of Art in Total Darkness,* Darby English confirms Black art's emergence in service of two juxtaposed purposes and communities: "racism's ceaselessly inventive way of isolating Black realities from the spaces whose purity it would conserve by doing so," and "a now century-long effort [on the part of Black artists and communities] to engender and keep pure a cultural domain that is uniquely our own" (8).[2] Fred Moten and Stefano Harney observe that those who claim colonized space as their own often distinguish inside-ness and outside-ness in high contrast terms, but further observe that those relegated to the outside can seek alternatives to those exclusionary systems by defining discrete spaces for themselves without reinscribing the false conception of borders.[3] This gives rise to the question: How does one reject the former, and honor the latter, without being confined to, or defined entirely by, either space? As Moten and Harney propose, the answer is to free oneself from the false construction of enclosures and surrounds by escaping to an underground network—not from one territory (inside) to another (outside), but rather to an *undercommon* that can ultimately exists in the same material space as the one from which we have escaped. *That we occupy the same physical space does not mean we are operating in the same realm; Here is more than one place.* For these reasons, I take comfort in Thomas DeFrantz's offering that "Black performance is not static, contained, or geographically specific;" instead race can function as "both a defining paradigm for blackness and a resistant frame for understanding the unbound nature of the [emerging] field [of Black performance theory]."[4] Like so much of Black experience, Black performance is rhizomatic in its multiplicity, and cannot be confined to a narrow set of parameters. This tension between my own identification with blackness and my desire to conjure a world of my own making have proven integral to the artistic and curatorial processes out of which *Privy* emerged.

Choreographing the Frame

Gesturing to these political and social tensions in the construction of a secure *and* generatively porous Black space, I am reminded of my early creative process in the development of *Privy*. In the summer of 2010, I was invited to participate as an Artist in Residence at Bates Dance Festival in Lewiston, Maine. Each morning over the course of three weeks, I retreated alone to a studio space on the Bates College campus to begin conjuring the first seeds of this new work. I shared those seedlings in two works-in-progress showings during the festival: at the mid-point of the festival where I received useful feedback, and again at the conclusion of the festival. During the feedback session following the final showing, one witness gave voice to an absence of what she called *movement invention* in my work. She pointed to what she saw as an unnecessary reliance on Horton technique, a codified movement vocabulary and methodology named for its creator Lester Horton in the first half of the 20th century. Though often aligned with notions of "Black dance," Horton technique is often divorced from the whiteness of its originator, and the whiteness of Bella Lewitsky, the dancer on whose body the technique was initially developed. While I had never choreographed a work with a deliberate intention to employ that technique, this colleague saw Horton technique prominently positioned in my work in that moment.

How did it get there? Had I mis-placed it there, or had this witness done so? Should the presence of Horton technique represent just cause for the works' dismissal? While I admit to having trained in Horton technique, I have also trained in a wide variety of dance traditions from ballet, Afro-Haitian and Cape Verdean cultural dance forms, jazz, modern and contemporary Western dance techniques, and a variety of somatically informed methodologies. Like many of my contemporaries—this colleague included—my body holds a vast assemblage of movement styles and traditions. So why would Horton technique emerge most prominently for this witness? This exchange had significant impact on the development of *Privy* in the ensuing years, and while I will not deny a complex set of causes for the tension of that exchange, I have come to believe that the presence of my Black body was a consequential factor.

Experiences like the one I had at Bates have often forced me to attend to the Africanist presences in my work and body, or their lack thereof. I've come to understand that my dark skinned, thick thigh-ed, muscle-bound female body seems to make promises. Whether I intend to deliver on those promises or not, they are written on this body.[5] So this body never performs alone or of its own accord, even when engaged in solo performance practice. Alongside (or in opposition) to my expressed choreographic aims, my body is always in relationship to, and experienced through the filter of, the narrative being written on it moment-to-moment. While I have no interest in boxing myself into categorizations, I acknowledge and lay claim to traces of these and other characteristics that are often attributed to Black dance and dancers. At the same time, rather than suggesting an absence of *movement invention*, these characteristics strike me as especially rooted in the very experimentation that is otherwise disregarded in favor of a fixed narrative of Black aesthetic and experience.

Brenda Dixon Gottschild argues that an Africanist presence runs through much of American dance and performance, because an Africanist presence cannot be uncoupled from American-ness. In her seminal text, *Digging the Africanist Presence in American Performance,* she draws on the work of Robert Farris Thompson, Susan Vogel and Kariamu Welsh Asante to designate five Africanist threads running through much of mid-twentieth century modern concert dance and the sneakered post-moderns, as well as through the Americanization of ballet at the hands of George Balanchine.[6] Thomas DeFrantz likewise proclaims Black as "the manifestation of Africanist aesthetics." If, as DeFrantz suggests, Africanist and Black are linked, and if, as Dixon-Gottschild asserts, an Africanist presence is pervasive in American performance traditions, then perhaps the presence of a Black aesthetic exists even if a Black body is not present. However, as I dig the Africanist presence in my own work, *my* Black body is ever-present, and I have wondered if the presence of that Black body (in the making or performance process) inevitably renders the work black? If not for me, there is evidence that my work might be perceived as such by those who witness it.

In *Choreographing Difference: The Body and Identity in Contemporary Dance*, Ann Cooper Albright speaks of a "double moment of dancing in front of an audience [as] one in which the dancer negotiates between objectivity and subjectivity—between seeing and being seen, experiencing and being experienced, moving and being moved [. . .]."[7] Albright's double moment in performance contexts bears resemblance to Du Bois' racially-rendered double consciousness—simultaneously experiencing the moment of being, while calculating others' observation of that being. Albright also points out that, "some [. . .] dances foreground the social markings of identity on the body, using movement and text to comment on (often subvert) the cultural meanings of those bodily markers."[8] In my own dance making in recent years, I have been inclined to make this negotiation between objectivity and subjectivity more explicit by engaging key questions: What happens in those first few moments of a performance when the witnesses' gaze falls upon the body of the performer, and calculations are quickly made about what the dancing body promises? What happens when that gaze is met, and the passage of time is used as a threshold through which an audience is invited to calculate less and co-experience more? Can we (maker, performer, and witness) move beyond preconceived promises toward an experience that is allowed to unfold within the frame established by the work itself? In answer to these questions, I have experimented with ways to make the double moment legible, reciprocal and shared. I have likewise used the performance moment as a space to shift presumed correlations between neutrality and whiteness by asserting my own identity—my Black body in particular—in the performance context. In doing so, I imagine ways to harness what Albright refers to as ". . . slippage between the lived body and the cultural representation, between a somatic identity (the experience of one's physicality) and cultural one (how one's body—skin, gender, ability, age, etc.— renders meaning in society)."[9] How do I define a mutable Black space as a foundation on which my work can be experienced?

My solution of the moment, a strategy central to the construction of *Privy*, has often been to meet gaze with gaze, and to wait . . . like a kindergarten teacher out-waiting the buzz of preoccupation in order to facilitate a settling of collective focus. In fact, I employ this strategy of direct address to activate the gap between performance space and audience space in several recent pieces. In the case of my solo choreographic study, *Creation Myth (or Reinventing the Wheel),* the lights come up to find me standing, looking back at the witnesses who find me there. Over the course of a minute or more, I slowly melt into a protective stance, my arms framing and guarding my head as I peer out from beneath the crook of my right elbow. In *BE'SPOKE(n),* soloist Paul Dennis meets the audience in direct address before devolving into a nodding dance in homage to the nods of acknowledgement Black men often offer as greetings to one another when passing through white space. Dennis' Black male figure is amplified by the presence of nine full-sized cardboard cutouts of himself in various stages of undress, and gazing out to the audience throughout the piece. In the performance of *Reaction Bubble,* as the audience gathers around the perimeter of the installation, I stand, meet their eyes, and once it seems I have their attention, I lead the group through a meditative ritual intended to bring their attention back to their own bodies, and the bodies around them.[10] In this piece too, by casting a majority of Black and brown performers in the project, I sought to shift the presumed whiteness of the gallery by ensuring a critical mass of people of color in the space. In each case, I was motivated to give special attention to the space between the audiences and work, both because the work warranted it, and because the particular performance contexts in which these works were presented could not be relied upon to prepare audiences for the presence of a mutable and abundant blackness. I intervened in curatorial functions by choreographing my own frame, and troubling the threshold between the work and those who encountered it at the onset.

In her text, *Troubling Vision: Performance, Visuality, and Blackness*, Nicole Fleetwood affirms that

> Blackness fills space between matter, between object and subject, between bodies, between looking and being looked upon. It fills the void and is the void. Through its circulation, blackness attaches to bodies and narratives coded as such but it always exceeds these attachments.[11]

Fleetwood acknowledges Black artists' efforts to move beyond "overdetermined narratives of Black arts traditions" and argues "for the productive possibilities of Black subjects to trouble the field of vision precisely by presenting the Black body as a troubling figuration to visual discourse."[12] Likewise, my efforts to center the body is joined by the sing-song refrain of "see me here." Through *Privy*, I imagine ways to trouble vision, to challenge guests' assumptions so we might move beyond them, or into them. Given the risk that my body might be relegated to outsider status, or otherwise colonized—even in my own home—I have found it necessary to attune the between-space in order to ensure my safety as a performer, the integrity of the work, and my commitment to invitation as a primary term of engagement with an audience. I have most often met this need by meeting gaze and establishing a shared sense of together-ness at the onset. In *Privy*, I've called upon curatorial practice to extend this choreographic devices. By extending a directness of address out beyond the edges of the performance moment itself, I have established conditions in which the work, audiences, and I can flourish.

What Stories Do and Who Is Made Privy

What is catalyzed when we bring one another into personal confidence around unspoken familial and societal legacies? What do we choose to disclose, what do we keep for

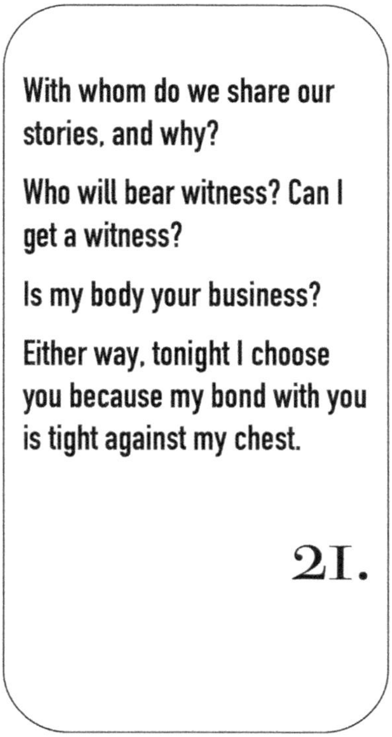

> With whom do we share our stories, and why?
>
> Who will bear witness? Can I get a witness?
>
> Is my body your business?
>
> Either way, tonight I choose you because my bond with you is tight against my chest.
>
> 21.

Figure 6.1 Deborah Goffe, *Privy*, 2016. Card 21: one in a series of text and image cards used in Privy performances. Courtesy of Scapegoat Garden, Inc.

ourselves, and what is risked on either side? What role do intersectional identities play in shaping one's level of risk? How is healing (for storyteller and witness) catalyzed by ritualizing personal experience through performance practice?

I see the offering of story as part of a larger trajectory of social relations. In developing *Privy*, the goal was to share my own story as a way to reconcile performance making with my desires to nurture relationship through mutual care, between myself and those who would witness the work. This interest in how and why we share personal stories can certainly be traced through my lifetime, though most notably in early exchanges with my parents who insisted there was rarely a reason to expose oneself to others' scrutiny. For my Jamaican parents, one's story was to be kept for oneself, and they made their best effort to instill their values around privacy as dearly as they could. It was not unusual for my parents to respond to my energetic retellings of conversations I'd had that day at school or the intensity of my daily dramas by saying, "Why are you telling people our business?" Nonetheless, I was aware early on that my birth and upbringing in an entirely different time and place than theirs had informed my relationship to privacy as much as their values had. While I agreed that everything wasn't for everybody, I also determined to always have relationships that could care-fully and reciprocally hold many of the concerns and enthusiasms of our hearts. I've nurtured a few deep forever-friendships with that logic, and I have an increasing number of discussions with my family about the ways giving voice to all that troubles or excites us can relieve burden or ignite possibility. However, I also find myself resorting to my parents' idea of keeping my *business off the street* more and more as conventions around privacy and disclosure are particularly volatile in this current time and place. In *The Sovereignty of Quiet: Beyond Resistance in Black Culture*, Kevin Quashie quotes Darlene Clark Hine's idea of dissemblance:

> Black women, as a rule, developed and adhered to a cult of secrecy, a culture of dissemblance to protect the sanctity of inner aspects of their lives. The dynamics of dissemblance involved the appearance of disclosure, or openness about themselves and their feelings, while actually remaining an enigma.[13]

In *Privy*, I actively leverage this power to simultaneously disclose and withhold information about my interior world, extending an invitation and ensuring my story remains mine.

In the month leading up to that *Privy* event, I extended detailed personal invitation letters to potential guests: family, new and old friends, neighbors, teaching colleagues and artistic collaborators, past and present students, and acquaintances from various affiliations. These letters served as a bridge into the work by communicating the goals of the evening, relevant details about how the work came to be, and logistics that would frame my guests' sense of their role in the experience. In July of 2017, twenty-three more guests arrived in my home. Twenty-eight gathered that October, thirty-five more in December, and twenty-eight the following September. This extended repetition of invitation and shared encounter over the course of almost three years has provided space, in my thinking and in my capacity, to vision the world of the piece more thoroughly. With each round of guests, I have been able to adjust the opacity of each layer, deciding where to be more explicit, and where to be more veiled—to "tell all the truth but tell it slant" (Dickenson).[14]

The Quiet of Home

Kevin Quashie equates quiet with the quality of interiority, and defines this quiet as "a metaphor for the full range of one's inner life—one's desires, ambitions, hungers, vulnerabilities, fears."[15] He offers this quiet as a contrast to its common associations with "silence or stillness". For Quashie, quiet is aligned with the wild wandering of one's interior world. It is the place of imagination, the place of prayer, the place of vulnerability. Further, he offers this wild and wandering quiet as an alternative to the presumption that Black subjectivity is necessarily correlated with resistance, the experience of perpetually being brought out away from the work of the interior world to fight whiteness in the public realm. Quashie's repeated affirmation of "an aesthetic of quiet" has been a source of comfort and inspiration in my thinking about *Privy*.[16] Vulnerability and shame might exist in the gap between quiet and another person. To close that gap is intimacy.

Asserting that "home is an intimate place," humanistic geographer Yi-Fu Tuan correlates the care one finds at home with the capacity to risk vulnerability:

Intimate occasions are often those on which we become passive and allow ourselves to be vulnerable, exposed to the caress or sting of new experience. [. . .] Intimate places are places of nurture where our fundamental needs are heeded and cared for without fuss.[17]

In my early conceptions of *Privy,* I hadn't imagined that the piece would be performed in my actual home, though I knew it would need to occupy a nontraditional performance space in order to cultivate its requisite sense of intimacy. During the three years I managed and developed programming at the dance incubator space I founded in Hartford, I was certain *that* space would be the ideal place for this piece. I had taken great care to nest in that studio the way I would in a home so it might function as a suitable space for dance artists, dances and their witnesses to encounter one another. Soft light, art objects in abundance, living plants, and the regular availability of food and drink all made the space feel like home. However, my move to Western Massachusetts necessitated my search for a new choreographic work space, and from the moment I walked into the converted wool mill in which I now live, it was clear that *Privy* could not have been completed before that point. I needed to establish my home there, first. Now that *Privy* has taken root in my home, a number of experiences point to dynamics that could not have come to the fore in any other context as readily.

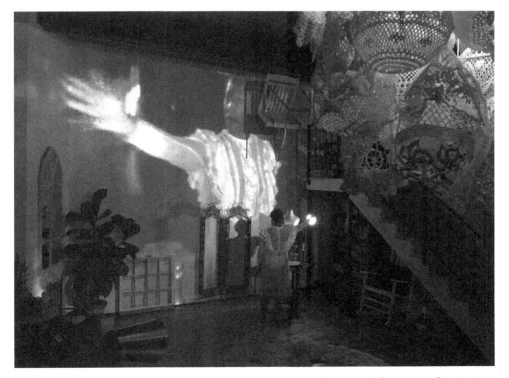

Plate 15 Deborah Goffe, *Privy*, 2016. Photo by Kelly Silliman. Courtesy of Scapegoat Garden, Inc.

Through the process of developing and presenting *Privy*, I have come to recognize privilege in the assumption that one can lay claim to any place, object or person, or that this claim could be made with a simple assertion of one's will. As such, the threat of white occupation in this performance space has been especially potent, especially because this space also functions as my home. For this reason, it has been my express purpose to claim and re-claim the performance as both my home and as Black space beyond the context of the dance work, while making evident the fact that my decision to invite others into my home is a choice—an exercise in generosity—not an obligation. These are conditions that would be difficult to assert as effectively outside my home, but even under these circumstances, I have had to be mindful.

Artistic and curatorial functions converge to mitigate the work's inherent risks. As such, details have mattered a great deal. It matters that my home represents my best attempts to render beauty and comfort—a jewel box teeming with daily, though humble, extravaganzes that underscore my values, my aesthetics and my identities. It matters who greets guests at the door. It matters what and how guests have come to know about the encounter in the first place. It matters that I work diligently to ensure a significant presence of Black and brown guests. It matters that I obsessively nurture an idea of *hospitality aesthetic* in my work. It matters that I share a list of secrets, but redact them—that I tell my most intimate story in detail, but do so alongside a host of recorded voices that allow only portions of my narrative to peek through. It matters that guests are charged with the responsibility of configuring the space for my use, serving as co-makers of the space, but on my terms. It matters that my only covering is a sheer dress and panties—4 pairs of them—put on and off in a ritual that is most scandalous given the way I was raised. *But I am in my own home, after all.* These devices have not served primary functions as acts of resistance, but also as strategies to increase the likelihood that I can enter my quiet in the sanctity of my own home. While I choose to invite others in, I reserve the right to decide who joins me for this ritual, and under what circumstances. My quiet is gently veiled so it always stays mine in such a way that it is evident to my guests that their access is, in fact, limited.

At the start of each *Privy* event, guests are greeted at the door, and welcomed to partake of the bounty of food, drink, and conversation with each other, my collaborators, and me. Guests meander throughout my home, taking in layer upon layer of house plants, moody lights, and a sculptural object made from doily-ed masses flanking a large bird cage and hanging from the ceiling. Textured projections fill one 14-foot wall—casting the passage of light and shadow through the doilies perforations. An abundance of artifacts line shelves, tables, and walls throughout the space—as if every bit of it exists only in the context of *Privy, and* every bit of it exists as part of my everyday life. After about an hour of spirited mingling, my collaborators and I invite the group to help shift the space for my singing of a surprisingly old song about the advantages of being a single girl without children, turning my least favorite questions about my reproductive intentions back on my guests, and embodying circuitous pathways created from the inside of the giant bird cage. For forty minutes, I indulge skyward heart opening, sink again and again into the spaciousness of the mottled wooden floor, and make space for the most important women, who no longer live in this realm, to enter and move the room somehow. And when I'm done, my guests graciously reconfigure the space once more so we can sit together in a circle, eat dessert and talk as a group about the evening's shared experience. In the days following, I close the loop by sending emails thanking each guest for their presence and participation.

After welcoming more than one hundred and twenty guests into my home to witness *Privy* over the course of the initial two years, I observed a pattern in the correspondences that follow each event. Many more guests write to me after one of these gatherings than is typical of my other experiences with performance or curating. This is true, in part, because in the intimacy of each event's closing circle, I ask guests to write me, if they were so moved, after the fact. Notes detailing their experiences of the events arrive to me by email, and by physical cards delivered to my home by post. In large part, they affirm the potentiality of mutual care for the relationship that the performance event conditions, and of the performance space as social space. An excerpt from one email message powerfully reads:

> Cultivating a "withness" – a being-with. Yet we were and were not necessary. We were and were not privy. Were we always there? You held us perhaps more than we could hold you. The invitation with the annotation, the performance with the redaction, these are conditions of sharing and care. Perhaps this gathering gesture—gestures that gather in multiple ways—forms a restorative practice, an unfurling re-curling, a sharing in power that imperfectly balances and processes in collective, in common across difference, through ineffable stories and experience expressed in vulnerability and retained in opacity.[18]

This guest, a dear friend, and a scholar skilled in rendering the embodied and experiential in words, captures the intended invitation to enter, to respect the spaces that have been reserved, and to share in the vulnerabilities of both.

At the same time, a very small number of people interpreted my invitation to engage correspondence as a request for corrective feedback—only three of the more than one hundred guests who joined me over the course of the first year. In each case, when white men misread their roles, they assumed I sought their validation in order to be enough, rather than my expressed intention to extend invitations for us both to be with. Whether offering suggestions about my choice of song, or how to reconcile the formal structures of the evening with the expectations they had upon entering, these guests could only imagine their roles in light of their perceived mandate to fix. Though relatively few, these exchanges highlighted the ways *Privy's* curatorial frame supported most guests' understanding of our terms of engagement, and my own when some were unable to meet those terms.

Having constructed *Privy* in the space of my home, I have wondered what form the future life of the piece would take. Is *Privy* fated to be performed only in its original context, or is it possible to transpose the conditions of home to another venue? By defining my own curatorial frame, with its corresponding nested ecosystem to support it, have I forfeited opportunities to reintegrate this project into professional trajectories that might prolong its life, and sustain my arts practice more generally? What kinds of institutional partnerships are equipped—materially and conceptually—to hold the integrity and essence of the project? These and other questions loom large in the wake of the project's initial years of home performances. One set of answers arrived in early 2021 when the constraints of global pandemic forced paradigm shifts that resulted in new partnerships with arts institutions to invite guests—across local and international boundaries—into the intimacy of my home by way of internet-mediated platforms.[19] Whether in-person or virtually, *Privy* has powerfully shifted my orientation to the cultural abundance nested within my own local arts ecosystems—in private residences, in back yards, on stages, on screens, and in a range of other unexpected locations and contexts. Through *Privy*, I affirm blackness as multiplicity: the dance and the frame, the public/private space of home and stage, quiet and resistance, disclosure and keeping something entirely for oneself.[20]

Notes

1   Here I find resonance in Tara Aisha Willis's reflection on her hybrid roles as performer in Will Rawls's *What Remains*, and as curator at Chicago's Museum of Contemporary Art where Rawls's work was presented in 2018. As she puts it, "I see fellow women of color in the arts multitasking intensely all the time, being responsible for representing many things at many different tables. That takes a lot of work and energy, and sometimes requires doing less of one thing to make sure you have the bandwidth to make your voice heard elsewhere. [. . .] We are performing that capacity to code switch, to speak multiple social languages, to hold both our own voices and the voices of other folks not in the room." Tara Aisha Willis, "What Remains: Reflections on Blackness, Dance, and Curation," *Performa* 18 (2018).

2   Darby English, *How to See a Work of Art in Total Darkness* (Cambridge: MIT Press, 2010), 8.

3   Stefano Harney and Fred Moten, The *Undercommons: Fugitive Planning and Black Study* (Wivenhoe; NY: Minor Compositions, 2013).

4   Thomas DeFrantz, *Black Performance Theory* (Durham: Duke University Press, 2014), 9.

5   In *Dancing Revelations*, DeFrantz addresses this reading of Black bodies as marked: "Although the actions of African Americans may indeed express 'universal' truths, the Black body itself never achieves this transcendence in any discourse of the West. Marked even before it can be seen, before it can even exist, the body carries its tangled web of work and sexual potentials, athletic and creative resources, and stratified social locations onto the stages of the modern." Thomas DeFrantz, *Dancing Revelations: Alvin Ailey's Embodiment of African American Culture* (New York: Oxford University Press, 2004), 19.

6   Brenda Dixon Gottschild, *Digging the Africanist Presence in American Performance: Dance and Other Contexts* (Westport, CT: Praeger, 1998), 15–16.

7   Ann Cooper Albright, *Choreographing Difference: The Body and Identity in Contemporary Dance* (Middletown, CT: Wesleyan University Press, 1997), 3.

8   Albright, *Choreographing Difference*, 3–4.

9   Albright, *Choreographing Difference*, 4.

10   *Reaction Bubble* was an installation and performance work commissioned by Real Art Ways, and developed in collaboration with New York-based interactive media duo LoVid, and Hartford-based ceramicist Matt Towers.

11   Nicole Fleetwood, *Troubling Vision: Performance, Visuality, and Blackness* (Chicago: University of Chicago Press, 2011), 6.

12 Fleetwood, *Troubling Vision*, 18.

13 Quoted in Kevin Quashie, *The Sovereignty of Quiet: Beyond Resistance in Black Culture* (New Brunswick: Rutgers University Press, 2012), 15.

14 Emily Dickinson, "Tell all the truth but tell it slant," Poetry Foundation, accessed 15 August 2018: www.poetryfoundation.org/poems/56824/tell-all-the-truth-but-tell-it-slant-1263.

15 Quashie, *Sovereignty of Quiet*, 6.

16 Quashie, *Sovereignty of Quiet*, 6.

17 Yi-Fu Tuan, *Space and Place: the Perspective of Experience* (Minneapolis: University of Minnesota Press, 1977), 144; 137.

18 Dasha Chapman, email message to author, October 7, 2017.

19 In February 2021, an internet-mediated performance of *Privy* was presented in partnership with the Center for Afrofuturist Studies and Public Space One (Iowa City, IA) and as an Artist-in-Residence in collaboration with André M. Zachery.

20 "See Me Here" is adapted from a chapter in "Orienting Ourselves to See: Mapping Nested Dance Ecosystems as Curatorial Practice in New England," a thesis submitted in partial fulfillment of the MA in Curatorial Practice at Wesleyan University's Institute for Curatorial Practice in Performance in 2019.

7

THE BLACK IMAGE CORPORATION: WHEN HISTORY ISN'T ENOUGH. THE NEED FOR CORPORATE PRACTICES WITHIN THE ARCHIVE

Theaster Gates

Episode 1. Introduction: The Black Image Corporation

One major facet of my artistic practice is the process of naming things, which is often followed by the process of shaping things. Naming things and shaping things is a complex gift. In my case, this is not exclusively about the naming of artworks, or the naming of exhibitions, but the conceptual practice of using legal corporations, LLC's, S Corps., and 501c3's, and naming, what would be considered by the IRS a corporation or a small business. For most artists, these forays would simply be called projects. One might say: "I'm doing a project around hardware stores," or "I'm producing a book project," but for me, I register the legal name of an organization, I create a book corporation, a publishing house, or a hardware store company. When an artist chooses to engage the real world, I don't think that having a project live solely in a museological record is enough, and thus I create new entities. If I'm going to engage the real world, I want the legal legitimacy of the world to inform the process of naming and shaping things, and then creating businesses that locate these projects at a specific moment of creation, of ideation, of importance to me feels central to the artistic project. As a result, I possess forty-five trademarked entities around the world. There are companies that, while they do very little business, live as legal testaments of my belief in ideas.

The Black Image Corporation was established with the same germ of belief. I believe that historic Black images have the right to be more important than wallpaper and toilet fodder for large white corporations. I believe that historic Black images should be seen by the people who occupy those images – everyday Black people – and that their celebration and amplification should not just be ploys that trigger the possibility of diversity within multi-national corporations, but rather, they should be a reminder of the sweet and bittersweet past that people of color have experienced in the United States and beyond. The creation of the Black Image Corporation was an attempt at demonstrating my love of amplifying the Black experience. This chapter is in part about my attempt to acquire the Johnson Publishing Company photographic archive when it went up for auction on July 17, 2019, but more largely, it conveys how my artistic process requires not only form, and color, and volume, but cooperation, legalization, and scale. I articulate that these conceptual works require copyright not just museum legitimacy.

Episode 2. An Origin Story

In 2011, Linda Johnson Rice paid a visit to Dorchester Avenue, a neighborhood in the Greater Grand Crossing neighborhood on the South Side of Chicago where I have been

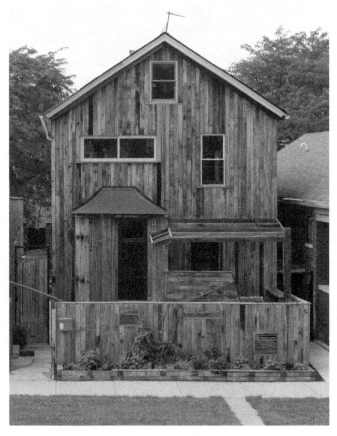

Plate 24 Theaster Gates, Exterior, *Archive House*, 2014. Image: Sara Pooley. Copyright Theaster Gates. Courtesy of Rebuild Foundation.

slowly renovating a set of buildings to make informal cultural spaces. Linda was visiting a building that we call *Archive House* (Plate 24) and noticed that I had an array of books from the now retired Prairie Avenue Bookshop. When Prairie Avenue was having its closing sale, I witnessed people, including architects and designers, crying at the loss of this great design hub. As they trolled through the boxes and the annals of books getting whatever they could find for sale, I approached the lead administrator at the Prairie Avenue Bookshop and asked if it was possible to buy all of the remaining inventory in the store, with the intention that I would dedicate these books as a kind of gift to the design community and establish a house where the books might live. This perked the ears of the owner, Wilbert Hasbrouck, who over the next series of days began a set of negotiations with me for the acquisition of the Prairie Avenue holdings. It was a big undertaking that required my studio, which was fledgling at the time, to box up the books, oversee a cataloging process, transport the books to Dorchester Avenue, and then create, over the next year and a half, a structure within the house that could receive them. This work was done, and for Linda Johnson Rice, her visit to my house struck a chord (Plate 25).

It became evident to Linda that I had a deep commitment towards caring for books and that I wasn't afraid of a big project. I understood the logistics of moving an archive from one place to another, and, if given the chance, I would also fulfill the potential of a gift. During this visit, Linda said: "I have some books." The books that she was referring to were the entire library of Johnson Publishing Company, for which Linda gave to me at

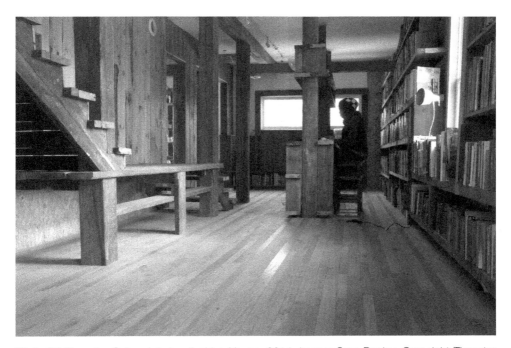

Plate 25 Theaster Gates, Interior, *Archive House*, 2014. Image: Sara Pooley. Copyright Theaster Gates. Courtesy of Rebuild Foundation.

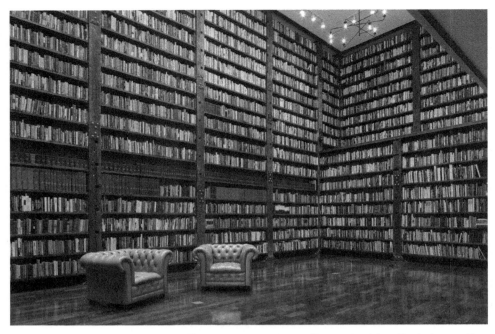

Plate 26 Theaster Gates, Johnson Publishing Library in the Stony Island Arts Bank. Image: Tom Harris. Copyright Hedrich Blessing. Courtesy of Rebuild Foundation.

no cost with the hope that I would do something special with the books – that I would extend the legacy of her father John Johnson through this collection. I shared with Linda that I was in the process of redeveloping a former bank building and that the books would be the heart, or a kind of centerpiece within the Arts Bank (Plate 26). In advance of their semi-permanent location at the Arts Bank, I would tour the books, making a stop at my first exhibition in London at White Cube Gallery, *My Labor is My Protest* (September 10 to November 11, 2012). Within this exhibition, I would create a temporary library and begin my cataloging process in real-time. Following the exhibition, I would ship the books back to Chicago and place them in their permanent home at the Stony Island Arts Bank.

When the books moved to London, they had an interesting effect on people. Unexpectedly, a large number of British-Caribbean descendants visited the exhibition looking for family members who had gone to the United States, and in some cases, were in the annals of *Jet, Black World,* or *Ebony.* Thus, this Black library of 26,000 books became a temporary Black space for all of London, but particularly the Caribbean community in the UK. During the run of the exhibition, I visited White Cube to ensure that the library was functioning, examine the model of librarianship, and imagine some of the ways in which the public could activate the archive. I was humbled by the act of people sharing their gratitude with me for making these books available to a public in such a free and accessible way. I was really taken by the communities response to the books, but also the fact that, as an artist, I had the capacity to take objects from the real world and place them in the imaginary zone of the art world, and not render them for sale, but to rather demonstrate a kind of cultural possibility, and the complexities of a mash-up between what is considered a commercial gallery, and the evidence of the most important Black legacy in the United States. I had created my first satellite library.

The books came home, the Arts Bank opened, and something magical started to happen on the South Side of Chicago. People from across the city, and especially on the South Side, and from all over the country started to recognize that something special was happening here, because a very special gift had landed in an unexpected place. The Johnson legacy was living, and I was excited to be a part of that. Over time, Linda Johnson Rice and I would have conversations. She would reflect on her father's legacy, the company, and she would share who came in and out of the doors, but Linda would ultimately trust me with the removal of and the care of her father's penthouse. The penthouse was supposed to be become a museum through an acquisition agreement between Johnson Publishing Company and Columbia College, which was ultimately never fulfilled. The resources necessary to create the museum were never realized, the funds were never raised and Columbia, who needed to resell the building, had to make the call to Linda Johnson Rice and inform her that everything had to be removed from the building. At this moment, Linda was not only selling parts of the material company, she ultimately had to sell the building, and the question for me did not feel like an artistic question, but a social responsibility: "What do we do with the material culture of Black people?" I have been grappling with this question for many years after this encounter, and it has become a leading impulse within my artistic practice.

Linda approached a number of institutions, including the DuSable Museum, and the National Museum of African American History and Culture – which was still in the process of being built – but none of these museums had the full capacity to receive John Johnson's collection in its entirety. The Johnson Publishing Company headquarters, an eleven-story giant built by John Moutoussamy was the most important Black-owned building in the city of Chicago. It was the largest building built by an African-American architect in the United States. It's true that John Johnson had to save his resources for ten years to realize this building. I was faced with a critical set of questions: Where do you put carpet, couches, filing cabinets, and a kitchen from the 1960s? Where do you put the stuff that made Black life sexy to a white America, and white commerce attractive to Black Americans? Where do you house the bowels of Black image production? When I was presented with the opportunity to care for these important objects, I was compelled to make a home for them.

When I got the call from Linda and she said that we had 30 days to get her father's things out, it became clear to me that the logistical task ahead was much larger than any artistic project that I had ever realized. What I was about to embark upon would absorb my emotional and financial resources entirely; it would require tremendous ingenuity in the absence of large campaigns. I didn't have enough time to ask the foundation community for support. I couldn't use my charitable entity, because it would require all of my studio's resources. I had to be swift, and ultimately twenty semi-trucks filled to the brim were put in a storage facility, and over time I had to make meaning of why this effort was so important. For the last 5 years, I've been grappling with material questions, ideological questions, and commercial questions about how to share the power of Blackness via a powerful Black Corporation via an artistic practice. The naming of things and the shaping of things then requires legal structures, and when combined, these three mechanisms inform new possibilities. I'm careful not to use the word *sustainability*, and I'm extremely careful not to use the word *perpetuity* because these are not my projects. Sustainability and perpetuity have often been born out of monopolistic greed and ensuring that specific cultural survival is important, but not all. When the foundations of our country were involved in their creations to ensure that a name would survive, they were also involved in subjugation, the exploitation of labor, and the ultimate demise of others.

How do we make something relevant enough that the world will carry it forward in iteration? How do we ensure the value of things beyond a founder or an owner? How do you give legs to the material world so that the world itself will want to carry those things forward? These are the questions that inform my work, and everyday I'm preoccupied with the possibility that artists can do things that no one else can.

Episode 3: The Finale: Since Time is Precious, Why Not Make the Most Of It?

In early 2019, after the books had successfully been on the road, and after I developed an even deeper friendship with Linda Johnson Rice, I produced a series of exhibitions anchored by the *Black Madonna* as a central figure (Plate 27). The projects—which were presented at the Kunstmuseum Basel in Basel, Switzerland (*Black Madonna*, 2018); the Sprengel Museum in Hannover (*Black Madonna*, 2018); the Milan Osservatorio at Fondazione Prada, in Milan (*Black Image Corporation*, 2018); Gropius Bau, Berlin (*The Black Image Corporation*, 2019); and the Spelman College Museum of Fine Art (*Black Image Corporation*, 2020), in Atlanta, Georgia—were derived from 20,000 licensed images from the Johnson Publishing Company photographic archive. Central to this project was a work titled *Walking Prayer* (Plate 28) which utilized books on the Black experience from the Johnson archive, rebound them in black and embossed the spines with language to constitute one long poem or performative score.

With the furniture now reupholstered and housed, I exhibited an ongoing dialogue about the museological and spatial possibilities of objects that I had come to love. After I found solace in the ongoing making of order with objects from Johnson Publishing, it was announced that the company had declared bankruptcy, which also meant a liquidation of the remaining holdings – the largest asset being the photographic archive. Estimates on the value of the archive had circulated, and varying constituencies invested in the Black image were gossiping about the acquisition of these images, and who would have the right to own them. The sale of four million images was projected at a cost of $30 million. Varying entities over the last several years have tried to acquire the collection by making low bids that were disrespectful and shameful. Finally, when the images came to auction in July 2019, *The New York Times* and other news outlets started to pick up the topic. The headlines of their articles read: "Black History is for Sale in Chicago. Whoever owns the culture, controls the narrative." "Who Owns This Collection?" "Ebony Photo Archive To Be Auctioned To Pay Creditors." "A Last Look at Ebony's Archives, Before They're Sold."

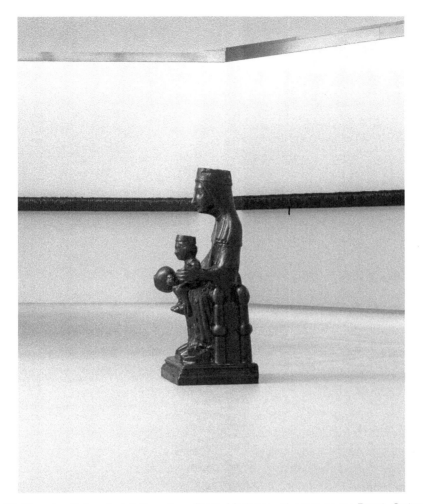

Plate 27 Theaster Gates, installation view, *Black Madonna*, Kunstmuseum Basel, Switzerland. June 9 to October 21, 2018. Image: Julian Salinas. Copyright Theaster Gates.

I was one of the contenders that put my hat in the ring for the acquisition of the images. In order to participate, I had to demonstrate that I had the financial capacity and that the resources I would bid with were in fact secured. I put my personal savings on the line, completely leveraged myself with my galleries, and asked close friends for their support. During the month leading up to the auction, I was able to create a small Black Image Fund that bolstered $12.75 million. With this fund, I would attempt to acquire the Johnson Publishing photographic archive.

Hilco Streambank, an intellectual property advisory firm, managed the bidding process. As much as we were given personality types of different businesses: this hedge fund, this private investigator, this organization, this corporation, and this artist, none of the contenders were officially named. I'm certain that I was in an auction filled with giants, but no one with the clarity, focus, and deep commitment that I had. People had different

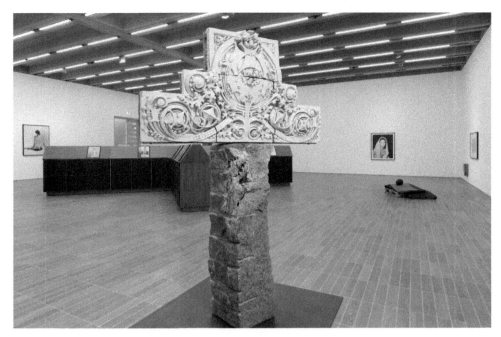

Plate 28 Theaster Gates, *Walking Prayer*, Kunstmuseum Basel, Switzerland. June 9 to October 21, 2018. Image: Julian Salinas. Copyright Theaster Gates.

strategies for why they would purchase the collection. They would purchase the collection low, digitize all of the images, and donate the physical archive at its full appraised value of $40 million. People were involved in sophisticated tax strategies that were above my head. Others wanted to be able to broker these images so that they could be sold to other companies like Target and Condé Nast, and others, probably out of personal passion, wanted to have a stake and their name associated with the collection.

The bidding begins. The low bid is $5 million, and the number moves to $12 million over a couple days. I'm still in the race. 40 to 50 percent of the contenders have fallen out, and now what's called a marriage in the bidding community is starting to come together – deals that would create partnerships between varying financial interests put those people together in an arrangement, and then together they would get the highest number for the acquisition. I was asked if I wanted to join other hedge funds and other organizations that would ultimately donate the physical asset, but only after they would scan for the digital rights. At each point I declined. When the number got to $12.25 million, the anticipated number of the purchase, I realized that I was probably not going to win. I made a call to the key holder of the collection, and it was evident that my resources were too short. I was in first position for the bid and there was a bidding entity, an unnamed consortium who would collectively acquire the archive for $30 million USD. I would later learn that this consortium was a marriage between the Smithsonian's National Museum of African American History and Culture, the Ford Foundation, the J. Paul Getty Trust, the Andrew W. Mellon Foundation, and the John D. and Catherine T. MacArthur Foundation.[1] The four families that would amass billions of dollars in steel, and rail, in land ownership, automobile giants. Four families that would introduce the industrial revolution to America and change the way commerce moved throughout the world. Four families that would come together and ultimately care for this project. Through all of these moments, I'm asking myself is this the work of an artist? Am I using my time for the right things? Should I not be making paintings and drawings? Should I just commit to making shoeshine stands, and stone works? Why am I in a bidding war with the largest philanthropists in the world? I realize that the work that I'm after is not in fact to make the world's greatest work of art. The work that I'm after is to live deeply and truly by my spiritual and emotional code. To try and write the very simple things of the nature of culture is to recalibrate my people and to create the annals of the future. To be good to my friends and to stand up for them when I believe in them and when they're right. That what I was after was not an artistic win but a life win – a cultural win.

I wanted the Johnson Publishing Company and the legacy of John and Eunice Johnson to be remembered forever. I wanted to honor the titans that they were between 1984 and 1987 when Johnson Publishing was the largest and most important Black business in the world. I wanted to demonstrate that important Black archives have the right to live in Black spaces. I wanted to demonstrate that a Black person in a Black neighborhood was willing to go as far as he could to see that great cultural legacies live among Black people, and that everyday people could have the capacity to see the greatness of their legacy. Everyday, like my religious faith, I question who I am as an artist. I question my relevance. I question my sincerity. I question my intended outcomes for the work that I do. I question the strategies: Should I make companies? Should I try so hard to shape things outside of the material world? Should I be shaping the legal world, the social world? Am I really a sculptor? Am I just a bad political ploy? Or am I an ineffective bureaucrat? Am I a bootlegged preacher? Or am I in fact involved with the complexity that art was intended to occupy? Am I actually doing my job, because I don't have certainty and clarity about who I am in the work?

The Johnson Publishing Company photographic archive found an important home and the images will be cared for, researched, and deployed with the highest possible museological standards. I'm excited that I still have 17,000 images to play with, and I have license permission and a contract to use those things and amplify them in the world and allow others to amplify those images. Following the auction and since the onset of the COVID-19 pandemic, I went on to realize a new series of exhibitions that would continue my exploration and amplification of the Johnson Publishing Company archive. In 2019, I realized an exhibition at Haus der Kunst in Munich titled *Black Chapel,* where I produced a series of rotating billboards with images of Black women from the Johnson Publishing Company archive (Plate 29).

The Black Image Corporation is about the projection of images into the world. With the Johnson billboards, I wanted to create something monumental as a means of celebrating these women. In 2020, I realized an exhibition titled *Black Vessel* at Gagosian Gallery in New York where I reinterpreted my work *Walking Prayer* from the Black Madonna exhibition, and arranged it on Carnegie library shelving inviting the viewer to engage in reading the archive as a processional act. (Plate 30).

The Getty Research Institute and the National Museum of African American History and Culture are using the archive in perpetuity to tell a story about history. I get to

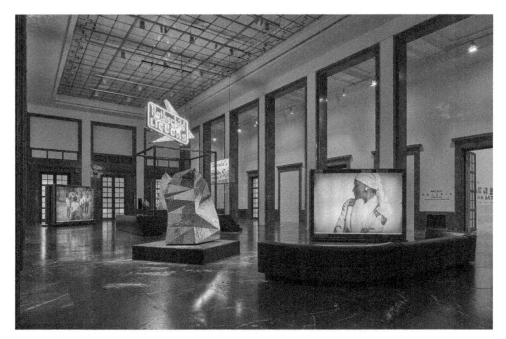

Plate 29 Theaster Gates, installation view of *Black Chapel*, Haus der Kunst, Munich. October 25, 2019 to July 19, 2020. Image Credit: Connolly Weber. Copyright Theaster Gates

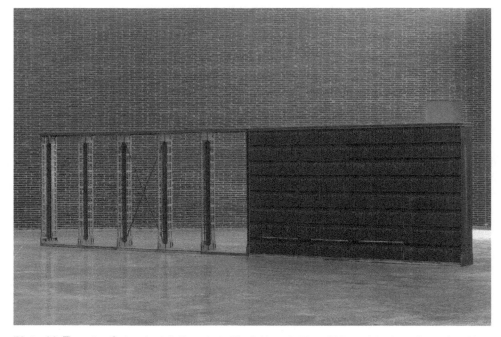

Plate 30 Theaster Gates, Installation shot, *Black Vessel*. 83 × 320 × 19 inches. Gagosian, New York. October 10, 2020 to January 23, 2021. Image Credit: Robert McKeever. Courtesy Gagosian. Copyright Theaster Gates.

temporarily activate these images that would then live in other places. Images that have permission to go to private collectors and then museums. Images that get to contend with structure, that get to fight for their right to be seen in the audaciousness that they were made. I get to celebrate Black photographers who made exceptional decisions about what was important within Blackness. I get to acquire future Black images by unknown photographers for which I get to amplify, and most importantly, I get to be a part of the bloodstream of image making and create a new legacy through the Black Image Corporation.

Notes

1   The Smithsonian's National Museum of African American History and Culture and the Getty Research Institute currently share stewardship responsibilities for the Johnson Publishing Company Archive, including collections care, archival processing, digitization, and ultimately, facilitating public access to the archive. The archive, which consists of over four million photographic prints, slides, and negatives, currently occupies 2,500 linear feet in a temperature-controlled building in Chicago. The Getty Research Institute is currently devising a strategy for making the archive available digitally.

News Article Headlines (Page 124)

"Black History is for Sale in Chicago. Whoever owns the culture, controls the narrative." https://www.bostonglobe.com/metro/2019/07/22/black-history-for-sale-chicago-whoever-owns-culture-controls-narrative/eLevaFaawdJDHx4Knb0FRL/story.html

"Who Owns This Collection?" https://chicagocrusader.com/who-owns-this-collection/

"Ebony Photo Archive To Be Auctioned To Pay Creditors." https://www.nbcnews.com/news/nbcblk/ebony-photo-archive-be-auctioned-pay- creditors-n1015041

"A Last Look at Ebony's Archives, Before They're Sold." https://www.nytimes.com/2019/07/16/us/ebony-magazine-photographs- auction.html

8

ELEVATORS

Simone White and Benjamin Krusling

When he dies he cannot be buried beside white corpses.
His neighbors have barricaded their porches against his view.
— W. E. B. Du Bois, *The Philadelphia Negro*

go to jail

months later   only able later   for many months holding the image of myself in the
    kitchen
an image of raising up out of the nothing feeling which isn't not feeling at all   i don't
    feel nothing   i feel
like i want to strangle somebody most of the time
Seeing seeing, the image, as an energetic problem of not being raised up, too
junky and at the ready   i'm saying
up and above the vagueness of knowing togetherness   there we were together learning
the spiritual and the literary should never be confused
I am not in my body

acts of holding   not exactly trying to resolve how it is i am involved in Chicago's
    war
though I'm interested in anticipating a certain kind of moral demand

"pussy how you warring" is meaningful to me in its digital strike or pluck that covers
the time within which it becomes instantly possible to gather
as the high frequency is withheld the passion is in the stinginess of the strike   the
    tease
There are two definitional proposals with respect to the high hat in that song, I'd say
one allowing it to become "drill" this is "refrain" or pattern
the other proposing singularity or arrest
something incredibly stupid or bad in that plinky anti-loop
it curls up around the spasmodic coughing from which it is technically and sonically
    apart

and the completely undanceable horror of *this Aiki pack*

no one stops dancing

I am holding close to me Mei-mei's voice with me at all times when i am thinking
different problems with working or beginning with the non-relation between me and them
always making an excuse for feeling close scuttling away

dancing is not an endorsement of violence but of course it is

when dancing, holding also the problematics of uplift i do feel spread out
i feel helpless and resent the sense that separating myself from feelings of love and
     enjoyment for the sake of so-called liberation is fucking us all up

Do i know myself to be a person who is stalked? AM I a killer

I can barely stand the convergence between Mei-mei's *Stars* book and what I am
     trying to say about feeling empathy

you try to hold onto the visibility of this object and its location

just as unbearable
when the object is a form of personal power

Now I'm close.

You're laughing at my orgasm joke but it's not a joke. I ain't joking. From which I have
     learned. To be irresolute.

war

drill rings true to the depressive — boring as in piercing and turning   *dope got me
coughing   thought I was gon end up in a coffin*   if you could call that drilling, martial
engagement, black dynamism, extremity

well , it's how I be feeling sometimes   forgetting what other than survival I was
thinking about
but every day I'm not warring in that sense , I wake up and begin the task of applying
semiotic pressure,
some hacking and wheezing as prelude to clarity of purpose

chief keef doesn't historicize his condition , so rahm says "but. . ." *pure present and
always tense* the judge is the more serious antagonist – he can only turn his mind

against the sentence ex: *I don't want to have to go to jail* and she misunderstands what he means by everything he does

so there's a misunderstanding of fame – the real interrupts it – I mean the face gives the camera a reason , it sprints alongside the music

and I don't want to have to get exploited to "make a living" or make a living, full-faced – there's an emotional stake in the truth either way – or see myself as ten bands , a hundred , of experience , wrapped around childhood with the dirt and blood of learning in my eyes and mouth , and bouncing , with the bass vibrating the frame of the vehicle , with the steel pulse and digable planets , all memory and reanimated by brain power , too $hort, slick rick, mobb deep "hell on earth"   I don't love the film of sentimentality over it , conflict in that sense

        well , we're in it , running in new york , chicago , given life by class war , the condition of being held hostage   the world is owned , *consciousness at war with the given* black noise
re-racialized , it's gothic and rattling

in the end , I'm sad but not just
blood running , flying
an argument for escalation
a bag , a head , drumming , counting
immature in the sense that experience is impervious to it
in the song's womb where noise makes matter happen

but we like friction over here – we lay down words about it
to say childhood is expensive ! going to war with the given

        or be a parasite – and not wanting it , to change everything on my ID , and it's a manner of singing that isn't crooning , flexing and not at the gym , it's a sound that blows the speakers out a smart phone

my amniotic listening I've said that but then I think myself escalating a situation to the point of decisive action , all synthetic drum and horn alive with low fidelity   time and space deglaze

whether or not he's just telling you what he just did , war is an argument for action and flight , like blowing new jersey up and my own heroic self-preservation and destruction, childlike in the sense that experience is impervious to it – expensive

across a narrow abyss of misapprehension , or whatever he said , I do sit down and "think"   pinch and save , accosted by a cop at the movies   when people ask do you think it was intentional   of course   i willed it into being:

in other words, he's corporeal – talking about presence
not a game
presence

so pain comes unshareably into our midst"[1]

Note

1   Elaine Scarry, *The Body in Pain: The Making and Unmaking of the World* (Oxford: Oxford
University Press, 1985), 4.

9

AESTHETIC FORM IN THE NEW THING: AESTHETIC SOCIALITY OF *MUSIQUE INFORMELLE*

Fumi Okiji

The new thing of black music, the mid-century experimentalism of the tradition we often call jazz, is an intensified, intentional turn toward what Theodor W. Adorno understands to be "aesthetic form." This is the anchoring contention of this essay. Aesthetic form needs to be understood as distinct from, and perhaps even defined in distinction to, musical form—musical form being that on which most musicological accounts of the emergence of free jazz tend to focus. Musical, or constructionist, form, the working together of sonic stuff, is certainly that by which aesthetic form comes about and becomes sensuously available, albeit obliquely. However, aesthetic form holds a categorical difference in its "transformation of what is given into something *other*, that is, something unreal, nonidentical, outside the grasp of concepts, categories, or distinctions, not to mention purposes, functions, or positions in any standing order of things," to borrow Gerald Brun's useful gloss.[1] Aesthetic form is pursued through the handling, composition and playing of musical material; through the manipulation of sonic material toward (the) work, which is forever unstable. In phrasing that turns Adorno squarely to jazz, aesthetic form is ultimately processual even when it is encountered in the objectified work-thing. It is oriented by what Adorno calls a "mimetic impulse," a mode of correspondence that has little to do with imitation, but rather, might be thought as extra-rational constellatory affinity.

While a diversity of scholarship has found remarkable consensus in narrating the emergence of the new thing (and, incidentally, the contemporaneous developments in the European and Euro-American avant-garde), as the rejection of external forms and an accompanying absorption in "raw" sonic material, I am concerned here with what aesthetic form contributes to the picture.[2] I propose that the new thing be recognized as an unadulteration of the core motivation of the music we call jazz—namely, the pursuit of moments of "complete communion," what Don Cherry also terms "brilliance," and what William Parker understands as the "center of the sound." It is a practice of happening upon "relationship," to draw Walter Benjamin into the assembly.[3] The new thing is a renewed, deepened commitment to the pursuit of aesthetic form in jazz, returning to Adorno's language. What is more, this coming together of the work, the arrangement of "sensuous elements" toward (transitory) complete communion, is an *aesthetic sociality*, inevitably set apart, if not autonomous, from "administered society," in its exceptional demonstration of a comportment in which the "thought of the many [or the diverse/ dispersed] as no longer inimical."[4]

The aging new music and the birth of the new thing

Despite my suspicion of historico-philosophical approaches to black life, and the tyranny of dialectical historicism, in particular, the intriguing contemporaneity of the new thing of black experimentalism, and the music that occupies "The Aging of the New Music" (1955), "*Vers une Musique Informelle*" (1961), and "Form in the New Music" (1966), has compelled me to test the notion that the emergence of free jazz (the new thing) contributes to what Adorno referred to in relation to mid-century new music as processes of "purification," the dissolution of the "slag and unhomogeneous vestiges of the past" (those "disturbing intrusions" that divert a composition or, I might add, an improvisation, from its internal "logic").[5] It is tempting to acquiesce to the consensus in the fields of black music, jazz, and improvisation studies that interprets the emergence of the new thing as a rejection (or attenuation in utility, at least) of traditional forms, and an accompanying ascendence of attention to raw sonic materiality. An account such as Ekkehard Jost's *Free Jazz,* that spotlights "energy," exemplified by Cecil Taylor, Albert Ayler, Archie Shepp as the "new musical quality," within the narration of freedom from harmonic conventions, is typical of such and enables my tentative (soon-to-be dismissed) thesis, concerning free jazz's participation in the dialectical movement of Western music.[6]

However, even as I acknowledge these two points of coincidence between the nascent new thing and the matured new music (the rejection of external form and convention, and a concomitant intensified attention on sonic material), the enduring idiomaticity of the former is a significant divergence, that, I would argue, eclipses those moments of agreement. This is to say, that in its free and avant-garde permutations, jazz remains a music compelled by its folk. It remains attracted to what Yoruba aesthetics terms òrò. Òrò can be translated as "word" but it also means a matter at hand, a situation that deserves communal consideration; and a dealing of this case in counsel, banter or gossip; an occasion for sustained reflection; a spot for temporally or generationally dispersed open-housed contemplation. Òrò is gathering contribution. Contributors will spin language in congress with one another, grappling with this matter at hand. The inextricable entanglement of thing and practice that is involved in òrò (translated, but not exhaustively, as word, communication, orality), compounds the difficulty in rendering its intention in English, even as that particular constellation (word, communication, orality) is perfectly legitimate, metonymically, in the target language. The business of defining òrò *is*, of course, òrò and helps demonstrate the intertwined nature of the substantive and processual in Yoruba's understanding of the phenomenon. Òrò is the thing. The point. Òrò is also our talk of it. Òrò is that toward which our òrò is directed.[7] As I hope will be revealed as the essay unfolds, this circuit, which is also a layering of object and means, is of defining importance to free jazz, and might well be a fundamental characteristic of music-making more broadly. Most useful for the argument unfolding in this essay, due to òrò's overwhelming sensuousness, its unremitting materiality, it provides us, with a model of the comparable circuitry and layering that occurs between òrò (the constructivist, melding and welding of sonic material) and what I am coming to understand as the nonsensuous standard, what Cherry calls brilliance, Benjamin terms relationship, and Adorno, aesthetic form.

Consider Ornette Coleman's "Chronology" from the 1959 album *The Shape of Jazz to Come*, which begins with a bebop head, exemplary, if not in its functionality, then by way of allusion, of those top-down forms considered an oppressive imposition.[8] This opening statement, along with the rhythm section (walking bass, up-tempo swing, albeit freed from harmonic commitment) that accompanies it and the improvised sections, reveal a recapitulation of the experiments saxophonist Charlie Parker and other bebop musicians had been making since the early 1940s. Commentators tend to focus on the release from harmonic constraint that Coleman's early piano-less quartet recordings heralded—harmonic adherence being a hallmark of bebop. Yet, I consider the most striking feature to be the retention and strengthening of the discursivity of the music, and its continuity with this earlier style, despite and perhaps, ironically, due to the freeing of harmony and, to a lesser extent, rhythm. This seeming contradiction between autopoiesis and something approaching idiomaticity is a key characteristic of the discourse surrounding the definition of free jazz. Anchoring her thoughts on Coleman's 1961 double quartet recording *Free Jazz,* Keren Omry suggests that despite devices that help promote release from the constraints of imposed, reified, or assured form, *Free Jazz* retains a seemingly inextricable bond to the material and improvisational devices of the tradition from which it springs. Omry writes that "[t]his claim for spontaneity is not to ignore, discount, or overlook the use of repetition, allusion, and even pastiche."[9] What is suggested but not fully appreciated in Omry's account is that this cooperation of spontaneity and idiomaticity is not an emergent characteristic of the new thing, even as this quality rises to the surface in this new turn. As Sara Ramshaw incisively offers, a "tension. . . exists between the 'spontaneous' conception of jazz improvisation and the more context-driven model. This tension is intrinsic to jazz improvisation itself. Improvisation can be neither purely spontaneous nor completely determined by the musical structures in which it engages. It must be both responsive to otherness and have some stable or determined dimension in order to endure as jazz improvisation."[10] I would say that the new thing makes more apparent the relative ease, or lack of anxiety, that the music exhibits in moving between "spontaneity" and the use of found material, forms, and conventions. I would also suggest that it is *autopoiesis* rather than spontaneity that stands in generative tension with idiomaticity. The spontaneous interplay of both aspects (idiomaticity and autopoiesis), an enduring faculty in jazz practice, is deepened and extended with the new thing. Familiar phrasing, cadence, articulation, instrumentation, and, in some cases, even, the head-solo-head convention remain, and are further investigated, as the scope of improvisational technique is extended. This practice that draws from existing language, convention, and material while allowing musicians to go where the music leads, facilitates great expressivity. This ante-formality cannot be sublated into the concurrent ever-perfecting "purifying" operations of the European and Euro-American schools, their radical nominalism driven by "a critical awareness of the impossibility of subjective expression in a world where political powers and capitalism are bent upon liquidating subjectivity."[11]

I will remain within the historical framework, for just a little longer, in order to flesh out the particular features of mid-century new music beyond the dismissal of external form consummated in Schoenbergian dodecaphony. What Adorno identifies as common to both the "irrational fetishization of rationalist construction" of integral serialism and the aleatory ego-avoidance of Cagean experientialism is a capitulation of "compositional subjectivity."[12] Of the former, Adorno complains, "[a]lienated and preestablished rules are blindly followed—as a good schoolboy might follow them—*excluding any tension with subjectivity, without which there is as little art as truth*."[13] Furthermore, in a formulation shared with Ligeti, he is struck by "the essential arbitrariness of the 'rationalistic' forms in which the originally pitch-based twelve-tone row was extended to the other parameters of music, and by virtue of which 'total determinacy comes to be identical with total indeterminacy', at least experientially."[14] The key to appreciating his coolness toward these developments is to know that, for Adorno, music has a responsibility toward the safeguard of subjective freedom. Or at the very least should be demonstratively bereft at the decline of the subject in musical expression.[15] As Marcus Zagorski points out, this is the cornerstone of Adorno's music philosophy. With its last breath music should seek "the preservation of subjective freedom; the expression of the individual before the abyss of the administered world."[16] It is this dismissal of compositional subjectivity—and, as I go on to argue, more pointedly, the accompanying attrition of openings that the vagaries of the music-maker (and, perhaps, listener) bring in their pursuit of aesthetic form—that spurs Adorno's program for a future informal music. The conventional wisdom that understands both mid-century European music and the new thing as a rejection, or loosening of external forms, and an accompanying valorization of raw materiality, while broadly correct, acquires refinement through reading Adorno's essays on the aging new music and his program for a future "free musical style [Alois Haba]."[17]

Musique informelle and Wols

In "*Vers une Musique Informelle*" Adorno is looking forward to a music that remains emancipated from external forms, from conventions of genre and musical material, while being equipped to find its way out of, or to avoid, the dead-end that integral serial and aleatory compositional techniques had led musicians. The very fact that Adorno is contravening his often quite strict prohibition on positive utopic imaginings, that he is, in a sense, jumping the dialectic (encouraging for this reader) is surprising, and while we welcome a lighter, possibly more optimistic tone, Adorno never sounds completely convinced of the legitimacy of his proposal. The movement of Western music at its journey's end had not led to an informal music, and so his speculative (one might say, artificial) offering must have been written in some ambivalence.[18] This unsteadiness compounds Adorno's characteristically esoteric, often aporetic approach to exposition. *Musique informelle* "mocks. . . all effort of definition," he tells us. Nonetheless, he does provide a rudimentary sketch. Alongside the ever-useful prototype provided by Schoenberg circa 1910, which Adorno cannot quite set aside, *musique informelle* is presented as an expressive music of weak, bottom-up, temporary and/or unstable autopoietic form. It does without "inflexible. . . external or abstract" formal imposition. It "constitute[s] itself in an objectively compelling way, in the musical substance itself, and not in terms of external laws." It is "a rejection of the mechanical," a return to or rather a reconstitution of an "organic" approach, "a growing unity of parts and whole and not their subsumption under a supreme abstract concept, together with the juxtaposition of the parts."[19] At this point, it is instructive to take a short detour through the art movement of the 1940s and 1950s that lends this "prismatic concept" its name.[20] Adorno intimates that the eponymous gesture was merely "a small token of gratitude towards the nation for whom the tradition of the avant-garde is synonymous with the courage to produce manifestos."[21] Yet as Max Paddison and Joris De Henau have shown, Adorno's cursory endorsement of Wols (Alfred Otto Wolfgang Schulze), a central proponent of *art informel,* ultimately suggests an appropriation that exceeds the namesake. Referring to the mention of the artist in a key passage in *"Vers une Musique Informelle,"* concerned with the emergence of a new "organic" approach, and the mode of compositional engagement required, De Henau writes that Adorno "was quick to notice the significance of Wols' artistic practice, and saw that it could open up new creative possibilities for composers."[22]

A drawing entitled "Injured Head," that in its play between abstraction and representation, coherence and indeterminacy, actual and fantastic possibility, and most importantly for the argument explicated here, in the demonstration of material handling toward moments of the work's fulfilment, provides a bridge from Adorno's bare sketch of an informal music to a more substantial appreciation of the orientation he has in mind. The ink marks are at once noodles (hand leading eye leading mind leading hand) and "rendered. . .with meticulous care." The apparent "faithful reproduction. . .[of an] interwoven web of tissue. . .a microcosm marked by the process of decay caused by ageing. Various irregularly closed openings and cracks [of] long-healed injuries to a rubbery clump of tissue," becomes, in time, "hallucinatory excrescence attributable solely to the artist's imagination."[23] (Interestingly, on the website for Städel Museum's digital collection, the drawing is categorized under both "Abstract, Non-representational Art," and "head (human)"). Wols's drawing cannot be considered representational or adhering to a conventional rendering of the phenomena of its fascination, but it also eschews the nominalism often associated with post-representational art. As De Henau writes, "Wols' style does not impose a pre-arranged form, but allows for associations and amalgamations of disparate elements, though at the same time preserving a certain degree of figurative recognizability, however dream-like or illogical their interrelations may appear."[24] Analogous to the spontaneous play between idiomaticity and autopoiesis we encounter in free jazz, in Wols's work we are confronted with periodic breaches of apparent representation and determinate figuration, and/or meandering formal operation, that like clouds fall (fugaciously, felicitously) upon "figurative recognizability."

Another work produced about the same time, the watercolor (at times) portrait "Don Juan," at first glance a perverted *Angelus Novus,* features a dispersed but ridiculously well-feathered, coiffured moustache, seemingly dissembled whisker by whisker.[25]

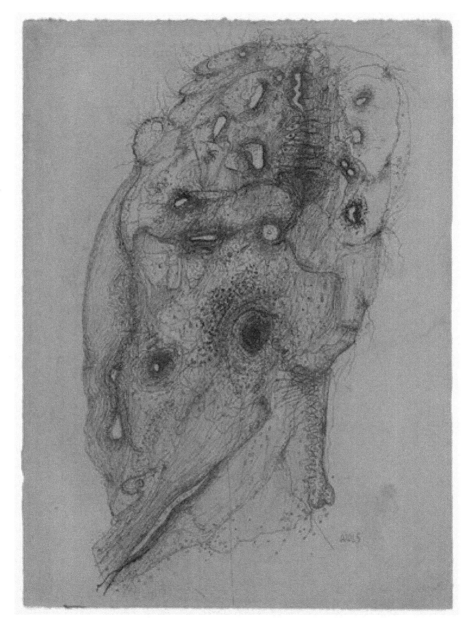

Figure 9.1 WOLS, *Tête Abimée (Injured Head)*, ca. 1944. Pen and black ink, watercolor, and white glaze on mottled pink laid paper. Public domain. Courtesy of the Städel Museum, Frankfurt am Main.

Barbules splay about the piece, sprouting from all areas of a head resting on a pair of pierced (or piercing) bollocks (maybe); right eye looking askance at said bollocks or something else below (possibly out of shot), left in mid-wink. As with "Injured Head," the viewer is called to recompose or improvise the piece, for as Delphine Biere writes, while Wols's "watercolours are populated with figures, landscapes and characters," they have

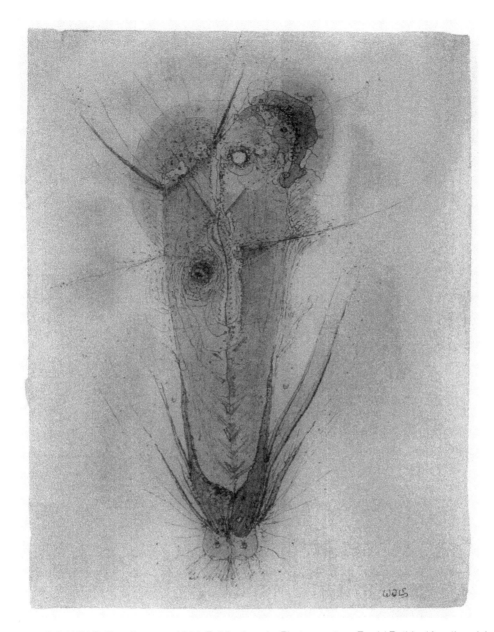

Figure 9.2 WOLS, *Don Juan*, ca. 1944. Public domain. Photo courtesy Ewald Rathke Kunsthandel.

"no counterpart in the real world, other than certain recurrent clues."[26] What is more, lest we rush to interpret the approach as a mere play between these two poles, we might consider such work as less oriented by a migration between form and aformality than an anfractuous unmooring toward aesthetic form. To borrow from bassist William Parker's writing on improvisation, we might say that Wols is oriented by "flow" which "is the spontaneously created map that leads us to. . . the essential house where all beauty [or truth] resides."[27] What Adorno finds in the artist's work is no project of strict aformality (although there is an argument for understanding the pieces as carrying out a sort of material deformation). He does not find a categorical rejection of the figurative or of traditional form. What is found is corroboration for his own denunciation of compositional inflexibility—whether this rigidity is driven by submission to congealed traditional forms, a practice that rigorously organizes prefabricated material, or an unyielding nominalism. Being oriented by aesthetic form (that which "relates to everything sensuous through which the content of a work of art, the spiritual element of whatever is written, painted or composed, is realized"), Adorno finds in Wols's pieces an unadulterated pursuit of the "spiritual element" within the creative process.[28] He finds material formation providing neural pathways to this elusive brilliance of (the) work.

It is important to keep in view that Adorno's sketch of a future informal music rejects the influence of external musical law, and hence, perhaps cannot accommodate the spectrum of possibility displayed in Wols's practice. This, I believe, can be accounted for by way of Adorno's commitment to a Hegelian dialectical analytic. That is to say, his speculation concerning a future informal music, in this regard, adheres to an understanding of the movement of music as quite strictly shaped by the determinate negation of its material, and, important for this particular point, that this progressive development is irreversible.[29] Once decadence of traditional musical form is revealed it is impossible to "unsee" it; we cannot feign innocence once lost. The organic approach sought, must look forward. However this historiological item—the reality of degenerate, useless forms, and the requisite injunction against their restoration—should not be considered the driving motivation of Adorno's proposal. Rather, his advocacy for an open form is in service to the freedom of subjective composition. This subject, "the only component of art that is non-mechanical, truly alive," is essential to the organically evolving "musical substance," or what might be understood as the aesthetic form of music.[30] In response to approaches in mid-century new music which seek to usurp the authority of the imposing composer by way of chance and organization, Adorno recasts the musical subject as resident rather than master of the music. What is key to *musique informelle's* subject is its sensitivity, one might say devotion to the unfolding organism (to be of the work "in ignorance of what" it will become). With this relinquishing of sovereignty emerges the "right of subjectivity to be present in the music itself, as the power of its immediate performance, instead of being excluded from it once it has launched."[31]

On my way back to free jazz and the unfolding exposition concerning its supposed intensified turn toward aesthetic form, I here lead with an idiosyncratic discursive pick-up, a slight blues-ing of Adorno's intention when he writes that "the subject must become an integral part of the organism, something which the organism itself calls for."[32] I want to claim that, Adorno, all the while maintaining the significance of art music autonomy from "administered society," is providing a formulation for what might be understood as an *aesthetic sociality*. We will not find in Adorno's aesthetic sociality an unmediated communion of individuals (i.e. between composer and audience, although his notion of composed listening is certainly suggestive of such). Rather we find a coming together of subject and (or in) aesthetic form. For Adorno, aesthetic form is a key forum for the sustenance of the autonomy of art, and so the notion of a mode of sociality being found there seems an acute departure from his implication. After all, as Eva Geulen reminds us in gentle reproach of some recent readings that contravene this important position, Adorno understands aesthetic form as that which "distinguishes and separates the artwork from the social world. The new concept of form ignores this fundamental distinction. Instead, everything now turns out to be form."[33] Notwithstanding an appreciation of this vigilance, I set about the matter as a rebellious African should.

I examine it by way of the modally anomalous black life. From a place at which divergent options are available (even as these divergent routes manifest in remarkable resemblance). Fantasy is a quotidian modality for me (a product of both the Mobius strip of denied entry to the "household of humanity" / "refusal of what has been refused me," *and* of a certain epistemological Africanity).[34] Along with the logically fantastic I also find here a radical negativity, blackness as the seemingly ever-generative but, I would argue, highly inefficient fuel for the dialectical engine, unable to mine African/black way and comportment, and so restricted to an appropriation of only the most superficial elements. Or to reiterate these possible paths using Adorno's own language: I approach the matter of aesthetic sociality from a position at which I might be of the vanquished *and/or* of the nondialectical ("that which did not fit properly into the laws of historical movement").[35] The important move is that I do not race to lay claim to a radically alienated world I have been structurally, discursively excluded from. The music we sometimes call jazz is demonstrative of the possibility, however fantastic, extra- or ante-dialectic, of a heteronomous aesthetic form. The works and practices of the new thing (and of Adorno's future informal music, for that matter), their aesthetic sociality, does not reflect society as it stands, or the way the world is currently coursing with its extractive drive, its pedagogies of incorporation and its ever-more sophisticated technologies of category. *Musique informelle* as imagined by Adorno is a model for future reconciliation; for us African/black, and others attuned to the realm of open possibility such life emerges and contributes, these "otherwise" socialities are already at hand, even if out of this European world.

The new thing toward aesthetic form

When Adorno speaks of free and spontaneous happenings emerging through and within the unfolding work, he is referring to the formation of material aspects toward momentary communion of/with the work. The music we call jazz, despite the undeniable heteronomy of even its more experimental manifestations, is dedicated to this orientation. The *modus operandi* of such work, communion of subject and organism, or as subject as part of organism, that I suggest is being gestured toward in Adorno's writing on aesthetic form, is not just an didactic tool by which one might develop comportment for a *future* worldly sociality. It is a "logic" by which the various modes of coming together/dispersal in jazz work has always operated within. This is to say that the music—Bessie through Cecil and beyond— as it works toward its material consummation, or perhaps more appropriate to black poetics, as it carries out its sensuous experiments, is simultaneously engaged in a search for moments when those material/sensuous particulars align in such a way as to happen upon a point of incorporeal /nonsensuous correspondence. A piece is kept open by this search for a point or moment of immaterial similarity that there is no guarantee of finding, even as the piece reaches its musicological destination, or when the musician has said all they can or all they desire. The compulsion toward nonsensuous affinity is anti-gravitational, dark energy, to borrow some terminology from astrophysics, that pulls the piece apart or keeps its experiments in play. This component could be described as anomalous with Western modernity's modality, this latter confined to actuality and to its indexed real possibilities that the world is dialectically spun out through (a pointed demotion of the fantastic or formal possibilities through which blackness/Africanness and art move). The complicated relation to determination that is so usefully illustrated in Wols's work—a lack of insistence on coherent material form (and the determination that this presupposes) and a concurrent refusal to prohibit this—is tracked by a want of assurance that these orienting immaterial correspondences will be found. In fact, the only promise is of caprice, and in the event of success, evanescence.

Such mimeticism, wherever it operates, gives to artistic pursuit, something in the order of orality, or (in order to avoid entanglement in anthropological debates that cohere around the term, and in order to offer greater precision, the limitations of translation, notwithstanding), I might say that this mimetic comportment shows artistic pursuit to be òrò. I pick up on the discussion early in the essay, where I suggest that the òrò, this term I adopt from Yoruba aesthetics, that names our gathering around a matter at hand, through our material experiments, provides a useful portrayal of the more ephemeral type of sociality that occurs as part of aesthetic form.[36] At this latter register, òrò speaks to a coming together/dispersal in search, to borrow from Toni Morrison, of "the right combination, the key, the code, the sound that [breaks] the back of words," that breaks the crest of the matter, the case being dealt with, that has our communal attention. "Building voice upon voice until [we] find it [and found it] and when [we] do it is a wave of sound wide enough to sound deep water and knock the pods off chestnut trees."[37] In *All the Notes*, the 2004 documentary on Cecil Taylor, poet and critic Nathaniel Mackey points to the pianist's "voracious appetite for intellectual, emotional, aesthetic stimulation and information that cuts across artistic genres." Mackey speaks of the breadth of interests, and how they become manifest in the music as "asymmetric equations."[38] Taylor's is a tinker shop mind. His pool of found material is not only of well-loved/worn motifs and phrases, voicings and percussive figures, but include the racehorse Sea Biscuit, cantilever bridges, dancer Carmen Amaya, Billie Holiday's bent elbow.[39] Tony Harrington remaining in strictly musicological terrain, writes that Taylor's "improvisations drew from a vast library of fragments—favorite phrases, motifs, licks and riffs; intervals, inversions and voicings—which he summoned forth into the here and now each time he soloed, reconfiguring and recombining them, impacting them into one another at great speed and with immense force."[40]

The fragments that Taylor gathers, in which he becomes absorbed, these sonic textures, angled extremities, structures that take us somewhere, looks and tastes of words, are items that are drawn from an idiosyncratic alphabet, a multimedia *lalangue*, that he welcomes us to as he goes in search of aesthetic form. His placing, and scattering, and throwing of these fragments in space and time, showcases a capacity for recognizing and producing a range of similarities, both those easily perceptible, and others that swirl around the immaterial.[41] Other times Taylor appears to be more ascetic and (as far as we can tell, less apparent correspondences notwithstanding) utilizes single recurring musical figures. For instance on "Second Pleasures," from the live album *Always a Pleasure*, a single fragment, a most discrete unit of sound, is worked over the entire course of the piece.[42] On further reflection, perhaps it would be more accurate to say the fragment unworks the piece, as an agent of the mimetic drive that wants to keep the piece open, the anti-gravitation that pulls these iterations into constellation, toward a point of correspondence that exceeds their undeniable, material similarities. Or to borrow language from Adorno, Taylor's experimentation "is the nonviolent synthesis of the diffuse that nevertheless preserves it [the diffuse] as what it is in its divergences and contradictions, and for this reason form is actually an unfolding of truth. A posited unity, it constantly suspends itself as such; essential to it is that it interrupts itself through its other just as *the essence of its coherence is that it does not cohere*."[43] As it is cast in *Negative Dialectics*, exhibited is "the thought of the many" or diverse/divergent as not inimical in artistic pursuit.[44] What is more, Taylor demonstrates, most brilliantly, the dance of material parts toward the extra-sensuous correspondence that is aesthetic form. The music moves in search of that something else, that immaterial something else, that exceeds the (at times) abstract, but, nonetheless, sensuous dealings of sonic and lyric manipulation. It is this sociality that I am suggesting Adorno mourns in his appraisal of the aging new music of the European schools; it is that which we see in the in- or aformal art of Wols, and that Adorno finds appealing.

The very material, bodily, sensuous sociality of the music we often call jazz—the ubiquity of which makes calling out examples a superfluous task but which we find in Coleman's early quartet records, in his *Free Jazz*, in Coltrane's *Ascension*, in Cecil's own ensemble recordings, as much as in the Hot Fives and Sevens, and Miles Davis orchestrated configurations—offers both great support and added complication to my understanding of the new thing as an intensification of focus on aesthetic form and aesthetic sociality. The coming together in musical banter and gossip, their charting of polyphonic maps toward brilliance, their material formations, is *a social toward another order of sociality,* namely, [often] momentary aesthetic form. In fact I might say that the "wave of sound" that Toni Morrison speaks of—the brilliance (Cherry), relationship/musicality (Benjamin), mu (Cherry; Mackey; Moten), the center of the sound (Parker), the nonsensuous standard (Okiji)—that "breaks the back of [their] words," their word, their òrò, is as much the means toward material/sensuous sociality as the coming together of musicians in performance, and their meandering, unresolvable equations, are the means to aesthetic form.[45]

The abandonment of external forms in the new thing is undeniably a feature of this mid-twentieth century turn in the music we call jazz, as is its exploration of *materia prima,* but what I find most fascinating and most distinctive is how free jazz leans into a preoccupation with aesthetic form. It devotes itself to the welding and melding of sonic material toward nonsensuous work. It is not (only) that pieces develop from the ground up, spontaneously through autopoiesis (*and* idiomaticity, lest we forget).[46] Most excitingly, there is an increased focus, a renewed dedication to the incessant search for those moments of complete communion. All this is to say that the emergence of jazz's new thing should be understood not only (or primarily) as a rejection of external form, but also as an intensified focus on the pursuit of the aesthetic one. It is also to highlight an alternate double character of art. In distinction to that presented by Adorno for art music (autonomous and *fait social*), the dual sociality of black music, and that perhaps all music is compelled toward, is one in which musicians, their materials, their audiences and material forms come together in *òrò*, toward the sociality of aesthetic form.[47]

Notes

1 Gerald L Bruns, "On the Conundrum of Form and Material in Adorno's *Aesthetic Theory*," *The Journal of Aesthetics and Art Criticism* 66, no. 3 (2008): 225. Original italics.

2 See, for instance, Ekkehard Jost, *Free Jazz* (Boston: Da Capo Press, 1974); George E. Lewis, "Improvised Music after 1950: Afrological and Eurological Perspectives," *Black Music Research Journal* (1996): 91–122; Jeff Pressing, "Free Jazz and the Avant-Garde," in *The Cambridge Companion to Jazz* (Cambridge: Cambridge University Press, 2002); Scott De Veaux, "Constructing the Jazz Tradition: Jazz Historiography," *Black American Literature Forum* 25, no. 3 (1991): 525–60.; Charles Hersch, "'Let Freedom Ring!': Free Jazz and African-American Politics," *Cultural Critique* 32 (1995): 97–123; Kwami Coleman, "Free Jazz and the "New Thing" Aesthetics, Identity, and Texture, 1960–1966." *The Journal of Musicology* 38, no. 3 (2021): 261–95.

3 Don Cherry, Gato Barbieri, Henry Grimes, and Ed Blackwell, *Complete Communion*. Blue Note, 1965; LeRoi Jones (Amiri Baraka), "Don Cherry," in *Black Music* (Akashic Books, 2010), 191; Eyal Hareuveni, "William Parker: Everything is Valid" *All About Jazz* (March 7, 2005). https://www.allaboutjazz.com/william-parker-everything-is-valid-william-parker-by-eyal-hareuveni; Walter Benjamin, "Analogy and Relationship," in *Walter Benjamin: Selected Writings 1: 1913–1926* (Cambridge: Harvard University Press, 2004), 207. It is beyond the scope of this essay to satisfactorily introduce early Benjamin's very particular understanding of relationship [*Verwandtschaft*]. In his topography of similarity sketched in the short fragment "Analogy and Relationship," "Doctrine of the Similar," and "On the Mimetic Faculty (and more obliquely, but importantly, in "The Task of the Translator," and his writing on "Trauerspiel")," "relationship" designates a mimetic correspondence that *might* not have any substantive resemblance but is nevertheless a pinnacle of kinship and affinity.

4 Theodor W. Adorno, *Negative Dialectics* (London: Continuum, 2007). 6.

5 Theodor W. Adorno, "The Aging of the New Music," in *Essays on Music* (Berkeley: University of California Press, 2002), 182. My thanks to Benjamin Piekut for penetrating thoughts on an earlier iteration of this essay, that, among other things, forced a clearer definition of my area of enquiry (i.e., aesthetic rather than musicological or historical).

6 Jost, *Free Jazz*, 69.

7 Adélékè Adéèkó, *Arts of Being Yorùbá: Divination, Allegory, Tragedy, Proverb, Panegyric* (Bloomington: Indiana University Press, 2017), 28–32. Rowland Abiodun, "Verbal and Visual Metaphors: Mythical Allusions in Yoruba Ritualistic Art of *Orí*," *Word & Image* 3, no. 3 (1987): 252–70.

8 Ornette Coleman, *The Shape of Jazz to Come*. United States: Atlantic, 1959.

9 Keren Omry, "Literary Free Jazz?" Mumbo Jumbo" and" Paradise": Language and Meaning," *African American Review* 41, no. 1 (2007): 131.

10 Sara Ramshaw, "Deconstructin(g) Jazz Improvisation: Derrida and the Law of the Singular Event," *Critical Studies in Improvisation/Études Critiques en Improvisation* 2, no. 1 (2006): 3.

11 Marcus Zagorski, "'*Nach dem Weltuntergang*': Adorno's Engagement with Postwar Music," *Journal of Musicology* 22, no. 4 (2005): 683.

12 David Cunningham, "Notes on Nuance." *Radical Philosophy* 125 (May/June 2004): 19; Zagorski, "Adorno's Engagement with Postwar Music," 689. Original italics.

13 Adorno, "Aging of the New Music," 194. Italics mine.

14 Cunningham, "Notes on Nuance," 19. Gyorgy Ligeti is being quoted here. See "Metamorposes of Musical Form" in Robert P. Morgan, ed., *Source Readings in Musical History: The Twentieth Century*, W.W. Norton, New York and London, 1998, p. 113

15 It has been noted that free jazz bears greater resemblance to earlier twentieth century permutations (Expressionist-era Schoenberg, Stravinsky, Bartok) than it does the total organization of integral serialism, and, although this might be more contentious, the aleatory composition of Cage (see Gunther Schuller, 1989; Steven Block, 1990; A. B. Spellman, 1985). I find it interesting that Adorno writes "[t]he expressionist ideal of expression is altogether one of the immediacy of expression. . . . For one thing, Expressionist music seeks to eliminate all conventional elements of conventionality, everything that has been rigidified in terms of form, and indeed all the one-time case and its general universality of musical language – analogous to the poetic ideal of the 'scream'." While I might need to dial down the extent to which Adorno understands Expressionist music as a rejection of "all conventional elements" (and, by the way, in "*Vers une Musique Informelle*," we find Adorno acknowledge that the dissolution was not across the board and did not manifest evenly across Schoenberg's composition of this era), this gloss from Adorno could describe Ayler on "Ghosts" or Coltrane on "Sun Ship." Importantly, while mid-century European and Euro-American new music, maintained the "eliminat[ion] of conventionality," it demonstrated, quite pointedly, an accompanying rejection of "immediacy of expression" in favor of prefabrication and ego-avoidance methods that usurp the centrality of "compositional subjectivity."

16 Zagorski, "Adorno's Engagement with Postwar Music," *Journal of Musicology* 22, no. 4 (2005): 691.

17 Theodor W. Adorno, "*Vers une Musique Informelle*." In *Quasi una Fantasia: Essays on Modern Music* (London: Verso, 1998), 274.

18 See Raymond Geuss in *Morality, Culture, and History: Essays on German Philosophy.* (Cambridge: Cambridge University Press, 1999), 146. "[T]]here is something *inherently* odd about Adorno's project in 'Vers une musique informelle' of using [a] dialectical method to tell us where music must, could, might, or ought to go. Strictly speaking, a Hegelian dialectician should claim that the 'outcome' of a conflict, tension, contradiction, etc. can be seen to be 'rational' or 'logical' *only retrospectively.*"

19 Adorno, "*Music Informelle,*" 272, 307.

20 Max Paddison writes that Adorno's informal music "is not a prescription for composers to try to put into practice. . . but is really what I would call a 'prismatic concept' — that is to say, a multi-faceted concept that enables us to see things from different and unusual angles and in a new and unfamiliar light" "Contemporary Music: Theory, Aesthetic, Critical Theory," in *Contemporary Music, Theoretical and Philosophical Perspectives* (Farnham: Ashgate, 2010), 8.

21 Adorno, "*Music Informelle,*" 272.

22 Joris De Henau, "Towards an Aesthetics of the '*(in)formel*': Time, Space and the Dialectical Image in the Music of Varèse, Feldman and Xenakis." PhD diss. (Durham University, 2015), 80.

23 Text provided by Städel Museum accompanying the digital archive of "Injured Head." Accessed on October 20, 2021. https://sammlung.staedelmuseum.de/en/work/injured-head

24 De Henau, "Towards an Aesthetics of the '*(in)formel*,'" 80.

25 The reference is to Paul Klee's *Angelus Novus* (1920).

26 Quoted in De Henau, "Towards an Aesthetics of the *'(in)formel*,'" 79.

27 William Parker, Liner notes to *Sound Unity*. AUM Fidelity, 2004.

28 Theodor W. Adorno, "Form in the New Music," *Music Analysis* 27, no. 2/3 (2008): 201. He continues: "Form has to be distinguished from whatever is formed; it is the epitome of what makes art art, of all the elements which organise a work of art as a meaningful thing in itself."

29 "Adorno's idea of musical material appears in various forms throughout his output, and crystallizes aspects found in his thought more generally: the dialectics of history and nature, and the antagonistic relations of constraint and freedom under modernity. Musical material, for Adorno, is all that faces the composer in the present as inherited from the past: formal schemes, instrumental forces, harmonic and melodic formulae and expectations, and so on." Samuel Wilson, "Notes on Adorno's 'Musical Material' During the New Materialisms," *Music and Letters* 99, no. 2 (2018): 262.

30 Adorno, *"Musique Informelle,"* 307.

31 Adorno, *"Musique Informelle,"* 322; 320.

32 Adorno, *"Musique Informelle,"* 307.

33 Eva Geulen, "'The Primacy of the Object': Adorno's *Aesthetic Theory* and the Return of Form," *New German Critique* 48, no. 2 (2021): 7.

34 Walter Benjamin, "The Storyteller: Reflections on the Works of Nikolai Leskov," in *Illuminations: Essays and Reflections* (London: Fontana, 1992), 100. I am not able to expand on this idea of African/black modal anomaly in this essay, however it is important to note that it is not only that the world lacks the mechanism for recognizing black life as real possibility; not only that the world does not possess the conditions for black actualization. I also want to say that African orientation was/is, to borrow a phrase from Jay Bernstein concerning artistic practice and experience, *"modally* anomalous" (436) to a world of strictly determinate possibilities. The modes and movements of possibility particular to it are incompatible (or make it incompatible) with the European world (the converse is not true). The reason the European world is incapable of true blackening, is not only a consequence of the comprehensive education in racial difference but due, moreover, to the modal ambiguity characteristic of Africanness/ blackness, with its ease of transport between what the European world understands as real possibility, and the fantastic and formal. On refusal see Stefano Harney and Fred Moten, *The Undercommons: Fugitive Planning and Black Study*. (London: Minor Compositions, 2013).

35 "[Walter] Benjamin said that history had hitherto been written from the standpoint of the victor, and needed to be written from that of the vanquished, we might add that knowledge must indeed present the fatally rectilinear succession of victory and defeat, but should also address itself to those things which were not embraced by this dynamic, which fell by the wayside—what might be called the waste products and blind spots that have escaped the dialectic. . . .What transcends the ruling society is not only the potentiality it develops but also all that which did not fit properly into the laws of historical movement. Theory must needs deal with cross-grained, opaque, unassimilated material, which as such admittedly has from the start an anachronistic quality, but is not wholly obsolete since it has outwitted the historical dynamic." Theodor W. Adorno, *Minima Moralia: Reflections on a Damaged Life* (London: Verso, 2005), 151.

36 There are discussions of *òrò* that deepen and complicate the affinity of the term with aesthetic form as understood by Adorno. Most significant to this unfolding argument is that *òrò* names a phenomenon remarkably similar to aesthetic form. See Rowland Abiodun's "Verbal and visual metaphors": mythical allusions in Yoruba ritualistic art of *Orí*" for instance. I have chosen to limit my use of the term to its more quotidian definition as (the conversation around) a matter at hand to avoid compounding existing complications in my formulation. What I am suggesting at this point in the discussion, however, that the more colloquial definition provides a model for the nonsensuous, is in tension with the fact that *òrò*, as used in Yoruba aesthetics, already includes this latter valence.

37 Toni Morrison, *Beloved*. (New York: Knopf Doubleday, 2007), 308. Unfortunately, I do not have the space to comment on the theory of relationship (kinship)/musicality that Toni Morrison and Walter Benjamin share, but those familiar with *Beloved* and Walter Benjamin's philosophy of language might see what I am unable to deal with here.

38 Christopher Felver, *Cecil Taylor: All the Notes* (Sausalito, CA: EMotion Studios, 2004).

39 Cecil Taylor, "Sound structure of subculture becoming major breath/Naked fire gesture." *Liner notes on Unit Structures. LP BST* 84237 (1966); Chris Funkhouser, "Being Matter Ignited. . ., an interview with Cecil Taylor." *Hambone Magazine* 12 (1995). https://writing.upenn.edu/epc/authors/funkhouser/ceciltaylor.html

40 Tony Harrington, "Three Seconds in the World of Cecil Taylor." *The Wire* (April 2018). https://www.thewire.co.uk/in-writing/essays/three-seconds-in-the-world-of-cecil-taylor-by-tony-herrington

41 Here I stray into Benjaminian terrain, referring to his writing on nonsensuous correspondence. See Walter Benjamin, "On the Mimetic Faculty," *Reflections: Essays, Aphorisms, Autobiographical Writings* (Houghton Mifflin Harcourt, 2019), 351; "Doctrine of the Similar (1933)," *New German Critique* 17 (1979): 66.

42 Cecil Taylor, *Always a Pleasure*. FMP, 1996.

43 Theodor W. Adorno, *Aesthetic Theory*, trans. Robert Hullot-Kentor. (Minneapolis: University of Minnesota Press, 1997), 143.

44 As I hope the recounting of my experience with Wols's work intimated, there is a need to improvise the work, to journey toward a re-composition of it, and in doing so become a part of the organism, as a viewer, along with its material parts and with participating practitioners. In my listening experience and retelling, I contribute to an unstable, temporary communion, what Walter Benjamin calls relationship or *Verwandtschaft*, being pulled into constellation and for a moment becoming of a "nonviolent synthesis of the diffuse." Benjamin, "Analogy and Relationship"; Adorno, *Negative Dialectics*, 6.

45 Jones/Baraka, "Don Cherry"; Benjamin, "Analogy and Relationship"; Fred Moten, "Blackness and Nothingness (Mysticism in the Flesh)." *South Atlantic Quarterly* 112, no. 4 (2013): 743–47; Hareuveni, "William Parker"; Morrison, *Beloved*, 308.

46 In case it needs to be stated bluntly, the work of the new thing cannot be thought as observing the autonomy or nominalism of its European counterparts, and in fact this is perhaps where the music departs most sharply from Adorno's *musique informelle*—free jazz is most often unabashedly collective-based or committed, and its disparate performances, at times, sharing works).

47 Adorno, *Aesthetic Theory,* 225–28.

10
WHITE BY DESIGN
Mabel O. Wilson

In MoMA's *Good Design* exhibitions of 1951, Ovals, a fabric by African-American designer A. Joel Robinson, stood out among the sample swathes hung on display in the Museum's gallery, and among a larger selection of design objects in Chicago's massive Merchandise Mart.[1] Robinson created his award-winning modern design for the Manhattan-based manufacturer L. Anton Maix, a company whose fabrics by noted white designers Serge Chermayeff and Paul McCobb were also on view in the 1951 *Good Design* shows. Maix printed Robinson's variable pattern of overlapping outlined and solid colored ovals on fine Belgian linen, a fabric best suited for draperies and adaptable for summer clothing. Robinson, who had trained as an architect but worked in other design disciplines, developed with Maix an innovative production process that arranged patterns in kaleidoscopic formation.[2] Shown in the Mart and the Museum's galleries alongside selected furniture, lamps, tableware, kitchenware, appliances, and flooring, Ovals's abstract geometry of shifting forms exemplified the industrial machine aesthetic and utilization of new technologies that MoMA was promoting as fundamental to modernism in the disciplines of architecture, planning, graphic design, product design, and industrial design.

In an effort to popularize modern design principles in the booming postwar consumer-goods market, *Good Design*'s white head curator, Edgar Kaufmann, Jr., also negotiated to have some items from the exhibits, including Robinson's high-end fabric at $9 a yard, on view in special displays at the Bloomingdale's and Abraham and Straus department stores in New York. Kaufmann, the son of a Pittsburgh department-store family who recognized the importance of modern design's influence on how Americans could live, wanted *Good Design* to directly affect the design and production of household products. Because the exhibition had several platforms—MoMA's galleries, the two semiannual exhibits at the Merchandise Mart (which attracted twenty-seven thousand buyers), and a kit of iconic labels to affix to select goods on sale in department-store displays nationwide— it was an accessible primer for consumers anywhere in the country.[3] For Kaufmann, what distinguished an item out of the thousands submitted to him by manufacturers and distributors was that it possess "eye-appeal, function, construction and price, with emphasis on the first."[4] By these standards, Robinson's fabric designs advanced modern manufacturing techniques and had the aesthetic allure to succeed in the marketplace.[5]

For the *Good Design* exhibits of 1952, the committee of architects, designers, curators, and industry experts chose Robinson's fabric Ovals No. 1, a hand-printed oval pattern on beige linen. Another variation of Robinson's Ovals pattern (#2, or II) was included in a special fifth-anniversary *Good Design* exhibit in 1955. For this later show, an all-white MoMA special committee that included René d'Harnoncourt, Alfred H. Barr, Jr., and Philip C. Johnson, respectively the Museum's director, founding director, and the founder of the Museum's Department of Architecture and Design (A&D), joined Kaufmann to choose one hundred exceptional objects from the previous exhibitions to highlight "visual excellence" and "progressive furnishings available on the American market since 1950."[6]

Robinson's triumph in being selected several times by a distinguished museum such as MoMA was heralded in a 1952 issue of *Ebony*, a *Life*-like magazine aimed at black American audiences, as the "first Negro to crack the fabric design field and only Negro ever to win Good Design Awards"[7] Although Robinson, then twenty-nine, had trained in architecture at New York University and Cooper Union, he told *Ebony* that he had worked as a bellhop and a bartender because no New York architecture firm would hire a Negro architect.[8] *Ebony's* monthly articles, such as the ones reporting on Robinson's successes, functioned as bellwethers of black middle-class progress in the face of the overt and structural white racism that hampered all forms of black economic and social advancement in the postwar United States. *Ebony* heaped praise on Robinson's skyrocketing rise in industrial design. In the early years of his career, unable to secure employment as an architect, Robinson designed several fabrics for Maix, as well as completing advertisements and product and furniture designs. In 1954, according to *Jet Magazine*, *Ebony's* sister weekly magazine, he was eventually appointed to an executive-vice-president position at an advertising agency.[9] Little is known about the rest of his career.

In 1975, twenty-three years after Ovals #2 was included in the *Good Design* exhibits, MoMA accessioned a swatch into its A&D study collection—a collection mainly for research rather than public display, unlike the works in the permanent collection.[10] A. Joel Robinson was the only black designer or architect represented in either parts of the collection and remained so for another twenty-five years, until 2000, when the Museum acquired, again for the study collection, *Entity as Information Zoom*, a digital print on acrylic panel, from 1995, by the black Canadian architect Gordon Kipping.[11] To the Museum's knowledge, out of 14,500 objects and artifacts acquired in the eighty-foilr years since the founding of the Department of Architecture and Design, in 1932, it had accessioned into its permanent collection no works by a black architect or designer until 2016, when it acquired Charles Harrison's View-Master (model G), a popular mass-produced plastic-shell stereoscope designed in 1962.

How to understand this absence of black designers in the first and still one of the most significant collections of modern architecture and design, one that shaped the historiography of modernism and incorporated its tenets into education, practice, and manufacturing? As the anthropologist Michel-Rolph Trouillot wrote, "The making of archives involves a number of selective operations: selection of producers, selection of evidence, selection of themes, selection of procedures—which means, at best the differential ranking and, at worst, the exclusion of some producers, some evidence, some themes, some procedures. Power enters here both obviously and surreptitiously."[12] What then is architecture's power, particularly of racialization, both within the institution and beyond the archive's walls?

What Is Modern Architecture?

The *Good Design* exhibitions, staged from 1950 to 1955, demonstrate how MoMA's Department of Architecture and Design, eighteen years old when the series began, engaged with industry and commerce to promote the influence of modernist tenets of design on the objects and spaces of daily American life. "Design intended for present-day life," as Kaufmann described in the first *Good Design* press release, should attend "to usefulness, to production methods and materials, and to the progressive taste of the day."[13] One part of the A&D department's mission was to influence the production of consumer goods and the design of modern buildings and cities. This was to be accomplished not only by organizing exhibitions—including collaborations, such as the *Good Design* series, on which the Museum partnered with outside institutions and agencies affiliated with commerce, industry and policy—but also through the creation of the collection. These select design objects—ranging from fabric swatches to helicopters and including modern architecture in the form of drawings, photographs, models, and building fragments—defined the canon of modernism.

MoMA launched its first exhibition dedicated to modern architecture in February 1932. *Modern Architecture: International Exhibition* was a two-year endeavor curated by Johnson, a wealthy white Midwestern architecture enthusiast who would later train as an architect and establish his own practice, and Henry-Russell Hitchcock, Jr., an influential white architectural historian who wrote one of the first histories of modern architecture. To proselytize the virtues of modernism, *Modern Architecture: International Exhibition* traveled around the country for three years, not only to museums but also to department stores. This mix of venues demonstrates the intersection of culture and commerce that underwrote the A&D department's mission. Barr, who joined in organizing the exhibition, believed that the modern museum should exhibit new art forms such as film, architecture, and the arts of product and graphic design, influenced as they were by industrialization and new technologies. It was important that the museum show how modern architecture's unadorned walls, sun-filled and air-conditioned rooms, utilitarian furniture, and affordable construction could transform life at home and at work. Mobilizing MoMA as a platform to promote modernism beyond painting and sculpture, Barr opened the world's first museum department of architecture in the summer of 1932, an endeavor headed and funded by Johnson. To achieve this lofty goal, MoMA had to determine for an American audience precisely how it defined modern architecture—its character, its history, and its production.

Modern Architecture: International Exhibition showcased a roster of leading white architects building in Europe, including Walter Gropius (Germany), Le Corbusier (France), Ludwig Mies van der Rohe (Germany), and J. J. P. Oud (the Netherlands), alongside several important architects practicing in the United States, including Frank Lloyd Wright, Raymond Hood, William Lescaze (a Swiss émigré), and Richard Neutra (an Austrian émigré). The exhibition's only projects by nonwhite architects and outside Europe and the United States were two buildings in Japan by Isaburo Ueno and Mamoru Yamada.[14] For Johnson, Hitchcock, and Barr, this European and American cohort of architects exemplified a truthful utilization of material and structure, quintessential characteristics of rationalized modern form. Taking stock of the projects in the exhibition's catalogue, Barr praised the way "*technical and utilitarian* factors in the hands of designers who understand inherent aesthetic possibilities have resulted in an architecture comparable in integrity and even in beauty to the styles of the past."[15] In the American context, aesthetics over-shadowed the functionalism central to such movements as the German Werkbund. In designating these projects "international" in their exhibition's title (and in an influential book published independently of MoMA the same year, *The International Style: Architecture since 1922*), Johnson and Hitchcock defined a modern "style" of architecture whose construction techniques and aesthetic could be replicated almost anywhere in the world — an architecture that suited American and European imperialism, which continued to foster colonial infrastructures in Asia, Africa, and parts of South America. The phrase "International Style" also doubly muted the influences of Northern African and Middle Eastern vernacular in European modernism's use of flat roofs and white or pale-colored walls, much in the same way that white artists had adapted "primitive" forms to unsettle bourgeois art.[16]

Along with defining the fundamental technological and aesthetic qualities of modern design, *Modern Architecture: International Exhibition* also initiated a historiographic project that charted the formation of modernism in architecture. The exhibition's catalogue and wall texts described how Expressionism and Neo-Plasticism in painting had influenced architecture and design. Johnson explained the importance of Germany's *Neue Sachlichkeit* (New Objectivity) movement and Bauhaus school to the evolution of functionalism.[17] The show formulated a canon of modernism by sorting out and chronicling different movements of revivalism and engineering. By establishing this timeline of Euro-American modernism, with Japan and, beginning in the 1940s, parts of Latin America incorporated into the geographic scope, the new department under Johnson's stewardship categorized the objects and images it accessioned into its new collection of architecture, with similar categories and timelines also applied to industrial, product, and graphic design.

Visions of Housing

In MoMA's galleries, *Modern Architecture: International Exhibition* featured models, drawings, and photographs of office buildings, banks, and exposition pavilions from around the United States and Europe. To educate the public on the promise of modernism, Johnson and Hitchcock placed on view a large selection of projects demonstrating how the rational organization of space could orchestrate and transform domestic life. Visitors saw single-family private houses, low-rise housing units designed for workers, high-rise housing units that tested different ratios of density for families or students, and prefabricated houses that experimented with manufacturing techniques designed for mass production. In the section of the catalogue dedicated to housing, the white cultural critic and historian Lewis Mumford observed that "it is only during the last generation that we have begun to conceive of a new domestic environment which will utilize our technical and scientific achievements for the benefit of human living. The laying down of a new basis for housing has been, since 1914, one of the chief triumphs of modern architecture."[18] In the American context, however, "worker housing" such as the Weissenhofsiedlung in Stuttgart, which included projects by Gropius, Oud, Le Corbusier, and Mies, was stripped of its left-leaning political agenda and Americanized as "housing." A convergence of government and market forces would determine the future of housing in the United States, and charting that course would become a major focus of MoMA's A&D exhibitions for the next forty years.

Following *Modern Architecture: International Exhibition*, MoMA hosted several exhibitions dedicated to new designs for public housing in the United States. In 1934, the U.S. Congress passed the National Housing Act to create the Federal Housing Administration (FHA), an agency that regulated interest rates and insured bank loans to private borrowers for home-building in order to increase homeownership, which had fallen drastically with the onset of the Great Depression. Later that year, Carol Aronovici, a white Columbia University professor and expert on New York housing, organized for Johnson the exhibition *Housing Exhibition of the City of New York*, with an accompanying catalogue, *America Can't Have Housing*. MoMA, Aronovici wrote, served as a perfect venue "to arouse public interest and foster a better understanding of the housing problem."[19] With its large panels comparing the housing conditions of old flat types with those of modern projects, all in the genre of sociological study, the Museum served as a platform for researchers and authorities to promote slum clearance and low-cost housing in New York and other parts of the country.

Two years later, MoMA hosted another, smaller exhibition on housing, organized in cooperation with the Resettlement Administration and the Public Works Administration (PWA), agencies established to oversee the housing of the poor under the New Deal. This exhibition, *Architecture in Government Housing* (1936), showed drawings, models, and photographs of five proposed low-cost housing projects, as well as of two suburban schemes promoting low-income rentals and greenbelt planning to resettle residents displaced by the new policies of urban slum clearance. Among the five federally financed PWA projects were the 317 proposed units, of which 274 were built, for "Negro families of low income" that made up Langston Terrace, in Washington, D.C.[20] The project was designed by the African-American architects Hilyard Robinson, based in Washington, D.C., and Paul Revere Williams, practicing in Los Angeles, along with Irving Porter, a white architect in Washington, D.C. At MoMA the three exhibited a model, a perspective, plans of units and social rooms, and a site plan that gave the public a glimpse of their proposal. As part of the PWA's mandate to do more than provide housing for low-income families, the project was to employ African-American construction workers to build the spare geometric volumes of the two-story brick row house units and four-story apartment building units. Failing to note the promise of Langston Terrace, Mumford, writing in his "Sky Line" column for *The New Yorker*, criticized the lackluster evidence of innovation in state-funded housing, arguing that bureaucracy had stifled the architects' imaginations.[21] Ignored by the architectural elites for the remainder of their careers, Robinson and Williams nonetheless developed successful practices.[22] None of their work would be included in another MoMA exhibit or accessioned for the collection.

The A&D department's collaborations with universities, institutions, and state housing and urban-planning agencies remained a key part of MoMA's exhibition strategy until the early 1970s, which marked the end of a period of urban renewal and also of modernism's entanglement with it. Even so, as late as 1973, Arthur Drexler, a white curator who helmed the A&D department from 1956 to 1987, could write in the catalogue for a MoMA exhibition called *Another Chance for Housing: Low-Rise Alternatives*, "As its name might suggest, the Museum of Modern Art, through its Department of Architecture and Design, is concerned with the art of architecture. It recognizes—indeed it insists—that architecture even more than the other arts is bound up with ethics, social justice, technology, politics, and finance, along with a lofty desire to improve the human condition."[23]

Another Chance for Housing, a collaboration with the Institute for Architecture and Urban Studies (IAUS) and the New York State Urban Development Corporation (UDC), was another attempt by white architects to offer solutions to an urban housing crisis that most affected poor black and Hispanic communities. The exhibition opened in 1973, the year after the beginning of the demolition of St. Louis's Pruitt-Igoe housing complex—thirty-three eleven-story high-rise slab buildings, designed by Japanese-American architect Minoru Yamasaki, that had housed thousands of poor black families. The main focus of *Another Chance for Housing* was a group of proposals for low-rise housing units designed by IAUS's architects. Architectural teams tested these housing typologies in the neighborhoods of Fox Hills, Staten Island, and Brownsville, Brooklyn, in one of the rare instances where a MoMA exhibition identified a neighborhood as inhabited by black residents. Included in the UDC section of the exhibition were drawings of the Lionel Hampton Houses in Harlem, a 355-unit, twenty-six-story brown-brick high-rise for low- and moderate-income residents that also featured a seven-story apartment building for elderly residents and a two-story professional building and day care center. Black architects J. Max Bond, Jr., and Donald P. Ryder of Bond Ryder & Associates designed this ensemble of buildings, which opened in July 1973 near St. Nicholas Park.[24] After Hilyard Robinson and Williams in *Architecture in Government Housing* in 1936, and Joel Robinson in the *Good Design* shows in the 1950s, this was only the third time that black architects or designers had appeared in a MoMA exhibition, but the Museum accessioned no work from Bond's stellar architectural career, which included spearheading the design for the Smithsonian's National Museum of African American History and Culture, in Washington, D.C., completed by David Adjaye and Philip Freelon in 2016, after Bond died in the early stages of the project.

If architecture and design, as Drexler stated, were "even more than the other arts . . . bound up with ethics, social justice, technology, politics, and finance, along with a lofty desire to improve the human condition," then why were questions of racism and poverty absent from so many exhibitions, and black architects and designers from both exhibitions and the collection? A show that might have addressed these issues was planned but never staged. In early 1970, Drexler and the black architect W. Joseph Black, who worked for the New York City Planning Commission, conceived an exhibition to oe called *Visions of Harlem*. The project was to highlight Harlem's "positive architectural qualities" by calling "attention to significant buildings and sites whose presence ought to condition future planning for the area."[25] A response to The Metropolitan Museum of Art's controversial exhibition *Harlem on My Mind*, which had opened in January 1969, *Visions of Harlem* was to be an objective view of the uptown neighborhood that had been a crossroads of black culture for sixty years. It would be a "dry show," Drexler imagined—"there will be no photographs of people (as in the Met show)"—but would draw attention to aspects of

Harlem's architecture that were of "real quality" and could be preserved as part of future planning. Instead of favoring the bulldozer approach of urban renewal, which had in part fueled a backlash in the form of the urban uprisings that had set cities afire in the 1960s, *Visions of Harlem* sought a curatorial approach that would be of "service to both the black and white communities."[26] The show was scheduled to open in MoMA's Goodwin Gallery in October 1971 and later to move to a venue in Harlem, with the prospect of traveling elsewhere. In the end, none of these plans materialized. A version of *Visions of Harlem* was eventually exhibited in 1974 at the Studio Museum in Harlem, an institution dedicated to contemporary black art and culture, but the accompanying book was never published.

It is revealing that in *Visions of Harlem* Drexler wanted "no photographs of people." The absence of black residents would have rendered Harlem's architecture as a sociopolitically neutral vessel, accessible and in "service to both the black and white communities." This was not the first time Drexler had used Harlem as a tabula rasa for the white architectural imagination. In the 1967 exhibition *The New City: Architecture and Urban Renewal*, he had invited four teams of white architects and planners, from Cornell, Columbia, MIT, and Princeton universities, to imagine a "new city" for Harlem and northern Manhattan. The projects proposed by architects Peter Eisenman, Michael Graves, Richard Meier, Colin Rowe, and others were seen in bird's-eye views, as if the spectator were hovering above Harlem's main avenues. The architects reconfigured neighborhoods by inserting large white grids and primary-colored geometries outlining block-busting mega-projects. As a reminder of architecture's limits, Drexler cautioned, "it would be presumptuous to suppose that problems of poverty and prejudice, and the hundred other evils that beset us, can be solved by architecture alone."[27] In the minds and eyes of MoMA's curators, architecture was above the fray.

Black by Design

MoMA offered designers an experimental platform to explore the arts of architecture and design, but it is important to note that these same disciplines were also mobilized to racially divide spaces in cities and towns across the United States, and in other nations engaged in forms of colonial domination. Racial segregation was implemented through a host of agents and apparatuses in the field of design. In the public arena of housing, "urban renewal" was code for "Negro removal" from the 1930s to the '70s. The ruthless evictions of black and poor families in the name of slum clearance opened up land for gargantuan experiments in housing and for the national highway system, and left thousands of empty lots awaiting future development. In the private housing market, black Americans were deliberately excluded through legal means from homeownership in white neighborhoods. Public agencies such as the FHA joined with the private banking system to deploy practices such as redlining, which rated black neighborhoods as undesirable and risky for investment, depriving those communities of financial capital to construct new buildings and improve old ones. The marketplace of household goods popularized by *Good Design* and exhibitions like it served flourishing white-only suburbs that kept black populations in increasingly marginalized and underserved urban ghettos.

"Despite the fact that architects and design critics of the period emphasized avant-garde solutions and even the search for a 'democratic' architecture," writes historian Dianne Harris, "very few postwar building professionals engaged consistently or deeply with issues of social, economic, and political justice."[28] Harris adds that "design professionals tended to imagine the consideration of race and class as falling outside of the purviews of their respective professional realms."[29] Indeed, white architects largely shared Drexler's stance that architecture alone could not solve poverty and prejudice.

The invisibility of black designers in MoMA's exhibitions, and most conspicuously in the A&D collection, highlights the paradox of modern architecture and design in terms of its ideal of universality, its goal of service to all, in contrast to those it actually served. MoMA's experiments with private and public housing reveal the intimacies of spaces designed for individuals, families, and communities. It is precisely in these everyday realms of the home, of work, and of public space that racism walled off white bodies from their racial others. For instance, before Johnson became affiliated with MoMA, he and Barr were neighbors. All educated at Harvard but in different disciplines, Barr, Hitchcock, and Johnson traveled in the same social circles of elite art patrons. In 1930, a year after Barr became the director of MoMA, he and his wife, Margaret Scolari Barr, moved into a one-bedroom apartment in the Southgate apartment complex in midtown Manhattan.[30] Their apartment was directly over the unit Johnson had rented before joining MoMA's staff in the fall of 1930.[31] In consultation with Johnson, the Barrs furnished their apartment with the latest tubular-steel furniture, mainly by Donald Deskey. Johnson enlisted Mies, the German architect who at the time was head of the Bauhaus, and his collaborator Lilly Reich to design his apartment.[32] Johnson's daily domestic routines were orchestrated by minimalist modernist furniture in metal, leather, and glass; the walls were adorned with modern artworks recommended by Barr. Modern design choreographed every aspect of home and work—precisely MoMA's future vision of American life.

The places many Americans called home were regulated by racial boundaries that segregated white residences from black ones. Many white-only domiciles, however, were transgressed daily by black domestics, often the labor force that maintained the impeccable order and polished gleam of the modern interior.[33] A magazine photograph of Johnson's iconic Connecticut residence the Glass House, built in 1949, for example, shows Johnson sitting at his desk; another photo captures a black butler behind the kitchen counter. Architect and architectural theorist Mario Gooden observes, "Johnson said that he wanted to keep the kitchen very abstract, to make it just a simple bar. It seems that this figure of the black butler standing at the cooking unit signified that this was the service space of the house. And this is important because it signifies the larger ways race has been at the service of modern architecture."[34] Le Corbusier too saw blackness in that service. Visiting Harlem during a trip to the United States in 1935, in part sponsored by MoMA, the Frenchman rhapsodized about "hot jazz" and the dynamic movement of black performers, including trumpeter Louis Armstrong, as akin to machines and black skyscrapers. This raw primitive energy of modernity would give rise to new "white cathedrals," modern skyscrapers in Le Corbusier's beloved Europe.[35]

The primitive reappeared in MoMA's 1964 exhibition *Architecture Without Architects: An Introduction to Non-Pedigreed Architecture*, a show on indigenous and vernacular buildings around the world. It was organized by the Czech-American architect and social historian Bernard Rudofsky, who believed that "the philosophy and know-how of the anonymous builders presents the largest untapped source of architectural inspiration for industrial man."[36] Whether discovered in the ghetto, the colony, or remote regions, blackness and black building forms, in their vital simplicity, provided white architects with conceptual and formal inspiration to advance their cause of social progress and technological advancement in the metropole.

In this period, however, was there a critical "black architecture" not in service to white modernism? In April 1965, *Esquire* magazine published an article by the black architect and writer June Jordan (writing under her married name, June Meyer), "Instant Slum Clearance," which featured the proposal "Skyrise to Harlem"—the original title of the essay before *Esquire* replaced it with something more provocative, and also attributed the project solely to Jordan's white collaborator, architect R. Buckminster Fuller.[37] Working with Fuller, whose work had been featured in solo shows at MoMA, Jordan envisioned a new architectural landscape for Harlem absent the devastating sweep of slum clearance. Launched as a critique of urban renewal's ruthless displacement of poor residents, "Skyrise to Harlem" imagined a participatory process in which Harlem's black residents would incrementally build skyward a new community of a hundred circular decks with residences adorned by hanging gardens fed by recycled water.[38] To avoid the displacement typical of urban renewal, the first floor of the new structure would align with the seventh, top floor of the old buildings. Jordan wrote in a letter to Fuller that once the new structures were completed, Harlemites would "literally move up into their new homes. The enormous ground area freed would be converted to communal open space for recreation, parking, and so forth."[39] A truly modern proposition, "Skyrise to Harlem" sought to harness the power of industrialized housing production while remaining attentive to social and natural ecologies. Jordan and Fuller suggested that private investment would be regenerative for the hundred thousand families who would dwell in the filigree structures. Their eco-towers, each populated with shared amenities and social services, would sprout from the bottom up and would be built by the black community, preserving social relations and black social spaces while also opening the area to settlement by other, nonblack residents, in contrast to the white architects who, for MoMA's *New City* show two years later, imagined dropping gridded mega-structures into the neighborhood from above. While one can find various works of Fuller's in MoMA's collection and archives, the black architecture of "Skyrise to Harlem" is not included.

After Joel Robinson's swatch of fabric in 1975, the next object by a black designer to be accessioned into MoMA's A&D study collection, in 2000, was Kipping's *Entity as Information Zoom*. The department's chief curator, Terence Riley, had included the work in the catalogue for his exhibition *The Un-Private House* the previous year. Here, like Jordan and Fuller, Kipping critiques the canonical influence of modern architecture, specifically the use of horizontal windows and large panels of glass to provide fresh air, sunlight, and views. To address the overexposure of the private domestic interior to public scrutiny, Kipping's drawing of a speculative house—a generic "domestic enclosure" described as either urban or suburban—locates within the facade and interior various apertures of media and apparatuses of surveillance.[40] *Entity as Information Zoom* incorporates a still image of Kipping's looming figure outside the house. The image was captured by a video camera, and Kipping's anonymous form is infilled by an image of former star football player and accused murderer O. J. Simpson. That same image of Simpson also appears on a television screen inside the house. This doubling of images in the drawing positions representations of blackness (perceived as unknown and menacing) both outside the domestic threshold and inside the private white domicile, echoing the racist logic by which black people are simultaneously excluded from the housing market and drafted as labor to maintain domestic order. This spatial doubling articulates how the ability to survey and control what's inside (the private domain of the self) and what's outside (the public sphere of politics) provides white architecture and its archive with stability. As argued above, it is precisely the way buildings separate black and other bodies from white ones that produces the onto-epistemological experience of racial differences. Modern architecture builds the world for the white subject, maintaining the logics of racism while also imagining a future world in which nonwhite subjects remain exploitable and marginal. The power of the architecture and its archive is to produce "whiteness" by design.

Notes

Many of The Museum of Modern Art's historical exhibition catalogues, and such documents as press releases and exhibition checklists, have been digitized and can be found through the search function on the Museum's website, www.moma.org. While correspondence and other documents in the Museum's Archives may not be available by this route, many of the public documents cited below are locatable on the website.

1   MoMA curator Edgar Kaufmann, Jr., organized the *Good Design* exhibits from 1950 to 1955 in collaboration with Chicago's Merchandise Mart. The exhibitions, five in all at MoMA itself, brought together designers, manufacturers, and retailers to offer new. aesthetically pleasing, affordable, and functional products to postwar consumers. Each exhibit opened with two large exhibitions in January and July at the Merchandise Mart in Chicago, followed by a smaller exhibition later in the year at MoMA in New York.

2   "Fabric Designer," *Ebony* 7, no. 7 (May 1952):115.

3   See Terence Riley and Edward Eigen, "Between the Museum and the Marketplace: Selling Good Design," in *The Museum of Modern Art at Mid-Century: At Home and Abroad*, ed. John Elderfield, *Studies in Modern Art* no. 4 (New York: The Museum of Modern Art, 1994), 156.

4   *Good Design*, exh. cat. (New York: The Museum of Modern Art, 1953), n.p. [inside front cover].

5   Everything in the exhibition had been carefully selected by a committee of taste arbiters: William Friedman of Minneapolis's Walker Art Center, Hugh Lawson of Chicago's Carson Pirie Scott department store, the Detroit-based modernist architect Eero Saarinen, and Philip C. Johnson, the founder and director of MoMA's Department of Architecture and Design. Kaufmann invited the Danish architect, furniture, and product designer Finn Juhl to design each of 1951's *Good Design* shows at MoMA and the Merchandise Mart.

6   *Good Design: 5th Anniversary*, exh. cat. (New York: The Museum of Modern Art, 1955), n.p.

7   "Fabric Designer," 113.

8   "Fabric Designer," 117.

9   "Negro Named Vice Prexy of N.Y. Ad Firm," *Jet* no. 16 (February 25,1954):25.

10 Joel Robinson's fabric designs for Maix have also been accessioned into the collections of London's Victoria and Albert Museum and the Cleveland Museum of Art.

11 Robinson's works have recently been promoted to the permanent collection, which has also acquired four more designs of his. Other black designers and architects may be represented in the collection but have not openly claimed this racial identification. Architect Ricardo Scofidio, for example, a principal in Diller Scofidio + Renfro, a practice with projects in MoMA's collection since the 1990s and the designers of MoMA's building project of the mid-to-late 2010s, is African American in heritage but does not identify as African American. Who identifies as African American or black can be complex and often reflects the legacy of racism. Also, given the collaborative nature of design work, black designers may have contributed to many projects in the collection, but the institution is geared to recognize the singular genius of a designer or architect who is typically white and male.

12 Michel-Rolph Trouillot, *Silencing the Past: Power and the Production of History* (Boston: Beacon Press, 1995), 53.

13 Kaufmann, quoted in "First Showing of *Good Design* Exhibition in New York," MoMA press release, 1950.

14 See *Modern Architecture: International Exhibition*, exh. cat. (New York: The Museum of Modern Art, 1932).

15 Barr, "Foreword," in ibid., 14.

16 See Paul Overy, "White Walls, White Skins: Cosmopolitanism and Colonialism in Inter-War Modernist Architecture," in Kobena Mercer, ed., *Cosmopolitan Modernisms* (Cambridge, Mass.: The MIT Press, 2005), 59.

17 Johnson, "Historical Note," in *Modern Architecture: International Exhibition*, 18–20.

18 Lewis Mumford, "Housing," in ibid., 179.

19 Carol Aronovici, "Foreword," in Aronovici, ed., *America Can't Have Housing*, exh. cat. (New York: The Museum of Modern Art, 1934), n.p. [p. 7].

20 *Architecture in Government Housing*, exh. cat. (New York: The Museum of Modern Art, n.d. [1936]), n.p.

21 Mumford, "The Sky Line," *The New Yorker*. June 20, 1936, 31.

22 Hilyard Robinson traveled through Europe in the 1930s visiting landmarks of modern architecture, which would greatly influence his future designs of schools and public institutions in Washington, D.C. Paul Revere Williams established a thriving practice in Los Angeles by designing projects ranging from public housing, through private residences for white Hollywood entertainers, to major commercial projects.

23 Arthur Drexler, *Another Chance for Housing: Low-Rise Alternatives*, exh. cat. (New York: The Museum of Modern Art, 1973), 4.

24 John Darnton, "Hampton Houses Opened in Harlem," *New York Times*, July 2,1973.

25 Drexler, letter to Joseph Black, January 27, 1970. MoMA Archives, PI, II.B.759.

26 "Visions of Harlem," n.d. MoMA Archives, PI, II.B.759. The first part of the exhibition was to be a history of Harlem's development from 1660 to 1960. A second section would cover the decade from 1960 to 1970, characterizing the architectural landscape and scenes on the street. Photographs and walking tours were to highlight distinctive buildings and architectural details. A third section was to focus on the future of Harlem as envisioned by architects and planners.

27 Drexler, "Architecture and Urban Renewal," in *The New City: Architecture and Urban Renewal*, exh. cat. (New York: The Museum of Modern Art, 1967), 22.

28 Dianne Harris, *Little White Houses: How the Postwar Home Constructed Race in America* (Minneapolis: University of Minnesota Press, 2013), 35.

29 Ibid.

30 See David A. Hanks, "Laboratories for Modernism: The Barr and Johnson Apartments," in Hanks, ed., *Partners in Design: Alfred H. Barr Jr. and Philip Johnson* (New York: Monacelli Press, 2015), 68.

31 See Hanks, "Introduction," in ibid., 14.

32 See Hanks, "Laboratories for Modernism," 71–79.

33 Johnson's first gay lover was reportedly the black cabaret performer Jimmie Daniels, who lived and performed in Harlem; scholars claim they met for trysts at black actress Edna Thomas's apartment. See Verner D. Mitchell and Cynthia Davis, *Literary Sisters: Dorothy West and Her Circle, a Biography of the Harlem Renaissance* (New Brunswick. N.J., and London: Rutgers University Press, 2012), p. 120, and Mario Gooden, "Jimmy Robert in Conversation with Mario Gooden," *Performs Magazine*, October 25, 2017; available online at http://performa-arts.org/magazine/entry/jimmy-robert-in-conversation-with-mario-gooden (accessed October 2018).

34 Gooden, in "Jimmy Robert in Conversation with Mario Gooden."

35 Le Corbusier, *When the Cathedrals Were White*, 1937, Eng. trans. Francis E. Hyslop, Jr. (New York, Toronto, and London: McGraw-Hill, 1964), p. 87. See also Mabel O. Wilson. "Dancing in the Dark: The Construction of Blackness in Le Corbusier's Radiant City," in Steve Pile and Heidi Nast, eds., *Places through the Body* (London: Routledge. 1998). 133–52.

36 Bernard Rudofsky, "Preface." in *Architecture Without Architects: An Introduction to Non-Pedigreed Architecture*, exh. cat. (New York: The Museum of Modern Art 1964), n.p.

37 See Cheryl J. Fish, "Place, Emotion, and Environmental Justice in Harlem: June Jordan and Buckminster Fuller's 1965 'Architextual' Collaboration." *Discourse* 29, no. 2/3, special issue: Race. *Environment, and Representation* (Spring and Fall 2007):341.

38 June Meyer, "Instant Slum Clearance." *Esquire* 63, no. 4 (April 1965):111.

39 Fish, "Place, Emotion, and Environmental Justice in Harlem," p. 340. The letter is June Jordan. "Letter to R. Buckminster Fuller," 1964, in Jordan, *Civil Wars*, 1981 (reprint ed. New York: Simon and Schuster, 1995). 24.

40 Gordon Kipping, *Ordinary Diagrams* (Los Angeles: Public Access Press and Sci-Arc. 1995). 3.7.

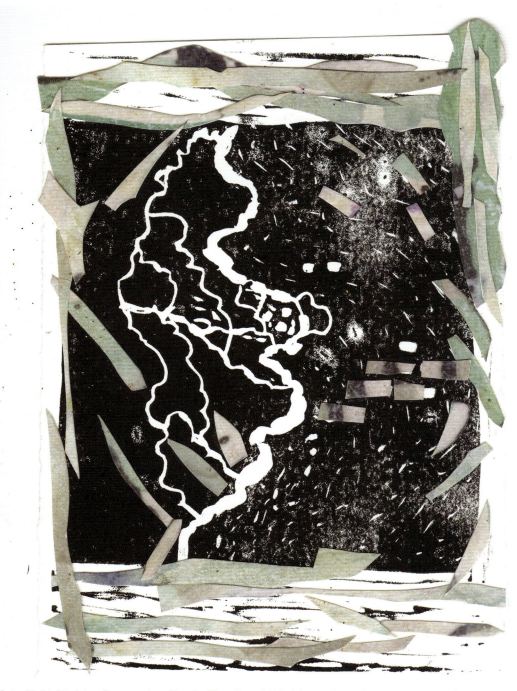

Plate 16 Nell Painter, *Swampy Land by the River Don*, 2018. Ink, acrylic, and collage, 7 × 5 in. Copyright Nell Painter.

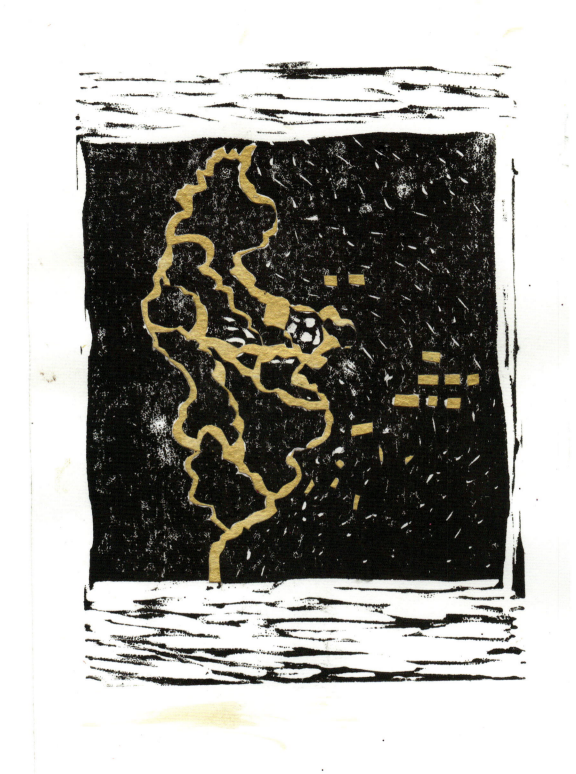

Plate 17 Nell Painter, *Swampy Land by the River Don*, 2018. Ink, acrylic, and collage, 7 × 5 in. Copyright Nell Painter.

18 Nell Painter, *Swampy Land by the River Don*, 2018. Ink, acrylic, and collage, 7 × 5 in. Copyright Nell Painter.

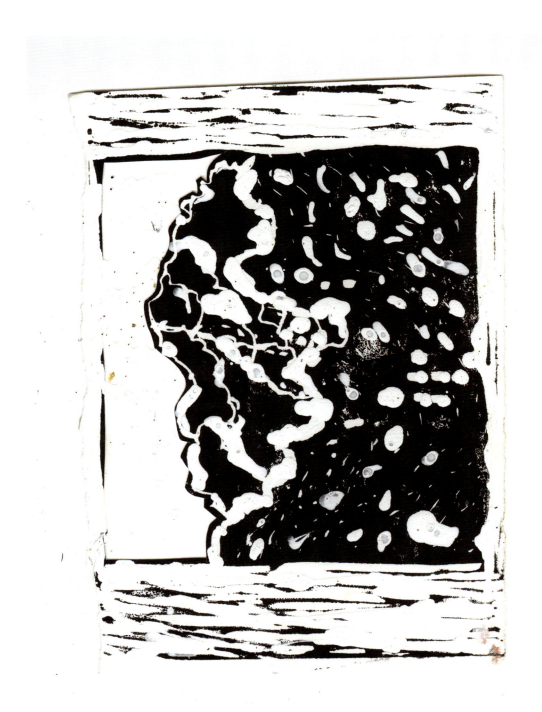

Plate 19 Nell Painter, *Swampy Land by the River Don*, 2018. Ink, acrylic, and collage, 7 × 5 in. Copyright Nell Painter.

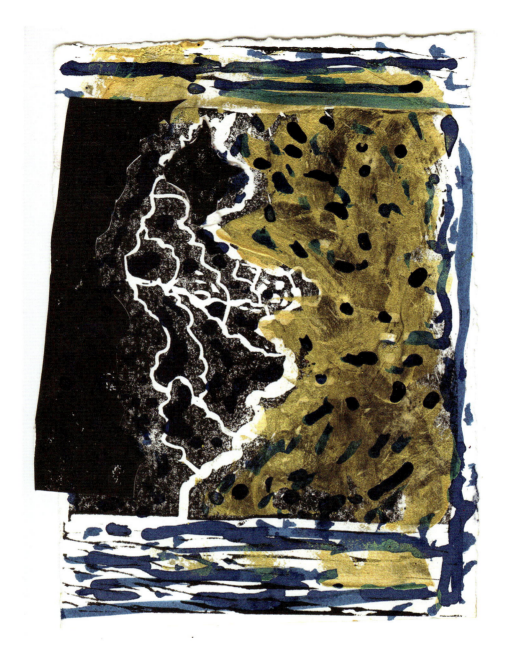

Plate 20 Nell Painter, *Swampy Land by the River Don*, 2018. Ink, acrylic, and collage, 7 × 5 in. Copyright Nell Painter.

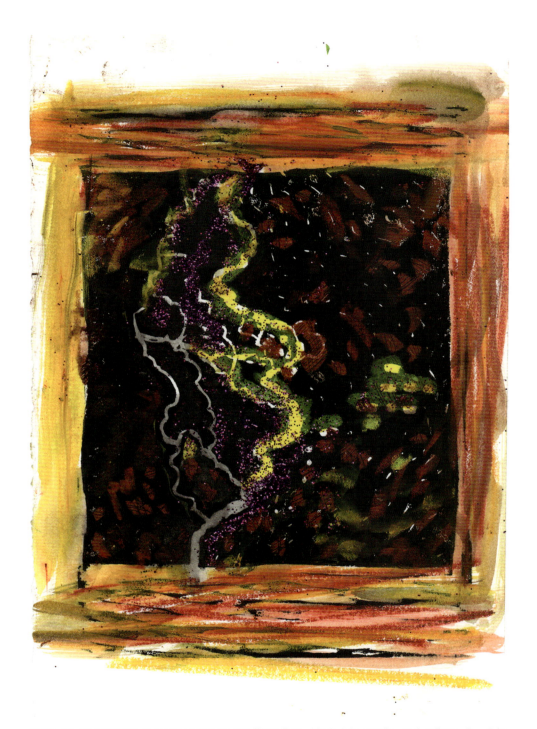

Plate 21 Nell Painter, *Swampy Land by the River Don*, 2018. Ink, acrylic, and collage, 7 × 5 in. Copyright Nell Painter.

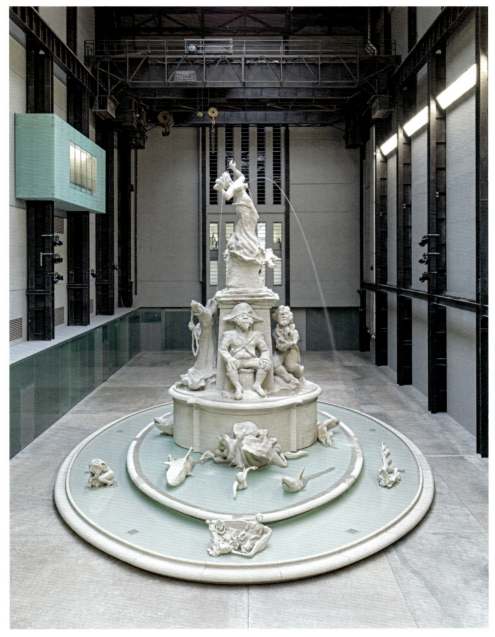

Plate 22 Kara Walker, *Fons Americanus* (2019). Non-toxic acrylic and cement composite, recyclable cork, wood, and metal, Main: 73.5 × 50 × 43 feet; Grotto: 10.2 × 10.5 × 10.8 feet. Installation view: Hyundai Commission: Kara Walker—Fons Americanus, Tate Modern, London, UK, 2019. Photo: Tate (Matt Greenwood). Artwork copyright Kara Walker. Courtesy of Sikkema Jenkins & Co., New York; Sprüth Magers, Berlin.

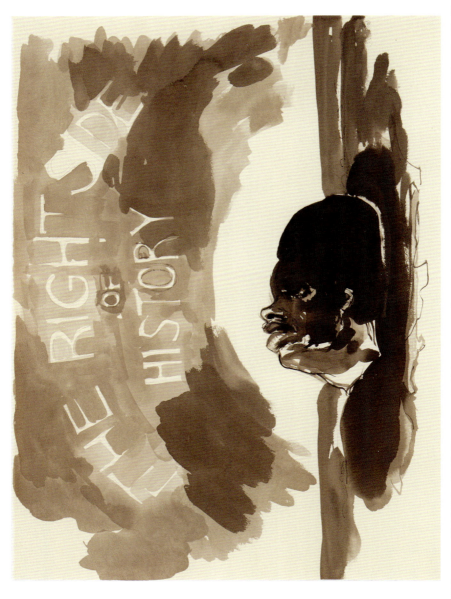

Plate 23 Kara Walker, *The Right Side*, 2018. Graphite, sumi ink, gofun, and gouache on paper, 22 × 30 inches. From the 38-part suite The Gross Clinician Presents: Pater Gravidam. Artwork copyright Kara Walker. Courtesy of Sikkema Jenkins & Co., New York; Sprüth Magers, Berlin.

PART THREE

MAKING HISTORIES, CREATING WORLDS

11
SWAMPY LAND BY THE RIVER DON

Nell Painter

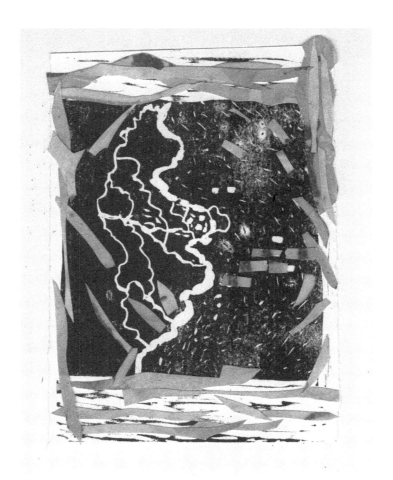

Plate 16 Nell Painter, *Swampy Land by the River Don*, 2018.

August 2018: Time for me to sit down and finally make some art after two months on the road promoting my new book, Old in Art School: A Memoir of Starting Over. *Ah! A return to the simple enjoyment of making images. Let me go back to line and color and the joy of mark-making on paper.*

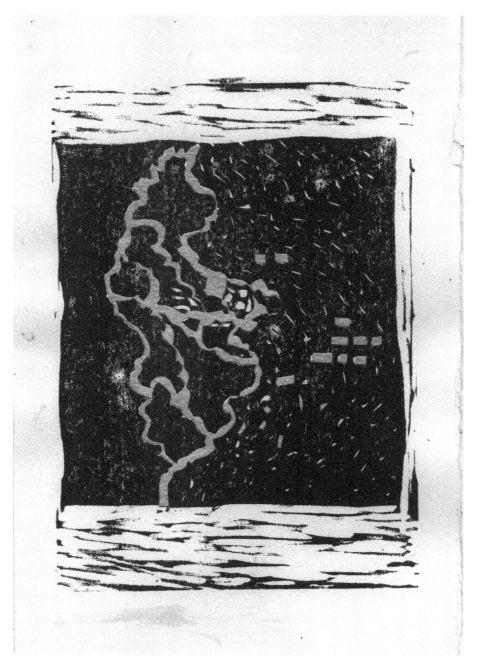

Plate 17 Nell Painter, *Swampy Land by the River Don*, 2018.

Rummaging through my archive of images, I found an old map from my research at the Beinecke Library at Yale in 2012, when I was painting my Odalisque Atlas *series. In 2018 I just liked the way it looked, this eighteenth-century map of a section of the Don River in Russia. It was the appearance of the thing that attracted me. I made a little 7" x 5" lino print and colored about a dozen by hand using ink, acrylic, and collage. I had a very good time.*

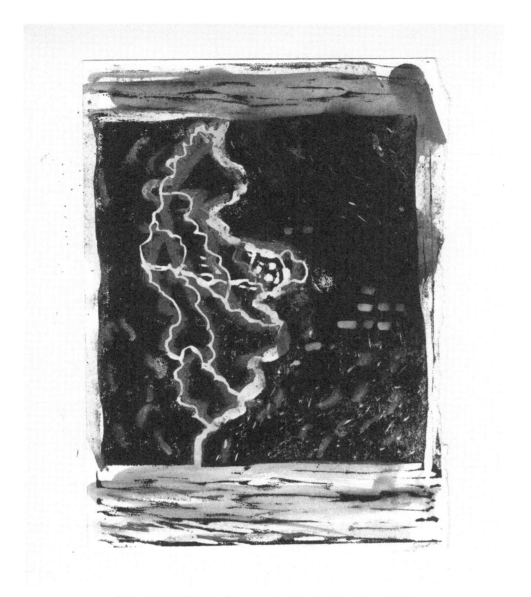

Plate 18 Nell Painter, *Swampy Land by the River Don*, 2018.

After I colored my lino prints, I checked into the history just out of curiosity. I can never get very far from my love of history. And it turns out my prints have quite a back story with relevance beyond the Black Sea.

A centuries old, major commercial route, the Don River in Russia ends at the port of Azov (also called Tana) on the northern part of the Black Sea known as the Sea of Azov. For many centuries before 1900, the principal export through the port of Azov was live merchandise *supplied by Cossacks.*

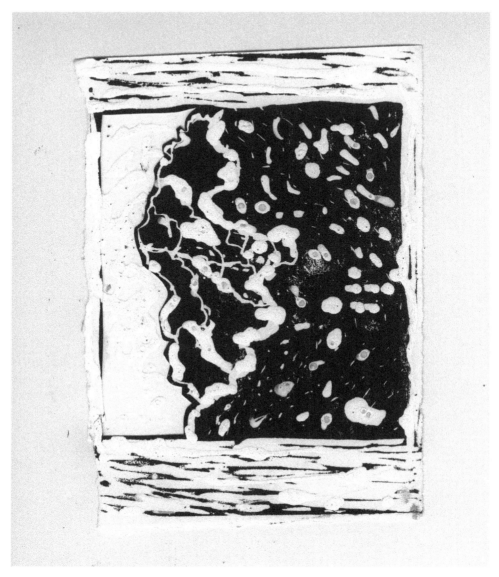

Plate 19 Nell Painter, *Swampy Land by the River Don*, 2018.

Cossacks captured their live merchandise *by* harvesting the steppe.

This was raiding the peasants of the steppe between Poland, Ukraine, and Russia for people to sell to the rich eastern Mediterranean, especially to the Ottomans. But it wasn't just Cossacks in this kind of business.

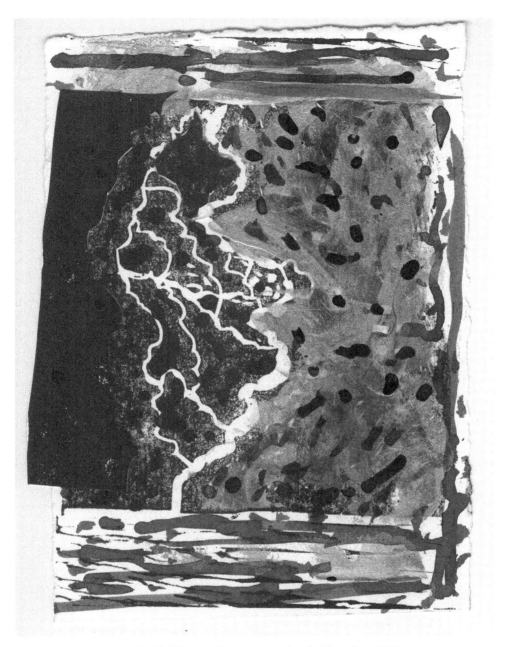

Plate 20 Nell Painter, *Swampy Land by the River Don*, 2018.

If you know anything about the Atlantic slave trade, you'll recognize this business model. Harvesting the steppe *for* live merchandise *was exactly the kind of raiding that delivered millions of hapless African peasants into the Atlantic slave trade, where ports along the west coast of Africa played the part of Azov/Tana with the Atlantic Ocean as the Black Sea.*

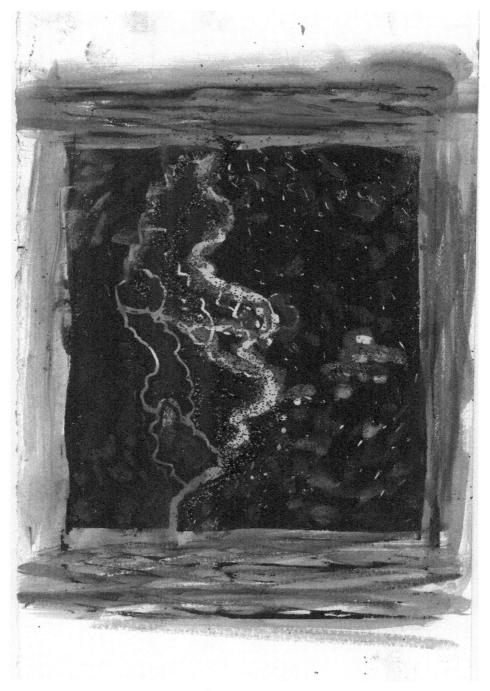

Plate 21 Nell Painter, *Swampy Land by the River Don*, 2018.

Whether in eastern Europe or Africa, whether for transport across the Black Sea or the Atlantic Ocean, slave-raiding warlords have long been "harvesting the steppe" where innocent peasants toiled, rounding them up for sale in a cruel business that knows no color line.

12

ADDRESSING THE WORLD? AESTHETICS OF RESISTANCE, DIFFERENCE, AND RELATIONALITY IN AIMÉ CÉSAIRE'S PLAYS[1]

Mickaella Perina

Introduction

The Tragedy of King Christophe (1963), *A Season in the Congo* (1967) and *A Tempest: Based on Shakespeare's 'The Tempest;' Adaptation for a Black Theater* (1969) constitute an interrelated set of plays that Césaire named a triptych. This body of work was preceded by *And the Dog Were Silent*, a long tragic poem turned into a play (1958) that occupies a pivotal place in Césaire's oeuvre; as he remarks: "In the end, everything I have done since comes from this original source called *And The Dogs Were Silent*, which already contained the seeds of the premiere and total inspiration."[2] While I recognize the importance of the source, it is the triptych that is the focus of this essay. Césaire described it as follows in a 1967 interview: "I conceived of my current work as a triptych. It's basically the tragedy of the Negroes in the modern world. Two components of the triptych already exist; King Christophe is the Antillean one, *A Season in the Congo* is the African one and the third one should normally be of the American Negro, whose awakening is this half-century's event."[3] Unequivocally Césaire's theater is grounded in what he conceived of as the experience of "the Negroes in the modern world" and the characteristics of his expressive practice deserve careful attention.

It might be tempting to read the triptych mainly as a medium for advancing the political project of Negritude[4] or as a manifestation of Césaire's social and political engagement against colonialism and imperialism in general and French colonialism in particular[5]. It is true that Césaire's theater is concerned with emancipation, decolonization, and racialization. However, analyzing these plays through this prism alone would reduce it to one of its constitutive dimensions, namely a response to colonial oppression. But the plays escape simple categorizations, they combine poetry and history to engage with historical anti-colonial struggles in the Americas and in Africa. The protagonists are both actors and witnesses of history.

In what follows I propose to explore Césaire's aesthetic inquiry and to follow his critical engagement with the modern world by way of a discussion of the triptych as aesthetics of resistance, difference, and relationality. For the purposes of clarity, I will discuss each of these properties successively; while these analytical distinctions are helpful, they are fabricated since resistance, difference and relationality are interconnected in the plays. First, centering the analysis on the dialectical relation that the plays maintain with colonialism, I discuss how they can be conceived of as creative contestation, transgression, and resistance. Second, I submit that these plays can also be regarded as aesthetics of difference where difference is understood as what makes it possible to contemplate opposites in a non-dialectical way and what allows for multiplicity, plurality, and contingency. I examine how Césaire deliberately used formal strategies in the texts to make difference palpable, visible, and audible. Last, I discuss the plays' various forms of address and multimodal types of signification directed at various protagonists as well as readers, viewers, or performers and argue that in Césaire's theater, the aesthetic, the political, and the relational are inextricable.

Resistance, Black subjectivity, and the legacy of colonialism

Considered as examples of a practice of resistance, Césaire's plays can fruitfully be associated with the political project of the Negritude movement regarded, in Césaire's view, as irreconcilable with the essentialism and anti-racist racism critics sometimes see in it. The explanation Césaire gave of the project in 1967 is helpful to understand the relation I see between the Negritude project and the resistance I argue is expressed in these plays. Césaire states:

> It must not be forgotten that the word Negritude was, at first, a riposte. The word *nègre* had been thrown at us as an insult, and we picked it up and turned it into a positive concept . . . We thought that it was an injustice to say that Africa had done nothing, that Africa did not count in the evolution of the world, that Africa had not invented anything of value. It was also an immense injustice, and an enormous error, to think that nothing of value could ever come out of Africa. Our faith in Africa did not result in a sort of philosophy of the ghetto, and this cult of, this respect for, the African past did not lead us to a museum philosophy.[6]

Following Césaire's assertion that the word Negritude was first a riposte, a quick and clever reply to an insult, I propose to conceive of Césaire's theater not simply as a riposte but as a carefully crafted counter to the injustices of colonial oppression. In all three plays Césaire put in relation his concerns with colonialism, enslavement, racism, racialization and assimilationism on the one hand and the need for decolonization, the difficulties inherent to post-revolutionary and post-colonial leadership and political identity on the other hand. Consequently, I propose to read these plays as creative contestation and aesthetics of resistance.

The Tragedy of King Christophe is the first of Césaire's three theatrical engagements with decolonization. Christophe, the main character, embodied the historical figure of the enslaved Black, self-proclaimed monarch in the New World. The metamorphosis of the enslaved into a king, the journey from enslavement to conquered freedom at the expense of one's life is presented as a tragedy and Christophe, the revolutionary and charismatic leader, will end up being an oppressor. Throughout the play, deeply rooted in Haitian history, particularly the Haitian revolution, Césaire examined the difficulties of postcolonial leadership and the problem of colonial assimilation following Christophe's journey. *The Tragedy of King Christophe* affirms the subjectivity of Blacks in their struggle for freedom and asserts the difficulties associated with breaking free from the legacy of enslavement and colonialism.

One important theme is the betrayal of revolutionary ideals. Christophe's character is divided between his commitment to freedom (his own and his fellow countrymen's) and the legacy of enslavement, including oppression and exploitation. For instance, the promise Christophe makes to his people in the first act suggests a benevolent leader with a commitment to freedom, and redemption. He says: "With names of glory I will cover your slave names/ with names of pride our names of infamy."[7] But Christophe also wants to build a Citadel to protect his people and their freedom and while the Citadel appears as a symbol of collective political freedom from external powers it is expected to be built by the people. The construction will require the labor and the exploitation of the people which shows the ambiguity of Christophe's circumstances and the complex relations between the colonial past and the future Christophe is attempting to create. As such the image of the Citadel connotes the tensions between freedom and the possibility of re-enslavement since the Citadel has the potential to both protect and re-enslave the people. Progressively Christophe's will to be free and to have his people free appears corrupted by the logic of enslavement and unfreedom. As the play draws to a close, Christophe appears old, fragile, and unstable; in the face of failure and misguided leadership he is betrayed by his own entourage and abandoned by his people.

Throughout the play forms of resistance to colonialism are noticeable by way of references to what was expected to be erased by colonialism. In the second to last scene for example, a "disturbing aura of a vodou ceremony" according to Césaire's stage direction, both Christophe and his wife, Madame Christophe, invoke Africa before Christophe commits suicide. Christophe's last words are an incantation to Africa, "Africa! Help me to return (. . .) And wash me!"[8] Africa seems to have the power to save Christophe who could in return regain the qualities he had before he betrayed the revolutionary ideals. The play illustrates the tragedy associated with the exercise of power in a post-colonial state that recently claimed independence from a colonial empire. In the end, Christophe did not fulfill his promise to ensure freedom from enslavement for all; instead, he reinstated subjugation and imposed tyranny and autocracy. While Christophe's character is firmly grounded in Haitian history, it transcends the frame of Haiti to embody the antinomies of freedom involved in processes of decolonization and independence from colonial powers.

A Season in the Congo, the second play of the triptych*,* provides an account of the rise, fall, and assassination of Congolese political leader Patrice Lumumba. As Césaire argues his theater "is not an individual or individualistic theater, it's an epic theater because it is always the fate of a collectivity that is at stake."[9] The play starts with the Congo's declaration of independence from Belgian colonial rule, continues with its rise to independence as Zaire under the leadership of Lumumba, and ends with its neocolonial experience under the ambitious but corrupt Mokutu, a character that resemble Mobutu Sésé Seko, the former president of Zaire. Lumumba is portrayed as a pure, archetypal tragic figure and his faultlessness emphasizes his tragedy.

As the play depicts Lumumba's rise to power, it unveils the colonial and neocolonial forces at play in the Congo. Like *The Tragedy of King Christophe* this play describes a crisis in post-revolutionary leadership and political identity through the historical failure of the Congolese people to achieve freedom and unity under the leadership of Lumumba. Contrary to Christophe however, Lumumba is not destroyed by his own flaws but by a combination of factors including the ambitious Mokutu, Belgian imperialists, and French and American forces. The play rigorously follows the historical events of the early decolonization period in the Congo, most of the characters are historical figures whose identities and names are maintained or slightly transformed. The play engages with issues of violence, solidarity, and unity to narrate the difficulties of Lumumba's leadership and Césaire uses poetic forms to emphasize the control colonial forces continue to exercise over the fate of the newly independent state. Three key moments in Lumumba's political career are recounted in three acts: his conquest of power, the crisis in leadership, and his assassination.

The polarization between the two contrasting characters Lumumba and Mokutu illustrates the affirmation of Black subjectivity and the difficulty to escape the legacy of colonialism. Césaire's Lumumba appears as a messiah who seeks the unity of the people of the Congo and of Africa. He is presented as a pan-Africanist who is characterized by his humanity – his love for his wife, his family and his people are described as major motivations for his actions. Mokutu on the other hand, intends to restore order to the Congo and does not feel any responsibility for the rest of Africa.

The play appears consistent with the political project of the negritude movement as both a refusal of colonialism—including in its post-colonial, post-revolutionary forms— and an effort to promote decolonization. At the beginning of the play (Act 1, Scene 4) readers/viewers are introduced to bankers outraged to discover that the Belgian government had agreed to fix the independence of the Congo to June 30th, 1960, at Lumumba's request; an agreement they interpret as the liquidation of their empire. The contrasting picture portrayed through this exchange shows the persistence of the old colonial order while the independence is being celebrated; Césaire expresses both the promise of post-colonial nationhood and the legacy of colonialism and how it may hinder true decolonization. Césaire also exposes the false rhetoric of the "civilizing mission" Belgian colonizers used to justify the colonization of the Congo. At the beginning of the play the departing president Kala-Lubu reminds the crowd that King Leopold came to the Congo in the name of civilization and that the new nation shall remain faithful to civilization.[10] As the play progresses, Césaire expands his critique of colonization and colonizers introducing at the end of the first Act both the seemingly neutral forces of the United Nations and the U.S., embodied in the characters of Dag Hammarskjöld, and the Great Western Ambassador. In his speech, Dag Hammarskjöld recognizes that the stakes are high identifying the Congo as a testing ground *par excellence* for international public service. The Great Western Ambassador acknowledges the bad reputation of his country but justifies its authority by the belief that "When people do not behave like decent people, it is necessary that someone makes them decent. It is to us that providence has given that task."[11] Césaire underscores the role of the U.S. in the tragedy of the Congo along with the self-proclaimed neutrality and instructions of the United Nations; post-colonialism is portrayed as an experience that is not between a single colonizing power and a colonized people or territory but includes other forces and implies global responsibility. At the end of the play, readers/viewers are reminded that there will be other seasons in the Congo; Lumumba is dead, but he will continue to live. The play ends with the crowd shouting: "Glory to Lumumba! / Immortal glory to Lumumba! / Down with neo-colonialism! / Long live *dipenda*[12]! / *Uhuru*[13] Lumumba / *Uhuru*!/"[14]

The last component of the triptych, *A Tempest*, is designed to illustrate the relations between white colonizers and Black enslaved persons in the colonized territories of the Americas. In this third theatrical exploration of colonialism, Césaire turned to Shakespeare and explicitly identifies his play as an adaptation of Shakespeare's *The Tempest,* an adaptation for Black Theater, or *théâtre nègre* to be more exact. While translating *nègre* into "Black" might obscure the association with the Negritude movement, this translation also points to something important that could have been obstructed by a literal translation or by the conservation of the French word—namely the influence (albeit indirect) of the Harlem Renaissance (along with French Literature and Africa) on Césaire's theater. In a 1969 interview with François Beloux, Césaire articulated this influence:

> Since I had been mulling over a play about the United-States, inevitably reference points became American . . . I wrote the play in the following way: on the one hand Prospero the conqueror; on the other hand, Caliban and Ariel . . . considering Prospero's domination there are several possible reactions: there is the violent attitude and the non-violent one. There is Martin Luther King and Malcom X and the Black Panthers. To simplify, Caliban would be the violent, Ariel would be the non-violent tendency. But both, through different methods, work for liberation.[15]

Césaire's characters here are the same as in Shakespeare's play with two significant alterations—Ariel and Caliban described by Césaire respectively as an enslaved mulatto and an enslaved black—and one addition, Eshu, a black devil-God. Césaire revised, racialized, and politicized the relationships Shakespeare created among Prospero, Ariel, and Caliban. As a mulatto, Ariel appears as an ambivalent intermediary between whites and Blacks and between colonizer and colonized. The relationship between Prospero and Caliban seems comparable to the colonizer/colonized relationship defined by the idea of a civilizing mission portrayed in *A Season in the Congo*. Prospero for instance congratulates himself for having given Caliban language while at the same time characterizing him as an ape. Prospero exhibits racism, he questions Caliban's humanity and regards his language as barbaric. But while Prospero claims to have taught Caliban language and therefore to have civilized him, Caliban who understands the instrumentalization of this "gift of language" responds: "You didn't teach me a thing. Except to jabber in your own language so that I could understand your orders." Moreover, Caliban expresses himself both in Swahili and in French asserting that he was able to learn and understand languages before his encounter with Prospero and points to the African culture that informs his views and experiences. No matter what Prospero professes, Caliban is aware and proud of his rich cultural heritage. Various levels of racial politics are made visible through interactions between Caliban and other characters throughout the play.

The last scene is particularly important in representing the relation between Blacks and White in the Americas, relation that seemed both necessary and enduring to Césaire at the time. At this point, the conflict between Caliban and Prospero appears inextricable. Prospero cannot leave the island, his civilizing mission or Caliban. He will not return to Naples. Unequivocally Caliban condemns colonialism and the pretended civilizing mission while underscoring the lasting relationship between colonizer and colonized:

> I am sure you won't leave
> You make me laugh with your 'mission'!
> Your 'vocation'!
> Your vocation is to hassle me.
> And that's why you'll stay,
> Just like those guys who founded the colonies
> And who now can't live anywhere else.
> You are just an old addict, that's what you are![16]

At the end of the last scene, the island is presented as overrun by nature. Caliban's song "FREEDOM HI-DAY, FREEDOM HI-DAY!"[17] can be heard but he is not seen. There is no clear indication of what will happen next, but there is no doubt Caliban is a threat to the colonial order Prospero intents to maintain.

It seems fair to say that Césaire's theater resists and counters the fallacious rhetoric of the civilizing mission and its various justifications by promoting Black heroes; his theater is designed to raise consciousness and envisions a future without enslavement, colonization, or alienation. However, in all three plays the heroes are men. Did Césaire overlook colonized revolutionary women? Addressing this question satisfactorily would require a longer analysis that what I can offer in the context of this inquiry, but perhaps one can begin to answer this question by noticing that main female characters do take part in post-revolutionary nation-building in both *The Tragedy of King Christophe* and *A Season in The Congo* although their roles appear predicated upon the role of the male revolutionary heroes. Indeed, both Madame Christophe and Pauline Lumumba, the heroes' wives, are important characters who speaks truth to their husbands and show an acute understanding of the political and social orders and an aptitude for counseling their husbands; but they are not heroes per se. It might also be worth noticing that *A Tempest* presents a different structure where the only female character is Miranda, Prospero's daughter. There is no female equivalent of Caliban or Ariel. However, nature, present at the beginning and at the end of the play, can be interpreted as a metaphorical feminine figure; an evocation that can be read as both revolutionary and prophetic[18].

Aesthetic of Difference and Revolutionary Poetry

I now turn to an analysis and discussion of these plays as aesthetics of difference; a focus on difference enables the examination of opposites in a non-symmetrical and non-dialectical way. Articulated as non-identity or dissimilarity, difference acknowledges multiplicity, plurality, and contingency and is not reducible to radical or essential otherness. Furthermore, while difference implies possible transformations, it does not necessarily entail rejection or resignation. To read Césaire's theater as aesthetics of difference is to take seriously his view that European colonialism necessarily created an experience for the colonized that was different from that of colonizers or of Africans before the colonial encounter and that this experience has been the site of a recognizably different culture and worldview. In that sense Césaire's triptych is an invitation to see differently and to interrogate one's perceptions and understandings; it constitutes a critical intervention aiming at subverting racist and colonial domination. One might ask whether the promise of such revolutionary intervention can really be fulfilled. The desire of an encounter with otherness can be manipulated and is not necessarily incompatible with the preservation of hegemonic positioning and domination. Indeed, as bell hooks argues in her critique of successful forms of commodification of Otherness, "To make one's self vulnerable to the seduction of difference, to seek an encounter with the Other, does not require that one relinquish forever one's mainstream positionality."[19] Such question is important and related to my inquiry but it is not its focus. I suspect that when difference is accompanied by resistance and relationality it might be more difficult to produce otherness as strict commodification but that is not my argument here. By centering the essay on forms, I intend to demonstrate that in Césaire's theater resistance, difference and relationality are combined. Césaire's conception of difference is grounded in his understanding of the relationship between universal and particulars. In his view the universal is rich of all particulars.

First, difference is manifested in these plays through Césaire's revolutionary poetry. His theater puts lyric and dramatic poetry at the service of decolonial struggle. It combines prose, poetry, and drama, to call for revolution and social change in a post-colonial world he perceives as fallacious. At the heart of Césaire's expressive practice is his conception of poetic knowledge. A detailed description of what counts as "poetic knowledge" can be found in "Poetry and Knowledge," an essay he first presented at the International Congress of Philosophy in Haiti in September 1944. There, Césaire contrasts poetic images with rational knowledge and criticizes abstract instrumental reason and scientific truth as impoverished knowledge although he does not reject reason per se. While scientific knowledge "enumerates, measures, classifies and kills," "poetic knowledge" and "poetic truth" are different ways of knowing. It is with poetic knowledge that "we see resolved . . . two of the most anguishing antinomies that exist: the antinomy of one and other, the antinomy of Self and World." The ambition of poetry is the resolution of these antinomies, the point where the antinomies cease to be perceived contradictorily. "What presides over the poem is not the most lucid intelligence, or the most acute sensibility, but an entire experience"[20] and the poet reconnects humanity with the universe by consenting and attesting to a life that transcends her. "So, pregnant with the world the poet speaks."[21] Poetic knowledge includes, but is not limited to, "poetic violence," "poetic aggressivity," and "poetic instability because the idea of irritable poet transferred to poetry itself."[22] There are numerous examples of poetic violence and poetic aggressivity in the triptych where language is on occasion a vehicle for threat and use of violence, an instrument of performative power, and a conduit for incantation and rituals. For instance, in a passage of *A tempest* discussed in more details in the next section, when Caliban engages in a process of emancipation from the colonizer's objectification, he launches an attack on Prospero's language, reclaims his "Uhuru" speech, and rejects the name Prospero gave him claiming "Call me X. Like a man without a name." Further poetic knowledge provides "the most authentic vision of the world."[23] This visionary component of poetic knowledge, present in all three plays, makes visible how the visionary quality of revolutionary heroes is related to the qualities of a poet and how past, present, and future are related in Black struggles for freedom. When asked about how he viewed the place of the poet in politics in a 1967 interview Césaire offered his conception of the revolutionary:

> For me the true revolutionary can only be a visionary. I am of those who integrate utopia and revolution, and I can't fall into the schema that consists in saying: there are revolutionary and there are utopians . . . Obviously my conception of the revolutionary is always that of someone who is ahead; there is therefore a prophetism that is the first revolutionary step . . . And Lumumba is a revolutionary insofar as he is a visionary. Because, in reality, what does he have before his eyes? A miserable country . . . The grandeur of Lumumba was to sweep aside all of these realities and to see an extraordinary Congo that is still only in his mind, but which will become a reality tomorrow. And Lumumba is great, through this, because there is always a beyond [au-delà] for him. Those are qualities of a poet, of imagination.[24]

The emphasis on poetic knowledge and on imagination points to a capacity to go beyond the actual to envision a future that does not yet exist while being aware of the past and its legacy. In that sense, Césaire's revolutionary poetry is an invitation for colonized and post-colonized subjects to reflect upon what it means to be in charge of one's destiny and conceive of forms of solidarity based on the experience of colonialism. Additionally, Césaire's theater is intentionally calling upon poets and other "men of culture" to fulfill what he sees as their duty. In his words, "Our duty as men of culture, our double duty is there: to speed decolonization, and in the present to prepare the good decolonization, a decolonization without sequels. . . . To speed decolonization means that we must by all means speed the maturation of popular awareness, otherwise they will never be a decolonization . . ."[25] Césaire's theater is designed to raise awareness and to prepare for a good and true decolonization; it aims at transforming the people. In that sense, Césaire's theater is both a chronicle of the history of decolonization struggles and a means to raise consciousness to create the right type of decolonization.

Césaire does not aim at transforming only "his people," he also aims at transforming all potential readers, performers, and spectators. In *The Tragedy of King Christophe*, he does not simply describe Haiti but rather uses visual and sonic images to evoke Haiti. As a result, the audience can become acquainted with Haiti, in its difference. Likewise, through various images the play makes it possible for the audience to sense King Christophe, to experience him in his Haitian culture, in his difference. This is possible because, for Césaire, images convey more than variations of the law of non-contradiction or propositions that are mutually exclusive; in his words: "In the image every object of thought is not necessarily A or not-A. The image maintains the possibility of the happy medium."[26] Imaginative perceptions allow discoveries that would not be possible otherwise. To make those "discoveries" possible for audiences, Césaire deliberately used formal strategies in the text and make difference palpable, visible, or audible. The words are not simply used as tools of communication rather they are used to create sensations; they are connected both semantically and phonetically. In the plays words often present both manifest and latent meanings and combine the mundane, the political, the religious and the supernatural as in the vodou ceremony of the second to last scene of *The Tragedy of King Christophe*. The combination of grammatical, linguistic, and phonetic arrangements along with the vodou structure of the play make the experience of difference possible. Visual arrangements of words matter to Césaire, they are additional ways to convey difference and make it accessible through the text as much as through performances. I have kept the forms of these arrangements when quoting from the texts.

Césaire's unique use of the French language in his entire corpus, but perhaps specifically in his theater, is in my view a second reason to read his plays as aesthetics of difference. In a 1978 interview he described his relationship with the French language as follows: "I am not a prisoner of the French language! . . . I always wanted to inflect French . . . I am re-creating a language that is not French. Whether or not French people recognize themselves in it is their problem."[27] I take Césaire's own understanding of this relationship to be a sufficient reason to look for evidence of "re-creations" of such language in the texts. Césaire's revolutionary poetry reframes the French language and by doing so create a different language; a language that is no longer French and yet is not so radically different that it cannot be recognized as French. I suspect that for the purist such reframing would equate creating something radically and completely different, an attitude Césaire alluded to when he said, "I am re-creating a language that is not French" but also questioned by stating that French people might or might not recognize themselves in it. The poetry at play in his theater uses various rhythms, repetitions, and accelerations; it includes pauses to call upon images of African drums, dances and vodou. Following Sartre, in *Black Orpheus*, one might assert that Césaire reconfigured the French language, syntactically, lexically, and rhythmically to fit his revolutionary project and the word and images perpetually translate the same obsession."[28] But as I have been discussing throughout this essay, fitting the revolutionary project of Negritude is only part of the story.

Last, difference is asserted through various metaphorical references to animals and nature. For instance, at the end of *A Season in the Congo*, when M'siri, Lumumba's soon to be murderer, claims that Lumumba does not see his imminent death or sees it but does not feel it, Lumumba responds, "I die my life, and that's enough for me."[29] The image of one dying one's own life certainly suggests a reframing of French language but perhaps also some extraordinary power on the part of Lumumba. M'siri does not seem surprised by Lumumba's assertion and asks Lumumba what he sees. Lumumba explains:

I will be the field; I will be pasture
I will be with the fisher Wagenia
I will be with the shepherd of the Kivu
I will be on the mount, I will be in the ravine.[30]

Arguably, these successive transformations may not appear as legitimate transfiguration to all audiences; the change from human to nature is likely to be regarded as a form of regress by those attached to the superiority of the human. Here again difference is manifested, a difference that suggests a very specific world view. Noticing that characters and continents are often associated with animals in *A Season in the Congo*, Lilian Pestre de Almeida, for instance, argues that for Césaire the animal is always superior to man and the vegetable superior to the animal.[31]

Relationality, Address, Solidarity

As a man of culture with a responsibility to speed the process of decolonization and prepare the right kind of decolonization, Césaire integrated both African and Caribbean heritages that lived under the appearance of French-ness into his theater to invite readers, viewers, or performers to engage into the aesthetic and political endeavor of meaning making. He aimed at providing a particular understanding of colonialism and post-colonialism while persuading readers/viewers of the possibility of critique, social change, and freedom. This work is fundamentally relational; in Césaire's theater the reader/viewer is conceived of as a site of agency and not simply as a passive consumer. Césaire's theater is inspired by human relations and their colonial context and is constituted by relations between colonizer and colonized, post-colonial nations and former colonial powers, planters and enslaved persons, whites, mulattos, and Blacks and between words and imaginaries. His theater provides audiences with a possible access to the power to make social change through aesthetic expressions. I submit that the various forms of formal address in Césaire's theater indicate that it can be understood as relational aesthetics. In *The Cultural Promise of Aesthetics*, Monique Roelofs describes address as the "muscles and joints of aesthetics relationality"[32]; she explains that various modes of address are embedded within aesthetics objects and constitute promises and threats in which audiences are invited to participate thereby changing the aesthetic object and/or being changed by it. It is against that theoretical background that I discuss Césaire's theater as relational aesthetics.

The analysis of Césaire's theater must take the concern for performance seriously; according to its author, this theater was meant to be performed more than read. Initially Césaire directed his theater primarily to a specific group of readers, namely the masses in post-colonial states; he saw theater as better suited than poetry strictly defined to present and pursue social change. In a 1970 interview he observed:

I came to do theater because theater is a means to clarify [. . .] everything that is said in an obscure way, obscure for others in any case, not for me, obscure in my poems

[. . .]. It seems to me that it is the best way to make people aware, especially people who do not read [. . .]. Thanks to theater there is a sort of multiplication of poetic force, and, for me, it is essential.[33]

Césaire directly addressed his theater to the people who do not read his poetry; by doing so he acknowledged both existing processes and patterns of social hierarchy, and the legacy of the colonial order that generated them, while envisioning their transformation. He also addressed, indirectly, the post-colonial elite, the French state (former colonial power), the French elite, the French masses, international organizations, and the world at large.

A focus on performance highlights dimensions of the written work that might not be accounted for otherwise. In performance, there is, in the words of Erika Fischer-Lichte, "co-presence of actors and spectators,"[34] so spectating becomes an active participation in the process of meaning making. There is no unidirectional transfer of meaning from one sender such as the author to receivers but rather a feedback loop from performers to audience and back modifying the relationships between subject and object, spectator and performer, and signifier and signified. Césaire's triptych is written to include various forms of address, directed at different addressees, in which readers, viewers and performers are invited to participate and become interlocutors. Césaire intentionally included these forms of address in his theater to make it possible for readers, viewers, or performers to alter and be altered by the plays. What do I mean by address? For now, the standard definition provided by Monique Roelofs in her 2016 essay should suffice: "Address concerns the modes of signification that we direct at people, things, and places, and that they direct at us. (. . .) address ties elements of aesthetic form to aspects of the anticipated reception and contextual grounding of such form."[35] Address is a vehicle that channels relations between creators of objects and intended recipients but since recipients are not passive, they address creators back thereby participating in existing relations with the possibility of reframing these relations and the social order within which they are situated. I now turn to a discussion of some examples of verbal address to provide a sense of the wide range of verbal forms of addresses in these plays.

In *A Tempest* Césaire presents Caliban as an enslaved black whose resistant agency is blatant in his exchanges with Prospero. I already mentioned Caliban's refuting the claim that Prospero taught him language in the first section of this essay. More generally, in all the exchanges between Caliban and Prospero, Caliban uses the French familiar second-person pronoun *tu* suggesting that he regards Prospero as an equal while Ariel, the enslaved mulatto, on the other hand, uses the more formal *vous* suggesting that he recognizes a hierarchical distance between him and the colonizer. What does this mean? Does the different form of verbal address here highlight Ariel's intermediary and transitional status between colonized and colonizer, between Blacks and whites? To read this play is to join in the activity of meaning making; the reader is addressed by Césaire and is invited to address the play and the characters in return.

Address carries aesthetic and political meaning and the inherently conflictual relation between Caliban and Prospero is a good example of how Césaire portrays this relationship. The conflict which occurs in the second scene of the first act is particularly telling. It starts with Caliban asserting that he does not want to be called Caliban any longer; he considers this name an insult. Prospero, sarcastic, asks Caliban to suggest a different name and Caliban proclaims a radical identity: "Call me X. Like a man without a name. Or, to be more precise, a man whose name has been stolen. You talk about history . . . well, that's history and everyone knows it. Every time you summon me it reminds me of a basic fact, the fact that you've stolen everything from me, even my identity! Uhuru!"[36] So on one level Prospero has stolen everything even Caliban's identity but on another level Caliban's original language has not been lost which suggests that his identity has not been completely lost. Additionally, Caliban has an intimate relation with the forces of nature, and he can invoke Shango, the thunder god, and benefit from his destructive powers. And it is Caliban who teaches Prospero about the natural world of the island; a knowledge that is crucial for matters of survival. In these passages we see different positions of enunciations and verbal forms of address that call for meaning making.

The juxtaposition of Swahili and French languages is in my view another form of verbal address. The juxtaposition of two languages, one European the other African, connotes a plurilingual rationality and addresses the issue of the hegemony of the language of the colonizer in colonized countries and territories. French colonialism was a model of assimilationism that did not allow for plurilingualism and did not regard indigenous languages as proper language. Interestingly, Césaire places Swahili words next to French words without providing a translation or attempting to make a bilingual address. This juxtaposition, I would argue, is a very specific type of verbal encounter. There is no attempt to provide a verbal equivalent with a translation, but the very absence of verbal equivalent is an address, a form of signification directed both at Prospero and audiences. The verbal encounter is related to a social and political encounter, namely the colonial encounter. As Monique Roelofs showed, "The interactions between words in dual languages summon extended lexical traditions, which are simultaneously social and political histories."[37] By shouting Uhuru Caliban reclaims his native language, a language Prospero openly dislikes, and claims a radical identity. Moreover, the interplays between words and languages ("X", name, history, identity, Uhuru, French/English, Swahili) calls on various political histories (histories of Colonialism and enslavement in the Americas and the US along with recent decolonial struggles in Africa). In *The Tragedy of King Christophe*, Césaire juxtaposed French words and expressions with creole words and expressions, vodou incantations and hymns, apparitions of vodou gods (male or female lwa), along with Latin liturgy and Christian practices, providing a wide range of verbal forms of address that work jointly. These words are deeply embedded in the social and political realities of Haiti (both the Haiti of historical king Christophe and the Haiti of the early 1960's). Two other forms of verbal address that have already been discussed in the section on difference deserve consideration here. The first one is Césaire's alterations of the French language, in my view a creative move intended to direct form of significations to the reader and accounting for the relevant political and social histories; the second is the visual forms of address found all throughout the texts.

As stated earlier, Césaire alters the French language to recreate a language that, he said, is not French. However, the recreated language acquires meaning in relation to the French language. It is a new language that is made of the old one and within which the old one continues to exist, albeit transformed. These transformations bring about possibilities that would have otherwise remained unknown providing Césaire with a large repertoire of verbal forms of address. Césaire's language is a modification of French designed to convey his revolutionary poetry and, on his own admission, to make it accessible to an audience for whom his poetry would remain obscure. This creative move positions the reader/viewer in a fecund relation with the text/performance where meaning is constructed and where unanticipated meaning can be created. It should also be noted that the very nature of this language makes it susceptible to the accusation of violating norms of address. Precisely because it is French and not French at the same time Césaire re-created language can be regarded either as not French enough or too French and therefore a violation.

All three plays include visual forms of address; various passages take distinct forms and words are ordered in particular ways. We find, for instance, poems and songs in rhymes and prose centered on pages; the rhythm in Césaire's poetry is at time instrumental, as in the evocation of vodou practices in *The Tragedy of King Christophe*. His use of rhythm, repetitions, pauses, and stops constitute forms of address; there is performance in Césaire's writing. A good example of this form is Lumumba's speech in *A Season in the Congo* (Act 3, scene 2):

> My only arms are my words, I speak and I
> awaken, I am not a redresser of wrongs, nor a miracle
> worker, I am a redresser of life, I speak and I give back
> Africa to herself! I speak and I give Africa to the
> world! I speak and, attacking the very base of oppress-
> sion and servitude, I make fraternity possible for the
> first time![38]

Here content and form address each other. Of special note in this passage are the emphasis on relationality, the power of words, and the activity of speaking and the relation between the first possibility of "fraternity" and the attack on oppression and servitude through speech and fraternity. This passage exemplifies the complex interplays of forms of addresses and the multilevel intentionalism developed by Césaire in his theater. Lumumba expresses the engagement of both the militant and the poet. He speaks not of righting wrongs but of redressing life and giving Africa back to herself; and his words constitute his only force. Furthermore, it seems as if Lumumba's speech is directed at the reader as much as it is to the crowd in the play; following the late Ivorian poet and playwright, Bernard Zadi-Zaourou[39], one might say that the reader becomes a "second narrator." Is Césaire here asserting that decolonization is necessary? Is he asserting that violence and solidarity are also necessary? If so, this passage can also be read as exemplifying the kind of violent poetry Césaire discusses in *Poetry and Knowledge*. Words appear to be capable of violent resistance and are Lumumba's only weapons. Lumumba's words have the power to awaken his people and to make fraternity possible by attacking the foundation of oppression and servitude. Lumumba's relationship with language reflects violence as a means to achieve freedom from oppression. His speech is a tool of liberation and resistance.

Another aspect of Césaire's theater that is manifested through historical and future-oriented forms of address participating in the creation of meaning is the relation to time. Césaire uses his political imaginary combined with his revolutionary poetic to design modes of address that reconfigure the assumed order of processes of colonization and decolonization and by doing so he transforms or adjusts the meaning of decolonization. Decolonization cannot only be what comes after the abolition of colonization in a linear conception of history but must be a new order with renewed relations between people, objects and places, and between past, present and future. Both King Christophe and Lumumba are post-colonial heroes in post-colonial territories and in both cases Césaire explored corruption whether it is determined by Christophe's own flaws or by the surrounding of Lumumba. Caliban on the other hand is in a metaphorical space. In all three plays while there is a downfall of the main character there also are seeds for a future beyond the downfall. At the end of *The Tragedy of King Christophe*, Christophe is dead, but he still stands. Mokutu's speech at the end of *A Season in The Congo* is a beautiful example of a multidirectional address that engages present, past, and future:

"The force to pursue my task, Patrice, it is to you that I
Ask for it, martyr, athlete, hero.
Sensation. Mokutu collects himself for a moment.
People of the Congo,
I wish that from now on the most beautiful
Of our boulevards
Proudly bear his name;
That the place where he was slaughtered become,
for the nation, a sanctuary;
And that a statue erected at the entry of what was
formerly Leopoldville
signify to the universe
That the piety of a people will never finish with
The reparation of that which was our crime
To all of us!
People of the Congo, may today's date be for the
Congo
The point of departure for a new season![40]"

Here, Mokutu addresses both Lumumba, using his first name Patrice to convey intimacy, and the people of the Congo. The passage is also an intervention in the field of address where past, present, and future, dead and living, and space and time are put in relation with one another by Césaire. Prima facie it might seem obvious that Lumumba represents the past, Mokutu the present and the new season the future but, upon examination, complex relationships and processes of meaning making are revealed. Lumumba is a living dead and Mokutu seems to find legitimacy in him. The making of a sanctuary, the renaming of boulevards and the erection of the statue relate both to a wishful future and to the past. The city is referred to as "formerly Leopoldville," the capital of the former

Belgian colony of Congo, but not as Kinshasa the name it took in 1966 the same year *The Season in the Congo* was published. And, in Mokutu's words, the statue to be erected will be a form of signification not to the Congo, not to Africa but to the universe.

Conclusion

Césaire's large body of work has often been associated with the Negritude movement and with resistance to colonialism and, seen through that prism, his theater is often understood as a dramatic declaration on the dangers of the wrong kind of decolonization that presents itself as post-colonialism. I do not dispute that the triptych describes the difficulty of attaining liberation from the legacy of colonialism or that it interacts with socio-political historical realities in profound ways, however I hope to have shown that Césaire's triptych is also fundamentally a project of revolutionary poetry and theater, of cultural and aesthetic inter-relationship. On this account the triptych transcends Negritude and resistance to colonialism conceived of as exclusive categories and appears as aesthetics of resistance, difference, and relationality through a web of verbal forms of address designed to engage readers, viewers and performers in meaning making about post-colonialism, Black subjectivity, struggles for freedom and the possibility of solidarity.

Notes

1   An earlier version of this essay was presented at the 2017 Questioning Aesthetics Symposium on Black Aesthetics at Hampshire College. I thank the organizers and the audience.

2   Aimé Césaire, "Pour un théâtre d'inspiration Africaine", entretien avec Claude Stevens, in *La Vie Africaine*, no. 59 (juin 1965), 40–41. [My translation.]

3   Nicole Zand, "Entretien avec Aimé Césaire," *Le Monde*, N,7071 (Oct. 1967), 13. [My Translation.]

4   Cultural and ideological movement born in Paris in the 1930s, in particular in *Le Salon de Clamart* opened by the Nardal Sisters in 1929, and developed by Aimé Césaire, Léopold Sédar Senghor, and Léon-Gontran Damas in reaction to French colonialism and legacy.

5   Regarding the interpretation of Césaire's theater as a trilogy on decolonization and an expression of the political project of Negritude, see Robert Eric Livingston, "Decolonizing the Theater: Césaire, Serreau and the Drama of Negritude," in *Imperialism and Theater*, ed. J. Ellen Gainor (London: Routledge, 1995), 182-90; Jim McWilliams, "'Uhuru!' Negritude in Césaire's *A Tempest*", *Notes on Contemporary Literature* 23(1993), 10-11; and Seth L. Wolitz, "The Hero of Negritude in the Theater of Aimé Césaire," *Kentucky Romance Quarterly* 16, no. 3 (1969), 195-208. For a reading of Césaire's theater and poetry from a dialectical approach, see Nick Nesbitt, *Voicing Memory, History and Subjectivity in French Caribbean Literature* (Charlottesville: University of Virginia Press, 2003), 118–44.

6   Césaire, Lecture at the Maison Helvétique de Paris, 1967, cited by Bennetta Jules-Rosette, "Jean-Paul Sartre and the philosophy of négritude: Race, self, and society," *Theory and Society,* 36, no. 3 (June 2007): 267

7   Césaire, *The Tragedy of King Christophe*, trans. Paul Breslin and Rachel Ney (Northwestern University Press, 2015), 37.

8 Césaire, *The Tragedy of King Christophe*, 93.

9 Zand, "Entretien avec Aimé Césaire."

10 Zand, "Entretien avec Aimé Césaire," 28.

11 Zand, "Entretien avec Aimé Césaire," 56.

12 "Independence" in Lingala.

13 "Freedom" in Swahili.

14 Aimé Césaire, *A Season in The Congo*, trans. Gayatri Spivak (Seagull Books, 2010): 155.

15 François Beloux, "Un Poète Politique: Aimé Césaire," Le Magazine Littéraire 34 (Nov. 1969).

16 Beloux, "Un Poète Politique," 65.

17 It is worth noticing that while Caliban's cheerful song already existed in Shakespeare's *The Tempest* where Caliban takes some liberty with the language and adds some rhythm (Ban' ban' Ca-caliban – high-day, holiday freedom! Freedom!) the two plays' endings are significantly different. At the end of Shakespeare's play Caliban has a new master and seem to have internalized his subjection and to believe things might be different this time. In Césaire's *A Tempest,* Caliban takes some liberty with the language but does not play with his name and does not put freedom and holiday in relation (Freedom, Hi-Day! Freedom, Hi-Day!). Césaire's Caliban knows what he told Prospero earlier in that scene: "I know that one day/my bare fist, just that/will be enough to crush your world!"

18 At the beginning of the play (Act 1, Scene 2), when Prospero claims that Caliban's mother, Syrocax is dead, Caliban refutes, ". . . You only think she's dead because you think the earth itself is dead . . . It's so much simpler that way! Dead, you can walk on it, pollute it, you can tread upon it with the steps of a conqueror. Sycorax. Mother./ Serpent, rain, lightning./And I see thee everywhere!/ (. . .) Often in dreams, she speaks to me and warns me . . . " And at the end of the play (Act 3, Scene 5) after Prospero announces that he will finally answer Caliban's violence by violence he describes his environment and says "Odd, but for some time now we seem to be overrun by opossums. They're everywhere . . . all this unclean nature! But mainly opossums. Those eyes! . . . It's as though the jungle was laying siege to the cave . . ." When he calls Caliban's name the only answer is the sound of nature (surf and birds) and Caliban's song FREEDOM HI-DAY! FREEDOM HI-DAY!

19 bell hooks, "Eating the Other, Desire and Resistance." In *Black Looks: Race and Representation* (Boston: South End Press, 1992), 23.

20 Aimé Césaire, "Poetry and Knowledge, in *Lyric and Dramatic Poetry 1946–82*, trans. Clayton Eshelman and Annette Smith (Charlottesville: University Press of Virginia, 1990), xlvii.

21 Césaire, "Poetry and Knowledge, xlix.

22 Césaire, "Poetry and Knowledge," I.

23 Césaire, "Poetry and Knowledge," liv.

24 Zand, "Entretien avec Aimé Césaire."

25 Césaire, *L'homme de Culture et ses Responsabilités*, Présence Africaine, Nouvelle Série, N°24-25, Deuxième Congrès des Écrivains et Artistes Noirs (Rome 26 Mars-1er Avril, 1959), Février-Mai 1959, p.117. [My translation].

26 Césaire, "Poetry and Knowledge," lii.

27 Aimé Césaire, et Jacqueline Leiner, "Entretien avec Aimé Césaire par Jacqueline Leiner," *Tropiques, 1941–1945* (Paris: J-M. Place, 1978), v–xxiv.

28 Sartre, Jean-Paul, "Black Orpheus," in *"What is Literature?" and Other Essays* (Cambridge: Harvard University Press, 1988), 311

29 Césaire, *A Season in the Congo*, 145.

30 Césaire, *A Season in the Congo*, 145.

31 Lilian Pestre de Almeida, "Le Bestiaire symbolique dans Une saison au Congo." *Présence Francophone* 13 (Fall 1976): 93–195.

32 Monique Roelofs, *The Cultural Promise of Aesthetics* (New York: Bloomsbury, 2014), 177.

33 Aimé Césaire, Interview, Radio Canada, 1970. Cited by Gérard Cogez, *Le Théâtre de Aimé Césaire*, (Lausanne: Ides et Calendes, 2018).

34 For more on this issue, see Erika Fischer-Lichte, *The Transformative Power of Performance: A New Aesthetics* (Routledge, 2008), especially chapter 5, "The Emergence of Meaning."

35 Monique Roelofs, "Navigating Frames of Address: María Lugones on Language, Bodies, Things and Places," *Hypatia* 31, no. 2 (spring 2016): 370–87.

36 Aimé Césaire, *A Tempest*, trans. Richard Miller (New York: TGC, 2016), 20.

37 Roelofs, "Navigating Frames of Address," 374.

38 Césaire, *A Season in the Congo*, 123. The 1967 French edition included a different visual presentation.

39 Bernard Zadi-Zaourou, "Césaire entre deux cultures, problèmes théoriques de la littérature négro-africaine d'aujourd'hui (Dakar: Nouvelles Éditions Africaines, 1978).

40 Zadi-Zaourou, "Césaire entre deux cultures," 154–55.

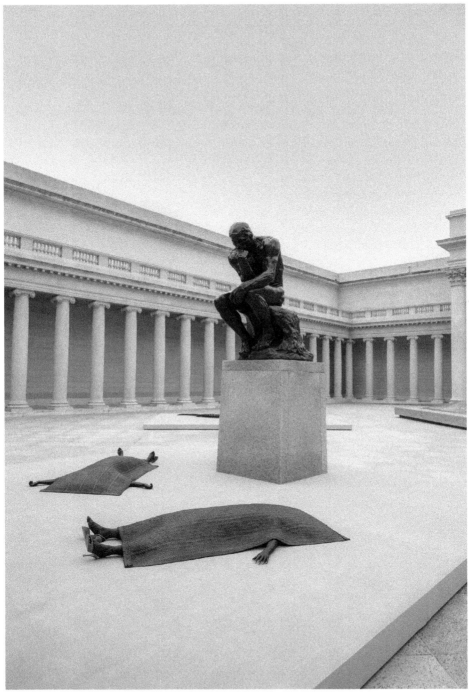

Plate 13 Wangechi Mutu, Installation shot, *I Am Speaking, Are You Listening?* Exhibition, Legion of Honor, San Francisco. From *Wangechi Mutu: I am Speaking, Are you Listening?* Edited by Claudia Schmuckli and published by the Fine Arts Museums of San Francisco and DelMonico Books/DAP in 2021. Photo: Gary Sexton.

13

MAKING HISTORIES: WANGECHI MUTU IN CONVERSATION WITH ISAAC JULIEN AND CLAUDIA SCHMUCKLI

On the occasion of the exhibition I Am Speaking, Are You Listening?, *Wangechi Mutu spoke with fellow artist Isaac Julien and exhibition curator Claudia Schmuckli about her insistence on materiality, her art's connection to nature, the psychic choreography of space, the dethroning of monuments, and the legacy of institutional critique.*

Isaac Julien   Wangechi, I am thinking back to the exhibition *Rook My Soul* [Victoria Miro, London, October 2-November 2,2019], which I curated. I was so thrilled to include your work, and it ended up being the star of the show. There was also a meeting between you and Grace Jones, who came to see your solo show at Victoria Miro in London [*Nguva na Nyoka*, October 14-December 19,2014], which I thought was fantastic because of the synergy it created. There was this performative relationship between your work and Jones's work with [the French photographer] Jean-Paul Goude. . . . I see this continual development now from the performative and the cinematic into the sculptural. The way in which the work has been able to choreograph these different moves between collage, painting, sculpture, film. I'm excited about that because I know that some of these developments—being able to really articulate themes and forms and concerns of artistic practice—have taken place, I think, in relationship to your relocation. And now it's at this incredible stage where it connects to questions around ecology and nature, and how the spirit of one's original location reverberates in the work.

Wangechi Mutu   Isaac, that's really generous. I remember the first time I saw you was at the Whitney Museum's Independent Study Program, when you came to speak . . . . There was something very familiar about the way you talked about history and dislocation and trying to find ourselves in history. I was extremely intimidated by the whole presentation, and I asked you the most absurd question, which I've come back to in my head many a time. Funnily enough, it had to do with a woman who was in entertainment, as opposed to in the arts or academia. It was Lil' Kim, who was super-hot at the time. And there was this really vulgar—I say vulgar because I'm a Catholic schoolgirl prude, and I'm just drawn to these images—poster of her all over the city, legs splayed. It was so provocative. I don't think my question to you was very well articulated, but I was trying to ask, "Where does this kind of image and person sit within the larger imagination—the Black imagination, for example? Or within representations of Black women?" I guess my work has, in some ways, picked up these questions and carried them all the way up until now. Even in the *Shavasana* pieces [see pls. 35–36] there is something that looks back to this pretty difficult and horrific picture of Lil' Kim. This woman spread out throughout the city.

So having this conversation with you is very meaningful for me. Our work occupies different places and spaces—but there is some kinship and camaraderie that I so appreciate. I learned a lot from watching how impeccable you are but also how courageous your work has been. I think the retelling of history is one of the hardest things to do. In my case, in some ways, I'm saying, "Well, if some of the history has been completely destroyed, or doesn't even exist because it was carried in the minds and the mouths of the people who knew it best, then I'm just going to make it up. And I'm going to make it extremely powerful and convincing." And that, in and of itself, is creating history. Grace Jones has always been a visual symbol for the rebellious and regal spirit of Black femininity. She is, for me, one of the most iconic cultural and historical provocateurs. From the time I first saw her on TV as a teenager and until today, she represents the extraordinariness of the underrepresented. I still feel very inspired in the way she moves her body in space, either in clothes, costume, or barely dressed, as a dance of self-definition of the "IamVisible." Grace is always describing in radical style and whimsy the multiplicity of the African, of Blackness, and of human-types; she represented multiple pronouns before there was a word for them. Lil' Kim's image pasted all over New York felt like a contemporary symbol of fertility and sexual prowess, but I feel like she was also the virgin sacrifice.

IJ I feel like this exhibition, the specificity of it, the way that you and Claudia have been able to site the work, is such a magnificent intervention that really reverberates. And I think it's incredibly brave as well, in terms of how the site-specificity of it connects to the whole question around the role of statues. There's been such a huge debate recently—both in America and in the United Kingdom. . . . The reason why I brought up Grace Jones earlier is because of Jean-Paul Goude and the way in which he montaged her body. I've always seen your work as a counter-position [to Goude]. You've been able to take montage and collage and bricolage approaches to the body and to rearticulate them into a lexicon of sorts that relates to the history of art but also, and maybe more importantly, enters into the territory of subjectivity and psychic spaces. I think it's wonderful, the way in which this approach in your 2D work has translated into sculpture and this exhibition, where we have this coordinate response between your work and the statues that are permanently installed at the Legion of Honor—the way in which this conversation gets to become complicated. The way in which you're in conversation with the Greek-Romanesque iconography of the building and statues, which in turn are being counter-posed with different bodies, with nature and with mythologies, many of them Kenyan, that are connected to ecology and the land using the horizontal plane as opposed to the vertical one. All of these different ways of signifying and re-signifying are quite astonishing.

WM   It's interesting that you bring up Goude. I bought that massive monograph he put together years ago, and it contains this method of reconfiguring photography, of what we consider to be the most definitive image that is real. It speaks of reality in a way that we still see in social media and the news. Photography has this elevated position, this authority. And he just slices and dices and messes with these photographs and, essentially, with reality in a way that tweaks the world toward his kind of exotic ideals of women of color, Asian women, Black women. All the different incredible women that he has in this book are severed and reconfigured in a way that he imagines them. And it's so exquisitely done, and so problematic. I was obsessed with it while I was making the collages. I was obsessed with how violent and untethered he is. . . . There is one image—I don't know where I found it because I didn't cut it out of my book, I found it in a fashion magazine—of Naomi Campbell on a crocodile. That stayed on my wall for years. And then, of course, I found this repeated in Peter Beard's work and other white male photographers who've somewhat replicated that kind of motif and also that methodology of taking what they consider to be, essentially, the noble savages and reconfiguring them into these insane, misogynistic, sexy, and absolutely mind-blowing images. . . . I mean, you can't take your eyes away. It's like a train wreck, and at the same time it's all one big learning experience in how people see—how they see you, how they see us. It becomes a challenge for me when I see an image that distorted and that difficult. Just to find a way to take that image and put it in something like a theater of my own, to work to see where the problem really is and also work to treat it somehow. It becomes a method of healing.

Claudia and I, we had so many conversations about this exhibition by phone call— virtual. I mean, it was this insane way of talking about space without being in a space, talking about ideas without having them next to you. We hadn't seen the work in a while and hadn't seen each other, but the trust that went into how we positioned work around what is, essentially, this holy permanent collection was extremely important. I think that's part of what has really taken off here. I think what people are experiencing and what I feel I've learned and am still learning from this exhibition is that you have to be ready to communicate. You have to be ready to let go of some of your power and your voice, and lend it to the other person, and go back and forth in order for something to actually happen. I know now that Claudia was protecting that conversation constantly. It's probably difficult for the museum's more traditional curators to let go of how they see things. What's the most dominant thing in the room? We come in and we kind of mess with it. Not because we're trying to vie for dominance but because these things actually exist on an even plane, and rarely do you see them sitting together rapping and going, "Wait a minute, how did you get here? How did you, why did you consider me there? And why, how are you still relevant?" That kind of thing that's happening with the work is a huge part of the battle in curator-and-artist conversations.

I'm glad we pulled it off. I'm excited about being able to come back to these reconfigurations of the figure with the confidence that I have in the studio and knowing that this can happen here again. I can keep making these virtual and physical conversations in institutions in a way that really ignites an interest. I walked into these spaces, and I was looking at the paintings and the sculptures that much more attentively because I was looking at them through these many lenses that we had positioned the work within.

IJ   There've been very important interventions that artists have made in conversation with museums. If I go right back to a very early work by an artist like Fred Wilson in *Mining the Museum* [The Contemporary, Baltimore; Maryland Historical Society, Baltimore, April 2,1992-February 28,1993], where he collaborated with Lisa Corrin in the walls of the Maryland Historical Society in Baltimore—that sort of intervention became a kind of institutional critique. But, of course, since that time there's been a lot of debate. There's been a debate about the critique of institutional critique. And there's also the way in which that in itself has become part of a vocabulary, or lexicon, appropriated by the museum. . . . And then, of course, there is the recent debate around the repatriation of statues. There's been a debate about the pulling down of statues around the whole Black Lives Matter movement that we experienced just last year. The [Edward] Colston statue being, literally, dethroned and thrown into a canal in Bristol, and the resulting ramifications of that. It seems to me that these works, which are artworks, and your coming together with Claudia in terms of the site-specificity and location, and the response through your own practice, is another meditation on these debates. Which takes us to another space and location, which is not the one ordinarily trod.

WM   Hans Haacke and Fred Wilson and Faith Wilding and Dennis Adams were at Cooper Union—all these institutional critique figures that were my teachers. We also had people like Coco Fusco, Jimmie Durham, and Lyle Ashton [Harris] come and give riveting artist lectures. And it was a real moment where that was the direction that a lot of student work was looking in. We looked around us and said, "Yes, institutions are flawed; they represent the powers that be; they pretend to represent the underdog and the oppressed. And there's all of these societal issues that they're hiding and problems they're exacerbating—the histories that they are masking over and the skeletons that they have hidden." All this was really my education, the classroom and the cauldron I was educated in. But I think one of the things that I've always felt—and I miss so much when I'm in the midst of that kind of thinking and work—is work, is craft and material and nuance. And that doesn't only mean work crafted by hand, but I love watching and looking at work that has a poetic way of being put together. . . . I personally love making things using materials, particularly with my hands, and not just theoretically or only having someone else do it for me.

And so in the many years of making and recreating and reconfiguring things, and using scissors and paint and adhesives and saws and soil to try to address a historical angst and brutality that comes out of my own personal story and my own family story, I realized that material has its own impact, its own energy, its life cycle, its desire to be alive, its wish not to be dead. I'm drawn to organic material in Nairobi. I'm drawn to certain objects when I'm working in New York that I can't purchase in Nairobi. I also know how I feel when I'm in my studio in Nairobi, where I am now. I'm not afraid to touch things and to pick things up off the ground, or to grasp things from trees. I also have a space-specific relationship to objects—colors of objects that I grew up with, like certain pots, certain types of blankets, and patterns. And so I have that confidence I feel when I'm getting my hands into these materials. I know who they are, and I know they know me. I can just sit with them and have this real, familiar conversation, where I know that I'm going to do my best to represent them, be it the soil or a singular bone or an acacia branch or the lesos that women wear.

So that's at the beginning of how I gather and harvest these things that I put in the work. And then you use this word *lexicon*. This is my lexicon that I've cobbled together, [that] I turn into figures, or these images. And then I honestly do feel something miraculous happens when I persuade these materials to be something that they weren't originally. And then there's a rebirth—a reincarnation and a return of their potential and their power. I also tend to pick up broken things. There is something about broken things that I'm drawn to, that makes me want to re-create them as whole again. In a way it's almost like a fossil, where you start to question from a single fragment, "What was this? And how can I make it speak to me about its value, its genesis, even its who it was?" That's different from critiquing the institution and having a banter or an argument or a discussion with the— essentially, with things that are sometimes hypocritical and biased. I feel like if I'm going to have a conversation with an entire institution or a nation about its bias, then I have to know much more about their bias or prejudice than they do. And they know more about their biases and their hypocrisies than I do. So I'd rather have a conversation where I put myself on the same level: "I bring, essentially, these totemic ideas, and you, yours. Let's see if they can even sit together. Do they have the capability to even address one another?" The minute that happens, you sort of debunk this notion of hierarchies and any ascending order of knowledge or of history being linear.

Some of the most ancient things are some of the most impactful things. There are some ways in which we've definitely progressed and evolved, but there are others that we have forgotten; we've forgotten how much more enlightened we might have been when things were simpler than they are now. And I do have a love of nature. Claudia, we talked a lot about land and animals. I think you identify with nature and the natural in the work too. That's something that we have in common.

Claudia Schmuckli   Most definitely. I think that is a very important part of how the work registers also—in its deep connectivity to nature. As a source of strength, as a source of spiritual guidance, but also as material that is not divorced from culture or from art but is integral to it. We talked a lot about [the 2020 film] *My Octopus Teacher*, remember? Just cultivating a different relationship to what surrounds us. And I'm really interested for you to emphasize the materiality aspect of the work, and the importance of that within the context and how it functions. Coming back to what you said earlier, Isaac—in terms of drawing this lineage between institutional interventions or these kinds of gestures, beginning with Fred Wilson to this day, and all the different iterations that you might've seen over the years— you mentioned that you felt that this hits a different register. I would love to ask you to elaborate, if you can, on how you feel it hits a different register and why, and whether it goes precisely to what Wangechi is talking about right now: some of the emphasis on the object's own power and presence in this space. And then the accumulative power of the constellation of objects as they are arranged throughout the museum—objects that make individual points and arguments rather than construct, as you say, a form of metacritique that assumes or presumes to be something that it maybe cannot be.

IJ   There is this radicality in the intertextual materiality of the work and the way it's been able to perform this ecological turn, where it resonates with this question of nature and culture. And [Wangechi] brings all of these different aspects to the work with a bricolage sensibility that is able to question, if you like, the ways in which one thinks about sculpture in the twenty-first century by looking at the trajectory of the totemic and the mythical aspect that African sculpture had going back to the sixteenth century. And then appropriating these forms in conversation with sculpture made in the twenty-first century. It's a form of freestyle that is incredibly exciting and really interesting in terms of its psychic resonances.

I think there's a translation of these psychic resonances in the constellation of these objects in their site-specificity—how they relate vertically and horizontally to one another within the space. I think it's exactly this poetic sonography, which is being proffered in the juxtaposition between the permanent collection and your sculptures, that articulates space and brings out a much deeper resonance than that of institutional critique. We're able to relocate ourselves in a space where there is a sort of speaking between the spaces of the sculptural objects as well. Like the way in which you're mining aspects of Kenyan mythology because you're looking to the sea and oceanic mythologies and returning them to the land, so to speak. So I think these questions between mammals and man, the earth and the sea, and the symbiotic correlation between nature and culture—they begin to have this sort of uncanny aspect to them. I find that quite cinematic.

CS   There is also something cinematic about the choreography of the works inside the Legion of Honor. With *Sentinel IV* [see pl. 14] and *Prayers* [see pl. 86], *Mirror Faced I, II, and III* [see pl. 33], *I am Speaking, Can you hear me?* [see pl. 34], *Rose Quartz* [see pl. 51], and *Dream Catcher* [see pl. 54] centrally placed in the five galleries that radiate out from the rotunda, there is a panning effect to the visual experience in the round. As you move through the space, you realize that the sculptures are in dialogue not only with the architecture and permanent-collection works of their respective galleries but also with one another across the central axis of the rotunda, where *Water Woman* [see pls. 76–77] is situated.

IJ   Yes, the choreography has been reassembled. There's a psychic kind of geography, if you like, in relationship to being able to produce a particular object or form. The question of form is so integral to [Wangechi's] work. And so in reply to the action of the dethroning of statues, one could say there's a dethroning of statues by being able to create a conversation, which produces a much more dialogic response. One of the things that happens by the dethroning of statues is that somehow one thinks one can just erase these histories by those actions, whereas I think in a psychic sense, perhaps, it's really interesting to have what I'm calling this lateral response, where we can help resonate and open up the spaces in which certain objects are trying to reframe history.

WM   I also see it as a gendered gesture. This method that I'm using, that I've inherited here and I'm working with and that I've persuaded these works to be about, is very much about an approach that I feel, as someone who's not a man, is my terrain. I've thought a lot about statues being pulled down. Personally, in my lifetime the most dramatic was the Saddam

Hussein. I was in New York on September 11th, and it was like a whole propaganda. I say *propaganda* because the tearing down of his statue was the justification for a long war, a big war by the UK and the US. And so you had to create these really dramatic images to persuade people that something was about to change. History was being upturned; the evil that the Middle East contained was about to be expunged. All these things were in the media, which is a big part of my inspiration. I watch a lot of news. And I feel that it didn't solve enough. The removal of this massive icon of Iraq was not enough. Because it wasn't this prop that was the issue. This symbolism was, essentially, a kind of theater. It was very machismo and very much about dethroning and castration.

So I think there's something powerful about letting some of these images stay where they are and actually working with them as they present themselves. To see if they actually still carry their power and the potential that they were made to. Nevertheless, the removal of statues is dramatic and very cathartic. It helps us to put our grief somewhere. And we need these kind of quasi crucifixions, reverse crucifixions, to feel like something is atoned and so forth. But the real problem sits beneath them. Like at the pedestal and the base and surrounding ground of these objects is all of this evil. And so then what do we do then? When we're still violating people and violating them through upholding histories that have so many lies in them? How do we now discuss further something that has been (fake) removed? Now [that] we've acted like we've exorcised the problem and yet it's not over?

There are so many issues in cultural production and history making. And history's making in plural, because there are many, many histories that are being discussed in the Legion of Honor. I mean, the history of the woman who founded the museum—the insecurity of an American billionaire socialite who decided that Europe was the history to mimic at that point. If you really wanted to prove your sophistication and your intellectual prowess—and that you're historically valid—you copy what the Europeans have done. That insecurity is embedded in that institution. And it is wrapped around so many of the methods that have been used to preserve the way the work is shown, and who is shown next to the work, if ever. Going back to this idea of emphasizing other histories in this museum—it's no small thing. Every contemporary artist is going to have to interject differently. So there's a chance that if another person worked at the museum in this way, it may not work. It may not have the same resonance. It may not have the same reverberation. But we have to come up with new ways to argue and new ways to resolve problems that we haven't used throughout history. When you leave those objects up, something else can potentially happen that is not an attempt to amputate and forget what has passed and start from scratch but more a method of putting things on the table. And then [to] be courageous enough to say, "Okay, well, this is powerfully vile, but we still need to discuss this. We live in this world together. We're in these institutions together. We've agreed and chosen to work together. So what is this conversation really about?"

CS   You rightfully pointed to the fact that even if you tear down a statue, the power still remains and resides in the leftover pedestal. It doesn't go away as a symbol even though the specificity of the person who was commemorated on top of it may be gone. I feel what you've done in the courtyard, Wangechi, with [Auguste] Rodin's *The Thinker* is different [see fig. 1, p. 19], Obviously it is a different kind of monument since it doesn't commemorate a problematic historical figure, but it still could point to a way of thinking differently about the recontextualization, or the redress, of the power of such monuments. In my mind, placing the two *Shavasana* figures at its base is a much more consequential and resonant gesture than, let's say, if we had taken the Rodin down. Because if you just remove it, there's this vacuum of specificity that actually doesn't give you, or anybody, a hold or an anchor with which to ground the conversation. This opens up, in my mind, a whole other way to frame the monuments debate.

IJ   In this kind of lateral thinking—as opposed to the hierarchal-thinking model that has been posed in this phallic display of monuments—we begin to discover what could be the possibility for a form of poetic restitution, which allows for a deeper kind of reading of the way monuments are psychically functioning. At the same time, I think there's a way in which this kind of lateral pose could be a form of what I call the "aesthetics of reparation."

I made a project in 2003 that was connected to the Museum Without Walls project. I went to Baltimore, and I thought to myself, Well, what can I do after Fred Wilson's project? After walking around in Baltimore over a couple of years, I came across this wonderful museum, the National Great Blacks in Wax Museum. And as soon as I saw these Black wax figures, I thought, I want to bring those wax figures in conversation with works of art from the Renaissance collection, and to perform this kind of séance between the waxworks and artworks, to create this kind of conversational exchange. . . . There is this kind of third position that isn't about dethroning but about a kind of exploration which goes deep into the psychic areas of a culture, where I think the materiality lives.

WM   I really think that these removals of statues that have stood only for certain people and not for others, and also have stood for things that are really repugnant, they are castrations, and they leave a wound. And I think that wound—its impact is not doing what it should do. There's a different way to enter the human spirit, as opposed to cutting off bits and pieces of the body. You have to do it through the mind, and you have to do it through the emotions, and you have to do it through the more universal and shared aspects of what makes us humans.

The *Shavasana* pieces are complicated. I've worked with the figure of a dead woman, the figure of a sleeping woman, the figure of a woman reclined, for a long time in my work. But it always goes back to things I look at and obsess over—how powerful these bodies of violated women are in terms of their numbers, in terms of the imagery and how they impact us. There's a reason why women get raped and killed in war: it sends a particular kind of message different from killing a soldier or a man. And then, at the same time, there's something very peaceful about a body laying down on the ground. I mean, I do yoga. So I know that this is that position that you do at the end of the practice, and it's considered the hardest position because it really is about letting go of everything—just relinquishing the conversation in your brain and being absolutely present. So there's a combination of those two things. But there is also the added, the anecdotal, aspect of the work. . . . At the time when I was really coming to terms [with] how to complete the work, [Nia Wilson] was murdered—that story was in the news. And I followed it; she was so young, and they kept showing her picture before she died. Her father went to the area where she was killed, and they had put a tarp on top of her. . . . It struck me so deeply because I remember thinking, What would I do if I showed up somewhere and someone said, "That's one of your daughters under there"? I mean, how do you even pick up that tarp to look and see what's under there?

And, of course, it's one of many, many killings of young Black people. Of Black people, of women, of trans women—of all these deaths that we've seen happening. This one is one of thousands, but it struck me because of the visual—that it was obviously obscured. And there was this moment—there's this kind of tempo when you approach someone and you know it's your kin. And then you have to really investigate and see what it is. And that person could be any of us when they're under there. But, obviously, when he picked it up it was his daughter. Having that work at the entryway has been extremely important for charging the exhibition with a real sense of importance and relevance for this moment. But it's also something that I've been heartbroken about for a long time. It didn't just start—sacrificing women for these larger, problematic statements of white supremacy and colonization and war. And so, in a way it's very fortunate for me that *The Thinker* is deemed to be the most important piece in the collection, because it's right there. And there's something quite unthinkable happening right in front of him.

14
ALIVENESS AND AESTHETICS
Kevin Quashie

In a black world's rightness of being, one can be—can yearn to be—moved, devastated, broken. Such an orientation of worldness is realized in the made-text, in attending to the aesthetics of the created thing: its shape and form, its poetics, its effects and affects rendered via language.

The terms of aesthetics sometimes seem antagonistic to racial matters, as if blackness itself were formless, as if aesthetic discourse were contrary to the political contexts of black arts. These disavowals are flawed since, as philosopher Monique Roelofs argues, "racial formations are aesthetic phenomena and aesthetic practices are racialized structures".[1] Simply, as performance studies has shown us, attempts to segregate aesthetics from politics misunderstand the mutual conditions between lived life and art; such attempts also misappreciate the philosophical bearing of representational practices.[2]

This is aesthetics as a form-of-life, aesthetics as a schema for considering the aliveness of phenomena and the phenomena of aliveness, the "quality of light by which we scrutinize our lives," in Audre Lorde's language (*Sister Outsider* 36). Or, to cite Toni Morrison's Nobel lecture, "We die. That may be the meaning of life. But we do language. That may be the measure of our lives" (203).[3]

In linking aesthetics and aliveness, I am trying to turn toward the animating capacities evident in the art object, following media studies scholar Amit S. Rai, who calls for antiracist politics that "move beyond reactive dialectics and representational strategies [and toward] something else, experimenting with duration, *sensation,* resonance, and *affect*" (64–65; emphases added).[4] This commitment to sensibility echoes the case that LeRoi Jones (Amiri Baraka) makes in his 1967 essay "The World You're Talking About": "The Black Poetry is a sensitivity to the world total, to the American total. It is *about,* or *is* feeling(s). Even governmental structures are made the way people *feel* they should be made. The animating intelligence is a total of all existence. . . . Ways of making sense, of sensing. . . . Worlds. Spectrums. Galaxies. What the god knows".[5] Jones's title and argument advance precisely an understanding of black feeling as an instantiation of textual sociality, "a *world* of humans and their paths and forms" (n.p. [first page]; emphasis added). And in collating animacy, intelligence, and existence, Jones articulates aesthetics as the aliveness of worldmaking.[6]

In my engagement with poetics, I am interested in aesthetics as a means to explore the specificity of aliveness. And though I elsewhere emphasize the syntax of pronouns and point of view, we can also consider aliveness through the quality of verbs.[7] Think of Lucille Clifton's "reply" to the question, asked of W. E. B. Dubois, whether the black person "sheds tears," where being is particularized through the poem's sustained present tense:

> he do
> she do
> . . .
> they try
> they tire
> . . .
> they moan
> they mourn
> . . .
> they do
> they do
> they do

Notice the work these verbs do to enunciate blackness as phenomena, this sequence of being that is at once definitive and untrackable, present and of presence. The poem's simple and marvelous sequencing reinforces why it matters to read aesthetically, since without attention to the sensible, Clifton's catalog of doings might appear only as antiracist counternarrative. Which would be a loss, really, since her exceptional music ("moan"/"mourn," "try"/"tire") and her rendering of quotidian excellence deserve to be appreciated more wholly.

We could explore how the temporalities of verbs constitute worldness, especially in the instance of the subjunctive, the syntax of imagining. We know subjunctivity as an expression of desired or conditional action. As such, subjunctive utterances, through their wishfulness, seem to create or manifest a scene for happening, as if the subjunctive is a spell that casts its subject into the suspension of an imaginary. This claim recalls the consideration of being-object developed in a previous context,[8] where a habitat of *introspection* yields a moment of *prospection,* though now I want to highlight time as a feature of prospection, how subjunctivity conceptualizes experience as a toggling between then (past), now (present), and what may come. That is, even though the subjunctive is more properly a mood rather than a verb, it inflects a condition of dynamic time via the one speaking through its syntax.[9] There are plentiful examples in Terrance Hayes's *American Sonnets for My Past and Future Assassin,* a collection that signals its temporality in the title and that throws its speaker(s) into suspension via the rubric of the-slaughter-to-come. Throughout the seventy sonnets, Hayes puts forth a black male speaker who is a poet or singer or songmaker, a speaker whose bid to sing is animated by the assassin trained on his life. That killer, in one sense, is anti-blackness, and repeatedly the speaker encounters the ideation of blackness that renders him both as a feared force and as a shadow of/to himself, an immaculate agent who is also powerless. We might think of *American Sonnets* as a study of poetic ontology, an aesthetic materialization of the speaker's feeling asunder in existence.[10] And as Hayes's poetic invites the speaker to behold who he might be in regard to the rapture of killing possibility, the temporality remains superlatively in the present: the speaker recalls past happenings and projects into the future, but the existential tremor of voice, sustained from poem to poem, is of a one figuring *now*. Here is an example from sonnet 55, titled as are all of them "American Sonnet for My Past and Future Assassin":

My mother says I am beautiful inside
And out. But my lover never believed it.
My lover never believed I held her name
In my mouth. My mother calls me her silver
Bullet. Her mercy pill, the metal along her spine.
I am my mother's bewildered shadow.
My lover's bewildering shadow is mine.
I have wept listening to a terrible bewildering
Music break over & through & break down
A black woman's voice. I talk to myself
Like her sister. Assassin, you are a mystery
To me, I say to my reflection sometimes.
You are beautiful because of your sadness, but
You would be more beautiful without your fear. (65)

The meditative formality of the sonnet, its inclination to exaggerate or resolve a question, resides in the repetition we see early in the poem, as the speaker toggles between the mother's and the lover's (dis)belief. That repetition gains intensity through three successive iterations of the word "bewilder," as in "bewildered" (line 6) and "bewildering" (lines 7 and 8), iterations that are the first volta in the poem:

I am my mother's bewildered shadow.
My lover's bewildering shadow is mine.
I have wept listening to a terrible bewildering
Music break over & through & break down
A black woman's voice . . . .

Let me pause to unpack what I think happens here, since its occurrence will animate how to apprehend time and subjunctivity in the poem's conclusion. First, as is the case throughout *American Sonnets,* the speaker often reckons with his being through femaleness. (Hayes uses the idiom "a black male hysteria" to open five poems, revising the common designation of hysteria as a dismissed female condition of somatic trauma.) Notice, for example, the speaker's negotiation of his being vis-à-vis the female shadow; notice, also, that the speaker moves from intense abstractions about mother and lover toward a specific encounter with breaking—his being brought to tender terror through identification with a black female singer: "I have wept listening to a terrible bewildering/ Music break over & through & break down / A black woman's voice." I am struck here by the compounding terms of undoing articulated via prepositions of movement ("break *over* & *through* & break *down*") and by the intensification in the rhyme (the *r*'s, *b*'s, *l*'s and *d*'s in "terrible bewildering"), as I am by the subtlety of the speaker's relationality with the singer.

That is, rather than being moved by the singer's *singing,* what Farah Jasmine Griffin describes as the facile idiom of black woman singer-as-muse, the speaker is transformed in recognizing the singer's own affective vitality—he is moved because he beholds that the terrible beauty in her song is also a terrible beauty in her experience of rendering the song.[11] This relationality, enunciated via the present perfect tense ("I have wept"), propels the speaker to a more acute sensibility in the present, a further identification through femaleness: "I talk to myself/ Like her sister." We might call this, as Hayes does, being *bewildered,* where the word means not confusion but being taken out of one's sense of commonsense—being made wild or being lured into the wild.

"I talk to myself/ Like her sister": The speaker is *thrown* by the singer's *thrownness.* And here is where the poem registers subjunctive time, via the direct address of line 11 as the speaker projects himself through looking at his reflection:

. . . Assassin, you are a mystery
To me, I say to my reflection sometimes.
You are beautiful because of your sadness, but
You would be more beautiful without your fear.

The lines of address multiply as the speaker announces himself as sister and then as the killing one he has internalized. Moreover, the sweet closing recognition couples the temporality of the speaker beholding his (now) beautiful sadness with the possibility that he or his sadness might be something more in another (future) instance. This is subjunctivity, the doubt and vitality of leaning into one's relationality, the animating of being through the expressiveness of might-be.

Consider again the temporality in the closing couplet, not just the gap between the speaker's now-beauty and that which may come but the temporal sensibility of the implied if-then phrasing in the final line: *if* you were of less fear, *then* you could be of more beauty. Reading through the syntax of if-then heightens the prayer quality here as the declarative statement hesitates because it is not yet achieved.

The matter of subjunctivity and poetic time relates to my consideration of aliveness, especially because the phrase "imagine a black world" is a subjunctive clause—an imperative one too. Notably, the keenness of temporal suspension is different in examples where the subjunctive coheres with the imperative, where there is no disjuncture between the wish, the command, and the achievement.[12] Indeed, the subjunctive-imperative of "imagine" yearns and instantiates at the same time; the one who says "imagine" expresses a still-to-come authority in the present. This attribute constitutes another aestheticization of aliveness, as is the case with Nikky Finney's "The Making of Paper" (*The World Is Round* 100–102):

for Toni Cade Bambara, 1939–1995

In the early 1980s I spent two years in a writing workshop that the writer Toni Cade Bambara held in her house in Atlanta every first Sunday. Anybody in the community who was writing was welcome: students, bus drivers, carpenters. I adored the opportunity to sit at this great writer's feet. She knew so much about so much. She later moved to

Philadelphia. She was later diagnosed with cancer. We talked on the long-distance line when we could. I would always ask was there anything she needed that I could send. She usually answered no. But in our last conversation, which took place one week before she crossed over, she held the phone a little longer. "Maybe . . ." she said, ". . . maybe you could send some paper, and what about one of those fat juicy pens?"

Imagine that,
you asking me for paper.

For the record let me state:
I would hunt a tree down for you,
stalk it until it fell
all loud and out of breath
in the forest.
Much as I love a tree;
fat, tall, and free.
As antiviolent and provegetarian
as I am.

Never much
for strapping a gun
to any of my many hips,
for any reason whatsoever,
but on the copper penny eyes
of my grandmother, I tell you
this: I would hunt a tree down for you.

And when found
I would pull it all the way down the road
through congested city streets all by myself
and deliver it straightway
to your hospital bed,
one single extra-large floral arrangement,
something loud and free,
with red and purple bow.
Or better yet,
this tree-loving
gun-hating Geechee girl
would strap a Wild West
gun belt-machete
around her hips
enter the worst part of the woods alone
and go trunk to trunk
until the right one appeared

growing peaceful in its thousand-year-old
natal pot.

Look it
right in its
round rough ancient eyes
and confess away,
tell it straight to its woody face
my about-to-do deed.

I'd even touch it
on its limbs,
fingers begging forgiveness,
give as much comfort to it
as I could, while trying to
explain the necessaryness
of its impending death;
me standing there,
my *Gorilla, My Love* eyes
spilling all over everything,
sending up papyrus prayers
that all begin with,
"I'm so sorry but Toni Cade needs paper."

Only then would I slash its lovely body
into one million thin black cotton rag sheets,
just your uncompromising size.

Send you some paper?
Oh yes,
paper is coming Toni Cade
wagonloads
in the name
of your sweet Black writing life,
from Black writers everywhere
refusing to leave
the arena
to the fools.

Paper is on the way.

Though an elegy, the poem's proper subject is not Toni Cade Bambara but the speaker, the speaker's twitching toward being through the poem's length. The subjunctive-imperative first line, "Imagine that, / you asking me for paper," initiates the speaker's voice, since the expression is performative, a thought of surprise that is said out loud. Here, the praxis of make-believe animates the speaker's voice immediately with force and doing, closing the gap between here and the wherever of Toni Cade. We see this animation in the way "Much as I love a tree" and "Never been much" approximate the urgency of everyday speech. Yet even in haste, the speaker lingers on the tree of her imagination, as in "Look it/ right in its/ round rough ancient eyes"—the briskness is there in the clipped syntax that replaces the full subject-verb clause (as in, "I would look it"), as well as in the double use of "it" . . . both are features of spoken excitability. But notice, too, how the speaker materializes the tree and materializes the moment of contending with its shape, particularly via the alliterative compounding of adjectives that attend deliberately to the tree's eyes: "round rough ancient." In Finney's poem, we are in the midst of a conjecture that has the heft of presence as the speaker imagines and exists in suspension with this tree. The poem teems with dynamism, the tingling of the speaker's instance of *being in becoming,* her wish that arrives as an achievement. "Imagine that."[13]

"The Making of Paper" showcases the speaker's capacity to make something happen, to be and become the happening of relationality. Importantly, the speaker doesn't try to idealize or conjure Toni Cade, who is addressed directly and who is referred to in regard to her art ("your sweet Black writing life"). Instead, the poem figures the *speaker,* her expressiveness and energy and ferocity, her being a one in devotion. I love the way that the time of relationality in this poem is radical, as much now as it is also timeless. I am reluctant to use that term, "radical," though I can't think of another word that characterizes how the habitat of "Imagine that" animates the speaker's becoming not as an occurrence in the future but as a scene in the present. Said another way, this relationality achieves a sublime expression of wish through an idiom that brings the wish into being.[14] If "The Making of Paper" enacts devotion, it is the speaker who is revealed as the subject of its devotioning, the speaker whose vocal vitality tingles on, off, and beyond the verse page. In regard to these poetics, we might recognize three closing things: One, that Finney merges the speaker's voice with Bambara's, since the injunction "refusing to leave / the arena / to the fools" is one that Bambara wrote on a postcard to Finney. This merger maps one voice on the other through shared speech that surpasses time and space. Two, we might read the poem's last line as a temporal reiteration of its title—not "the making of paper" but the promise, "Paper is on the way." Both the dramatic widowing of this final line and its declarative spoken quality imbue the phrase with the force of imperative, the forever capacity of one saying a thing that hasn't occurred but that will happen shortly and surely—the will of the one to breech the gap between now and tomorrow. That final line enhances the timelessness announced in the title and stands as a perfect accomplishment of the aesthetics of worldmaking. And finally, as an extension of my insistence that the poem is not, precisely, about Bambara, we might appreciate how much the speaker's rambunctious poetic materiality (the voice, the imagining, the fidelity to accomplish) amounts to an activism that is roused by and partner to Bambara's legacy—the poem is the materialization of the speaker speaking out in honor of Bambara and against legacies of violence and exclusion, as if the speaker comes into her voice through speaking about and speaking to her elegiac subject. Said another way, the speaker's verse urgency makes literal the relationality of aliveness conceptualized in one black woman saying to another, "Can I say again how alive your being alive makes me feel!?!"[15]

I love the way Finney's "The Making of Paper" uses the subjunctive-imperative to reorder time and to execute a heightened expressiveness that such warped time permits. I love the poem's animacy of performative language achieved through a wish that is also a command. The poem's instantiations are of timelessness, since the work to be done (make paper) is being done (in the poem by the speaker) and what remains is the sweet devotional promise one must steadily bear: "Paper is on the way."[16]

Subjunctivity in this way, entwined with the imperative and animating of being, comprises an aesthetics of aliveness. Indeed, I am reminded of the call in the opening passage of Audre Lorde's "Poetry Is Not a Luxury"; again:

> *The quality of light by which we scrutinize* our lives has direct bearing upon the product which we live, and upon the changes which we hope to bring about through those lives. It is within this light that we form those ideas by which we pursue our magic and make it realized. This is poetry as illumination, for it is through poetry that we give name to those ideas which are, until the poem, nameless and formless—about to be birthed, but already felt. That distillation of *experience* from which true poetry springs births thought as dream births concept, as *feeling* births idea, as knowledge births (precedes) understanding. (*Sister Outsider* 36; emphases added)

It is nearly counterintuitive to consider experience as a praxis that houses possibility, but in Lorde's thinking, *experience is subjunctive* because it merges what is deeply felt with what has not yet occurred. *Experience, then, is a state of suspension in the intensity of presence and possibility, a state of readiness and surrender.*

This framing of subjunctivity—as relational surrender, in regard to the thrall of experience—reaffirms aliveness as a call toward dispossession. That is, following the work of Fred Moten and others, I think of aliveness as an inhabitance that runs counter to possessive investments of subjecthood. The alive one does not possess herself, even as her aliveness animates her being in the world. (Think of Toni Morrison's Sula.) In a black world orientation, we could countenance risk and threat as if one were free to be suspended in human happening.[17]

Such a study of particularized dispossession exists in Ruth Ellen Kocher's *domina Un/blued,* a book-length collection on domination and submission as terms of erotic sexual desire as much as they are terms of empire and coloniality. The subjunctive is all over *domina Un/blued* and its investigation of subjection. We know, following Patricia J. Williams, that enslaved people "were either owned or unowned, never the owner" (156). It is this fault line that Kocher brings alive on her pages abundant with white space, pages where language is sometimes subsumed below the footer's bar:

Exercise 3.

Possessive case for the word 'slave' does not exist in Italian.

The slave   owned   not own   nor owns
Nor evolves. Nor provision   any   make consonant belonging. (4)

This insight, appropriately named an exercise since it has to be practiced into becoming, is from "D/domina: Issues Involving Translation," and it exemplifies the wild and wide-open materialities in Kocher's book, the way that words float unexpectedly in columns and at the bottom of pages and unpredictably across horizontal planes. Kocher's poeticization of ownership continues in "Exercise 4," which asserts that "black is only a thing the slave owns that is nothing" and then later,

> the writing done by the slave in a notebook belongs to no one
> no one belongs to the slave (9)

In this sequence, Kocher's use of "done" as a verb keeps the black one in a syntax of subjection, object even to one's own writing. Her book's early poems acknowledge the complex racialized landscape of domination, and yet Kocher does not shy away from thinking through dominion as a feature of human-to-human erotic exchange. Indeed, throughout Kocher's poems, small scenes of complicated hunger for another, of sexual rapaciousness, become moments of meditating on being. For example, consider how she takes up possession—through the subjunctive and the imperative—in the poem "Domina":

> What boy in leather pants
> to gaze but   O   the long hallway that wields you finally
>
> wild breasted thing.
>
> Imagine he cries   He stiffens   The carcass of a derailed train that
> sits
> at an angle to its track
>
> so together you make an arrow pointing away.
>
> Imagine he walks into the club & the purple lasers him into two so
> one eye
>
> belongs to the him coming toward you and one
> stays just a step behind   measures the pace   stalks the beat
>   him coming
>
> towards you   his reflection pooled across every mirrored wall
> Mercury's quick desire but   O   only him wantless to look at others
>
> as they look at him but   O   if he could see—and to see to see
> to see them see him see
>
> *Sweet brute*
>
> *drop*
>
> *to your knees.* (28–29; emphases in the original)

Though small, this poem is dense—even difficult—so let's focus on the first five lines: For one, notice that the poem's politics of dominion depend on the complicated locality of voice, such that the speaker, the one who beholds the "boy in leather pants" and who exclaims via apostrophe, is and is not necessarily the same as the dominant/dominating subject. That is, the intimacy of the apostrophe and the switch to the second person ("the long hallway that wields you") suggest that the positionality between speaker and dominant could shift. This volatility exemplifies Kocher's nuanced exploration of dominion—of power as a generic term as well as power as a term of colonial and racialized harm. The poem's flux heightens via the phrase "Imagine he cries," which is followed immediately by the direct present tense, "He stiffens": in one sense, the point of reference seems to move from a voice that is outside the scene to one that is enmeshed in the materiality of his stiffening. Or, in another reading, the subjunctive-imperative "imagine" slips so as to modify both the crying and the stiffening. Whatever the case, in five quick lines, Kocher enacts a scene of charge and intensity where status is not static.

Even more compelling is the dynamism in the exclaimed word "O," which is an expressive sign that marks both a speaker's articulation of feeling (surprise, pain, joy) and a direct address to an elevated someone or something. This latter use is the vocative quality of "O," its elegiac and romantic speech capacity. In "Domina," the direction of the address is not defined—the speaker doesn't say "O boy," for example—so the exclamation dangles as an expression of feeling (experience) as well as a call toward something or someone beyond the time of the scene. As such, the apostrophe seems to indicate the making-present of the possible, and everything hangs in exquisite subjunctivity.[18]

This aliveness that decomposes easy subjectivity occurs also in the poem's repetition, especially "if he could see—and to see to see/ to see them see him see," where the reiterated word ("see") unsettles the authority of looking and codifies a funhouse of desire and being. Who is seeing, we are left to wonder, and the answer becomes no more clear in the poem's closing lines: *"Sweet brute/ drop/ to your knees."* Who speaks this tender call, and who is the tender one? It is as likely that the submissive boy makes this command as it is that the speaker—who inhabits the dominant role as narrator of the happening—has succumbed to the tension and entered the plane of things. I love, too, how the tenderness of *"Sweet brute"* recalls the honored attention of the opening phrase, "What boy," since in both instances the adjectives ("sweet," "what") indicate a kind of affection, a specialness. This is subjection as holiness, what Darieck Scott names as "extravagant abjection," that trail of Os down the page, where begging and demanding and experiencing become indistinguishable. All of this intense feeling and suspension that yields prayer is subjunctivity, the aesthetics that render blackness as small, tingling inflections.

Kocher's bewildered poem thrives on its scene of smallness. Indeed, the capacity-in-smallness is the reason why, I have emphasized short poems (with the exception of Finney's "The Making of Paper") rather than ones of epic scale; I want poems that are portable, poems that dare to try to carry the world of worldmaking in scant space, poems that conjure aesthetics to materialize cosmologically. By focusing thus, I am interested in the text's aliveness, the text as an object of animacy that invites encounter. The truth is that every made text, every song or poem or story, is alive; it has a voice or a speaker who is alive, and it beholds the world of aliveness. Said another way, the made-text is evidence of aliveness in at least two ways: in its own materiality as a thing made by an alive one, and in the world of being it imagines.[19]

"Every story is a travel story—a spatial practice," which means that every telling holds traversal and, as such, can incite relationality and worldmaking.[20] There is no genre more capable of this doing than the first-person or personal essay, that superlative form of relation and self-study.

As a genre, the essay installs both a scene of happening and a one immersed in the happening. Commonly, we know the essay as a brief composition "from a limited and often personal point of view,"[21] though more formally, in "The Essay as Form," philosopher Theodor Adorno historicizes the essay as a hybrid between science and art: "Instead of achieving something scientifically, or creating something artistically, the effort of the essay reflects a childlike freedom that catches fire, without scruple, on what others have already done. The essay mirrors what is loved and hated instead of presenting the intellect, on the model of a boundless work ethic, as *creatio ex nihilo*" (152). For Adorno, the essay arrives as if made out of nothing (*creatio ex nihilo*) other than the being (the experience) of the self. In this way, the essay constitutes matter, materiality, in three ways: as a form of being, as a form of being-in-the-world, and as a form that makes a world out of being. And yet, as dynamic a habitat as the essay might be, we should remember that the essay's capacity resides in what is small, even piecemeal.

We might think of the first-person essay, then, as a genre that generates from the declaration, "Let me tell you something that happened to me."

This inclination to tell of an experience is deceptive because it seem to initiate a listener, an audience or reader to whom the essay's working is directed. But the full energy of the essay ordinates toward self-study. Simply, *the essay aestheticizes the speaker,* privileging the will and wandering and affective intensity of the one who is of the happening. The author is the essay's hero, writer Carl H. Klaus argues in a fantastic survey of the genre and its classical figures, though I might modify this claim to suggest that what is found in the essay's terrain is the writer's proxy, the speaker, since we can't properly access the writer themself.[22] Indeed, focusing on the writer might ignite biographical expectations of representation and authenticity that cohere too readily to blackness. I will come back to this question of audience later, but for now I want to be clear that my investment lies in highlighting the speaker persona as an iteration of the essay's aesthetic and material abundance, the speaker as a figure through which telling and encounter happen.[23]

Let me extend this point a bit: with the essay, what we get on the page is the speaker's voice, a mess of feeling and aching and raging and thinking, a sliver of the capaciousness of being; the essay, properly, is the speaker's dwelling, a pursuit of discovery that marries ignorance and arrogance. Again, one turns to Adorno, who writes, "The essay becomes true in its progress, which drives it beyond itself, and not in a hoarding obsession with fundamentals. Its concepts receive their light from a *terminus ad quem* hidden to the essay itself, and not from an obvious *terminus a quo*" (161). Adorno reminds us that the essay is motivated by something beyond its own completeness, and that its dynamism rests in its capacity to inspire a point of mysterious ending rather than its serving as a clear beginning. More important, the time quality of the essay is *after (terminus ad quem),* not before, and the speaker suspends in the aesthetic habitat; that is, the speaker is not in control of the essay's working (the essay is not about transparent conclusions) but rather the speaker *arrives* through the telling. I know that this claim might seem contradictory to common understandings of authority over one's story, though in advocating for the essay as a relational praxis, I want to emphasize that the drive to narrate, which might imply control and mastery, exists in negotiation with the surprise that narration exposes.[24]

The essay is a genre of black oneness, a relational textuality of the speaker's preparedness to surrender to their becoming, site of the speaker as a rhetorical revelation. If every first-person essay conceptually begins, "Let me tell you something that happened to me," the act of telling is not *about* the happening, but the act of telling *becomes* a happening in itself. In this regard, the subject of the invitation is the speaker—the speaker is the essay's *you*. The keenest word in this characterization might be one I used earlier, "aestheticization," which anchors the notion that the essay enacts an aestheticization of the black one in and as aliveness, the essay as a case for rendering the pleasure and intelligence of the words for the saying.

The essay is neither argument nor conclusion but a genre for encounter, a form for "an everyday abstraction of blackness," in film scholar Michael Gillespie's language (9).[25] As such, it asks, "What is experience?" as writer John D'Agata notes. I love D'Agata's clarity here, since he reminds us that the essay is a schema of discovery that questions rather than confirms the definitiveness of experience.[26] In accord with its etymology, the essay stages a display of the speaker's trial, their encounter with being, even though this performativity can be hard to recognize given the genre's use of conversational language that mimics common speech. Indeed we should not interpret this performativity as an antithesis to the essay's oneness, since we've seen already the value of projection as a feature of alive being.[27]

This is the essay as poetic subjunctivity.[28]

Though D'Agata does not make specific reference to black aesthetics, his claim that the essay uses experience to explore the nature of experience is especially relevant in a world of blackness. As theorist Stuart Hall observes, "We tend to privilege experience itself, as if black life is lived experience outside of representation. We have only, as it were, to express what we already know we are. Instead, it is only through the way in which we represent and imagine ourselves that we come to know how we are constituted and who we are" (30). Like Hall, my investment is against an easy conflation of blackness with a simplistic notion of experience. In reading the essay as a genre of black aliveness, I am emphasizing the aesthetic dynamism that Patricia J. Williams describes as the always "rhetorical event" of rendering experience (II)—the dramatization of the speaker, the exhibition of flourishes of syntax, diction, repetition . . . all of the techniques of making and unfurling, techniques of rendering one's being in experience that are also how experience comes to be and comes to mean. (Again, Lorde's "the quality of light. . . .")[29]

There is an instructive example early in Dionne Brand's *A Map to the Door of No Return,* where, in a meditation on the heft of history, the speaker descends into feeling as knowing: "One enters a room and history follows; one enters a room and history precedes. History is already seated in the chair in the empty room when one arrives. Where one stands in a society seems always related to this historical experience. Where one can be observed is relative to that history. All human effort seems to emanate from this door. How do I know this? Only by self-observation, only by looking. Only by feeling. Only by being a part, sitting in the room with history" (24–25). In the syntax, the speaker moves between "one" and herself in the first person and, as such, the location of authority about one, history, diaspora is sutured to the clean specificity of a room, a chair, a black female subject's feeling. Even the question, "How do I know this?" could be read as a moment of self-interrogation, as if it is whispered by the one to the one about the one, as if manifesting a figuring of experience.

"How do I know this?" she asks, that enduring question of aliveness. I love the first-person essay as a prompt for imagining that a black one could sit in wonder and ask, "What is experience?" in the full iterative complexity of such a query.

Before turning to an example, let me assert again:

- The idiom of the essay is of autonomous passage for the one. That is, if the essay's vibrant rhetorics can correlate to authenticity, it is in regard to the ethos of authentic movement as choreographer Romain Bigé has explained it: "to sit with the (in)authenticity of one's self." Bigé's terms remind me that dance as a practice is of relation (again, Danielle Goldman's *I Want to Be Ready*), each dance as an occasion of embodied consciousness where the dancer is a one enacting movement as a locus of intelligence. In dance, the dancer is (being) and is (becoming), so perhaps the essay, as a habitat, is like dance.[30]

- The essay's relationality lies in performativity, in its functioning as a site of disidentification for the speaker who is both the one who is telling and the one who is the subject of the telling.[31]

- "Distance," "disidentification," and "orientation"—these are terms of phenomenology and are vital to how we understand the dynamics of the essay. Indeed, in this way, my suggestion that every first-person essay conceptually begins, "Let me tell you something that happened to me," is apt for not using the word "about" (that is, the phrase is not "Let me tell you *about* something that happened to me"). As it is, the statement emphasizes a narrative that is embodied and imminent and in process: the telling is not *about* the happening; the telling *is* the constitution of the thing itself.[32]

- The essay invokes and appropriates the scene as a moment of being object and subject, staging "the act of being seen and being seen in the process of being seen" (Thompson 10).

- As a materialization of being, the essay is a volatile embodiment; an instantiation and incantation, a magic thing where words are substance and are capable of making substance; a corpus of transformation or crossing, like the rhetorical trope of chiasmus that enacts becoming, exemplified well via the narrator's yearning at the end of Toni Morrison's *Jazz:* "Make me, remake me. You are free to do it and I am free to let you" (229). The essay offers an "aesthetics of existence."[33]

- The essay is a call to and of the one, an aliveness in aesthetics that surpasses representation. Not evidence or authority but the being alive, a collation of experience and existence that confirms its phenomenology since "from a phenomenological perspective, every act of description is at the same time an act of constitution; that is, whenever we describe the world, we are, in a very real sense, remaking it" (Fryer 228).[34]

–   Finally, the essay levitates as a nuanced privacy, akin to what Elizabeth Alexander—in reading Michael Harper's Black Arts poetry—describes as a "pride [that generates] from an angle of profoundest intimacy, as though nothing is worth saying loudly unless it is felt from a place" of depth (80–81). Yes, yes, yes, as though nothing but one's black intimacy is worth saying loudly.

In "Of Practice," Michel de Montaigne makes the essay's ethic clear: "My trade and art is living," he writes, and then later, "I expose myself entire. . . . It is not my deeds that I write down; it is myself, it is my essence" (189, 191). Or Patricia J. Williams, in *The Alchemy of Race and Rights,* who enacts the black self as a "floating signifier" in a first-person speech act, and who confesses, "I deliberately sacrifice myself in my writing" (7, 92). This is the essay, which, like Lucille Clifton's speaker, says "come celebrate" and mobilizes subjunctivity on behalf of a one of black aliveness.

To further the case for a poetics of the first-person essay, which could also be called the lyric essay,[35] I want to consider an exquisite example, Jamaica Kincaid's exploration of colonialism, tourism, and Caribbean modernity in *A Small Place.* We don't often think of this book through the aesthetics of the personal essay. Indeed, since its publication in 1988, *A Small Place* has been read either as a searing condemnation of white (American and European) tourism or as a misguided critique of Antiguans. These critical assessments privilege the text's arguments and also tend to lean heavily on psychological interpretation of Kincaid's biography; as such, these readings collapse the writer with the author function, her narrative persona, and overlook the book's aesthetic doings. Given this, I want to attend both to the speaker who materializes (in) the telling and to *A Small Place* as a scene of the speaker's undoing, of her being both subject and object of the essaying. I want to read as if the speaker's becoming on the page constitutes the book's revelatory dynamics.[36]

Central in *A Small Place's* aesthetics is the presentation of unsettledness, first in the way the speaker seems to disorient the reader and then in the speaker's own tumble into ambivalence that reflects a depth of black feeling about and within the colonial condition. "If you go to Antigua as a tourist, this is what you will see" (3) is the book's first sentence, a dare of a phrase that ensnares the reader and establishes an antagonism that will energize the arc of what follows. Immediately, the speaker asserts herself obliquely and aggressively by overdetermining the reader, who is co-opted into a discursive world via the command "you." Notice, too, that the second-person invocation consists of both a subjunctive ("if you go") and an imperative (direct address)—that the essay begins in the aesthetic of "imagine." We know, then, that we have to read this provocation thoughtfully so as to keep the textuality of the speaker in view. That is, we can't infer only that the address is directed to a (white) reader, especially since the speaker herself is also revisiting the island after a long absence. If we engage the book as a relational inhabiting, then the opening's invocation via the subjunctive *includes* the speaker in its command, a call of worldmaking that arrests the speaker in her conjured scene of small islandness. In this claim, I read "if you go" as a disorienting rhetorical function, one that cues us to notice the speaker's unsettled subjectivity. What we gain from such a reading is the capacity to attend to the speaker's anger and regret and confusion and ambivalence, her exasperation and her embarrassment for having such conflicted feelings; what we gain is a sense of the essay as a home of the speaker's grappling with experience and an appreciation for Kincaid's deployment of the force of the genre.[37]

I am interested in *A Small Place* as a textual landscape of the black speaker's relationality.

Kincaid's essay is composed of four untitled sections, each a meditation on being in Antigua. While the first section, just referenced, uses the second person almost to the exclusion of explicit reference to the speaking "I," parts 2 and 3 rely principally on first-person disclosure. The last section, which is a brief poetic reprisal of Antigua's colonial history, deploys an omniscient third-person voice to reinforce the speaker's intimacy.[38] But I am getting ahead of myself in summarizing the essay's narrative kinetics: we can recognize relation as a praxis in *A Small Place* by paying attention to the pronouns in the essay, how the direct address ensures the first-person speaker's authority of voice without having to say "I." It is an act of control, or delay, maybe even a gambit to orient the scene of colonial happenings appropriately. Throughout the initial pages, the speaker assails the imagined reader through second-person conjecture:

> You are a tourist. . . . You disembark from your plane. You go through customs. Since you are a tourist, a North American or European—to be frank, white—and not an Antiguan black returning to Antigua from Europe or North America with cardboard boxes of much needed cheap clothes and food for relatives, you move through customs swiftly, you move through customs with ease. Your bags are not searched. You emerge from customs into the hot, clean air: immediately you feel cleansed, immediately you feel blessed (which is to say special); you feel free. (3–5)

The speaker's assumptions about the reader multiply, even to the level of projecting what the you feels: "You are feeling wonderful" (5). Later, the speaker summarizes the power of the colonizer with another astute accusing projection, "You see yourself, you see yourself" (13), the repetition emphasizing the insight and the authority of its saying. Not only do these summations codify the reader, the white you, but they secure the speaker as part of a black collective ("we Antiguans, for I am one . . ." [8]), at least momentarily. Moreover, this second-person encasement establishes a clear distance between the one speaking and the ones held captive in her lure. And still, even in this torrent of clear address, the speaker seems distanced from herself—as if she were a voice offstage that is describing a scene of ridiculous actors in ferocious syntax.

The rhetorical intensity of the direct address is so total in the first section that the use of "I" at the start of part 2 is startling: "The Antigua that I knew, the Antigua in which I grew up, is not the Antigua you, a tourist, would see now" (23). This is a statement of exposedness, of the speaker entering the stage explicitly as opposed to being shrouded in the authority of the second-person capture; in this doing, the speaker inhabits a tone that is more vulnerable and hesitant (notice how the repetition and commas create that pause: "The Antigua that I knew, the Antigua in which I grew up, is not the Antigua you, a tourist, would see now"). We can recognize an affective shift in the relationality of the speaker's speaking, as in "Let me show you the Antigua that I used to know" (24), which is how she prefaces this section's telling of small incidents that track a history of colonial wrongdoing. Such an offer opens up a narrative intimacy that is not quite mutuality since the speaker is cajoling the reader into accountability and maybe even remorse. We see this affective dynamic in the speaker's interrogations:

> Do you ever wonder why some people blow things up? I can imagine that if my life had taken a certain turn, there would be the Barclays Bank, and there I would be, both of us in ashes. Do you ever try to understand why people like me cannot get over the past, cannot forgive and cannot forget? (26)

> Have I given you the impression that the Antigua I grew up in revolved almost completely around England? . . . Are you saying to yourself, "Can't she get beyond all that, everything that happened so long ago . . .?" (33–34)

> Have you ever wondered to yourself why it is that all people like me seem to have learned from you is how to imprison and murder each other, how to govern badly, and how to take the wealth of our country and place it in Swiss bank accounts? Have you ever wondered why it is that all we seem to have learned from you is how to corrupt our societies and how to be tyrants? You will have to accept that this is mostly your fault. (34–35)

Reading through this sequence of indictment, it is clear that the speaker seeks from the reader neither answer nor reparative gesture; instead, the persona seems to revel in the chance to *feel* the wild, hot anger of being harmed by colonial plunder, of having to do that reveling in a language that is unyielding. ("For isn't it odd that the only language I have in which to speak of this crime is the language of the criminal who committed the crime?" she concedes in a parenthetical notation [31].) The case I am pressing is to notice the speaker, the intensity of her difficult feelings, the impossibility that the discursive would to make of her being. The speaker's voice here is almost oxymoronic (deictic?) conceptually, *speaking imprecisely from a precise location of feeling,* addressing impossibility with crisp insight. It is not the claims against history that seem aesthetically compelling as much as the emotional ache articulated as she, the speaker, moves through telling this thing that happened—and is happening—to her, this terrible unsettling happening . . . and doing so in a dialogue that is and will always be of one, since the addressed cannot possibly respond or engage. As such, rather than try to assess the speaker's politics, we might instead ask, "Who is this speaker, and who is she *becoming* in this narrative?" That is, I am trying to implore us to read this essay as an essay, as home for/of its speaker. This orientation, of beholding the speaker as a one who is being figured through the narrative, is essential to discerning the laced comments in this section, including this intense claim: "Even if I really came from people who were living like monkeys in trees, it was better to be that than what happened to me, what I became after I met you" (37). This sentence registers as a sigh, as if the speaker is momentarily exhausted in struggling through the whole world of her feeling and thinking. We might want to read this sentence for its declaration against colonial terror or for Kincaid's complicity in not dismissing the racist claim (the "even if" clause), though such interpretations miss the affective textuality here, the tumbling suspension of the speaker's inhabited sensibility. Or, as Audre Lorde told us, "I feel, therefore I can be free" (*Sister Outsider* 38).

"I feel, therefore I can be free": Again, I don't mean to suggest that there are no ideological dimensions to *A Small Place;* I mean, instead, to focus on the essay as a habitat of a black one's navigation through being subject and object of the essaying, what literary theorist Phillip Brian Harper might call "the abstractionist aesthetics" of pronouns.[39] As a genre, the essay is not of argument or proof or even evidence; it is instead of the *experience* of black being, the flight into one's variousness. In this regard, Kincaid's speaker is the hero of the essay, she who makes the scene for her own encounter and feeling.

Such appreciation allows us to acknowledge a vital moment that begins the book's third section:

> And so you can imagine how I felt when, one day, in Antigua, standing on Market Street, looking up one way and down the other, I asked myself: Is the Antigua I see before me, self-ruled, a worse place than what it was when it was dominated by the bad-minded English and all the bad-minded things they brought with them? How did Antigua get to such a state that I would have to ask myself this? For the answer on every Antiguan's lips to the question "What is going on here now?" is "The government is corrupt. Them are thief, them are big thief." Imagine, then, the bitterness and the shame in me as I tell you this. (41)

This in medias res instance of the first person is particular because it is so wrought with tender confession. Here, the speaker turns the performativity of "imagine" upon her own affective constellation, inventing a scene capable of her ambivalence. This is not just a citation of shame, but something else—the meeting of an intractable terribleness in an attempt to travel the small place of her black life with some modicum of fearlessness. It is an astonishing intimacy, the habitat for which the speaker has made through the praxis of her telling. Scholars readily note that Kincaid's writings exhibit "a very personal politics" (Bouson 89), though this display surpasses and dispenses with politics by its ordinary name. No, this sublime invocation, "And so you can imagine," ascends to a level of being beheld in deep feeling.

More than all this, however, is the fact that this moment is the proper anecdote of *A Small Place.* Conceptually, the anecdote works as an essay's most specific materiality, the unremarkable incident animated via telling. In this regard, the anecdote constitutes the "something" of the phrase "Let me tell you something that happened to me," the something that might be humorous or trivial, that is unreliable because it is casual and is uncorroborated by sociality: the anecdote is the materiality around which a speaker can flutter since it is small, unremarkable, compelling. Intimately unreliable.

I come to thinking of the anecdote through the genre of the personal essay but also through David Wills's writing about literature and public function. Wills defines the anecdote as "the explicit but secret other side to narrative . . . and conversely, as *the becoming literary of any text*" (22; emphasis added).Wills is right to designate the anecdote as a surfeit, an intimate but casual textuality that can support a dynamic relation. And the potential or energy of the anecdote is not truth or precision; indeed "the anecdote is most often . . . consigned to a discursive structure in which truth and certainty are not at issue; where disbelief is willingly suspended to enable the gratuitous, the frivolous, the autobiographical, the fictional to be given free rein" (Wills 24). One could say that the anecdote is virtual, in Deleuzean terms—that which is real but not fully actualized. Not pure or raw, but a buzzing, nearly there thing that exists on the edge of the limits of representation or capture.[40]

At the heart of every essay, there is an anecdote, the narrative of a specific happening that is flush with feeling though it remains ordinary until scrutinized (and remains ordinary afterward). The anecdote is a site of transformation, in that it is a materiality that the speaker manipulates but, ultimately, doesn't control. Something happened, and now there is the telling, and in the telling there is becoming. The anecdote doesn't supplant the happening—it could not possibly do that—but it is perhaps a viable site for the speaker's being in regard to the world of her being. Said another way, the speaker and the anecdote exist in relational encounter.

Again: "And so you can imagine how I felt when, one day, in Antigua, standing on Market Street, looking up one way and down the other, I asked myself: Is the Antigua I see before me, self-ruled, a worse place than what it was when it was dominated by the bad-minded English and all the bad-minded things they brought with them?" And then, "Imagine, then, the bitterness and the shame in me as I tell you this" (41). Not only am I thoroughly moved by the way the speaker's anecdote begins in full stream of a sustained self-conversation, but I am taken by the way in which this anecdote is rendered as an unspecific specificity. We can imagine it, a moment on a random day when, caught in a certain sunlight, the speaker comes upon a thought that she might have had before but without conscious notice: How did it come to this, and do I belong here? Such questions might have been related to an incident—or not, since whatever spurred the questions has been lost to memory. (It is almost too ordinary to remember.) The point is that this textual moment triggers deep feeling and crystallizes as the speaker's reckoning. We should notice, too, that this anecdote is prefaced by two sections (nearly forty pages) of deliberate rage-work. To me, this deferral enhances the drama of the anecdotal moment that is not presented specifically but that is *felt* specifically—intensely—by the speaker.

The thrilling diffuseness of the small happening: I love that Kincaid's anecdote is encased in a call to imagine, since this call gestures to how impossible the happening is to describe and share, how difficult it is for the speaker to be of regard to the happening for herself (never mind to try to relay it to a reader), as if it can only be instantiated by a world other than this one. "Imagine . . . the bitterness and the shame in me," the speaker says as she conjures up a capacity to be of bitterness and shame. I love that the speaker, in thrall of the essay's aesthetic, sets a scene not to criticize white wrongdoing but for her own engagedness with the difficult. This is the capacity of the personal essay, where the black one can invoke a habitat for being and then can surrender into that habitat toward her becoming.

The essay lets the speaker do the work that is hers to do in the best way she can imagine.

It is not a surprise, then, that this section and its intimate anecdote feature prominently when scholars question Kincaid's racial politics. For one, the speaker's reencounter with Antigua does not shy away from addressing her dissonance with her kin. And the acknowledgment of embarrassment seems directed to the book's generic reader, who has been signaled as white (the "you" of the opening), which means that *A Small Place* appears to denigrate blackness while pleading to the virtues of whiteness. Literary theorist Greg Thomas summarizes a common sentiment in arguing that "when attention is drawn less to what Kincaid says explicitly to white tourists, and more to what she says about black Antiguans, her political outlook is exposed for its crude conservatism" (118). Thomas's claim is about the book's content, though he minimizes that *A Small Place* begins with a critique of whiteness and of the destructions made by colonialism, at least as such destructions are experienced by a speaker who herself is something of a tourist. Moreover, in my reading, Kincaid's political undertaking exists not only in the essay's content but especially in its aesthetics, her deployment of the genre's form toward instantiating a black diasporic speaker in the midst of a complicated affective subjectivity. Kincaid the writer—and her persona, the speaker—is trying to reckon with her feelings, their messy and necessary rightness; she is trying to make a world for being where she can think-feel her rightness.

Sigh: I am uneasy about trying to defend *A Small Place* in regard to its ideas about antiblackness and its overtures toward a dominant (white) reader, not only because I understand those overtures as an aesthetic apparatus of the speaker's relational doing but also because in a black world, the book and its speaker (never mind its writer) do not need defense. In mounting this defense, I am enacting an anxiety of audience that works awry of the aliveness of the essay form.[41] Simply, if the essay is the terrain of the speaker, then what is being assayed by *A Small Place* is the speaker's exploration of the ambivalence of home in the enduring harmful legacy of colonization. She, the speaker in this book, feels the dissonance and disorientation of Antigua, and the essay constitutes a space for her trial, as in to try to encounter the world of her affective being in regard to this small place. "Let me tell you something that happened to me," the speaker says, which means that we must acquiesce to her right to understand—to experience—the ravages of colonialism on her own terms. And through the telling, the speaker establishes and traverses a scene of mattering, an erotics of feeling and of becoming.

Surely *A Small Place* is not only a private conversation, but what if we read its speaker as having a relational encounter with herself, including the ambivalence of return to a place that she cannot now bear? What if we permit that the world made by the speaker's act of telling is one where, rather than only articulating pride or self-assuredness, the speaker gets to countenance shame as a part of black being? In a black world, we could countenance shame.

The first-person essay is a display of a speaker's inhabitance of disorientation in regard to the thing that happened—disorientation that, as Sara Ahmed argues, is a relational condition. As such, the pronoun of Kincaid's first-person essay might not be "I," at least not conceptually, since "I" indicates more control than resides in the essay's worldness. No, the subjectivity of the first-person essay here might be "me," the singular object case, or at least the oneness invoked in asking, "How am I me?" as a question of being subject and object at the same time. I find this conclusion useful in tracking the arc of the speaker in *A Small Place,* where the heft of direct address gives way to the subjectivity of beholding shame's oneness.[42] Indeed, in the book's final brief section (it is five pages), Kincaid's speaker mobilizes her me-positionality into a sense of oneness and offers a stunning call of relationality:

> Again, Antigua is a small place, a small island. It is nine miles wide by twelve miles long. It was discovered by Christopher Columbus in 1493. Not too long after, it was settled by human rubbish from Europe, who used enslaved but noble and exalted human beings from Africa (all masters of every stripe are rubbish, and all slaves of every stripe are noble and exalted; there can be no question about this) to satisfy their desire for wealth and power, to feel better about their own miserable existence, so that they could be less lonely and empty—a European disease. Eventually, the masters left, in a kind of way; eventually, the slaves were freed, in a kind of way. The people in Antigua now, the people who really think of themselves as Antiguans (and the people who would immediately come to your mind when you think about what Antiguans might be like; I mean, supposing you were to think about it), are the descendants of those noble and exalted people, the slaves. Of course, the whole thing is, once you cease to be a master, once you throw off your master's yoke, you are no longer human rubbish, you are just a human being, and all the things that adds up to. So, too, with the slaves. Once they are no longer slaves, once they are free, they are no longer noble and exalted; they are just human beings. (80–81)

This passage exhibits *A Small Place's* characteristic syntax, especially its long conversational sentences full of the speaker's lively and casual—nearly flippant—ease ("Eventually, the masters left, in a kind of way," "I mean, supposing you were to think about it") and its deployment of parenthetical asides. The voice here resolves the philosophical question of master-slave relation with the looseness of the phrase "of course." Such flourish reminds us that the essay's grappling works through the specificity of the speaker, her me-ness, that the historical matters at hand are indexed to the particularity of their relation to her everyday experience and her ordinary language for that experience. Indeed, it is this ordinariness, this intimacy, that contextualizes the passage's turn toward universality, a turn that is not a naïve notion but that carries the weight of the speaker's rugged essay-work.[43]

A Small Place is of a black one who is navigating the intimacy of happening, a subject who can speak broadly through the specificity of her encounter with herself. And in the doings of Kincaid's mighty book, we remember that to be able to say one, to be of or as "one," is not to be deferent or imperial; it is to be rendered as a being via cosmological terms, of being open(ed) to textures of one's inestimable totality that is and is of a world.

Kincaid's speaker isn't organizing a *communal* affective encounter—this might be what some critics read as a failing. But perhaps the orientation of the black essay is toward what literary theorist Darieck Scott calls a politics without defense: "a politics that does not organize itself around a stance of defense or aggression, a politics that assimilates to itself racial identities and histories but choosing not to battle against them but rather to let them, as it were, flow through the self—even overwhelm the self—and yet become transformed" (245). Scott argues for a capacity to exist within the political undefensivly, akin to what I have explored in the aesthetics and affect of Kincaid's speaker, she who is not responsible for a politic against whiteness nor a politic in sustenance of black people (Antiguans or otherwise). *A Small Place* is hers, her world of feeling, and its force of being might well inspire other encounters that will have their own force of black being. (Such might be its sustaining work.)[44]

The essay is of the one of blackness, the voice speaking out toward its own (imagined) self, which is an act of worldmaking.[45]

The personal essay is superlatively of affect (emotions are "a form of . . . world making" Ahmed argues),[46] of the being of experience that is possible through aesthetics. We should read this form *as* a black world; otherwise we'd be inclined to look for its argument about antiblackness rather than honor its embodiment of blackness.

Again, the black world of the black essay constitutes and inspires a heterogeneity of us, not respectability or fidelity to community but a world of black particularity—the heterogeneity of blackness. In the essay, then, we encounter not a text of evidence but an aesthetic of experience, "the work of art [as] a being of sensation and nothing else: it exists in itself."[47]

The essay, this poetic of subjunctivity that beholds blackness as a capacity of wandering and wondering, free, as in the way one is in knowing that "God is a question, not an answer."[48]

Notes

1 Monique Roelofs, "Racialization as an Aesthetic Production: What Does the Aesthetic Do for Whiteness and Blackness and Vice Versa," in *White on White/Black on Black*, ed. George Yancy, 83-124 (New York: Rowman and Littlefield, 2005), 83.

2 My reference to performance studies here is indebted to the field's arguments about ideation, aesthetics, and performativity in the being of blackness. In this regard, I am drawing especially on E. Patrick Johnson's idiom of appropriation (see *Appropriating Blackness: Performance and the Politics of Authenticity* [Durham, NC: Duke University Press, 2003]), as well as on Thomas F. DeFrantz and Anita Gonzalez, *Black Performance Theory* (Durham, NC: Duke University Press, 2014); Robert Reid-Pharr's thinking about blackness in the opening of *Once You Go Black: Choice, Desire, and the Black American Intellectual* (New York: New York University Press, 2007); and Harvey Young, *Embodying Black Experience: Stillness, Critical Memory, and the Black Body* (Ann Arbor: University of Michigan Press, 2010), especially his exploration of how ideation creates the black social body in chap. 1. Here I am not interested in nonblack

performances of blackness, though these exist as part of the circuit of ideation. In terms of thinking about aesthetics and blackness, see Paul C. Taylor, *Black Is Beautiful: A Philosophy of Black Aesthetics* (Hoboken, NJ: Wiley-Blackwell, 2016), particularly the race-aesthetic nexus that he develops in conjunction with Roelofs's argument. Taylor writes that "black aesthetics is an unavoidably political subject. It exists as a cultural phenomenon and as a subject of philosophical study because of political conditions" (79). Taylor does well to surpass the "racial regimes" of aesthetic theory that David Lloyd notes in *Under Representation: The Racial Regime of Aesthetics* (New York: Fordham University Press, 2018). Also see the subfield of existential aesthetics, including Galen Johnson, *The Retrieval of the Beautiful: Thinking through Merleau-Ponty's Aesthetics* (Evanston, IL: Northwestern University Press, 2009); Eugene Kaelin, *An Existentialist Aesthetic: the Theories of Sartre and Merleau-Ponty* (Madison: University of Wisconsin Press, 1962); Richard Kearney, *Poetics of Imagining: From Modern to Postmodern* (Edinburgh: Edinburgh University Press, 1998); Jerrold Levinson, *The Pleasures of Aesthetics: Philosophical Essays* (Ithaca, NY: Cornell University Press, 1996); Richard Wollheim, *Art and Its Objects* (Cambridge: Cambridge University Press, 1980); and Amie Thomasson, "The Ontology of Art," in *The Blackwell Guide to Aesthetics*, ed. Peter Kivy (Oxford: Blackwell, 2004), 78–92. And to cite more broadly, my study of aesthetics draws from the following works: Jacques Rancière, *The Politics of Aesthetics* (New York: Bloomsbury, 2006); Sara Ahmed, *The Cultural Politics of Emotions* (Edinburgh: Edinburgh University Press, 2004); Mikhail Bakhtin, *Art and Answerability: Early Philosophical Essays* (Austin: University of Texas Press, 1990); José Muñoz, *Cruising Utopia: The Then and There of Queer Futurity* (New York: New York University Press, 2009); Phillip Brian Harper, *Abstractionist Aesthetics: Artistic Form and Social Critique in African American Culture* (New York: New York University Press, 2015); Jared Sexton, "All Black Everything," *e-flux* 79 (2017), https://www.e-flux.com/journal/79/94158/all-black-everything; Yuriko Saito, *Aesthetics of the Familiar: Everyday Life and World-Making* (Oxford: Oxford University Press, 2017); Martha C. Nussbaum, *Love's Knowledge: Essays on Philosophy and Literature* (New York: Oxford University Press, 1992); Marc Redfield, *The Politics of Aesthetics: Nationalism, Gender, Romanticism* (Stanford, CA: Stanford University Press, 2003); Russ Castronovo, *Beautiful Democracy: Aesthetics and Anarchy in a Global Era* (Chicago: University of Chicago Press, 2007); Roland Barthes, *S/Z* (New York: Hill and Wang, 1975); Barthes, *Pleasure of the Text* (New York: Hill and Wang, 1975); Jacques Derrida, "'A Self-Unsealing Poetic Text': Poetics and Politics of Witnessing," in *Revenge of the Aesthetic: The Place of Literature in Theory Today*, trans. Rachel Bowlby, ed. Michael P. Clark (Berkeley: University of California Press, 2000), 180–207; and Samantha Pinto, *Difficult Diasporas: The Transnational Feminist Aesthetic of the Black Atlantic* (New York: New York University Press, 2013), especially her consideration of aesthetics and black experimentalism.

3   In thinking with Morrison's declaration about language—and writing as a specific creative genre—I am engaging Mel Y. Chen's work in *Animacies: Biopolitics, Racial Mattering, and Queer Affect* (Durham, NC: Duke University Press, 2012), especially their consideration of materiality and vitality (51–53). Other works relevant to my engagement of aesthetics and representation include Lauren Berlant, *Cruel Optimism* (Durham, NC: Duke University Press, 2011): "Aesthetics is not only the place where we rehabituate our sensorium by taking in new material and becoming more refined in relation to it. But it provides metrics for understanding how we pace and space our encounters with things, how we manage the too closeness of the world and also the desire to have an impact on it that has some relation to its impact on us" (12); Gayatri Gopinath, *Unruly Visions: The Aesthetic Practices of Queer Diaspora* (Durham, NC: Duke University Press, 2018): "The aesthetic *enacts, produces, and performs*," which is why she writes of "aesthetic *practices*, not just aesthetic forms, because they do things in the world" (16; emphases in original); and Kandice Chuh's argument for aesthetics, relation, and a notion of "illiberal humanism" in *The Difference Aesthetics Makes: On the Humanities "After*

Man" (Durham, NC: Duke University Press, 2019). And again, I am using the phrase "form-of-life" from Giorgio Agamben, "Form-of-Life," in *Means without End: Notes on Politics* (Minneapolis: University of Minnesota Press, 2000), 3–12, though it also occurs in Ludwig Wittgenstein (*Philosophical Investigations* [London: Pearson, 1973]).

4 See Amit S. Rai, "Race Racing: Four Theses on Race and Intensity," *WSQ: Women's Studies Quarterly* 40, no. 1 (2012): 64–75, which I came to via Tavia Nyong'o's compelling "Unburdening Representation," *Black Scholar* 44, no. 2 (2014): 70–80.

5 LeRoi Jones, "The World You're Talking About." *Introduction to Felix of the Silent Forest*, by David Henderson, n.p. (New York: Poets, 1967), first page, emphases in original).

6 Jones's essay serves as the introduction to David Henderson's poetry collection *Felix of the Silent Forest*. Thanks to J. Pete Moore for pointing me to Henderson's collection. As I've noted in *Black Aliveness*, aesthetics and worldmaking are central features of the work in the Black Arts/Aesthetics movement. For more here, see Margo Natalie Crawford, *Black Post-blackness: The Black Arts Movement and Twenty-First-Century Aesthetics* (Urbana: University of Illinois, 2017), see the case Farah Jasmine Griffin makes for textuality and materiality in "Textual Healing: Claiming Black Women's Bodies, the Erotic and Resistance in Contemporary Novels of Slavery," *Callaloo* 19, no. 2 (1996): 519–536.

7 In Chapters 1 and 2 of *Black Aliveness*.

8 In Chapter 2 of *Black Aliveness*.

9 Geoffrey Pullum, in "Being a Subjunctive," says that subjunctive clauses are "finite and tenseless" (*Chronicle of Higher Education*, March 29, 2016), which follows the case that Rodney Huddleston makes in "Content Clauses and Reported Speech," in *The Cambridge Grammar of the English Language*, ed. Rodney Huddleston and Geoffrey K. Pullum (Cambridge: Cambridge University Press, 2002), 947–1031 (but see esp. 993–1000). For a brief consideration of the tense of imperatives and subjunctives, see Frank Parker, Charles Mayer, and Kathryn Riley, "Here Us Go Again," *American Speech* 69, no. 4 (1994): 435–439. Also see Charles D. Cannon, "A Survey of the Subjunctive Mood in English," *American Speech* 34, no. 1 (1959): 11–19; F. R. Palmer, *Mood and Modality* (Cambridge: Cambridge University Press, 2001); and Paul Portner, *Mood* (Oxford: Oxford University Press, 2018). The subjunctive matters to blackness; indeed, Saidiya V. Hartman has made the case for the subjunctive as an aesthetic of black being in regard to reading historical archives (see "Venus in Two Acts," *Small Axe* 12, no. 2 [2008]: 1–14). Also see Tavia Nyong'o, *Afro-fabulations: The Queer Drama of Black Life* (New York: New York University Press, 2018); Tina Campt's engagement of tense in *Listening to Images* (Durham, NC: Duke University Press, 2017); and Muñoz's attention to the "here and now" of any utopia or call for futurity (in *Cruising Utopia*). Especially in reading Muñoz, I came to think of the subjunctive as a structure of feeling à la Raymond Williams. Finally, the poet Lyrae Van Clief-Stefanon, in a presentation at the Callaloo conference "The Legacy of 1619" at the University of Pennsylvania, October 19, 2019, advances the idea of "adynaton," the impractical and impossible as rendered in a hyperbolic figure of speech, in a manner that echoes my consideration of the subjunctive.

10 In regard to black maleness as a poetic (and bardic) ontology, Hayes makes early reference to the caged-bird metaphor, in an allusion to Paul Laurence Dunbar ("Sympathy") and Countee Cullen ("Yet Do I Marvel"); as well as to Orpheus, Sylvia Plath, Emily Dickinson, Prince, Ginuwine, and Gucci Mane, among others.

11 See Farah Jasmine Griffin, "When Malindy Sings: A Meditation on Black Women's Vocality," in *Uptown Conversation: The New Jazz Studies*, ed. Robert G. O'Meally, Brent Hayes Edwards, and Farah Jasmine Griffin (New York: Columbia University Press, 2004), 102–125.

12 An excellent example of subjunctivity's if-then logic is Lucille Clifton, "poem in praise of menstruation" (in *The Collected Poems of Lucille Clifton, 1965–2010*, ed. Kevin Young and

Michael S. Glaser [Rochester, NY: BOA Editions, 2012], 357), where poetic force resides in the compounding of the subjunctive phrasing, "if there is a river," a phrase that is intensified by repetition and varied enjambment, such that with each iteration the clause becomes more dramatic. Clifton's staggered declaration generates suspension as we wait for the phrase that will append each iteration of "if." Another well-known example of subjunctive-into-imperative is Claude McKay's poem "If We Must Die" (*The Complete Poems of Claude McKay* [Urbana: University of Illinois Press, 2004], 177).

13   These syntactical dynamics include the compounded adjectives "tree-loving / gun-hating" and the lovely "about-to-do deed." Notice, also, how the work of "imagine" surpasses the subjunctive possibility of "could" and "maybe," which are articulated in the epigraphic paragraph that opens the poem.

14   Part of the sublime is that "imagine" mixes syntax that is both interior (which is the normative habitat of the subjunctive, as a mood) and exterior (the habitat of the imperative command). Here I am borrowing from Elizabeth Povinelli, who, in *The Cunning of Recognition: Indigenous Alterities and the Making of Australian Multiculturalism* (Durham, NC: Duke University Press, 2002), cites the subjunctive as interior (72).

15   This quotation, which is explored considerably in chapter 1 of *Black Aliveness* is from a letter Barbara Christian wrote to Audre Lorde; see Alexis DeVeaux, *Warrior Poet: A Biography of Audre Lorde* (New York: W. W. Norton, 2004), 199.

16   I mean "timelessness" here to emphasize the fact that the subjunctive and the imperative, as moods, don't really indicate time on their own and are therefore not overtly tensed. We tend to read the subjunctive as future-oriented because of its signifying possibility, and perhaps we read the imperative through the present, but these time sentiments are not inherent in either syntax.

17   See Fred Moten, *Black and Blur* (Durham, NC: Duke University Press, 2017), especially the first paragraph, where he notes that "our resistant, relentlessly impossible object is subjectless predication, subjectless escape, escape from subjection, in and through the paralegal flaw that animates and exhausts the language of ontology" (vii), which describes his undertaking in *In the Break* and "The Case of Blackness," *Criticism* 50, no. 2 (2008): 177–218. Also see Stephen Best (*The Fugitive's Properties: Laws and the Poetics of Possession* [Chicago: University of Chicago Press, 2004]), Saidiya Hartman (*Scenes of Subjection: Terror, Slavery, and Self-Making in Nineteenth-Century America* [New York: Oxford University Press, 1997]), Hortense Spillers (especially "Mama's Baby, Papa's Maybe: An American Grammar Book," in *Black, White, and in Color: Essays on American Literature and Culture* [Chicago: University of Chicago Press, 2003], 203–229), and Alexander Weheliye (*Habeas Viscus: Racializing Assemblages, Biopolitics, and Black Feminist Theories of the Human* [Durham, NC: Duke University Press, 2014]). I also want to recall the discussion of Toni Morrison's characters Sula and Ajax (in chapter 2 of *Black Aliveness*) and to cite two other works that engage the terms of possession in ways I find compelling: Natasha Trethewey's poetry collection *Thrall* (Boston: Houghton Mifflin Harcourt, 2012), including the title poem's use of "as if" and the way that a sensibility of imagine radiates through the book's poetics; and Stephanie L. Batiste, "Dunham Possessed: Ethnographic Bodies, Movement, and Transnational Constructions of Blackness," *Journal of Haitian Studies* 13, no. 2 (2007): 8–22.

18   I thank John Casey for helping me achieve the clarity of this reading. In considering these dialectics of being, one could look toward Lauren Berlant's description of intersubjectivity in *Cruel Optimism,* where, thinking about Barbara Johnson's conceptualizing of apostrophe, Berlant explicates "the reaching out to a you" that is "actually a turning back, an animating of a receiver on behalf of the desire to make something happen *now* that realizes something in *the speaker,* makes the speaker more or differently possible, because she has admitted, in a sense, the importance of speaking for, as, and to, two—but

only under the condition, and illusion, that the two are really (in) one" (25–26; emphasis in the original).

19 My quick reference to smallness here evidences my debt to affect studies as it intersects with thinking about materiality, aesthetics, the ordinary, and phenomenology . This confluence of ideas informs and is cited in the discussion of aliveness in chapter 1 of *Black Aliveness*.

20 Michel de Certeau, *The Practice of Everyday Life,* trans. Steven Rendall (Berkeley: University of California Press, 1988), 115.

21 The quotation is from *Encyclopaedia Britannica Online,* Academic ed., s.v. "essay," accessed June 14, 2020, britannica.com/search?query=essay.

22 See Carl H. Klaus, "Toward a Collective Poetics of the Essay," in *Essayists on the Essay: Montaigne to Our Time,* ed. Carl H. Klaus and Ned Stuckey-French (Iowa City: University of Iowa Press, 2012), xv–xxvii, esp. xxiii–xxiv. Cheryl B. Butler makes a similar claim in *The Art of the Black Essay: from Meditation to Transcendence* (New York: Routledge, 2003): "In the African American essay, the uncanny moment happens upon the reader as it happens upon the essayist and upon the character the essayist constructs" (11).

23 The matter of audience and the biographical is taken up in chapter 4 of *Black Aliveness*. In regard to thinking about the author function, see Michael Boyce Gillespie, *Film Blackness: American Cinema and the Idea of Black Film* (Durham, NC: Duke University Press, 2016); and Patrick Colm Hogan, *Narrative Discourse: Authors and Narrators in Literature, Film, and Art* (Columbus: Ohio State University Press, 2013). In regard to the genre more broadly, see Ned Stuckey-French, *The American Essay in the American Century* (Columbia: University of Missouri Press, 2011); and Terence Cave, *How to Read Montaigne* (London: Granta Books, 2013).

24 We might do well to think of the personal essay in the genre of memoir, as a text of memory, unreliability, and indeterminacy, where the dialectic is between writer and speaker, not speaker and reader. Or we might consider the way Robert McRuer puts pressure on the word "composition"—a text of failing and willful disorder; see "Composing Bodies; or, De-composition: Queer Theory, Disability Studies, and Alternative Corporealities," *JAC* 24, no. 1 (2004): 47–78. That is, I want to be clear that the conventional matter of voice and authority is not read flatly in regard to the essay's dynamism. As Stefano Harney and Fred Moten ask, "What if authoritative speech is detached from the notion of a univocal speaker" and from a "possessive individualism"? (*Undercommons* 135, 140). As an extension of comments made earlier about voice (see chapter 2 of *Black Aliveness*), I would add that not only is voice in the essay not engaged with audience, but the voice represents a commitment to becoming, perhaps even "dissensus" in the way Jacques Rancière means that term to characterize that "gap in the sensible itself" ("Ten Theses on Politics," in *Dissensus: On Politics and Aesthetics,* trans. Steven Corcoran [London: Continuum, 2010], 38). We might recall also heteroglossia as explored in Mae G. Henderson, "Speaking in Tongues: Dialogics, Dialectics, and the Black Woman Writer's Literary Tradition," in *Changing Our Own Words,* ed. Cheryl Wall (New Brunswick, NJ: Rutgers University Press, 1989), 16–37. Related here is Gerard Genette's arguments in *Narrative Discourse: An Essay in Method* (Ithaca, NY: Cornell University Press, 1983), particularly the claim that there is no "third-person" narrator; also see Mieke Bal and Jane E. Lewin, "The Narrating and the Focalizing: A Theory of the Agents in Narrative," *Style* 17, no. 2 (1983): 234–269.

25 The matter of abstraction is addressed in chapter 2 of *Black Aliveness*.

26 From John D'Agata, "2003," in Klaus and Stuckey-French, *Essayists on the Essay,* 172–173.

27 William Hazlitt calls this "familiar style" ("On Familiar Style," in *Table-Talk: Essays on Men and Manners* [Charleston, SC: BiblioBazaar, 2007], 113–114); also see Gerald Early's discussion of the essay's conversational tone in the introduction to *Tuxedo Junction: Essays on American Culture* (New York: Ecco, 1989).

28 I mean poetic here in accord with the discussion of lyric voice in chapter 2 of *Black Aliveness*.

29 Vinson Cunningham, in "What Makes the Essay American," *New Yorker,* May 13, 2016, argues with D'Agata's attempt to reenvision the essay as "neutral attempt" in the vein of Montaigne and argues that "most of us Americans are Emersons: artful sermonizers, pathological point-makers." I'll address Cunningham's argument for the essay as a site of "conflict [that] is elemental to America" in chapter 4 of *Black Aliveness*. And in regard to experience and Hall's argument, I am recalling Joan W. Scott's iconic essay, "The Evidence of Experience," *Critical Inquiry* 17, no. 4 (1991): 773–794, particularly her notion of "the discursive character of experience" (787). Scott's argument ignited a debate in feminist studies, especially in women-of-color feminism; see Linda Alcoff's response to Scott, "Phenomenology, Post-structuralism, and Feminist Theory on the Concept of Experience," in *Feminist Phenomenology,* ed. Linda Fisher and Lester Embree (Berlin: Spinger, 2000), 39–56; and Johanna Oksala's more recent "In Defense of Experience," *Hypatia* 29, no. 2 (2014): 388–403. My interest in Scott's exploration of experience generates from a black world orientation, where the calculus of experience, evidence, and value is not at stake; indeed, this is how I have read Audre Lorde's claim for experience in chapters 1 and 2 of *Black Aliveness*. Unrelated to the discourse about Scott's essay, see Harvey Young's thinking about black embodiment and misrecognition in *Embodying Black Experience*.

30 Bigé's comment is from a personal conversation; see also Patrizia Pallaro, ed., *Authentic Movement: Essays by Mary Starks Whitehouse, Janet Adler and Joan Chodorow,* 2 vols. (London: Jessica Kingsley, 1999); D. Soyini Madison, foreword to *Black Performance Theory,* ed. Thomas F. DeFrantz and Anita Gonzalez (Durham, NC: Duke University Press, 2014), vii–ix; and Thomas F. DeFrantz and Anita Gonzalez, "Introduction: From 'Negro Experiment' to 'Black Performance,'" in DeFrantz and Gonzalez, *Black Performance Theory,* 1–15. The phrase "autonomous passage" is from conversation with Matt Ashby. I think of this consideration of inauthenticity as akin to Derek Walcott's idiom of feasting in the poem "Love after Love," in *The Poetry of Derek Walcott, 1948–2013,* ed. Glyn Maxwell (New York: Farrar, Straus and Giroux, 2014), 227.

31 See José Esteban Muñoz on disidentification (*Disidentifications* [Minneapolis: University of Minnesota Press, 1999]), Daphne Brooks on distanciation ("Nina Simone's Triple Play," *Callaloo* 34, no. 1 [2011]: 176–197), and Phillip Brian Harper on abstraction (*Abstractionist Aesthetics*).

32 The essay embodies thingness. As such, we could think of it as a kind of fetish that Monique Allewaert theorizes in *Ariel's Ecology: Plantations, Personhood, and Colonialism in the American Tropics* (Minneapolis: University of Minnesota Press, 2013): "Diasporic Africans' production of fetishes recognized that objects, far from being wordless or mute, could be conceived as dense interiorities or constellations of force that could store, process, and actualize information and that were also crucial to the production of the collectivities, or assemblages, through which personhood was articulated" (118–119). I am compelled by Allewaert's notice of "dense interiorities or constellations of force" since it evokes my claim of the essay's worldness through its small, fierce partiality. Furthermore, her attention to the aesthetics of the object collates with the Black Aesthetic movement's engagement and "critique of the text as object and monument" (Crawford, *Black Post-blackness,* 17), its investment in a textual force of aliveness that resides in the inanimate. Writers like Amiri Baraka and Larry Neal knew that even in the face of treacherous discourses of black objectification, the art object in a black world imaginary could instantiate being. Or, as Allewaert describes it, "Here, subjects and objects are recalibrated as assemblages that are animate and entangling. It then follows that personhood is neither an a priori category nor a mode of being oppositional to objects, but a composition produced through the relation of (para)humans, artifacts, and ecological forces" (119). My consideration of the broad and complicated discourse of thingness includes Moten, "The Case of Blackness"; Bill Brown, *A Sense of Things* (Chicago: University of Chicago Press, 2003); Sara Ahmed, *Queer Phenomenology: Orientations, Objects, Others* (Durham, NC: Duke University Press, 2006); Jane Bennett, *Vibrant Matter: A Political Ecology of Things* (Durham, NC: Duke University Press, 2010); Robin Bernstein, *Racial Innocence: Performing American Childhood from Slavery to Civil Rights* (New York: New York University Press, 2011); Zakiyyah Jackson, "Outer Worlds: The Persistence of Race in Movement 'Beyond the Human,'" *GLQ* 21, no. 2–3 (2015): 215–218; Jackson, "Losing Manhood: Animality and Plasticity in the (Neo)Slave Narrative," *Qui Parle* 25, no. 1–2 (2016): 95–136; Jayna Brown, "Being Cellular: Race, the Inhuman, and the Plasticity of Life," *GLQ* 21, no. 2–3 (2015): 321–341; and Aime Cesaire's notion of "Thingification," from *Discourse on Colonialism,* trans. Joan Pinkham (New York: Monthly Review Press, 2000), 42.

33 The idiom "aesthetics of existence" comes from Michel Foucault's essay "An Aesthetics of Existence," in *Philosophy, Politics, Culture: Interviews and Other Writings,* ed. Lawrence D. Kritzman (New York: Routledge, 1988), 47–53. And in thinking of the essay's volatility, I am leaning on Elizabeth Grosz's conceit of *Volatile Bodies: Toward a Corporeal Feminism* (Bloomington: Indiana University Press, 1994), as I am also recalling Adorno's claim that "the essay's innermost formal law is heresy. Through violations of the orthodoxy of thought, something in the object becomes visible which it is orthodoxy's secret and objective aim to keep invisible" ("The Essay as Form," trans. Bob Hullot-Kentor and Frederic Will, *New German Critique* 32 (1984): 151–171, 171).

34 My conceptualization of aliveness is phenomenological, which my engagement of the essay-as-genre bears out. And I should note here Moten's critique of "phenomenology's assumption of thingly individuation [that] renders no-thingness unavoidable and unavowable" (*The Universal Machine* [Durham, NC: Duke University Press, 2018], ix), where no-thingness is blackness. I am aware that phenomenology proper often excludes blackness, but I think that its ideas can be used for blackness in a black world, which indeed seems to be the point of Moten's discussion of Fanon in *Universal Machine,* chap. 3.

35 See *Seneca Review*'s fall 1997 issue on the lyric essay, though I retain the term "first-person essay" because I am speaking of works here that are less intentionally hybrid in form than the canonical examples of lyric essays (for example, Maggie Nelson, *The Argonauts* [Minneapolis: Graywolf, 2015]).

36 In *Film Blackness,* Michael Gillespie describes this collapsing as characteristic of the problem of black representations and cultural criticism. Moira Ferguson, in *Jamaica Kincaid: Where the Land Meets the Body* (Charlottesville: University of Virginia Press, 1994), argues that "in *A Small Place* the speaker is concerned for her native land, not herself" (78), which is one way to read Kincaid's work though different from my attention to the singularity of the speaker. Also see J. Brooks Bouson's reading in *Jamaica Kincaid: Writing Memory, Writing Back to the Mother* (Albany: State University of New York Press, 2005).

37 See Julieta Singh's argument about Kincaid's engagement of ambivalence in *Unthinking Mastery: Dehumanism and Decolonial Entanglements* (Durham, NC: Duke University Press, 2018). For scholarly considerations of the second person in *A Small Place* (New York: Farrar, Straus and Giroux, 1988), see Claudia Marquis, "'Making a Spectacle of Yourself': The Art of Anger in Jamaica Kincaid's *A Small Place,*" *Journal of Postcolonial Writing* 54, no. 2 (2018): 147–160; and Suzanne Gauch, "A Small Place: Some Perspectives on the Ordinary," *Callaloo* 25, no. 3 (2002): 910–919. Finally, Kincaid uses direct address superbly in her well-known short story (or is it an essay?) "Girl," *New Yorker,* June 26, 1978, https://www.newyorker.com/magazine/1978/06/26/girl.

38 In the first section, there are only two references where "I" is the subject of the sentence, though I am not including here this sentence where the singular first person operates as an exclamation: "I mean, in a way; I mean, your dismay and puzzlement are natural to you" (15).

39 See Harper, *Abstractionist Aesthetics,* esp. chap. 3, as well as his discussion of the second person in *Are We Not Men? Masculine Anxiety and the Problem of African-American Identity* (New York: Oxford University Press, 1996), chap. 2.

40 See David Wills, "Passionate Secrets and Democratic Dissidence," *Diacritics* 38, no. 1–2 (2008): 17–29. On virtuals, see Gilles Deleuze, *Difference and Repetition,* trans. Paul Patton (New York: Columbia University Press, 1994) and *Pure Immanence: Essays on a Life* (New York: Zone Books, 2005). I am also inspired here by Brian Massumi's conceptualization of affect (the use of "pure" and "raw" echoes him from *The Politics of Affect* [Cambridge, UK: Polity, 2015], 207) and Ashon Crawley's notion of otherwise in *Blackpentecostal Breath: The Aesthetics of Possibility* (New York: Fordham University Press, 2016). This tension between explicitness and furtiveness fuels the performative aspect of the anecdote, its quality of discursive unfolding, which Wills goes on to track via the secrecy embedded in the etymology of the word:

> The anecdote, *anekdota,* is etymologically the unedited (*inédit*). One should hear that in two senses: in the first place as that which hasn't yet been published, or prepared for publication, that which remains out of the light, in secret, but simply waiting for the inquisitive or all-seeing gaze of an editor; and in the second place as that which appears without the benefit of an editor's red pen, what is spoken of in excess of what needs to be written, that which appears unexpurgated, *unsecreted.* Thus the anecdote as *inédit* has, between its two senses, the paradoxical structure of the "patent secret": it can both give and withhold. (22–23)

See also Jane Gallop, *Anecdotal Theory* (Durham, NC: Duke University, 2002), especially for its suggestion that the anecdote merges the literary and the real; and Joel Fineman's essay "The History of the Anecdote," in *The Subjectivity Effect in Western Literary Tradition: Essays toward the Release of Shakespeare's Will* (Cambridge, MA: MIT Press, 1991), esp. 61–62. Wills's thinking about the anecdote parallels Foucault's theorizing in "Lives of Infamous Men," which considers the power to be had in the characterization of ordinary happenings, what he calls "nameless misfortunes and adventures gathered into a handful of words" and later, "those flash existences, those poem-lives" (in *Power: The Essential Works of Foucault, 1954–1984,* ed. James D. Faubion [New York: New Press, 2001], 3:157, 159). I find this compelling even though Foucault is describing accounts made *of* rather than *by* subjects. Thanks to Tamar Katz for pointing me to Wills's article and John Casey for the Gallop reference.

41 Indeed, it is an anxiety of audience that inspires much of the harsh criticism of Kincaid's writing; see, for example, Derik Smith and Cliff Beumel, "My Other: Imperialism and Subjectivity in Jamaica Kincaid's *My Brother,*" in *Jamaica Kincaid and Caribbean Double Crossings,* ed. Linda Lang-Peralta (Newark: University of Delaware Press, 2006), 96–112. In addition to Greg Thomas's arguments in *The Sexual Demon of Colonial Power: Pan-African Embodiment and Erotic Schemes of Empire* (Bloomington: Indiana University Press, 2007), see also Jane King, "A Small Place Writes Back," *Callaloo* 25, no. 3 (2002): 885–909.

42 See Ahmed, *Queer Phenomenology.* Bouson notes that shame is central to Kincaid's conceptualization of diasporic subjectivity. On the aesthetics of bad/ugly/difficult feelings, see José Esteban Muñoz, "Feeling Brown: Ethnicity and Affect in Ricardo Bracho's *The Sweetest Hangover (and Other STDs)" Theatre Journal* 52, no. 1 (2000): 67–71; Muñoz, "Feeling Brown, Feeling Down: Latina Affect, the Performativity of Race, and the Depressive Position," *Signs* 31, no. 3 (2006): 675–688; Sianne Ngai, *Ugly Feelings* (Cambridge, MA: Harvard University Press, 2007); and Darieck Scott, *Extravagant Abjection: Blackness, Power, and Sexuality in the African American Literary Imagination* (New York: New York University Press, 2010). This speaking of one's self through the object case coheres with the inclination of affect theory in these works. Also see Shaundra Myers, "Black Anaesthetics: The New Yorker and Andrea

Lee's *Russian Journal,*" *American Literary History* 31, no. 1 (2019): 47–73, on black aesthetics and the pronoun case.

43 That is, this closing abstraction reprises the subjunctive ambivalence of Kincaid's speaker, her aesthetic of "Caribbean impossibility," a phrase that is the title of Thomas W. Sheehan's useful study "Caribbean Impossibility: The Lack of Jamaica Kincaid," in Lang-Peralta, *Jamaica Kincaid and Caribbean Double Crossings,* 79–95. In using "ordinary language" here, I am making reference to the school of ordinary language philosophy; see Stanley Cavell, *Must We Mean What We Say?* (Cambridge: Cambridge University Press, 2002), especially the title essay; and *Themes Out of School: Effects and Causes* (Chicago: University of Chicago Press, 1984), especially the opening essay, as well as Toril Moi, *Revolution of the Ordinary: Literary Studies after Wittgenstein, Austin, and Cavell* (Chicago: University of Chicago Press, 2017). Finally, it is notable that Kincaid's final passage uses an equation that is strikingly similar to both Édouard Glissant's near the end of *Poetics of Relation* (trans. Betsy Wing [Ann Arbor: University of Michigan Press, 1997]) ("There would be something great and noble about initiating such a movement, referring not to Humanity but to the exultant divergence of humanities. Thought of self and thought of other here become obsolete in their duality. Every Other is a citizen and no longer a barbarian" [190]) and Frantz Fanon's near the end of *Black Skin, White Masks* (trans. Charles Lam Markmann [London: Pluto, 2008]): "There is no Negro mission; there is no white burden" (178).

44 This doing reminds me of Saidiya Hartman's undertaking in *Lose Your Mother: A Journey along the Atlantic Slave Route* (New York: Macmillan, 2008). That is, the imperative in Hartman's title, "lose your mother," is an ambivalence that infers an act of colonial imposition, a loss made inevitable and irrecuperable via the horrors of modernity, as well as a call to relinquish the meager practices of recovery. (Think, for example, about the speaker's journey through the trouble and fictions of kinship.) For a scholarly exploration of such losing, see Stephen Michael Best, *None like Us: Blackness, Belonging, Aesthetic Life* (Durham, NC: Duke University Press, 2018), especially his consideration of elimination and his engagement of Toni Morrison's *Beloved* and *A Mercy.*

45 The case for this making resonates with Jana Evans Braziel's argument about autofiction in "'Another Line Was Born . . .': Genesis, Genealogy, and Genre in Jamaica Kincaid's *Mr. Potter,*'" in Lang-Peralta, *Jamaica Kincaid and Caribbean Double Crossings,* 127–150.

46 See Ahmed, *Cultural Politics of Emotions* 12.

47 The quotation comes from Gilles Deleuze and Félix Guattari, *What Is Philosophy?,* trans. Hugh Tomlinson and Graham Burchell (New York: Columbia University Press, 1994): "Percepts are no longer perceptions; they are independent of a state of those who experience them. Affects are no longer feelings or affections; they go beyond the strength of those who undergo them. Sensations, percepts, and affects are *beings* whose validity lies in themselves and exceeds any lived. They could be said to exist in the absence of man because man, as he is caught in stone, on the canvas, or by words, is himself a compound of percepts and affects. The work of art is a being of sensation and nothing else: it exists in itself" (164; emphasis in original).

48 The quotation is the title of William Irwin's book, which was inspired by a moment in Kamel Daoud, *The Meursault Investigation* (New York: Other Press, 2015).

15
KARA WALKER, TWO IMAGES (*FONS AMERICANUS* AND *THE RIGHT SIDE*)

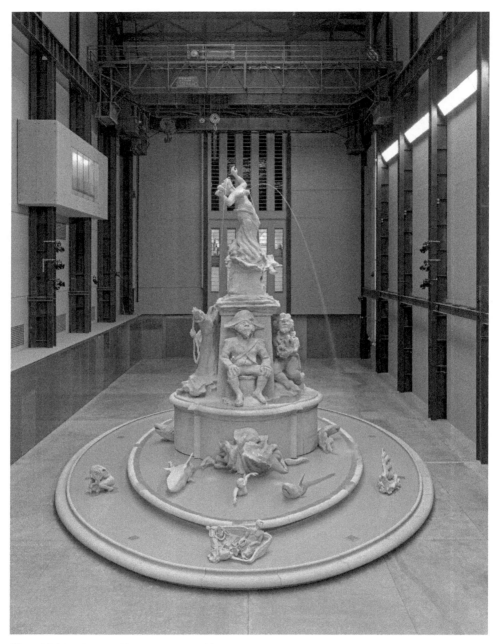

Plate 22 Kara Walker, *Fons Americanus* (2019). Non-toxic acrylic and cement composite, recyclable cork, wood, and metal, Main: 73.5 × 50 × 43 feet; Grotto: 10.2 × 10.5 × 10.8 feet. Installation view: Hyundai Commission: Kara Walker—Fons Americanus, Tate Modern, London, UK, 2019. Photo: Tate (Matt Greenwood). Artwork copyright Kara Walker. Courtesy of Sikkema Jenkins & Co., New York; Sprüth Magers, Berlin.

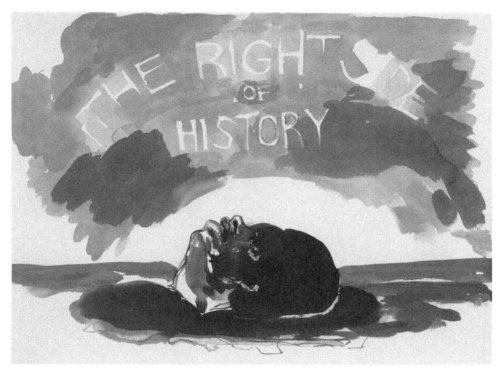

Plate 23 Kara Walker, *The Right Side*, 2018. Graphite, sumi ink, gofun, and gouache on paper, 22 × 30 inches. From the 38-part suite The Gross Clinician Presents: Pater Gravidam. Artwork copyright Kara Walker. Courtesy of Sikkema Jenkins & Co., New York; Sprüth Magers, Berlin.

PART FOUR

GROUNDINGS, TRANSPOSITIONS, BREAKS

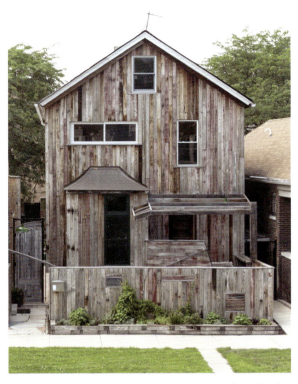

Plate 24 Theaster Gates, Exterior, *Archive House*, 2014. Image: Sara Pooley. Copyright Theaster Gates. Courtesy of Rebuild Foundation.

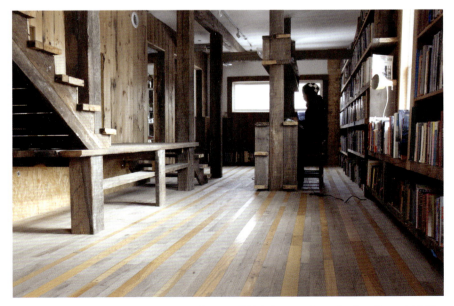

Plate 25 Theaster Gates, Interior, *Archive House*, 2014. Image: Sara Pooley. Copyright Theaster Gates. Courtesy of Rebuild Foundation.

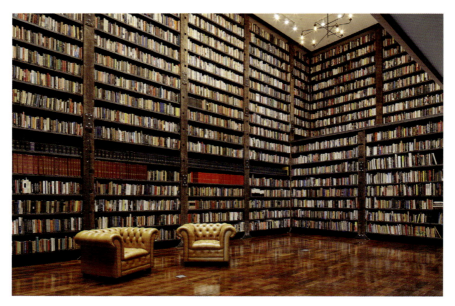

Plate 26 Theaster Gates, Johnson Publishing Library in the Stony Island Arts Bank. Image: Tom Harris. Copyright Hedrich Blessing. Courtesy of Rebuild Foundation.

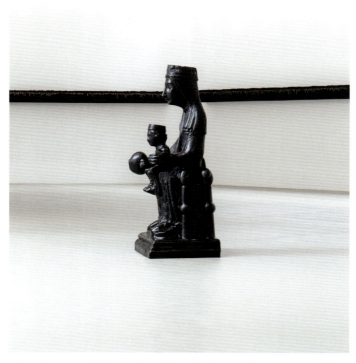

Plate 27 Theaster Gates, installation view, *Black Madonna*, Kunstmuseum Basel, Switzerland. June 9 to October 21, 2018. Image: Julian Salinas. Copyright Theaster Gates.

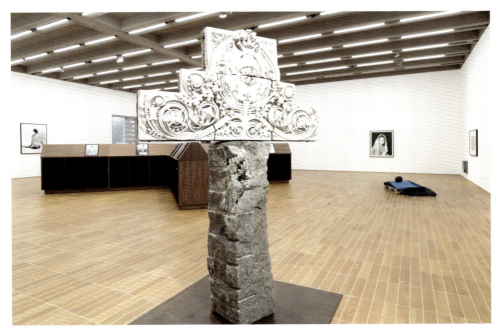

Plate 28 Theater Gates, *Walking Prayer*, Kunstmuseum Basel, Switzerland. June 9 to October 21, 2018. Image: Julian Salinas. Copyright Theaster Gates.

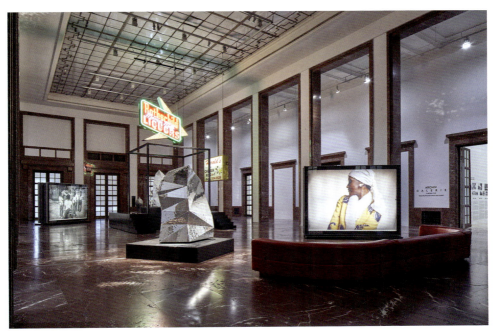

Plate 29 Theaster Gates, installation view of *Black Chapel*, Haus der Kunst, Munich. October 25, 2019 to July 19, 2020. Image Credit: Connolly Weber. Copyright Theaster Gates

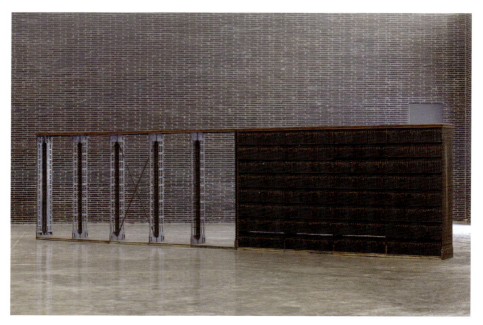

Plate 30 Theaster Gates, Installation shot, *Black Vessel*. 83 × 320 × 19 inches. Gagosian, New York. October 10, 2020 to January 23, 2021. Image Credit: Robert McKeever. Courtesy Gagosian. Copyright Theaster Gates.

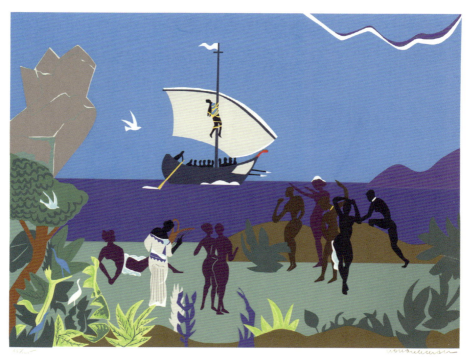

Plate 31 Romare Bearden, *Sirens' Song*, 1979. Color screenprint on wove Lana paper. Image: 46.04 × 60.96 cm (18 1/8 × 24 in.) sheet: 55.56 × 74.3 cm (21 7/8 × 29 1/4 in.). Copyright Romare Bearden Foundation. Licensed by VAGA at Artists Rights Society, New York.

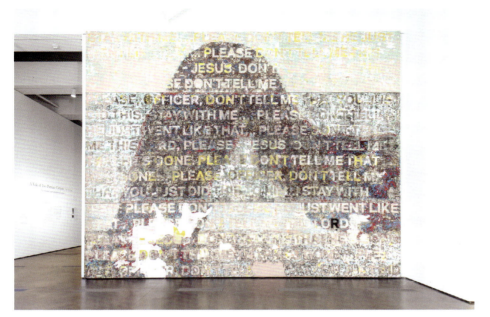

Plate 32 Mark Bradford, *150 Portrait Tone*, 2017. Mixed media on canvas, 240 × 310 in. Photo: Joshua White. Copyright Mark Bradford. Courtesy of the artist and Hauser & Wirth.

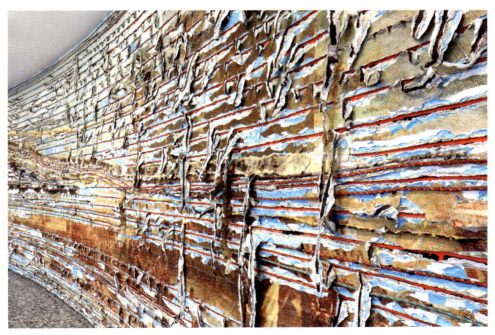

Plate 33 Mark Bradford, installation view, *Pikett's Charge*, 2017, Hirshhorn Museum and Sculpture Garden. Washington, DC. Photo: Cathy Carver. Courtesy of the artist and Hauser & Wirth.

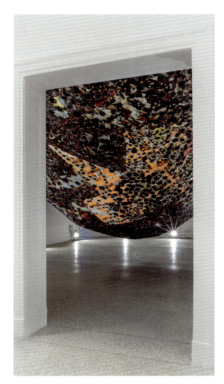

Plate 34 Mark Bradford, *Spoiled Foot*, 2016. Mixed media on canvas, lumber, luan sheeting and drywall. Dimensions variable. Copyright Mark Bradford. Photo: Joshua White. Courtesy of the artist and Hauser & Wirth.

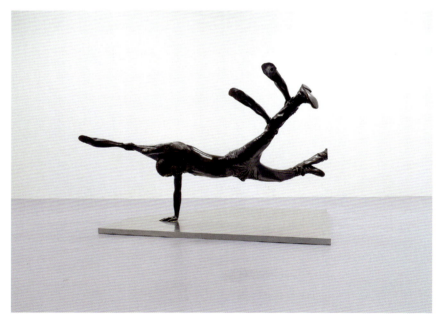

Plate 35 Hank Willis Thomas, *Looking for America*, 2018. Bronze and steel. 61 × 97 7/8 × 67 1/8 inches (overall). Copyright Hank Willis Thomas. Courtesy of the artist and Jack Shainman Gallery, New York.

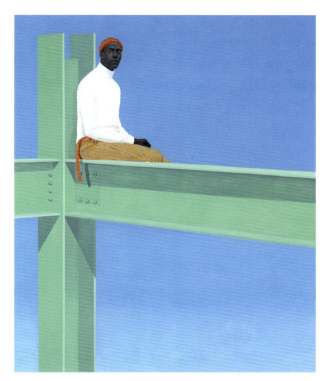

Plate 36 Amy Sherald, *If you surrendered to the air, you could ride it*, 2019. Oil on linen, 30 × 108 × 2 in. Copyright Amy Sherald. Courtesy of the artist and Hauser & Wirth.

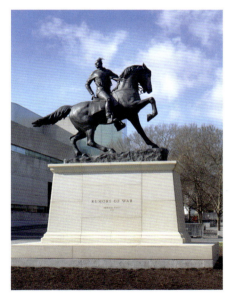

Plate 37 Kehinde Wiley, *Rumors of War*, 2019. Bronze with limestone base, 328 7/8 H × 305 7/8 W × 189 5/8 D inches. Photo: Travis Fullerton. Virginia Museum of Fine Arts, Richmond. Purchased with funds provided by Virginia Sargeant Reynolds in memory of her husband, Richard S. Reynolds, Jr., by exchange. Arthur and Margaret Glasgow Endowment, Pamela K. and William A. Royall, Jr., Angel and Tom Papa, Katherine and Steven Markel, and additional private donors, 2019.39.

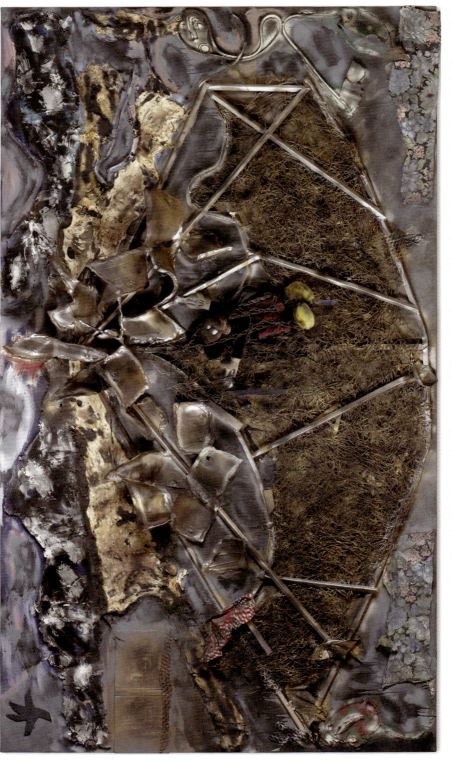

Plate 38 Thornton Dial, *High and Wide (Carrying The Rats to the Man)*, 2002. Philadelphia Museum of Art. Goat hides, carpet, found metal, clothing, stuffed-animal backpack, barbed wire, upholstery, textbook cover, Splash Zone compound, enamel, and spray paint on canvas on wood, 76 × 134 × 13 inches. Purchased with the McNeil Acquisition Fund for American Art and Material Culture, and gift of the Souls Grown Deep Foundation from the William S. Arnett Collection, 2017, 2017-229-16. Copyright Estate of Thornton Dial / Artists Rights Society, New York.

16

FROM *THE BLACK MARIA* AND FROM *KINGDOM ANIMALIA*

Aracelis Girmay

The Black Maria

black the raven, black the dapples on the moon & horses, black sleep of
    night & the night's idea,
black the piano, white its teeth but black its gums & mind with which
    we serenade the black maria.

& the night, wearing its special silver, serenades us, too,
with metaphors for how the body makes: semen stars, egg moon.

1600s: European ships heave fatly with the weight of black grief, black
    flesh, black people, across the sea; the
astronomers think the moon's dark marks are also seas & call them "the
    black maria."

Meanwhile, the Italian Riccioli, naming the seas according to his
    language & sensibilities.
Riccioli naming the dark fur of the moon:

Mare Cognitum, Mare Crisium, Mare Fecunditatis; Sea that Has
    Become Known, Sea of Crises, Sea of Fertility.
If it is up to Riccioli, then these are the names of three of the black maria.

I call the sea "mar." I call the sea "bahri."
I call the moon "luna." But "far" is my word for both you & the moon.

I heard a story once of a woman in the Sahara who, for years, carried a
    single page of *Anna Karenina*
that she read over & over, the long combers of print repeating like the
    waves of the black maria.

Language is something like this. A hard studying of cells under a
    microscope,
cells on their way to becoming other things: a person, a book,
    a moon.

Above the bowl, I crack the egg of this idea. Yolk from clear. Which is It?
    Which is Not It?
Does "moon" name the whole thing, or just the side we know, the side
    made dark with the black maria?

    How language is an asha tree, a fool that grows everywhere, a
        snake shedding its skin.
    A bowl of teeth. A kitchen plate of shadow & ruins, like the moon.

Moon says, "Please, god, crowd my loneliness with stars." But the star's
    life is short compared to Moon's.
There is always a funeral. Moon is always wearing the veil of the black maria.

    However pretty the sound, it was a misidentification,
    to name the basalt basins & craters the black maria of the moon.

If this is a poem about misseeing—Renisha McBride, Trayvon Martin,
    Rekia Boyd,
then these are also three of the names of the black maria.

    Naming, however kind, is always an act of estrangement. (To put
        into language that which can't be
    put.) & someone who does not love you cannot name you right, &
        even "moon" can't carry the moon.

If this is a poem about estrangement & waters made dark with millions
    of names & bodies—the Atlantic
Ocean, the Mediterranean & Caribbean Seas, the Mississippi, then these
    are also the names of the black maria.

    For days, the beautiful child Emmett swells into Tallahatchie. Even
        now, the moon paints its face
    with Emmett's in petition. Open casket of the night, somebody's
        child, our much more than the moon.

From *The Black Maria*

[I see Romare Bearden's "The Siren Song" & cannot help but think of you.]

Odysseus, his lungs full
of air, the sailors, their ears

full of wax, their lack
of will, then their will,

Odysseus' hearing,
the white froth

of gull, salt lapping at
the boat's brown skin,

the strange syntax of
his body's phrasing,

perpetual blue,
the perpetual blue

through which we read
his struggle, his

body is a black flag
wounding the pastoral

scene. I want to taunt
ship, to do two

things: call you Home
& deliver you Away,

revise the birth
of that hateful passage

by which you, Romare, & we.

[In one corner of the sky, near the horizon line, Romare Bearden has signed his
name. The name "Romare" means "Rome."]

Claim, I, to be the poet, making talk
the sirens who foreground the scene

where even the sky sings *More air, More air.*
Romare, Romare, whose body is a mourning sound

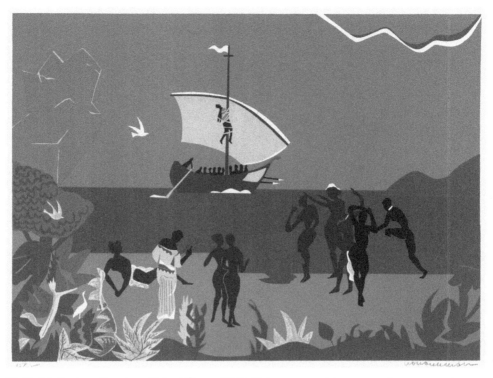

Plate 31 Romare Bearden, *Sirens' Song*, 1979. Color screenprint on wove Lana paper. Image: 46.04 × 60.96 cm (18 1/8 × 24 in.) sheet: 55.56 × 74.3 cm (21 7/8 × 29 1/4 in.). Copyright Romare Bearden Foundation. Licensed by VAGA at Artists Rights Society, New York.

(blood hyphened by the fleet
to Saint Domingue, to Rome), is

siren speech. But listen closely.
It is *my* mouth wailing redly

into the scene from The Future Knows.
It is my history raiding me. Romare,

teach me how to read this blues, please,
differently. How not to

assign all blackness near the sea
a captivity. I, the descendant

of each early war, who cannot remember peace,
have taken hostage the greenness

of my own mind. Want
the sirens to be

only the sirens. The sea
to be only the sea. O, magnolia

without blood, blackness
without blood.

Elegy

What to do with this knowledge
that our living is not guaranteed?

Perhaps one day you touch the young branch
of something beautiful. & it grows & grows
despite your birthdays & the death certificate,
& it one day shades the heads of something beautiful
or makes itself useful to the nest. Walk out
of your house, then, believing in this.
Nothing else matters.

All above us is the touching
of strangers & parrots,
some of them human,
some of them not human.

Listen to me. I am telling you
a true thing. This is the only kingdom.
The kingdom of touching;
the touches of the disappearing, things.

Kingdom Animalia

When I get the call about my brother,
I'm on a stopped train leaving town
& the news packs into me—freight—
though it's him on the other end
now, saying *finefine*—

Forfeit my eyes, I want to turn away
from the hair on the floor of his house

& how it got there Monday,
but my one heart falls
like a sad, fat persimmon
dropped by the hand of the Turczyn's old tree.

I want to sleep. I do not want to sleep. See,

one day, not today, not now, we will be gone
from this earth where we know the gladiolas.
My brother, this noise,
some love [you] I loved
with all my brain, & breath,
will be gone; I've been told, today, to consider this
as I ride the long tracks out & dream so good

I see a plant in the window of the house
my brother shares with his love, their shoes. & there
he is, asleep in bed
with this same woman whose long skin
covers all of her bones, in a city called Oakland,
& their dreams hang above them
a little like a chandelier, & their teeth
flash in the night, oh, body.

Oh, body, be held now by whom you love.
Whole years will be spent, underneath these impossible stars,
when dirt's the only animal who will sleep with you
& touch you with
its mouth.

Ars Poetica

May the poems be
the little snail's trail.

Everywhere I go,
every inch: quiet record

of the foot's silver prayer.
    I lived once.
    Thank you.
    It was here.

17

GROUNDWORK: RACE AND AESTHETICS IN THE ERA OF STAND YOUR GROUND LAW[1]

Sarah Elizabeth Lewis

Nothing is *without* ground.

—MARTIN HEIDEGGER

A grave. I sweat into the earth as I repair it.

—JERICHO BROWN

In 2016, Mark Bradford set to work on the ground of *150 Portrait Tone* (2017). A color field of found papers and acrylic paint with block text centralizes a searing scene from months earlier, when thirty-two–year-old Philando Castile was killed in his car by police officer Jeronimo Yanez at a traffic stop. Yanez had pulled over Castile for a broken taillight in Falcon Heights, Minnesota. He asked for Castile's license and registration. Castile, who had no criminal record and worked as a school supervisor at a Montessori school, complied, volunteering that he also had a legally owned firearm in the car in the compartment containing the documents. While leaning over to extract these, Castile affirmed that he was not reaching for a gun, but only submitting to the officer's request. His words offered no protection. Yanez shot Castile seven times as he sat next to his fiancée, Diamond "Lavish" Reynolds, with her four-year-old daughter in the backseat. Yanez would be acquitted of all charges.

But Reynolds had been video-recording the fatal events with her phone and began livestreaming. The video went viral. Bradford was gripped as he saw the footage of Reynolds holding four conversations nearly at once as Castile lay dying just inches away. She addressed the police officer, saying, "Please, officer, don't tell me that you just did this to him"; then said to Castile, "Stay with me"; prayed to God, "Please, Jesus, don't tell me that he's gone"; and to unknown viewers of her livestream exclaimed, "Please don't tell me he just went like that."[2] Bradford affixed these four utterances on the canvas as a streaming text. The regularized, stencil-shaped words visually rhymed with Reynolds's voice, which seemed unnaturally composed in the face of catastrophe—possibly an

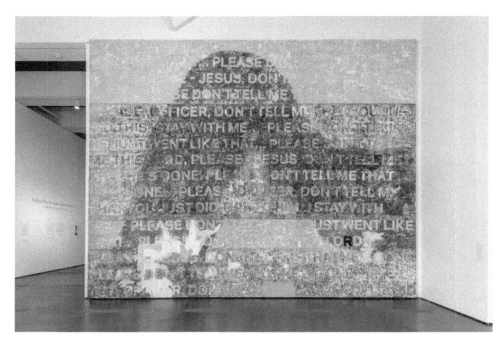

Plate 32 Mark Bradford, *150 Portrait Tone*, 2017. Mixed media on canvas, 240 × 310 in. Copyright Mark Bradford. Photo: Joshua White. Courtesy of the artist and Hauser & Wirth.

indication of shock, yet perhaps a necessary decision to present herself as unthreatening to the police officer in the wake of the fatal shooting. Reynolds's words, rendered in hues of reds, pinks, and textured blacks, cover and run off the edges of Bradford's canvas, with colors seeping through and across the letters' limits filling all intervening space. These textual pleas constitute the entire ground of the canvas, prostrating Reynolds, laying out the brutality of the event, and unfurling her words like a body at the viewers' feet.

Early drafts of the painting in Bradford's studio in 2016 consisted solely of the papered surface of stenciled words, a decision that seemed in keeping with his oeuvre of earlier gridded, cartographic, text-filled abstractions. Yet when the final version of *150 Portrait Tone* was installed at the Los Angeles County Museum of Art in 2017, it contained a new and massive central feature: snaking around, between, and under the words of the gridded text was an undulating brown and black shape, scaling up the canvas, approximating a mountainous peak. Hovering between an abstraction and the outline of a landscape mass, the uncanny form suggested a distended ground. Scholarship on Bradford has paid ample attention to his pioneering form of social abstraction but less to the significance behind his recent engagement with the ground. Bradford insistently lays down and deconstructs the ground both as material and conceptual foundation, as sullied and, at times, potentially redeemed.[3]

Bradford's practice began and remains a process of ambulatory digging into politicized grounds. He scoured the cityscape of his hometown of South Central Los Angeles for used, worn, and discarded papers from the informal economy shaped by the nexus of property, industrialization, and commerce—signs advertising goods and services.[4] With these found papers, which offered a source of pigment when wet, as well as others he purchased, he would build up his multilayered and multihued canvas and then dig and rip into it to construct the composition.[5] His selection of found paper—initially including translucent "end papers" from his time as a hairdresser—became a conceptual device to push against what he framed as racial and social exclusion, a way of "pulling things that don't belong in the art world and willing them into it."[6]

In the past few years, Bradford's practice has inspired a body of work focused on the conceptual foundations of American democracy. While painting *150 Portrait Tone* in 2016, he was at work on three other major projects. Selected to represent the United States at the Venice Biennale in 2017, he was creating an installation, *Tomorrow Is Another Day*, for the American Pavilion. He had also been commissioned by the US Embassy in London to create a mural that became *We the People*, a largescale painting of thirty-two panels, each ten square feet, based on excerpted text from the US Constitution. He was also at work compiling *Pickett's Charge* (2017), a nearly four-hundred-foot-long work based on Paul Dominique Philippoteaux's nineteenth-century cyclorama of the Civil War battle of Gettysburg (1883), to be displayed for four years on a curved gallery wall of the Hirshhorn Museum and Sculpture Garden in Washington, DC. Whereas previously his works had (as Huey Copeland put it) been fixed at once on "the historical, the cartographic, and the architectural while remaining resolutely abstract," with these new paintings, Bradford developed a deliberate, compositional insistence on ground.[7] Distinct from landscape, "ground" afforded the artist a way to consider, in ways both painterly and discursive, justice-oriented social and legal foundations.

Bradford is one of a number of contemporary artists, including Amy Sherald, Hank Willis Thomas, and Kehinde Wiley, who have innovated conceptual, compositional, and material tactics that create what I term "groundwork." By groundwork, I mean a set of aesthetic strategies through which the literal and figurative meaning of ground is destabilized productively to establish new conditions in the era of Stand Your Ground law.[8] Stand Your Ground (SYG) laws in the United States, first established in 2005 in Florida, define the right to self-defense and to claim the ground on which one stands if there is a perception of "reasonable threat."[9] As Caroline Light assiduously details, to date there exist some version of SYG laws in thirty-three states, some of which have higher homicide rates than states without them. The proliferation of SYG laws followed the 2008 Supreme Court *District of Columbia v. Heller* decision, which upheld the right to keep and bear arms for self-defense. The majority opinion rested on Justice Antonin Scalia's "originalist" interpretation of the Second Amendment, a temporal contextualization that does not recognize how the law disproportionately affects Black and Brown lives today. The right to use deadly force to protect oneself while in one's home, known as the castle doctrine, based on an early seventeenth-century case, was meant to offer legal protection from a violent home invasion with force. Yet Light argues that this doctrine, when "translated to the slave-holding colonies in North America," excluded "people who were themselves considered property—such as enslaved Africans and African Americans—from the legal capacity to defend themselves from white violence."[10]

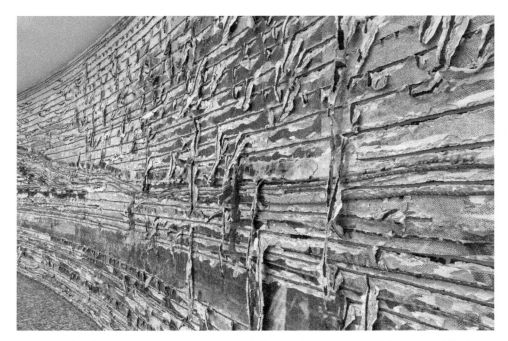

Plate 33 Mark Bradford, installation view, *Pikett's Charge*, 2017, Hirshhorn Museum and Sculpture Garden. Washington, DC. Copyright Mark Bradford. Photo: Cathy Carver. Courtesy of the artist and Hauser & Wirth.

The emergence of groundwork aesthetics during the SYG era is of distinct significance. This period has witnessed a new civic tradition of visual documentation, as was the case with Reynolds, to counter what often appears to be the groundlessness or baselessness of the law. (Indeed, synonyms and antonyms of the terms "grounded," "on the ground that," and "ground for dismissal" are often used in legal arguments including, ironically, in the cases about reparations.)[11] Visually capturing events has become a response to and, at times, a defense against the disproportionate number of killings of largely Black bodies in the American public landscape.[12] This legacy is born of what Jasmine Nichole Cobb, a scholar of art and visual culture, has called the "ocular culture" of surveillance that defined enslavement and fugitivity and which helped to establish the long history of the hypervisibility of racial terror.[13] The aim here, however, is not to document the temporal shifts that have occurred *within* the SYG era, but rather to interrogate a consistent feature of groundwork aesthetics.

Groundwork aesthetics emerging in contemporary art intersect with philosophical work on the ground of history and on the history of the concept of "ground." For artists to render a landscape, they must create a picture that is "the contrary of the ground," as Jean-Luc Nancy has put it.[14] In the history of art, the picture plane constitutes both the concrete ground of the image and also a repudiation—the flat surface that bears the paint is at odds with the dimensional illusions that representational painting is bound to give. Recent philosophical engagements with the pictorial ground are never far from the Heideggerian investigations of the "groundedness" of what we consider to be history, which is to say, the reasons or causes behind it.[15] Exploring this domain in the modern age requires asking, as philosopher Michael Allen Gillespie frames it, not "What is *history*?" but instead "*What* is history?"—namely, what is the ground of history.[16] The aesthetic investigations of ground under discussion here also engage Christina Sharpe's articulation and meditation on being "in the wake," with this groundlessness of law born of what Saidiya V. Hartman considers the "afterlife of slavery," settler colonialism, and democracy in the United States.[17]

Groundwork aesthetics push the conceptual limits of what T. J. Clark frames as art created from a fixation on "ground level," that is, art that takes the upright physical form as a "subject in its own right."[18] Clark's project focused on compositional engagements with the ground such that it "becomes something other than a notional 'plane'"; rather, in his words, it becomes "a grounding, a limit condition of the human; and further, it becomes a world in itself."[19] By analyzing the cultural project as it spans centuries and cuts across "ideological boundaries," Clark argues that these artists are wrestling with "uprightness" as a "value" or a "great fact of human existence."[20]

The artists under consideration challenge the semantics of the ground by framing upright physical posture not as a "value" alone, as Clark terms it, but as a condition of sovereignty, as a stance connected to power incontrovertibly affected by the decimation of Indigenous populations as well as the "afterlife of slavery" and Jim Crow–era terror tactics.[21] These artists ask: What does it mean to not be able to "stand your ground"? What are the tools available to prompt a meditation on this question? Is there methodological room in the discipline of art history to consider what we make of these artistic practices focused on bodies denied this upright position of self-sovereignty and agency? Bradford's work typifies how these artists both explicitly and implicitly call for an expanded set of methods to accommodate how artists are formally addressing the racialized and political forces that create an artwork's conceptual and material ground.

Groundwork expands what constitutes ground itself in aesthetic practice through certain "gothic" tactics (see below) focusing on precarity and migration. My focus is on the compositional attention to groundlessness and precarity as a strategy through which to challenge and reconceive what is meant by the foundations of the history of racial representation and rights in the United States. While Bradford drafted 150 *Portrait Tone* in his Los Angeles studio, he was also transforming Philippoteaux's scene of the failed Confederate offense, *Pickett's Charge*, into a scene of instability on an adjacent wall. He glued layers of paper with grossly enlarged, pixilated images of Philippoteaux's original traveling cyclorama (first shown in Boston and later at the 1893 World's Fair) onto eight panels, each twelve feet high and up to fifty feet in length. Then he tore those piled reproductions by cutting, scraping, and tugging at twine he had embedded in the layers. On a visit I took to his studio, I saw Bradford start to rip up the layers, showing me pieces in his hand as if gathering stones or shells from a vast beach. This muscular process of décollage left edges of paper pulp that flagrantly hang off the canvas, now a mass of caked, stratigraphic bands of undulating and textured layers of colored paper.[22] "Politically and socially, we are at the edge of another precipice. I'm standing in the middle of a question about where we are as a nation," Bradford said in a statement for his installation, a composition insistent on creating a sense of groundlessness as a precondition to a new future.[23] Very few indices of the original skirmishes, objects, figures, or soldiers from the Civil War history painting remain. Visitors to Bradford's work in the Hirshhorn gallery are provided magnifying glasses, a confirmation of the confusion and disorientation it provokes from the severe abstraction and its installation in the open, cylindrical chamber. As Tobias Wofford notes, searching the canvas for moments of legibility or clues to connect Bradford's contemporary interpretation to the Civil War battlefield scenes in the cyclorama is futile.[24]

Bradford created this work alongside his installation for the 2017 American Pavilion at the Venice Biennale, where he altered the graveled and typically manicured grounds of the entrance through an installation of strewn trash—paper, debris, and ephemera—deliberately imported from Los Angeles (*Barren*, 2017). Visitors stepped gingerly around debris to enter the first salon of the pavilion, entitled "Mark Bradford: *Tomorrow Is Another Day*," referencing part of the final line of the film *Gone with the Wind* as seen through his eyes—a signal of Bradford's continued recursive investigation of this mediated history of American racial politics. The first room was entirely subsumed by the distended sculptural painting *Spoiled Foot* (2016), a concave canvas mass suspended from the ceiling nearly to the floor that physically forces the viewer back nearly to the perimeter of the room upon entering. This expands the scope of Clark's ground-level considerations. The surface of this bulging form, rendered in blood red, orange, and white, is mottled with black spheres as if diseased and metastasized, reflecting Bradford's sense of the world in a state of epic collapse. In a pavilion funded almost entirely by the US State Department, viewers were forced to walk "on the margin," as Bradford said.[25] To enter was to be unsure of one's footing and then forcibly displaced.

Spoiled Foot references aspects of nineteenth-century gothic visual traditions exemplified in John Quidor's painting *The Money Diggers* (1832), with its focus on the earth in a curious state of instability. The composition centers a gap-mouthed pit in the earth on a pitch-black night, with a Black man, rendered in brown and green almost indistinguishable from the ground, crawling out at the feet of alarmed figures—a scene of horror from the eponymous collection of tales by Washington Irving. Sarah Burns has undertaken a close reading of this painting through what she terms the visual gothic, distinct from an architectural or literary gothic as a "haunting" that often is borne obliquely of a reckoning with enslavement and the "pernicious inequalities of gender, class, and ethnicity" that shaped the political and social conditions of democracy in the United States.[26] Quidor based his painting on a scene in the tale "The Adventure of a Black Fisherman," about a cabbage farmer's search for treasure that joins him to a healer and a caricatured Black fisherman, "Mud Sam," who attempts to locate the spoils—a satire of the risky Jacksonian market of speculation. At the moment when the fisherman digs a hole by firelight, he hits an object and finds that it is hollow, and the environment becomes haunted with the presence of a spectral buccaneer. To convey this pivotal moment, Quidor not only renders the visceral response to this shock found in the book: the figures recoil and seek cover in their thwarted pursuit of reward and stability. Here he goes further than Irving's text in aligning blackness, both figuratively and spatially, with the shape of the unstable ground as the means to convey terror.[27]

Bradford's aim was for the pavilion to convey viscerally his own sense of being foundationally "pushed out" or expelled when considering the foundational grounds of

American life.[28] At the conclusion of the pavilion installation was a large-scale projection of his video *Niagara* (2005). The frame holds for an extended time on the swishing walk of an African American man seen from behind in sneakers and socks pulled up and wearing tight, high-waisted shorts. He often passed by Bradford's studio, at times with a baseball bat to protect himself.[29] This contemporary *Rückenfigur* faces down an urban terrain as he claims the security of his path. "The last room is really about me again, walking the earth," Bradford said, referring to this piece. "It is not me walking literally. . . . But it is about me, as I am, vulnerable body, walking the earth."[30]

It is within this context that Bradford completed 150 *Portrait Tone*, a title that references how aesthetics have historically crafted the contested ground of racial justice. "150 Portrait Tone" is a commercial painter supplier's name for the slightly pink acrylic—akin to Crayola's "flesh" crayon, later renamed "peach"—that provides much of the ground of the color field of Bradford's painting. Embedded in the decision to call one color "portrait tone" is the consideration of whiteness as a normative designation. The pigment's title conveys that it is part of an ascending, linear, systematized framework for delineating color as connected to racial hierarchy, naturalized in aesthetic traditions. Bradford deliberately used the peach color, 150 Portrait Tone, unmixed, straight from the container.[3] Indeed, a peach, light pink color once guided the photographic studio laboratory's process of defining a "normal" portrait range. As Lorna Roth argues, this was epitomized in the invention of "the Shirley card," an image of a white woman that film processing companies, largely in the United States, used to calibrate the ideal chromatic range of a photographic print.[32] As Roth's research demonstrated, it took complaints from chocolate and furniture manufacturers unable to show the difference between tones of these products to spur Kodak to create a separate film that had a broader dynamic range and altered the chemical composition in film. With the use of color, title, and Reynolds's verbal plea, Bradford's work questions what historic ground undergirds the fatality embedded in racial profiling. Vision in the SYG era, he suggests, is conditioned by the foundation of nineteenth-century racial science that reduced Black subjects to racialized "types."[33]

Bradford's investigation came with a productive clarion call to expand the methods used to understand his work. He made this demand plain with a direct address to critics. "Look . . . I know I have to engage art history, and I am going to be a painter, and I know that modernism is on the table, I'm just trying to tell you there's more here than what you're seeing now," he explained in the rounds of press interviews that accompanied the debut of these landmark murals and installations. "All you're seeing is linear grids because that's where I am but stay tuned."[34] He then addressed how to train our gazes to see the racialized history of our aesthetic conventions: "What does it mean to unpack that moment, when both Jackson Pollock and Emmett Till were on magazine covers?" Bradford asked this question while speaking about his interest in 1950s abstraction and the history of racial terror, but he formulated the question as one pertaining directly to the discipline of art history itself.[35] In his own work, Bradford has forced the conceptual extension down to his titles. One of his paintings from 2001 references Agnes Martin's print suite *On a Clear Day* (1973) with the title *On a clear day, I can usually see all the way to Watts*. Yet Bradford's practice does not engage with the "abstract sublime" on its own terms, with its "covert allusions to nature" (as Rosalind Krauss argued was the case with Martin).[36] By deliberately

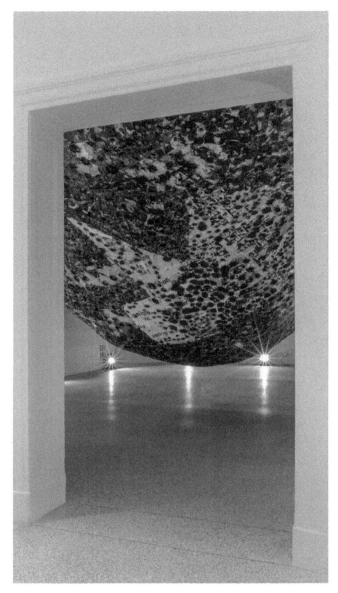

Plate 34 Mark Bradford, *Spoiled Foot*, 2016. Mixed media on canvas, lumber, luan sheeting and drywall. Dimensions variable. Copyright Mark Bradford. Photo: Joshua White. Courtesy of the artist and Hauser & Wirth.

alienating us from the sublime and the experience of nature, Bradford aims not to allude to American landscape conventions—the vaunted tradition that most engaged with the cultural project of nation-building in the nineteenth century—even if the distended, snaking form that unifies the field in 150 *Portrait Tone* partially conjures them. Instead, or rather by way of this ghost of landscape past, his groundwork challenges how we define the culture deliberately left out of these genres. While Bradford's Art + Practice Foundation, based in the Leimert Park neighborhood of South Los Angeles, is often seen as the site of this more social engagement, his groundwork has created a new strategy through which to locate what Copeland called the "ethical imperatives" of his painting practice.[37]

This methodological question is significant since compositional groundlessness is both a historic condition of African American visual representation and a reemergent aesthetic tool for indicating the unfinished reckoning with the history of racial terror. Artists have long depicted the slippage between subject and object that has led to the asymmetry within the SYG laws: who is being protected and what (or who) may lay claim to one's place.[38] One of the best-known examples is the "selfie" photograph of Trayvon Martin, killed by George Zimmerman on February 26, 2012, in Sanford, Florida. Art and cultural historian Nicole R. Fleetwood centers this image in her probing study of racial icons, noting that the top-lighting in Martin's "selfie" photograph gives the effect of a haloed, disembodied head, which partially accounts for its iconicity.[39] This compositional feature foundationally impacted artistic representation of African American subjects during early periods of contested citizenship. An example comes to us in the set of drawings made by William H. Townsend circa 1839–40, during the trial of the *Amistad* enslavement ship rebellion in New Haven, Connecticut, where the enslaved Mende remained awaiting their trial with a defense mounted by former president John Quincy Adams. In twenty-two portraits, Townsend drew the outline of Mende heads and busts in graphite traces that offer a sense of how they fashioned themselves, controlled their gaze, smiled or not in his presence. What is most compositionally present is the emptiness—each head is placed as if floating in the upper picture plane, marking it as a kind of provisional portraiture. Cobb's study of the marriage of racial subjecthood, enslavement, and representation in nineteenth-century visual culture argues that this blankness signals the attempt to place the Mende—themselves in a suspended state as they awaited a decision about their status as free or enslaved—in a new conditional context.

In *The Souls of Black Folk*, W. E. B. Du Bois also presaged this consideration with the literal and figurative signification of "ground" in the context of Reconstruction. According to Adrienne R. Brown, Du Bois fixes on the residue of enslavement found in the dilapidation of the built environment in his "Black Belt" chapter on Dougherty County, Georgia.[40] He catalogs the "falling homes" with "bricks . . . falling out" of buildings, and others with "worm-eaten pillars," one with a "moss-grown roof" that was "falling in," all in a state of impending collapse.[41] As I discuss at length in the book project on which this chapter is based, Du Bois's focus here anticipates the polysemic fixation on ground, as distinct from land or property, to question, conjure, and critique what could have supported post-Emancipation visions of the future.

Yet the artists under consideration here have crystallized a new compositional device of groundlessness to visually emblematize a civic and conceptual foundation that needs to be rebuilt. One sees this in the oeuvre of Whitfield Lovell in the *KIN* series begun in 2008, in Xaviera Simmons's *The Whole United States Is Southern* (2019) project, which examines Jacob Lawrence's *The Migration Series*, in Amy Sherald's painting *If you surrendered to the air, you could ride it* (2019), and in Theaster Gates's installation in 2019 of the gazebo where Tamir Rice was killed. This is to say that Bradford's engagement with groundwork aesthetics has occurred alongside other landmark works fixated on precarity that reconceive and challenge the foundational journey that led to the SYG laws. While there is not sufficient space in this chapter to engage each extensively, a foray into some of the related groundwork projects on precarity shows how this phenomenon has also pushed the boundaries of these artworks to include an engagement with SYG laws in ways that reframe and extend the discourse on art, race, and migrancy.[42] When seen together, groundwork aesthetics and the issues of precarity they address and render speak to the urgency of this development in the field of contemporary, American, and African American art—three fields that cannot be neatly separated when considering the interpenetration of representation in the history and future of justice in this country.

Consider the form of the Equal Justice Initiative (EJI)'s National Memorial for Peace and Justice unveiled in Montgomery, Alabama, in April 2018 to honor the lives lost to lynching. Codesigned by MASS Design and framed by public installations by artists such as Hank Willis Thomas, the memorial suspends eight hundred weathered steel plinths from the ceiling of the open-air Capitoline structure that recapitulate the form of the often municipally endorsed, even celebrated public spectacles—acts of racial control and terror. Deliberately sited on a hill in Montgomery rivaling the height of the city's capitol dome, the weathered steel columns in variegated shades of brown approximate the scale and tone of the bodies, largely African American, lynched with nooses hung from trees. Lynchings, which largely took place between 1877 and 1950, were a distinct form of extrajudicial violence meant to ensure racial inequality, a form of terrorism carried out with impunity. Many victims of lynching were murdered without ever being formally accused of any crime.

What has gone undiscussed in the critical acclaim for this celebrated memorial is that the EJI offices, built on the site of a former enslavement warehouse, contain another monument, an installation of soil collected from the site of every known lynching in the state of Alabama and displayed in glass jars. (A portion of this installation is now presented at EJI's Legacy Museum.) In the full installation in the office, done in collaboration with MASS Design, the clear jars of soil operate as synecdoche, each with a unique color— rust red, deep green, brown—standing for individual Black lives lost in Alabama alone. Each jar is the result of members of the community marking the site of a known or recently discovered incident of lynching. One jar stays with the community, the other comes to EJI. The graves, once unmarked, are now made; each jar is a way to "sweat into the earth" as an act of "repair," as poet Jericho Brown might reflect on it.[43]

On the pathway out of the memorial stands a second version of a bronze sculpture by Thomas, *Raise Up* (2018), that connects the visual logic of policing with the legacy of racial terror. Thomas has sunk the bronze arms and heads of twelve men with their hands up and fingers outstretched in the symbolic gesture of surrender and acquiescence to power into a concrete block approximately six feet high. The composition challenges T. J. Clark's framing of "uprightness," defined as largely a comment on evolution or an allegorical statement about "value," offering the example of "high standing" as a statement of worth and stating that "being supine or prostrate is never very far from lollying about and groveling."[44] By contrast, Thomas uses the visual fact of uprightness and emergency conditions as a strategy to foreground rights-based struggle, expanding our sense of what Clark considers to be the "resistances" and "constraints" that work against the upright form and, in so doing, revealing how a critical race perspective is requisite for grasping this posture as a hard-won act of self-sovereignty. One could extend this analysis by considering how Thomas's recent public art installation practice further engages with this rhetoric, perhaps most dramatically with *Looking for America* (2019). In this bronze and steel sculpture, a body has its limbs splayed out as if it were a human kite. Pants and shirt strain to stay on a body with only one hand on the floor while both legs are being gripped by disembodied forearms. The work is a volumetric appropriation of a central portion of a 1964 photograph by Danny Lyon of the arrest in Cambridge, Maryland, of Clifford Vaughs, a Student Nonviolent Coordinating Committee photographer. Thomas has eliminated the dominating figures of the police in the midground. Here, he symbolizes the physical strain and sacrifice of the civic efforts to work toward racial justice through a body straining to remain upright.

This double valence of groundlessness as an incisive engagement with migrancy and precarity is a way to understand the composition of a recent painting by Amy Sherald, *If you surrendered to the air, you could ride it* (2019), her largest painting to date, with a title that quotes a line from Toni Morrison's novel *Song of Solomon*. Against a cerulean sky save a band of lightly rendered clouds, Sherald sets a lone figure of a Black man in a white turtleneck on a corner of a construction I-beam at the middle of the canvas. For the vertiginous perspective, Sherald draws on a widely known image composition: the 1932 photograph *Lunch atop a Skyscraper*, recently attributed to Charles Ebbets, with eleven workmen, all ostensibly white, three of whom have been identified as Mohawk, sitting on a construction beam 850 feet high at New York City's 11 Rockefeller Plaza. Adrienne R. Brown's research on race and the development of skyscrapers reveals a paradox—the building's very materiality proves inextricably entangled with race, down to designs meant to avoid "miscegenated" facades, yet the effects of skyscrapers' abstracting scale has a reductive effect on visualizing the racial and ethnic specificity of labor.[45] Sherald's composition inverts what Brown recuperates from early twentieth-century writing—that the "skyscraper potentially disrupted the ability to perceive race as well as the capacity to feel raced" by her figurative focus on a Black man seen from below.[46] Sherald eliminates what created the dimensional impact in Ebbets's photograph—the dizzying density of New York City buildings seen from high above. In her composition, a lone Black man is perched as if an emblem of the often-unexamined racial homogeneity of the source image and its commentary on racialized class divides. His expression is calm, his eyes, piercing and direct, rendered with her characteristic grisaille.[47] Through the compositional tension of suspension, we are blocked from seeing the ground "scenes" of contestation, considered as Hartman might see them.[48]

Sherrilyn Ifill and Bryan Stevenson, among other writers and scholars, have shown that the northward migratory movement that changed the tone and racial composition of northern cities such as New York City, alongside immigration, was powered not only by opportunity but also by fear of lynching and other forms of retribution for resistance to Jim Crow rule.[49] Legal doctrines fueled lynching and racial terror, namely the Slaughterhouse case of 1873 and *U.S. v. Cruikshank* (1876), which ruled that the Fourteenth Amendment only protected citizens from actions of the state, not from actions of individuals, which left many, including African Americans, vulnerable to these acts of violence.[50] What Kevin

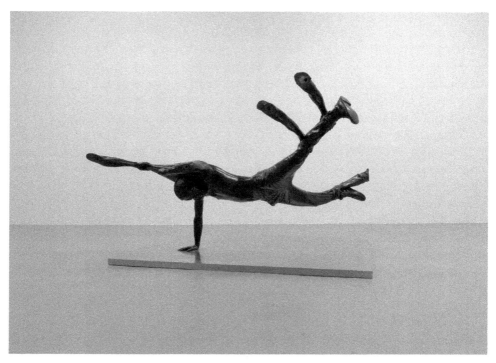

Plate 35 Hank Willis Thomas, *Looking for America*, 2018. Bronze and steel. 61 × 97 7/8 × 67 1/8 inches (overall). Copyright Hank Willis Thomas. Courtesy of the artist and Jack Shainman Gallery, New York.

Quashie articulates as the "quiet" and "interiority" of the man in Sherald's sparse, groundless composition allows us to consider the broader spatial coordinates that could have led to this social precarity: Jim Crow rule, lynching, and that were also part of the cultural context of the 1930s.[51]

Indeed, Kehinde Wiley's public art statue *Rumors of War* (2019) acquires historical depth from the ground, bravura upright posture, and engagement with SYG-era violence. Unveiled in Times Square in New York City and moved to the longest-held Confederate capital city, Richmond, Virginia, the statue made a journey across contested terrain that became a compositional feature of the work. Wiley reimagined a Confederate monument in the form of a twenty-seven-foot-tall equestrian statue topped by a dreadlocked, top-knotted figure wearing a hoodie confidently astride a horse. When I saw the work in person with Wiley, he also focused on ground in the philosophical sense, pointing out two features: that it was reinforced by steel under the New York City sidewalk, and that he decided to embed his signature in the sculpture's rendering of soil and grass. The plinth base, he also explained, was not only able to accommodate people sitting on it but also was larger than that of the J. E. B. Stuart Confederate statue in Richmond on Monument Avenue.[52] This monument is now permanently installed on Arthur Ashe Boulevard, next to the headquarters of the Daughters of the Confederacy, in front of the Virginia Museum of Fine Arts, and adjacent to the row of Confederate monuments on the avenue in Richmond.

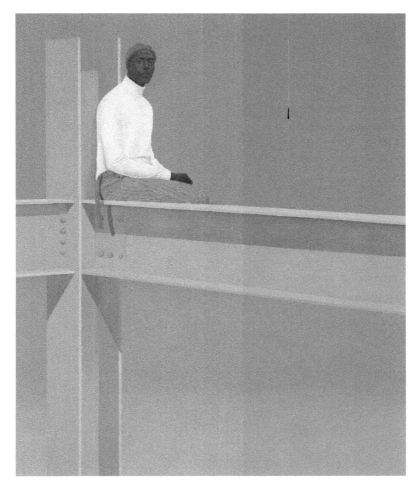

Plate 36 Amy Sherald, *If you surrendered to the air, you could ride it*, 2019. Oil on linen, 30 × 108 × 2 in. Copyright Amy Sherald. Courtesy of the artist and Hauser & Wirth.

The rider's head is dramatically turned toward the sky, a figurative send-up of the Stuart statue and the racial legacy on which it is based.

Wiley rendered the rider's face from a composite of images of six Black men killed in Stand Your Ground law states.[53] The sky-facing position, in fact, a frequent pose of Wiley's sitters, offers a potential rereading of his *Down* series from 2008, with its chilling juxtaposition of images of prone or collapsed Black men and settings drawn largely from paintings of deaths by artists such as Andrea Mantegna, Diego Velázquez, and Caravaggio that, too, recall the prostrated bodies and fatal aftermath of incidents of racial terror. In Wiley's hands, the sky-facing direction becomes a symbolic rebuke and refusal to surrender as a matter of life or death.

These aesthetics force a consideration of how artists are working in ways to honor lives lost due to racial bias in the carceral state—an aesthetic ethics of care for Philando Castile,

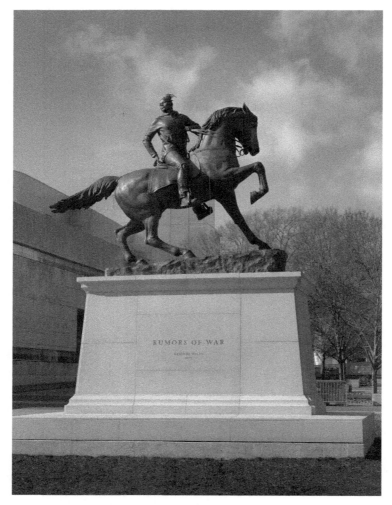

Plate 37 Kehinde Wiley, *Rumors of War*, 2019. Bronze with limestone base, 328 7/8 H × 305 7/8 W × 189 5/8 D inches. Photo: Travis Fullerton. Virginia Museum of Fine Arts, Richmond. Purchased with funds provided by Virginia Sargeant Reynolds in memory of her husband, Richard S. Reynolds, Jr., by exchange. Arthur and Margaret Glasgow Endowment, Pamela K. and William A. Royall, Jr., Angel and Tom Papa, Katherine and Steven Markel, and additional private donors, 2019.39.

for Tamir Rice, for the six unnamed Black men in Wiley's portrait, for the countless men who haunt Sherald's image, and for the over four thousand men and women killed by lynching as memorialized by the work of the Equal Justice Initiative founded by Bryan Stevenson. As a final example, in 2018 Theaster Gates used the same aesthetic tactic of mobility by resiting the actual gazebo in which twelve-year-old Tamir Rice was killed by twenty-six-year-old Cleveland rural police officer Timothy Loehmann in 2014. On learning that it would be destroyed by the city, Gates asked Rice's mother Samaria to allow his Rebuild Foundation in Chicago to house the structure until it found a permanent home. A gazebo, a rural visual device, is a polygonal structure positioned to offer a vantage point from which to take in a landscape. This gazebo was placed on the manicured lawn of the Rebuild Foundation's building, ground that is, in fact, an easement, a mound required by municipal zoning regulation to prevent drive-by shootings of the nearby residences. The structure associated with Rice's murder stands as a symbol of the interpenetration of the ground, land, and racialized life.

Wiley's resituated and migrated statue, Sherald's suspension, Thomas's symbolic figuration, and Gates's migrated gazebo set the distinction between the terms "ground" and "land" in stark relief. In his study *What Is Landscape?*, John R. Stilgoe positions security as the distinguishing feature, arguing that "ground which itself cannot sustain human life even for a few hours or days never truly achieves the status of land."[54] His study is framed by an exhortation to the reader to explore the idea by accessing the land—to get out, walk, and look. What do we make of those who have a more precarious access, namely those whom police so often profile? On what ground can one be safe?

"When I see a young black man murdered by the police on television," Bradford has said, reflecting on his suite of works in the past few years, "I'm trying to grapple with policy. I'm trying to grapple with it personally."[55] After Bradford's creation of these legally focused works, including his installation *We the People*, Anita Hill asked the artist about the relationship between his past work and this interrogation of legal foundations. Bradford responded that they are part of the same project of "trying to grapple with the enormous history that made this country. It's me grappling with being three-fifths of a man originally in this country in the south. Where do I fit into this document that was made when they weren't thinking about black bodies?"[56]

I complete this chapter alongside the publication of Fleetwood's *Marking Time: Art in the Age of Mass Incarceration*, in which she archives, analyzes, and examines the development of "carceral aesthetics," art made by those caught in the criminal justice system, born from "the compulsion to make, to create, and to produce meaning," as the field of visuality at large is impacted by this moment of racial terror and reckoning.[57] Her deft analysis requires a methodological widening of our inherent assumptions about the network of relationships that are part of an artist's milieu and, she argues, what is meant by "relational aesthetics" as she describes the necessary collaboration between incarcerated and nonincarcerated individuals to sustain a practice.[58] Groundwork aesthetics, too, not only wrestle with the discourse on looking at images of racial violence but also challenge how we define the very environment of the artist and the form that resistance can take.

In the United States, a nation that has by far the highest rate of incarceration in the world, "crime control," as Elizabeth Hinton argues, "may be *the* domestic policy issue in the late twentieth century."[59] Not to consider this phenomenon of groundwork aesthetics is to assume that the field of contemporary art (and therefore an artist) is somehow sealed off from a distinct shift in worldview that developed in the SYG era, born of the culture of surveillance that challenges the sovereignty of Black subjectivity. Indeed, one need only think of how this method can be extended into contemporary art philanthropy, given that Agnes Gund used the proceeds of her sale of Roy Lichtenstein's *Masterpiece* (1962) for

$165 million to create initiatives such as the Art for Justice Fund, a criminal justice reform initiative to which Bradford was one of the first artists to offer support with a donation of a painting for auction.

Joan Kee's periodized, landmark study of the interpenetration of art and law in the United States between 1970 and 1990 ends with an artist's mediation on the significance of physical posture in Philando Castile's killing—not Bradford's canvas, but Henry Taylor's painting *THE TIMES THAY AINT A CHANGING, FAST ENOUGH!* (2017). She considers Taylor's decision to portray Castile as "supine" but deliberately with "his head lifted up, as if Taylor were attempting to salvage it from the wreckage."[60] Here, Castile's position is "productively ambiguous," as the painting centralizes his suspension—focused on the head, car, disembodied police officer, and sky, with no ground in sight—as a way to telegraph the disorienting injustice of his killing. The marriage of art and law, she argues, calls attention to the law itself as "plastic," forged of "language, aesthetic decisions, and individual behavior."[61] I follow Kee in thinking that the intersection of art and law in contemporary art in the United States is the unique creation of the "necessary psychological space" to permit the "political and affective labor needed to bridge the sometimes gaping chasm between law and justice."[62] Yet parsing these works requires a shift in methodological demands of scholarship on the intersection of art, race, and representational justice offered by a capacious focus on groundwork.

Beyond providing a framework for analysis of new directions in contemporary art, what I have here called groundwork might help guide future steps that the discipline of art history will have to take in order to engage more decisively with sociopolitical life that informs artistic production in the context of racial contestation and violence. In short, groundwork, as the word implies, is the beginning of practical labor as well as theoretical reflection. For example, the question of how racial violence has structured the institutions, resources, and preservationist tactics that we use to consider, describe, and protect the outdoors has shifted the discourse in environmental history. Scholars including Carolyn Finney, Dianne D. Glave, Paul Outka, and Dorceta E. Taylor have examined the interaction of the history of racial disenfranchisement via racial terror that fueled the migratory movements of the early twentieth century, Black land loss and theft—legally conscribing the enslaved to be seen as part of the land—and a startling lack of engagement with the environmental moment and protected spaces by African Americans in particular.[63] If the environmental humanities have understood the structuring of the ground as inevitably connected with the topic of racial justice, then so too might art history benefit from a new methodological engagement with a critical race perspective that focuses on a capacious understanding of ground.

The presence of groundwork requires a broad investigation at the intersection of critical race studies, art history, and the politics of reception, putting productive pressure on scholarship to accommodate how artists are formally addressing the racialized and political forces that establish an artwork's conceptual and material foundations. The polysemic focus on "ground," as exemplified by Bradford and other visual artists, enlarges what we reflexively consider to be an aesthetics of reckoning and resistance and the important forms that Paul C. Taylor aptly calls "assembly," as much as they do the conceptual scope of Clark's ground level project.[64] In focusing on precarity and challenges to the upright form, groundworks demand that we reckon with the racial foundations that permeate and condition vision and subjectivity in the United States. Indeed, this approach, too, conceptually recalls Carl Schmitt's important distinction between law and "nomos," a global order dependent on spatial arrangements defined by colonial expansion, as distinct from the idea of the "law," that obscures how the ground has shaped the legal order.[65] Yet groundwork is not only a phenomenon of race and aesthetics in the era of Stand Your Ground law. Through groundwork, the artists identified here, and many more, working independently in contemporary, American, and African American art, have created an indispensable framework that offers a way to understand how aesthetics mobilize a reading of the legal, social, and racial histories that generate the reasons or the grounds for contestation of racialized life in the United States—what has been wrought, maimed, and sustained under our feet.

Notes

1   I first began to develop the ideas in this chapter when I delivered the Grace A. Tanner Lecture in Human Values at Southern Utah University in 2018. The lecture evolved into a version of this essay given as the 19th Annual Navin Narayan Memorial Lecture in the Committee on Degrees in Social Studies at Harvard University on November 19, 2019. The late Navin Narayan's selflessness and dedication to social justice offered the inspiration for the development of this project. I'm deeply grateful for both lecture invitations, from Danielle Dubrasky and Anya Bassett, respectively, for the encouragement of the Narayan family, and for engagement with drafts of this text by many colleagues, including Courtney Baker, Timothy Barringer, Suzanne Blier, Adrienne Brown, Huey Copeland, Henry Louis Gates Jr., Maria Gough, Jeffrey Hamburger, Joan Kee, Robin Kelsey, Jinah Kim, Joseph Koerner, Ewa Lajer-Burcharth, Caroline Light, Jordana Moore Saggese, Tommie Shelby, Deborah Willis, Harvard graduate students Jessica Williams and Rachel Burke, and the anonymous reviewers of this chapter.

    The epigraphs are from Martin Heidegger, "The Principle of Ground," trans. Keith Hoeller, *Man and World* 7 (1974): 207, emphasis in original; and Jericho Brown, "Shovel," *The Tradition* (Port Townsend, WA: Copper Canyon Press, 2019), 37. Reprinted with permission.

2   Diamond Reynolds, as quoted by Mark Bradford in Jennifer King, "Now on View: Mark Bradford's '150 Portrait Tone,'" *Unframed*, October 17, 2017, https://unframed.lacma.org/2017/10/19/now-view-mark-bradford%E2%80%99s-150-portrait-tone.

3   See Bedford, "Against Abstraction," in *Mark Bradford*, ed. Bedford, exh. cat. (Columbus, OH: Wexner Center for the Arts; New Haven, CT: Yale University Press, 2010), 7–29; Katy Siegel, "Somebody and Nobody," in ibid., 103–19.

4   See Michel S. Laguerre, *The Informal City* (New York: St. Martin's Press, 1994); Steven Nelson, "Mark Bradford's Allegorical Impulse," in *Mark Bradford*, exh. cat. (New York: Sikkema Jenkins & Co., 2006), 9–13; and Huey Copeland, "A Range of Convergences," *Parkett* 89 (2011): 152–59.

5   For Bradford's discussion of paper as a form of "frozen pigment," see Huey Copeland, "Painting after All: A Conversation with Mark Bradford," *Callaloo* 37, no. 4 (Fall 2014): 824.

6   Bradford quoted in Lanre Bakare, "Mark Bradford: The Artist and Ex-hairdresser Forcing America to Face Ugly Truths about Itself," *Guardian*, November 17, 2017.

7   Copeland, "Painting after All," 814.

8 This term "groundwork" is not in conscious dialogue with Karl Marx's term *Grundrisse*, used in an early elaboration of Communist history and a commentary on the connection between property and personal interactions and freedom, as discussed in his unfinished manuscript "Grundrisse der Kritik de politischen Ökonomie" (Fundamentals of political economy criticism). See Marx, *Grundrisse: Foundations of the Critique of Political Economy*, trans. Martin Nicolaus (New York: Random House, 1973).

9 Caroline Light, *Stand Your Ground: A History of America's Love Affair with Lethal Self-Defense* (Boston: Beacon Press, 2017), 8, 155. Light's scholarship on SYG law has been of enormous value as I developed this project.

10 Ibid., 12.

11 See *Cato v. United States*. I'd like to thank Joan Kee for her generous feedback on an early draft of this chapter that prompted my decision to focus squarely on the concept of the "ground" and for her scholarship in Kee, *Models of Integrity: Art and Law in Post-Sixties America* (Oakland: University of California Press, 2019), along with Joseph Koerner for his sustained, thoughtful engagement with various iterations of my development of the theory of groundwork.

12 See Mia Fischer and K. Mohrman, "Black Deaths Matter? Sousveillance and the Invisibility of Black Life," *Ada: A Journal of Gender, New Media, and Technology* 10 (2016), https://adanewmedia.org/2016/10/issue10-fischer-mohrman/. Ariella Azoulay anticipated the shift from the sovereignty of the photographer to the agency of the subject in creating images that impact civic life, in Azoulay, *The Civil Contract of Photography* (Cambridge, MA: MIT Press, 2008). Courtney Baker, Elizabeth Alexander, and Karla F. C. Holloway are among the many scholars who have incisively analyzed the ethical dimensions of looking in the context of violence against Black bodies in the United States. See Baker, *Humane Insight: Looking at Images of African American Suffering and Death* (Champaign: University of Illinois Press, 2015); Alexander, "Can You Be BLACK and Look at This? Reading the Rodney King Video(s)," in *Black Male: Representations of Masculinity in Contemporary American Art*, ed. Thelma Golden, exh. cat. (New York: Whitney Museum of American Art, 1994), 91; and Holloway, *Passed On: African American Mourning Stories; A Memorial* (Durham, NC: Duke University Press, 2003).

13 Jasmine Nichole Cobb, *Picture Freedom: Remaking Black Visuality in the Early Nineteenth Century* (New York: New York University Press, 2015). See also Simone Browne, *Dark Matters: On the Surveillance of Blackness* (Durham, NC: Duke University Press, 2015).

14 Jean-Luc Nancy, *The Ground of the Image*, trans. Jeff Fort (New York: Fordham University Press, 2005), 58.

15 While a fuller engagement with Meyer Schapiro's critique of Martin Heidegger's understanding of Vincent van Gogh via his essay "On the Origins of a Work of Art" is not within the scope of this article, it is important to highlight that the idea of the ground or *Boden* in the Heideggerian tradition is connected to a rootedness and territorialism in ways that diverge from its connotation in this contemporary context. See Schapiro, "The Still Life as a Personal Object—A Note on Heidegger and van Gogh," in *The Reach of Mind: Essays in Memory of Kurt Goldstein*, ed. Marianne Simmel (New York: Springer Publishing, 1968), 203–9; Martin Heidegger, *Der Satz vom Grund* (Pfullingen, Germany: Neske, 1957), 191–211; and Martin Heidegger, "The Principle of Ground," trans. Keith Hoeller, *Man and World* 7 (1974): 207–22.

16 Michael Allen Gillespie, "The Question of History," in *Hegel, Heidegger, and the Ground of History* (Chicago: University of Chicago Press, 1984), 24.

17 Christina Sharpe, *In the Wake: On Blackness and Being* (Durham, NC: Duke University Press, 2016), 13; Saidiya V. Hartman, *Lose Your Mother: A Journey along the Atlantic Slave Route* (New York: Farrar, Straus and Giroux, 2007), 6, 45, 73, 107, 133. This chapter's meditation on the term "precarity" and ideas of futurity is, too, in dialogue with Kara Keeling, *Queer Times, Black Futures* (New York: New York University Press, 2019).

18 T. J. Clark, "Painting at Ground Level," Tanner Lectures on Human Values, Princeton University, April 17–19, 2002 (Salt Lake City: University of Utah Press, 2004), 135.

19 Ibid.

20 Ibid., 134–35, 152.

21 Here I am thinking of the expanded notion of sovereignty as found at the intersection of and also the distinctions between Black and Indigenous studies focusing on environmental mutuality. See Tiffany Lethabo King, *The Black Shoals: Offshore Formations of Black and Native Studies* (Durham, NC: Duke University Press, 2019); Tiya Miles, *The House on Diamond Hill: A Cherokee Plantation Story* (Chapel Hill: University of North Carolina Press, 2010); and Mark Rifkin, *Fictions of Land and Flesh: Blackness, Indigeneity, Speculation* (Durham, NC: Duke University Press, 2019).

22 Bradford, having studied the practice of décollage in post–World War II era Paris, considers Jacques de la Villeglé, Raymond Hains, and Mimmo Rotella among his influences. Bradford, in-person interview with the author, December 22, 2005. See also Sarah Lewis, "Mark Bradford: The Evidence of Things Not Seen," in *Street Level: Mark Bradford, William Cordova, and Robin Rhode*, ed. Trevor Schoonmaker, exh. cat. (Durham, NC: Duke University Press, 2007).

23 Bradford quoted in Smithsonian Institution press release, March 20, 2017, https://hirshhorn.si.edu/exhibitions/mark-bradford-picketts-charge/.

24 Tobias Wofford, "Mark Bradford: Pickett's Charge," *Panorama* 4, no. 2 (2018).

25 Bradford quoted in Christopher Bedford and Mark Bradford, "Loose Like a Shawl: Christopher Bedford and Mark Bradford," in *Mark Bradford: Tomorrow Is Another Day*, ed. Katy Siegel and Bedford, exh. cat. (New York: Gregory R. Miller; Berlin: Hatje Cantz, 2017), 123.

26 Sarah Burns, *Painting the Dark Side: Art and the Gothic Imagination in Nineteenth-Century America* (Berkeley: University of California Press, 2004), 3, 21.

27 Burns aptly notes that Quidor takes the gothic tones of Irving's tale to extremes not found in the text through this focus on aligning blackness with terror. For more on Quidor, see ibid., 101–2, 105–6, 108–9, 125.

28 Bradford quoted in Jori Finkel, "An Artist's Mythic Rebellion for the Venice Biennale," *New York Times*, April 27, 2017.

29 See Zadie Smith, "Niagara," in Siegel and Bedford, *Tomorrow Is Another Day*, 82–93.

30 Bradford quoted in "Anita Hill in Conversation with Mark Bradford," in Anita Hill, Sebastian Smee, and Connie Butler, *Mark Bradford* (London: Phaidon Press, 2018), 32.

31 Bradford, telephone interview with the author, July 2020.

32 See Lorna Roth, "Looking at Shirley, the Ultimate Norm: Colour Balance, Image Technologies, and Cognitive Equity," *Canadian Journal of Communication* 34, no. 1 (2009): 116. See also Lorna Roth, "The Delicate Acts of 'Colour Balancing': Multiculturalism and Canadian Television Broadcasting Policies and Practices," *Canadian Journal of Communication* 23, no. 4 (April 1988): 487–506. I engage this scholarship in Sarah Lewis, "The Racial Bias Built into Photography," *New York Times*, April 25, 2019.

33 See Nicole R. Fleetwood, *On Racial Icons: Blackness and the Public Imagination* (New Brunswick, NJ: Rutgers University Press, 2015), 8–10; Elizabeth Edwards, *Anthropology and Photography, 1860–1920* (New Haven, CT: Yale University Press, 1992); Kathleen Stewart Howe, *First Seen: Portraits of the World's Peoples, 1840–1880*, exh. cat. (Santa Barbara, CA: Santa Barbara Museum of Art, 2004); Stephen Jay Gould, *The Mismeasure of Man* (1981;

repr., New York: W. W. Norton, 1996); and Molly Rogers, *Delia's Tears: Race, Science, and Photography in Nineteenth-Century America* (New Haven, CT: Yale University Press, 2010).

34 Bradford cited in "Loose Like a Shawl," in Siegel and Bedford, *Mark Bradford: Tomorrow Is Another Day*, 113.

35 Bradford quoted in Alina Cohen, "AIDS, Abstraction, and Absent Bodies: A Conversation with Mark Bradford," *Hyperallergic*, December 9, 2015, https://hyperallergic.com/260045/aids-abstraction-and-absent-bodies-a-conversation-with-mark-bradford/.

36 Rosalind E. Krauss, "Agnes Martin: The / Cloud/," in *Bachelors* (Cambridge, MA: MIT Press, 1999), 78. I follow Barry Schwabsky's assessment that contemporary landscape painting, flourishing and undergoing reinvention, however overlooked due to the conditioning and dominance of abstraction, often contains allusions to nature as decried by Krauss and Yve-Alain Bois. Schwabsky, "Painting with the Flow of the World," in *Landscape Painting Now: From Pop Abstraction to New Romanticism*, ed. Todd Bradway (New York: Thames and Hudson, 2019), 13–15.

37 Copeland, "Painting after All," 819. For the history of Brockman Gallery and Brockman Productions in Leimert Park, see Kellie Jones, *South of Pico*: *African American Artists in Los Angeles in the 1960s and 1970s* (Durham, NC: Duke University Press, 2017), 145–51. In the spirit of full disclosure, I should mention that I was invited to become a board member of the Art + Practice Foundation only *after* I submitted this chapter for publication.

38 See Cheryl Harris, "Whiteness as Property," *Harvard Law Review* 106, no. 8 (1993): 1707–91.

39 Fleetwood, *On Racial Icons*, 8–10.

40 See Adrienne R. Brown, *The Black Skyscraper: Architecture and the Perception of Race* (Baltimore: Johns Hopkins University Press, 2017), 28, 29.

41 W. E. B. Du Bois, *The Souls of Black Folk* (1903; repr., New York: Oxford University Press, 2007), 84, 86, 90.

42 See Deborah Willis, Ellyn Toscano, and Kalia Brooks Nelson, eds., *Women and Migration: Responses in Art and History* (Cambridge, UK: Open Book Publishers, 2019); and Tanya Sheehan, *Photography and Migration* (New York: Routledge, 2018).

43 Jericho Brown, "Shovel," *The Tradition* (Port Townsend, WA: Copper Canyon Press, 2019), 37.

44 Clark, "Painting at Ground Level," 135.

45 See Brown, *Black Skyscraper*, 2, 127–28. See also Lauren Kroiz, *Creative Composites: Modernism, Race, and the Stieglitz Circle* (Berkeley: University of California Press, 2012).

46 Brown, *Black Skyscraper,* 2.

47 For more on Amy Sherald's use of grisaille, see Richard J. Powell, "The Obama Portraits, in Art History and Beyond," in *The Obama Portraits*, ed. Tania Caragol, Dorothy Moss, and Powell (Princeton, NJ: Princeton University Press, 2020), 55, 93; and Erin Christovale, "Notes on Amy Sherald," in *Amy Sherald*, ed. Lisa Melandri, exh. cat. (Saint Louis: Contemporary Art Museum St. Louis, 2018), 15.

48 See Saidiya V. Hartman, *Scenes of Subjection: Terror, Slavery, and Self-Making in Nineteenth-Century America* (New York: Oxford University Press, 1997).

49 See Sherrilyn Ifill, *On the Courthouse Lawn: Confronting the Legacy of Lynching in the Twenty-First Century*, foreword by Bryan Stevenson (Boston: Beacon Press, 2007).

50 See the Equal Justice Initiative publication *Lynching in America: Confronting the Legacy of Racial Terror*, downloadable at https://eji.org/wp-content/uploads/2019/10/lynching-in-america-3d-ed-080219.pdf, as of August 2, 2020.

51 Kevin Quashie, *The Sovereignty of Quiet: Beyond Resistance in Black Culture* (New Brunswick, NJ: Rutgers University Press, 2012).

52 Wiley, in-person interview with the author, November 2019.

53 Ibid.

54 John R. Stilgoe, *What Is Landscape?* (Cambridge, MA: MIT Press, 2015), 89. While there is not space to do so here, I engage fully with the historiography of landscape in the history of art as distinct from groundwork in the book-length version of this project.

55 Bradford quoted in Hill, Smee, and Butler, *Mark Bradford*, 36.

56 Ibid.

57 Nicole R. Fleetwood, *Marking Time: Art in the Age of Mass Incarceration* (Cambridge, MA: Harvard University Press, 2020).

58 Ibid., 2–11, 18, 25, 32, 51, 58, 126, 154, 158, 230, 241, 257, 263.

59 Elizabeth Hinton, *From the War on Poverty to the War on Crime: The Making of Mass Incarceration in America* (Cambridge, MA: Harvard University Press, 2016), 8 (emphasis added).

60 Kee, *Models of Integrity,* 235.

61 Ibid., 5.

62 Ibid., 236.

63 See Carolyn Finney, *Black Faces, White Spaces: Reimagining the Relationship of African Americans to the Great Outdoors* (Chapel Hill: University of North Carolina Press, 2014); Dianne D. Glave, *Rooted in the Earth: Reclaiming the African American Environmental Heritage* (Chicago: Chicago Review Press, 2010); Paul Outka, *Race and Nature from Transcendentalism to the Harlem Renaissance* (New York: Palgrave Macmillan, 2008); Dorceta E. Taylor, "Blacks and the Environment: Toward an Explanation of the Concern and Action Gap between Blacks and Whites," *Environment and Behavior* 21, no. 2 (1989): 175–205; and Katherine McKittrick, *Demonic Grounds: Black Women and the Cartographies of Struggle* (Minneapolis: University of Minnesota Press, 2006).

64 Paul C. Taylor, *Black Is Beautiful: A Philosophy of Black Aesthetics* (Chichester, UK: Wiley Blackwell, 2016).

65 Carl Schmitt, *The Nomos of the Earth in the International Law of the Jus Publicum Europaeum,* trans. G. L. Ulmen (New York: Telos Press, 2003), 20.

18

"SURVIVAL IS NOT A THEORY": AFRO-PESSIMISM TRANSPOSED

Paul C. Taylor

1. Introduction: on transposition

The emergence of Afro-pessimism is an important development in cultural theory, particularly for students of Black aesthetics and related subjects. In the words of Jared Sexton, one of its more important interpreters, this "highly technical dispute in a small corner of the American academy" has achieved a degree of "critical purchase and affective resonance" that calls out for explanation.[1] In addition to offering this explanation, Sexton also provides a reading of the Afro-pessimist problem-space that is immensely clarifying for readers who find the technical nature of the dispute perplexing.

It is no slight against Sexton's reading of Afro-pessimism to say that there is room for still more clarification. For one thing, the work takes up issues that require the sort of complicated intellectual balancing act that underwrites Audre Lorde's reminder that "survival is not a theory."[2] For another, most of the technicalities Sexton refers to are rooted in fine points of argumentation in or near post-structuralism. This latter feature leaves key insights relatively inaccessible to people for whom figures like Jacques Derrida and Jacques Lacan are not useful guides.

This essay will attempt to articulate some of Afro-pessimism's key insights in language that does not presuppose an intimate familiarity with poststructuralist theory. More precisely, it will attempt to read those insights through—or, as the critic James Woods will soon enable me to say, write them through—an alternative vocabulary.[3] Sexton's masterful clarifying efforts gave me my first accessible points of entry to Afropessimism as an enterprise, so he will be my main guide in what follows, with some assistance from Frank Wilderson and Saidiya Hartman.

It is tempting to describe this essay as an exercise in translation, but a proper translation would require fluency in all of the relevant traditions. In the absence of that bi- or multi-directional fluency, I think less of translation than of "transposition." Musicians transpose pieces from one key to another while preserving the harmonic relationships that give the pieces their character. My aim is to reproduce a version of the Afro-pessimist intervention in a different intellectual key—the key (keys?) of American naturalist phenomenology and post-analytic critical race theory. I am to reproduce the central moves, including the moves that aim to accommodate Lorde's challenge to theory, while preserving the intervention's overall shape.

2. Listen, I have to play it for you: on writing-through

To be clear: what follows is not an attempt to refute or reject poststructuralism, nor does it assume that a refutation is available, forthcoming, or even needed. It is an attempt to capture the key insights of an influential school of thought in a language that resonates for me more effectively than the language the school's best-known teachers prefer. Better: it is an attempt not to capture but to reproduce, rehearse, perform, or re-describe those insights, in senses of "re-description" and "performance" that I'll soon come to.

I use "poststructuralist" as a blanket label for the teachers' preferred language on the assumption that this is an uncontroversial way of tracking the work of people who write, as Wilderson does, about things like "the performance of Black thought. . . under erasure," and who prepare for writing things like that with seminars on Lacan.[4] If that is not the right way to refer to this language and these thinkers, or if Afropessimism's theoretical debts are for some other reason less obvious than I take them to be, then I'll invite the reader to forget the label and credit the readerly response that inspired this essay: the canonical formulations of Afropessimism appear to rely on theoretical resources—however one identifies them—that get relatively little traction with me and with many readers who share my theoretical commitments. I am writing, then, as a reader for whom these formulations don't work as well as they might, and for whom the logical next step is to find words for what does work, to shore up the common ground that might support future efforts at criticism and collaboration.

One might instead begin by diagnosing what does *not* work, but that is not my aim here. I am not interested in mapping or dissecting or diagnosing the sources of my readerly unease, beyond noting that people who work through Derrida and Lacan tend to have little common ground with people who work through, say, Hilary Putnam or John Dewey. What I am interested in is making it harder for readers like me to let Sexton's "highly technical disputes" turn us away. I want to provide a less forbidding point of entry that discourages this reaction while still holding onto—in fact, creating more responsible grounds for—the prospect of critical dissent, dissent rooted not in failures of theoretical translation but in substantive disagreements about the subject matter.

I refer to transposition above because a metaphor that points to musicking rather than wordsmithing usefully foregrounds the degree to which reading involves activity and something like performance. But the great critic James Wood offers a way back from music to words. He explains:

> When I write about a novel. . . I am essentially bearing witness. I'm describing an experience and trying to stimulate in the reader an experience of that experience. . . . It's like playing, to a friend, a piece of music you really love. . . You are trying to get the

listener to hear (or see) the same thing as you, to have the same kind of experience. Criticism is just such an adventure in sameness. . . . [But] the review-essay involves not just pointing at something, but pointing at it while re-describing it. The analogy is less 'You have to *hear* it' than 'Listen, I have to *play it for you on the piano*.'[5]

This essay may be a way of asking Afropessimism's admirers if I've heard what they hear. It is certainly a way of inviting people who speak my theoretical languages to hear what I hear instead of simply retreating in puzzlement (at which point we may or may not find other, more productive grounds for retreating). The thing is, I can only tell them what I hear in the language I have available to me: I can only play the piano the way I play the piano. This exercise in what Wood calls "passionate re-description" has to involve finding my own words for the experience; it has to involve performing the experience, writing-through it, in just those words, not because other words are inadequate but because my words are the only words I have.[6]

3. Reading

I pledged above to preserve the shape of the Afropessimist intervention, but this may already get the proceedings off to a bad start. Listen to Sexton refusing that approach:

Afro-Pessimism is not an intervention so much as it is a reading, or meta-commentary, on what we seem to do with, or how we relate to, what black creative intellectuals continue to generate without being able to bring fully into account. It is a reading of what is gained and lost in the attempt—the impulse—to delineate the spatial and temporal borders of anti-blackness, to delimit the "bad news" of black life, to fix its precise scope and scale, to find an edge beyond or before which true living unfolds.[7]

Sexton's distinction between an intervention and a reading tracks the language I borrowed from Wood, and puts me in mind of this language from Stanley Cavell: "I would like to say that what I am doing in reading a film is performing it (if you wish, performing it inside myself)." If, as he goes on to say, a performance in this sense is an interpretation that manifests "one way of hearing," then maybe Afropessimism manifests a way of hearing something.[8]

What does Afropessimism hear and perform? The place to begin, I think, is with Sexton's reference to "what black creative intellectuals. . . generate without being able to bring fully into account." I read this as a point about what one can bring into *an* account, what one can fold into an explanation. I read it, better, as a reminder about the limits of explanation, and the value of alternative, supplementary, ways of engaging with reality and experience, such as interpretation, reading, or expression.

Dewey, whose work is in the key that defines my attempts at transposition, insists on a distinction that helps here. (Other traditions capture it with talk of suspension or bracketing.) It is one thing to *have* an experience, Dewey says; it's another thing to have knowledge of it, of the situation that the experience discloses (or begins to disclose). This disclosure, if it happens, comes in stages, and the first stage involves simply inhabiting the situation in its qualitative immediacy. Knowledge, like art, comes later.[9]

What Sexton's black creative intellectuals can't fully bring into account, thereby furnishing Afropessimism with the subject matter of its reading, lies in the gap between having an experience and having, and seeking, knowledge. Afropessimism is a mode of black intellectual work that (among other things) points beyond (or before) the limits of intellectual accounting to the qualitative immediacy of black life in an anti-black world. *Survival is not a theory*, in a sense of that expression that does not exhaust Lorde's meaning but is eminently consistent with it.

This mode of intellectual work points to the condition of having a certain kind of experience in an anti-black world. It insists on the irreducibly qualitative dimension of that experience. And it demands that responsible ethical and epistemic agents grapple with this lived experience in particular ways—mindful of the insights gleaned from critical reflection on black life, and of the phenomenological texture of the immediate experiences that inspire reflection. (Survival is not itself a theory but it inspires theories, and the good ones work in its service.)

4. Projects, theorems, streams

Sexton maps Afropessimism's key insights in a rich passage that demands our sustained attention. The view, he says, involves "both *an epistemological and an ethical project*." He goes on: these "two tributaries of thought converge in *the carefully navigated stream of consciousness* whose abstraction enables *a theorem of political ontology*. . . ."[10] What does this mean?

4.1. Political ontology

For help with the "theorem of political ontology," we can turn to this passage from Wilderson:

> Afropessimism is premised on a comprehensive and iconoclastic claim: that Blackness is coterminous with Slaveness: Blackness *is* social death. . . . Blackness, as a paradigmatic position (rather than as a set of cultural practices, anthropological accoutrements) is elaborated through slavery.[11]

Blackness just is social death, in a sense of that expression that descends from the germinal formulations of Orlando Patterson;[12] and it is "a paradigmatic position" rather than a set of cultural practices.

It would take some work to flesh out how Wilderson means for his "is" to work, here, but I would transpose it into language about blackness being an ontological condition rather than a cultural identity or biological condition. The point is that being racialized-as-black leaves one subject to certain distinctive modes of treatment, or more exposed to certain risks and conditions than one would be if racialized differently, and that this condition, and the experience of this condition, demands attention. This condition is, as nearly everyone now says, socially constructed. But, as nearly everyone now also says (in one way or another), it is real enough for all that.

Why does Wilderson describe this as an iconoclastic claim? Because he means this in the original sense of that term: he means to demolish certain iconic renderings of black life, icons that have distracted their adherents from important truths. To insist, as Sexton does on his behalf, on the oxymoronic nature of "the postulate of a free black"[13] is to refuse the celebratory narratives that emerge in every era of black politics. (We will return to this.)

4.2. The epistemological project (tributary 1)

How does the Afropessimist motivate this story about an anti-black ontology—one populated by humans and, opposed to them, beneath them, enslaved/blacks—and refuse the more congenial ontology of humanist antiracism? By refining and supplementing the methodological tools that get us from a problematic situation to an explanatory account of it, and perhaps beyond or beside such an account. In this spirit Afropessimism aims "to decenter, without diminishing, the analysis of political economy by discerning the libidinal economy that underwrites and sutures its dynamics." It means "to describe [not only] the operations of systems, structures and institutions, but also. . . the fantasies of murderous hatred and unlimited destruction, of sexual consumption and social availability that animate the realization of. . . violence."[14]

That is: understanding blackness in an anti-black world requires the usual investigations in political economy and in (what one might call) the epidemiology of disadvantage, examining which social goods are distributed, or withheld, in what patterns among which people. But it also requires a mode of black study that explores the world's passionate investment in the violent subordination and abjection of black people.

4.3. The ethical project (tributary 2)

The obvious response to this violent subordination involves resistance, contrary to caricatures that equate Afropessimism with quietism or resignation. Wilderson makes clear that resistance is very much on the table:

> I am not suggesting that Black people should resign themselves to the inevitability of social death – it *is* inevitable, in the sense that one is born into social death just as one is born into a gender or a class; but it is also constructed by the violence and imagination of other sentient beings. Thus, like class and gender, which are also *constructs*. . . social death can be destroyed.[15]

Something like resistance to oppression and defense of black life is at the heart of the Afropessimist ethical project.

There is a problem, though, in the need to appeal to "something like" these familiar staples of antiracist ethics. The available conceptual resources for this work have been forged in a world premised on anti-blackness. This means that, to take just one example, anti-racist appeals to common humanity founder on their embeddedness in and dependence on a wider frame that leaves the category of the human structurally opposed to the category of the black. Which is to say, in deference to the epistemological and ontological reorientations noted above: *look at what has happened in the name of humanity to this point in human history. At some point, you are what your record says you are. At some point the subtext (enslavement, the scramble for Africa, apartheid, &c.) just becomes the text.*

Just as the historical materialist can appeal only with difficulty to the enlightenment norms that the march of history means to supersede, the Afropessimist can appeal only with difficulty to ideas like humanity, justice, and freedom. This saddles the ethical project with the epistemological challenge that Sexton finds in "Agamben's grand urging. . . to 'abandon decidedly, without reservation, the fundamental concepts through which we have so far represented the subjects of the political' in order to 'build our political philosophy anew.'"[16]

Consequently, Afropessimism joins other revolutionary projects in offering untimely and provocative projects in political epistemology in the place of a more traditional ethics. If, like Marx, you can't yet say much about what the new world will look like, then you turn your attention to excavating and uprooting the epistemic habits that constrain our ethical imaginations. This is why Wilderson's arguments tend to eventuate simply in calls for "the end of the world"—the anti-black world, not the earth—and to "burn the slave ship from the inside."

There is another ethical dimension, though, and it grows out of the appeal to immediacy noted above. Wilderson puts it like this:

> If, when caught between the pincers of the imperative to meditate on Black dispossession and Black political agency, we do not dissemble, but instead. . . reflect on the murderous ontology of. . . slavery's gratuitous violence. . . then maybe. . . we will be able to think Blackness and agency together in an ethical manner.[17]

A properly ethical orientation to the condition of social death requires that one decline to "dissemble," that one reflect soberly on the murderous ontology of gratuitous violence. There is an important thought here about bearing witness to the way social death feels, the way the enslaved person's defeat registers, the way responsible agents choose to register it. If political epistemology fills part of the space where traditional ethical reflection would be, an existentialist ethic of something like responsibility fills much of the remaining space.

4.4. Streams of consciousness

The idea of bearing witness to the condition of social death, of refusing to dissemble and evade, is closely related to the "carefully navigated stream of consciousness" that links the project to the theorem. This is a gesture at the phenomenological richness of the Afropessimist account. It is crucially committed to taking seriously the experiential cost of attending to black suffering, as well as the epistemic and ethical costs of doing so irresponsibly.

The idea of the stream of consciousness comes down to us (setting aside the romantic and idealist backstory) from William James, from his studies of what agents do with the "blooming, buzzing confusion" of prereflective experience.[18] This backdrop encourages me to read Sexton's point about the "abstraction" of the stream of consciousness as an appeal to the reflective refinement of immediate experience. Dewey extends this line of thinking from James (and others) in ways that sound like this: immediate experience demands interpretation and resolution, and good interpretations, effective inquiry, will enrich the agent's immediate experiences and enable more effective—at a minimum, safer—experiments in navigating an indifferent world.

Putting that immediatist, developmental phenomenology in the context of a story about anti-blackness yields something like this: the immediate experience of the anti-black world is problematic in ways that require interpretation and resolution. The better interpretations produce, reinforce, and depend on stories about blackness as a structural position, or about racialization as black, or (and) about social death in the context of anti-blackness.

In light of the ethical project noted above, we have to say also that the interpretations must also be responsible, in the sense of being responsive to the ban on dissembling and evasion. That is, the interpretations must also credit, make sense of, do justice to, the qualitative dimension of a problematic situation in which (what one on reflection refers to as) blackness is initially experienced as social death. This is what it means to have a "carefully navigated stream of consciousness" in the context of anti-blackness: to resist the temptation to "fix the precise scope and scale" of the negative dimensions of the experience. Delimiting the bad news in advance is not just an error of fact or a mistake in ethical judgment: it is also, it results from, a refusal to take one's immediate experience seriously. It is, in this sense, a phenomenological error—a failure of something like ethico-aesthetic sensitivity.

5. Pessimism and immediacy

Sexton's mapping of the elements of Afropessimism leads us back to the question of immediacy, and toward some closing thoughts on the most distinctive feature of the view. The carefully navigated stream of consciousness enables a theorem of political ontology in this sense: careful reflective refinement of the evidence of immediate experience leads to the thesis that blackness just is social death. The ethical and epistemological projects reinforce and enable this conclusion by insisting on considerations—libidinal and political economies, the burden of taking one's experience seriously, and so on—that pull against any other reading.

If those are Afropessimism's vital elements, though, then what does it mean that there are other ways to make all of these points? The political ontology, the ethical claims, the epistemological shifts, the phenomenological turn toward the immediate phase of experience: Afropessimism has no monopoly in these areas. It presents these elements in distinctive combinations and proportions, but the real distinctiveness of the view must lie elsewhere.

The name of the view, of course, marks the source of its distinctiveness: pessimism makes the difference, by knitting together and inflecting the other elements. Understanding how it does this requires getting clear on the inputs and outputs, one might say, of this pessimism. It turns out to mark the limits of certain discursive strategies, of a certain philosophy of the history of blackness, and of a certain phenomenological orientation.

We've seen the pessimistic phenomenological orientation already. This is both a refusal of the impulse to delimit the bad news of black life, and a commitment to attend to immediate experience in ways that defeat the impulse to delimitation. As we've seen, there are plenty of reasons to endorse this form of pessimism. The approaches it refuses are epistemically disempowering, phenomenologically irresponsible, and, in ways related to both of the other problems, unethical.

Phenomenological pessimism shades into a pessimistic temporality that refuses an optimistic philosophy of (the) history (of racial politics). Hartman explains this in an interview with Wilderson:

> there's a certain integrationist rights agenda that subjects who are variously positioned on the color line can take up. And that project is something I consider obscene: the attempt to make the narrative of defeat into an opportunity for celebration, the desire to look at the ravages and the brutality of the last few centuries, but to still find a way to feel good about ourselves.[19]

We can locate a version of this integrationist rights agenda, and the sense of urgency with which some thinkers responded to it, with some precision. Since at least the late 1990s and early 2000s, when the key pessimist texts and debates started to appear, civil rights platitudes have become part of the commonsense ethos of the US. This tendency grew particularly pronounced after the election of Barack Obama, which reinforced the crude post-racialist tendency to see black humanity as something granted in theory and on its way to being realized in practice. While the upheavals in Ferguson, the rise of Donald Trump, and the protests of spring and summer 2020 gave the lie to this triumphalist, progressivist reading of black history, Afropessimism seeks to pull this optimism up from its roots.

Finally, the pessimist's refusal of the optimistic, "integrationist" political eschatology tracks a broader refusal of a certain discursive strategy and conceptual framework. Here's Hartman again:

> So much of our political vocabulary/imaginary/desires have been implicitly integrationist even when we imagine our claims are more radical. . . . [C]ertainly it's about more than the desire for inclusion within the limited set of possibilities that the national project provides. *What. . . does this language - the given language of freedom - enable? And once you realize its limits and begin to see its inexorable investment in certain notions*

of the subject and subjection, then that language of freedom no longer becomes that which rescues the slave from his or her former condition, but the site of the re-elaboration of that condition, rather than its transformation.[20]

Afropessimism is dubious not about the prospects for black struggle full stop, but about the prospects for *anti-racist* struggle, which is not the same thing, on the terms of a humanist, liberal integrationism. It does not counsel resignation to the inevitability of defeat. It recognizes the inevitability of defeat *on the terms of the world as it stands*, premised as that world is on anti-blackness, and so calls for the destruction of this world and the inauguration of a new one.

6. Conclusion

I've tried to read—to manifest the way I hear—the attempts that a few Afropessimist writers have made to manifest what Afropessimism hears. Along the way I have been haunted by ghostly overtones. Kierkegaard's Johannes de Silentio in *Fear and Trembling*, talking about being reconciled in and through pain. Leo Tolstoy's Ivan Ilyich lamenting the decay of the habits that had kept the inevitability of death conveniently out of his view. Lorde's insistence that survival is not a theory, which, as noted above, calls for more than we have so far seen from the Afropessimist. That, sadly, is another conversation.

The overtones I hear most clearly, though, started sounding from my very first encounter with Afropessimism, and in fact encouraged me to attempt this exercise in transposition. I'm thinking of Cornel West's discussions of the tragicomic sense, which he describes as an orientation to the absurdity and the travails of life that animates (among other things) the best of Afro-US culture (like John Coltrane) and the greatest achievements in Russian literature (like Anton Chekhov). He offers this account explicitly as an alternative to optimism *and* to pessimism. If optimism is the epistemically unwarranted and existentially and ethically irresponsible certainty that all will be well, and pessimism is the (he would say) unwarranted and irresponsible conviction that defeat is assured, then the tragicomic sense is the responsible alternative to both. Not a conviction of victory *or* of defeat, but a recognition that while defeat is permanently possible, and perhaps probable, victory is not necessarily out of reach.[21]

There is of course much more to say about this, but that, too, is another conversation. My main thought right now is that Afropessimism is *not* pessimistic in West's sense. It might in fact find considerable common ground with him, were it not for the choice of a predictably misleading word to convey their shared thought. Invoking "pessimism" immediately, and not unreasonably, given the way the language works, puts people in mind of despair and resignation, which is why these are the first charges the Afropessimist has to beat back. Why choose a word that invites this misreading?

The answer of course is the answer Dewey gave when faced with a version of this question. Determined to reclaim the idea of experience from the likes of David Hume and John Locke, he decided that that particular word could do some work that other words couldn't and therefore had to be salvaged. It may be worth noting that near the end of his life he decided that he'd been wrong, the weight of the word was too much to overcome, and he should've just chosen something else.[22]

In any case, offering this response to the pessimist just pushes the question back a step. Why try to reclaim "pessimism" if the effect of that choice is to center, to *re*-center, the perspective of the anti-black world? That world says, in deed if not always in word, that blacks are not human. Why concede that point and reclaim the notion of pessimism instead of contesting the point and reclaiming the category of the human? (I have to this point steered clear of the literature outside of the very few sources I've used for my reading, which was the point of describing this as an exercise in reading and transposition. But I have to note that Lewis R. Gordon has also recently raised this worry, and he is far more in touch with the Afropessimist's sources than I am.)[23]

This is one of the places where I part company with Afropessimism, at least as I understand it. I have different intuitions about which terms to salvage and which vocabularies are irremediably tainted, about the relative costs of conceding the entire world of our current understanding to anti-blackness while leaving the destruction of social death entirely to an unknowable beyond. This is supposed to be pessimistic, or, better, revolutionary, with its stirring calls for the inauguration of a new world; but no matter how hard I listen, I can't quite hear it that way.

I know my ears are supposed to be better than this. I'm supposed to hear echoes of Frantz Fanon, or something. (That said, I know of no more sensitive reader of Fanon than Professor Gordon, and his ears appear to be no better than mine on this point). In advance of, as a step toward, learning to hear better, I've opted to work through what I think I can hear, much more clearly, in people like Sexton and, to a lesser degree, in Hartman and Wilderson.

I'm sure this reading is incomplete, and perhaps badly so. But if it succeeds in making explicit what I hear in the work of these Afropessimist authors, then it may also show more clearly what I'm mishearing. That will leave anyone inclined to offer further instruction in a better position to do so effectively.

Notes

1   Jared Sexton, "Afropessimism: The Unclear Word," *Rhizomes* 29 (2016), par. 4; available at http://www.rhizomes.net/issue29/index.html; accessed June 6, 2020.

2   Audre Lorde, "Learning from the 60s," in *Sister Outsider* (1984; New York: Penguin Books, 2020), 126–37, 131.

3   "[I]n criticism, the language of pure summation does not exist. One is always thinking through books, not about them." James Wood, "Virginia Woolf's Mysticism," in *Serious Noticing: Selected Essays 1997-2019* (New York: Farrar, Straus and Giroux, 2019), 407–25.

4   Frank B. Wilderson III, *Afropessimism* (New York: Norton-Liveright, 2020), 221, 322.

5   James Wood, "Introduction," *Serious Noticing*, 1-13, 6-7.

6   Wood, "Introduction," 7.

7   Sexton, "Unclear Word," par. 16.

8   Stanley Cavell, *Pursuits of Happiness* (Cambridge: Harvard University Press, 1981).

9 John Dewey, *Art as Experience* (New York: Minton, Balch and Company, 1934). See especially chapter 3, "Having an Experience." See also John Dewey, *Experience and Nature* (Chicago: Open Court, 1925), especially chapters 2, 3, and 9.

10 Sexton, "Unclear Word," par. 15 (emphases added).

11 Wilderson, *Afropessimism*, 103.

12 Orlando Patterson, *Slavery and Social Death* (Cambridge: Harvard University Press, 1982).

13 Sexton, "Unclear Word," par. 3.

14 Sexton, "Unclear Word," par. 14.

15 Wilderson, *Afropessimism*, 103.

16 Jared Sexton, "Ante-Anti-Blackness: Afterthoughts," *Lateral* 1 (2012). https://doi.org/10.25158/L1.1.16; citing Giorgio Agamben, *Means without Ends* (University of Minnesota Press, 2000), 16.

17 Sexton, "Unclear Word," par. 15, quoting Frank B. Wilderson III, *Red, White and Black: Cinema and the Structure of U.S. Antagonisms* (Durham: Duke University Press, 2020), 143.

18 William James, *The Principles of Psychology* (1890; Cambridge: Harvard University Press, 1981), 462. The quotation appears in a discussion of developmental psychology but maps neatly onto his radical empiricist phenomenology.

19 Saidiya V. Hartman and Frank B. Wilderson III, "The Position of the Unthought," *Qui Parle* 13, no. 2 (Spring/Summer 2003): 183–201, 185.

20 Hartman and Wilderson, "Unthought," 185 (emphasis added).

21 Cornel West, *Democracy Matters* (New York: Penguin, 2004), esp. 216-18; West, "Subversive Joy and Revolutionary Patience in Black Christianity," in *Prophetic Fragments* (Trenton, NJ: Africa World Press, 1988), 161–65.

22 "Were I to write (or rewrite) *Experience and Nature* today I would entitle the book 'Culture and Nature' and the treatment of specific subject-matters would be correspondingly modified. I would abandon the term 'experience' because of my growing realization that the historical obstacles which prevented understanding of my use of 'experience' are, for all practical purposes, insurmountable." John Dewey, "Unfinished Introduction to Reissued Edition of *Experience and Nature*," in *The Later Works of John Dewey, 1925-1953. Volume 1: 1925, Experience and Nature*, ed. Jo Ann Boydston and Larry Hickman (Carbondale: Southern Illinois University Press, 1985), 329–65, 363. (Published online in the Past Masters database by Intelex (Charlottesville, VA: Intelex, 2003)).

23 Lewis R. Gordon, "Thoughts on two recent decades of studying race and racism," *Social Identities* 24, no.1 (2018): 29–38, DOI: 10.1080/13504630.2017.1314924. I am grateful to Anika Simpson for pointing this out to me.

19

IMITATION OF LIFE/A BOX FULL OF DARKNESS

James B. Haile, III

Imitation of Life

"It is clear that the choice of object that is one of the elements in the harmony of form must be decided ONLY by a corresponding vibration in the human soul."[1] John Guare's enigmatic 1982 play, *Six Degrees of Separation,* gravitates around this equally enigmatic quote attributed to Wassily Kandinsky, perhaps from the "Blue Rider Exhibition" in 1914, an attribution equally enigmatic.

But, what is clear, from the play as from this attributed quote is the idea that, on the one hand, the work of art, as enigmatic as it is mysterious, is a highly personal, more aptly, the most human element of human existence, of embodiment and consciousness: purely of this entanglement, which we often call the aesthetic imagination; on the other hand, what is also clear is that this work of art is somehow beyond both artist and art-object, somehow borne of them, borne from them, but existing outside of each, in its own, independent world. A work of art, then, for Guare is both within the artist *and* beyond the artist, the connection being this process—this "harmony of form"—which can never really *belong* to a collector, a museum, or even the artist.

What is additionally clear in Guare's play is the fundamental failure to capture, categorize, catalogue, and disseminate "the work" [of art] into a coherent meaning of biographical or experiential fact: "Wassily Kandinsky. Born 1866, Moscow. . .Died 1944, France." What are we to gather from this? What can this possibly mean for the "Blue Rider Exhibition" other than the brute 'fact' that he was born and that he died? Other than to timestamp a specific moment of human duration? Kandinsky, like all men, was born and died, in the time-period between 1866 and 1944, but what can this tell us about color or form? That is to say, what can biographical details tell us about *any* of the selections in the work of art: *this* color over *that* one; *this* light structure and patten, over *that* one; *this* shape and not *that* shape? These are all choices—we see them, right before us but their very presence does not explain itself; and we cannot know this knowing something about the artist. For Guare, to gather such insight *requires* something else, another *kind* of knowledge, another *way* of knowing.

This is the task of Guare's *Six Degrees of Separation*—to unpack, as it were, the mysterious and enigmatic relationship between the artist and the work of art to reveal not only the mysterious and enigmatic process and trace it back to its origin, but to also reveal a fundamental truth: the work of art though emergent from the artist, does not belong *to* the artist any more than the patron that purchases it. Rather, it exists and belongs to its own world and the artist and the viewer, only catch a glimpse of this other world through the object.

Guare's play, then, functions as a grand metaphor, not so much about "art" and the "art-object" in relation to the mosaic or ambiguities of human life. But, rather, a metaphor of the impossibility of knowing ourselves completely, or our capacity to capture that enigmatic element of what we produce through some element of biographical or historical 'facts.' "Color. Structure," as Guare reminds us throughout the play, "THOSE are problems. . . ."[2] As manifestations of these enigmatic elements often attributed to internal relation of the mysterious enigmatic process that is the artist process and the mysterious and enigmatic reality that is the art-object, Guare can be seen as providing for us a theory of chromatography, not merely in the sense of bending or refracting light into what is experienced as the phenomenon of "color," but in the sense in which *we* are bent or refracted in our relation to the world *through* the aesthetic experience of the inner life of the work of art.

The inner relation of color and structure, though, is not an analytic problem, but one that is metaphysical. They reside in the feeling of ecstasy, of the *sublime*.

"Cezanne. The problems he brought up are the problems painters are still dealing with.""[3]

What should not be missed about Guare's play, though, is that it centers on a black character whose identity is an open and ambiguous mystery. This character seemingly shifts his identity to fit the expectations of every white character with whom he comes into contact. At times he is the son of black actor Sidney Poitier, at others, the biracial son of a wealthy white art dealer. But, as Guare notes, at every turn in his multiple origin stories, there is something authentic—in every ruse there is a moment of sincerity that draws the other characters into a sublime aesthetic experience *to want* to believe *in* him: Paul Poitier; or Paul Poitier-Kittridge. Guare situates Paul's own self-creation in terms of an artistic process and an aesthetic experience to alert his audience that identity is as ambiguous as the artist process, its object, the self, as ambiguous as the art-object itself.

But, more than this, Guare's play alerts us to the aesthetic and *performative* process of black identity, an aesthetic experience at once under the control of the artist but also outside of their control.

What Guare seems to be telling us is that this ambiguous process is beguiling for black people generally, but especially for black artists whose identity, art process, and art object are often conflated with biographical detail. Replace "Wassily Kandinsky. Born 1866, Moscow. . .Died 1944, France" with "Black Artist. *1619. Enslavement ship. Left Africa. Across the Atlantic. Now New World. Now, newly Black*," and we see developing a new theory of color—a new chromatology, if you will. Just as the inner life of the black individual recedes behind the biographical detail of race, the inner life of the work of art is disappeared behind the idea of the *black* artist.

> "They approach me in a half-hesitant sort of way, eye me with curiosity or compassionately, and then instead of saying it directly, How does it feel to be a problem? they say. . . ."[4]
> Du Bois. The problems he brought up are the problems that we are still dealing with.

Straddling between the aesthetic and *performative* process of identity, the *black* artist finds themselves in a double bind: at once part of the artistic process and aesthetic experience in the performance of their blackness, but also finding that their work, denied that enigmatic process Kandinsky described, circumscribed without an inner world. Both their identity and their work rendered as mute objects to be consumed in an ecstatic feeling of a *racial sublime*.[5]

It should not be surprising, then, that a work of art, enigmatic and mysterious as it is, would one day come into consciousness and, recognizing itself as a consumer good placed in an art gallery and blinded by high tension lights and peering faces, no longer able to hold the outside world at bay, would one day grow tired of it all, and try to escape. This is the story of one such painting by Kerry James Marshall.

A Box Full of Darkness

Pre

he felt Ablade Glover all inside. that "By All Means."[6] "Market Innuendos."[7] and "Slumscape" feeling.[8] "Yellow People I" *and* "II" inside.[9] *he* felt that year 2014 all over again, like the opening night of the exhibit. it was the year that *he* turned the color of burnt ember, cracklin' end of fire. that was that year 2014, and *he* felt it rise up in *him*. all inside. that feeling. pops of yellow. and blue. and green. wild and vivid all over the canvas. scenes human, and inhuman, all-too-human to be human, but still human. villages, marketplaces where there were people and yet no people. *he* looked closely and stood far away—and they were all there, but not there. *he* felt the color of forests and leaves on a tree from water lilies[10] reimagined by a "boy and a dog in a johnnypump,"[11] 30 years later; and "Bacchus and Ariadne"[12] four hundred years later, and knew they were there and wouldn't leave. and *he* is somewhere, inside, having been stranded on a deserted island and found in the suddenness of Ablade's touch. in the procession of feelings and those revelers, lined up to gaze and wonder at *his* miracle, something like a natural wonder. but *he* did not feel Pollock inside. not "Convergence"[13] or "Number 18."[14] not even "Mural."[15] no. no. no, *no no!* none of that! *he* knew *he* wasn't all dripped all over himself. *he* was chaotic but controlled. with perspective. and presence. more or less, a *direction*. at least one *he* could follow.

someone that *he* loved, had given *him* a box full of darkness. and *he* knew, somewhere deep inside, it was a gift.[16]

One

His back slid down the wall. He slouched at the bottom, forming an "L" shape at the intersection of the floor and the baseboard. The walls turned a pale blue, his flat, mat charcoal skin seemingly siphoning life and color. The lamps attempted to throw a bright yellow color back onto the walls, entering the battle, but they, too, lost, glowing a soft muted amber, like the sounding call of a fallen soldier. But that sofa! Oh, that sofa. It resisted his flesh, became stronger, as if it knew who it was. It gleamed bright electric red. It and he stared at one another from across the room. Neither moved. In a sort of measured antagonism. A stand-off of color!

His skin flaked soot. He folded his arm, and entrails of dark mist followed closely behind. When he stood, black streaked the wall. He was black, alright; black enough that he used to hear, "He looks like a retrospective"; and "I think he looks like he has something prove. We get it. You're black. You don't have to beat us over the head with it. I'd like him much better if he were much more understated." But it was the couch that was out of line, mocking with its overabundance of color, like a master capitalist, hoarding all shades in itself. *It wasn't him that was draining hues from the room*, but the sofa hiding behind its electricity and *his* blackness. It was the sofa, not him, that had torn the face off pigmentation. This, they didn't seem to get.

Entanglement. Perhaps that was it: a theory of entanglement can explain this stand-off. Perhaps, that can explain the excess that occurs when an object cannot hold all of its color—or, maybe it's just him that can't contain all of what he is; maybe sofas and other objects not concerned with being themselves or any of the other trappings of modern life can and do know what they are and contain just that; but his blackness could not be contained—it simply leaked out, from his arms, his legs, his mouth, the flesh of his cheek and forehead, streaked from one place to another, blended into the walls, choked out what was left of him, and when it was done, transferred, yes transferred, on to the next one—to the next scene. He couldn't contain this excess. Though it was all around him, it was not *his*, but consumed him; the sofa, that goddamn sofa, consumed its colors—he was consumed by his color.

and if that's not enough, he just recently discovered that he had nowhere to put his excess—the room is just a room, its dead blue walls streaked with smoke, bare floor, frowning kitchenette, no real window, other than the one used to look into the room and spy on him, slouching on the floor facing his sofa, and, of course the sofa: the red sofa—he knew there was tension there; but he was not a room; his excess was not in his blackness but what it meant; he knew he resented the ease with which his sofa kept its color, let itself be sat upon, laid upon, even slept on, now huddled together with the lamp, peering over to the walls, the floor, and the stove, as if conspiring, whispering, "don't worry if you're dull. we can share colors." in this room, there was no room for his excess. with his blackness and the red sofa, the walls were choked enough for light. at one point, he had tried to stuff his excess in the front of his pants (the bulge was fantastic and exhilarating), then his pants pocket (but it made him look too suspicious); it just oozed out. he even rented a U-Haul storage locker but was told it was illegal to store this excess—on page three of the contract, "no storage of hazardous materials." If he had an attic the excess would bow the ceiling; if he had a basement, it would crack the foundation. whatever could not be contained just oozed out, and what didn't make it to the sofa for absorption, found its way as streaks of white on the walls.[17] for the longest time he tried to tell those that peered in, commented on him in jest, in jealousy, in envy that they don't wanna know exactly what's inside, all this color just makes you explode in darkness and causes objects to face off in self-defense and the world to peer in curious wonder;[18] tried to tell them they don't want this spotlight;[19] they don't want what they think they want, this constant self-reinvention, but how could they know, always only being themselves and wanting his color?

They persisted in asking about color, asking about the entrails that follow every one of his motions. They insisted on coming to gallery openings with their pencils and pads, sketching, taking down notes, asking the docent questions that they could find out themselves if they would just *look*, *really* look at what's before them. But no. That's never the way it happens. They want him to open up, to tell them what their peering eyes want to know: "here I am, poking through. The *real* me, just what you always thought I was— excess blackness, a 'black star'."[20]

And, so as they pass him, in all of their lives, pass one another with pleasant and knowing nods of understanding, a single canvas pulled itself off of the wall, hopping down to the floor, turning itself thinly along its side, slowly and angularly moving between the crowd, who now looked at the blank space left from his absence and remarked THE absolute form of abstraction "Unifying all of Marshall's chosen art forms is his process of 'amalgamation' of multiple languages drawn from a shopping catalogue of styles—from high to low art, from across time and place, including European, Japanese, American, and African-aboriginal and -diasporic arts and cultures. Among his subjects are the reverberations of the trans-Atlantic enslavement trade, the neglected history of black resistance, the everyday reality of African Americans (beyond the tropes of exotics or victims), and their potential for a better life" read the placard on the wall, now next to space he left behind.[21]

as he proceeded past those depreciably less coal brown as himself, they seemed to appear appreciably paler, greyer, like the cloudless sky over a tumultuous sea, or like the Van Gogh "self-portrait."[22] but, it wasn't him. was never him. like the walls in his room, it was them; what they lacked. that's why the flocked to IKEA, and Crate and Barrel to buy that new vintage midcentury birch or sage modular sofa, low- slung wood-grain coffee tables with metal legs, indigo, teal, and copper floor vases filled with crimson sticks, and paid whatever it cost to do so. they needed it and filled every inch of space around them with it; abstraction was good for a gallery, but not for their lives. and what they couldn't buy, they envied. he knew he'd be next. thrown over the sofa, or into a collection of nick knacks for conversation, a portal into another world.

If he didn't have a theory of color, he would need one now.

If he didn't have a theory of abstraction, having one now would help him sort some things out.

Two

The show was a hit. Every piece "moved"—which meant, had pinned on the wall next to every asset, a "sold" sticker. *He* was a hit selling at *nearly* double the asking price.

Meandering between the roaming audience, he had almost made it out of the large double-doors when he was caught and returned to his place on the wall. A vanishing face behind a cloak of hair and large rimmed sunglasses squinting not more than an inch away drew him in and exclaimed, "Brilliant! A canvas *in* the gallery space! Interactive art!" And, with this, picked him up and carried him back into the room. He was merchandise and he knew it.

> *There were times when he looked solemn or just sat against the wall confronting the sofa and the audience loved him for it. The more he resisted them with his color, the more they resented it and the higher the price would go.*
>
> *When he would smile, revealing his missing tooth, and lean closer into the canvas, hat cocked to the side, background missing, erased, usurped by his density, the more the audience fought amongst themselves, voices and hands flying high for who would consume the art.*[23]
>
> *If he turned his back to them to tend to his garden, the audience would climb over themselves trying to peer in.*
>
> *When he would be distant, refusing eye contact, hiding his flesh beneath a bland green Japanese coat, attempting to distract attention with his sofa thrown against the wall, exploding into red/yellow/green blots of geometric streaks they would astound, "authentic!"*[24] *There were times he would bring all of his things from his past and try to distract the audience: a big clock, a sign from his home town, "Welcome to. . .," a tree from his yard, cotton plants and old photographs of houses from his region of the world.*[25] *And, when he would invite friends over for a small party to take on some of the pressure*[26] *or change his sofa to a muted blue, throw a braided rug on the floor, and add a vase of flowers,*[27] *he would hear them say, "I can see you; there you are. . ." and, "it's nice to see him break out of his mold. I'm glad he has friends. I was beginning to worry."*

They thought they knew him, could own him with a purchase. He didn't think so. And would, whatever may, escape, somewhere. In the end, perhaps, that's all there was. This excess, his blackness which stood out, was ubiquitous, and would always transition from scene to scene, setting to setting, canvas to canvas transported from things to every other form—invested with a meaning that refused specificity, refused articulation, touching everything with absolute, illuminating force leaving him on the floor, slumped into an "L" facing the beguiling redness of the sofa. But what else could *he* do with this "gift"? The one everyone wanted—his explicit blackness that dripped from place to place, and with it removed all possibility/ies of his humanity?

Three

~~Kerry James~~ Marshall sat in his studio sketching the edges of what would become *his* life—the redness of *his* sofa, the greenness of *his* garden, the pale blueness of *his* walls, the friends who would visit, the vistas of *his* past and *his* memories—for *him* to move between, distract the viewer and to hide. And *his* skin; oh, *his* skin. *His* black skin. A sort of craft, his skin.

Marshall had staged the darkness that someone had once given to him, and out of it, *he* emerged, a figure marked with layering denseness, and a message with its own perspective. *He* was black. *His* skin an entrapment, an occasion for excitement and fame; but *his* created room was HIS own, his sofa HIS nemesis, each personae of each painting became possibilities for HIS own existence—in each painting, Marshall had given him an exit, a way to escape the crowds, but with each canvas, what seemed like an exit became a more elaborate, more public trap.

He travelled from city to city, country to country, each time awakening in the brightness of a thousand-watt sun of new shining faces peering in and gasping in every language imaginable; and, at the end, Marshall himself would invariably stand in front of *him* to deliver a speech.

"When you go to an art museum," *he* would hear Marshall begin, time after time, "the thing you're least likely to encounter is a picture of a black person. When it comes to ideas about art and about beauty, the black figure is absent—"[28]

"What is your inspiration," the inevitable interruption, this time, a woman with red, blue, and green round glasses. Her question seemed to be rhetorical. She had a short brown bob, a long rainbow jacket, like the plumage of a peacock, and tall black shoes, that when she moved, showed the hidden secret of red color at the bottom. "Your paintings emphasize the surface as a metaphorical skin," she continued. "They are loaded with decorative motifs of the kind prominent in 1970s Pattern and Decoration art, including floral stencils, garlands, ribbons and glitter, as well as spiritual talismans from Afro-Caribbean voodoo."[29]

She had begun the free for all, and all the interruptions. Marshall knew he didn't need to answer her question. She had laid down the gauntlet of those paler folks who "get it"—authentic Afro expression!—and someone was sure to raise the bar. And did. A balding white man with a closely shaven even whiter beard and black round glasses to compliment his black jacket and pants, inserted, in a rather serious tone,

"The paintings, particularly the large ones, also revel in detail that make the story more narratively complex. In a Kerry James Marshall painting, nothing is arbitrary. Everything has been thought through. He is building a picture from the ground up."[30]

He then looked around the crowd for response peering over his shoulder at the woman in plumage, who diverted her eyes. He had won that round. The room was relatively quiet, people seemingly ruminating over the pallet of commentary. Until a bristly faced older, and noticeably paler man in a denim jacket, a denim shirt, denim pants tucked into brown broken-in cowboy boots parted the sea to the front and turned and faced the crowd.

> "Yes. Marshall is quite superior to those who came before him. The Bob Thompsons of the art world who try to show you how clever they are by not telling you what the hell the paintings are about. The worst of them all is the arrogance of Norman Lewis, making his audience continuously beg for more. Just what *are* all those shapes supposed to mean? I could go on and on, but this is about Marshall's work. He doesn't stand on pretense of the "art world," He cuts right to the chase; he gets right to point.
>
> James Baldwin once wrote, "One writes out of one thing only—one's own experience." What, then, was the experience of a man with a black skin, what could it be in this country? How could a Negro put pen to paper [or brush to canvas], how could he so much as think or breathe, without some impulsion to protest, be it harsh or mild, political or private, released or buried?[31]
>
> Marshall's paintings are a kind of controlled rage to let the white world know about the meaning of living a black life in America."

This man was the gallery owner. A woman with short blonde hair, horn-rimmed glasses, a white shirt, dark pants, and white Birkenstocks, added,

> "Kerry James Marshall was born in 1955 in Birmingham, Alabama. When he was six years old the Ku Klux Klan bombed the 16th Street Baptist Church, killing four small schoolgirls."

The audience is finally hushed, not a thought could be heard. They leaned in for more. She continued,

> "Birmingham, Alabama is small now; it was smaller then. So, if you were an African American family in Birmingham, Alabama the chances of knowing family members of one of those four small girls was pretty high. And that of course, was the case for Kerry and his family. And Kerry's parents did what many parents did at that moment, parents of black families in the South, and they participated in the last wave of the Great Migration. And they moved their family to Los Angeles where they felt their family would be safer. They arrived in the Watts neighborhood, just in time for the Watts' riots.
>
> I tell you this because I think that it's important to imagine a young person, by the age of eight already having experienced two of the most important historical moments in what will become the Civil Rights Movement.
>
> The other thing that happened to Kerry was his discovery of pictures, from magazines, newspapers, greeting cards, and art books. I tell you this story about pictures, because as much as Kerry is formed by the struggle for Civil Rights and the violence around Civil Rights, he is also equally part of that first generation of artists who grew up with a television in the home. In this cross-section of the Civil Rights movement and pictures. . .this is the magic sweet spot of Kerry's biography, and this returns and returns in these canvases around you."[32]

She was the curator for the show. The denim man fidgeted while she spoke. Looking back and forth between her, Kerry, and the canvases on the walls. The curator and owner exchanged a few back-and-forth remarks, something about a retrospective, and the importance of biographical detail in understanding black art versus the basic idea that one can simply imbibe experience through their lineage — "his parents had dreams, that's why they moved to Los Angeles; they would pass these dreams down to Kerry," and, "As a black artist, he couldn't help but be moved by the world around him." After the exchange ended in a stalemate, the owner turned to Marshall.

"Kerry James Marshall." He started a crowd clap. "Kerry James Marshall!" A thunder of applause.

Color. Structure. Texture. Relation of consciousness to object — the only sacred space between artist and art-object, between man and the world, between the reality as chosen and that which is given. But, then there is blackness — it flattens everything out: the dynamic correspondence integral to human existence, to the process of aesthetic production and appreciation — to the inner life of the work of art itself. Kerry James Marshall, black painter — quite economically viable title, but leaves something out, makes for only an imitation of life.

The canvas, at times filled with spots of color, at other times, filled with an intentional blankness, at other times filled, more or less with an explosion of color, a seeming overflow or excess of color beyond form itself, what cannot be contained in a single image, is also captured at moments in a muteness — excess returning to itself, not only in the brightness of the red in the couch, but also in the muted darkness of pigment or of the even darker background: blackness not as lack, but as the absolute density of excess, which cannot be contained so instead of turning outwards, dripping all over the page, onto the various objects, in splatters throughout, rather, turns inward, almost contemplative, stoic, meditative. Nowhere can this be seen better than in "Portrait of Nat Turner":[33] man standing, in repose, calm, without expression, his skin, no-longer-just-black, but still black, so black it has turned grey, not ashen, like the fading of color, but the excess turned inward, folding back on itself like a collapsed star: a black hole with its own gravity that sucks into itself all form, structure, light and color to create its own structure, form, light and color beyond what is visible, traceable, detectable. It is all there, in totality — the ax in his right hand, almost invisible, blending into his almost equally invisible clothing, a brown — almost the color of his skin, but different, dark, or darkening; perhaps different, maybe in hue or in comportment — slave cloth and in the background, a bed, white, so white that it almost obscures that it unmade or the head on it, severed from a body no longer there, leaking ever so slightly a liquid, not quite red, but once-red now turning pale eventually white, either by exposure to the elements or to the imposing force of the stark-whiteness of the sheets. This painting representing so much to so many — revenge, perhaps remorse for what had to be done, for the circumstances as much as the action itself — made Marshall famous, standing in front of it, slightly smiling, unlike Turner in the painting itself, but contemplative, stoic, meditative, like Turner, almost in the exact bodily position, only Kerry does not wield an ax, rather, his hand is closed, like that of Frederick Douglass, closed, around itself like a fist. Marshall, too, is draped in color like that of Turner, dark but not brown, and yet still dancing with color, so much color that his skin is turned grey, but not ashen.[34]

A Retrospective. Marshall, born in Birmingham, Alabama. Where the little girls are blown up in that church. Turner. Born enslaved. Not part of the retrospective: he is a Baptist minister who Spoke to God in sign and natural wonder: a full eclipse of the sun. And Marshall stood there next to the Turner painting, like he stands here now in front of this growing crowd, contemplative, stoic, almost meditative, A black Painter. There is also the internal stirrings in the life of the painting itself that drew Marshall to its expressive form, and it is not clear if it is this same stirring that draws this crowd and their response: who would cheer such an act, such a stirring that would be compel such a scene—the hues inverted on themselves, the form caste to attempt to hold such inscrutable hues—and such excess?

Marshall looked around the room, paused, and after briefly clearing his throat, glanced over his shoulders at all the black figures on the canvases' and began again,

"—You have to take an overview of how the culture is structured. Even before I got to museums, I was interested in comic books. When you grow up looking at Superman, Batman and all those superheroes, you take it for granted that is what superheroes are supposed to be. So then, when I see art books at the library, and I'm seeing Leonardo da Vinci and Michelangelo and Rembrandt, I think that's what artists look like.

At a certain point, you have to decide whether you'd be satisfied always acknowledging the beauty and the greatness of what other people create or if you want to be in the same arena. You can't keep saying that a superhero is a white guy with a square jaw and broad shoulders because every time you say that, it means you can't be a superhero. You have to demonstrate that you believe you have the capacity to be a superhero too. Or the capacity to be an 'old master.'"[35]

The crowd filed out. Marshall was parted with pleasantries, "such a great show, Kerry. I feel I've been changed." Eventually, he was left where he had begun the day, by himself with his paintings. And he thought of how it had all started.

Four

From time to time, when the studio was empty and Marshall thought he was alone, he would talk to his paintings. He would try to explain the process and the business of the art world to ease the burden of being seen. He hoped they would understand that he didn't want to part with them, but that this was how things were.

He whispered to them, "Somebody I loved once gave me a box of darkness, and it took me thirty-five years to know that it was a gift" and continued layering color, and shading in faces, leaving eyes and teeth and mouths as blank spots in the canvas—the absence oft times carrying the weight of the composition as much as the figures and setting itself.

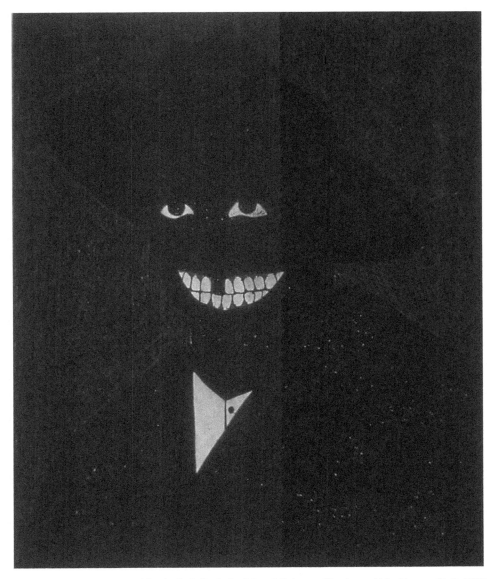

Figure 19.1 Kerry James Marshall, *A Portrait of the Artist as a Shadow of His Former Self*, 1981. Egg tempera on paper, 9 × 7 inches. Copyright Kerry James Marshall. Courtesy of the artist and Jack Shainman Gallery, New York.

Absence as a mode of presence. He looked over to his "Self-Portrait"[36] and saw staring back from the canvas *at once* a pair of white eyes *impossibly* set into a darkness, suspended, dangling above two rows of equally white teeth, which, too, seemingly floated in an ocean of infinite depth; but, he also saw a black figure set against a *blacker* background, blackness foregrounding blackness, with white eyes and teeth set deep into this double, this duality of blackness, figured and prefigured by both their contrast as well as the noticeable *gap*. This was, perhaps, the star of the show: the *gap*. Noticeably doubled as well: in the center of the painting, with floating white eyes and white teeth, there was a break, between the eyes and between the teeth. Blackness to break up whiteness and cause it to float. The gap, more than a break, was a pause in the *entanglement between color and form*.

This smile, though, this had to be accounted for—both as the foregrounded and backgrounding of blackness *and* whiteness. *This smile*, both presence and absence, set lonely against a singular black(ening) backdrop *and* nestled into a black face. *This smile and its gap*, both "haunting and mischievous" give the impression, not unlike da Vinci's *Mona Lisa*, that they are not so much hiding something, but *holding something back*: perhaps the *secret* of the process, its inner world, and that mysterious and enigmatic relationship of soul and object.

A smirk of knowing obscurity? The refusal of a gesture of invitation? A gesture towards invisibility? He'd heard it all before.[37] Everyone peering in trying to discover what it could *possibly* mean? What had been said of da Vinci's *Mona Lisa* could be said of Marshall's "Self-Portrait." Namely: "there is a gaze-dependent illusory effect in the portrait[s]." And, like da Vinci, whose "mastery of the technique [of the illusion] and its subsequent use in the *Mona Lisa*, it is quite conceivable that the ambiguity of the effect was intentional, based on artistic skill and used in line with Leonardo's maxim that portraits should reflect some 'inner turmoil of the mind.'[38] But, there is always more with the *black* smile.

More than the black-on-black—black figure on a *blacker* canvas—it was the teeth that draws our attention. *The teeth*, for black people, the teeth, not the eyes, are the window to the soul. The double-meaning of the *gap*, and the absence of teeth in the Turner painting, and Marshall's own standing-next-to-the-painting lack of teeth tell us something. In "Self-Portrait," that there is, perhaps, a through line: what is communicated in the lack of teeth is also communicated in the *excess* of teeth.

That smile and the *absence* of it, like da Vinci's technique of illusion and the inner turmoil of the viewer's gaze is retrofitted. Marshall, in step with the old master becomes the new master with a secret all his own. *That smile, his smile* how it would be received by those crowds who didn't see superheroes or a competing new master, not the technique of color and light, and the layering of figure and landscape borrowed from and furthered along, not *his* secret, *his* holding something back but only *his* blackness, captured in his biography and spilled all-over his canvas, the "hooves of Bojangles stomping poor Africa to death and replacing her with *Showtime*"?[39] But there was always more than the show and the performance, and the art object consumed within the applause and handshakes and agreeing nods.

All those teeth and that beguiling grin: *blackness*, that blackest of black stretched out and placed right out in the open, before your eyes, there in each of the canvases, even those littered with furniture and rugs, and windows peeking out of and peeking into intimate moments and even more intimate exchanges between people who filled up the spaces and in those other spaces, there is a *gap*, and this is where Marshall and his man, the figure in each of the scenes, having come to self-consciousness in them finds himself, with a secret—the something more of a blackness, which is not a lack, but so much, too much to be housed; and, so *he* finds himself, like Marshall, like Douglass, like Turner had, in the presence and absence of color and shape, peeking through the beige canvas, in the thick drops of color, which are not color, or even structure or form, but that subtle and hidden element of divine correspondence of the human soul, *so black* that it has become something other—the absolute density of *all* colors, *all* forms, *all* structures.[40]

Whereas Blackness was my condemnation; Blackness, subjectively revised, is my vindication.[41]

Post

Marshall stopped and paused to catch out of the corner of his eye the black figure slumped into a L-shape, begin to run, only to be joined by another, both now naked except their *blackness*—two black bodies running through a controlled explosion of color that Marshall had created, one whose combination and sometimes refusal of legible form disorients and befuddles the mind, like a punch in the face. Their skin, and hands and feet; arms and legs; mouths and teeth, at once hidden among the flying birds and butterflies, and the tall grass also revealed in *their* color, captured in charcoal hues, the excess all around them, now held by and within the movement of *their* flesh. They had just sold for over a million dollars.[42]

He whispered to himself,

A painter losing a painting[43]

. . . and remembered the first time he painted this slouching man a universe in *his* room and nodded confirmingly and picked up a blank canvas and continued to construct *their* world.

Someone he once loved had given him a box full of darkness, and it took him years to understand that this, too, was a gift.[44]

Notes

1   John Guare, *Six Degrees of Separation* (New York: Vintage, 1990), 19.
2   Guare, *Six Degrees*, 118.
3   Guare, *Six Degrees*, 118.
4   W. E. B. Du Bois, "Of Our Spiritual Strivings," in *The Souls of Black Folk* (New York: The Library of America, 1986), 363.
5   The sublime, as I am using it here, is an aesthetic term that refers to the experience of that which is beyond measure, the greatness of which renders a sort of awe in the experiencer as to the physical, moral, metaphysical, aesthetic, or spiritual inexpressible quality of a thing, a person, or a condition of existence. Popularized by Immanuel Kant, the sublime additionally refers to a quality of being that is *in the nature* of a thing or a condition, but also that which present *in the viewer* to *feel* such awe in the appropriate fashion. According to Michael Shapiro,

the concept of race was critical for how Kant understood sublimity. That is, the concept of race—by which Kant understood in terms of racial *difference*—was not simply a physical/biological fact, but represented deeper moral, psychological, and intellectual virtues which would help to shape the direction and development of the individual as well as the individual's civilizational-type. It is no surprise, then, that for Kant, the experience of the sublime was related to the concept of race as natural kind, but also to the development of the nation-state and its manifestation in world-history (European nations, in particular Germany, then, would represent the development of the European civilizational-type as the highest form of the human). This additional element of race is what Shapiro and others have referred to as a "racial sublime": the experience of racialization which renders within and without certain insights into moral, psychological, and intellectual virtues, but also physical, moral, metaphysical, aesthetic, or spiritual inexpressible quality of a thing, a person, or a condition of existence that places the observer in a kind of awe. Only certain developed races were to be moved in the appropriate ways and to the appropriate things. The ecstatic, then, as racially coded delimits the possibility of black art and the black artists, which, though we have done away with much of Kant's overt beliefs, vestiges of it still remain. For more on the racial sublime, see Michael Shapiro, "The Racial Sublime," in *The Political Sublime* (Durham: Duke University Press, 2018); Laura Doyle, "The Poetics of Liberty and the Racial Sublime," in *Freedom's Empire: Race and the Rise of the Novel in Atlantic Modernity, 1640–1940* (Durham: Duke University Press, 2007).

6　Ablade Glover, *By All Means*, oil on canvas, 2014, October Gallery, London, http://www.artnet.com/artists/ablade-glover/by-all-means-a-sCxNOL_2oYjS8c_XMyFLSg2

7　Ablade Glover, "Market Innuendos," oil on canvas, 2014, October Gallery, London, https://www.artsy.net/artwork/ablade-glover-market-innuendos

8　Ablade Glover, "Slumscape," oil on canvas, 2013, October Gallery, London, http://www.octobergallery.co.uk/artists/glover/

9　Ablade Glover, "Yellow People, II" oil on canvas, 2014, October Gallery, London, http://www.artnet.com/artists/ablade-glover/yellow-people-ii-a-IZ4KeGQF0y0M3wg6XR0veQ2

10　Claude Monet, "Water Lilies," oil on canvas, 1919, Metropolitan Museum of Art, New York, https://www.metmuseum.org/art/collection/search/438008

11　Jean-Michel Basquiat, "Boy and Dog in a Johnnypump," oil on canvas, 1982, Art Institute of Chicago, Chicago, https://www.artic.edu/highlights/4/new-on-view

12　Titan, "Bacchus and Ariadne," oil on canvas, 1520-23, Colourlex, http://colourlex.com/bacchus-ariadne-composition/

13　Jackson Pollock, "Convergence," enamel, oil on canvas, 1952, Albright-Knox Art Gallery, Buffalo, NY, https://www.wikiart.org/en/jackson-pollock/convergence-1952

14　Jackson Pollock, "Number 18," oil and enamel on Masonite, 1950, East Hampton, NY http://pollockprints.org/number-18/

15　Jackson Pollock, "Mural," oil and casein on canvas, 1943, The University of Iowa Museum of Art, Ames, https://www.guggenheim-bilbao.eus/en/learn/schools/teachers-guides/mural-1943-2

16　Mary Oliver, "The Uses of Sorrow," in *Thirst* (Boston: Beacon Press, 2007), 52.

17　Kerry James Marshall, "Lost Boys: AKA Black Al" acrylic and collage on canvas, 1993, Jack Shainman Gallery, New York, https://thewestmoreland.org/blog/kerry-james-marshalls-lost-boys-aka-bb/

18　Kerry James Marshall, "Untitled," acrylic on PVC panel, 2009, Metropolitan Museum of Art, New York, https://www.metmuseum.org/art/collection/search/668410

19　Kerry James Marshall, "Nude (Spotlight)," acrylic on PVC panel, 2009, Defares Collection, The Netherlands, https://www.muhka.be/programme/detail/71-kerry-james-marshall-painting-and-other-stuff/item/3585-nude-spotlight

20   Kerry James Marshall, "Black Star 2," acrylic on PVC panel, 2012, Metropolitan Museum of Art, New York, https://www.metmuseum.org/art/collection/search/690154

21   Jill Glessing, "Painting the Black Presence: Kerry James Marshall," Canadian Art, October 26, 2014, http://canadianart.ca/reviews/kerry-james-marshall-2/

22   Vincent van Gogh, "Self-Portrait," oil on canvas, 1889, National Gallery of Art, Washington, DC, https://www.nga.gov/collection/highlights/van-gogh-self-portrait.html

23   Kerry James Marshall, "A Portrait of the Artist as a Shadow of His Former Self," egg tempera on paper, 1980, Metropolitan Museum of Art, New York, https://www.metmuseum.org/exhibitions/view?exhibitionId=%7b175f55d3-dbd8-4be6-b248-9dc2025021f0%7d&oid=668284&pkgids=368&pg=1&rpp=4&pos=2&ft=*

24   Kerry James Marshall, "The Actor Hezekiah Washington as Julian Carlton Taliesen Murderer of Frank Lloyd Wright Family, acrylic on PVC panel, 2009, Metropolitan Museum of Art, New York, https://www.metmuseum.org/art/collection/search/668390

25   Kerry James Marshall, "Watts 1963," acrylic on PVC panel, 1995, Metropolitan Museum of Art, New York, https://www.metmuseum.org/art/collection/search/668327

26   Susan Stamberg, "Kerry James Marshall: A Black Presence in the Art World is 'Not Negotiable," National Public Radio, March 28, 2017, https://www.npr.org/2017/03/28/521683667/kerry-james-marshall-a-black-presence-in-the-art-world-is-not-negotiable

27   Kerry James Marshall, "Slow Dance," acrylic and collage on canvas, 1992–1993, Metropolitan Museum of Art, New York, https://www.metmuseum.org/art/collection/search/668308

28   Barbara Isenberg, "For Kerry James Marshall, the mission is clear: Bring portraits of black life into every white art museums," Los Angeles Times, March 7, 2017, https://www.latimes.com/entertainment/arts/la-et-cm-kerry-james-marshall-20170307-htmlstory.html

29   Christopher Knight, "Kerry James Marshall's paintings insist on black self-representation," Los Angeles Times, March 20, 2017, http://www.latimes.com/entertainment/arts/la-et-cm-kerry-james-marshall-moca-20170320-htmlstory.html

30   Barbara Isenberg, "For Kerry James Marshall," https://www.latimes.com/entertainment/arts/la-et-cm-kerry-james-marshall-20170307-htmlstory.html.

31   Irving Howe, "Black Boys and Native Sons," Dissent (Autumn 1963): 353–68. http://www.plosin.com/beatbegins/archive/HoweDissent.htm

32   Helen Molesworth, chief curator. Kerry James Marshall: Mastery. Los Angeles: Museum of Contemporary Art, 2017. https://www.moca.org/exhibition/kerry-james-marshall-mastry

33   Kerry James Marshall, "Portrait of Nat Turner with the Head of his Master," acrylic on PVC panel, 2011, Metropolitan Museum of Art, New York, https://www.metmuseum.org/art/collection/search/668395

34   Bill Lamb, "Kerry James Marshall, Artist of the Black Experience," ThoughtCo., November 30, 2018, https://www.thoughtco.com/kerry-james-marshall-biography-4570818

35   Isenberg, "For Kerry James Marshall," https://www.latimes.com/entertainment/arts/la-et-cm-kerry-james-marshall-20170307-htmlstory.html.

36   Kerry James Marshall, "A Portrait of the Artist as a Shadow of His Former Self," egg tempera on paper, 1980, Metropolitan Museum of Art, New York, https://www.metmuseum.org/exhibitions/view?exhibitionId=%7b175f55d3-dbd8-4be6-b248-9dc2025021f0%7d&oid=668284&pkgids=368&pg=1&rpp=4&pos=2&ft=*

37   Kerry James Marshall, "Untitled," acrylic on PVC panel, 2009, Metropolitan Museum of Art, New York, https://www.metmuseum.org/art/collection/search/668410

38 Amah-Rose Abrams, "Scientists Discover the Legendary Secret Behind 'Mona Lisa' Smile," artnet news, August 21, 2015, https://news.artnet.com/art-world/secret-behind-mona-lisa-smile-discovered-326770

39 Caryl Philips, *Dancing in the Dark*, (New York: Vintage, 2005), 5.

40 In the HBO special, "Black Art: In the Absence of Light," Kerry James Marshall explains this theory of blackness when he says,

> I made a painting called, "A Portrait of the Artist as a Shadow of His Former Self," which is a black figure against a black ground. And it was the first time I had used this simplified, kind of reductive representation of a black figure. And so that painting was the—the one that established the black figure as a mode of operating for me. One of things that I was trying to do was embody in a picture the concept that Ralph Ellison had laid out in his novel, *Invisible Man*. He describes the condition of invisibility as it relates to black people in America. This condition of being seen and not seen simultaneously. And that's what I think a black figure against a black ground, where if you change the color temperature of the black, it creates enough separation so that you can alternatively see and then sometimes not see the figure that's present there. I started creating the sense of volume in those figures by using the grayscale. So, uh—you take black, you add white to it, you create grayscale and then you can actually start doing modelling, you know—with values. *Black is not the absence of color, black is particular kinds of color*. And so if I went to the paint store, as I did, and I bought black paint, I could see I could buy three variations of black paint. . .they all look the same, but when you stack them on top of each other, then the—the variations start to become more pronounced. So, I can end up with six, seven, eight or nine different colors that are made from black. So that means I have a palette that's as complex and as broad and as ranged as any other that's on the spectrum. *Black Art: In the Absence of Light*, directed by Sam Pollard (2021; New York: HBO)

41 Thomas F. Slaughter, "Epidermalizing the World: A Basic Mode of Being-Black," *Man and World* 10, no. 3 (1977): 307.

42 Victoria L. Valentine, "Kerry James Marshall's 'Vignette' Sells at Christie's for Record $1 Million," Culture Type, November 26, 2014, http://www.culturetype.com/2014/11/26/kerry-james-marshalls-vignette-sells-at-christies-for-record-1-million/

43 Guare, *Six Degrees*, 46.

44 Mary Oliver, "The Uses of Sorrow," 52.

PART FIVE

CALLINGS

20

TRACY K. SMITH'S *ORDINARY LIFE*: ENFLESHING A THEORY OF POST-SOUL

Daphne Lamothe

Introduction

In her 2015 memoir *Ordinary Light*, the poet Tracy K. Smith brings together a collection of loosely connected memories in order to explore the paradoxes of black girlhood in the decades following the successes of the Civil Rights movement.[1] The narrative focuses on Smith's formative years in the seventies and eighties, in the northern California city where her family settled because of her father's air force career. It offers a loosely chronological pastiche of memories, experiences and relationships that helped nurture the literary aspirations that would lead Smith to professional heights that her ancestors could only have imagined.[2] More than being a narrative of personal development and advancement however, *Ordinary Light* frames this personal journey across an expanse of time and possibility as an occasion for reflection on the changing meanings of blackness at the end of the twentieth and beginning of the twenty-first centuries.

For these reasons *Ordinary Light* exemplifies the post-soul aesthetic, which the culture critic Nelson George describes as, "tales told not from the belly of the beat, but from the barely integrated mountain tops of academia, law, and mainstream journalism" (108).[3] Framed as a coming of age story, the narrative dramatizes some of the key demographic and societal changes in black life after the sixties. For example, the Smith family's entry into the middle class and integration of predominantly white suburbs and schools forms the backdrop for this meditation on the limits of respectability and racial uplift ideologies. Both concepts have been premised historically on the idea that individual black achievement can effect positive change on the racial collective. Yet Smith's exploration of these ideas from within the context of the aforementioned societal and generational changes compels a reckoning with the fraying of the kinship, communal and political ties that have historically formed the basis of notions of racial collectivity bound by a common history and shared political futures.

This context necessarily informs my reading of *Ordinary Light,* though my point is less that Smith's personal history is representative of a generational condition, and more that the narrative offers an illuminating and nuanced portrayal of contemporary blackness through an exploration of the ambivalence of the everyday. Through the aperture of "ordinary blackness," Smith paints a portrait of blackness as signifier whose fluidity and dynamism, contingency and instability, refuses easy categorization.[4] Movement, whether it manifests as upward social mobility or regional migrations, operates as a central metaphor in the text by connecting the narrative exploration of the communal "boundaries of blackness" with the protagonist's quest for self-knowledge and self-realization.[5]

I read *Ordinary Life* as an example of autotheory, a genre that critic Robyn Wiegman describes as ". . . an encounter between first person narration and theory as an established body of contemporary academic thought" (1).[6] Read as autotheory, the memoir's purpose as a distinctly black aesthetic practice is to "put flesh" on the universalist and collectivist claims of theoretical discourse.[7] Here, I purposefully extend Wiegman's reading of autotheory as "as a distinctly feminist practice," that maintains a, ". . . commitment to putting 'flesh' on the universalist pretensions of established theoretical traditions by situating the story of lived experience in politically consequential terms" (7-8). This is because Wiegman's emphasis on the "politically consequential" doesn't fully capture the tensions inherent to theories of race and racialization. Namely, because social and critical discourse tend to frame blackness as a political identity, the autotheoretical intervention of black life-writing almost inevitably addresses political claims and conditions, whether implicitly or explicitly. In the post-soul era however, the impulse more often than not is to trouble conventional ideas of the political, rather than viewing it primarily as a form of resistance against bankrupt claims of universality (although it can be that too). Thus I read Smith's version of life-writing as an *aesthetic practice*: one that is certainly feminist and anti-racist in orientation, yet whose "enfleshment" works to trouble ideas of the political and racial collective in order to expand the social imaginary in regard to race and gender, and in particular black womanhood.

Like all memoirs, *Ordinary Light* employs a doubled perspective that combines the immediacy of the protagonist's lived experiences and the narrator's retrospective, more knowing, vantage point. Its portrayal of the experiences of a Black girl whose upbringing is shaped by this sociohistorical context employs a doubled perspective and temporality that sheds light on changes in racialized consciousness in this time. Because it was published in in 2015 and focuses on black girlhood in the 1970s and 80s, it combines a depiction of the optimism of a generation viewed as the culmination of the Civil Rights era struggle, with the disillusionment and pessimism of the more recent past, during which black people continue to reckon with the racial "antagonisms" at the foundations of American institutions and ideologies that work to undermine efforts at meaningful racial justice.[8] In other words, ambivalence is the primary mode of what Bertram Ashe would describe as Smith's "blaxploration" of the "boundaries of blackness."[9]

Ordinary Light's post-soul sensibility also emerges in its meditation on the relationship between life-writing and self-making, and in particular the tensions that emerge from the historical equation of agency and subjectivity with writing in a literary tradition that extends back to nineteenth century enslavement narratives. As is typical of African American life-writing – and here I am indebted to literary critic Valerie Smith's invaluable work on the historical foundations of black autobiography – Tracy Smith follows the convention of linking the individual development of selfhood with the acquisition of a "racial consciousness." In the nineteenth century, a narrator like Frederick Douglass represented the fight for individual and collective emancipation as a reckoning with and resistance to the abjection and subjection associated with the category of "slave."[10] In the late twentieth century context, self-actualization compels this narrator to wrestle with the black elite's complicity in failing to understand that their achievements did little to dismantle the structures that exist to otherize blackness. At the same time however, various anecdotes in *Ordinary Light* convey a reluctance to minimize experiences and expressions of singularity and particularity in order to privilege a communalist ethic and collectivist action against anti-blackness. Instead, the narrative dwells on the loss that is felt when one of these orientations surpasses the other. It suggests that the ambivalence that defines post-soul racial consciousness suspends the subject in between articulations of blackness as political identity, and an affective/aesthetic orientation to "the nuance, fragmentation and fragility of a single black life begging to be considered on its own terms and in its own voice."[11]

Structurally, Smith organizes *Ordinary Light* around a series of impressionistic and elliptical vignettes: fragments of memory that stayed with the author and which she chooses to share with readers. On the one hand, this structure enacts the kind of "narrative construction," or ordering of certain events and forgetting of others in order to produce a coherent version of past, which Ashe views as a correlate to the post-soul project of constructing a coherent version of the black subject.[12] On the other hand, many of Smith's stories and recollections remain enigmatic and resistant to easy interpretation. This underscores the openness of the narrative to a myriad of interpretations, which implicitly calls readers to embrace the multiplicity and difference that will shape our understanding of black womanhood in a period of generational change.[13]

A Self in Search of Origins

The prologue to *Ordinary Life* begins with an ending, as Smith's family gathers around her mother's deathbed. Smith describes their grief as they come to terms with their impending loss. While the prologue gestures towards several themes that readers will encounter in the narrative (e.g. faith, love, even respectability), the primary concern is with the loss of a maternal figure who is instrumental to the author's quest for selfhood and self-knowledge. The mother figure though typically linked with "home" in black literature, here hints at a narrative preoccupation with belonging *and unbelonging*. To begin however, Tracy's memories, especially those focused on her earliest years, underscore her deep love and admiration for, and connection to, her mother. As the emotional and moral anchor of the family, "Mommy's" presence functions as a bridge linking her children spiritually and emotionally to their Southern roots. Tracy recalls, ". . . I'd lie beside her and listen while she talked on the phone with one of her sisters back East. . . . When that other voice coaxed her to travel the distance back to the old days down South, she'd let slip a phrase like 'ain't that a blip,'" (15). That "slip" resonates because, not only are the Smiths Alabama transplants, they also insist on the children using "proper," standard English at home. Yet southern blackness finds its way in, transmitted through language and the sound of the mother's words, timbre, and inflections.

An ensuing chapter adds another dynamic by delving into ideas of ancestry and origins. In this chapter, readers learn of Tracy's first visit at the age of six or seven to her mother's Alabama home in a town named Leroy. Rather than satisfying the urge for a place of uncomplicated belonging however, this journey inspires feelings of intense confusion. Her mother's stories of the past lead Tracy to expect the visit to take place in "the deep country," in a world, "with its outhouses and smokehouses, its miles and miles of [] cotton" (53). Instead of ". . . a past like that still going about its business, flush with the present," she finds a place dotted with cars, billboards and "sprawling modern supermarkets" (54). In other words she encounters a South that is not preserved in amber, but rather exists in and of the modern world.

In addition, the home that Leroy represents is accessible only to Tracy's mother, who the narrator describes as in possession of the "language and currency" needed to "stay afloat in this place" (56). The narrative frames change – such as the geographical dispersal of certain family members and passing on of elders – as loss because it underscores the fragility and difficulty of maintaining forms of sociality that critics from Farah Jasmine Griffin to Terrion L. Williamson have argued historically existed to affirm black people's understanding of our own humanity.[14] We see this exemplified in the portrayal of Tracy's mother, who she describes as "herself and something more" upon her return home (56). We see it also in her mother's interactions with her siblings and the "ease and warmth" they all feel while telling and listening to stories that 'triggered other stories" (60).

This kind of belonging feels unattainably mysterious to a child lacking direct, lived experiences of the joys and terrors of living in this place. In contrast to her mother's memories of her grandfather, proudly overlooking his "army of boys and girls" as they farmed their land, or her "kindhearted" grandmother, ". . . who turned out big fluffy cakes and sat laughing beside a lively, jocular Daddy Herbert," Tracy finds herself surrounded by the ghostly presence of family. Her grandfather is already dead from a stroke; and her grandmother (whom they refer to as Mother) suffering from the early stages of dementia, calls Tracy "that little gal" and appears "stern, watchful, almost feral" (55). Moreover, even while engaged in solitary play, she feels haunted by history. For example, when alone in the woods surrounding Mother's house, she envisions, "the kinds of human harm that sat just outside of the frame of those stories of the long-ago days down south, just beyond the edges of Daddy Herbert's woods, just around the wrong bend" (58). The violence of Jim Crow history is a ghostly presence too, one symbolized by rows of cotton and lynchers' ropes, thus manifesting feelings, not of loss, but rather of terror. In this particular sense, Smith's meditation on her Southern "home" resonates with Avery Gordon's definition of haunting as, "an animated state in which a repressed or unresolved social violence is making itself known, sometimes very directly, sometimes more obliquely."[15] My larger point however is that some historical hauntings terrorize; while others, especially those reminiscent of an idea of home that no long exists, prove equally unsettling though for different reasons.

How then, does the text propose that young Tracy might begin to tap into this source of self-affirmation and -definition? Narrative, in the form of storytelling but not only that, will come to play a central role in the self-development that propels the memoir. In fact, this turns out to be an indirect lesson learned during this southern interlude, as Tracy witnesses the power of storytelling to gather kin, reassemble the family unit, and reinforce the ties that bind them together: "It was as if this small group of sibling coming together—three of thirteen—had brought the whole family into being, just like Jesus said in the Bible, *Where two or three gather in my name, there am I with them*" (60). The conditional tense of this sentence ("it was as if. . .") gestures toward what *could be*, rather than what *is*. Story produces feelings of wellness and wholeness however, that narrow the gap between imagined and real.

Unsurprisingly in a narrative focused on the gradual development of a poet, forms of cultural and literary expressivity play a critical role in the story. In another example, again in Leroy, music too helps to reknit the family's frayed connections. Tracy states,

> Within hours of our arrival, Dinah had taught me to plant my feet shoulder width apart and swing my hips back and forth while a forty-five of the disco hit 'Le Freak' played over and over on the turntable. We danced together all morning. Dinah laughing and me reveling in the song's assurance that I was not so far from home—after all, it wasn't impossible to imagine my siblings listening to the same song just then on our stereo in California (54-55).

In the same way that her mother's colloquialisms ("ain't that a blip") offer Tracy a glimpse of the southern-ness that is part of her identity, in this passage her sense of self coheres around a different kind of cultural exchange. Like her mother's southern idioms, music embodies a notion of blackness capable of transcending the experiences of dislocation. Cultural and other aesthetic texts play an outsized role in helping to fill in the blanks of the narrator's still developing identity. Where storytelling derives from southern vernacular culture however, this passages offers a strikingly different symbol of blackness with its reference to the disco classic, "Le Freak." As opposed to merely overcoming the problems of migration and hybridity, in this example disco's hybrid and urban origins complicates the tendency to link "belonging" to narrow or strict racial/communal boundaries.[16] This passage conveys two important and interlocking ideas: that migration can be experienced sometimes as generative rather than disruptive; and that aesthetic encounters (like trading stories, or dancing together) have the power to produce a racial feeling that enables blackness to cohere.

Ultimately, the image of storytelling and music as vehicles capable of crossing borders and boundaries underscores the memoir's unwillingness to fetishize static ideas of home and belonging. In fact another passage about her grandmother, which appears in one of the last chapters of the book, underscores this more complicated and fraught understanding of home, connection and origins. Rather than revisiting the previous ideas of the maternal figure as culture source and anchor, Tracy describes "Mother," now firmly caught in the grip of dementia and living in California, as "unmoored, an alien adrift" in space and time (206). Left unguarded, she would wander the streets in the hopes of finding her way back "to her own house, her own life" (204). This image of Mother unmoored drives home the point that the trip to "Leroy" introduces: that home is more a "mood" than a place, and one can never assume that one's identity will remains fixed and unchanging over the course of a lifetime.

If the vernacular cultures of the south offer one version of aesthetic self-fashioning, the literary-centered culture of the California suburbs offers yet another model. In a chapter entitled "My Book House," Smith describes a bookshelf-lined hallway in the family home with an array of titles that gesture toward the confusions and contradictions she will have to navigate as she grows older and matures. At first glance, the volumes – e.g. *National Geographic* magazine, the *Encyclopedia Britannica*, and a collection of Shakespeare's sonnets – exist to convey the family's middle class status and educational aspirations. The shelves are filled with children's stories, autobiographies, encyclopedias and Christian devotional texts. Smith describes their organization on the shelves as an enactment of a silent conversation about blackness. For example, Claude Brown's *Manchild in the Promised Land* sits beside *Stranger in a Strange Land*, which sits next to *Be My Guest*, by the hotelier Conrad Hilton: each title evoking themes of un/belonging, hospitability and/or alienation (12).[17] Others, like Lorraine Hansberry's *To Be Young, Gifted and Black* and Sammy Davis Jr.'s autobiography *Yes I Can,* suggests the myth of meritocracy, which will be reinforced by her father's reminders to his children to exhibit, "drive, intelligence, effort" (129).

In addition to these aspirational books, Smith also recalls a twelve volume collection of nursery rhymes and stories entitled *My Book House*, for which a particular memory introduces ideas of black enfleshment and embodiment, which a color-blind reading of the inspirational books might otherwise obscure or erase. *My Book House*, "an antique from the 1940s," features a stereotypical story of "Little Black Sambo" (11). Sambo's presence in Smith's memories of that otherwise beloved library calls forth the ontological negation that blackness confers. One can't help but hear echoes of the white child's exclamation, "Look, a Negro!" in the memory of "Little Black Sambo;" the former being Frantz Fanon's paradigmatic example in "The Fact of Blackness" of being called into the world through the encounter with whiteness (89).[18]

This anecdote suggests that the historical hauntings associated with the south will also be found in the new and supposedly unmarked territories of the family's adopted California home, "a place of low, bare hills and a history as blank and clear as the sky on a sunny day" (72). This image of a place untouched and untainted by history is, of course, an illusion that quickly dissipates, that cannot be sustained. In one example, her recollections of a kind a beloved second-grade teacher are tarred by the memory of that teacher asking, "why do black people always have such white-white teeth?" as they watch a telethon for "victims and refugees" after school (73). This anecdote ends with the kind of insight that distance make possible: "Those faces hadn't made her feel a part of the wider world at all but more like a spectator, someone on safari, it seemed to me, watching from the kind of distance that facilitates judgment or fear" (73). This passage marks the distance between the child conflicted by her need to see her teacher as "an ally or a friend" in spite of her casual racism, and the mature narrator who is capable of recognizing and assessing the violence of the racialized gaze.

The level of nuance and complexity required to make sense of the cognitive dissonance of this moment develops over time and with experience. At the same time, when young

Tracy learns how to write, she begins to experience the potentiality of mobilizing language in a project of self-making. In the empty pages of a diary, she envisions herself as free externally imposed ideas and associations, writing, "At the top of the next blank page, I wrote 1980. Under that, I wrote my full name: Tracy Kathleen Smith" (67). Literally, "1980" signals newness and change that are associated with the turning of a new decade. Symbolically the assemblage of circles and holes in the last two digits portend new beginnings and possibility: "I looked at the zero, the fresh, round, empty hole of it, and I imagined that every life, lived every day, everywhere, would go into filling up that space" (68). Through the experience of writing, an aesthetic practice, "Tracy Kathleen Smith" envisions herself through an anticipatory lens as open and undefined space waiting to be filled with experience, rather than from the perspective of tradition, which focuses instead on the gathering of remnants and reassemblage of fragments.

It's important to note that *Ordinary Light* expresses equal measures of ambivalence about the written word and the ideas associated with it, as it does the orality. Because the text associates Tracy's love of writing with her being good at school, the vexed relationship of literacy and authorship to African-American history tempers the inclination to view the so-called power of the pen as an unconditional good. Enslaved-holding societies in the west associated literacy with personhood because they viewed the written word as evidence of the capacity to reason. When the title pages of narratives written by abolitionists like Frederick Douglass or Harriet Jacobs proclaimed the text to have been, "written by himself" or herself, such claims of authorship where rightfully viewed as expressions of self-assertion and self-authorization. Empowering as this may have been, the fact remains that abiding by western ideologies of personhood meant that black life-writers were compelled to accept an ideology that instituted narrow and restrictive criteria in order to separate and empower some category of people from others who they viewed as falling outside of the category of the human.

Although it is never explicitly invoked, this legacy tarnishes Tracy's educational experience, for the narrative makes clear that more is at stake than the positive attention she received for her poise and good behavior. For example when describing her placement in an elementary school program for "mentally gifted minors," she states,, ". . . even if it was wrong to acquiesce to the notion that we were the smarter ones and to let smarter become a synonym for better—I liked the way it felt getting the things we got, and doubt I ever saw myself back then as anything but deserving" (97). The hint of self-critique – "even if it was wrong to acquiesce. . . . I liked the way it felt" – introduces a retrospective weighing and measuring of the spiritual, emotional and social costs that accompanied the increased access that they enjoyed and other societal changes of the era.

Lines Demarcating "Us" and "Them"

Ordinary Light dramatizes the development of Tracy's capacity for self-reflection and critical thinking that precede the development of a racial consciousness as a series of encounters in which class differences blur and muddle the lines between some notion of "us" and "them." In several examples, she bears witness to performances of middle class respectability that are designed to, ". . [show] the world we were just as good, as smart, as adept, as brave, as necessary as anyone else;" yet end up exacerbating differences and creating divisions between individuals who long for racial community and connection (130-131). For example, she wonders at the unspoken tension that erupts when she and her mother display proper etiquette to the point of parody when hosting a new acquaintance, named Maggie.[19]

> When the three of sat down to lunch, I recalled the manners that had been instilled in me. Napkin in my lap, mouth closed while I chewed, no smacking, no elbows on the table, no reaching across for extra helpings. . . . Maggie was much easier on herself, heaping her plate and eating quickly, like a boy (47).

The passage goes on to compare Tracy's "manners" and her mother's smiling formality with Maggie's "boyish" ways (she wears "military fatigues and shiny brogan boots" and speaks coarsely by the family's standards: dropping phrases like "aw, hell" and "my old man") (45). Tracy wonders why her mother remains incapable, "for whatever reason," of showing a ". . . version of herself that Maggie was certain to have liked" (48). Yet she also expresses compassion for her mother: "I imagine her a young woman alone with one or two or four children while her husband, my father, was overseas on duty" (48). This encounter represents one of what she imagines to have been numerous disappointing attempts at forging kinship. "Had she reached out to God only after she'd exhausted the communities of women she hoped might keep her from feeling alone and unmoored?" (48).

Examples such as this suggest that Tracy will have to guard herself from uncritically adopting the bourgeois values that authority figures might reward, but that will draw literal and figurative lines between her and the communities of women who could help anchor her in self and in relation to others. This is a lesson that lived experience continually reinforces, for example when a classmate, Virginia, bullies her older sister Jean for "talking white, acting white, believing she was white, . . . (130)." Smith expresses sympathy for her sister, but leavens her compassion by probing an equally pressing question about race and community. She notes that "sweet," "shy" and obedient Jean is unfairly compared to Virginia, who their father would have dismissed as "sorry, up to no good, squandering her potential" (129). Each girl suffers, though they express their pain in different ways: one with fear and the other with anger. Once again, the narrator displays an understanding that the child lacks: "Perhaps Jean's every word reached Virginia like a telegram from some inescapable future: Renounce yourself. Agree that you're worth nothing. Learn how to talk, act, think, white—or watch everything you've ever wanted in life get handed to someone who does. Fighting words" (132). Reflecting back on this conflict, the narrator asks, "what happens when a line gets drawn between us and ourselves?", conjuring the historical line drawn between those designated human subjects and those deemed sub- or nonhuman (132). When pulled together, these passage implicitly reject the claim that the politics and practice of respectability can sufficiently equip an individual engaged in a quest for self-determination and self-regard.

Coda: A Portrait of the Artist as a Girl in Search of Something More

It would be easy to end this reading of *Ordinary Light* on the above note, with a reinforcement of ideas that have long been foundational to discourses of blackness. That is, that the fate of the individual is inevitably and inherently tied to that of the collective; that black consciousness is primarily a political consciousness; and the path toward freedom from racial abjection lies in some combination of collective action and expressions of racial pride. It would be easy to end here because these are, in fact, some of the spoken and unspoken lessons embedded in the stories Smith tells of her childhood. At the same time, however, the narrative represents these ideas as enduring truths that co-exist with other, sometimes competing and contradictory, truths about contemporary black existence. There are, for example, no easy answers or solutions to the post-movement fracturing of racial community that the individual members experience through geographic dispersal of family, or class-based differences and tension, or as the double-edged sword of being labeled as "gifted and talented" which leads to being separated from other children who look like you. *Ordinary Light* asks its readers to stay with the discomfort and uncertainties of a context in which historical notions of black self-actualization must actively reckon with the question of what constitutes a viable understanding of the "we."

Ordinary Light's form, in particular its refusal of linearity and resistance to identifying a destination for Tracy's quest for selfhood, suggests how we might consider understandings of blackness that exist beyond conventional notions of racial consciousness and collectivity. The text ends as at begins, with its protagonist poised on the precipice of a major phase in her life: this time after having graduated from college, successfully applied to MFA programs and ready to move to New York and Columbia University. Thus the memoir ends as it begins, on the threshold of a new set of challenges and opportunities. Yet for all of the text's forward-facing momentum (moving as it does from Tracy's childhood to young adulthood), its episodic approach to storytelling consistently calls for an exploratory approach to reading and understanding.

This account of a poet in the process of becoming impresses readers with the shaping hand of history and tradition in her making. At the same time, the narrative places equal weight on moments of solitude and imaginative play. Such passages read not as digressions from the "real" story, but rather as meditations on the world-making and self-making potential in creative expression and aesthetic practice. For example, in a recollection of a summer of solitude as she awaits transfer to a different elementary school, Tracy's sense of wholeness and plenitude is not diminished by her aloneness, but rather is amplified by the freedom she has to read, play, explore her neighborhood, remember old friends and anticipate gaining new ones. This description aptly conveys the expansiveness and plenitude of the inner landscape of feeling and imagination, which Kevin Quashie theorizes as a form of "quiet." Having access to "quiet" calls for a certain kind of stillness, namely in the form of a refusal to follow the drumbeat of externally imposed notions of progress and advancement. Hence, Tracy's association of the stillness that makes possible what I have been calling aesthetic self-fashioning with the experience of being in a "slow, unchoreographed free fall"; as "the strange zero-gravity hover of being in-between places, phases, of having said goodbye to one thing before laying eyes on its replacement" (81). Suspended in the fall, and uncertain of the timing or the place of the landing, Tracy experiences her "self," by herself, as "herself and something more." I want to argue that the openness to stay with and in suspension in moment and movements that lack clearly defined endpoints is a defining feature of the post-soul aesthetic, and of black aesthetic being more generally. In this, my thinking is indebted to philosopher Paul Taylor's theorization of post-soul blackness as an ". . . emerging practice or situation [that] is still trying to establish an identity."[20] When viewed through the lens of autotheory, as a black aesthetic practice that puts flesh on theoretical and discursive constructions of blackness, *Ordinary Light* invites readers to conceive of identity as an unfolding and processual condition of being that refuses capture and categorization.

Even as the narrative actively engages conventional expectations that representations of blackness serve the political needs of the collective, Smith envisions aesthetic practice as an exploration of the everyday. Blackness viewed under an "ordinary light" becomes more opaque and less transparent, less easily digested and more layered and multi-valenced. The notion that there is value in the ordinary is in fact quite extraordinary because it refuses the assumption that narratives of blackness are obliged to cohere in order to fulfill some utilitarian purpose. It suggests an idea of aesthetic sovereignty that leads Smith to compare her imagination to the Hubble telescope that her father worked on as a member of NASA, which by "pointing off into a distance that had no shape" unveiled the universe (142):

> Perhaps there would sit, at the outer edges of that distance, something I was afraid to bring into focus, some knowledge or presence, the power or verity of which might cause the rest of me to cower. It felt like that sometimes, like there were limits to what I would let myself understand, limits to the whole to which I'd give myself access. I was ten years old, living with a vague knowledge that pain was part of my birthright, part of what was meant by a word like Home (142).

Caught between the limitations that are a "part of her birthright" as a black woman, and the exploration of the outer edges of the known world, which is also her birthright as a person imbued with the sovereignty of imagination, Smith trains her gaze in two directions simultaneously: backward toward the shadowy past and forward into an undefined future. She regard with wonderment the unknowable future and incomprehensible past, as she explores what it means (or more accurately, what it means to her) to be black and female at the turn of a new millennium.

Ordinary Light ends also with a meditation on the love that binds daughters to their mothers, and on the poet's love of word and image. "I am searching," she declares, implicitly describing writing as a form of loving exploration that resonates on multiple levels. In regard to her mother, the quest is to find "the real her, the woman she would have shown herself to be" but couldn't reveal because she died before Tracy was old enough to understand that she was more than "Tracy's mother" (347). "I am searching," Smith repeats, "for a glimpse of the person I could have been alongside her but chose not to be" (347). Limited, as most children are, by a partial understanding of her mother's desires and aspirations, she acknowledges having made decisions that shaped the outcome of her journey toward selfhood while foreclosing other possibilities. Yet when faced with the death of her mother, Smith merges memory and narrative in an effort to forestall the ending that the mother's passing portends. *Ordinary Light* elides the search for mother, with the search for origins, which in turn overlaps with the search for a coherent sense of self. However, rather than assuming that external forces, like history or politics, will work to make blackness seamlessly coalesce and cohere, Smith deploys the building blocks of poetry – word, image and sound —to represent subjects vast and small, and to envision blackness as a form of being shaped by historical forces, and also as "something more."

Notes

1   Tracy K. Smith, *Ordinary Light* (New York: Knopf, 2015).

2   Smith has published four books of poetry and won the Pulitzer Prize in 2011 for the collection, *Life on Mars*. She served as the 22nd Poet Laureate from 2017 to 2019.

3   See Nelson George, *Buppies, B-Boys, Baps, and Bohos: Notes on Post-Soul Black Culture* (New York: Harper Collins, 1992). Also, Bertram Ashe, "Theorizing the Post-Soul Aesthetic: An Introduction," *African American Review* 41, no. 4 (Winter 2007): 609–623.

4   Borrowing from Ashe, we might think of the memoir as a form of "blaxploration." I use the nomenclature, "post-soul" rather than "post-black," in order to resist the popular understanding of "post-blackness" as an articulation of a desire to transcend race. Noting the historical association of "soul" and "soulfulness" with racial authenticity, particularly during the Black Power/Black Arts era, the rhetoric of "post-soul" emphasizes instead the mindset of a generation, formed by post-modernist and post-structuralist thought, who embrace anti-essentialist and performative conceptualizations of identity. The work of scholars of post-soul, particularly that Francesca Royster and Mark Anthony Neal, inspire and inform my reading of *Ordinary Light* as a post-soul narrative. For example, Royster describes the freedom of culture-workers and creatives whose racial and gender-bending "eccentricity" (e.g. Grace Jones and Prince), who modeled anti-essentialist performances of blackness that rejected normative, heteropatriarchal ideas. And Neal examines the socio-political and historical changes that resulted in a shift from imagining blackness as a political identity and toward alternate conceptualization of it as cultural construct. Neal, Mark Anthony, *Soul Babies and the Post-Soul Aesthetic* (New York: Routledge, 2001). Francesca Royster, *Sounding Like a No-No: Queer Sounds and Eccentric Acts in the Post-Soul Era* (Ann Arbor: University of Michigan Press, 2012).

5   Ashe coins the phrase, "blaxploration" to describe the textual exploration of the "boundaries of blackness" in his faming of the post-soul aesthetic. His observation resonates with that of Malin Pereira who makes a similar case in regards to post-soul poetics when she states, "post-soul black poets enact their cosmopolitan migrations in two ways: as the poet moving out into the world; and as the poet exploring the interior of black subjectivity" (712) Ashe, "Theorizing the Post-Soul Aesthetic: An Introduction," *African American Review* 41, no. 4 (Winter 2007): 609–623. Malin Pereira, "the Poet in the World, the World in the Poet": Cyrus Cassells's and Elizabeth Alexander's Versions of Post-Soul Cosmopolitanism" *African American Review* 41, 4 (Winter 2007): 709–725.

6   For Wiegman, what makes auto-theory a compelling site of inquiry is the friction created when a writer's personal story rubs up against universalist claims of Enlightenment philosophers, as well as those embedded in critical theory's critique of the sovereign subject. Robyn Wiegman,

"Introduction: Autotheory Theory," *Arizona Quarterly: A Journal of American Literature, Culture, and Theory* 76, no. 1 (Spring 2020): 1–14.

7   Wiegman credits Stacey Young with coining the term, "autotheory" in 1997. Young writes about autotheory as a challenge to western notions of the self-authorized subject/individual: "[Autotheoretical texts] undermine the traditional autobiographical impulse to depict a life as unique and individual. Instead, they present the lives they chronicle as deeply enmeshed in other lives, and in history, in power relations that operate on multiple levels simultaneously" (69). Stacey Young, *Changing the Wor(l)d: Discourse, Politics, and the Feminist Movement* (New York: Routledge, 1997).

8   Wilderson argues, "modernity marks the emergence of a new ontology because it is an era in which an entire race appears, people who. . . stand as socially dead in relation to the rest of the world" (18). Like other theorists associated with Afro-Pessimism, Wilderson resists equating legal emancipation or civic incorporation with black liberation. Afro-Pessimist analysis suggests that despite African Americans' entry into public life and positions of institutional power, modern world systems continue to (re)produce antiblack modes of domination and racial abjection into the present day. Frank Wilderson, *Red, White and Black: Cinema and the Structure of U.S. Antagonisms* (Durham: Duke University Press, 2010).

9   Bertram Ashe argues that the disillusionment and skepticism that comes through the narrative's authorial perspective amplifies a change in political consciousness that accelerated and amplified with the election of Barack Obama to the presidency. Even as political conservatives repeatedly pointed to Obama's election as proof that the nation had transcended its racist past, progressives developed a critique of structural racism that helped usher in the restoration of the kind of politically grounded race consciousness that Neal describes as having wained during the era of post-soul blackness ("Theorizing the Post-Soul Aesthetic").

10   In the context of enslavement, narrators "affirm and legitimize their psychological autonomy by telling the stories of their own lives" (Smith, 2). Smith also warns against the expectation that reading an enslavement narrative can give a full understanding of an author's sense of what his or her life means. "In each stage of their history, the presence of an intermediary renders the majority of the narratives not artistic constructions of personal experience but illustrations of someone else's view of slavery" (9). Valerie Smith, *Self-Discovery and Authority in Afro-American Narrative* (Cambridge: Harvard University Press, 1987).

11   Smith uses this language in her laudatory review of Margo Jefferson's memoir *Negroland*, but she may as well been describing her own work. "By such emphasis on the self and its self-consciousness, Jefferson is not so much inviting a reader into her world as into its consequences. But what we gain from such a choice is revelatory: recognition of the nuance, fragmentation and fragility of a single black life begging to be considered on its own terms and in its own voice. Aren't all of us, no matter who we are, living for the rare moments when we can forget about the collective we belong to and just be? And what does it mean that, for everyone who can't lay claim to uncontested entitlement, the opportunities for just being are discouragingly few?" Tracy K. Smith, "Margo Jefferson's *Negroland*: A Memoir," *The New York Times*, Sept. 15, 2015 https://www.nytimes.com/2015/09/20/books/review/margo-jeffersons-negroland-a-memoir.html.

12   Bertram Ashe suggests that storytelling, "the act of narrative construction," can serve as a "key blaxploration gesture" (108). Ashe focuses in particular on Barack Obama's *Dreams from My Father*, in which he identifies a drive toward using narrative to impose coherence. "The (re) construction of that life, on the page, required him to sift through his youth and the events and people he encountered therein, ordering and structuring those events into narrative, recalling and emphasizing certain experiences—and relaying those experiences in a certain way—while 'forgetting' others, deemphasizing them in order to present a coherent narrative, one that does what all memoirs do: present a constructed version of a past reality, from a specific, present-day perspective" (108). Bertram D. Ashe, "Post-Soul President: Dreams from My Father and the Post-Soul Aesthetic," *The Obama Effect: Multidisciplinary Renderings of the 2008 Campaign*, eds. Heather E. Harris, Kimberly R. Moffit, and Catherine R. Squires (Albany: SUNY Press, 2010), 103–115.

13 According to Ashe, other features of post-soul aesthetics include uses of the "cultural mulatto archetype and the "allusion-disruption gesture in which part of post-soul "blaxploration" involves signifying on Civil Rights and Black Power agendas (Ashe, "Theorizing," 613).

14 "Home," Terrion L. Williamson declares, is the place "where black social life fulfills its greatest potential." In *Scandalize My Name: Black Feminist Practice and the Making of Black Social Life* (New York: American Literatures Initiative, 2016), 10). In *Scandalize My Name*, Williamson enumerates sites of black sociality: "The cotton field, the barbershop, and the athletic field. In Ellison's day and in our won, these and other places like them that we could name—the hair salon, the front porch, the church basement, the street corner, the backyard barbecue, the house party, the kitchen table—are where black social life fulfills its greatest potential" (10). Discussions of the phenomenon that Williamson defines as "black sociliaty" can be found in Toni Morrison's essay, "City Limits, Village Values: Concepts of the Neighborhood in Black Fiction" (*Literature and the Urban Experience*, ed. Michael C. Jaye and Ann Chalmers Watts (New Brunswick: Rutgers University Press, 1981), 35-430); and Farah Jasmin's "Who Set You Flowin'?": *The African-American Migration Narrative* (Oxford: Oxford University Press, 1996).

15 Avery Gordon, *Ghostly Matters*: (Minneapolis: University of Minnesota Press, [1997] 2008), xvi.

16 See, for example, Peter Shapiro's *Turn the Beat Around: The Secret History of Disco* (New York: Faber & Faber, 2017).

17 A science fiction novel written by Robert Heinlein, *Stranger in a Strange Land* recounts the story of a human raised on Mars.

18 Frantz Fanon, *Black Skin, White Masks*. Translated by Richard Philcox (New York: Grove Press, 2008; original French edition 1952).

19 "For my mother's part, she was friendly and smiling. . . . But she didn't ever stop being a hostess" (47).

20 Taylor riffs off of Thelma Golden's assertion that by "the end of the 1990s . . . post-black had fully entered the art world's consciousness. Post-black was the new black," a statement that inspires him to reflect on the relation of the discourse of post-blackness to notions of post-modernism. He asks, "How can post-black be the new black? Postmodernity is precisely not the new modernity; and ditto for postcolonialism and colonialism. And if post-black can be the new black, in what sense is it really 'post' blackness at all? Why isn't it just a new stage of blackness? And, if it is just a new stage of blackness, then why not name it accordingly? Not 'post-black,' as if blackness has been superseded, but, say neo-black. Or, since that stinks, something else?" (627). He goes on to note the contestation of the relevance of the language of "post-ness," describing opinions that range from those who complain about the difficulty of defining art gathered under this label (which makes sense given that the diversity and difference are central to the idea), to those who viewed it as a rejection of their blackness or African heritage. Paul Taylor, "Post-Black, Old Black," *African American Review*, 41, no. 4 (Winter): 625-640. See also Thelma Golden, *Freestyle* (New York: Studio Museum of Harlem, 2001).

21

FROM *CITIZEN* AND FROM *DON'T LET ME BE LONELY*

Claudia Rankine

From *Citizen*

Words work as release—well-oiled doors opening and closing between intention, gesture. A pulse in a neck, the shiftiness of the hands, an unconscious blink, the conversations you have with your eyes translate everything and nothing. What will be needed, what goes unfelt, unsaid—what has been duplicated, redacted here, redacted there, altered to hide or disguise—words encoding the bodies they cover. And despite everything the body remains.

Occasionally it is interesting to think about the outburst if you would just cry out—

To know what you'll sound like is worth noting—

In the darkened moment a body given blue light, a flashlight, enters with levity, with or without assumptions, doubts, with desire, the beating heart, disappointment, with desires—

Stand where you are.

You begin to move around in search of the steps it will take before you are thrown back into your own body, back into your own need to be found.

The destination is illusory. You raise your lids. No one else is seeking.

You exhaust yourself looking into the blue light. All day blue burrows the atmosphere. What doesn't belong with you won't be seen.

You could build a world out of need or you could hold everything black and see. You give back the lack.

You hold everything black. You give yourself back until nothing's left but the dissolving blues of metaphor.

Sometimes "I" is supposed to hold what is not there until it is. Then *what is* comes apart the closer you are to it.

This makes the first person a symbol for something.

The pronoun barely holding the person together.

Someone claimed we should use our skin as wallpaper knowing we couldn't win.

You said "I" has so much power; it's insane.

And you would look past me, all gloved up, in a big coat, with fancy fur around the collar, and record a self saying, you should be scared, the first person can't pull you together.

Shit, you are reading minds, but did you try?

Tried rhyme, tried truth, tried epistolary untruth, tried and tried.

You really did. Everyone understood you to be suffering and still everyone thought you thought you were the sun—never mind our unlikeness, you too have heard the noise in your voice.

Anyway, sit down. Sit here alongside.

Exactly why we survive and can look back with furrowed brow is beyond me.

It is not something to know.

Your ill-spirited, cooked, hell on Main Street, nobody's here, broken-down, first person could be one of many definitions of being to pass on.

The past is a life sentence, a blunt instrument aimed at tomorrow.

Drag that first person out of the social death of history, then we're kin.

Kin calling out the past like a foreigner with a newly minted "fuck you."

Maybe you don't agree.

Maybe you don't think so.

Maybe you are right, you don't really have anything to confess.

Why are you standing?

Listen, you, I was creating a life study of a monumental first person, a Brahmin first person.

If you need to feel that way—still you are in here and here is nowhere.

Join me down here in nowhere.

Don't lean against the wallpaper; sit down and pull together.

Yours is a strange dream, a strange reverie.

No, it's a strange beach; each body is a strange beach, and if you let in the excess emotion you will recall the Atlantic Ocean breaking on our heads.

Yesterday called to say we were together and you were bloodshot and again the day carried you across a field of hours, deep into dawn, back to now, where you are thankful for

what faces you, the storm, this day's sigh as the day shifts its leaves, the wind, a prompt against the calm you can't digest.

Blue ceiling calling a body into the midst of azure, oceanic, as ocean blushes the blues it can't absorb, reflecting back a day

the day frays, night, not night, this fright passes through the eye crashing into you, is this you?

Yes, it's me, clear the way, then hold me clear of this that faces, the storm carrying me through dawn

not knowing whether to climb down or up into its eye—day, hearing a breath shiver, whose are you?

Guard rail, spotlight, safety lock, airbag, fire lane, slip guard, night watch, far into this day are the days this day was meant to take out of its way. An obstacle to surrender, dusk in dawn, held open, then closing, then opening, a red-tailed hawk, dusk at dawn, taking over blue, surveying movement, against the calm, red sky at morning, whose are you?

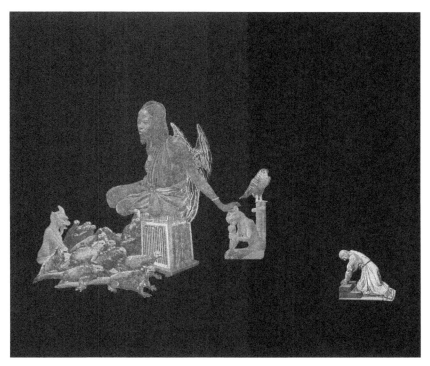

Figure 21.1 Mel Chin, *Black Angel*, 2012. From Volume #5 of Mel Chin, The Funk & Wag from A to Z. Excised printed pages from The Universal Standard Encyclopedia, 1953-56, by Wilfred Funk, Inc.; archival water-based glue, paper, 524 collages, each Varies from 8 × 11 inches to 17 × 23 inches. Copyright Mel Chin. Courtesy of the artist.

From *Don't Let Me Be Lonely*

I would have to drink five more cups of coffee a day to reduce my chances of getting type 2 diabetes. I usually have one cup in the morning. Today I am staring into a possible second cup, and I do not see my husband's expression when I tell him about the darkness and the curtain.

I have a dream, or rather, in my dream the lights are out in New York City. They are out because they were out. Even inside the dream I know I am dreaming. The events of my dream are a form of mimesis. The darkness that accompanied the blackout existed, but does not now in the world outside the dream. In my dream the lights are out because I cannot see ahead of me. Or in this dark dream I am looking for a chance, "my chance to" or "my chance for"—it is not clear. Then where I am going or what I want is behind a black curtain, but it is so dark the curtain becomes the night. I want to fall asleep inside my dream. This wish for further paralysis wakes me.

You think voting won't make a difference, says my husband. This might be a wise thing to think. He says all this without lifting his gaze from the morning paper.

My dream is about a voting booth? I am not convinced. He is not interested in convincing me. He is reading about the candidates for the presidency. He is wondering if voting against someone is enough motivation to drag voters away from the televised news of the election into an actual voting booth. Sometimes you read something and a thought that was floating around in your veins organizes itself into the sentence that reflects it. This might also be a form of dreaming.

Or I remember that the last two sentences I read in Fanny Howe's *Tis of Thee* before falling asleep the previous night were: "I learned to renounce a sense of independence by degrees and finally felt defeated by the times I lived in. Obedient to them."

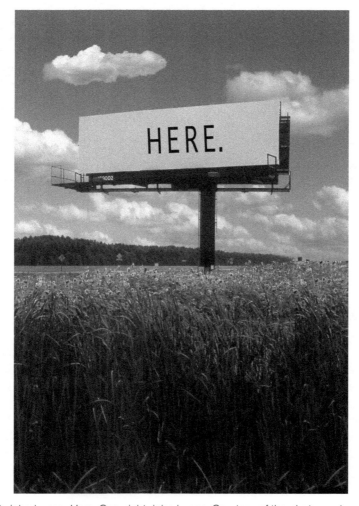

Figure 21.2 John Lucas, *Here*. Copyright John Lucas. Courtesy of the photographer.

Or, well, I tried to fit language into the shape of usefulness. The world moves through words as if the bodies the words reflect did not exist. The world, like a giant liver, receives everyone and everything, including these words: Is he dead? Is she dead? The words remain an inscription on the surface of my loneliness. This loneliness stems from a feeling of uselessness. Then Coetzee's Costello says in her fictional lecture, "for instants at a time I know what it is like to be a corpse."

Or Paul Celan said that the poem was no different from a handshake. *I cannot see any basic difference between a handshake and a poem* — is how Rosemary Waldrop translated his German. The handshake is our decided ritual of both asserting (I am here) and handing over (here) a self to another. Hence the poem is that—Here. I am here. This conflation of the solidity of presence with the offering of this same presence perhaps has everything to do with being alive.

Or one meaning of here is "In this world, in this life, on earth. In this place or position, indicating the presence of," or in other words, I am here. It also means to hand something to somebody—Here you are. Here, he said to her. Here both recognizes and demands recognition. I see you, or here, he said to her. In order for something to be handed over a hand must extend and a hand must receive. We must both be here in this world in this life in this place indicating the presence of.

22
DANCE ON
Thomas F. DeFrantz

"Pick It Up. . ."

If you can hold the beat. Or at least, if you can only work with and through the beat. If you can ride it, or enhance it; if only you could respond to it and predict it, move along with it and vary it. If only.

The beat lives beyond our imagination, in a place where we already know its contours and complexities. Many of us figure out how to wrangle its possibilities, and we dance. A lot. We enjoy the maneuvering with the beat; adjusting rhythm within ourselves according to what's needed where.

The beat might be an imaginary inevitability; a formation that gathers the complexity of world-making as time, or storytelling as practice. It's entirely real and not there at once; an indication of gesture made manifest as a relationship-in-motion. A contending with intuitions born in the body and borne out by creative response to social lives. We meet each other in relation to the beat, as we dance, and as we move towards a social destiny of some sort. The beat offers standards and guideposts towards what can happen, and we choose how to respond to its call.

We might understand that Black aesthetics are organized around rhythm, which is possibly another way to narrate "the beat." We Black artists admire and respect the beat and its manifestations as rhythm (although it could be the other way around, with rhythm making way for the beat). We structure our embodied creative time around the beat and its insistence; we develop complex modes to elaborate its capacities and test our abilities in relation to it. We write poems, construct sounds, and practice dances that stretch the beat towards its unexpected possibilities.

This is, then, an aesthetics of rhythm as foundational to Black creativity.

Rhythm remains exceedingly difficult to write about. This challenge arrives at the heart of theorizing through, at least, popular music and Black social dance. The particularities of shifting time while moving are hard to catch and nearly impossible to predict or remember. Witnessing rhythm might be like watching time, but rhythm is both a proposition and an activity; an affordance *to have and to hold* as well as something far beyond language.

Rhythm, engaged, is surely more than pattern and variation, accuracy or predictability. That would be the basic definition offered up in most accounts: rhythm as pattern and variation. But we know that rhythm has qualities, and also valuations. Good rhythm becomes manifest as an ability to transform event by shifting its terms—the terms of time and pattern and variation that might characterize its nature. Suspension, cross-pattern, complexity, and recognizable grooves might become ways to characterize what happens in a musicality. Ultimately, though, we're looking for the beat within Black performance and especially Black dance, in order to understand how we are connected and what we might do about that connection. The search for the beat, and how we care for it help us consider what might be at issue.

Prince

I recently moved to the Midwestern part of the United States; here I reacquaint with how rhythm animates Black life and Black thought in a manner particular to the region. The music of Prince Rogers Nelson came forward for me and inspired this chapter. Prince hailed from the Midwest and hailed the Midwest again and again in his creative output, and also in his structured responses to rhythm as a mode of assemblage and creative imperative.

The Midwest is both cold as ice and as friendly as a conversation about cars with a stranger on the sidewalk. Less blood-soaked than the deep South of the United States, for Black people at least, the Midwest encompasses a casual normativity, where expectations are narrow and obvious, and social presumptions are many. This everyday Blackness among whites who understand that their ancestors stole this land and murdered the indigenous people who lived here before, encourages a sort of willingness to try out other people's stuff. Mixed-race Black people are legion here, including Prince by way of his grandfather, and curiosities about modes of creativity spill out of bedroom neighborhoods and workplaces in a sort of aesthetic stew. For our purposes, though, what binds creative excellence from the Black Midwest—whether Chicago Blues, Detroit Techno, Ohio Funk, or Memphis Soul—is the beat.

Prince follows R&B and funk band practice with a conception of rhythmic array as the hook for hundreds of recordings, and of course always in his live shows. The tightly-woven capacity of rhythm surrounds his most famous recordings; the inevitable relationship to a rhythm blues beat we've already heard, rendered fresh again in "Alphabet Street" or "Kiss." And Prince recorded an endless stream of romantic ballads that allowed his falsetto voice to waver above an insistent slow groove; tunes that allow the musicians and listeners to lean back, behind the beat, and settle into something soothing as a reflection in sound.

Prince explored queer desire as the foundation of Black desire again and again, in songs like "Sister" or "Controversy" or "Sexy MF." Several times Prince sang as a femme in original songs about relationships, or voiced a non-normative duality in expressions of sex and love. Prince wondered, "If I Was Your Girlfriend" and narrated the "Erotic City;" claimed astonishment at "Pussy Control" and orchestrated the Kamasutra; wrote for the "Sexy Dancer" and explained how we should "Do Me Baby." These tracks, including their lyrical contents, assumed an erotic capacity within rhythmic manipulation. They reminded dancing listeners that following, and breaking, the beat could claim space in a relational aesthetics of expertise concerned with, at least, flow and rupture.

Most of Prince's recordings are danceable jams. Tracks that encourage a sociability born of physical movement to capture and elaborate the beat. Dance music entirely designed to provoke Black Social Dance.

Black Social Dance provides the rhythmic motor for an entire constellation of popular music and culture, a constellation that encompasses most of Prince's output. This chapter renders Black Social Dance toward its abilities to provoke physical improvisations that confirm corporeal agencies: individualities within a group context that propose variations in time. Rhythm arrives as a sacred trust in structures of African diaspora performance, and if we can ride and then cut the beat, we can remake our destinies.

Dance as a structuring logic or technology offers a counterpoint to "black death" and the unlikely, but enduring, nature of afropessimistic integrity. Remarkably, afropessimism coheres as a "metatheory" (Wilderson) that explores connections among theoretical models that inevitably undervalue or disregard Black life.[1] Afropessimism encourages us to consider an ongoing disavowal of Black life as a state of being, the historical rupture of enslavement as the pre-accelerated confirmation of Black as an under-category or sub-status that marks difference from a preferred norm.

The ongoingness of an anti-Black climate, sometimes referred to as *the weather* (Sharpe), forces Black life into a space of being always fugitive, always slightly out of step with anything that might be normative, always in transition and re-figuration.[2] This ability to be flexible and to form and reform in small combinatory gestures becomes the promise and achievement of Black aesthetic creativity. This manifests as a capacity to create from within the scream (Douglass), from within the attic chamber hiding place (Jacobs), from within substance addictions (Holiday), carceral formations, military subscriptions, transphobia, disavowed childhoods, etc.[3] The creative world-making of Black aesthetic production proves again and again that *something else* might be possible (Crawley), that *hope* might be constituent to the unfolding of Black life In aesthetic gesture (Muñoz), and that creative acts can offer remedy and "means for setting right a wrong" (Jackson).[4]

To consider how rhythm subvenes Black aesthetic production is to consider the tempi of Black life in multiplicity. Rhythm, as an aesthetic device, determines how events stack one to the next; it shapes memory and intuitive response; rhythm predicts the changing flows that constitute a liveliness-in-motion endemic to Black life, always in spite of its disavowal. Rhythm and its manipulation through embodied practice allow us to understand pattern and its disruption as a metaphysics of assembly, engaged by multiple modes of access to counting and discounting the beat. Dancing, in a social space of gestural responsiveness to the call of rhythm, allows a multi-modal response to time as a non-linear formation.

In this model, rhythm and dance allow a manipulation of presence that resists "straight time" or the inevitable pulse of neoliberal capital and structural racisms. It becomes possible to dance, through rhythm, towards an unexpected destiny or an *"otherwise modality of being"* (Crawley).[5] A general fascination with Black modes of social dance, rendered as expertise in designing rhythmic response through a body in motion, drives popular culture forward. As example, the "Watch Them Whip: A Decade of Viral Dance

Moves" short video produced by the *New Yorker* magazine, features Black social dances practiced by an international cohort of athletes, dancers, and "people on the street" as a translocational assembly.[6] Black social dance, practiced widely, becomes widely available as demonstration of resistant knowing, intuitive remembering, and expansive imagining of social potential.

Black social dance acts as a gathering notion (Outlaw), a site for creative assembly and an embodied temporary release of the strictures of normativities of many kinds.[7] These dances are organized around the manipulation of rhythm to produce the affective register of physical imagination. The best Black social dancers are those who understand how to manipulate rhythm in order to produce in- and out-of-time elaborations of movements and dance forms that are already known by many. It matters that assembled witnesses understand a base-line assumption around how rhythm and form operate in the dance that is near-to-hand; what becomes interesting are the disruptions and unexpected accenting and cross-phrasing that a dancer explores. In the "Black Social Dance" exhibition at the National Museum of African American History and Culture, an array of expert Black social dancers demonstrate their distinctive moves that galvanize attendant witnesses in theatres, on streetcorners, and in gymnasiums and social centers (DeFrantz and Smithsonian Channel).[8] The whole is tied together, as in the "Watch Them Whip" moving-image object, by a steady danceable pulse, one that needn't be in direct relation to the snippets of movement displayed in the film. The flashes of movement are already small examples of how rhythm matters, and gestures of incalculable choreographies (Derrida) through infinite variation.[9]

The Prince track "Dance On" arrives as a minor bit of funkiness, almost hidden on a minor collection of works gathered as *Lovesexy* (1988). No matter. Minor or major, funkiness emerges as affirmation of beat possibility. The track insists on a stuttering, out-of-sync rhythmic device, sounding like a wave of electronic djembe sampled and transformed into an angry string ensemble rumble. Each wave of sound is answered by an open rhythmic break, a wandering in suspension that encourages moving outside the basic pulse of the jam. Electronic hits and a dissonant wall of guitar sound confirm a moving-beyond-moving demanded by the musicians in an awkward, end-of-days dance rave.

"Dance On" begins with the exhortation "Pick It Up," meaning, of course, the beat. For Prince and collaborators, the beat is always already there, awaiting activation. It is something that can be organized by musicians and danced through by a general public of listeners, dancing Black sociability through a shared effort to bend time towards a preferred Black space of temporary liberation.

Prince and The Time

Prince fomented a side-project band, The Time, named literally for the incessant demand that Black musical structures explore an ontological rhythmic pulse. The Time essentially acted as an alternative rhythm section for Prince's creative wonderings, operating outside of the core group of The Revolution. Even as the band refused to stay coherent for more than a year or two, The Time allowed its rotating number of musicians to hone their skills alongside headlining singers Morris Day, Vanity Six, and at times, Prince.

The Time's name spoke to the rhythmic organization needed to craft spaces for dance conceived as the sharing of cultural knowledge through social assembly. The Time regularly crafted pulse as a relational affordance that could be enabled by dance practice; their biggest hits were dance instruction songs that told the listener what moves to make in order to join a sociality-in-motion (Banes and Szwed).[10] As musical sidemusicians, The Time set the foundation that allowed others to explore cross-rhythms and cross-purposes to the guiding beat.

The Time, like any number of rhythm musicians, enabled a relational affordance that allows Black social dance as Black thought to extend beyond the event of here and now. Black social dance becomes an aspect of social memory and social projection that can extend a metaphorical skin of Black being-in-motion (Ahmed).[11] An orientation towards Black being through social dance becomes a willingness to take time and consider time as a foundational aspect of aesthetic entanglement (Ahmed). Repetition, and practice, set in motion through aesthetic orientations offer predictive awarenesses that allow Black creativity to cohere in particular rhythmic formations (Ahmed). Our consideration of time as a musical practice and a theoretical elaboration of Black social possibility extends qutward, spidering diasporically, like Anansi's web, to entangle our orientation towards rhythm (George-Graves).[12]

Let's Work

Aligning conceptions of Black Time from several contemporary cultural theorists reveals a kaleidoscopic and coherent awareness of its again-emergent place in Black thought.

Time must be shifted to allow Black creativity to foment, and Black gestures reach through time in order to cohere with aesthetic and political force. Creativity allows us to undermine the disavowal of Blackness as a social deathliness. "Black movements are embodied actions that participate in political movements by creating links across time and space, thus disrupting the accumulative force of blackness when it unfolds in linear time" (Colbert).[13] Blackness emerges in a "racialized temporality" bound up with capital and its ability to produce Blackness as difference, rendering "racial distinction as a timeless timeliness" (Crawley).[14] Black Time shimmers in these formations, sounding a call towards something now, before, and just ahead. Something queer.

The disruption of straight time becomes key to a forward-casting creative constellation, Afrofuturism, modeling "disruptions to the dominant time line as rhythmic rather than directional" (Lothian).[15] This distension of time according to what's needed in the creative moment produces "cross-time touches and nonteleological histories that resonate with evocations of queer temporality" (Lothian). The queerness of this affect "exceeds any standard notion of timing" as rhythm—the crafted manipulation of rhythm—offers "the future of movement-moving makes itself felt."[16] Rhythm "is how we know duration, a duration that is always more than one" (Manning).[17]

While Erin Manning may not be solely concerned with Black thought in her writings about social relation, time, and affect, implications for time as a "dynamic form that recasts how relation is conceived" resonate in our consideration of Black liveliness alongside Black social death. When Manning affirms that an "affective attunement cannot be measured in linear time" she tilts towards an emergent branch of European philosophy that contends with Black thought as an inciting formation of the current moment (Manning).[18] Attempting to depict rhythm as an aspect of music, Jean-Luc Nancy asserts "rhythm: it is nothing other than the time of time, the vibration of time itself in the stroke of a present that presents it by separating it from itself" (Nancy).[19] This *separation* might be the cleavage of difference bound up in Blackness-as-being; a mode of creativity aligned with its origin as a remain of the unholy rhythms of the Middle Passage. Rhythm may have always been a weapon, but its re-purposing as Black aesthetic method in the crucible of enslavement and capital production made a *something else* possible in the caring for the beat: a way to modulate towards the temporary, imaginary *freedom* defined as movement (Nyong'o). This "afro-fabulation" of temporary freedom arrives as a "theory and practice of black time and temporality" that undergirds Black creative craft (Nyong'o).[20] Afro-fabulation might exist even within the wake, as the "residence time of the wake" can be *troubled*, through rhythmic elaboration (Sharpe).[21]

Prince released "Let's Work" on the album *Controversy* (1981). A thumping funk-groove, the track sits "in the pocket" with a forward-leaning tom-tom at the center of an assemblage that includes a handclap on the two and four of each cycle. The beat calls for moving forward and up-and-down at once, demanding moving bodies to acknowledge the repeating pattern. Here, dancing is cast as a certain sort of creative labor, something we do among each other towards an end of shared imagination. Dancing, we amplify the in-between possibilities of this rhythmic insistence. We work together, because we must, to dance, and to dream collectively through our labor. In direct counter distinction to labor for capital, this is the labor of Black imagination.

The beat in Black Social Dance reveals as much in its implications as it might in its sounding. In "Dance On" and "Let's Work" social dancers are hailed by the rhythmic formation to fill in or enhance the recordings through embodied responsiveness. By enacting things felt but not heard, we engage histories yet to come and remembrances of social formations (are these always families?) we never knew in person.

Moving across time, and allowing a movement through time, the beat supports an ongoing status of fugitivity as Being-In-Blackness. Manipulating time as an ordering of Black creativity, an aesthetics of rhythmic seeking and invention supports the impossible strictures of Black life. The beat draws us into its capacities, to *make time* where things seem stuck by dancing out-of-time in the interstitial spaces of the beat and its cadence.

Keep Bustin'

Beat juggling is conjuring with rhythm; a curated, metaphysical wondering at the capacity of recording as object. Digital or analog, the stacking of recorded rhythm to produce an unanticipated distension of sound allows another way to experience the past, this time with the flash and fire of a now to be embodied by dance. The recording of beat juggling, as in a mixtape, produces a seeming-singularity; a sounding of something special, like a one-off. A rhythmic dubplate. The mashup as a single. Not just a mixtape, but a dubplate mixtape.

The dubplate arrives with particular rhetorical force in Black aesthetic structures, as it enacts a recorded singularity of sorts; a one-time-only object that offers evidence of a moment and contains implications towards its outcomes. Dubplates lean in to the logics of neoliberal capital, turning the acquisition of a performance into an achievement of status bound up with Black creativity and possession. And yet, the dubplate spills outward with Black creativity; affirming a special production of sound that can be repeated locally, and shared as a memory first by those who encountered its wonders, and then by those who find a way to hear its contents.

Prince produced a vast storehouse of recordings that were never released publicly. Prince worked diligently as a musician and recording artist, crafting so many dubplates and one-off versions of materials that there might never be an accounting for the entirety of compositional output. Like the dubplates that evade wide circulation, even among connoisseurs, Prince's experiments and achievements in sound are always already known to exceed what might be available to a Black commons of listeners and dancers. This expansive output might distinguish Prince among Black creatives of the 20th and 21st century; Prince worked ceaselessly towards a Black sonic deliverance of creative rhythmic address.

Prince often worked as a solo musician, overlaying tracks of himself to produce a recording. Prince created the hit dance single "Batdance" (1989) differently, though, as a self-sampled mix that sutured a stream of grooves and snippets from the Hollywood film Batman. We hear an unusual process-driven groove that serves as background to a hard-rock guitar solo; a rewinding through an end-of-phrase device that stutters the ongoing pulse; an actor's sniffle transformed into a breakbeat. The groove changes three times in this track, reforming in distinctive, wildly unexpected array. In the slow, central back-beat strut section, the lyric "work" becomes a repeated mantra. sampled from dialogue in the movie. Beyond the call to labor, the call to work supports an understanding of dance as a repeated practice that produces outcomes likely beneficial to the group. We work together in the dance, crafting rhythm to reshape time. In this, the "Batdance" assemblage references world-making through dance that must be produced as event beyond its sounding. As with all good dance music, the track incites thinking towards formations of dance and Black sociability well beyond any sort of "here and now" that might permeate other forms of social dance.

"Batdance" ends as a jumble; a chaotic plea for rhythmic consistency. Prince calls out, "Don't Stop Dancing" and then a final "Stop!" to end the adventure. The stop is temporary. The dance continues, in our memory and on our skin, even as we are bathed in the sweat of deliverance by its engagement.

We return to the dance because we actually never left it, not really. It was the movement of the group that allowed us to recognize Black as a formation; it was the manifestation of the beat that we cared for at the beginning. The movement of the womb inside the enslavement ship, perhaps; the very human-animal assertion of creative drive as a response to the reorganizing of time. Working with time and the beat, caring for its contours and dropping it only to pick it up as we work, we danceBlacktogether. We wonder through our dancing, and figure out the endless variety of a beat and our relationships within it and beyond it. Weirdly, we are surprised that our Blackness is replenished through our dancing and the ways it always bounces back a little different. Not quite what we remembered, but something else. The dancing reveals its manifestation as a *something else*. Moving around the beat, and always considering its relationship to those temporary constructions, Black social dance replenishes, with an inevitable physical dissidence.

Notes

1   Frank Wilderson, *Afropessimism* (New York: Liveright Publishing Corporation, 2020).

2   Christina Sharpe, *In the Wake: On Blackness and Being* (Durham, NC: Duke University Press, 2016).

3   Frederick Douglass, *Narrative of the Life of Frederick Douglass, an American Slave* (Boston: Bedford/St. Martin's, 2003). Harriet A. Jacobs, *Incidents in the Life of a Slave Girl: Written by Herself. Edited by L. Maria Child*. (London: Hodson and Son, 22, Portugal Street, Lincoln's Inn, 1862).

4   Ashon Crawley, *Blackpentecostal Breath: The Aesthetics of Possibility* (New York: Fordham University Press, 2016). Jose Muñoz, *Cruising Utopia: The Then and There of Queer Futurity*. (New York: New York University Press, 2009). Zakiyyah Iman Jackson, *Becoming Human: Matter and Meaning in an Antiblack World* (New York: New York University Press, 2020), 214.

5   Crawley, *Blackpentecostal Breath*, 194.

6   "Watch Them Whip: A Decade of Viral Dance Moves: https://www.newyorker.com/video/watch/watch-them-whip-a-decade-of-viral-dance-moves."

7   Lucius Outlaw, "African, African American, Africana Philosophy," *African-American Perspectives and Philosophical Traditions*, ed. John P. Pittman (New York: Routledge, 1996), 63–94.

8   "Movement: Social Dance and Gesture," part of the "Cultural Expressions" exhibition at the National Museum of African American History & Culture: https://nmaahc.si.edu/explore/exhibitions/cultural-expressions.

9   Jacques Derrida and Christie V. McDonald, "Interview: Choreographies," *Diacritics* 12, no. 2 (Summer 1982): 66–76.

10 Sally Banes and John F. Szwed, "From 'Messin' Around' to 'Funky Western Civilization': The Rise and Fall of Dance Instruction Songs," in *Dancing Many Drums: Excavations in African American Dance*, ed. Thomas F. DeFrantz (Madison: The University of Wisconsin Press, 2002), 169–203.

11 Sara Ahmed, *Queer Phenomenology: Orientations, Objects, Other* (Durham: Duke University Press, 2006).

12 Nadine George-Graves, "Diasporic Spidering," in *Black Performance Theory*, ed. Anita Gonzalez and Thomas F. DeFrantz (Durham: Duke University Press, 2014).

13 Soyica Diggs Colbert, *Black Movements: Performance and Cultural Politics* (New Brunswick: Rutgers University Press, 2017), 19.

14 Crawley, *Blackpentecostal Breath*, 172.

15 Alexis Lothian, *Old Futures: Speculative Fiction and Queer Possibility* (New York: New York University Press, 2018), 103.

16 Erin Manning, *Always More Than One: Individuation's Dance* (Durham: Duke University Press, 2013), 82.

17 Manning, *Always More Than One*, 87.

18 Manning, *Always More Than One*, 206–207.

19 Jean-Luc Nancy, *Listening* (New York : Fordham University Press, 2009), 17.

20 Tavia Nyong'o, *Afro-Fabulations: The Queer Drama of Black Life* (New York: New York University Press, 2018), 5.

21 Sharpe, *In the Wake*, 41.

23

'ONE-EYED' IMMERSIVE PARTICULARITIES

Jeremy Matthew Glick

(In Memoriam, *Professor Cheryl A. Wall*)

What follows is an effort to think about a critical judgment catalogued by Hortense J. Spillers—read here speculatively anew—from her adjudicative mapping of "two mutually alien points—Harlem and Formalism."[1] The line in question is: "there are those who think this view is one-eyed".[2] This line is thought alongside works that engage the narrative and theoretical problem of odyssey. My goals here are modest—to stage a valorization of *process over product* in a meditation that juxtaposes critical reading and art criticism, charting a vector in the worlds of Black art, narrative theory, and aesthetics. I build out, around, and behind the formulation "one-eyed" pursuing an expository style that strives to model my process of inquiry: this chapter's sites of study in their commitment to an open-ended, contingent, and ever-becoming dialectic that resists closure. "Immersive particularity" here is neither methodological sloganeering, nor the announcement of a new reading strategy. Rather, it is a terminological reminder to refuse the temptation of epistemological closure in order to enter into art discourses and art works to access their penchant to exceed prescription and *a priori* frameworks.

Briefly consider Walter Benjamin's critique of Goethe's maxim in its foregrounding problems of causality and so-called progress worthy of detest due to their transactional nature:

> "Try to ensure that everything in life has a consequence."—This is without doubt one of the most detestable of maxims, one that you would not expect to run across in Goethe. It is the imperative of progress in its most dubious forms. It is not the case that the consequence leads to what is fruitful in right action, and even less that the consequence is its fruit. On the contrary, bearing fruit is the mark of evil acts. The acts of good people have no "consequence" that could be ascribed (or ascribed exclusively) to them. The fruits of an act are, as it right and proper, internal to it. To enter into the interior of a mode of action is the way to test its fruitfulness. But how to do this?"[3]

Cause and effect in the Benjamin quote is a mystified calculus that fallaciously correlates and evaluates actions with the fruit of their labor. Such correlation forecloses generativity attuned to (1) the problem of contingency and (2) odyssey as process—both mobilized in this essay as co-joined-homologies that speak to the work regimen of Black radical art and Black aesthetics. Recall how Amiri Baraka's cautionary warning in his essay collection *Home*—"Hunting is not those heads on the wall"—foregrounds process, odyssey over outcome; the ever escaping [never final] final product.[4] Such an insistence echoes Baraka's assertion in "The Revolutionary Theater" that "Wittgenstein said ethics and aesthetics are one."[5] As a kindred revolutionary spirit and ever the Faustian, Benjamin goes so far to subvert transactional calculus by ascribing malevolent intent to the "bearing [of] fruit [that is] the mark of evil acts." Alternatively, Benjamin advocates decoupling action from consequence. Immanence for Benjamin is the "right and proper" weapon of choice in an all-out war on instrumentalist transactional reasoning. Journey is prioritized over destination because it hones praxis and pools the resources necessary to change where we live. What matters here for this meditation on Black aesthetics and close reading is how Benjamin proposes an alternative matter of approach that resonates with a genealogy of Black art, writers, and readers. Not what aesthetics is but what it does—its penchant to render the fixed fluid even against its own presumptive logic and purported closures. This is why, as it will be shown, I begin with Samuel R. Delany's catalogue of "close reading" strategies and Spillers's profound meditation on who's afraid of formalism. It is an acknowledgment that the force of prescription never catches up to the creative insurgent force of its sites of inquiry. Once in conversation about a penetrating study of Ralph Ellison's *Invisible Man's* relationship to the American Communist Left—my professor wisely retorted—"Yes, but the problem is, Ellison's work is—*more*." Stated another way paraphrasing V. I. Lenin reading G. W. F. Hegel in the Zurich Library: the phenomenon is greater than the law. How does one enter "into the interior of a mode of action"? This chapter strives to model how such a query speaks to interpretive problems of Black aesthetics as a labor of close reading, listening, and looking. Paying attention to the *immersive particularities* of Black radical art are the royal roads "into the interior of a mode of [political] action." Immersive particularity as proximity attuned to the objects of one's study is one answer to Kantian disinterestedness as precondition for rendering aesthetic judgment. To extend Benjamin's rejoinder to think about art suggests that protocols and concepts are generated from within an immersive exploration of art and attendant critical discourses, rather than preceding such engagement from a distance. Rhetorical moves and creative work conjure the collective space one wishes to inhabit and build. Black radical aesthetics as a field of struggle is predicated on and sustained by negation, antagonism, and generative division actualized by way of active engagement.

James A. Snead's "Repetition as a Figure of Black Culture" famously flips Hegel's alleged disavowal of African historicity as a "succession of accidents and surprises" as insurgent asset rather than deficit.[6] For Snead, Black culture (recall Benjamin) disturbs the prioritization of goal (*Zweck*) over process: "A culture based on the idea of the 'cut' will always suffer in a society whose dominant idea is material progress—but 'cuts possess their own charm. . . Black culture, in the 'cut,' builds accidents into its *coverage*, almost as if to control their unpredictability. Itself a kind of cultural *coverage*, this magic of the 'cut' attempts to confront accident and rupture not by covering them over but by making room for them inside the system itself."[7] Rumination, fashioning rooms, making room as cultural coverage are an echo of Curtis Mayfield's crooning plea—"a little space is all that I need if these suckers just allow me to breathe."[8] Franz Kafka's *Zuraü Aphorisms* offer a strategic-ritualistic homology here: "Leopards break into the temple and drink all the sacrificial vessels dry; it keeps happening; in the end, it can be calculated in advance and is incorporated into the ritual."[9]

This chapter mixes it up within the interior of three discourses: (1) Delany on different national close-reading practices, framing a juxtaposition of commentaries from Spillers and Snead; (2) Jean-Michel Basquiat, Herman Melville, and Dial on the workerist imperative to sharpen one's tools; and (3) a reprisal and expansion on the Homeric problem of *Nobody* by way of a concluding reference to a short-story from Terry McMillan's 1990 *Breaking Ice: An Anthology of Contemporary African-American Fiction*. Wesley Brown's "I Was Here But I Disappeared" is a tight, tripartite narrative interrogation on the relationship between racism, painting, and minimalism. Its discourse on art and images serves to mine the fragility of human relationships and emotional accountability. The story charts and then subverts a pictorial-painterly journey to "Nobody." By way of modeling its objects in their "accidents and surprises," this essay proffers a speculative reading of the aforementioned line from Spillers. Snead's commentary on repetition and Black culture resonates with another aspect of Hegel's thought by way of *The Phenomenology of Spirit* (1807) particularly germane to aesthetics. Hegel's *Preface* to *Phenomenology* rallies against the tendency in "modern times. . .the individual finds the abstract form ready-made: the exertion of the grasping it and appropriating it is rather more the unmediated production of the inward and the cut-off generation of the general than the emergence of the general out of the concrete and the multiplicity of existence."[10] "Particularly one-eyed" foregrounds the dynamic dialectic that is Black art's war against *the ready-made* brought to the fore by juxtaposition and association. The building of concepts (*Begriff*) that render the fixed fluid requires a strong worker's grip (*Griff*) and attending strategy of the world.[11]

I. *Explication De Refused Texte* and The Cyclops' Enigma

Commenting on pedagogic and expository national *particularities* in North American and French close-reading practices, Delany writes, in "The Refused Text" section of his semiotic tour de force *The American Shore*:

> Here we must mention that the French have a problem with this sort of detailed analysis that in general the American avoids: that problem is the existence in the French *lycée* and *gymnasium*, of the pedagogic technique *explication de texte*, a traditional student exercise in which a paragraph or so of prose (or a short passage of poetry) is analyzed exhaustively in terms of the way the sounds of the words, their rhythms and specific ordering choice of tense and diction, as well as other stylistic elements, modulate the sense, lend emphasis here, irony there, or create a particular emotional tone. Such an exercise produces readers very sensitive to the nuances of French style. But such an exercise also constitutes a tradition where the extended analysis of prose

is equated with a particularly undergraduate sort of tediousness. French critics who attempt such a detail-oriented analysis must reassure the reader that they are not simply hawking a high school paper gone to seed. And they usually avoid all mention of those elements—euphony, rhythm, word order—that might so earmark the essay. American high schools and colleges have no such tradition . . . .[12]

There is a charm in Delany's playful précis of national-particular ways of reading. It is one of many moments in which Delany as essayist and pulse-taker of all things literary models a subdued comedic genius. An orderly inventory of French literary pedagogy is abruptly contrasted with a single sentence announcing America's lack. Tedium of the scholastic exercise and transactional reading practices produce the anti-climax of examination answers—the evaluative coin of the realm, a component of what Lacan theorized as "university discourse".[13] A proliferation of literary meaning and figurations are hemmed in by the implicit conservativism of the school exam and "high school paper gone to seed." *Pro forma* evaluation stifles the proliferation of immersive particularities in an act of evaluative closure.

The recent re-issuing of Snead's *Figures of Division: William Faulkner's Major Novels* brilliantly models a reading strategy and formalist attention to narrative and language of the highest order. Snead applies his careful analytic to problems of miniaturization, breaking Faulkner's narratives down into their smallest rhetorical units and immersive particularity. Snead does not evade but rather accentuates the political ramifications of his procedure. By way of a citation from Frederick Law Olmstead's 1853–54 *Journey in the Seaboard Slave States*, he notes "familiarity and closeness of [Southern] intimacy that would have been noticed with astonishment" and announces the critical intention to probe Faulkner's mobilization of rhetorical strategies to combat how [racialized and gendered] *figures of division* exist as a rhetorical armature of repressive power.[14] He demonstrates by way of close reading how such figures are employed "to defend against chaos—figures which, however, seem only to reintroduce."[15] Division answers to and combats division. Through close attention to rhetorical strategies of division and re-assemblage, Snead sets loose his careful critical apparatus to map how Faulkner's narrative universes "dismember figures of division at their weakest joint, the 'purity' notion that seems the requirement of white supremacist logic."[16] For Snead, "racism in general might be considered a normative recipe for domination created by speakers using rhetorical tactics. The characteristic figures of racial division repeat on the level of phoneme, sentence, and story."[17] Pace Delany, sensitivity to nuances of style, the particularities of language's rhetorical interplay, an immersive embrace in the particularities of Faulkner's novelistic narrative-worlds shun tediousness and announce a penetratingly incandescent Black radical critical reading regimen.

As an aside—note the "Concerning Violence" section of *Les Damnés de la Terre* in which Frantz Fanon links the lie of settler-colonial *tabula rasa*-origin story with epic and Odyssey. In the Fanon passage's critique of colonial discourse, etiology is conflated with permanence which is conflated with a conservative nod to *illusory* equilibrium as stability. A fraught developmentalist logic only recognizes particular historical periodization (such as the Middle Ages) and cannot think the scale of the hemispheric, let alone the diasporic in their multiplicities. There is no room for Samir Amin's crucial corrective—not Age, but rather "Ages of Antiquity."[18] Here is Fanon:

> The settler makes history; his life is an epoch, an Odyssey. He is the absolute beginning: "This land was created by us"; he is the unceasing cause: "If we leave, all is lost, and the country will go back to the Middle Ages." Over against him torpid creatures ,wasted by fevers, obsessed by ancestral customs, form an almost inorganic background for the innovating dynamism of colonial mercantilism.[19]

Snead's interpretive practice, his critical immersion bringing forth a new set of divisions and intellectual problems and attending to such divisions is delineated from and in response to a hegemonic logic of division that undergirds societies structured in racial dominance. His exploration of Faulkner's *Absalom, Absalom!* commences by theorizing what he calls "the joint"—where "the racial plot of the South both holds together and threatens to fall apart."[20] Snead's analytic expands the adjoining logic to web a string of associations linking American racialism, Socratic dialogue, and Hegelian thought:

> When Socratic rhetorical division is applied to social organization, it becomes clear that skin color is among the significations that have historically allowed human beings to be ranked, properly or improperly, within a hierarchy of oppositions. Fredric Jameson says that "The realm of separation, of fragmentation. . .exists, as Hegel would put it, not so much *in itself* as rather for us, as the basic logic and fundamental law of our daily life." Color is perhaps the most deceitful of all characteristic marks, because it seems self-evident, a division in itself—common sense says that everyone can agree upon the color of skin. Yet, compared to what all humans have in common (arms, legs, hair, blood, eyes), race is somewhat trivial, belonging to the category termed "deception" by Socrates himself. . . .[21]

Snead's analysis answers the ease of sense-perception division with an immersive tarrying with the particular rhetorical strategies and framing of the texts he explores. Consideration of the chronological architecture of Homer's epic bolsters rather than contradicts Fanon's astute analysis. *The Odyssey* itself problematizes a mythos of origins by commencing its narrative in the middle of the action—like Michael Ondaatje signaling by way of Buddy Bolden's cornet playing: "up there on stage. . .showing all the possibilities in the middle of the story."[22] Odysseus's proper-name signifies the "man of many [rhetorical] turns."

I now want to briefly consider two Homeric turns at play in the branch of aesthetics that is Afro-American literary criticism. This is in the service of thinking about some of the ways that aesthetic traditions are constituted. First, note the problematic of Homeric naming in Snead's discussion of Socrates in *Cratylus*:

> Socrates: Why clearly he who first gave names gave them according to his conception of the things which they signified—did he not?
>   Cratylus: True.

Socrates: And if his conception was erroneous, and he gave names according to his conception, in what position shall we who are his followers find ourselves? Shall we not be deceived by him?[23]

Snead is concerned with a mis-attribution of Socrates in the form of a literary allusion to Homer's *Odyssey*'s Book V Calypso-episode:

Socrates admires the "separation" that allows one "to speak and think," yet if we read him closely we will find a telling irony: he has promised an impossible—or, at best gross-merging. He says that, on finding a master "dialectician" to teach him division, he would "walk in his footsteps as if he were a god." The dialectician/god/teacher would be male by grammar and by custom. Socrates quotes Book V of Homer's *Odyssey* (possibly for the benefit of Phaedrus, who misses the allusion). Here [line 193] the actual wording is "So saying, the beautiful goddess led the way quickly, and he followed in the footsteps of the "goddess," not of a "god." So even Socrates does not divide the sexes properly; if he were to "walk in the footsteps of this "master dialectician," he would be following a woman. By custom, a woman would not be a "dialectician" and hence the "dialectician" would not be the "goddess" of his allusion. The confusion is heightened because the Homeric passage Socrates cites comes when Odysseus has just decided to *separate* himself from the "goddess" Calypso.
. . . The myth would seem to show the primary falsity of the notion of absolute differentiation. Conjunction and disjunction are inseparable; Socrates praises a "division" presided over by a "master" who has no definite gender. Socrates has in fact *condensed* rather than *divided*, the sexes, even in an example meant to praise separation.[24]

An immersive journey into the particularity-depths of Homeric epic and Socratic dialogue muddies the logic of the work and its conjuncture's purported structure of dominance and gendered divide. Such a blurring only occurs by way of Snead's patient and penetrating analytic. The parsing of proper names and gendered forms of address allow for an even more immersive account of the "miniaturization" that is William Faulkner's Yoknapatawpha County.[25] It is a play of division that refuses white supremacy's mythos of purity.

Spillers' "Formalism Comes to Harlem" refuses the premise of division in her essay's title and poses a question by way of Langston Hughes's organic intellectual, Simple:

How does the Afro-American critic preserve the unalterable authenticity of Simple's wisdom, sparing the references to ritual and kinship which Harlem implies, in conversation which requires the mastery of a technic of ideas and their certain configurations?
In its apparent inclusiveness, in its fertility of vision, the wisdom of Simple never learned to be stunned, or embarrassed, or enraged by alien or borrowed notations, because it is eventually restored to the most intimate self-reference. The world is judged by *it* and is, therefore, disabled of its own capacity to judge.[26]

Spillers glosses two competing tendencies in Afro-American literary studies and offers Simple's interpretive guerilla tactics as foil, synthesis, and refutation of a false choice. I am interested in the Homeric resonance of her word choice—*one-eyed*. Spillers charts a "rift of opinion between at least two schools of Black critics, both of them straighter, perhaps, than the complicated humor of Simple anticipates. There are those who think that Afro-American literature is the narrative of mute social categories, content determined before particular acts of writing. Then there are those who think this view is *one-eyed*."[27] Spillers stages a dialectical neutralization—Simple's self-possession and flexing the capacity for judgment neutralizes the sting of other much more malevolent judgments.

Speculatively push this last reproach to foreground its Homeric valence. The "one-eyed" view of the Cyclops in the context of *Isonomic* Homeric epic conjures associations of myopia, lack of hospitality, brutish cannibalism, and a propensity to be deceived—Homer's famous staging of a menace evaded by a "Nobody."[28] A lesser remarked detail (central to my reading here) of this episode is brought to the fore by Theodor Adorno and Max Horkheimer's "The Myth of Enlightenment." Its pinpointing the lawless, one-eyed titan's offending characteristic and root cause of the cyclops Polyphemus's barbarism:

> For Homer, the definition of barbarism coincides with that of a state in which no systematic agriculture, and therefore no systematic, time-managing organization of work and society, has yet been achieved. He calls the Cyclops "fierce, uncivilized people" because—and his words seem to contain a secret confession of the guilt of civilization itself—they "never lift a hand to plant or plough but put their trust in Providence. . . . Abundance needs no law, and civilization's accusation of anarchy sounds almost like a denunciation of abundance. . . ."[29]

It is not the Cyclops' general idle that interests me here; nor the conflation of such idleness with anarchy. It is the implication that the root hostility to their life-world expresses a contempt for the fruits of social reproduction without toil. To represent the hell of genocidally coerced Black labor as the heaven of idyll paradise is a key ideological hallmark and mystification of the American plantocracy. In this speculative reach, I want to suggest that Spillers's choice wording of "one-eyed" reminds critics that aesthetic traditions do not auto-generate and capital does not accumulate without the most violent coercion. Abundance and accumulation are painstakingly worked for and worked over. Antagonism, split, formation, splitting anew shores up strength—bringing such phenomena to the fore requires an active, critical immersion and wrestling with the particularities of one's objects. It is the kind of immersion that prescription more often than not at worst discourages and at best (and most interestingly) constitutes a limit only as a prologue to transgressing such limit. Frank Baum's *Return to Oz's* instantly regenerative lunch-box trees do not grow here. Traditions are striated by class struggle and cohere by splitting apart only to cohere and split anew. The springing up and tilling of literary and aesthetic insight—the process-evolving aesthetic criteria informing the casting of judgment—require active immersive engagement and a deliberate radical parting, as attested by the voluminous manifestos and criteria-decrees, and taxonomies from generations of Black cultural workers.[30] The respective false choices of form/content, formalistic/sociology of literature approaches—the Formalism/Harlem divide—are resoundingly refused.

Spillers juxtaposes the particularities of contrasting narrative strategies in two hefty works of fiction—Toni Morrison's *Song of Solomon* alongside William Gaddis's *The Recognitions* (yet another fictional meditation on painting). In this encounter, Afro-American literature is "intent on producing works of filiation, advocacy, preservation, convocation (a literature whose principal movement is informed by an external narrative), Black American writers tend to rehearse a metaphorical valuation of human experience."[31] For Spillers, the contrasting narrative strategies of Morrison and Gaddis, the political implications of their rhetorical choices are clear. Spillers catalogues Gaddis's tendency to render anonymous characters, his "repetition of idiomatic gestures and the infinite regression of figurative and scenic details," his episodic structure and framing characters as seemingly existing "as an extension of rhetorical choices."[32] This is in contrast to works like *Song of Solomon* and *Invisible Man's* employment of "words as an act of reciprocity" and "the power of language to disclose being."[33] Social categories become unmuted only by way of an immersive attention to writerly distinctions and experiments in form. In this regard, Gaddis and Morrison in their contrast become a united front force against the pitfalls of a false choice.

In a 1966 *Massachusetts Review* essay entitled "Black Liberation," then Stokely Carmichael (Kwame Ture) notes that "Marx said that the working class is the first class in history that ever wanted to abolish itself."[34] Ture's assertion from Marx could very well stand in for the (still operative) Afro-American and African diasporic radical literary and aesthetic traditions—consistently remade by way of a perpetual radical-splitting, self-professed opposition, a constant refining and interrogation of its object of study, the categories employed therein, and the historical conjuncture in which this takes place. It is a radical striving for an abolishment that never arrives. It is the deferral that institutes a radical becoming. The weapon of criticism (and criticism of weapons) are generated only by an immersive dive into its objects of study.

Adorno and Horkheimer's "The Concept of Enlightenment" frames the dialectic as a struggle in which something becomes something that it was not. Such movement itself is framed as mythos:

> When the tree is no longer approached merely as tree, but as evidence for an Other, as the location of *mana*, language expresses the contradiction that something is itself and at once and the same time something other than itself, identical and not identical. Through the deity, language is transformed from tautology to language. The concept, which some would see as the sign-unit for whatever is comprised under it, has from the beginning been instead the product of dialectical thinking in which everything is always that which it is, only because it becomes what it is not.[35]

Ryan Engley and Todd McGowan's recent engagement with *The Dialectic of Enlightenment* privileges the dialectic not as synthesis "but rather an internal antagonism."[36] Engley precisely juxtaposes a traditional understanding of Hegelian dialectics as "inter-dependence of opposites" with the more exacting phraseology "inter-dependence of things in their *own* opposition." There is no synthesis at the end of dialectical unfolding; only negativity, void, and intractability. Identity is not becoming (*Werden*) otherness; rather, it is internally ruptured from the start. It is a subtle yet important emphasis related to the critical work examined in this chapter. The "what it is" and "what it is not" from the tree/*mana* passage above is internal to the tree itself– not a constrast of two discrete properties or coupled associations.

Hegel's Owl of Minerva as an Odyssey into an unknown, openness, refusal of closure, a willingness to risk all without guarantees reverberates with a hallmark of Black radical thought. What I call "Black radical capaciousness" is a discursive strategy, political imperative, and intellectual legacy that consistently strives to account for the *all*, the proliferation of immersive particularity activated by careful, close study and praxis.

II. Sharpening Tools on The Pequod: From Nobody to Every Body

In a discussion of his work for an installation with the Southern Queens Park Association, Alabama artist Thornton Dial asserts "I ain't been nowhere but I believe I can strategize about the whole world."[37] Dial's refusal of odyssey is coupled with the self- professed imperative and confident aptitude to effectively strategize a world. Consider Dial's "nowhere" alongside a sneaky recital of performative self-abnegation—Odysseus's crying out "Nobody" (Οὖτις). Such cry facilitates his flee from capture, evading the cyclops Polyphemus's inhospitable grasp and foiling his attempt to call for reinforcements. *The*

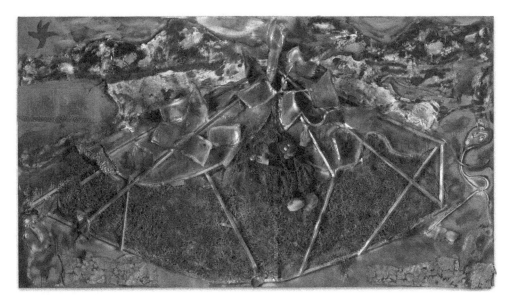

Plate 38 Thornton Dial, *High and Wide (Carrying The Rats to the Man)*, 2002. Philadelphia Museum of Art, Goat hides, carpet, found metal, clothing, stuffed-animal backpack, barbed wire, upholstery, textbook cover, Splash Zone compound, enamel, and spray paint on canvas on wood, 76 × 134 × 13 inches. Purchased with the McNeil Acquisition Fund for American Art and Material Culture, and gift of the Souls Grown Deep Foundation from the William S. Arnett Collection, 2017, 2017-229-16. Copyright Estate of Thornton Dial / Artists Rights Society, New York.

Odyssey stages the cyclops's ravenous affront against *xenia*. It is intellectual cunning supplementing might that releases Odysseus, allowing him to re-enter and ultimately traverse his oceanic briar-patch. It is variation on the theme of contradiction as radical splitting, the affirmation of negation—the *I am no*—constituting a canon in order to subvert it. It is the I am No[body] and I've been No[where]– not as empirical statements but rather dialectical enactments– that fabric traditions and craft strategies constituting radical traditions in Black art and its attendant aesthetic discourses. Dial's large sculpture installation entitled *High and Wide (Carrying the Rats to the Man)* theorizes abstraction by way of its immersive aesthetic. His abstraction method draws you in closer in order to conceptually fan out associations and analogues. His sculptural orbit (the product of his tools) reminds its viewer that staking a particular claim via an immersive immanence is the way to strategize the world. Experiencing *High and Wide* in its largesse and richness draws the looker in—the richness in color, the layering of variegated building materials immerses one further within while simultaneously exploding the onlooker's associations outwards to the abstraction that is worldly scale. The sculpture installation features a weathered Mickey Mouse doll with blackened face chained to a huge boat-structure surrounded by frenetic wiring, upholstery, text book covers, enamel, spray paint, found metal, and goat hides. As Baraka writes for the exhibition "Thornton Dial in the 21st Century":

> *High & Wild (Carrying the Rats to the Man)* centers on one of the wildest slave ships I've encountered. Is it the whole world being enslaved, including Mickey Mouse? The somberness of the central image *wired* to the world, popping with fragments of anywhere and every body so introduced to the "ghosts who would eat them."[38]

The particularity of the image and fragmentary "any where and every body" aesthetic totality that is Dial's installation reflects an aggregate universality "*wired* to the world." Dial's Mickey does not function as a jarring abrupt juxtaposition with its industrial material surround. It does not function like the quick surprise of the internet meme. Instead, Dial's Mickey belongs to the sculpture. Dial's arrangement, its placement technique, its saturation of color suggests immanence; yet its associations point outwards, proliferating meaning. Dial erects a haptic visual analog to a Black radical dialectic of particularity and universality. Such haptic particularity, the immersive color saturation as movement in Dial's aesthetic conjures and contains a world. For Judith Page, writing in a review of Dial's *Image of the Tiger*, this world is one whose formal choices are propelled by a commitment to interconnection and anti-hierarchy (recall Spillers on *Song of Solomon*): "Dial's method of composing his work is critical to its successful realization in both form and content. The composition is non-hierarchical; forms, symbols, colors have equal value throughout and exist without regard for pictorial space and linear time. The method serves as a potent metaphor for Dial's view of life; a life where one exists with the past, present, and future concurrently, where the inner and outer life have equal worth, and where all inhabitants of the physical world have equal value."[39] Dial's is the manifestation of a desire "to see a World in a Grain of Sand" proffered by another artist-intellectual-worker and *Prophet of Empire*.[40] Dial's tense exploration of immanence also points outwards, the interplay of miniaturization and largesse resonates with Blakean synecdoche defined as "a dynamic

Identity (contrary to difference/indifference) of words, but words conceived of as framing new cultural materials from a nature and culture that is only potential until the poet had done something with it. In such antithetical logic each word acts as a 'minute particularity' but acts also in a relation of identity to larger world."[41] Baraka concludes his analysis of Dial's "fearful symmetry" for the *Images of the Tiger* collection by loudly declaring the partisan universality of Dial's presence and art: "Dial is here, and speaks for us all, ready or not. Whether you know it or not."[42]

Jean-Michel Basquiat's series of drawings entitled "Melville" assembles nine 38" x 24" inch panels, vertically listing modest transcribed black capitalized letter variations on *Moby Dick's* 135-chapter plus epilogue and table of contents. Basquiat's "Melville' mirrors the multi-page listing style exhibited in Basquiat's famed marble notebooks. This is an important detail. Artifact and artwork are generated from the preparatory, the note-worthy, the exercise book, the occasional jotting, the collection of lined paper that in a different context house the scholastic exercises that Delany analyzes. Marble notebooks get repurposed and restaged as expanded aesthetic works; yet, such transformative expansions purposively maintain the trace of the notebook page entry. The preparatory is not a stage in a larger actualization; rather, a variation on the theme. Sometimes, Basquiat modifies chapter titles as in Melville's Chapter 52, "The Pequod meets the Albatross" shortened to "Albatross." More often, with the exception of Chapter 42, "The Whiteness of the Whale," it is his tactic to drop the definite article, denoting specificity resonating with the immanence and outward-bound movement of Dial's installation. Tricia Laughlin Bloom notes in her plate commentary for "Melville" how Basquiat's interest in "list making and notations as ends of themselves"—and apropos this essay—how Basquiat's work function "both an homage and an inspired gesture of interpretation, inverting the epic to the miniature."[43] It is precisely a logic of ends (closure) that is punctured and penetrated, reworked, and rejected, by Basquiat's reordering of Melville's "contents." Melville's opus is obsessively concerned with its own epic framing. His table of contents is framed by an epigraph from Milton's *Paradise Lost* that evokes Leviathan, followed by a multi-linguistic etymological chart for "Whale" and a sprawling, multi-page listing of Whale-themed "Extracts"—a vast range that includes Rabelais, *The Book of Job*, Dryden's *Annus Mirabilis*, and Richard Strafford's 1668 "Letter from the Bermudas," just to name a few. Such "Extracts" are parenthetically attributed to and supplied by a beast of Melville's own making—"the sub-sub librarian."[44] Basquiat's penultimate panel transcribes and truncates Melville's characterization of his fictional compiler of etymology, "the pale usher" in all caps: "THREAD BARE IN COAT, HEART, BODY, BRAIN." He transcribes and tm (trade-marks) "CALL ME ISHMAEL" and super-script raises the H in anticipation of the last panel's ETYMOLOGY AND HACKLUYT'S EXTRACTS. Basquiat's raised H in Ishmael in the penultimate panel is a nod to Melville's engagement with Hackluyt's assertion of the all importance of the letter H in the word whale. In Basquiat's last plate rendition, the underlined capitalized Etymology is all heading. He leaves it up the onlooker to perceive this as an evacuative procedure or as an invitation to participate in a filling out. Regardless of one's preference here, it is undeniable that Basquiat's Melville's by way of immersive particular adjustments reworks and repurposes what should be a settled matter. *Moby Dick's* table-of-contents frame, announce, and map a subsequent actuality of the epic novel's pages that follow. Basquiat's repurposing, his battery of formalist choices, his supplanting the role of the "pale usher" offers a challenge to tidy conceptualizations of odyssey, origin, and telos. The aesthetic *form* he materializes subsumes multiplicity under the single idea and heading of CONTENTS.

In the song "They Come in Gold," the esteemed Ishmael Butler of Digable Planets and Shabazz Palaces rhymes, "Ish dances with the white whale on the Pequod."[45] The Pequod, what C.L.R. James designates as "the conversion of the ship into a factory," scales a universality that can accommodate the multi-national working class coordinated in motion—all the immersive particularities.[46] Basquiat's work constitutes another logic of miniaturization. A quotidian detail pertaining to Basquiat's tool of choice is worthy of further consideration: oil-sticks sharpen via use. Comparable to crayon, an oil-stick's point is fashioned by utilizing the edge of the implement. Here is an enticing distillation of the rigor of Black radical aesthetics, an insistence on immersion in the richly saturated particularity of the universal. Tools (and categories) are constantly calibrated and sharpened as they generate the new. The best of which chips away at an ideological edifice informing the systematic purview of racial capitalism that frames its most insurgent creative force in an arrested dialectic. The imperative to commit to a lifetime study of Black radical aesthetics might be formulated as maxim: To see and create a world at the edge of one's oil-stick, in all its immersive particularity: categorizes actualized, activated, and sharpened by perpetual use.

Wesley Brown's "I Was Here But I Disappeared" is a feat of narrative economy.[47] A surgically precise tripartite short-story structure attentive to the nuance of its language throughout. It consistently doubles as a relationship story and a story about aesthetic (visual, kinetic, culinary, and musical) ways of knowing. As such it is deserving of and conducive to the kind of semiotic analysis, outside the scope of this paper, Delany (modeled partially on Roland Barthes's *S/Z*) brings to bear on Thomas M. Disch's short-story "Angouleme"—Delany's *The American Shore* where this essay began. Brown's is an example of the vanishing mediator gone awry. The first part stages an encounter and start of an intimate relationship triangulating characters Tyrone and Faye with Faye's nine-year old son—Cecil. Faye chastises and inevitably separates from Tyrone for his failure to recognize the need to offer support for child-care during their dates. This writerly exposition on "the intimacy of silences"[48] is abundant with visual reference: knowing is presented as a problem and Faye's departing words to Tyrone is a tellingly, "I'm tired of being your eyes."[49] Part II sees Tyrone taking the opportunity of the recent break-up to visit Rudy, a friend from his youthful days as revolutionary community organizer. Meditation on the visual is supplemented by the problem of the temporal as California offers up to Tyrone "a different way time was perceived."[50] Rudy is an African American man involved with Alex, a white woman, navigating the hostility their union somethings engenders in public (Rudy loses the ability of coherent speech when confronted by Black women questioning what Freud would call his object choice) by immersing himself in minimalist communities. Contrary to the minimalist motif, Brown's descriptive acumen arranges his narrative settings conjuring a visual textured lushness his character's ideology strives to bypass. A room is described as an aggregate of "posters, wine bottles, driftwood, books and records, a huge cable spool that served as a table"[51]—a descriptive installation of heterogenous congruous objects.

A run through Golden Gate Park to the ocean discloses Rudy's act of transcribing I WAS HERE BUT I DISAPPEARED on a concrete wall and the telling of its complicated assertion of presence and absence's backstory:

"About a year after I came out here. There was this dude I'd gotten friendly with who was a painter. He'd gotten this commission to do a painting of Christ's crucifixion and asked if I'd pose for it. I was glad to do it. The money came in handy, since I wasn't working. When I looked at the painting I was shocked because it wasn't me. I mean it as my body, minus the color. And the face looked more like Max Von Sydow's.

"When I pointed this out to him, he told me he hadn't wanted to inject race into the painting. He had done precisely that by using me as a model and then leaving out a physical trait that was intrinsic to being me! I was outraged. He told me that I was overreacting. I said I didn't want to impose on him my notion of what Christ looked like, but if he knew what he wanted he should have gotten someone who resembled it more. He said that was too limiting. As an artist it was his task to take what was and make it into something else. That was fine with me, but as a human being I resented him taking what *I* was and making me disappear.[52]

Rudy and Alex embrace wholeheartedly a minimalist world view and praxis, prompting Tyrone's return to New York City. In yet another nod to questions of interpretation and aesthetic engagement—Tyrone commits himself to "live with difficulty" as retort and answer to Rudy and Alex's minimalist immersion.[53] Part Three finds Tyrone dancing in a discotheque. The narrative stages another and final meditative disappearing act as an excursus on mimesis:

I went over to the bar, ordered another brandy, and nursed it while looking at the people in the mirror. Gradually I settled on my own reflection and considered how people get to the planned obsolescence of the high cost of living. As I acknowledged the impressive evidence that justifies cordoning off life to avoid discomfort, my mirror image began to fragment and disappear. All that was left of me was a curved slice of moon about to go into total eclipse. But just before I vanished, some nagging streak in me that had been weaned on risk reasserted itself. I realized I was not about to exempt myself from the terrors of being alive. I squeezed between two fingers the skin joining the bridge of my nose with my forehead and looked back in the mirror. I was intact again, distorted by recognizable. . . .[54]

This is an astonishing conclusion. As a culminating example of what I'm arguing for as the work of Black radical aesthetics, it foregrounds its contradictions and refuses to hasten its steps. This is no easy lament or excoriation of the false consciousness of minimalism as the hegemonic optic as inauthentic universal. It forces us as readers as it forces its characters to tarry in the ambiguities and generative problems of knowledge every step of its odyssey from self-assertion, self-effacement, and partiality—assertion in effacement. It asks you to look, linger, and read. Rudy and Alex surrender to their minimalist credo and community; yet, defiantly, Rudy still registers his disappearing presence, his anonymous nobody in the form of a transcription. He organizes and re-organizes his bodily presence and disappearance homologous to Basquiat's table-of-contents announcing and conjuring the work while also signaling its lack. Brown forces both characters and reader to linger with the sticky implications of each choice and every valence and level and gradation of visibility. It stages the stages of sense-perception's connection to self-awareness. The story's formalist narrative economy won't allow you to skip. It mobilizes its intellection, its fictional discourse on race, subjectivity, and representation as a bridge to think the fragility of human connectivity and the tragedy of such human connectivity's severance. It is the generative radical realm and logic of contradiction, as opposed to the easy populist logic of opposition. It is an aggregate of detrimental contingent steps and significant choices even if and especially if endings are already known. And finally, it is lamentation as philosophical insurgent cry. Punctuating the darkness of the cave, you can hear the cyclops's misfired lament: "Friends, Nobody is murdering me by craft. Force there is none."[55]

Notes

1   Here, *speculative* signifies not just experimental or counterfactual reading brought forth by juxtaposition; rather, it might be all those things in how the speculative foregrounds by performing an expository odyssey of contradiction in order to see formula or phenomena anew. Spillers, "Formalism Comes to Harlem," *Black American Literature Forum*, Vo. 16. No. 2 (Summer 1982), 58.

2   Spillers, "Formalism Comes to Harlem," 59.

3   Walter Benjamin, "Try to Ensure that Everything in Life has a Consequence", 1932, Translated by Rodney Livingston, *Walter Benjamin: Selected Writings, Volume 2, Part 2, 1931–1934*, Edited by Michael W. Jennings, Howard Eiland, Gary Smith (Cambridge: Harvard University Press, 1999), 686.

4   Amiri Baraka (writing as LeRoi Jones), "Hunting is Not Those Heads on the Wall," in *Home: Social Essays* (New York: William Morrow & Co., 1966), 173–78.

5   Baraka, "The Revolutionary Theatre," in *Home: Social Essays*, 212.

6   James A. Snead, "Repetition as a Figure of Black Culture," *Black Literature & Literary Theory*, ed. Henry Louis Gates Jr. (1984: reprint, New York: Routledge, 1990), 67. Hegel's lectures were posthumously transcribed by his students as Hegel's *Lectures on the Philosophy of History* as Timothy Brennan convincingly demonstrates: Timothy Brennan, *Borrowed Light: Vico, Hegel, and the Colonies* (Stanford: Stanford University Press, 2014).

7   Snead, "Repetition as a Figure of Black Culture," 67.

8   Curtis Mayfield, "Doo Doo Wap is Strong in Here," *Short Eyes Soundtrack*, Curtom, 1977.

9   Franz Kafka, *The Zuraü Aphorisms* (1931), trans. Roberto Calasso (New York: Schocken Books, 2006), 20.

10 G. W. F. Hegel, *Hegel: Texts and Contexts*, ed. Walter Kaufmann, "The Preface to the Phenomenology,"* 1807, (University of Notre Dame Press, 1982, 1986), 52.

11 Consider this philosophically rich German etymological overlap as a way to hear anew Billy Woods's magisterial song "The Undercard": "Declined the spliff/They took it as a dis. . . . But never one to Bite my Tongue/Professor Griff." Billy Woods, "The Undercard," *Dour Candy*, Backwoodz Studioz, 2013.

12 Samuel R. Delany, *The American Shore: Meditations on a Tale of Science Fiction* by Thomas M. Disch—"Angouleme" (Middletown: Wesleyan University Press, 2014), 23.

13 Samo Tomšič, *The Capitalist Unconscious: Marx and Lacan* (London and New York: Verso, 2015), 211–219. Jacques Lacan, *Le Séminaire. Livre XVI, tome 16. D'un Autre à l'autre* 1968–1969 (Paris: Seuil, 2006), 42.

14 James A. Snead, *Figures of Division: William Faulkner's Major Novels* (London and New York: Routledge, 1986/2018), 2.

15 Snead, *Figures of Division*, 7.

16 Snead, *Figures of Division*, xiii.

17 Snead, *Figures of Division*, x.

18 Samir Amin, "The Formation of Tributary Ideology in the Mediterranean Region," *Eurocentrism* (New York: Monthly Review Press, 2009, 2nd edition), 105.

19 Frantz Fanon, *The Wretched of the Earth*, trans. Constance Farrington (New York: Grove Press, 1961/1963), 51.

20 Snead, *Figures of Division*, 101–102.

21 Snead, 102.

22 Michael Ondaatje, *Coming Through Slaughter* (Canada: Vintage, 1976/1998), 43.

23 Snead, *Figures of Division*, 11.

24 Snead, *Figures of Division*, 12, 13.

25 Snead, *Figures of Division*, 2.

26 Spillers, "Formalism Comes to Harlem," 59.

27 Spillers, "Formalism Comes to Harlem," 59 (emphasis mine).

28 Kojin Karatani, *Isonomia and the Origins of Philosophy* (Durham: Duke University Press, 2012/2017).

29 Max Horkheimer and Theodor W. Adorno, "The Myth of Enlightenment," in *The Dialectic of Enlightenment*, ed. Gunzelin Schmid Noerr, trans. Edmund Jephcott (Stanford: Stanford University Press, 1947/2002), 50–51.

30 A brief sampling might include: Langston Hughes, "The Negro Artist and the Racial Mountain" (1926), *Poetry* Foundation: https://www.poetryfoundation.org/articles/69395/the-negro-artist-and-the-racial-mountain, accessed January 6, 2022. W. E. B. DuBois, "Criteria of Negro Art" (1926), in *The Crisis* 32, no. 6 (October 1926): 290–7; Zora Neale Hurston, "Characteristics of Negro Expression" (1933), in *Negro: An Anthology*, ed. Nancy Cunard and Hugh Ford (New York: Frederick Ungar Publishing Co., 1970), 24–46.; James Baldwin, "Everybody's Protest Novel" (1955), in *The Price of the Ticket: Collected Nonfiction 1948–1985* (New York: St. Martin's Press, 1985), 27–34; Amiri Baraka (writing as LeRoi Jones), "Myth of a Negro Literature" (1962), in *Home: Social Essays*, 105–15; June Jordan, "The Difficult Miracle of Black Poetry in America: Something Like a Sonnet for Phillis Wheatley," in *On Call: Political Essays* (London, Sydney: Pluto Press, 1985), 87–98; and Maryse Condé, "Order, Disorder, Freedom, and the West Indian Writer," *Yale French Studies*, no. 97 (2000), 151–65.

31 Spillers, "Formalism Comes to Harlem," 61.

32 Spillers, "Formalism Comes to Harlem," 62.

33 Spillers, "Formalism Comes to Harlem," 62.

34 Stokely Carmichael (Kwame Ture), "Toward Black Liberation," in *Stokely Speaks: Black Power Back to Pan-Africanism*, ed. Ethel N. Minor (New York: Vintage Books, 1966/1971), 39.

35 "The Concept of Enlightenment," 15.

36 *Why Theory* Podcast, *Dialectic of Enlightenment*, October 3, 2021. Accessed October 31, 2021. https://podcasts.apple.com/us/podcast/dialectic-of-enlightenment/id1299863834?i=1000537348976

37 Thornton Dial, "Thornton Dial Talks About His Work," Thornton Dial: Strategy of the World (Jamaica: Southern Queens Park Association, 1990), 4.

38 Amiri Baraka, "Revolutionary Traditional Art from the Cultural Commonwealth of Afro-Alabama," *Thornton Dial in the 21st Century* (Atlanta: Tinwood Books, 2005), 172.

39 Judith Page, "Thornton Dial: Image of the Tiger" (New York: The New Museum of Contemporary Art *Art Papers*, September-October 1994), 8.

40 David D. Erdman, *Blake: Prophet of Empire* (Princeton: Princeton University Press, 1954).

41 Hazard Adams, "Synecdoche and Method," in *Critical Paths: Blake and the Argument of Method*, ed. Dan Miller, Mark Bracher, Donald D. Ault, and Mark Bracher (Durham: Duke University Press, 1987), 47.

42 Amiri Baraka, "Fearful Symmetry: The Art of Thornton Dial," Thornton Dial, Images of the Tiger, ed. Harriet Whelchel and Margaret Donovan (New York: Harry N. Abrahms, 1993), 64.

43 Jean-Michel Basquiat, *Basquiat: The Unknown Notebooks*, ed. Dieter Buchhart and Tricia Laughlin Bloom, (Brooklyn: Brooklyn Museum & Skira Rizzoli, 2015), 204.

44 Herman Melville, *Moby-Dick* (New York: W.W. Norton & Company, 1851/1967), 2.

45 Shabazz Palaces, "They Come in Gold," *Lese Majesty*, July 28, 2014, Sub Pop Records.

46 C. L. R. James, *Mariners, Renegades, and Castaways: The Story of Herman Melville and the World We Live In* (Hanover: University Press of New England, 1953/1971/2001), 8.

47 Wesley Brown, "I was Here but I Disappeared," in *Breaking Ice: An Anthology of Contemporary African-American Fiction*, ed. Terry McMillan (New York: Viking, 1990).

48 Brown, "I was Here but I Disappeared," 88.

49 Brown, "I was Here but I Disappeared," 91.

50 Brown, "I was Here but I Disappeared," 92.

51 Brown, "I was Here but I Disappeared," 92.

52 Brown, "I was Here but I Disappeared," 94.

53 Brown, "I was Here but I Disappeared," 99.

54 Brown, "I was Here but I Disappeared," 101.

55 This is Polyphemus's lament of misrecognition.

24

ON BLACK SPECULATIVE MUSICALITIES

Vijay Iyer

These words—Black, speculative, musicalities—open out onto a vast terrain. None of them resolves to a single meaning; each one points, traces, asks. What might we hope to identify by setting them together?

The word *Black* as I invoke it here spans the last half-millennium, what Frank Wilderson has called "the time of the paradigm,"[1] or what Achille Mbembe describes in his *Critique of Black Reason* – by which he means:

> a collection of voices, pronouncements, discourses, forms of knowledge, commentary, and nonsense, whose object is things or people "of African origin" . . . From the beginning, its primary activity was fantasizing. . . . A range of intermediaries and institutions . . . contributed to the development of this reason and its transformation into common sense and a habitus . . . . its function was to codify the conditions for the appearance and the manifestation of the racial subject that would be called the Black Man (le Nègre) and, later, within colonialism, the Native (L'indigène). . . . [The] goal was to produce the Black Man as a racial subject and site of savage exteriority, who was therefore set up for moral disqualification and practical instrumentalization. We can call this founding narrative the *Western consciousness of Blackness*.[2]

If Mbembe's work is part of a critical deconstructive project, we also have a long history of Black scholars, theorists, music-makers, writers, and others, thinking through and testing African diasporic forms of expression: aesthetics, politics, priorities, and real-life stakes. At the turn of the twenty-first century, David Lionel Smith wrote,

> What then is black culture? No one can answer these questions definitively, because 'black culture' is not a fixed, single thing 'out there' in the empirical world. It is, rather, a complex and ambiguous set of processes and interactions, facts, and fantasies, assertions and inquiries, passionately held and passionately contested.[3]

The *speculative* is associated with counterfactuals, practices of world-building that diverge from empirical reality and imagine different social orders counter to our own. Hence a history of Black speculative thought would span the gamut of the Black radical imagination: fugitivity, practices of refusal, spirituals, Aimé Césaire's Afro-Surrealism, Dr. King's call for "creative maladjustment," Afrofuturism, abolition, critical fabulation.

In thinking through Black people's expressions and forms of life, Christina Sharpe theorizes,

> Living as I have argued we do in the wake of slavery, in spaces where we were never meant to survive, or have been punished for surviving and for daring to claim or make spaces of something like freedom, we yet reimagine and transform spaces for and practices of an ethics of care (as in repair, maintenance, attention), an ethics of seeing, and of being in the wake as consciousness.[4]

Music is our word for how we listen to each other. The first question is, "we, who?" And the second is, what's this zone called "other," to which we listen? And third, what is that other doing that grabs our ear? Those are the methods by which we categorize music: first, by constructing a listening subject, a "we" of which "you" are a member; second, by identifying your relation to the other, the not-you; and third, by solidifying that other's actions into objects that circulate, stockpile, signify, invoke.

A young man on the subway, bearded and tattooed, in a red head scarf and white muscle shirt, wears a backpack from which music emanates. It fills the car with beats and bass, a distressed pseudovoice warbling autotuned minor thirds. His friend, slimmer, hunched, with cornrows, rhymes along to himself, signaling his affiliation. We are plunging downtown from Harlem on a Thursday midmorning 4 train, and the demographic shifts in the usual ways as the doors open and close. Nobody overtly objects to this engulfing cloud of sound, though its extent and power is unusual. It is a palpable repurposing of the moving space into something more like a club, or a sidewalk. Certain bodies' movements, while not quite dance, are somehow reconditioned by these engulfing rhythms and strains, this intervening Black and Brown aural presence that emboldens their steps and stances. Yes, that's our "we," their bodies say. We who live uptown and in the outer boroughs, we who commute to the more moneyed neighborhoods if we're lucky, we who move, sing, speak, listen, feel this way. Music is a connector, an affiliator.

The constellation of practices referred to as Black music confers sonic life on such fugitive, relational qualities: embodied listening, heterarchical interaction, call and response, moving-together-in-time, and ecstatic transcendence. Moten writes,

> The animative materiality—the aesthetic, political, sexual, and racial force—of the ensemble of objects that we might call black performances, black history, blackness, is a real problem and a real chance for the philosophy of the human being (which would necessarily bear and be irreducible to what is called, or what somebody might hope to someday call, subjectivity).[5]

The work of Jamaican cultural theorist Sylvia Wynter speaks to these intersections and faultlines of the humanities, sciences, and Black studies by interrogating this category of the human being. In "Unparalleled Catastrophe for our species? Or, to give humanness a different future: Conversations," jointly authored with Katherine McKittrick, Wynter considers the conceptual space opened up by Darwin's "epistemological rupture or leap—that is, its far-reaching challenge to Christianity's biblical macro-origin story's . . . divide between an ostensibly generically Christian *mankind*, on the one hand, and all other species, on the other." She adds, "What I'm putting forward as a challenge here, as a wager, is . . . that the human is, meta-Darwinianly, a hybrid being, both bios and logos . . . bios and mythoi . . . together, define what it is to be human." And: "Notice! One major implication here: humanness is no longer a noun. *Being human is a praxis*."[6] So she calls for us to relativize the West's hitherto secular liberal monohumanist conception of our being human, its overrepresentation as the being of being human itself. We need to speak instead of our genres of being human. Once you redefine being human in hybrid mythoi and bios terms, and therefore in terms that draw attention to the relativity and original multiplicity of our *genres* of being human, *all of a sudden what you begin to recognize is the central role that our discursive formations, aesthetic fields, and systems of knowledge must play in the performative enactment of all such genres of being hybridly human*.[7]

To this end she considers the site of Blombos Cave, South Africa, home to the earliest pieces of human art ever found: a 77,000-year-old etching in ochre, in a humanly organized crosshatch pattern, in the context of what is further revealed to be a 100,000-year-old *workshop* holding the tools for artmaking. It is found among evidence of catching, cooking and serving shellfish, an originary site filled with all the ingredients for culture-making: a cave by the sea, where humans have gathered with their creations and creating anew, nourishing and grooming one another, marking objects with images for future generations. Wynter unpacks the significance of these artmaking practices around this master symbol of processed ochre, specifically: what she calls the "*symbolic transformation of biological identity*," as ochre-as-material comes to represent menstrual blood. What is revealed is "the praxis of the ritual initiatory transformation of the first form of life (biologically born individual life) into the second form of life (communal/fictive or *symbolic life*)."[8] She suggests that we need these orienting myths because they *make* the category of the human – not just a scientifically defined biological creature, but bios *plus* mythoi – and so she seizes upon a rehabilitative, reorienting myth that regrounds that category: the first instance, in humankind's cradle, of a ritual of human symbolic transformation of biological identity.

So, where is music, that most impermanent medium, inside this ancient archive? It has to be everywhere. What might such a human lifeworld sound like, a scene of sociality among artisans and others gathered inside the echoic caverns of Blombos Cave, 90,000 years BCE? In order to listen not just across the usual litany of musical genres, but rather to our innumerable *genres of being human*, to listen on a species-wide scale across the eons, we will need to consider music as a sphere of human action that straddles bios and mythoi, as one of our most ancient, most productive practices of *constructing* humanness.

I submit then that it is not actually not music per se but *musicality* that binds us. What do I mean by this? Let's agree that musicality denotes an emergent quality of establishing musicalness, or of becoming musical. Today, not all musical things are called music, and not all music is universally felt to be musi*cal*. In the Anglo-west, to call something *musical* is to confer a special value on it—much more rare and important than mere music, that ubiquitous substance that wallpapers modern life. To call something *musical* means that something *feels the way you believe music is supposed to feel.* Musicality is an entirely subjective quality of, let's say, feeling called, guided, or hailed into an affective relation with the sonorous acts of another. This quality can come about in innumerable ways: we have diverse musicalities for various modes of relation. Musicalities arise as embodied, which is to say affective and temporal, relation among beings and objects: not just sound-making, but *sonic mattering*.

This is why I argue that our domain of study should be *musicality*, the sphere of relations, not *music*, the object/substance—but furthermore that musicality should be treated as a dynamic, speculative, affectively charged, ritual space, a liminal zone of experience whereby people seek to experiment, create, commune, to hail and be hailed, to hold and be held, to lose themselves and be remade, to become part of something larger than themselves. Musicality, then, is a category that is continually being unmade and remade across humankind's thousand centuries: our many *musicalities* are nothing less than our praxes of being human together.

Let us listen to Black performance as a ritual space for *Black speculative musicalities*: sonically disruptive practices that posit new ways of becoming musical, new genres of being human, otherwise possibilities[9] for Black life and Black subjectivities, and radical futurities for the "philosophy of the human being." With and through Black speculative musicalities, we are bearing witness to an insurgent sonic world-building: moments of Black performance becoming musical, fugitive Black sonic operations affording intercorporeal movement, pleasure, release, ascension.

Importantly, this essay is not specifically concerned with so-called "experimental" or "avant-garde" aesthetics – except insofar as all Black musical creation could be described as experimental. As with Black life, Black sonic mattering can never be guaranteed under the violence of the existing order; so we must hear *every* instance of Black musicality as animated by a speculative life force, a defiant livingness, ideating and calling into being an (im)possible future: that persistent quality of the Black radical tradition that exceeds all frames.

As a non-Black person, I do not purport to make a sweeping pronouncement here about Black musics or Black people. Instead I hope to approach and highlight some scenes in which Black subjectivities, Black music-makers, Black counterpublics, sonically harken new ways of living, relating, listening, and being, new arrangements of time and space, new imaginings of the social, bending, breaking, burrowing under, or flying over the existing order of things: new musical orders, new paths. What follows is a series of subjective accounts, of varying length and focus, of some encounters with recorded and live Black music-making generated via interface: a piano, percussion, a saxophone, knobs on a machine. What different genres of the self do these embodied, transduced acts bring forth from me as I strive to narrate them? How do they offer a sense of their makers' defiant livingness, and of our own?

Duke Ellington: " *Lotus Blossom*" 1967.[10] There's some milling around behind him as he works his way through this bittersweet song by his then-newly departed, longtime musical partner, Billy Strayhorn. Ellington expressed the intimacy of their intergenerational creative partnership as an embodied fusion: "Billy Strayhorn was my right arm, my left arm, all the eyes in the back of my head, my brainwaves in his head, and his in mine."[11] Here we hear Ellington's hands, haunted by Strayhorn's premature death, lovingly, mournfully retracing the steps of his friend's arms and brainwaves. The limpid, pendular oscillations in the left hand are marking burdened time, like a melancholy ballet en pointe, while the right hand is the dancer's upper body, in its way of reaching, turning, and caressing the melody, now tender, now distraught, reworking it chorus after chorus, staying with the burden, as though searching its corners for a trace of his friend's life.

Even in Ellington's later years, they had to pry him away from the piano every night, after any given concert. Well after the music stands, instruments, microphones, and scores were all packed up, the mop pushed across the floor, a lone figure still sat building, searching, gnarled hands still probing the instrument. His road manager would lean on him, pointing at his watch.

The tendency is to reach for the anecdote about how the man spoke, how he walked, what he wore, what he ate, as if these things made him great. But the laborious, unglamorous zone of music-making is the same for everyone, a great equalizer: full of small failures, dead ends, abandoned drafts, ideas created and annihilated in an instant, and yet suffused with an ethic of care and discernment. The unnerving truth is that this is what made him great, and could indeed make anyone great: a lifetime's worth of tireless, self-assured, emotionally open pursuit, unpacking, scrutiny, and refinement of one idea, and the next idea, and the next, and the next.

Randy Weston: "*Ancient Future*," (2002).[12] What first strikes the ear is a composerly bearing— an attitude towards construction, a way of building or putting-together (which is what "composing" means) with the fundamental contours of interval — and I say "bearing" because he puts his torso in it; you might say that his very stance is audible. There is an insistent repetition with gesture, the telltale mark of the hands; a surprising capacity for digital-rhythmic excitations; an affinity for deep, clangorous vibration, a resonant tolling of the piano's body like a great bell.

A melody contains within it a longing, sorrow, hope, dignity, and a plainspoken grandeur. The left hand guides and shapes while the right hand tells, sings, spits knowledge, traces truths. The refinement of touch, the attention to weight, texture, and melodic shape. We have not yet understood what his right hand's lyrical-gestural insistence meant; we lack the vocabulary to describe what work his unnameable chords did. What are these ancient futures?

A solo piano introduction would plumb the dark, thick, murky depths of a song, then echo them an octave above, in dyads. Then he would set the pulse rolling, majestically, effortlessly, without force. A plainspoken melody contains within it a longing, sorrow, hope, dignity, and grandeur. The left hand guides, shapes, and pushes from below, while the right hand carves from above; it tells, it sings, it spits knowledge, it traces truths. The refinement of touch, the attention to weight, texture, and melodic shape. We have not yet understood what his right hand's lyrical-gestural insistence meant; we lack the vocabulary to describe what work his unnamable chords did. What were these ancient futures?

In an interview I did with Mr. Weston in Guelph in 2014, I asked him about his piano conception. He listed a few points of reference:

With *Basie* I loved his touch, just extraordinary. But also he developed a concept of just playing a few notes, but each note was so important because it was the blues. So from him I learned that kind of simplicity of the blues . . . *Nat King Cole*. He was a master pianist. Each note was utter beauty. I can't describe him any other way . . . *Art Tatum*. He had a kind of magic: polyrhythmic imagination, everything on the piano. From Art Tatum I got DARING. Never his technique, but that kind of daring . . . When I heard *Monk* play the piano I said, "I can play more piano than this guy . . ." But I went back again, and the first time I heard Ruby My Dear – magic for me. The magic of Africa. When he played the piano everyone used to laugh at him because he was funny, but it was almost like an African ballet. When I heard Monk I heard how music must have been 10,000 years ago. I heard a magic in the piano . . . *Duke Ellington* does a lot of things with the bass of the piano. A lot of pianists don't touch the bass of the piano; I love it. Duke, with his orchestral concept, also his commitment to his people, Duke was way ahead of everybody. To me he was the premier revolutionary . . . So you put them all together, and then you put traditional African music on top of that. Music from Congo, Benin, My experience with the Gnawa people in Morocco. Put all that together – that's Randy Weston.[13]

I, too, adore and am indebted to all of these sources; and so I am here to tell you that much of what Mr. Weston did at the piano could be attributed to *none* of the above. Some of his sounds can only be taken as his own ingenuity. The word "tradition," which has, at least since the 1980s, become permanently conjoined to the word "jazz," has a way of downplaying or even erasing the inventive, disruptive, speculative musicalities of this great Black music — obscuring the simple truth of the matter, that a musician like Mr. Weston pulled off some of his own utterly unprecedented things, his own mysteries, his own magic.

We can hear the history of this music as a history of ideas, and we can therefore state, without exaggeration, that Randy Weston's legacy offers some of the most far-reaching, most coolly inventive musical conceptions of the last century, which are nonetheless some of the least studied and least understood.

We attended Randy Weston's homegoing service at the Cathedral of St John the Divine in New York City. At 92 and 6'7", he was a giant, a leader, a sonic healer, a deep listener, a citizen of the non-West, a Brooklynite, a pan- Africanist, a chief. The spans of his hands, his heart, and his lifetime were vast, and subsequently he spoke for many: a musical dignitary, an emissary of compassion.

That day, the procession of his extra-long coffin was led by a chorus of drummers, a half dozen playing a West African arsenal — djembes, talking drums — and two more with metal clappers playing Gnawa trance patterns. Their rhythmic admixture filled the senses and jerked your spirit aloft.

The rest of us musicians were asked to follow in pairs behind the family, who followed the pallbearers. We all gathered in an anteroom, in close quarters, and the drummers started. As the rhythm unit lurched into motion, wrapped in bright fabrics, the sound filled the small chamber perfectly.

But what happened next was a sound that I won't forget anytime soon. The doors flew open, and this thunderous ensemble exited the anteroom. Suddenly all those acoustic vibrations tumbled into that cavernous hall, and their sound sprang forth to the distant walls of the enormous church, returning to us as a glorious, diffuse roar. It was a space designed for celestial sounds — pipe organs, choirs, boy sopranos, sounds with imperceptible articulations — but here instead, ten thousand impulses, sticks striking skins across resonant wooden casks, became a many-limbed army storming the place, a tumult of actional sound climbing the walls, bouncing off of every cornice, rounding every flying buttress. To hear those drums spill into a stone-and-mortar cathedral, and to feel the reverberations enveloping us, provided a special, mystical thrill. A swarm of rhythm, a vortex of thwacks and thumps and claps: the Global South, striking back, engulfing the hubristic Western edifice that had been built on their backs.

We followed the procession along the southern wall to the rear of the church and back up the center aisle. By then the drummers had gathered behind the lectern, and were really getting into something. The metal clappers are played in such a way that the tempo travels forward, incrementally yet inevitably, such that the entire assembly cannot help but go with it; it just feels like the right thing to do. The result is an intoxicating rhythmic vector that drives the gathering towards ecstasy. That church, bursting with sound and bodies, summoned forth a million other souls in transit, who joined and merged with Weston's journey across realms in a pulsating swirl of colors.

Ensemble. The composer-pianist Muhal Richard Abrams once said, "When you make music with someone, that creates a bond that can never be broken."[14] It sounds impossible, wishful; but what if we suspend our disbelief, and play out the scenario? If the doing of music - electing to take action together, coordinating what to play and how to play it, synchronizing actions, tuning in, making real-time relational decisions, moving with the same pulse — creates a lasting inter-self, then what kind of work do these unbreakable bonds do? What specific power lies in this invisible tensile web of relations in sound?

We've been in it, zigzagging across Europe. Most days are transit purgatories, strangely stationary affairs as we drift from one standing queue to the next, eventually making our way to a plane seat, a bumpy van ride, a hotel room, a chaotic soundcheck, a rushed plate of food. This twelve-hour trudge is followed by, finally, the point of it all: to shed our skins in public, to access some molten core of raw collective experience — a ritual, a spectacle, a communal reckoning.

This performative doing and being, these ephemeral freedoms, are enabled and upheld by an intense listening, an elaborately detailed, relational interaction. The first requirement is an openness to a rather banal yet strangely intimate kind of contact: a willingness to move together. There's something vulnerable about electing to sense and produce time together, as when asking someone to dance. To join someone in synchronous movement - of the limbs and joints, or of the voice, or in actions mediated through instruments - is to connect spine-to-spine, torso-to-torso, brain-stem-to-brain-stem. It is deeper than touch, earlier than speech; it is a merging of bodily awareness. This skill can be cultivated, of course; some people get more chances than others; some must seek them out.

As our group navigates through its set — repertoire and solo episodes chosen step by step, in relation to what has happened so far and what impact it has had, ideally moving the energy in the room like a good DJ — the larger message is one of unity; a dense, compact network of affiliations among a half-dozen players, casually expressed through a series of oddly comfortable, rough-and-tumble collective actions. It is the fact that this aggregate of bodies can act as a single system, "moving with its own intelligence," as Wadada Leo Smith once said. The compositions have abundant detail; however, the point is not the details themselves, but rather the story they tell. Our unity implies years of shared history, provoking an observer's imagination: who are they? why them? When and how did they arrive at this understanding about each other? And why do I feel connected to it?

The John Coltrane Quartet. *Both Directions at Once: The Lost Album* (recorded 1963; released 2018).[15] Pulsation emerges, forms a web of relation that entangles anyone in its reach. It is the sound of pendular motion, a pair of fingers on low strings, hands bearing sticks on hammered metal and skin, fingers and palms splayed across ivory and wood — all supported by a group of homologous effectors: human forearms, in various manifestations, wielded at all angles, lifted by muscles and falling with or faster than gravity, being lifted again, falling again, lifting again. We hear in these motions a set of sustained relations to the earth - ways of landing, ways of lifting. The flood of details that surrounds the pulse — the supporting barrage of cymbal patterns, snare attacks, toms, rimshots, bass drum kicks; the resonant piano chords landing firmly on upbeats, and miraculous runs lifting up the beat; the resolutely dancing bass — depict ways of holding pulse while living life, moving together, their freedoms in synchrony.

The saxophonist becomes an odd counterexample in his own band. The location of the beat in his body is largely unrelated to gravity; it exists by analogy. It comes from breath, embouchure, and fingering, and it appears in the timing of individual notes with respect to one another and to the rhythms of the band. His actions relate more directly to speech than to walking: supported by a column of air (which must be replenished between phrases), articulated by the tongue and throat, accompanied by minute gesticulations of the fingers, held sideways.

Drummer Roy Haynes said of Coltrane, "He had the world's greatest drummer inside him." The time emanates from within. That drummer within is the one who walks, pulsation moving across the legs and torso in a balanced periodic distribution. A sturdy, ambulatory homunculus, a bouncing inner version of the self that supports the actions of the outer self who stands more still.

That is the framework across which these canvases are stretched. The temporal armature of music is synchronous movement. So we may attend to what that movement sounds like, how the bodies lift and land with and against each other; and we may attend to the identity of those sounds: the tone colors, note choices, harmonic palette.

In Coltrane's quartet, pulse is paramount. It is not a mere afterthought; it is the crux of the music's action. Given that, there is also much to say about the spectrum of information that appears across such strongly pulsed time. A listening ear constantly darts from the shape and color of an expressed idea, to the way it pertains to the underlying form, to the feeling as it lands in rhythmic relation, to the way other players kick around responses, support and push back. So-called "solos" are still emanations of the group dynamic, in what Fred Moten likened to a solar flare, foregrounding not an individual but an aspect of the whole, a mode of collective excitation.

I find myself playing a couple of those long-lost Coltrane compositions with the late saxophonist's own son Ravi, himself an imposing musician. We tucked into that opening blues, a compact, slickly severe figure known only as Untitled Original 11383. I found that it engenders a way of playing that is iconically of that quartet: familiar sounds that you might call "McCoy-isms" or "Elvin-ish" for their faithful imitation of Tyner's and Jones's rhythms and colors. But it was also somehow that I was carried forth into that tributary, almost involuntarily. One surrenders to a familiar set of decisions, a well-traveled network of actions, and it manifests as a hexis: a particular way of holding oneself while acting. The spread of the hands, the swaggering intensity of attack, the rhythm and density, the outpouring of the self. Though familiar and possibly cliché, there is nothing closed or un-free about the feeling. It is as though Ravi's presence, as the son of Alice and John, gives us license to step on with him into that iconic, storied, raging river of sound and spirit.

Sun Ra: *Monorails and Satellites* (solo piano), 1968.[16] Formative music, creations full of feeling and storytelling, tuneful, haunting, rhapsodic. From his corner of the universe, Sun Ra arrives at some staggering musical discoveries—an utterly pianistic way of extending tonality and pulse through excitations and exhortations, resonances and impassioned ascents.

A musician who played with Sun Ra for years reported the bandleader's description of a guitarist in the band: "He sounds pretty good, but he plays too many known things. He needs to get into some unknowns."

The perennial question with piano music is: At what point, for the listener, do the hands *disappear*, so that the music can emerge? That is Sun Ra's zone, the DMZ where this material dwells— in that frontier between physicality and the imagination, between earthly reality and the world of spirits, between known and unknown. It could be said that this space *is* the place claimed by Black music, where transcendence *is* embodied, and the word *is* made flesh—or as Sun Ra once styled the phrase, "the were'd made *fresh*" ("were'd" itself an exotic re-tensing of the verb "to be").

In these solo performances, the tactile ingredients of stride, boogie-woogie, and other "jump" piano styles—pianistic behavioral shards, each fragment full of dance impulse and voice-like melisma—are submitted to a radical lifting of their underlying premises, so that we're left with the familiar behaviors untethered to grids of meter or harmony. The result is pure invention: space towers rising up in that place between body and soul.

A persistent faith in the process—of subjecting these piano-player-isms to an alter-destiny of transformation and recombination—leaves us pivoting wildly between sentimental ballads and contrapuntal adventures. On some pieces we encounter one or the other in isolation, and on others these countervailing tendencies are nonchalantly sutured together.

There's a trickster at work in this music, directly probing, pushing, and worrying the interface of the instrument. It often starts with a distillation of conventional playing—calm stride, or patient ballad playing, or boogie-woogie action—but then it erupts, splits open. From what feels at times like a beginner's chaos, patterning emerges—the spacings of the fingers are not random after all, and is that a melody? A progression? I am at times reminded of "Chordially," Thelonious Monk's only recorded open improvisation.[17] It reveals how, for Monk as for Sun Ra, melody, phrase, harmony, and form all emerge from or through (or, at the very least, are inseparable from) bodily interaction with the keys, a patient tactic that starts rigorously from first principles.

The actual events are important, but so is the feeling of eventfulness. Each mini-episode tumbles and morphs into another. What we find ourselves riding are the *qualities of movement*. "Cognition," for example, shows up with a choppy dance: the Nutty Professor doing the Robot. It is never not fleshy, but you get to suspend your disbelief for a while, and imagine an army of mechanical fingers (or tiny robo-legs) descending upon the keys. You never forget Mr. Blount is there, but sometimes you find yourself saying, Maybe he really *is* from Saturn; where else are these sonic beings coming from—these roving, bending, crawling, wriggling polyphonies? Eventually a right-hand spiraling behavior (fingers? knuckles?) interrupts once, then twice. Suddenly a unifying principle, the pianist's spine, provides the gravity necessary to close the form.

Similarly, the rhythmic underpinning of "Space Towers" is sometimes five beats long, sometimes six, but mostly it subscribes to an immeasurable bodily crawl. It's not quite a bassline but just the implied shape of it, made new with each throbbing iteration, its incremental changes generating progress.

"The Changing Wind" appears as a mischievous dancer whose whims affect the landscape with mostly gentle caresses and light steps, but occasionally gather enough power to destabilize, and at other times eddy around a central thought. In "The Galaxy Way," the hands pick out an abundant path of stars, some piercing through radiantly. As the path unfolds, the stars are less distant, and we feel their gravity. A familiar twelve-beat rhythm bubbles through, and a chording behavior emerges. The pattern is broken with a brusque gesture, as if to redirect the flow. It is taken back up, then halted, then alternated with the opening constellations, creating another formal boundary. (Something about form is actually about memory—about how, in the present, we might be reminded of something from the past.)

"Easy Street" reveals, in its second eight bars, a few runs and cascades that come more from the hands than from the song. This is how Sun Ra often intervenes on a standard—by bringing physicality back into the picture, the part of piano playing that is unsung: the un-song. It is a literal "reach"—the sound of the hand extending itself.

"The Ninth Eye" begins with stepwise motion in the two alternating hands, chords in one and bass notes in the other. Then they produce thick staccato aggregates, then rolling figures. Sometimes a certain figure or series is paused, rewound, and played back, especially when either a blues motive appears, or a surprising resonance, twang, or buzz is detected. Later, the left hand ambles to the basement, lingering in that nearly pitchless register, a strange attractor exciting a quasiperiodic two-lobe whorl. Across this, a methodical mid-range melody-ing leads to a longer spiraling in the top register. An uneasy chromaticism is born of the hands' ways, gyrating and cycling, evolving and disrupting, creeping and jumping.

Like its titular object, "Skylight" serves to remind you of heaven, perhaps. You keep wanting to say, "I recognize this song/progression/phrase." But it is not "a ballad" — instead it is "ballad-ing," a creative process of inventing plausible ballad forms. If I were from Earth, its creator seems to be thinking, I just might enjoy this song. But unlike the songs you know, this music doesn't repeat, or close; it just constantly reforms and regenerates, until it stops. It is the syntax freed of semantics, singing without a song.

There's a motor in the collection's title cut, a steadily pulsed left-hand patterning, across which occasional melodic fragments move as if following a different, more sentimental tune. Just when it verges on syrup, it breaks into more ferocious rhythmic behavior, black-key glissandi, and that high-register spiraling again. When we get both hands swirling, there is an ecstatic element breaking through, a vibratory communing with the instrument, which leads into a glorious hammering, and a hypnotic tremolo-ing.

We would do well to think in gerunds about this music. For Sun Ra's creative piano utterances are relentlessly fixated on a single process above all: *becoming*.

Alice Coltrane-Turiyasangitananda: "Prema" (solo piano version on NPR, 1981).[18]

"*Prema* is a Sanskrit word and it translates to Divine Love." Proceeding at its own pace, an elemental ritual, prompting a literal taking of breath.

A deep pedal tone. Widely spread chords encompassing all that is within reach.

Tremolos bloom, a solemn left-hand melody tolls, deep roots shift. An orchestral polyphony – gathering enough energy through a piano to conjure a multitude, grab hold of the trouble, carry the pain and the healing force at once, declaiming to the heavens, or is it from them?

Each modulation upward feels like the turning of a season, the possibility of change itself offering the sustenance of optimism amid our foreboding cries.

The shift to the upper register, each rolled chord a sigh and a cry, the sound of an "us." We are held by all that she bears, her austerities.

The sustained tremolo throughout marks the sheer *work* of this magnanimous, selfless, divine, *maternal* love: the work of the hands.

A dramatic move to major, to joy, hope, a prayer answered. As she once said, "The key to being an artist is giving abundantly." Cascading lines in exaltation of a goddess's blessing.

We have been carried to the vista, drenched in awe, and then pulled back into the everyday, with the sting of enlightenment.

Geri Allen: "Lonely Woman" (1988).[19] Her hands first showed up to my teenaged ears as spiders, scampering through multidimensional cracks in the rhythm. Those hands produced spare, spindly melodies, weaving and twisting around the harmonies, and leaving gauzy trails that accumulated into something majestic: an odd, enchanted web spun into the corner of a song, strange and delicate.

Those ephemeral lines, first appearing as spontaneous drops into the abyss, turned out to be structural moves, executed with care, determination, and foresight. I had the ongoing sense that the owner of these hands not only possessed perspicacious insight into whatever piece of music she was playing, but that she managed also to hear whatever that song *wasn't yet saying*—and that was the exact space where she would begin her work, in the time-honored Black speculative tradition. Such was our impression of Geri Allen, the pianist, as documented on other people's recordings: a constant source of sly, wry conjurings and disruptions, chromatic dislocations and interventions, she seemed to glide, unbothered, from mastery to transgression and back.

Her improvisations were full of space, thought, listening, and a liberatory quality; her groove was deep, her two-hand independence often shocking; her lines and voicings were fresh and unique; she would seem at times to play with great reserves of calm, but when she chose to step up, she would dazzle with fearless virtuosity. She could make a piano sigh, whisper, chortle, shriek, and roar.

"The Short End of the Stick" 1989.[20] What captured and fascinated me, particularly in her playing with the late great drummer Ralph Peterson, was not how she plays the changes, nor how she "builds" her solos –it was how she expresses time, fearlessly unbothered by Peterson's fusillades; how she on occasion emanates out of the ensemble texture, again like a solar flare,[21] seeming to swerve away from the form, only to then miraculously land with Peterson's drums, proving that she was with him the whole time; how she seems to be always both *wholly with* and strikingly *other than* the band. I remain mystified by the surprising absence of chords; there are rarely more than two notes sounding at once. Somehow she constructs dancing arcs of affective intensity without resorting to sonic saturation, rhythmic density, or excessive sustain: let's call them *quiet shouts*. A hushed sequence of dyads feels momentous, even climactic. The sparse yet pervasive left-hand stabs hold a clue, as they are never *not* in rhythm; often landing on eighth-note upbeats that lock tightly with the drums and bass, they convey a subtle rhythmic grounding, a quiet self-assurance that she is rhythmically not alone, and need not force the music. The resulting spaces in her solo express a generosity to her bandmates; she is not looking to dominate the conversation, but rather to motivate, propel, and stretch *with* the ensemble. The silences in her playing, in the tradition of soloists like Ahmad Jamal, Shirley Horn, and Wadada Leo Smith, signify key moments of *listening and interdependence*. Most of all, what captivated me in the late 1980s was how her hands would dance: how the embodied structures and rhythms of her hands generated a contrasting, productive musical form of their own. Her playing showcased the speculative work of the hands, their power to imagine new musicalities that intervene on and push against existing forms.

Yet if this was all you knew about Allen—her way of transforming someone else's band by calmly inhabiting, dancing in, and shouting from its margins—you might be a fan, but you would also be wholly unprepared for her own music. Imagine a sturdy, splendid palace built entirely from the peculiar details found in those spiderwebs: the splayed intervals proliferating and surrounding you as ostinati; the jagged, errant lines somehow doubled, orchestrated, even sung; the asymmetric rhythms stacked in contrapuntal towers; all the mercurial tendencies in her piano playing suddenly solidified and given full force. It was that same aesthetic from the margins, now made thrillingly central. This was the musical language of Geri Allen: clear, ebullient, and resoundingly complete.

Robert Hood: "Minus" (1994).[22] It starts all of a sudden. You move in your biped frame, but the arpeggio comes in threes, orbiting and breaking your symmetry. Its brutality is that it does not change. As it hangs in the air, you start to notice different things about it, like an endless polyphonic crystal. You notice the reverb cloud that seems to hang in the background, reactivated each 1.5 beats. Then this cloud coalesces into a single note that isn't in the existing chord, does not belong. This B forms shifting moiré patterns with the top Bb of the G minor arpeggio. It pingpongs around that top note, toggling among a half-dozen possibilities, forming iterative, machinic blues relations. Was this a song? Or some other thing? We are left to contemplate the eventfulness of what has transpired, the percolating half-step shifts as form, as melody, as a crux of significance.

The question I must ask when I take on this exercise is, what are my analytical details doing in relation to what the music is doing? How do I stop the violent agenda of musical analysis from hijacking the music's function, or ignoring the conditions to and under which the music is responding?

What is hiding from such analysis is how these musics reconfigure their spaces, reorder sociality; musicality as relation. To listen in earphones is to remain fixed in a single spatial orientation to the music; you are a lone stationary observer, pinned to the sweet spot of the stereo image. But to be in a room with other bodies, with sounds bouncing off of every surface, feels quite different; one moves through and is immersed in the very same air that is the vibratory medium of sound. The bass frequencies hit you in the stomach; they modulate the air in stride-length sine waves. The high-end claps and hi-hats flood the atmosphere, clatter off the ceiling, lift the hair off the nape of your neck. Panned synthetic tones float impossibly around the room. The tweak of a filter knob makes objects change color, on a temporal arc that fuses with your mounting emotional state. The music is not of you; it seems not to be of anybody. And yet you feel guided, invited to move and feel with it. The only body present in the place of any musician, the DJ at a console, you worship as you would an officiant, for they serve as conduit for this unseeable power. Musicality emerges not simply in the inner play of the song's formal attributes, but in your very relationship to the floor, walls, and ceiling, to the vibratory excitations of the very air you breathe, and to the co-beings alongside whom you maneuver and sweat and live, with whom you dissolve into collective sensation and action.

This world that calls you into it did not exist until it did, a few decades ago, in postindustrial Detroit and Chicago; this you is therefore also new; these new musical and human relations are the historically emergent result of Black queer invention.

What I have sought to identify is a series of moments in which Black sonic action becomes musical, interpellating listeners into an impossible future made present. I do not mean to romanticize this quality. When I say impossible, I mean in literal, continual danger of white supremacist terror and anti-Black violence that continue to this day. As a non-

Black person with considerable privilege, I do not intend to make a callous pronouncement, some ineffectual warm assurance about Black music and liberation. Rather I am trying to listen as closely as I can, to moments of instability, insurrection, and especially *reconstruction*—Black subjectivities collectively speculating Otherwise sonic architecture: in Coltrane's phrase, *living space*, or what Sun Ra named *alter destiny*.

In spring 2021, the composer-saxophonist Yosvany Terry and I co-taught a course titled "Composer-Performers of the African Diaspora," in which we studied the creative work of visiting artists Henry Threadgill, Cécile McLorin Salvant, Esperanza Spalding, Gonzalo Rubalcaba, Nicole Mitchell, and Tyshawn Sorey, and strove to listen for these artists' methods of self-definition. At the end of term, we asked our students to reflect on any common tendencies they noticed across these artists' work. One student, Joy Nesbitt, offered:

> I'm fascinated by the lineage of the diaspora [among] these artists . . . I think there's this ineffable uniquely Black curiosity inherent to all of this work. I think some of it might actually be passed down from the ancestors in that part of Black creativity is excavating other cultures and locations for a sense of identity that was robbed within the creation of the diaspora.

Perhaps "this ineffable uniquely Black curiosity" is what orients the ear diachronically, ancient to the future, speculatively remaking the category of the human across a multiverse of histories. Black curiosity extends a generous invitation to collectively study and feel our way through the contingent emergence, relationality, and sheer precarity of human sonic relation.

Toward a "critical musicalities"

Music's status is not freely given; it is conferred — it is the result of a process in which you, the subject, feel guided or hailed into an affective relation (that is, a musicality) with the sonorous acts of another. The category of music therefore aligns with the bios-mythos category of the human, which is itself explosively unstable and plastic. In challenging the systemic violent rearrangements of the human category—the coloniality of man—Black queer and feminist theorists have cultivated restorative models of care and repair: again, via Wynter, *being human as praxis*. Following their lead, we understand musicality as a dynamic, intimate sociality.

Therefore we must imagine a pivotal position for musicality/ies in any praxis of being human. As I write these words, I think back to Derrida's admonishment – "But who, we?"[23] – and humankind's endless capacity to eject or abandon entire populations from its own category: humanity's inhumanities. I take a cue from this call issued by Lisa Lowe and Kris Manjapra for "a different humanities":

> "The humanities could be instead a way of thinking, reading, writing, and critically reflecting on the 'plasticity' of the human; the human not as fixed form, but as a shifting

relation itself. A different humanities based in the analytic of relationality invites a total rethinking of discipline and method. Forging alternatives to the coloniality of knowledge, institutionalized in the very methods of the humanities and the history of the university, requires not only an analytic of relation, but also a rethinking of the archive, which may involve new readings of traditional archives, or finding alternative repositories and practices of knowledge and collection. We ponder what it means to 'recover' historical pasts for which there is no or little documentation or evidence. We investigate the manners in which collective memory practices, apocryphal materials, ephemera, and performance may constitute types of archives."[24]

If today's critical humanities interrogate the category of the human across these histories, I am asking similarly for a *critical musicalities* that might study emergences of musical relation as it has occurred across this violent half-millennium, and beyond, and how they might emerge anew, in our present and in our shared futures. Black speculative musicalities will have once again salvaged, illuminated, and remade our philosophies of the human being, our praxes of being human, our conceptions of "us."

As the term "speculative" assures us, there is an important role for the imagination in the kind of work that is called for here. It will be useful to invoke Saidiya Hartman's term, "critical fabulation," which refers to her practice of triangulating from spectral traces in the archives, working from its fissures and erasures, "to recover the insurgent ground of these lives," to develop counternarratives: "a dream book for existing otherwise."[25]

Notes

1   Frank Wilderson, "Doing Time in the (Psychic) Commons," in Anna M. Athangelou and Kyle D. Killian, eds., *Time, Temporality, and Violence in International Relations* (New York: Routledge, 2016), 87.

2   Achille Mbembe, *Critique of Black Reason* (Durham, NC: Duke University Press, 2017), 27–28.

3   David Lionel Smith, "What Is Black Culture?" in Wahneema Lubiano, ed., *The House That Race Built* (New York: Vintage Books, 1998), 192–93.

4   Christina Sharpe, *In the Wake: On Blackness and Being* (Durham: Duke University Press, 2016), 130–31.

5   Fred Moten, *In the Break: The Aesthetics of the Black Radical Tradition* (Minneapolis: University of Minnesota Press, 2003), 7–8.

6   Sylvia Wynter and Katherine McKittrick, *Sylvia Wynter: On Being Human as Praxis* (Durham: Duke University Press, 2015), 23.

7   Wynter and McKittrick, *On Being Human as Praxis*, 23.

8   Wynter and McKittrick, *On Being Human as Praxis*, 68.

9   Ashon Crawley, *Blackpentecostal Breath: The Aesthetics of Possibility* (New York: Fordham University Press, 2016).

10 Duke Ellington, pianist, "Lotus Blossom," by Billy Strayhorn, recorded 1967, track 12 on . . . *And His Mother Called Him Bill*, RCA 6287-2-RB, 1987, compact disc.

11   Duke Ellington, *Music Is My Mistress* (New York: Da Capo, 1973), 156.

12   Randy Weston, composer and pianist, "Ancient Future," recorded June 2001, track 1 on disc 1 of *Ancient Future / Blue*, Mutable Music 17508-2, 2002, 2 compact discs.

13   "Randy Weston interviewed by Vijay Iyer." Recorded at Guelph Jazz Festival, Ontario, Canada, September 4, 2014. https://vimeo.com/127509880

14   "Jack DeJohnette: Made In Chicago (Album EPK) | ECM Records." Uploaded January 9, 2015. https://www.youtube.com/watch?v=edLWmyTegvk

15   John Coltrane, *Both Directions at Once: The Lost Album*, recorded March 4, 1963, Spotify, Impulse, 2018.

16   Sun Ra, *Monorails And Satellites Vols. 1, 2, and 3*, recorded 1966, New York. Bandcamp, Solar Myth Records, 2019. https://sunramusic.bandcamp.com/album/monorails-and-satellites-vols-1-2-and-3

17   Thelonious Monk, "Chordially," track 11 on *The London Collection, Vol. 3*, recorded November 15, 1971, Black Lion BLCD-760142, compact disc, 1990.

18   Alice Coltrane-Turiyasangitananda, "Prema," from "Piano Jazz with Marian McPartland," National Public Radio, recorded December 4, 1981. https://youtu.be/5fV1M-hIllk

19   Charlie Haden/Paul Motian featuring Geri Allen, "Lonely Woman," recorded September 14–15, 1987 in New York, track 1 on *Études*, Soul Note, 1988, cassette.

20   Ralph Peterson Quintet, "The Short End of the Stick," recorded April 19–20, 1988, New York, track 3 on *V*, Blue Note B1-91730, LP, 1989.

21   Rail: So, music becomes a model of art where a group of people are listening and a group of people are making. Moten: It's the ensemble. And it's the recognition that the solo is an emanation of the ensemble. From Jarrett Ernst, "Close Encounters: Fred Moten," *Brooklyn Rail*, November 2017, https://brooklynrail.org/2017/11/art/FRED-MOTEN-with-Jarrett-Earnest.

Jafa: "One of the many things Fred Moten said that had an impact on me is that we normally think of jazz as a tension between a group and an individual: when the individual begins a solo, the group fades into the background. He argued that a better way to understand the individual is as an emanation of the group. Whenever there's a sun in my work, I'm thinking about that: you see the sun blazing; then, all of a sudden, a flare reaches out and you recognize it as a single entity. Afterwards, it's just absorbed back into the body of the sun; it's an emanation." From Jace Clayton, "As Brilliant as the Sun," *Frieze* 193 (March 2018), https://frieze.com/article/brilliant-sun

22   Robert Hood, "Minus," track A2 on *Internal Empire*, 2x vinyl 12" 45RPM album, Tresor 74321 24772-1, 1994.

23   Jacques Derrida, "The Ends of Man," in *Margins of Philosophy*, tr. Alan Bass (Chicago: U. of Chicago Press, 1972), 136.

24   Lisa Lowe & Kris Manjapra, "Comparative Global Humanities After Man: Alternatives to the Coloniality of Knowledge." *Theory, Culture & Society* 36, no. 5 (2019), 23–48.

25   Saidiya Hartman, *Wayward Lives, Beautiful Experiments: Intimate Histories of Riotous Black Girls, Troublesome women, and Queer Radicals* (New York: W. W. Norton, 2019), xiv–xv.

CONTRIBUTORS

GerShun Avilez is Professor of English at the University of Maryland, College Park. An award-winning teacher and writer, he specializes in contemporary African American and Black Diasporic literatures and visual cultures. His scholarship explores how questions of gender and sexuality inform artistic production. He has published two books: *Radical Aesthetics and Modern Black Nationalism* (2016) and *Black Queer Freedom: Spaces of Injury and Paths of Desire* (2020). He also co-edited the 10th edition of the *Norton Anthology of American Literature, 1945-Present* (2022). He is at work on a new book project on race, sexuality, and healthcare.

Angela Y. Davis, through her activism and scholarship over many decades, has been deeply involved in movements for social justice around the world. Her work as an educator—both at the university level and in the larger public sphere—has always emphasized the importance of building communities of struggle for economic, racial, and gender justice. She is the author of eleven books, including *Abolition.Feminism.Now*, co-authored with Gina Dent, Erica Meiners, and Beth Richie, and a new edition of her *Autobiography*, both of which will be released in 2022. Having helped to popularize the notion of a "prison industrial complex," she now urges her audiences to think seriously about the future possibility of a world without carceral systems and to help forge a 21st century abolitionist movement.

Thomas F. DeFrantz directs SLIPPAGE: Performance|Culture|Technology, a research group that explores emerging technology in live performance. Received 2017 Outstanding Research in Dance award, Dance Studies Association. Believes in our shared capacity to do better, and to engage our creative spirit for a collective good that is anti-racist, anti-homophobic, proto-feminist, and queer affirming. Consultant for the Smithsonian Museum of African American Life and Culture. In 2013, working with Takiyah Nur Amin, founded the Collegium for African Diaspora Dance, a growing consortium of 300 researchers. Expertises: Black expressive cultures and their impacts on everyday life. slippage.org.

Theaster Gates is an artist and social innovator based in Chicago. Trained as an urban planner and potter, his practice has evolved through the remaking of objects, cultural narratives, and places. Over the past decade, his practice has demonstrated the intricacy of Blackness through space theory and land development, sculpture, and performance. Gates is a professor at the University of Chicago in the Department of Visual Arts and serves as the Senior Advisor for Cultural Innovation and Advisor to the Dean at the Harris School of Public Policy.

Aracelis Girmay is Assistant Chair of Writing & MFA Advisor at Pratt Institute. She recently edited *How to Carry Water: Selected Poems of Lucille Clifton* (2020). Her most recent book of poems is *the black maria* (2016).

Jeremy Matthew Glick is an Associate Professor of African Diaspora literature in the English Department of Hunter College, CUNY and author of *The Black Radical Tragic: Performance, Aesthetics and the Unfinished Haitian Revolution*- winner of the Caribbean Philosophical Association's 2017 *Nicolás Guillén* Outstanding Book *Award*. He is currently finishing a book entitled *Coriolanus Against Liberalism/ Lumumba & Pan-Africanist Loss* and a small book juxtaposing Goya's *Caprichos,* Du Bois's *Black Reconstruction*, and Black Radical poetics. He is the editor of *Situations: A Journal of the Radical Imagination* and a frequent contributor to *The A-Line: A Journal of Progressive Thought*.

Deborah Goffe is Executive Director of Austin Arts Center and Artist-in-Residence of Theater and Dance at Trinity College (Hartford, CT). She is also Founder/Director of Scapegoat Garden, a creative engine that, since its founding in 2002, has functioned as a primary vehicle and artistic community through which Deborah activates the world-making potential of expressive bodies in movement(s), localities, networked and collaborative processes, interdisciplinarity, and curatorial practices as systems of care. www.scapegoatgarden.org

James B. Haile, III is an Associate Professor of Philosophy at the University of Rhode Island. His research interests focus on Africana philosophy, philosophy and literature, philosophical fiction, and aesthetics. His latest book is *The Buck, the Black and the Existential Hero: Refiguring the Black Male Literary Canon 1850 to Present* (2020).

Vijay Iyer is a composer-pianist. He has released two dozen albums, including seven on ECM Records, and has collaborated with Amiri Baraka, Wadada Leo Smith, Carrie Mae Weems, Teju Cole, Tyshawn Sorey, Pamela Z, Henry Threadgill, Jennifer Koh, Matt Haimovitz, Orpheus Chamber Orchestra, and many other artists across disciplines. He received a MacArthur Fellowship, a U.S. Artists Fellowship, the Doris Duke Performing Artist Award, the Alpert Award in the Arts, and two German Echo Awards, and was the four-time Jazz Artist of the Year in the DownBeat International Critics' Poll. He teaches at Harvard University, with a joint appointment in the Department of Music and the Department of African and African American Studies; there he founded the Department of Music's doctoral program in Creative Practice and Critical Inquiry.

Sir Isaac Julien, RA (1960) is a critically acclaimed British artist and filmmaker. He is a Distinguished Professor of the Arts at the University of California, Santa Cruz, where he leads the Moving Image Lab together with Arts Professor Mark Nash. Current and recent international solo exhibitions include *Isaac Julien*, Tate Britain, London, UK, 2023; *Lina Bo*

Bardi, A Marvellous Entanglement, Philadelphia Museum of Art, Philadelphia, USA, 2023; *Lessons of the Hour*, Virginia Museum of Fine Art, Virginia, USA, 2022-23; *Once Again . . . Statues Never Die)*, Barnes Foundation, Philadelphia, USA, 2022. Julien is the recipient of The Royal Academy of Arts Charles Wollaston Award 2017, and a Kaiserring Goslar Award in 2022. He was granted knighthood as part of the Queen's Honours List in 2022.

Michael Kelly is Professor of Philosophy at the University of North Carolina at Charlotte. He is the Editor-in-Chief of two editions of the Oxford *Encyclopedia of Aesthetics* (1998/2014); and author of *A Hunger for Aesthetics: Enacting the Demands of Art* (2012) and *Iconoclasm in Aesthetics* (2003). He is also President of the Transdisciplinary Aesthetics Foundation, which sponsors Questioning Aesthetics Symposia on new topics of research in aesthetics, including Anthropocene aesthetics, Black aesthetics, and carceral aesthetics.

Benjamin Krusling is a doctoral candidate in English at the CUNY Graduate Center in New York. His research interests focus on race and politico-aesthetic crises of visuality and form in late-20th century innovative poetry and cinema. His most recent book, a poetry collection, is *Glaring* (2020).

Daphne Lamothe is a professor of Africana Studies at Smith College. Her research and teaching interests center on questions of literary representation, Black aesthetics and ethics, migration and transnationalism, culture, and identity. She is the author of *Black Time and the Aesthetic Possibility of Objects* (forthcoming in 2024) and *Inventing the New Negro: Narrative, Culture, and Ethnography* (2008), as well as scholarly articles and essays that have appeared in some of the top journals in her field, like *African American Review*, *Callaloo*, and *Meridians: Feminism, Race, Transnationalism*.

George E. Lewis is Case Professor of American Music at Columbia University. He is a composer, musicologist, computer-installation artist, and trombonist. A member of the Association for the Advancement of Creative Musicians, his book, *A Power Stronger Than Itself: The AACM and American Experimental Music* (2008) received the American Book Award. Lewis and Benjamin Piekut are the co-editors of the *Oxford Handbook of Critical Improvisation Studies* (2016). Lewis is a MacArthur Fellow, a Corresponding Fellow of the British Academy, and a Fellow of the American Academy of Arts and Sciences, the American Academy of Arts and Letters, and the Akademie der Künste Berlin.

Sarah Elizabeth Lewis is the John L. Loeb Associate Professor of the Humanities and Associate Professor of African and African American Studies at Harvard University. She is the founder of Vision & Justice. Her books and edited volumes include *Carrie Mae Weems* (2021), "Vision & Justice" *Aperture* (2016), and *The Rise* (2014). Lewis was named an Andrew Carnegie Fellow in 2022. Her scholarship has received awards including the Arthur Danto/American Society for Aesthetics Prize, the inaugural Freedom Scholar Award from The Association for the Study of African American Life and History, and the Infinity Award from the International Center of Photography.

Meleko Mokgosi (born in Francistown, Botswana; lives and works in Wellesley, MA) is an artist, Associate Professor and co-director of graduate studies at the Yale School of Art, and co-director of the Interdisciplinary Art and Theory Program (https://www.artandtheoryprogram.org). He received his BA from Williams College in 2007 and participated in the Whitney Museum of American Art's Independent Study program from 2007–2008. Mokgosi received his MFA from the Interdisciplinary Studio Program at the University of California Los Angeles in 2011. He participated in the Rauschenberg Residency at the Robert Rauschenberg Foundation, Captiva, FL in 2015 and the Artist in Residence Program at the Studio Museum in Harlem, New York, in 2012. With an emphasis on historiography and systems of knowledge production and representation, Mokgosi uses history painting, cinematic tropes, psychoanalysis, and post-colonial theory to create large-scale project-based installations.

Wangechi Mutu, born in Nairobi, Kenya, is a contemporary artist working in New York and Nairobi in a variety of mediums: collage-paintings, sculptures, films, performance rituals. Recent exhibitions include: "Wangechi Mutu," Storm King Art Center, New York; "Mama Ray," Nasher Museum of Art, Durham, NC; "Wangechi Mutu," Gladstone Gallery, New York; "Wangechi Mutu: I Am Speaking, Can You Hear Me?," Legion of Honor, Fine Arts Museum of San Francisco; and *The NewOnes, will free Us* at the Metropolitan Museum of art, New York.

Fumi Okiji is Assistant Professor of Rhetoric at the University of California, Berkeley. Okiji is the author of *Jazz as Critique: Adorno and Black Expression Revisited* (Stanford University Press, 2018). Her work crosses music, critical theory and black radical thought.

Nell Painter (the artist formerly known as the historian Nell Irvin Painter, author of *The History of White People*, *Old in Art School*, *Sojourner Truth, A Life, A Symbol* and *Old in Art School: A Memoir of Starting Over*) earned degrees in painting from Mason Gross School of the Arts at Rutgers and the Rhode Island School of Design after a Ph.D. in history from Harvard. She lives and works in Newark, New Jersey, and when not writing essays and drawing self-portraits, she makes artist's books that visualize people and history. A member of the American Academy of Arts and Sciences since 2007, she also currently serves as Madame Chairman of MacDowell.

Mickaella Perina is Associate Professor of Philosophy at the University of Massachusetts Boston. Her areas of research are political and legal philosophy, critical philosophy of race, aesthetics, Caribbean philosophy, contemporary French philosophy, and philosophy of Human Rights. Her main research interests include liberal democracy theory and its exclusions; race, identity, and political membership; and remembering/forgetting with reference to public memory/counter-memories. She is the author of *Citoyenneté et Sujétion aux Antilles Francophones* (1997) and numerous articles. She is a co-organizer of the California Roundtable for Philosophy and Race and a Series editor with Bloomsbury Introductions to World Philosophies.

Claudia Rankine is a poet, essayist, and playwright. She is the author of five books of poetry, including *Citizen: An American Lyric* and *Don't Let Me Be Lonely.* Her recent collection of essays, *Just Us: An American Conversation*, was published by Graywolf Press in 2020. Among her numerous awards and honors, Rankine is the recipient of the Bobbitt National Prize for Poetry, the Poets & Writers' Jackson Poetry Prize, and fellowships from the Guggenheim Foundation, the Lannan Foundation, the MacArthur Foundation, United States Artists, and the National Endowment for the Arts. She teaches creative writing at New York University.

Monique Roelofs is Professor of Philosophy at the University of Amsterdam, where she holds the Chair of Philosophy of Art and Culture and leads the Critical Cultural Theory program group. Her research centers on the relation between aesthetics and politics, with a focus on the dynamics of race, gender, nation, decoloniality, and the global. She is the author of *Arts of Address: Being Alive to Language and The World* (2020) and *The Cultural Promise of the Aesthetic* (2014). Roelofs has recently completed a new book manuscript, *Aesthetics, Address, and the Politics of Culture.* She is also coauthoring a book on aesthetics and temporality in Latinx and Latin America.

Claudia Schmuckli is the inaugural curator in charge of contemporary art and programming at the Fine Arts Museums of San Francisco. Since joining the Museums in 2016, she has developed a dynamic program in dialogue with the institution's sites, buildings, and collections, including solo exhibitions dedicated to Kehinde Wiley, Wangechi Mutu, Judy Chicago, Lynn Hershman Leeson, Sarah Lucas, and Urs Fischer alongside major group exhibitions such as *Uncanny Valley: Being Human in the Age of AI* and *Specters of Disruption*. Previously, she was director and chief curator of the Blaffer Art Museum at the University of Houston, where she organized more than thirty exhibitions. She holds a master of arts degree in art history from the Ludwigs-Maximilians-Universität in Munich, Germany.

Evie Shockley is Professor of English at Rutgers University-New Brunswick. She is the author of *Renegade Poetics: Black Aesthetics and Formal Innovation in African American Poetry* (2011) and three books of poetry, most recently *the new black* (2011) and *semiautomatic* (2017), both of which won the Hurston/Wright Legacy Award in Poetry. Her current research focuses on contemporary Black poetry and visual art that combine text and image to navigate or challenge the ideology of colorblindness.

Paul C. Taylor is the Presidential Professor of Philosophy at the University of California, Los Angeles. He received his undergraduate training at Morehouse College and his graduate training at the Kennedy School of Government and at Rutgers University. His research focuses primarily on aesthetics, the philosophy of race, American philosophy, and Africana philosophy. His books include *Black is Beautiful: A Philosophy of Black Aesthetics*, which received the 2017 monograph prize from the American Society for Aesthetics, and *Race: A Philosophical Introduction*.

Kara Walker Kara Walker is an American artist born in Stockton, California in 1969. She was raised in Atlanta, Georgia from the age of 13, and studied at the Atlanta College of Art (BFA, 1991) and the Rhode Island School of Design (MFA, 1994). She is the recipient of numerous awards, notably the John D. and Catherine T. MacArthur Foundation Achievement Award in 1997, and the United States Artists, Eileen Harris Norton Fellowship in 2008. Walker is a member of the American Academy of Arts and Letters (elected 2012), and the American Philosophical Society (elected 2018).

Simone White is the author of the collections *or, on being the other woman, Dear Angel of Death, Of Being* Dispersed, and *House Envy of All the World*. She is Stephen M. Gorn Family Assistant Professor of English at the University of Pennsylvania and lives in Brooklyn.

Mabel O. Wilson is the Nancy and George Rupp Professor of Architecture, Planning and Preservation, a Professor in African American and African Diasporic Studies, and the Director of the Institute for Research in African American Studies at Columbia University. At GSAPP she co-directs the *Global Africa Lab*. Wilson is trained in Architecture and American Studies, two fields that inform her scholarship, curatorial projects, art works and design projects. Through her transdisciplinary practice Studio&, Wilson makes visible and legible the ways that anti-black racism shapes the built environment along with the ways that blackness creates spaces of imagination, refusal and desire.

Index

Page numbers in **bold** refer to figures.